Kaleidoscope of POLAND

Poznaj Polskę

Kaleidoscope of
POLAND
A CULTURAL ENCYCLOPEDIA

OSCAR E. SWAN with EWA KOŁACZEK-FILA

with a Foreword by Adam Zamoyski

Prolog
PUBLISHING

Cover art:(*Top row, left to right*) St. Mary's Basilica, photo by Peter Kracht; Tamara de Łempicka, *Autoportrait*, (Self-portrait in the green Bugatti), 1925. © Tamara Art Heritage. Licensed by www.MuseumMasters.com, courtesy of Marilyn Goldberg; Wooden church in Bączal Dolny; Ludwika Nitschowa (1889–1989), *Warszawska syrenka*, photo by Dixi, CC BY-SA 3.0 (creativecommons.org/licenses/by-sa/3.0/) via Wikimedia Commons. (*Bottom row, left to right*) 2006 Peace Race, Dippoldiswalde, Germany, photo by Harald Weber, CC BY-SA 3.0 (creativecommons.org/licenses/by-sa/3.0/), via Wikimedia Commons; Old Town, Warsaw, photo by Peter Kracht; Maria Wodzińska, *Portrait of Frédéric Chopin*, 1836; "Małe Zabi Oko," Rafał Kozubek, CC BY-SA 3.0 (creativecommons.org/licenses/by-sa/3.0), via Wikimedia Commons

This edition first published 2015 by PROLOG Publishing,
ul. Bronowicka 37, 30-084 Kraków, Poland.
Printed in Kraków, Poland, by Zakład Graficzny Colonel S.A.
Copyright © 2015, University of Pittsburgh Press
All rights reserved

Printed on acid-free paper
ISBN 978-83-60229-46-0

In the 210th anniversary of his death, I invoke as patron for the present endeavor the assiduous eighteenth-century chronicler of the customs of the *saskie czasy* (Saxon times), Jędrzej Kitowicz (1728–1804), who more or less single-handedly introduced the cultural chronicle into Polish letters, hoping that in so doing I may be able to channel in some measure that observer's sharp eye for culturally significant detail and his encyclopedist's penchant for cataloging it.

Contents

Foreword by Adam Zamoyski, ix
Preface, xvii
Acknowledgments, xxi
Polish Pronunciation, xxiii
Timeline of Polish History, xxv
Note about the Entries, xxvii

Timeline of Polish Historical Months, 309
Timeline of Polish Literary Figures Cited, 311
Timeline of Polish Rulers, 313
Major Polish National and Regional Uprisings, 317
Important Twentieth-Century Conferences Affecting Poland, 319
English Index, 321
Polish Index, 335
Illustration Credits, 363

Kaleidoscope of Poland

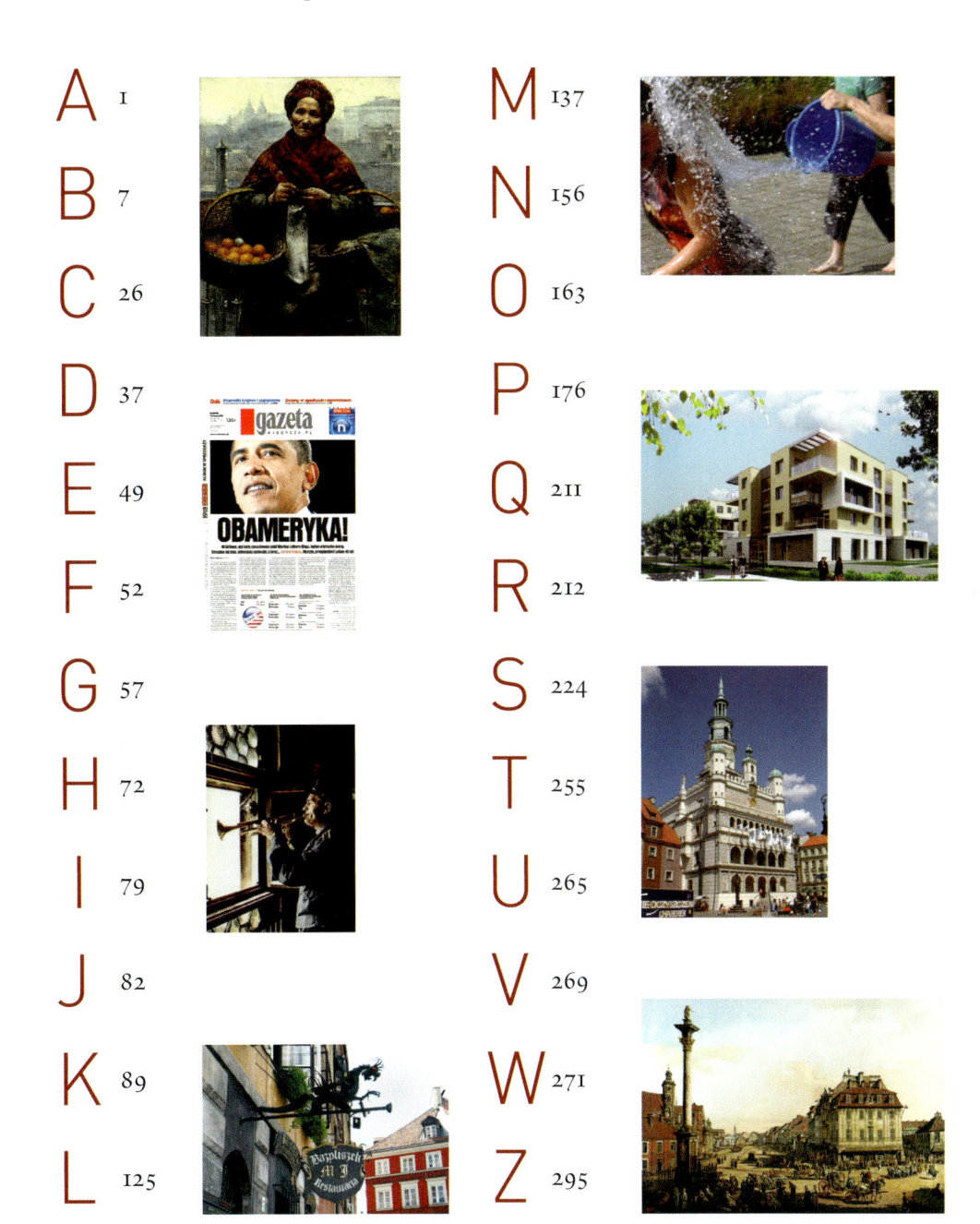

A   1

B   7

C   26

D   37

E   49

F   52

G   57

H   72

I   79

J   82

K   89

L   125

M   137

N   156

O   163

P   176

Q   211

R   212

S   224

T   255

U   265

V   269

W   271

Z   295

Foreword — Overview of Polish History
Adam Zamoyski

There are people who have educated themselves entirely by dipping into encyclopedias. This might sound eccentric, but it is actually not a bad way of approaching some subjects. One reference leads to another, which raises questions that can only be satisfied by a third and a fourth, curiosity is generated naturally, and the process can become compulsive. The greatest art experts notoriously acquire knowledge through often haphazard contact with works of art and the study of peripheral topics. And historians are forever deepening their understanding of a given field by wandering down apparently irrelevant avenues of investigation.

Stuffed with information ranging from the arcane to the banal, this book provides rich grazing for such rumination and makes for an effortless and entertaining way of discovering Poland. But all this information is useless without any fundamental terms of reference or some kind of road map.

The lives of Copernicus, Chopin, and Marie Curie; the fact that the Poles invented the oil well, saved Europe from Islam in 1683 and from Bolshevism in 1920, led the way in parliamentary democracy and were the first to give women the vote; the heroics of Polish airmen and soldiers in World War II; the extraordinary achievement of bringing down communism by Solidarity; Lech Wałęsa; and Pope John Paul II are of little significance if they cannot be placed in context and woven into some greater narrative.

To do so is not easy. Histories based on litanies of kings, queens, heroes, and battles are undone by the fact that the more concise they are, the more dates and unpronounceable names they feature per page. Any synthesis must either leave out the detail that so often counts for a great deal, or be so comprehensive that it defeats any but the most dedicated reader. Yet Poland is less suited to easy classification than most European nations, and requires a great deal more explanation.

It became a recognized European state over a thousand years ago, and for much of that time it was one of the most extensive. It began as a kingdom, but was subsequently split up into smaller units. These were reunited and added to, making it the largest dominion in Europe. It then turned itself into a parliamentary democracy with an elected king. Two hundred years later it was swallowed up by its neighbors and disappeared from the map altogether for over a century. It reemerged as a sovereign state in 1918, only to be taken apart once more in 1939. In 1945 it became a dependency of Russia, and finally regained its independence in 1989 as one of the half-dozen largest states in Europe by territory and population.

Such a stark résumé of its historical trajectory reveals a lack of continuity that defies easy narration: Poland cannot be treated just as a geographical entity or as a political one. If one wishes to provide some kind of narrative one therefore has to set it within different parameters. It is perhaps easiest to think first and foremost in terms of a society, and to trace its progress as that of a family, whose fortunes vary from generation to generation. It is out of such ups and downs, and in the way they are dealt with, that the character of a family emerges. And the more of them it has to contend with, the more distinctive that character, or set of characteristics, becomes. Taken together, they can replace geography and ethnicity to provide the template onto which the information in this volume can be spread.

The first recorded major political act in Polish history was its conversion to Christianity in the year 966. This *was* a political act, because it was not so much the result of a spiritual epiphany as a clearheaded decision by Prince Mieszko I of the Polanians to bring the people he ruled into the modern world in its evolving Western embodiment, a world they could either join or be overwhelmed by. It was a decision dictated by much the same logic as was the more recent one to join the European Union. By accepting Christianity, Mieszko took his Polish realm into Europe as it was then constituted.

At the same time, he and his successors vigorously resisted incorporation into the German empire, which is what had happened to Poland's southern Czech neighbors. They displayed a similar attitude toward the other power governing the European world, the Church of Rome. The rulers of Poland enthusiastically embraced all its institutions (spiritual considerations apart, these provided education, inward investment, technical innovation, a legal system, channels of communication with the outside world, etc.). But they fought long and hard to ensure that Polish bishops would be nominated by them, not by the Pope, who merely sanctioned their choice. They also tolerated and even encouraged the presence of large numbers of Jews, who were allowed to practice their religion publicly and live with fewer restrictions than in other countries, as well as Muslims, who were admitted to the nobility on an equal basis.

This jealously guarded sense of autonomy was reflected within the state itself, in the shape of strong regional loyalties. While the Polish realm continued to grow in size throughout the Middle Ages, partly through conquest, but mostly through adhesion by marriage or other means, it did not coalesce into a strong state. In the year 1138 the kingdom was actually divided into six duchies, some of which were further subdivided. The rulers of these duchies all accepted that they belonged to the *Corona regni Poloniae*, the Polish political community, but kept their independence within it. The trend throughout the rest of Europe was toward greater centralization and extension of royal power; the Poles chose instead a model of loose association of nominally autonomous provinces. This centrifugal tendency and fierce regional loyalties were to remain a constant in Polish political life, and had a major impact on how the Polish state would develop and on its relationship with the rest of Europe.

In the course of the fourteenth century the Polish lands were reunited under one crown and reemerged as a large and powerful kingdom whose alliance and support were courted by other powers. But it was still not a centralized state, like most comparable European kingdoms. It was a collage of several provinces with lesser or greater degrees of autonomy, and in 1386 it was linked by dynastic ties to the large Grand Duchy of Lithuania, which kept its own political structures and even its titular ruler despite being part of the Polish realm. Ethnic Poles were in a minority in this state, and they coexisted on an equal footing with Lithuanians, Ruthenians, Jews, Armenians, Tatars, Germans, and lesser numbers of Hungarians, Italians and Scots.

The difference between the Polish view of things and that governing other states became very clear at the Council of Constance in 1414. This had been meant to deal with purely religious matters, but soon turned into a discussion about jurisdiction, relations between church and state, and the laws governing interstate relations. This shift in emphasis was brought about mainly by the Polish delegation, led by the rector of Kraków university, Paweł Włodkowic (Paulus Vladimiri). In his indictment of the Teutonic Order, which had charged the kingdom of Poland with supporting pagans against Christian states, he argued that since every man is a son of God, every man has certain "natural" rights, whatever his religion. It therefore followed that every state, which was no more than a community of people, had certain "natural" rights as well, and that these rights should be inviolate, even to supposedly higher agencies such as the papacy or a concert of Christian European states. His colleague, another professor of Kraków university, Stanisław of Skalbmierz, took this further, arguing that all international relations should, like those between individuals, be governed by universal laws. The Poles were turning into the awkward squad, out of step with the rest of the European regiment. But during the sixteenth century it looked as though that step might change.

Polish society embraced the art and learning of the Renaissance with greater enthusiasm than did most nations, particularly in northern Europe. The idea that reconnecting with the intellectual and aesthetic achievements of the classical world would give rise to a new international cultural space, defined by reason and eternal artistic rules, was appealing. It raised the possibility of arriving at a system by which the states of Europe could coexist in greater harmony, based on the application of Aristotelian principles. Thinkers and writers such as Erasmus of Rotterdam found a great following in Poland, where many embraced his view of the world, and were eagerly trying to implement it.

Poland was already, to all intents and purposes, a very loosely federated constitutional monarchy with extensive civil liberties. The only cement binding it together was the monarchy itself. When the reigning dynasty died out, in 1572, it became necessary to replace it.

What the Poles did put in its place was a political experiment of extraordinary ambition and originality: the Commonwealth. This was essentially a republic with a king elected by universal suffrage of the nobility, who were the political nation. He reigned but could not rule without the support of a parliament consisting of two chambers: an elected Sejm and a senate. Civil and religious liberties were guaranteed, as were the legal rights of all minorities, to the extent that over a dozen languages were allowed to be used in a court of law.

It was more than a constitutional arrangement: it was the embodiment of a political culture which had been evolving gradually over the centuries, one built on the rights of the individual, based on local assemblies which elected deputies to the national congress. And embedded in it was the layering of loyalty according to personal circumstances. A man could be *civis Polonus*, *natione Lithuanus*, *gente Ruthenus*, which meant that he was ethnically Ruthene, came from the Grand Duchy of Lithuania, and was a Polish citizen. He might add to this another layer of self-definition, that of religion, which introduced a further division of loyalty.

The theological disputes that rent the Christian church during the Reformation were well represented, with every conceivable sect finding refuge in Poland. As well as being home to large colonies of Muslim Tatars, it had also become a haven for Jews who had been progressively forced out of most European states since the end of the thirteenth century. By the sixteenth, the overwhelming majority of all the Jews in the world had settled and built up their own institutions there, with the result that from then on the history of Poland became inextricably linked with that of the Jewish diaspora.

Such a society could only function given a fundamental consensus and large doses of idealism, or perhaps naïvety. But, in spite of a great deal of vociferous quarrelling, function it did, for a time.

The problem with this utopian arrangement was that it was predicated on the idea that others must hold the same values. In a work entitled *O naprawie Rzeczypospolitej*, published in 1554, Andrzej Frycz Modrzewski argued that unjustifiable war should be recognized as a crime, and that there should be an international court of judges to intervene when tensions between states began mounting in order to prevent conflict breaking out.

Ironically, the following century, the seventeenth, was to see some of the worst bloodshed in Europe as wars of religion engulfed most of the Continent. These wars hardly affected Poland, which continued along its own chosen path regardless. This was not conducive to the development of a strong political unit, and Poland soon found herself surrounded by states with larger armies and deeper war chests. This was to have fatal consequences, particularly when the system itself began to malfunction.

The ensuing period, from the mid-seventeenth to the mid-eighteenth centuries, is traditionally viewed as that of the country's great decline, both moral and physical. The majority of Polish society took the view (motivated more by reluctance to pay taxes and the fear of absolutist government than by any political philosophy) that central government is a bad thing, that state organs inevitably encroach on personal liberties, that standing armies are a threat to these, and that most of the needs of society could be dealt with at the local level, with the necessary taxes set, militias raised, and judges elected by regional assemblies. They carried this so far that, abusing a deputy's right to veto legislation, they managed to immobilize the nation's legislative and executive body and render the king powerless. For a time, Poland virtually ceased to function as a state at all. While the rest of Europe mocked, the supporters of this view held that this was her greatest safeguard, arguing that since she threatened nobody, her neighbors had no reason to attack her.

Many could see the fallacy of this but clung to idealistic solutions. One of the most prominent, the ex-king of Poland and subsequent king of Lorraine Stanisław Leszczyński, saw in the great philosophical revolution taking place in Europe in the first half of the eighteenth century a chance to move away from the pattern of continual wars and to build a political space in which peace and civil liberties could thrive. In 1748 he wrote a memorandum on the subject which he himself called "a Utopian, pan-European project."

Others abandoned such traditionally utopian views and opted for a total overhaul of the whole system that would turn Poland into a modern state that could stand on its own, with a proper administration and army. They sought to reeducate the nation and to marry the best Polish political traditions to the ideas of the European Enlightenment in order to create robust political structures. This was no easy task, made no easier by the fact that Poland's powerful neighbors interfered in order to prevent her from becoming an effective state. But under the leadership of King Stanisław II Augustus, in the space of a few decades the reformers did manage to transform the country. Their reforms took in the state administration, the fiscal system, the coinage, the law, the army, infrastructure, industry and canals, and, most important, the creation of a nationwide modern educational system. All this was to have a fundamental influence on what would happen to Poland and the Poles over the next two hundred years.

The American War of Independence and particularly the French Revolution of 1789 had a greater resonance in Poland than almost anywhere else in Europe. They were seen as kindred movements, emanations of the same old Polish ideals of liberty, and harbingers of a new dawn presaging a place in the sun for the renewed Poland. A major landmark in that process of renewal was the voting by the Sejm of a new constitution in 1791. But the following year Russia invaded and Poland was partitioned among her three neighbors, initiating a curious new stage in her history, that of a nation without a state.

A struggle for the recovery of independence

began almost immediately. Yet the "national insurrection" that broke out under the leadership of Tadeusz Kościuszko in 1794 was in effect as much an extension of the French Revolution and part of a universal war against despotism as a purely national struggle. Thus at the very moment when the cause of Polish national liberation was born it had an internationalist element to it.

Perhaps more important, it had a profoundly spiritual base. The faith in sacrifice to the motherland was intensified by the fact that it had been ravished and murdered, giving it a Christ-like aura which demanded not vengeance but selfless devotion. The nation these patriots were fighting for was based not on ethnic or religious or political parameters (how could it have been, given the multi ethnic and religious makeup of the Polish Commonwealth?) but on a somewhat poetic and spiritual imagining of the Polish community.

The disappearance of Poland from the map coincided with the birth of the Romantic Movement and a flowering of art, music, and literature, all of which was dedicated to the cause of restoring a Polish state. Revolutionary activity and uprisings went hand in hand with this — the paintings of Piotr Michałowski, the music of Fryderyk Chopin, and the poems of Adam Mickiewicz are simply the most eminent and striking examples. Mickiewicz actually turned the Polish cause into a redemptive religion for the whole of humanity, and over the next hundred years Poles would take part in every single national liberation movement or revolution in the Western world, always under the slogan "For our freedom and yours." These supranationalist ideas persisted even in the face of mounting nationalist pressures on all sides.

From the moment they seized their pieces of the old Polish state, all three partitioning powers made it to a lesser or greater extent their policy to destroy Poland as a national organism. The Austrians adopted ostensibly the least aggressive approach, by trying to drive a wedge between the gentry and intelligentsia on the one hand and the peasantry on the other. The Russians concentrated on heavy-handed methods of reducing the influence of the Catholic Church and eradicating the Polish language. The Prussians applied the most extreme policies, underpinned by arguments of German racial superiority, banning the use of Polish speech in public, using economic sanctions against Polish farmers and producers, and bringing in large numbers of German colonists who were supposed to gradually turn their share of the former Polish state into a bastion of Germandom.

Not surprisingly, these threats provoked a number of initiatives in defense of Polish nationality, centered on the language, history, and literature. With the emergence of ethnic self-awareness among the Lithuanians, Belorussians and Ukrainians, and the political mobilization of the Jewish population in the area, which split between the rival movements of Zionism and the socialist Bund, by the end of the nineteenth and the beginning of the twentieth centuries a new trend in Polish nationalism began to call for a more ethnically based and defensive vision of Polishness. This was not as biological or doctrinaire, let alone as violent, as similar movements in other European countries, most notably France and Germany, but it did show some of the same symptoms — the ugliest of them being widespread anti-Semitism. Yet this trend remained in the shadow of the continuing Romantic tradition, as embodied by the political giant of the day, Józef Piłsudski, who saw himself as fighting not just for Poland, but for a free Lithuania, Belarus, and Ukraine as well, and a comfortable homeland for all the minorities inhabiting the area, particularly the Jews.

The independent Polish state that emerged after 1918 was very much of its time in most respects, and its political trajectory resembled that of many other European countries of the period: imperfect democracy gave way to authoritarian government with a preponderant influence of the army; political oppositionists, particularly socialists and communists, were persecuted, anti-Semitism thrived, the Ukrainian minority was harshly treated, and so on.

But one of the most striking aspects of the period of independence between 1918 and 1939 is the way in which Polish society, including large proportions of those who were of Lithuanian, Ukrainian, Jewish, and German origin, asserted itself to create not the most efficient *state* but a very strong and highly successful *community*, whose achievements in the spheres of social benefits, education, emancipation of women, and so on are quite remarkable. And so was the richly avant-garde literary and artistic flowering. The traditions of past centuries reappeared in strength, which was to prove providential.

From the first days of their invasion of Poland, on September 1 and 17, 1939, respectively, Nazi Germany and Soviet Russia set in motion astonishingly similar programs aimed at destroying the very existence of the Polish nation. They were based on the decapitation of society through the liquidation of political, religious, and social elites; the undermining of social solidarity by setting one group or minority against another; and the gradual murder or brutalization of the masses. Through its client regime in Poland, the Soviet Union was able to carry on this work even after the cessation of hostilities in 1945. In addition, between 1939 and the mid-1950s the whole area was methodically ethnically cleansed of its minorities — Jewish, Ukrainian, German, and the rest.

But while all this succeeded in wiping out a huge proportion of the population and tearing apart the sinews of civil society, these processes did not manage to destroy the national sense of community that had grown up prior to 1939. Throughout the period of communist rule, up to 1989, that community manifested itself in various ways, coalescing around the Church and any other institutions that were allowed to exist, continuously asserting its values even within the parameters set by the communist regime.

It drew moral and financial support from émigré communities around the world, in centers such as London, Paris, New York, Chicago, Buenos Aires — communities which themselves created elaborate self-support systems, with their own universities, schools, free press, and publishing houses, not to mention both charitable and commercial institutions providing everything from health care to professional guidance. At the apex of this emigration stood the Polish government-in-exile in London, at the very least a symbol of resistance and continuity.

When, after 1989, the Polish people did recover a state that they could call their own, they did not hold back on celebrating all the symbols of sovereignty. But in contrast to almost all the other countries emerging from under Soviet domination following 1989, mainstream Polish society adopted a supranationalist outlook. This manifested itself in large-scale migrations, not just for work but also for study, and an enthusiastic response to the opportunities offered by membership of the European Union and of NATO. It also resulted in a marked diminution of what had in effect been largely political support for the Catholic Church. It was also strikingly in evidence with regard to eastern neighbors whose territories include areas that had once been Polish and contain sizable Polish minorities. Within weeks of its formation in September 1989, the Polish government initiated diplomatic relations with what were then still the Soviet Republics of Lithuania, Belarus, and Ukraine as though they were already sovereign states, declaring that it recognized their possession of formerly Polish territory and authority over their Polish subjects. This was entirely in conformity with the age-old Polish view that boundaries matter less than the people who live on either side of them. For it is as difficult today as it ever was to define with any precision where Poland begins and ends.

Any brief overview of a thousand years in the history of a country or a people cannot escape the charge of being facile. It cannot help but leave out much that is both creditable and discreditable, much that is positive and much that is negative, fail to address a number of major issues, and generally lay itself open to criticism. But short of writing a whole book on the subject, I can see no better way of introducing a novice into that curious sphere that is "Poland" than by sketching some of the characteristics of those that inhabit it — those characteristics which I believe have defined them, shaped their history, and allowed them to survive so many defeats, a good many of which were self-inflicted. More than most nations, it is first and foremost a community, and in many ways, Poland is best considered more as a state of mind than as a place or a nation.

This book is full of insights into that state of mind. As such, it is an absolute must for anyone meaning to visit the country, do business there, or gain some idea of what has been going on in that part of the world for centuries — in an accessible and pleasurable way. But its usefulness is by no means confined to novices. Even after decades of living with and struggling to understand what "Poland" really is, I will be quietly dipping into it to find out things I never got round to inquiring about.

Preface

Poland celebrated the twenty-fifth anniversary of its emergence from communism on June 4, 2014. After the "partially free" elections of June 1989, and the "free" ones of 1990, Poland has emerged in the twenty-first century as a regular Western European country of nearly thirty-eight million people, eventually a member of NATO and the European Union, and is today an economic powerhouse with a firm sense of where it has been, what it is doing now, and where it is going. Since it first emerged on the pages of history in 966, Poland's territories have radically ebbed and flowed, and its fate has waxed and waned, but it has never lost its sense of cultural identity. With Poland having survived its often tumultuous history into the twenty-first century as a state intact, with a raison d'être that has never been stronger, now is a good time to trace the outlines of what it is that crucially comprises Polish history and culture, in its aspects both sublime and mundane.

The *Kaleidoscope of Poland* contains short articles on major events, personages, commonplaces, and accomplishments from the more than thousand-year-old record of Polish history and culture, along with a selection of articles on lesser-known but equally noteworthy Polish-related topics. The name "Polska" (Poland) has at its root the word *pole* (field), but in fact the country is much more geographically diverse than the word implies. Accordingly, much attention is devoted here to the country's physical characteristics — its rivers, lakes, seacoast, mountains, wildlife, climate — and also its ethnicities. In all, this book gathers together around one thousand capsules of knowledge about Poland that are known to many or most Poles, but which will probably be unfamiliar to people outside the country, no matter how generally well educated they might be. Some relate to "high" culture, others to "low," some to old culture, and others to new. In all, there are about as many entries here as there are years of Polish history — 1,048, counting back from 2014 to 966 AD, when the Polanian prince Mieszko I accepted Christianity from Czech missionaries.

This book can be used for reference, or it can be read from cover to cover, as I hope most people will do. It will be of particular interest to tourists and foreign residents in Poland who want to acquire a broader context for the many unfamiliar cultural terms they will encounter while in the country. Many topics are contained within other topics, greatly adding to the overall topical coverage; for example, the *warszawska pielgrzymka* (Warsaw pilgrimage to Częstochowa) — Poland's longest regularly-held religious walk — is described under the town Częstochowa — an encouragement for the reader to cover this work page by page rather than topic by topic, and to liberally consult the cross-referencing index, both Polish–English and English–Polish, at the end before deciding that an item is missing.

The *Kaleidoscope* is appropriate as a supplementary text in courses on Polish history, literature, culture, and in Polish-language courses, where increasing emphasis is placed on not only linguistic but also cultural fluency. Both tourists and serious students of Polish culture will want to know, for example, that the *bajgiel* (bagel) was developed in Kraków; that the Polish army uses the world's only two-finger salute; that Europe's largest bat sanctuary is in an abandoned Nazi system of underground bunkers, now on Polish soil; that the international word *vodka* ultimately comes, via Russia, from Polish *wódka*; and so on.

Poles seem to have a greater affinity for accumulating and making use of points of shared knowledge about their country's history, culture, and geography — so-called cultural *topoi*, or commonplaces — than do people of many other nationalities. For example, many Poles would be able to reel off a list of their country's highest mountain peaks, something few Americans would be able to do for their country. To an outsider it sometimes seems as though Poles are able to communicate with one another in a secret code by relying on their store of common points of historical knowledge. Polish journalists are notorious for using without explanation phrases like *ksiądz Ściegienny* (Father Ściegienny), *pięść Gołoty* (Gołota's fist), or *wóz Drzymały* (Drzymała's wagon), confident that a typical readership will know who or what is meant. Newcomers to Poland invariably have trouble remembering whether a given *powstanie* (national uprising) was the *listopadowe* (November) one, or the *styczniowe* (January) one; or which *wydarzenia* ("incidents," i.e., official code for political protest riots) were *marcowe* (March), *grudniowe* (December), *sierpniowe* (August), or *czerwcowe* (June). To the extent that such terms, opaque to the outsider, are identified and explained here, this work functions as a Polish "cultural decoder."

A certain number of entries have been included on the basis of the author's personal judgment as to an item's inherent interest, whether or not it is known to the average person on the Polish street. For example, the *Kaleidoscope* becomes richer through the inclusion of Elżbieta Drużbacka (ca. 1695–1765), the first Polish woman writer of note and an early feminist; Jakub Frank (1726–1791), the colorful founder of a breakaway mystical Jewish sect; and Wanda Landowska (1879–1959), who more or less single-handedly rescued the harpsichord from oblivion. Other names are chosen from among cultural figures known to almost everyone in Poland. There are so many of them that painful decisions had to be made regarding whom to include. Among those not making the cut, but who arguably could have, was Izabela Lubomirska, the "blue marquise," one of the richest women in eighteenth-century Europe, founder of a distillery that is still in existence, who at one point owned, among other palatial residences, the immense baroque palace in Wilanów, one of Poland's most valued architectural treasures, and who sent her laundry to be done in Paris (wouldn't we all like to?). In the final analysis, being extravagantly rich was judged not to count as a ticket of admission. A more recent candidate on the wrong side of the cusp of inclusion was computer visionary Jacek Karpiński (1927–2010), whose minicomputer, operating system, and digital scanner were a dozen or so years ahead of their time, but who never got financial backing because of bureaucratic wrangling in communist Poland's centralized planning system. Karpiński was simply born in the wrong country, or, let us say, in the right country at the wrong time. Many figures are ones most Poles would just as soon forget — for example, gray ghosts from Poland's communist past like Bolesław Bierut, Konstanty Rokossowski, or Mieczysław Moczar.

My areas of relative expertise are Polish language, literature, film, and "culture." Specifically, it is not history. However, several historians have read and commented on the manuscript, and I am fairly confident that thanks to their help I have not done any major injustice to this subject. At the same time I stress that I am not concerned with presenting the latest interpretation of the many chestnuts in the fireplace of Polish history. Rather, I have endeavored to convey the traditional things that Poles know about their history from having learned them in school. I have no interest here in undermining, say, Tadeusz Kościuszko's role as leader of the first major Polish national insurrection, or in delving into the true motivations behind the peasant Bartosz Głowacki's snuffing out the wick of his captured cannon in Kościuszko's uprising.

Of course, what a Pole has "learned in school" can be radically different depending on whether he or she went to school before or after the fall of communism in 1989, and in such instances I try to be responsive to what is being taught currently.

I have tried not to let this work turn into just another tourist guide, but I nevertheless felt that certain aspects of Polish reality were worth highlighting or cataloguing on their own merits, for example, popular kinds of Polish *grzyby* (mushrooms) or *pierogi*, the things one can buy in a *kiosk*, or trends in Polish store names. Additionally, it was felt that certain prominent features of the Polish language itself — such as its wildly complicated numeral system, its system of grammatical cases, or its unique category of "masculine personal nouns" — deserved comment. Since language is the entry point to much of what counts as culture, whenever specific terms are involved, I give both the Polish word and its English correspondent, for example, *oświecenie* (the Enlightenment), *Środa Popielcowa* (Ash Wednesday), *gest Kozakiewicza* (Kozakiewicz's gesture), and so on. In general I try to use Polish proper names wherever possible, making an exception mainly in the instance of the capital city Warsaw.

To aid readability and ease of reference, entries are short, on the level of a brief encyclopedia entry or an extended dictionary definition. In addition to the limit of one thousand entries — more or less — I aimed for 150 words as the limit for an entry's length, even on such outsized topics as the Second World War, Polish-Jewish relations, or the Polish educational or banking systems; and I often trimmed or split entries to aim for this limit, which I ended up having to relax in many instances. The reader should not infer any valuational implications from the length of entries. Often minor topics are more in need of detailed explanation than major ones.

One may occasionally be struck by the accidental juxtaposition of entries. For example, the eminent fifteenth-century chronicler Jan Długosz is sandwiched here between the 1980s *disco polo* dance craze on the one hand and the interwar right-wing politician Roman Dmowski on the other. Political activist and newspaper publisher Adam Michnik appears next to the national bard Adam Mickiewicz. Such juxtapositions, in which all of Polish history and culture from its beginnings to the present day are jumbled together — mirroring Polish contemporary cultural reality — gave rise to the description of the present work as a *kalejdoskop* (kaleidoscope). Within this framework, I have endeavored to make sure that each individual entry is well researched, accurate, and representative of the composite thing that is Polska.

Almost any of the topics chosen here for brief description could be expanded into a full-length book, and many have been. Even *niedźwiedź Wojtek* (Wojtek the Bear) has had half a dozen books written about him. The *Kaleidoscope* gives only a topic's barest outline, an encouragement to its fuller investigation elsewhere. I ask for the reader's indulgence if some particular topic of interest has not been selected; if one or another favorite subject has not been fleshed out to his or her satisfaction; or if some topic of special interest to the author does not awaken in the reader the same amount of enthusiasm.

Finally, I am cognizant of the topicality and ephemerality of some of the *Kaleidoscope*'s entries on recent popular culture. As a visitor to Poland since 1967, I am well aware how things once considered virtually iconic of the country can quickly pass into oblivion — for example, *książeczki autostopowe* (hitchhiking booklets), elevator keys, or returnable seltzer water siphons. Nevertheless I felt it was important to describe here the characteristic aspects of Poland as it exists in the summer of 2014, without worrying overly about whether, say, Doda's love life may have undergone radical transformation by the time this book falls into the hands of a future reader; or whether Wilhelm Sasnal, to take only one example, may have been dropped by fickle art critics.

Acknowledgments

The *Kaleidoscope* originally grew out of my online Polish–English dictionary, of which Nicholas Reimer was and still is the highly skilled and creative programmer. There came a point when I realized that many of the words and phrases I was collecting required more by way of cultural or historical commentary than lexical, and that they merited placement in their own dedicated work. The draft for this work was completed under a generous fellowship from the Międzynarodowe Centrum Kultury (International Center of Culture) in Kraków, Professor Jacek Purchla, director. I am grateful to many people for taking an interest in this project and generously devoting their time to reading entries and both suggesting new ones and correcting existing ones, but above all to the following persons: Ewa Bachmińska (Poznań/Utica), Katarzyna Dziwirek (Łódź/Seattle), Monika Franczak (Kraków), Mirosław Koziarski (Szczecin), Bogusław Kubiak (Opole), Tomasz Łysak (Warsaw), Robert Rothstein (Amherst), Izolda Wolski-Moskoff (Warsaw/Columbus), and three superb but anonymous readers for the University of Pittsburgh Press. Finally, the manuscript was vetted by a panel of Polish experts in their fields in the course of the symposium "Recovering Forgotten History," sponsored by Łazarski University of Warsaw and the Ministerstwo Kultury i Dziedzictwa Narodowego (Ministry of Culture and National Heritage), among others, held in Kraków in May 2012. The incredibly generous and meticulous commentators on my work were Krzysztof Łazarski (Warsaw), Andrzej Nowak (Kraków), and Jakub Tyszkiewicz (Wrocław). Thanks especially to Professor Andrzej Kamiński of Georgetown University for including this work for discussion at this conference. The index was compiled with the help of Sophia Hinkle with support from the University of Pittsburgh's Russian and East European Studies Center.

Unless otherwise noted, photographs and illustrations are taken from Wikimedia Commons, which is a wonderful resource. The pencil drawings of Polish rulers are from Jan Matejko's *Poczet królów i książąt polskich* (Gallery of Polish Kings and Princes, 1891–1892); and many additional illustrations come from Matejko's prodigious output. Other work is given credit to the extent possible. Polish spelling and orthography follow the choices made by the Polskie Wydawnictwo Naukowe (Polish Academic Publishers) on its web-based Portal Wiedzy.

My main cultural consultant on this project, Ewa Kołaczek-Fila of Kraków, on whose editorial assistance, critical commentary, and cultural acumen I rely throughout, could practically claim the rights of a coauthor. She contributed to the better elucidation of many items, ruthlessly critiqued my style and occasional habit of treating certain serious topics too lightly, made a number of suggestions for new entries (like *Biała Dama*, "White Lady," and *śpiący ryczerze*, "slumbering knights"), and vetoed certain favorites of mine, such as the 1960s Bytom rock-and-roll singing sensation Karin Stanek. She was overruled in the case of the flamboyant Violetta Villas and occasionally elsewhere. In short, ultimate responsibility for the text, editorial decisions, and for any remaining inaccuracies, are mine alone, but Ms. Fila's dedication to this project was crucial to its seeing the light of day, and I am forever grateful to her.

Polish Pronunciation

Polish sounds are not hard to produce, but the orthography can be daunting. The reader unfamiliar with the sounds of Polish should refer to this brief overview by bits, in reference to selected names and terms of interest.

These letters are pronounced more or less as their English equivalents are: *b, d, f, g, k, l, m, n, p, s, t, z*.

Vowel Sounds

The Polish vowels have only one pronunciation. Except for the nasal vowels ę and ą, which are long, vowels are all of the same short length. They are not glided, as *o*, *u*, and *i* are in English.

a	like *a* in f*a*ther: t*a*k, "yes"
e	like *e* in b*e*t: l*e*k, "medicine"
i	like *ee* in cr*ee*k: pl*i*k, "file"
o	like *o* in c*o*ke: l*o*t, "flight"
u, ó	like *oo* in l*oo*t: l*u*t, "soldier"; lód, "ice" (these words are both pronounced the same)
y	like *i* in p*i*t: b*y*t, "existence," rhymes with *bit*
ą	like *om* before *p, b*: dąb [domp], "oak"
	like *on* before *t, d*: kąt [kont], "corner"
	like *ong* (ŋ) before *k, g*: mąka [moŋka], "flour"
	otherwise like the nasal vowel in French *sont*: są, "they are"
ę	like *em* before p, b: sęp [semp], "vulture"
	like *en* before t, d: tętno [tentno], "pulse"
	like *eng* (ŋ) before k, g: lęk [leŋk], "fear"
	otherwise like the nasal vowel in French *vin*, "wine": kęs, "bite"
	ę is pronounced like *e* in final position: chcę [chce], "I want"

XXIII

Consonant Sounds

c	like *ts*: *c*o [tso]
ch and *h*	like German *h*alt, but not as harsh: *ch*yba, "probably"
cz	like *ch* in *ch*alk: *cz*as "time"
j	like *y* in *y*oke: *j*ak, "how"
ł	like *w* in *w*ish: *ł*yk, "swallow" (rhymes with *w*ick); da*ł*, "he gave" (rhymes with *c*ow)
r	lightly trilled, as in Spanish: *r*ok, "year"
w	like *v* in *v*at: *W*awel, "Wawel"
rz and *ż*	like *s* in trea*s*ure: mo*rz*e, "sea"; mo*ż*e, "maybe" (pronounced the same)
sz	like *sh* in *sh*ould: *sz*um, "noise"

The Consonant Spellings

ć, ci-	like "soft" *ch*, more or less like *ch*eek: *ć*ma, "moth," *ci*cho, "quiet"
dź, dzi-	like "soft" *j*, more or less like *J*eep: wie*dź*ma, "witch," *dzi*k, "boar"
ś, si-	like "soft" *sh*, more or less like *sh*eet: *ś*miech, "laughter"; *si*to, "sieve"
ź, zi-	like "soft" *zh*, more or less like *z* in a*z*ure: *ź*le, "badly"; *zi*ma "winter"
ń, ni-	like "soft" *n*, more or less like *ny* in ca*ny*on: koń, "horse"; *ni*e, "not"

Voiced consonants are devoiced in final position, so that **b**, **d**, **dź**, **g**, **w**, **z**, **ź**, **rz/ż** are pronounced, respectively, as **p**, **t**, **ć**, **k**, **f**, **s**, **ś**, **sz**; see ług [łuk], "lye"; paw [paf], "peacock"; nóż [nusz] "knife"; and so on.

Timeline of Polish History

840–900	The rise of Polanian tribes around Gniezno and the formation of the Piast dynasty.
966	*chrzest Polski* (Christianization of Poland). Acceptance of Christianity by Mieszko I.
1138–1320	*rozbicie dzielnicowe* (division into districts), according to the testament of Bolesław the Wrymouth.
1333–1370	*Kazimierz Wielki*. The reign of Kazimierz the Great, the last of the Piast rulers.
1377–1596	*Jagiellonowie*. The Jagiellonian dynasty.
1410	*bitwa pod Grunwaldem* (Battle of Grunwald). Polish forces defeat the Teutonic Knights under King Władysław II Jagiełło.
1569	*unia lubelska* (Union of Lublin). The Polish-Lithuanian Commonwealth is formed during the reign of King Zygmunt II August.
1655–1660	*potop szwedzki* (Swedish Deluge). Wars with Sweden devastate the country.
1683	*odsiecz wiedeńska* (Relief of Vienna). King Jan III Sobieski leads a multinational army to defeat Turkish troops besieging Vienna.
1772, 1773, 1795	*rozbiory* (the partitions). Three successive partitions divide Poland among Russia, Prussia, and Austria. Poland disappears as an independent state.
1794	*insurekcja kościuszkowska* (Kościuszko Insurrection). Tadeusz Kościuszko fails in his revolt against Russia.
1807–1815	*Księstwo Warszawskie* (Duchy of Warsaw). A small client state of France is created by Napoleon.
1815–1831	*Królestwo Kongresowe* (Congress Kingdom). Following Napoleon's defeat in Russia, a Russian-controlled Polish puppet state is created at the Congress of Vienna.
1830–1831	*powstanie listopadowe* (November Uprising). Following the uprising's fall, Poland becomes increasingly administratively incorporated into the Russian Empire.
1863–1864	*powstanie styczniowe* (January Uprising). The brutally crushed revolt leads to mass repression, expropriation of property, and emigration.
1918	*traktat wersalski* (Versailles Treaty). Poland regains statehood following World War I.
1919–1921	*wojna polsko-bolszewicka* (Polish-Bolshevik War). Recently arisen Poland successfully beats back an invading Bolshevik army.
1939–1945	*druga wojna światowa* (World War II). Hitler's invasion of Poland touches off World War II. The 1939 Molotov-Ribbentrop Pact divides Poland between Germany and Russia.

1945	*konferencja jałtańska* (Yalta Conference). Poland is ceded by the great powers to the Soviet sphere of influence. The eastern *kresy* (borderlands) are ceded to the Soviet Union, while German territory in the west is given to Poland.
1945	*konferencja poczdamski* (Potsdam Conference). Poland's western border is set at the Oder-Neisse line, creating the so-called "recovered territories," formerly belonging to Germany.
1947	*wybory 1947* (1947 elections). Falsified elections install a communist government.
1952–1989	*Polska Rzeczpospolita Ludowa (PRL)*. The official years of "communist Poland."
1956, 1968, 1970, 1988	*rozruchy, strajki, protesty* (major workers' and student protests and strikes).
1978	Cardinal Karol Wojtyła is elected Pope John Paul II.
1981–1983	*stan wojenny* (martial law). The Solidarity trade union is outlawed and its leaders are interned. Lech Wałęsa wins the Nobel Peace Prize in 1983.
1989	*rozmowy Okrągłego Stołu* (roundtable discussions). Discussions lead to power-sharing between communists and the opposition, and the office of president is reconstituted.
1990	*wolne wybory* (free elections). Lech Wałęsa is elected the first post-communist president of Poland.
2004	*Unia Europejska*. Poland's accession to the European Union.
2010	*katastrofa pod Smoleńskiem* (Smolensk air disaster). Ninety-six people, including President Lech Kaczyński and his wife and most of the Polish General Staff, perish in a bad-weather air crash near Smoleńsk, Belarus.

Note about the Entries

An encyclopedia is something that can be read just as easily from back to front or front to back. However, one of the features that distinguishes the *Kaleidoscope* is its elaborate system of **blue-tinged cross-references**, encouraging the curious reader to "dip in" to the *Kaleidoscope* at any point and read it in a zig-zag, following the cross-references, which are supplemental to the English and Polish indexes at the back of the book, wherever they lead. The system looks a bit like Wikipedia's hyperlinks, which are also **highlighted in blue**, but here the cross-references circle around to eventually converge on the thing that is Poland. They are inspired by the sense that everything in Polish history and culture one way or another, sooner or later, leads to everything else.

Kaleidoscope of
POLAND

A

"Ala ma kota" (Ala has a cat). The first line of a famous Polish *elementarz* (ABC book) by Marian Falski, first appearing in 1910, and periodically renewed and updated to the present day — over eighty editions in all. It was the first Polish children's book to be published after World War II. In addition to the traditional stories of Ala, Ola, Janek, and the merry dog As (Ace), the 1945 edition added references to soldiers returning home and families resettling to the so-called *ziemie odzyskane* (recovered territories) in the west. References to the Falski reader occur everywhere. A recent one appeared in the film *Rewers* (Reverse), Poland's candidate for the 2009 Oscars, in which the villain seducer Falski is asked by the mother of the shy young woman who is a book editor whether he is related to the famous Falski. A popular contemporary series of books for teenagers by Małgorzata Budzyńska, written in the form of notes taken by a thirteen-year-old "Ala Makota," cleverly builds on the title.

Alibabki. A wholesome female popular vocal group originating out of the *harcerstwo* (scouting) movement, the Alibabki had their recording debut in 1963 and their heyday through the 1970s, officially disbanding in 1988. Their name is based on a pun: besides connoting Ali Baba and the stories of Scheherezade, *babka* can mean "lass." They might remind Americans of the Lennon Sisters of *The Lawrence Welk Show*. Often appearing as a backup group for headliners, they are sometimes used in period film soundtracks to lend the flavor of the 1960s–1970s. Among their best-known songs are "Kwiat jednej nocy" (One-night flower) and "Kapitańskie tango" (Captain's tango). Their "Przeleć mnie," based on a racy double entendre, made people think twice about their carefully cultivated wholesome image. A similar but less long-lasting group of this time were the Filipinki, coming out of Szczecin.

Anders, Władysław (1892–1970). A profile in honor. Commander of a cavalry brigade at the start of World War II, General Anders was captured and imprisoned by the Soviets. Following the *układ Sikorski-Majski* (Sikorski-Majski Pact, 1941), he was allowed to form a Polish army, one of the few people ever able to hold his own when negotiating head-to-head with Joseph Stalin. Friction with the Soviets led to his army's evacuation, along with some twenty to fifty thousand Polish civilians (estimates vary), through Azerbaijan into Iraq and Palestine, where in 1943 he formed the II Korpus Polski (Second Polish Corps) out of detachments of Polish soldiers fighting across north Africa. The corps numbered around fifty thousand when it was shifted to the Italian campaign in 1944, independently capturing Ancona and crucially helping the British to achieve victory at Monte Cassino, suffering heavy losses. By this time Anders and his men were fighting only for their honor, no longer for their country, as the *kresy wschodnie* (eastern borderlands) whence most came had been ceded to Stalin by the United States and Great Britain at the Tehran Conference (*konferencja teherańska*) of 1943. In 1946 Anders and most of his men were demobilized and stayed permanently in Great Britain, for which the Polish government stripped him of his citizenship. To appease Stalin the British shamefully did not allow Anders's troops to participate in their victory parade. He is buried, according to his wishes, with his men in the Polish cemetery at Monte Cassino. See also: mak; Wojtek, niedźwiedź Wojtek.

Andrzejewski, Jerzy (1909–1983). One of the most important postwar Polish writers, Andrzejewski got his start as a Catholic author before the war, but later joined the communist bandwagon in the 1950s to subsequently become one of the most active spokesmen for the democratic opposition in the 1970–1980s. At all periods his characters face moral choices in a shifting world. His short story "Złoty lis" (The gold fox), about the stifling of the imagination of the young by the socialist ideology, heralded the Polish *odwilż* (thaw). As a novelist of the 1970–1980s, Andrzejewski experimented with new narrative forms. Two of his works were turned into films by Andrzej Wajda, the classic *Popiół i diament* (Ashes and diamonds, 1958), about the postwar communist takeover, and the less well-known novella *Wielki Tydzień* (Easter week, 1995), about the powstanie w getcie warszawskim (Warsaw Ghetto Uprising) of 1943.

andrzejki (Saint Andrew's Eve, November 29). A young people's party with games held at the end of the Church calendar, the last time to celebrate loudly before the beginning of Advent.

Historically, *andrzejki* were girls' parties at which any of a dozen or so fortune-telling methods were used to predict marriage and husbands. The corresponding night for men used to be *katarzynki* (Saint Catherine's Eve, November 24), but it has fallen out of fashion. A popular fortune-telling method is *lanie wosku*, the dripping of melted candlewax through the eye of a key into cold water, then casting the shadow from the wax shape upon a wall (pictured) to interpret its symbolism. Another method is to leapfrog all the left shoes of the party over one another from the front of the house to the back, with the first shoe over the rear threshold signaling the one most likely to get married. It works.

Antek. In a story that is known (or used to be) to every Polish schoolchild, the bright young protagonist in an 1880 positivist (i.e., progressive and philanthropical) story by Bolesław Prus (1847–1912) tries to overcome the limiting circumstances of being born in a backwards nineteenth-century Polish village. At the end, his uncertain future lies before him as he heads out of the village for the city. A less fortunate nineteenth-century childhood literary character is Janko Muzykant (Janko the Musician), the pathetic underdeveloped boy in an 1879 short story by Henryk Sienkiewicz, who has a natural talent for music, but is beaten to death for theft by a constable when the curious Janko takes the manor-house butler's fiddle off its hook. "Antek" was made into a 1971 television film (a still is pictured) by Wojciech Fiwek.

Apel Jasnogórski (Jasna Góra Appeal). Part of the *Jasnogórskie śluby narodu polskiego* (Jasna Góra Vows of the Polish Nation, written by Cardinal Stefan Wyszyński), the Apel is a brief prayer directed to the Matka Boska Królowa Polski (Mother of God, Queen of Poland), recited daily at 9:00 p.m. at the Jasna Góra monastery in Częstochowa on behalf of the Polish nation, begun in 1953. The prayer is recited on the thirteenth of the month in most Polish churches, and it is broadcast daily by church-affiliated radio and television stations. Its main words: "Maryjo, Królowo Polski, jestem przy Tobie, pamiętam, czuwam" (Mary, Queen of Poland, I am with you, I remember you, I am vigilant).

araby, polskie konie arabskie (Polish Arabian horses). Few nations enjoy as high a reputation as horse-breeders as Poland with its Polish Arabians, whose breeding stock with its carefully maintained bloodlines traces back to the eastern estates of the wealthy eighteenth-century magnates. The offspring of the three state-owned stud farms — the oldest being in Janów Podlaski — command staggering prices from the *sławni i bogaci* (rich and famous) at yearly auctions. They were an important source of hard-currency income during the PRL (communist Poland). Prices of over $200,000 are typical; the record-holder was the *klacz* (mare) Penicylina (Penicillin), which sold for $1.5 million in 1985. Polish Arabians are a good all-around horse, more muscularly built and less fragile than the English thoroughbred, which are slimmer and taller. Still, Arabians are a good short-distance racehorse, and they can be seen in action at the main Polish racetrack in Służewiec, in the Mokotów district in southern Warsaw.

architektura drewniana (wooden architecture). Poland, and southern Poland in particular, is a repository of some of the best examples of monumental wooden architecture in Europe. In practice this usually means churches, taverns, manor houses, windmills, and other structures, the oldest of which survive from the fourteenth century. Various regions of Poland have their own *szlak architektury drewnianej* (trail of wooden buildings) for tourists. The movement in Poland to preserve old wooden buildings is among the most active in Europe. Many historic wooden structures are preserved in *skanseny*, i.e., outdoor building museums; others are slowly rotting where they stand. The wooden architecture of southern Poland as a collective is on UNESCO's list of world heritage sites. *Wooden church in Bączal Dolny.*

architektura romańska, gotycka, renesansowa, barokowa (Romanesque, Gothic, Renaissance, baroque architecture). Early Polish buildings are often classified as one of these four chronologically listed styles. The Romanesque style (ca. 1000–1200) or "castle" architecture, replicates common geometrical shapes, as though one were building with large oblong, conical, and cylindrical blocks. Example: the eleventh-century rotunda of Saint Nicholas in Cieszyn. Gothic architecture (ca. 1200–1400) uses high vaulting arches, stained-glass windows, and pointy towers reaching for the sky. Renaissance architecture (ca. 1400–1600) in Poland followed Italian models. It is associated with replicated round arches, arcades, and the multi-storied pointy-topped verdigris towers of sixteenth- and seventeenth-century churches and *ratusze* (city halls); see the ratusz in Poznań. Town houses (*kamienice*) often have ornately decorated facades. The baroque style grows out of the Renaissance by adding dramatic flourishes, embellishments, and anything to strike the eye.

arianie, bracia polscy (Arians, Polish Brethren). Arianism was a form of anti-Trinitarianism (i.e., Unitarianism) taking its name from Arianus of Alexandria, who was excommunicated from the Roman Church in 321 for questioning the divine nature of Christ. During the fifteenth- to sixteenth-century *reformacja* (Reformation) and into the seventeenth century, the Arian doctrine was popular in many parts of Poland. The Arians were socially radical and were active publicists, calling for the separation of church and state, the abolition of class structure, and the equality of men and women. They experimented in communal living and rejected the special position in the Church of the Virgin Mary. An Arian offshoot called the *bracia polscy* (Polish Brethren) centered in Raków founded an internationally influential academy and printery. They were persecuted by both Catholics and Protestants, and their expulsion from Poland in 1658 (most went to Holland) broke radically with the Polish tradition of religious tolerance.

Armia Krajowa (AK) (Home Army). The Polish underground military organization during World War II operating in the years 1939–1945 on the territory of occupied Poland. It was the military wing of the Polish underground resistance, loyal to the *rząd na uchodźstwie* (government in exile) in London. The AK numbered around 250,000–300,000 soldiers. It was the initiator of *akcja Burza* (Operation Storm), leading to the 1944 powstanie warszawskie (Warsaw Uprising). After the war AK members were persecuted and often imprisoned, even executed, especially those who did not immediately lay down their arms; see *żołnierze wyklęci* (excommunicated soldiers). It is said that the AK was the best organized of all national resistance movements in World War II. *Armband worn by members of the AK.*

Armia Ludowa (AL) (People's Army). A relatively small communist partisan army operating on the territory of German-occupied Poland in 1944. It was created by the Krajowa Rada Narodowa (People's National Council), a Soviet-supported organ of the Polska Partia Robotnicza (Polish Workers' Party) under Bolesław Bierut. One of its aims was to usurp the legitimacy of the *rząd na uchodźstwie* (government in exile) in London. It was engaged in both sabotage and direct engagement with the Nazi occupiers, and in combating the activities of the Armia Krajowa (Home Army) loyal to London — including denouncing them to the Nazis. After seven months the AL was folded into the Polish army, that the Soviet Union created mostly out of freed prisoners, and renamed the Wojsko Polskie (Polish Army). Some AL officers were active in the postwar government. Lesser officers went into the state security services and the Milicja Obywatelska (Citizens' Militia, i.e., the police).

arrasy wawelskie (Wawel tapestries). One of the world's most valuable collections of Belgian tapestries, interwoven with threads of silver and gold, and the only items remaining of the original interior decoration of the Wawel royal castle in Kraków. Most were manufactured in Brussels at the order of King Zygmunt II August in 1550–1565. During World War II they were transported to Canada for safekeeping and were returned to Poland in 1961. *Conversation between God and Noah.*

Arrinera. The less-than-fetching name of Poland's combined answer to the Maserati and the Batmobile, this high-performance sports car, designed from scratch by England's Lee Noble, was unveiled in 2012. It is the first specifically Polish production automobile since the Polonez went off-line in 2002. The standard model will be able to develop 640 hp and attain a speed of 350 km/h (220 mph). Not skimping on any detail of materials, style, technology, or luxury appointments, the basic version of the Arrinera is expected to sell in the comparatively modest range of $160,000. Now all the country needs are some roads to drive it on.

aspekt dokonany i niedokonany (perfective and imperfective verbal aspect). As in other Slavic languages, Polish verbs distinguish between verbs that describe an action as such (imperfective), and as an accomplishment (perfective). Perfective verbs, describing successfully accomplished acts, occur in only the past or future tense, a distinction that tends to leave non-Slavs perplexed. For example, imperfective *czytać*, "read," refers to a not necessarily conclusive activity in present, past, or future, while its perfective partner *przeczytać*, "read through," typically refers to an action that either has just been or soon will be conclusively accomplished; its present tense is logically excluded. Example:

> *Czytałeś tę powieść?* (Were you reading/did you ever read that novel?)

> *Przeczytałeś tę powieść?* (Did you get that novel read? Did you finish reading it?)

See also **rodzaj męskoosobowy; język polski, języki słowiańskie; przypadki gramatyczne**.

autostop (hitchhiking). A unique idea from the **PRL** (communist Poland). In the 1950s–1980s it was possible (even for foreigners) to buy, for a small price, a hitchhiker's booklet and to register as an official Polish *autostopowicz* (hitchhiker). One merely had to prove possession of a modest bank account for handling emergencies. Registration provided hitchhiking insurance. The booklet contained coupons graded according to kilometers traveled, which drivers could collect and redeem for chances for prizes at the end of the year. The cover of the booklet had a red circle on it that the hitchhiker would wave at passing motorists as an enticement to stop. Hitchhiking was a cult phenomenon of the 1960s–1970s. A popular book, TV series, and movie titled *Podróż za jeden uśmiech* (Travel for one smile), by Adam Bahdaj, encouraged the youth of the 1960s–1970s to go "gdzie oczy poniosą" (wherever your eyes take you). In her song "Autostop," pop singing sensation Karin Stanek radically urged Polish youth to head out on the road and not worry about the morrow. Although hitchhiking is still legal in Poland, nobody much does it, and hitchhiking booklets are collected as mementos of the past. Long-distance carpooling is often arranged over the internet.

B

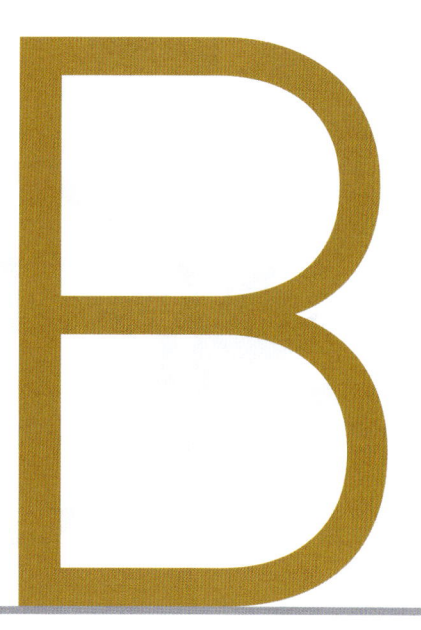

baca (senior *góral*, "highlander" shepherd). The highlander shepherds of the Tatra Mountains (**Tatry**) have a rigid hierarchical order, consisting of: *baca* (chief shepherd, pictured); *juhas* (assistant to a *baca*); *honielnik* (assistant to a juhas); *owcarek* (assistant to a honielnik). Jokes featuring interactions between a baca and a tourist (in góral speech, a *ceper*), a policeman, or a shopkeeper are a staple of cheap jokes, the humor often coming from the baca's regional speech or from his supposed carnal proclivity for his sheep.

Bacciarelli, Marcello (1731–1818). Rome-born court painter to King **Stanisław II August Poniatowski**, in charge of royal portraiture and curator of the king's art treasures. Bacciarelli remained in Poland after the king's abdication in 1795, and through the art school he founded he had a major influence on Polish painting in the early nineteenth century. Bacciarelli painted everything, from historical scenes to ceiling decorations, but his special talent was in portraiture. He left more than thirty portraits of King Stanisław II August Poniatowski alone. *Self-portrait.*

7

Baczyński, Krzysztof Kamil (1921–1944). The most promising poet of the doomed World War II generation of Polish artists who came of age at the outbreak of the war. Baczyński published around five hundred poems during the war in limited illegal self-published editions, on romantic and apocalyptic themes, including the willingness to sacrifice himself for the sake of an ideal Poland. In this sense his work harks back to the Polish Romantics of the nineteenth century. Baczyński was active as platoon commander in the **Armia Krajowa** and died from a sniper's bullet during the **powstanie warszawskie** (Warsaw Uprising). His wife Barbara was killed shortly thereafter.

bajgiel (bagel). A bread product that has taken the United States, Canada, and other countries by storm over the last forty years or so, developed by **Kraków** Jews in the sixteenth century as a softer and more sliceable variety of *obwarzanek*. It is usually boiled briefly before baking, making it chewy. The consistency of an obwarzanek is more like that of a bread ring or soft pretzel, and its dough is usually twisted, whereas bajgiel dough is not always. As it developed outside Poland, the bagel became softer and easier to slice. *Bajgle*, like obwarzanki, come in plain, salted, poppy seed, and sesame seed.

Balcerowicz, plan Balcerowicza (Balcerowicz Plan). Leszek Balcerowicz (b. 1947) is an economist, former president of the Narodowy Bank Polski (National Bank of Poland), and a one time representative to the **Sejm RP** (parliament). He was the minister of finance (1989–1991, 1997–2000) under whose leadership the Polish economy was changed from a socialist central-command model to a Western-style free market one. The plan Balcerowicza was a bite-the-bullet approach, widely called "shock therapy," aimed at stabilizing the Polish currency by letting it float freely, no matter the short-term social costs. The plan was predictably unpopular with the public — the slogan of the day was "Balcerowicz musi odejść!" (Balcerowicz must go!) — but it was internationally recognized as effective, and was copied in several of the other former Eastern Bloc countries.

"Ballada o Janku Wiśniewskim" (The ballad of Janek Wiśniewski). A **Solidarność** (Solidarity) protest ballad commemorating the killing (alongside others) in **Gdynia** of eighteen-year-old Zbigniew Godlewski by army bullets during the shipyard protests of December 1970 (see **Stocznia Gdańska**; *grudzień 1970, wydarzenia grudniowe*). The author of the song did not know the victim's name, and so made one up. Godlewski was placed on a door and carried by workers down the street in a procession toward city hall, a scene immortalized in **Andrzej Wajda**'s film *Człowiek z żelaza* (Man of iron). A long-awaited major film version of the December events, *Czarny czwartek: Janek Wiśniewski padł* (Black Thursday: Janek Wiśniewski has fallen), by Antoni Krauze, came out in 2011. The scene pictured here is from that movie. Despite Wiśniewski's being partly fictional, a street in Gdynia is named after him. Streets in Elbląg and Zielona Góra are named after him under his real name, Godlewski.

Bałtowie (Baltic tribes). The Balts originally inhabited a broad strip of territory along the **Bałtyk** (Baltic Sea) in the north of contemporary Poland and farther east. The first attempt to baptize the Balts in the tenth century by **Święty Wojciech** (Saint Adalbert) met with failure (to put it mildly – they beheaded Wojciech). In Eastern Prussia the Balts were forcibly baptized and to a large extent wiped out in the fourteenth century by the **Krzyżacy** (Teutonic Knights), although the Prussian language (*język pruski*) died out completely only in the eighteenth century. The only surviving Baltic languages are *litewski* (Lithuanian) and *łotewski* (Latvian), spoken in the roughly equal-sized countries of Litwa (Lithuania) and Łotwa (Latvia). The Baltic languages are cousins to the Slavic languages – unlike Finnish and Estonian, which, although geographically Baltic, are non-Indo-European, very distantly related to Hungarian.

Bałtyk (Baltic Sea). The Baltic is the Mediterranean of the north, being surrounded, except for a few shallow openings to the North Sea, by land belonging to nine different countries, including Poland and Germany to the south. Some 250 rivers flow into the Baltic, the largest of which is the Polish **Wisła** (Vistula). The Baltic is about half as salty as the ocean because of all the rivers flowing into it and its cold temperature, which does not favor large-scale evaporation and concentration of minerals. It is less than pristine and is often described as a ticking time bomb because of the slowly deteriorating barrels of poisonous chemicals dumped into it after World War II.

Bamber, Bamberka. **Poznań**-area historical slang for settlers from the Bamberg, Germany, area who were brought to Poland in 1719–1753 in order to occupy Polish villages decimated by war and cholera. The Bambrzy, small in number, were resented for being given concessions in preference to Polish peasants, as a result of which they were relatively prosperous. Eventually,

KALEIDOSCOPE OF POLAND

although still aware of their heritage (a Bamber cultural society exists, sponsoring yearly festivals), they were culturally assimilated, a process made easier by the fact that they were Roman Catholic. *Poznań Bamberka well sculpture.*

Banach, Stefan (1892–1945). Poland's most famous mathematician, founder of the Lwów school of mathematics and an important contributor to set theory and other branches of mathematics. Banach was a self-taught mathematical prodigy in Kraków. He received his doctorate from Lwów University, without completing formal course work, for his published thesis containing the basic outlines of functional analysis, a new branch of mathematics that he founded. At least eighteen theorems or concepts in mathematics bear his name.

---

bankowość (banking). The Narodowy Bank Polski (NBP, National Bank of Poland) was founded in 1945, with predecessors going back to 1828. It is responsible for issuing currency and controlling monetary policy. The Bank Gospodarstwa Krajowego (National Bank for the Economy) handles EU funds for the government. The bulk of the Polish banking system was privatized beginning in 1989, with most of the system ending up in foreign hands. The Powszechna Kasa Oszczędności, Bank Polski Spółka Akcyjna (Universal Savings Bank, Bank of Poland, Inc., PKO BP SA), a prominent remnant of the former system, is part of the UniCredit group. The once regional Bank Śląski (Silesian Bank) is owned by the Dutch ING group and has gone national, as has Poznań's Bank Zachodni Wielkopolski Bank Kredytowy (BZ WBK; Western Bank, Greater Poland Credit Bank). Once hard to find, banks now line some downtown streets from one end to the other.

---

bar mleczny (milk bar). Milk bars are a traditional Polish fast food outlet that flourished especially in the PRL (communist Poland). They are fewer now than formerly, but they still hang on. Some are private and some are partially supported by the government as a means of providing simple, nutritious, "home-cooked" food to retirees and other low-income persons. Originally they specialized in milk, egg, and vegetarian dishes, but most now serve meat as well. In fact, *mleko* (plain cold milk) is the one thing one cannot usually get in a milk bar. But try Inka brand *kawa zbożowa* instead. Orders are placed, and food is served, across a counter, usually by an older woman. Milk bars are a great social leveler, as one may find a retiree, a laborer, a student, and a professor partaking of the same simple fare, often at the same table. Not only milk bars but also other less expensive eating establishments such as *jadłodajnie* (eateries) have a more or less stable menu of so-called *dania barowe* (bar dishes).

Baranów. The epitome of a magnificent late Renaissance-style castle/palace, sometimes called *mały* Wawel (little Wawel), located near Sandomierz in southeast Poland, owned over the centuries by some of the most illustrious aristocratic families in Poland: the Leszczyński, Wiśniowiecki, Lubomirscy, Sanguszko, Małachowski, Potocki, and Krasicki families. Today it is owned by an agency for industrial development in Warsaw, which has restored it to its former splendor, running it as a hotel, museum and, on occasion, a movie set.

Barańczak, Stanisław (1946–2014). Poznań--born poet, literary critic, and translator, one of the major poetic voices of the postwar generation, referred to as the Nowa Fala (new wave) of Polish writers. A founding member of **KOR** (Workers' Defense Committee) and active in the political opposition, Barańczak was fired from the faculty of Adam Mickiewicz University in Poznań in 1977 for his political activities, but was later reinstated. However, in 1981 he accepted a position at Harvard University, where, in increasingly poor health until his death, he wrote poetry, translated Shakespeare into Polish, and was active as a literary editor. His book *Chirurgiczna precyzja* (Surgical precision) won the 1999 **Nike** book award.

barok, literatura barokowa (baroque literature). The baroque trend in literature (late sixteenth century through the seventeenth century) was characterized by extreme formal complexity and technical dexterity, using striking juxtapositions, comparisons, inversions, and other means designed to amaze the reader. In Poland, baroque poetry was of exceptionally high quality and creativity, its most important exponents being the metaphysical-religious poet Mikołaj Sęp-Szarzyński (1550–1681), the well-traveled introspective Daniel Naborowski (1573–1640), the sophisticated roué courtier Jan Andrzej Morsztyn (1621–1693, pictured), and the moralizing classicist Wacław Potocki (1621–1696). In oratory, **Piotr Skarga**'s *Kazania sejmowe* (Sermons to the **Sejm**) are emblematic of the period and its issues. **Jan Chryzostom Pasek**'s (ca. 1636–1701) memoirs, while of this time, besides being written in prose, stand outside the baroque mainstream for their naïve primitivism.

barszcz, barszcz biały, barszcz czerwony (borscht, white borscht, red borscht). In some parts of Poland, the south especially, one has to specify *barszcz czerwony* (red barszcz, pictured) or *barszcz biały* (white barszcz), one having nothing to do with the other except for being soups. Barszcz czerwony is a clear soup made from beet roots, while barszcz biały is basically the same as *żurek*, but made from a fermented wheat starter instead of rye. The red tends to be associated with **Boże Narodzenie** (Christmas), the white with **Wielkanoc** (Easter), although this is not a hard and fast rule. *Barszcz ukraiński* (Ukrainian borscht) is a multi-vegetable soup (no beans, please) made as much with cabbage as with beets. *Barszcz litewski* (Lithuanian borscht) is similar to Polish barszcz czerwony, but richer and more substantial, with vegetables, mushrooms, and even meat added.

Batory, Stefan (1533–1586, ruled 1576–1586). After Anna Jagiellonka (1523–1596) was crowned queen (with the rights of king), the Polish nobility under Jan Zamoyski selected Stefan Batory of Transylvania to be her husband and king. While the marriage was a disaster, Batory is considered to have been one of the best of the Polish elected kings, especially in a military capacity. He reorganized the army (including establishing the famed Polish hussars, *husaria*) and conducted victorious campaigns against Muscovy, then ruled by Tsar Ivan IV (the Terrible). In 1579 he raised the Wilno Jesuit College to the level of a university, the second-oldest Polish university after Kraków's and the alma mater of innumerable Polish notables. The university carried his name up until 1939. In 1988 George Soros founded the Fundacja Batorego (Batory Foundation) to promote democratic institutions in Poland and throughout central Europe.

Baudouin de Courtenay, Jan (1845–1929). Polish linguist and Slavist, pioneer of phonemic and morphophonemic theory. Warsaw-educated, Baudouin de Courtenay was an early champion, alongside Swiss linguist Ferdinand de Saussure, of synchronic linguistics, as opposed to the mostly historical linguistics practiced theretofore. He established the influential Kazan' school of linguistics in Russia. Three major phonological schools developed out of his work, the most important internationally being the Prague school. Baudouin de Courtenay was a strong supporter of the revival of smaller ethnic groups, and he was an active practitioner of Esperanto (see Zamenhof, Ludwik).

bazyliszek (basilisk). Warsaw's answer to Kraków's *smok wawelski* (Wawel dragon). The legendary basilisk is a greenish monster, half rooster, half reptile, but larger and more frightening, with a gaze that freezes people dead. One once took up abode in Warsaw beneath Krzywe Koło (Crooked Wheel) Street, and terrorized its citizens by coming out at night, looking at them, and stealing their treasure. Finally, a *szewc* (cobbler) draped himself in mirrors and made his way down to the monster's lair. As soon as the basilisk took a look at himself in the mirror he himself became frozen into stone, thus ridding Warsaw of the problem. The mayor had three daughters for the cobbler to choose from for marriage, and with one of them he founded the Bazyliszek restaurant, still standing in Warsaw's Starówka (its sign is pictured). At least, that is the restaurant's version of the story.

Beck, Józef (1894–1944). An aide to Józef Piłsudski in the latter's First Brigade in 1914–1917, Beck was active in the government after World War I and helped organize the *przewrót majowy* (1926 May coup d'état) that put Piłsudski in power. After Piłsudski's death in 1935 he shared power with Edward Śmigły-Rydz and President Ignacy Mościcki in the *sanacja* (return to health) regime. From 1932 on, as Poland's minister of foreign affairs, Beck was the main architect of Poland's foreign policy, aiming for a delicate balance between German ambitions and those of the Soviet Union. On the eve of World War II he successfully negotiated defense treaties with England and France that, even if those countries did not follow through on their obligations, formally brought them into the war with Germany after it attacked Poland in 1939. Beck followed the Polish government into exile in Romania, where he died of tuberculosis.

Beksiński, Zdzisław (1929–2005). Sanok-born artist of the macabre, surreal, and evil forebodings, especially well appreciated in Japan, but also highly collected in the United States and Europe. Many considered Beksiński to be Poland's most outstanding contemporary artist. Said to be amiable and jovial in private despite his morbid subject matter, Beksiński's family was marked by tragedy. His wife died of cancer in 1988, and his son committed suicide a year later. In 2005 the artist himself was brutally stabbed to death in his home during a senseless robbery by the teenage son of a friend — to whom he had apparently refused a request for a trivially small amount of money. *Untitled*, 1984.

Belweder (Belweder Palace). Built in 1818–1822 near Łazienki Królewskie (Łazienki Park) in Warsaw, Belweder served various purposes until it became the Polish presidential residence in the early part of the twentieth century. It was especially associated, first, with the powstanie listopadowe (November Uprising, 1830) and the attempted assassination of Archduke Constantine; and later, in the twentieth century, with Marshal Józef Piłsudski, who died there in 1935. Beginning with Lech Wałęsa's presidency (elected 1990) the function of presidential residence was taken over by Pałac Namiestnikowski (Viceroy's Palace), now Pałac Prezydencki (Presidential Palace), on Krakowskie Przedmieście street, Belweder being used for national ceremonial occasions and as the residence of visiting dignitaries. However, as of this writing Belweder has been taken over by President Bronisław Komorowski as his official residence, pending repairs at the Presidential Palace.

Bem, Józef (1794–1850). Polish general during the failed 1830–1831 powstanie listopadowe (November Uprising), sometimes called the *bohater trzech narodów* (hero of three nations). Bem joined the Wielka Emigracja (Great Emigration) in Paris but then returned to action as a leader of the 1848 Hungarian uprising, making him as much of a Hungarian national hero as a Polish one, if not more so. He then converted to Islam, along with six thousand other Polish soldiers, and joined the Turkish army under the name Murat

Pasza. He died not in battle but of malaria, and is buried in Tarnów, where he was born. A famous elegy, "Bema pamięci żałobny rapsod" (Funeral rhapsody in memory of General Bem), was written by Cyprian Kamil Norwid in 1851.

Berling, Zygmunt (1896–1980). A deserter to the Soviet side in World War II, Berling eventually was nominated (by Joseph Stalin himself) to be general of the Soviet-led (and cynically named) Tadeusz Kościuszko Infantry Division, which fought alongside Soviet troops as the front moved toward Warsaw and, eventually, north to the Baltic seacoast and on to Berlin. It was Berling's army that was camped on the other side of the Wisła River during the powstanie warszawskie (Warsaw Uprising) in 1944 while the Germans pounded the city to shreds. Suspected of trying to aid the Poles (this is still debated), Berling was recalled to Moscow until the end of the war. After the war, he continued to be active in the Polish army and government, retiring in 1953.

Beskidy (Beskid Mountains). The Beskids are a series of mountain ranges of the outer Karpaty (Carpathians), about six hundred kilometers long and fifty to seventy kilometers wide. In Poland they run from the border with Ukraine in the southeast all the way to the Brama Morawska (Moravian Gate) above the Czech Republic. The highest peak is the barren Babia Góra (Witches' Mountain) on the Slovak-Polish border at 1,725 meters. The Beskids include among its ranges the Bieszczady in the far southeast. To the south of the Beskids lie the Tatry (Tatras).

Biała Dama (Lady in White). Every self-respecting castle has a ghost, and many Polish castles lay claim to the Biała Dama, a noblewoman dressed in white who climbs out of her portrait and walks down the stairs and into the night to be met by a mysterious rider on a coal-black charger. What happens after that is anyone's guess; however, see *Szał uniesień*. She is back in her portrait by morning. Castles in Łańcut, Nieborów, Rydzyna, and Kórnik all claim White Ladies as their own. A good one to know is Julia z Lubomirskich Potocka of Łańcut, whose mother, Izabela Lubomirska, founded a distillery around 1764, which nearly 250 years later produces a luxury vodka (*wódka*) under the name Biała Dama. This is also the name of a rich cheesecake, a famed Kraków street mime, at least two darkly pessimistic rock songs, and some other things besides. *The Biała Dama of Kórnik, Teofila Potulicka*.

Białoszewski, Miron (1922–1983). Experimental and provocative poet, playwright, and actor who emerged after the *odwilż gomułkowska* (Gomułka Thaw) in 1956 to develop a broad following. Some of his poems depend on linguistic jokes; others are only two lines long; all are language-centered, as if language were the only thing one can hang on to, although their syntax is often unfathomable. His poems often invoke unpoetic objects and highly colloquial speech. Despite his cult following as an iconoclastic poet, Białoszewski's most lasting work is his still widely read memoirs of the powstanie warszawskie (Warsaw Uprising), *Pamiętnik z powstania warszawskiego* (1970), in which he had taken part. His memoirs were controversial, since he described the events of the powstanie warszawskie without pathos or mythologizing, in the language of the street.

Białowieża, Puszcza Białowieska (Białowieża wilderness preserve). In Poland and Belarus there extends a large remnant of the original primeval forest that once covered northern Europe, 1,460 square kilometers in all, of which 580 square kilometers are in Poland. It is named after the village within it of Białowieża (White Tower) and is a UNESCO World Heritage Site. To protect the ecology, it may be visited only on foot, by bicycle, or in a horse cart. The forest was ready-made for partisan activity in World War II; see **Bielscy, bracia**. It is home to abundant animal and plant life (with over three thousand species of mushrooms alone), and includes herds of the forest's signature species, *żubry* (wisent, or European bison, pictured), which once inhabited the whole of northern Europe but which had died out in the wild by the 1920s. The present herd was bred from a stock of only twelve remaining individuals preserved in zoos. The *żubr* is not the same as the *tur*, another wild but now extinct kind of European bison. See also *tarpan*. The *puszcza* is under constant pressure from those who want to manage or manicure it, and those who want to let it develop it in its natural untrammeled state.

Białystok. The largest town in the Polish northeast. Białystok is next to the border with Lithuania and numbers around 295,000 inhabitants. It lies close to the **Puszcza Białowieska** (Białowieża wilderness), what is left of the last remaining primeval forest in Europe. Białystok's economy is enhanced by being located along the Saint Petersburg–Berlin railway line and along the Via Baltica highway, connecting Warsaw with Estonia. While the town itself is uninspiring, the Białystok area itself has a number of imposing and well-preserved former residences of the *magnateria* (Polish magnates), foremost among which is that of the locally prominent Branicki family (pictured). The bialy, a chewy New York roll with a poppy seed–, sesame seed–, or onion-filled depression in the middle, originated among Białystok Jews. See also: **Zamenhof, Ludwik**.

Biblia (Bible). The first known Polish translation of the Bible is the beautifully illuminated Biblia królowej Zofii (Queen Zofia's Bible, pictured), commissioned in 1453–1455 by the fourth wife of King **Władysław II Jagiełło.** Only an incomplete version of the Old Testament remains, in language heavily influenced by the Czech on which the translation was undoubtedly based. The first printed Polish Bible was Biblia Leopolity

(Leopolita's Bible, 1561), an anonymous translation of the Latin Vulgate named after its editor from Lwów. Seemingly the first Bible anywhere to be translated in its entirety from the original Hebrew, Aramaic, and Greek was the protestant Biblia brzeska (Brześć Bible, 1563), followed by various other protestant translations. The Jakub Wujek Bible (1593–1595), based on the Vulgate, became the standard Polish Roman Catholic biblical text for the next 367 years. The first Catholic Bible in Polish to be based on original sources was the Biblia Tysiąclecia (Bible of the Millennium, 1965; see Tyniec).

Bielscy, bracia (Bielski brother partisans, active 1941–1944). A remarkable story, virtually unknown in Poland before being brought to world attention by the 2009 film *Defiance* (*Opór*). The Bielski brothers were Jewish Polish citizens living near Nowogródek in today's Belarus who, when the Nowogródek ghetto was being liquidated, fled to the Białowieża forest with about forty others and organized what turned into a vast group of Jewish partisans operating throughout Lithuania and Belarus, of whom over 1,200 survived the war, including two of the four Bielski brothers, who eventually settled in New York and ended up operating a trucking business. Their leader was Tevje Bielski, who had been a corporal in the Polish army. The bracia Bielscy are controversial in Poland because of their support of the Soviet counteroffensive against Polish partisan groups. Their participation in the *zbrodnia naliboska* (Naliboki massacre, 1943), in which 129 Polish villagers were murdered, is alleged but unproven.

Bierut, Bolesław (1892–1956). A major actor in the communist takeover of Poland following World War II. President of the Polish communist puppet regime from 1947–1952, head of the communist party from 1948–1956, Bierut was handpicked by Joseph Stalin. His first major achievement was the falsification of the *wybory 1947* (1947 elections) to the Sejm (parliament). The Bierut years were ones of severe political repression, increasing dependence on the Soviet Union, and the imprisonment of tens of thousands of political prisoners, particularly members of the wartime underground resistance. He personally signed the death sentences of many prominent political prisoners. Bierut died unexpectedly and mysteriously during his attendance at the 1956 Moscow Communist Party congress at which Nikita Khrushchev denounced Joseph Stalin. A malicious rhyming couplet of the day went: "Do Moskwy pojechał dumnie, z Moskwy wracał w trumnie" (He went to Moscow in pride, and returned from Moscow in a coffin).

Bieszczady (Bieszczad Mountains). In Poland, the Bieszczads are the mountains of the Podkarpacie, the far southeastern Polish Karpaty (Carpathians). Most of the Bieszczads are in Ukraine. The tallest peak in Poland is Tarnica at 1,346 meters. For Poles, the Bieszczady, while actually in the southeast, function as a kind of "Wild West,"

by reputation attracting recluses and people escaping society and the law. A particularly barren stretch of the Bieszczady, above the timberline, is called the *połonina* (high pastureland, pictured).

Located near Żnin in present-day Kujawy, it has been a major archeological site and popular excursion destination since its discovery in the 1930s. Its reconstructed walls and chambers attract numerous festivals, historical reenactments, and occasional use as a movie set. *Reconstruction of the gate into Biskupin.*

bigos (hunters' stew). An old Polish-Lithuanian dish and staple of contemporary Polish cuisine — the Polish national dish if there is one. It was supposedly first concocted by the future king Władysław II Jagiełło, who served it to a hunting party. It is made on a sauerkraut base (washed to get some of the salt out) to which various meats and sausages are added, along with dried mushrooms, onions, and sometimes prunes. Red wine may be added. Family fights break out over whether to add tomatoes (of course not). Bigos is best when allowed to sit and stew for several days before serving. Practically no winter's entertainment passes without a pot of bigos simmering on the stove, and it is also a staple of *jadłodajnie* (eateries). It can be kept going indefinitely by constantly adding to it and then putting it on the balcony overnight to freeze. A lyrical description of bigos may be found in Adam Mickiewicz's *Pan Tadeusz*, book IV, in which the cabbage is described as "entering the mouth of its own accord." Figuratively, *bigos* means a hodgepodge, or a big mess.

Biskupin. A prehistoric lake village (established ca. 700–650 BC, abandoned ca. 500 BC) on the cusp between the Iron and Bronze Ages belonging to the so-called *kultura łużycka* (Lusatian culture), about whose ethnicity little is known.

bloki z wielkiej płyty (concrete slab apartment house blocks). This was the main architectural approach to satisfying the mass housing needs in Poland from the late 1960s through the early 1990s, and the majority of apartments constructed with this method still stand because they are solidly built, if not always beautiful. The prefabricated construction method was relatively quick if expensive. Often the building would be up, and people would have moved in with the finishing work (e.g., flooring, plumbing, and cabinetry) still needing to be completed. People tend not to live in *bloki z wielkiej płyty* by choice, but most are located near good public transportation, parks, playgrounds, and other amenities.

KALEIDOSCOPE OF POLAND

By unfair reputation, in recent years bloki z wielkiej płyty are associated with so-called *blokersi*, i.e., the young urban unemployed and disaffected, who sit outside on benches all day with their chums, drinking beer, swearing, leering at girls, and listening to hip-hop.

"Bo zupa była za słona" (Because the soup was too salty). The best-remembered of several billboard slogans from 1997 promoting a nationwide campaign against domestic abuse, showing the bruised faces of women and children. The brainchild of the Niebieska Linia (Blue Line) organization for aiding victims of family violence, the campaign is credited for bringing the problem to broad national attention, although the posters came under criticism for supposedly attacking the institution of marriage and promoting a negative view of men. The slogan entered the national idiom without, however, causing a decline in reported instances of family violence.

---

bocian (stork). Storks are a model bird, bringing good luck to wherever they nest. They are especially common in north-central Poland and in the east, where people try to attract a stork to nest on a telephone pole by putting up a metal framework to support the nest (a stork "starter kit"). Storks don't sing but make a distinctive throaty crackling sound (*kle kle kle*). They follow the farmer as he mows to catch frogs in the grass. They are monogamous and, like good parents, they do not push their offspring out of the nest at the first opportunity, but allow them first to get their wings. A live camera feed from a stork family's nest in Przygodzice (west-central Poland) may be seen at any time at http://www.bociany.ec.pl. In the winter all one sees is an empty nest. Storks winter in Africa and return to the same nest each spring, carrying a new crop of Polish babies in their beaks.

Bodo, Eugeniusz (Bogdan Eugène Junod, 1899–1943). One of the most popular film actors and singers of the pre–World War II period, especially in light forgettable musical comedies. He is sometimes compared to France's Maurice Chevalier. Bodo is also an emblem of the innumerable personal tragedies the war indiscriminately meted out. In 1940 he fled the German occupation to Lwów, where he was arrested by the Soviet NKVD for being a "socially suspect element" and sentenced to five years at hard labor in the Gułag. Having a Swiss passport, which he thought would save him, Bodo was not covered by the Sikorski-Majski Pact of 1941 (see *rząd na uchodźstwie*). He died of starvation while being transported to a labor camp in the north of European Russia and was buried in a common grave. A monument and symbolic grave marker was dedicated to him in 2011 in the Russian town of Kotlas near Arkhangelsk.

Bogurodzica (Mother of God). A medieval chant arising in the thirteenth through fifteenth centuries, showing thematic elements of the

Eastern Church, including the iconic figure *deisis*, portraying Christ enthroned, flanked by the Virgin Mary on one side and John the Baptist on the other. By improbable legend, it was authored by Święty Wojciech. The Bogurodzica is the oldest complete piece of Polish poetry. Designed to be sung or chanted, it served as the de facto national anthem of early Poland. According to fifteenth-century historian Jan Długosz it was sung by Polish-Lithuanian troops before the battle of Grunwald in 1410. Together with the anonymous medieval poem "Żale Matki Boskiej pod krzyżem" (Lament of the Mother of God beneath the cross) and the early veneration of the icon Matka Boska Częstochowska, it reflects the special status in Poland of the Virgin Mary (*kult maryjny*, "Marian cult") from the earliest times. The Bogurodzica's first lines are:

> Bogurodzica dziewica,
> Bogiem sławiena Maryja
> U twego syna Gospodzina
> Matko zwolena, Maryja!
> Zyszczy nam, spuści nam.
> Kyrie eleison.

> Mother of God, Virgin
> By God glorified Mary
> Through your son the Lord
> O chosen mother, Mary!
> Obtain for us, come down to us.
> Kyrie eleison.

Bolek i Lolek (1963–1983). A popular television cartoon series for children, in which the two titular boys hardly ever speak, but have adventures in their backyard and around the world. Other favorite children's series were *Zaczarowany ołówek* (Enchanted pencil, 1964–1976), about a boy, his dog, and a pencil that materializes everything it draws; *Reksio* (1967–1988), about the adventures of the dog Reksio and his animal and human friends; and two animated teddy bears: *Miś Uszatek* (Teddy floppy-ears, 1975–1987) and the French-Polish coproduction *Miś Coralgol* (1967–1974), both intended for preschoolers.

All of these appeared in the *dobranocka* (nighty-night) time slot on TV, as a sign for children to go to bed. A popular comic strip of the times was *Kajko i Kokosz* (1968–1972), a pair of ancient Slavic warrior buddies, differing greatly in personality and physique, who have adventures in both the past and future. A notable museum of Polish *dobranocki* from the PRL (communist Poland) is located in Rzeszów.

Bolesław I Chrobry (Bolesław the Brave, 967–1025, prince from 992 to April 19, 1025, king for three months, until June 17, 1025). Son of Mieszko I and Dobrawa, Bolesław accepted a ruler's crown from the Holy Roman Emperor Otto III at the *zjazd gnieźnieński* (Gniezno Synod) in 1000 (a date remembered by many because of its roundness), but was officially crowned king by the Pope, just before his death. A brilliant military tactician, he greatly enlarged Polish territory in the east, occupying Kiev at one point in 1018. According to legend he nicked his sword on the golden gate of Kiev, the sword becoming the Polish coronation sword known as Szczerbiec (Old Nick). However, the coronation sword by that name in Wawel castle dates from the thirteenth century, is not nicked, and the golden gate was built later. But for all that . . . under Bolesław I, Poland became a European power to be reckoned with.

Bolesław II Śmiały (Bolesław the Bold, ca. 1042–1082, ruled 1076–1079). The son of

Kazimierz I Odnowiciel (Kazimierz the Restorer), Bolesław II was active in restoring and building churches and monasteries following the collapse of the *reakcja pogańska* (pagan revolt), while neglecting Polish interests on the Baltic coast. He introduced Polish coinage on a broad scale, establishing mints in **Wrocław** and **Kraków**. Bolesław II was forced to flee Poland following a nobles' revolt in 1079, sparked by his rash assassination of **Stanisław**, Bishop of Kraków, later canonized as a saint. Bolesław, not a saint himself, was succeeded on the throne by his brother, Władysław Herman.

Bolesław III Krzywousty (Bolesław the Wrymouth, 1086–1138, ruled 1107–1138). Bolesław III spent his reign defending Poland's territory in the west and establishing Polish rule and Christianity in **Pomorze** (Pomerania). He established in his *testament* (will) the principle of dividing Poland into *dzielnice* (districts), each to be ruled by its own prince, his sons. The assignment as to district was made according to seniority, with the currently eldest prince being given domain over the rest, with his seat in **Kraków**. If the aim was to avoid internecine fighting among the princes, it did not work. The resulting situation, known as *rozbicie dzielnicowe* (division into districts), lasted for 182 years. It was left to **Władysław I Łokietek** (Władysław the Short, reigned 1320–1333) to put the pieces mostly back together — except for **Śląsk** (Silesia), which had become vassalized by Bohemia, and much of Pomorze, now ruled by the **Krzyżacy** (Teutonic Knights).

Bona Sforza, królowa (Queen Bona Sforza, 1494–1557). Well-educated, politically astute, and conniving Milan-born queen of Poland-Lithuania from 1518; wife of **Zygmunt I Stary**; mother of **Zygmunt II August**, the last of the Jagiellonian kings (**Jagiellonowie**). An important sponsor of Polish culture, Queen Bona introduced many Italian customs to the Polish court, especially Italian cuisine, including many vegetables new to the Polish palate (called to this day *włoszczyzna*, "from Włochy," Italy). At odds with her son, the king, over his marriage to Barbara Radziwiłłówna, she left Poland for her native Italy, where she was fatally poisoned on behalf of Philip II of Spain, to avoid his having to repay his debts to her. Out of this debt has grown the contemporary idiom *sumy neapolitańskie* (Neapolitan sums), meaning immense sums of money owed that will never be collected.

Borowski, Tadeusz (1922–1951). Poet and short-story writer of the immediate postwar period. Both he and his fiancée were caught separately in Warsaw *łapanki* (roundups) and sent to the Auschwitz-Birkenau *obóz koncentracyjny i zagłady* (concentration and extermination camp). He was later transferred to Dachau, from which he was liberated by the American army. His fiancée also miraculously survived the war, and the two married. Borowski returned to Poland and became one of the so-called *pryszczaci* (young, pimply-faced supporters of the communist regime). His best-known prose works, describing dispassionately what everyday life was like in Auschwitz, belong to the canon of world Holocaust literature. Best known is his story "Proszę państwa do gazu" (This way to the gas, ladies and gentlemen), in the collection *Pożegnanie z Marią* (Farewell to Maria). Tragic-ironically, Borowski died of self-inflicted gas poisoning just as his life seemed to be getting back to normal.

Boruta, diabeł Boruta (devil Boruta). Boruta is a devil who inhabits the lower levels of the royal castle in Łęczyca (in the center of Poland above Łódź), and he has grown into the virtual symbol of the town. Boruta is more mischievous than evil. He takes on various forms to elude detection, besides his main identity as a mustachioed nobleman. He is endowed with superhuman strength and a prodigious capacity for drink. Boruta is not to be confused with his sometimes drinking partner Rokita, a brigand and Robin Hood–type devil inhabiting swamps and marshes.

Boże Ciało (Corpus Christi). A major Roman Catholic holiday celebrating the Last Supper, held sixty days after Wielkanoc (Easter). Corpus Christi is a Polish national holiday marked by street processions and, in villages, by ribbon- and flower-bedecked main roads. The procession, bearing the Najświętszy Sakrament (Blessed Sacrament, i.e., communion bread) and preceded by *feretrony* (portable holy images), stops at four different stations along the way while excerpts from the four Gospels are read. The procession is often led by girls in regional costume. One of the most colorful such processions, attracting tourists, is in Łowicz. *Corpus Christi procession in Stargard.*

KALEIDOSCOPE OF POLAND 21

"Boże coś Polskę" (O God who has defended Poland). A religious song, the words for which were written in 1816 by Alojzy Feliński, in commemoration of the Russian tsar Alexander's creation of the Królestwo Polskie (Kingdom of Poland). Over the years the words have been altered to suit the times, and the song acquired a strong aura of combined patriotism and religious fervor. It was sung by insurgents in the 1863 **powstanie styczniowe** (January Uprising) and was a candidate for selection as the Polish national anthem in 1918. More recently, it was an anthem of the **Solidarność** (Solidarity) trade union movement. The original first stanza is:

> Boże, coś Polskę przez tak liczne wieki
> Otaczał blaskiem potęgi i chwały
> I tarczą swojej zasłaniał opieki
> Od nieszczęść, które przywalić ją miały.

> Oh God who, through numerous centuries,
> Has surrounded Poland with the light of your power and glory,
> And, with the shield of your protection,
> Has shielded it from misfortunes that were to have brought it down.

Boże Narodzenie (Christmas). Christmas in Poland is a religious and national holiday accompanied by many traditions, including *prezenty pod choinkę* (presents under the Christmas tree), **Wigilia** (Christmas Eve Supper, which starts with the *pierwsza gwiazdka*, "first star"), *łamanie się opłatkiem* (the breaking and the sharing of an *opłatek* or Christmas wafer, pictured), *pasterka* (Christmas Eve service), the singing of *kolędy* (Christmas carols), and a possible visit from Święty Mikołaj (Santa Claus, Saint Nicholas), alternatively: Gwiazdor, although by tradition he is supposed to come on **mikołajki** (December 6). Traditionally *kolędnicy* (carolers) began caroling on the second day of Christmas. When sharing the Christmas wafer, a person will take a small portion for him- or herself and give the remainder to the next person, conveying to that person an appropriate wish for the coming year — who then acts similarly in turn with the next person.

Bóg, Honor, Ojczyzna (God, Honor, Fatherland). The official (from 1993) — and, some would say, quintessentially Polish — motto currently appearing on the standards of the Wojsko Polskie (Polish Army), pictured, its origins stretching back to Napoleonic times and earlier. During the Second Republic (interwar Poland) the motto was simply "Honor i Ojczyzna" (Honor and the Fatherland). The latter is at present the name of a popular (they say) street rap group promoting in their lyrics a primitive xenophobic skinhead ideology. See also: **honor**.

Brama Morawska (Moravian Gate). An approximately sixty-five-kilometer stretch between Poland and the Czech Republic, separating the **Karpaty** (Carpathian Mountains) to the east and the **Sudety** (Sudeten Mountains) to the west. The Moravian Gate offered a natural trade route connecting northern Europe with the south. More than that, it is said to have been one of the main trails by which man out of Africa made his way to the north. The historical *szlak bursztynowy* (amber road; see *bursztyn*) passed through the Moravian Gate, as did the Czech missionaries who baptized Poland in the late tenth century.

bruderszaft. The traditional ceremony of going over to a first-name basis with someone, abandoning the formal pronouns of address, *pan, pani* (sir, madam), thereafter using instead informal *ty* (you) and the verb forms that go with it. Bruderszaft is traditionally accompanied by entwining right arms and drinking a draft of vodka, exchanging kisses three times on alternate cheeks. Colloquially the ceremony is called *brudzio*. Some guides to Polish etiquette have prematurely declared the death of this custom. The relationship of people on first-name and other bases in Poland is so complicated that it has yet to be adequately described.

Brzechwa, Jan (Jan Wiktor Lesman, ca. 1898–1966). A skilled translator of foreign poetry into Polish, Brzechwa (the pen name means "arrow shaft") is mainly remembered as the author of clever children's verse, rich in fantasy and wordplay, most of it still in print, and much of which has become part of the Polish idiom. Most renowned is **"Chrząszcz brzmi w trzcinie"** (The beetle buzzes in the reeds), beginning with the lines of a now classic Polish tongue-twister. A popular series of books describe the doings of Pan Kleks (Mr. Inkspot), head of a magical academy. In the 1980s many of Brzechwa's poems were made into animated films, as was the poem "Pchła szachrajka" (The swindler flea). Brzechwa's *Kaczka dziwaczka* (The oddball duck) seems especially to appeal to Polish children. Guitarist Andrzej Chochół has recently set twelve Brzechwa poems to music in different styles, from classical to hip-hop.

Brzeziński, Zbigniew (b. 1928). Poland has done its share in providing other countries (particularly Israel) with government leaders. Zbigniew Brzeziński was the US national security adviser under President Jimmy Carter during a time of momentous events in such countries as Afghanistan, Iran, and China. His father, a career Polish diplomat, was posted on the eve of World War II to Canada, where the family settled. As security adviser, Brzeziński assisted in fashioning the Camp David Egypt-Israel peace accord and in signing the Strategic Arms Limitation Treaty (SALT) with the Soviet Union. His daughter Miki is a well-known American journalist, author, and commentator. Polish-born Israeli politicians include David Ben-Gurion

(1886–1973); Menachem Begin (1913–1992); Yitzhak Shamir (1915–2012); and Shimon Peres (b. 1923). Golda Meir, 1898–1978, was born in Kiev, and Prime Minister Benjamin Netanyahu's father, also active in politics, was born in Poland. *Polish-born Zbigniew Brzeziński plays chess with Polish-born Monachem Begin at Camp David.*

"**Budujemy nowy dom**" (We're building a new house). A propaganda slogan of the 1950s, encouraging people to pitch in and help with the massive rebuilding of war-destroyed Poland, especially Warsaw. This was also the title of a popular song of *socrealizm* (socialist realism) on the same theme, whose first lines were:

> Budujemy nowy dom
> Jeszcze jeden nowy dom
> Naszym przyszłym lepszym dniom
> Warszawo!
>
> We're building a new house
> One more new house
> To our future better days
> Oh Warsaw!

A song in a similar vein is "Pieśń o cegle" (Song of the brick), taking off from Aleksander Kobzdej's iconic image *Podaj cegłę* (Pass a Brick; see *socrealizm*), revived in big-beat form in the 1980s by Izabela Trojanowska. A motto on the empik building in central Warsaw still prominently proclaims "Cały naród buduje swoją stolicę" (The whole nation is building its capital), although the capital has long since been "built," and then some.

Bug. A river in eastern Poland 772 kilometers long, of which 363 kilometers form part of the Polish-Ukrainian and -Belarus border). It is the fifth-longest Polish river and the fourth largest in volume, ahead of the Narew. It turns west and flows into the Narew about twenty-five kilometers north of Warsaw, and the combined river flows into the Wisła near Nowy Dwór Mazowiecki. The expression "między Odrą a Bugiem" (between the western Odra and the Bug) arose as a postwar propaganda metaphor for referring to Poland in its readjusted boundaries. This is a somewhat less ambitious description than the fifteenth-century slogan "Polska od morza do morza" (Poland from sea to sea), when Polish territory stretched briefly (1416–1484) between the Baltic and Black seas. The phrase is used today to refer ironically to Polish ambitions as a world power.

Bulla gnieźnieńska (Gniezno Papal Bull). An 1136 papal edict nullifying the authority of the Magdeburg Church over the Polish Church, which thereby became independent. Not that this edict nullified German pretensions toward Polish lands. The *bulla* is written in Latin, but it contains around four hundred Polish place and personal names, inaugurating the history of Polish orthography and topography.

bursztyn (amber). Bursztyn is petrified pine sap used for centuries in jewelry and folk medicine. The amber found along the Bałtyk is the most highly prized in the world, and Poland is in possession of the most generous deposits.

The *szlak bursztynowy* (amber road) was a trade route between the Baltic Sea in the north, the Brama Morawska (Moravian Gate), and Roman Acquilea on the Adriatic Sea, dealing primarily in amber, but also in honey, slaves, beeswax, and other commodities; see Brama Morawska. The center of the amber trade was Gdańsk. Trade along the amber route decreased from the fourth century on. Its precise route is not known. Especially prized are instances of insects trapped inside the amber (pictured).

Burza, akcja (Operation Storm, or Tempest, 1944). As the Soviet army drove the Germans back west and appeared ready to cross into prewar Polish territory (the *kresy*) at the end of World War II, the Armia Krajowa (Home Army) opened an offensive against the retreating Germans with the aim of "welcoming" the Soviet Army with the country already in Polish hands. Its most prominent undertaking was the powstanie warszawskie (Warsaw Uprising) of 1944 under General Tadeusz Komorowski, doomed by the lack of support from the Soviets and the Allies, and the still overwhelming strength of the Germans. *Akcja Burza* achieved its goal of liberating a number of cities but ultimately fell victim to the might of the Soviet army and the brutal pacification methods of the Soviet NKVD (security services) as they swept into Poland.

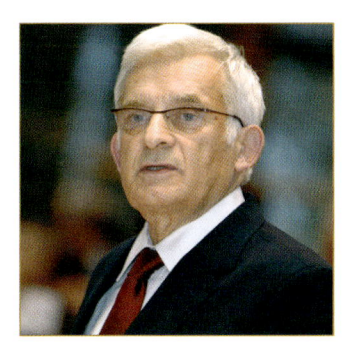

Buzek, Jerzy (b. 1940). A chemical engineer by training and a professor in Częstochowa and Opole by profession, Buzek was active in the political opposition of the 1980s, including the Solidarność (Solidarity) trade union movement. In 1997 he was elected to the Polish Sejm RP (parliament), and soon afterward was appointed Polish prime minister (1997–2001). In 2004 Buzek was elected to the European Parliament as a delegate from Śląsk (Silesia). In 2009 he was elected twenty-fourth president of the European Parliament, the first former Eastern Bloc member to hold that position. His daughter Agata Buzek is a film and theater actress, selected at the Gdynia Film Festival as best Polish actress of 2009 for her role in the film *Rewers* (Reverse).

Bydgoszcz. Located on the Brda River not far from Toruń on the Wisła, Bydgoszcz is a town of nearly 360,000 inhabitants in historic Kujawy, one of the most productive agricultural regions of the country. The area is known for its good soil and for a wide variety of midsize industries. It has a number of higher educational institutions, including a well-regarded music academy. Alongside Bydgoszcz is situated the Kanał Bydgoski (Bydgoszcz Canal, pictured). Built in 1773–1774, it links the Wisła and Odra rivers via the Brda, Noteć, and Warta rivers, and is the oldest active artificial waterway in Poland. Bydgoszcz area farmers were active during the early Solidarność (Solidarity) period. Their leaders were brutally beaten by police at a meeting in March 1981 in what became known as the *prowokacja bydgoska* (Bydgoszcz provocation), an omen of the *stan wojenny* (martial law) proclaimed later that year.

KALEIDOSCOPE OF POLAND

C

całowanie w policzek, podanie ręki (cheek-kissing, hand-shaking). As a relatively new but now firmly entrenched phenomenon, women friends kiss upon meeting after a certain while apart, often three times on alternating cheeks (less often twice, sometimes only once). Traditionally cheek-kissing was practiced mostly among relatives and very close friends, including males. Professionally, one shakes a woman's hand the same as a man's (a woman offers her hand first to a man). Among working-class men, hand-shaking upon meeting up is the norm, even upon each new day.

całowanie w rękę (hand-kissing). In Poland the tradition of a man kissing a woman's hand as a sign of respect was practiced more in the past century (especially pre-1989) than in the present, where it mostly holds on in the countryside and among blue-collar workers. Nevertheless, one observes hand-kissing in Poland more than elsewhere, and in some formal situations it is practically obligatory. The context is almost always indoors. Younger male relatives sometimes kiss the hand of an older female relative (e.g., one's mother-in-law) upon greeting. When a man presents an award to a woman in a formal ceremony, hand-kissing is probably expected. When a man asks a woman to dance (and she accepts), he may kiss her hand afterward as he takes her back to her table. Polish women do not expect such behavior from foreigners; indeed, younger women tend to view the custom as patronizing.

Canaletto (1721–1780). An Italian artist, born Bernardo Bellotto. Already renowned in Italy as a prolific painter of small-format urban landscapes, Canaletto was brought to Poland by King **Stanisław II August Poniatowski**, where he remained. Abroad, Canaletto is known as Venice's best-known painter. In Poland his name is linked to his finely detailed depictions of late eighteenth-century Warsaw, so realistic that they were used after World War II as guidelines for the reconstruction of the war-destroyed *Stare Miasto* (**Starówka**) and the streets Krakowskie Przedmieście and Nowy Świat leading up to it. *Canaletto,* Krakowskie Przedmieście, Warsaw.

Cepelia (Centrala Przemysłu Ludowego i Artystycznego) (Central Office of the Art and Folk Industry). Formed in 1949, Cepelia is an umbrella organization selling the products of several hundred folk art cooperatives around the country. It used to be associated with cheap tourist trinkets. Now privatized, it has stores in all major Polish towns and cities, selling high-end folk art: sculpture, furniture, paintings, dolls, jewelry, fabrics, tapestries, folk costumes, paper cutouts (*wycinanki*), and more. A successful venture was the resurrection of the prewar ceramics industry in Bolesławiec, German *Bunzlau,* whose pottery products with the trademark peacock-eye pattern (pictured) are recognized, sold, and collected around the world. Another prized Cepelia product is handmade heirloom lace with a two-hundred-year tradition behind it, from the Silesian **Beskid** village of Koniaków, used on napkins, handkerchiefs, tablecloths, *czepki* (married women's caps), and — recently and controversially — women's intimate apparel.

chasydyzm (Hasidism). A mystical sect of orthodox Judaism with its origins in eighteenth-century Poland — primarily in Podole (Podolia, now Podilia in Ukraine). Hasidism was a back-to-basics movement against the rabbinical establishment. Its main founder was Rabbi Israel Baal Shem Tov (1700–1760). Another important founder was Elimelech Weisblum (1717–1786), whose grave in Leżajsk is visited yearly by Hasids from around the world. Hasidism is pantheistic. It emphasizes direct contact with God and the enjoyment of life through song, dance, and ecstatic prayer. Important roles are played by the *cadyk,* or charismatic leader, and by the study of the body of mystical medieval writings known as the *kabała*. Hasidism continues to thrive today in around thirty communities around the world, independent but sharing an underlying philosophy and ritual. Hasids are active in preserving, both in the home and for religious purposes, the Yiddish language, a recognized minority language in Poland that is based on medieval German vernacular.

Chełmoński, Józef Marian (1849–1914). A realistic painter of genre scenes of the Polish countryside and the village. After studying and traveling extensively in Europe, he returned to paint scenes of Polish rural life. His paintings often have the kind of iconic quality that makes them popular reproduction (or parody) pieces, such as, for example, his 1875 *Babie lato* (*Indian summer*), pictured.

chleb i sól (bread and salt). A folk song from the **Kujawy** region runs "Mamy soli, mamy chleba . . . Mamy wszystko, co potrzeba" (We have salt, we have bread, we have everything we need). Throughout Slavic lands bread and salt are ceremonially presented to distinguished guests as a sign of welcome and symbol of respect for God's bounty. In Poland the custom is primarily observed at weddings, when the *para młoda* (newlyweds) are presented with a large round loaf with a salt pit dug into the top as they enter the dining area after the wedding. Bread and salt are also part of the traditional Easter basket. Throughout their history, Poles may have lacked for this or that, but hardly ever for bread and salt. Good Polish bread is the one thing Poles in emigration miss most. Bread is treated with virtual religiosity. Bread crumbs are traditionally swept up after a meal. Before slicing a fresh loaf, women of older generations will often make the sign of a cross on it with their knife.

Chocim, bitwa pod Chocimiem (Battle of Chocim, 1621, 1673). Two enormous battles, some fifty years apart, between forces of the Polish-Lithuanian Commonwealth and the Turkish army at Chocim (Ukrainian: Khotyn) in present southwest Ukraine. At that time Chocim was a fortress on the southeast frontier of the Polish-Lithuanian Commonwealth bordering the Turkish Empire (pictured). Both times Polish forces were victorious. In the 1673 encounter some thirty thousand Polish-Lithuanian troops led by *hetman wielki koronny* (Hetman of the Crown) Jan Sobieski (later crowned King **Jan III Sobieski**) defeated a Turkish force of around thirty-five thousand, capturing an immense number of prisoners and amount of arms and equipment. A major role in the victory was played by the Polish *husaria* (hussars), considered at the time the best cavalry in Europe.

Chopin, Fryderyk (Polish: Szopen; 1810–1849). Polish pianist of French extraction, and Poland's most famous composer. He was born in Żelazowa Wola, fifty kilometers west of Warsaw. Chopin left Poland in 1830 and became part of the **Wielka Emigracja** (Great Emigration) in Paris, where his fame as composer, virtuoso performer, and teacher of the rich and famous steadily increased. He carried on a long and tempestuous relationship with the French woman writer George Sand, his senior by several years, while his health steadily deteriorated, apparently from tuberculosis. When Chopin died, his body was buried in Paris but his heart, sealed in a jar of cognac, was smuggled into Warsaw and interred in a pillar at the Holy Cross Church. Chopin composed two piano concertos, but he is best known for the original harmonies and tempos, and the frequent moodiness and unexpected emotional turns, of his shorter pieces: polonaises, scherzos, mazurkas, études, and preludes. The year 2010 in Poland was designated "rok Chopina" (the year of Chopin), with many commemorative events. Two of Chopin's most recognizable works are "Etiuda rewolucyjna" (Revolutionary Etude) and "Marsz żałobny" (Funeral March).

Chopin, Konkurs Chopinowski (International Chopin Piano Competition). Held every five years since 1927, it is the oldest and one of the most prestigious such competitions in the world, and one of few devoted to the works of a single composer. The 2005 winner was Rafał Blechacz of Bydgoszcz, the first Pole to win since Krystian Zimerman in 1975. The 2010 laureate, on the two hundredth anniversary of Chopin's birth, was Yulianna Avdeeva of Russia. *The 2010 competition logo.*

Chrystus Frasobliwy (worry-worn Christ). Having its origins in medieval iconography, the image of "worry-worn" (alternatively, "sorrowful," or "pensive") Christ, sitting with head in hand and with a crown of thorns, is one of the most commonly executed versions of Christ in Polish folk art, and is often depicted in a *kapliczka przydrożna* (roadside chapel). *Chrystus Frasobliwy in Cisna (in the Bieszczad Mountains).*

"Chrząszcz brzmi w trzcinie" (The beetle is buzzing in the reeds). The classic Polish tongue-twister, from a poem by Jan Brzechwa (1898–1966), often brought out to show foreigners how hard Polish is to pronounce. In fact, there are many much harder Polish tongue-twisters than this. Brzechwa's initial couplet reads: "W Szczebrzeszynie chrząszcz brzmi w trzcinie, i Szczebrzeszyn z tego słynie" (In Szczebrzeszyn a beetle buzzes in the reeds, and Szczebrzeszyn is famous for it). In the actual town of Szczebrzeszyn a piece of wooden statuary has been erected to commemorate the titular *chrząszcz* (pictured). He looks more like a cricket than a beetle.

KALEIDOSCOPE OF POLAND

chrzest Polski (baptism of Poland, 996). The acceptance of Christianity by the Polanian prince **Mieszko I** in 966 is taken as the beginning of Poland's history as a Christian nation in the sphere of the western (Roman) Church. The struggle between Christianity and pagan religions, especially among the Baltic tribes, lasted to varying degrees for several more centuries. According to national mythology, Mieszko's decision to accept the cross through Bohemia rather than from Germanic lands, by marrying the Czech princess Dobrawa, was politically motivated: Mieszko wished to deprive the Germanic people of an ideological basis for expanding eastward into Polanian territory. The precise location of Mieszko's baptism is not known; putatively it was in Ostrów Lednicki, an archeological site that is today's Poland's largest open-air museum.

ciasta, ciastka (cakes, pastries). Poland is known for its many *ciasta* (cakes) and *ciastka* (pastries). The term *ciastko* often designates a pastry in the French or Viennese style, in Poland available at a *cukiernia* (sweet or confectionery shop); but it can also designate what amounts to a cookie, although for that *ciasteczko* is often used. Common generic varieties of one or the other include *babka* (cream-filled cake), *bezy* (meringues), *biszkopt* (sponge cake), *ciasto drożdżowiec* (yeast cake), *faworki* (sugared fritters), *jabłecznik* (apple cake), *keks* (fruitcake), *kremówka* (cream puff), *makowiec* (poppy-seed cake or roll, pictured), *mazurek* (cake layered with jam), *murzynek* (brownie), *napoleonka* (eclair), *pączki* (doughnuts), *piernik* (gingerbread), *placek* (flat-cake with fruit on top), *przekładaniec* (layer cake with fruit filling), *ptyś* (puff pastry), *rolada* (rolade), *sernik* (cheesecake), *strucla* (stollen), *szarlotka* (charlotte, applesauce cake), *tort* (iced layer cake). Given such variety, it is surprising that Polish cooking does not have a product like deep-dish American pie.

Ciechocinek. A town of around eleven thousand inhabitants south of **Toruń** along the **Wisła**, Ciechocinek is one of Poland's most popular spas and curative resorts, known for its saline thermal springs, said to be good for curing arthritis, rheumatism, cardiovascular and respiratory diseases, "women's diseases," and afflictions of the nervous system. Ciechocinek is one of around fifty localities in Poland officially designated as an *uzdrowisko* (spa) according to government criteria. Many have the name "Zdrój" (spring/spa) attached to their name, as in Krynica-Zdrój. Dolny Śląsk (Lower Silesia) has more spas than any other region. *The tężnia (salt-evaporating tower) in Ciechocinek.*

ciupaga (mountaineer's ax, alpenstock). A combined walking stick, mountain-climbing tool, and weapon for hacking or throwing, the ciupaga was the favorite weapon of the legendary Tatra Mountain *zbójnicy* (brigands), the most famous of whom was the *harnaś* (brigand chieftain) **Juraj Janosik**, a historical Robin Hood–like figure of Slovak background. Today one may buy souvenir *ciupagi* (probably not good for real hacking and head-splitting, as most have wooden "blades") at tourist outlets all over the south of the country.

cmentarz (cemetery). Polish cemeteries are tightly packed, well visited, and carefully tended. On **Dzień Wszystkich Świętych** (All Saints' Day, November 1) and Dzień Zaduszny (All Souls' Day, November 2), the latter a successor to the pre-Christian ceremony **Dziady** (Forefathers Eve), they are ablaze at night with votive candles. Two well-known Polish cemeteries with imposing grave markers and mausoleums, the resting places of prominent military, political, and cultural figures, are the Powązkowski in Warsaw (founded 1790, pictured) and the Rakowicki in **Kraków** (founded 1803). Both are known by the names of the main streets on which they are located. Historically important Polish cemeteries in the *kresy* (former eastern Poland) are the Cmentarz na Rossie in **Wilno** and the Cmentarz Łyczakowski in **Lwów** (Ukrainian L'viv). For self-evident reasons, many Polish cemeteries have special sections containing rows of tombstones of war dead. Larger city cemeteries have Jewish sections with often imposing statuary. Smaller, separate Jewish cemeteries, called *kirkuty*, are numerous throughout Poland but, lacking a supporting Jewish population, are mostly neither active nor well tended.

cmentarze radzieckie w Polsce (Soviet cemeteries in Poland). The remains of some 650,000 Soviet soldiers killed in World War II in the offensive of 1944–1945 rest in some 638 cemeteries across Poland. Officers are usually buried separately, while rank-and-file solders may lie in common graves. The largest such cemetery in terms of area is in Warsaw alongside Pole Mokotowskie (Mokotów Field), containing the remains of 24,468 soldiers. Poland and Russia each allocate around $1,000,000 for the cemeteries' yearly upkeep. Visitors from Russia often remark that Soviet graves in Poland are better kept than those in Russia. Most Poles recognize the bravery and sacrifice of the Soviet soldiers who died freeing the land of the Nazi occupier, and treat these grave sites with the respect they deserve. Increasingly, Poles visit Soviet cemeteries on **Dzień Wszystkich Świętych** (All Saints' Day) and light votive candles on graves or next to the commemorative obelisks.

Conrad, Joseph (1857–1924). A unique story in world literature. Born Józef Korzeniowski, Conrad was raised by an uncle in **Kraków** after his parents were exiled to Russia for antigovernment activity. As a seventeen-year-old he left Poland for Marseilles, France, and became a sailor. He later joined the British merchant marines and rose to the rank of captain. His trips throughout Central America, Africa, Australia, and the Far East provided material for his later novels and short stories. In 1894 he settled in England and began to write under the name Joseph Conrad. Though he spoke with a thick Polish accent, by the time of his death he was considered one of the most distinctive English stylists. He is recognized today as one of the pioneers of literary modernism and a forerunner of the French existentialists. His most famous books are *Lord Jim* and *Heart of Darkness* (in Polish, *Jądro ciemności*). Both are mentioned as literary sources for Francis Ford Coppola's 1979 Vietnam War film *Apocalypse Now*.

Curie, Maria Skłodowska (1867–1934). Polish-born physicist and chemist, a pioneer radiologist, and two-time recipient of the Nobel Prize, the first in 1903 in physics, together with her husband Pierre, and the second by herself in chemistry, in 1911. Curie discovered two new elements, radium and polonium (the latter named after Poland); coined the term "radioactive"; and revised the scientific understanding of matter at its most basic level. She was the first female Nobel laureate, is the only woman to have received it twice, and thus far is the only person to have received it in two different scientific disciplines. She was the first woman in France to earn a PhD in physics, and the first to teach at the Sorbonne. Although also claimed by France, where she rests with her husband in the national Panthéon as the only woman interred there on her own merits, in 2011 she was selected in a plebiscite conducted by the Muzeum Historii Polski (Museum of Polish History) as the "Polka wszechczasów" (Polish woman of all time). She has appeared on no fewer than eight Polish postage stamps. The element polonium, which she discovered, is highly poisonous and is widely suspected to have been used by the Soviet KGB to kill defector Alexander Litvinenko in London in 2006.

Cybulski, Zbigniew (1927–1967). Nonconformist film and stage actor who cultivated the style on-screen and off of a "rebel without a cause." He was often compared to America's James Dean. Like Dean, he also died senselessly, in his case in Wrocław while trying to leap onto a moving train while drunk. He is still thought of as one of the best actors of the postwar generation. Two of his best roles were Maciek Chełmicki in *Popiół i diament* (Ashes and diamonds, 1958, pictured), by Andrzej Wajda, and Wiktor Rawicz in *Jak być kochaną* (How to be loved, 1963), by Wojciech Jerzy Has. Since 1969 the Zbigniew Cybulski Prize is awarded to the most promising young Polish actor. Cybulski's trademark dark glasses were not an affectation (suggesting injury from gas in the sewers of Warsaw during the **powstanie warszawskie**, the Warsaw Uprising of 1944) but masked a sensitivity to light, shared by his distant relative, General **Wojciech Jaruzelski**.

cyganeria krakowska (artistic Bohemia of Kraków). The term refers to a group of modernistic, nonconformist artists, rejecting middle-class values and living a life demonstrably at odds with the community around them, seeming to spend most of their time in *kawiarnie* (coffee houses), endlessly talking. Preferred dress was a romantic cape, wide-brimmed cap, and fantastic necktie. In Poland this term is usually connected to **Kraków** and the **Młoda Polska** (Young Poland) generation of artists gathered around its theoretician Stanisław Przybyszewski (1868–1927), meeting most prominently in the coffee house Jama Michalika (Michalik's Cavern), with its trendsetting Kabaret Zielony Balonik (Green Balloon Cabaret, 1906–ca. 1912), established by literary critic Tadeusz Boy-Żeleński. The café (pictured) is still doing business on Floriańska Street in Kraków, but more sedately.

Cyrankiewicz, Józef (1911–1989). The brainy, tough, and seemingly indestructible (today one might say "Teflon") communist party careerist who held the office of Polish premier in the **PRL** (communist Poland) from 1947–1970, with a short break in 1952–1954 as vice premier. Having a background as a wartime prisoner in Auschwitz (where he acquired the habit of shaving his head), Cyrankiewicz had no problem using force to quell civil disturbances in **Poznań** in 1956 (*czerwiec 1956, wypadki czerwcowe*) or in Warsaw in 1968 (*marzec 1968, wydarzenia marcowe*). Responding to the former situation, Cyrankiewicz uttered the deathless words, "Let every provocateur or madman be certain that whosoever raises his hand against the people's government will have that hand cut off by that government." Cyrankiewicz gave the orders to the army to fire live ammunition at protesting workers in **Gdańsk** and **Gdynia** in 1970 (see *grudzień 1970, wydarzenia grudniowe*). After that he was gradually shunted aside from positions of true power. He died in 1989 and never lived to see the collapse of the communist regime he helped to create and perpetuate.

cystersi (Cistercian Order). An offshoot of the Benedictine monks, the Cistercians were important in the Middle Ages in promoting science, culture, agriculture, and crafts. They established a large number of imposing monasteries and churches in Poland beginning in the twelfth century, many of which are still standing, often in out-of-the-way places, hence not often visited. Most of the ones still in use are in the south. A favorite tourist route taken by *pielgrzymki* (pilgrimages) is the so-called *szlak cysterski*

(Cistercian route), linking important Cistercian monasteries. *Cistercian Abbey in Wąchock (in southeast Poland)*.

Cytadela Warszawska (Warsaw Citadel). An infamous fortress, prison, and place of execution for political prisoners built in the center of Warsaw by Russian tsar Nicholas I in the 1830s after the failed **powstanie listopadowe** (November Uprising, 1830–1831). The Citadel housed a sizable permanent garrison of Russian troops. Following World War I, it continued to be used by the Polish army as a garrison and arms depot. Today it houses a mixture of military and civilian organizations as well as a museum. Other famous "citadels" built in the nineteenth century by the partitioning powers are Fort Winiary in **Poznań** by Prussia and the Cytadela lwowska (in **Lwów**, Ukraine) by Austria. All today are in various states of disrepair and dismemberment. *A portion of the Cytadela Warszawska*.

czarna porzeczka (black currants, *Ribes nigrum*). Whereas apricots and peaches barely grow in Poland, with its moderate climate and sandy soil, the country is one of the world's premier berry-growing regions. The queen of Polish berries is the black currant, which grows almost everywhere but especially in central Poland, where large plantations help to make Poland the world's number-one producer of both red and black currants. Not far behind, in second place worldwide, are raspberry (*malina*) and strawberry (*truskawka*) production. Poland is also a major apple exporter. Currants take the place in Poland of the berry slot filled in the United States by the cranberry. Like cranberries, they are rich in antioxidants and good for curing urinary infections. More importantly, they make excellent jams, jellies, and sweet sauces, and are good for eating by themselves. Poles are prodigious drinkers of juice, and *sok z czarnej porzeczki* (black currant juice) is foremost among them, almost a national symbol.

Czartoryscy, rodzina (Czartoryski family). An influential and numerous magnate family of ancient Lithuanian lineage, related to the Jagiellons (see **Jagiellonowie**), and active in Polish political

34 KALEIDOSCOPE OF POLAND

life up through the beginning of World War II. The Czartoryski palace in Puławy is now a major research library. Izabela Czartoryska (1746–1835) founded in Puławy what grew into the first Polish national museum, now in Kraków. Her son, Adam Jerzy Czartoryski, was tsarist Russian foreign minister and, later, leader of the Polish émigré community in Paris; see Wielka Emigracja. *Czartoryski coat of arms (Pogoń, Knight in chase).*

---

czerwiec 1956, wypadki czerwcowe (Poznań June 1956, the June incidents). A general strike and street demonstrations in 1956 in Poznań against living and working conditions and repressive communist government rule, brutally suppressed by the police and some ten thousand soldiers, causing fifty-eight documented fatalities. The strike originated in the venerable Cegielski Metal Factory, at the time called the Joseph Stalin Metal Works. The Poznań incidents, in their aftermath, helped to accelerate liberalizing changes within the communist party, including the election of Władyław Gomułka as first party secretary and the release from arrest of many political prisoners, including Cardinal Stefan Wyszyński. The Poznań "incidents" (they were so called by the authorities to belittle their significance) were portrayed in the 1996 film *Poznań 1956*, by Filip Bajon.

---

czerwiec 1976, wydarzenia czerwcowe (June 1976 events). A sudden unannounced increase in food prices in the latter part of June 1976 provoked spontaneous worker strikes and protests throughout Poland, most notably at the Ursus tractor factory in Warsaw and in Radom, where workers burned down the communist party headquarters and cut the main railway line to Warsaw. The protests were put down by the police and special detachments of the Służba Bezpieczeństwa (security service). Several thousand workers were jailed, fined, imprisoned, and fired from work with no chance of employment elsewhere. The workers' legal defense and financial assistance was undertaken by opposition political leaders, who formed KOR (Komitet Obrony Robotników, Workers' Defense Committee). This was a major turning point in the emerging anticommunist movement, for once uniting the interests of workers and intellectuals.

Czerwone Gitary (The Red Guitars). An easy-listening, politically correct rock band with their heyday in the 1960s and 1970s. They were roughly on the model of and contemporaneous with the Beatles, although unlike them they still do concerts. They are often played on the radio. Among their best-known songs (of which most Poles would be able to hum a few bars) are "Anna Maria," "Dozwolone od lat 18" (Only for eighteen and older), "Kwiaty we włosach" (Flowers in your hair), "Matura" (High school exam), and "Takie ładne oczy" (Such pretty eyes). Two other groups of roughly the same time period are Trubadurzy (Troubadours) and Tercet Egzotyczny (Exotic Tercet).

Częstochowa. Poland's thirteenth-largest city, Częstochowa is a city of around 240,000, located on the Warta River in mid-southern Poland. Częstochowa's industry is largely connected to metal-smelting. The town is a major religious center and destination of *pielgrzymki* (pilgrimages) from all over Poland, which come to visit the Jasna Góra monastery and view the miracle-working icon of the Matka Boska Częstochowska (Mother of God of Częstochowa). From the year 2013 they have been able to view the world's largest statue of Jan Paweł II, standing at 13.8 meters. Częstochowa has one of Poland's largest Jewish cemeteries, or *kirkuty*.

Czterej pancerni i pies (Four tankers and a dog, 1966–1970). One of the Poland's all-time most popular television series, directed at an audience ready for lighter war-related fare. Made primarily for a youth audience, the series tells of the fictional, occasionally raucous adventures of a Polish-Russian-Georgian tank crew and its canine mascot Szarik as they fight in the Soviet-led First Polish Army across Poland up to the Baltic seacoast and then east to Berlin in the final days of World War II. Their tank is named "Rudy." For a long time the series was rebroadcast yearly, and it was highly popular both in the Soviet Bloc countries and, in video rerelease, among Poles abroad, despite its propagandistic underpinnings and many historical falsifications. The series helped launch the film career of one of the country's major film actors, Janusz Gajos — pictured here with Szarik and Rudy — who played the role of tank leader Janek.

---

czyn społeczny (organized community service). A method of forced volunteerism used through the 1970s during the PRL (communist Poland), employing shock-troop "volunteers" to finish social projects said to be "above and beyond the plan." In actuality this usually involved work on projects the plan had not foreseen the need for, or had fallen behind on. Most often they were organized by schools or factories. People would gather on Sundays or other days off (Saturdays then were not generally "off") in order to work on construction projects of communal use (like social halls or sidewalks), to help collective farms with seasonal farm work, or to catch the pernicious *stonka ziemniaczana* (Colorado potato beetle). *A czyn społeczny underway in Maków Mazowiecki.*

---

36 KALEIDOSCOPE OF POLAND

D

"**Daj, ać ja pobruszę, a ty poczywaj**" (modern transcription of original *day ut ia pobrusa i ti poziwai*, "Here, let me grind, and you take a break"). This oldest recorded Polish sentence dates from 1270 and was entered in a Latin volume preserved in a Cistercian monastery near Henryków, not far from Wrocław. Commentators find significance in the hominess of the context, in which a dutiful husband seemingly offers to spell his wife with the household chores. *Monument in Henryków to the first Polish sentence, 1270.*

Dama z łasiczką (Dama z gronostajem) (*Lady with an Ermine*, also known as *Lady with a Weasel*). The only painting in Polish collections by the Italian Renaissance painter Leonardo

37

da Vinci, and one of the most valuable Polish museum holdings. Looted by the Nazis in World War II (see the 2014 American film *Monuments Men*), it is now housed in the Czartoryski Museum in Kraków — though Poles complain that it is perpetually traveling on loan to somewhere else. Executed in oil on wood in ca. 1483–1490, it most likely portrays Cecilia Gallerani, a mistress of Ludovico Sforza, holding an animal whose species remains a mystery. The portrait easily compares in its artistry to the Louvre's better-known *Mona Lisa*. A popular 2004 heist movie, *Vinci*, portraying the portrait's theft, was filmed by Juliusz Machulski. Following the film, Vinci became the name of the special police unit tasked with recovering stolen works of art, who were instrumental in recovering the "Arbeit macht frei" sign when it was stolen in 2009 from the Auschwitz-Birkenau museum in Oświęcim.

dania barowe (bar dishes). In less expensive establishments, including *bary mleczne* (milk bars) and *jadłodajnie* (eateries), among other items one will usually encounter a more or less fixed menu of traditional Polish food items — the kind Poles serve in their own homes, including *zupy* (soups) such as *barszcz* (beet soup) and *żurek* (sour-bread soup); *bigos* (cabbage or hunter's stew), *kasza gryczana* (buckwheat groats), *golonka* (pigs' knuckles), *gołąbki* (stuffed cabbage), *gulasz* (goulash), *kopytka* (potato dumplings), *kotlet schabowy* (wiener schnitzel), *pierogi* (filled dumplings), *placki ziemniaczane* (potato pancakes), *naleśniki* (crêpes), *omlet* (omelets), and *surówka* (grated raw carrots, beets, cabbage, or other vegetable). The typical drink/dessert is *kompot*, a thin liquid made from boiling fruit, with pieces of the fruit left in it (watch out for pits). Some bars cater to older citizens not wanting to cook but who still appreciate nutritious food, by offering take-home meal plans.

Dar Pomorza (the frigate *Gift of Pomerania*). A stately three-masted schooner built in 1910 in Hamburg, Germany, and alternately owned by Germany, England, and France. It was bought by Poland in 1929 with money raised by communities along the Baltic seacoast, to be commissioned in 1930 as a training ship for the Polish navy. It spent World War II interned in Sweden. In the 1970s *Dar Pomorza* took part in international tall-ship races, finally winning the Cutty Sark trophy in 1980, two years before its official decommissioning. It is now a floating museum in Gdynia, its home port, having been replaced as a naval training vessel by the Gdańsk-built *Dar Młodzieży* (*Gift of Youth*) — also a three-master. Another Polish sailing ship — TMS *Fryderyk Chopin* — offers the Szkoła pod Żaglami (School under Sails) to high school–age passengers who attend regular classes while visiting foreign ports and helping out on board.

dąb Bartek (Bartek the oak). Bartek is an oak tree growing in the *województwo świętokrzyskie* (Holy Cross Voivodeship) near the village of Bartków. It is an officially designated *pomnik przyrody* (monument of nature). Bartek is estimated to be 645–670 years old, which would place its origin at the time of Kazimierz III Wielki (Kazimierz the Great). Some think it is even older than that.

The oak is showing signs of decrepitude, despite intensive therapeutic efforts to protect it from the ravages of time. Bartek is not the oldest living Polish tree. That would be a common yew (*cis pospolity*), estimated to be around 1,300 years old (hence older than the Polish state itself) growing in Henryków in Dolny Śląsk (Lower Silesia), coincidentally the same town where the oldest Polish sentence was recorded (see "Daj, ać ja pobruszę, a ty poczywaj").

Dąbrowska, Maria (1889–1965). Writer of psychologically perceptive short stories and novels between the two wars and afterward. She lived in Warsaw throughout and after World War II. A religious agnostic, Dąbrowska was deeply humanistic and socially committed to human rights. Under Communism her writings counseled commonsense accommodation to the new social/political reality, while reaching out to people in need. Her most lasting work is the four-volume multigenerational novel *Noce i dnie* (Days and nights, 1932–1934), turned into a twelve-part 1975 film by Jerzy Antczak, more popular than the novel itself, called Poland's version of *Gone with the Wind*. Dąbrowska kept a daily journal throughout her life, describing her life and the events around her. It was published in five volumes in 1988.

Dąbrowski, Jan Henryk (1755–1818). A general under Tadeusz Kościuszko during the insurek-cja kościuszkowska (Kościuszko Insurrection) of 1794. Dąbrowski was later organizer of the Legiony Polskie we Włoszech (Polish Legions in Italy) under Napoleon Bonaparte in Italy in 1796, with the aim of eventually fighting to regain Polish independence. Dąbrowski later took part in Napoleon's unsuccessful Russian campaign of 1812. His raising of the Italian Legions inspired Józef Wybicki's song "Jeszcze Polska nie zginęła" (Poland has not yet perished), i.e., the Mazurek Dąbrowskiego (Dąbrowski mazurka), which is today the Polish national anthem.

Demarczyk, Ewa (b. 1941). Torchy Polish vocalist from the 1960s through the 1990s, a dramatic lyrical interpreter of difficult poetry, one of the most important figures of the Polish postwar musical stage. Nicknamed the *Czarny Anioł* (Black Angel), Demarczyk was long associated with Kraków's Kabaret pod Baranami (Cabaret under the Rams). She appeared in major venues worldwide, including Carnegie Hall in New York. Among her best-known songs are "Karuzela z madonnami" (Merry-go-round with Madonnas), "Groszki i róże" (Polka dots and roses), "Grande Valse Brillante," and "Taki pejsaż" (Such a landscape). Extremely religious, Demarczyk has lived the life of a recluse for the past several years, even her whereabouts being unknown.

demoludy (people's democracies). A colloquial pejorative term for the countries of the Soviet Bloc, an abbreviation of *kraje demokracji ludowej* (countries of people's democracy). Most commonly the term applied narrowly to the Soviet *satelity* (satellites): Bulgaria, Czechoslovakia, East Germany, Hungary, Poland, and Romania. Albania and Yugoslavia were also *demoludy*, but not in the Soviet *obóz* (camp, bloc). In all of the other countries komunizm (communism), usually going by the name *socjalizm* (socialism), was imposed by Soviet-installed puppet regimes, in most cases backed by Soviet forces stationed in the countries. The closely guarded border separating the demoludy from the Zachód (West) was referred to by Western leaders as the *żelazna kurtyna* (Iron Curtain), a term attributed to Winston Churchill, but actually existing earlier. The Soviet Bloc, and then the Soviet Union itself, began to fall apart toward the end of the 1980s, due to many combined forces, but mostly because of lack of economic viability.

Deyna, Kazimierz (1947–1989). Outstanding Polish soccer player of his generation, a still-remembered midfielder capable of scoring from all parts of the pitch. Deyna was a member of the national team in the early 1970s during its glory years, in which Poland won an Olympic gold (1972) and silver (1976), and a bronze in the 1974 world championships. He died in an alcohol-fueled automobile crash in the United States. As a professional he played for Manchester City in England and, later, for the San Diego Sockers in the United States. Deyna shared his glory with other members of the 1974 national team, the names of which many Poles would still be able to reel off, including Grzegorz Lato, who scored the most goals of any player in the 1974 World Cup, including Poland's crucial goal against Brazil for the bronze medal (Deyna and Lato are pictured here just after it). In 2008 Lato was elected president of the PZPN (Polish Football Association). See also: piłka nożna.

---

dialekty regionalne (regional dialects). The main dialect regions in Poland are those of Wielkopolska (Greater Poland), Mazowsze (Mazovian), Małopolska (Lesser Poland), Śląsk (Silesia), and the Podhale region (High Tatra Mountains, Tatry). Because of a uniform educational system and the reach of the mass media, standard Polish is spoken with barely noticeable differences in pronunciation (more in vocabulary than anything else) from place to place. A feature named after the Mazury region, but now mainly encountered in Podhale, is *mazurzenie*, under which *ż* (zh), *sz* (sh), *cz* (ch), and *dż* (j) are pronounced *z*, *s*, *c*, and *z*, respectively, while *rz* remains *rz*. For example, under mazurzenie, *czapka* is pronounced "capka," *szyja* as "syja," and *żurek* as "zurek." The pronunciation of final *ą* as *om* (*drogą*, "drogom") is common in Wielkopolska, Śląsk, and in some other places. In standard Polish, final *ę* is pronounced "e": *idę*, "ide"; "idę" or, worse, "idem" are considered mistakes by language purists.

---

disco polo. A dance and music craze that hit Poland in the 1980s and 1990s, growing out of traditional local wedding bands but with electronic instruments. The music, often of poor quality but with a steady beat, is not especially different from Western disco music. At Polish weddings and other gatherings, disco polo dancers of all ages typically gather in a circle around a constantly changing center couple. A prominent figure in the "movement" was Shazza (Magdalena Pańkowska, pictured), who billed herself as the *królowa* (queen) of disco polo, and besides that is thus far Poland's only disco polo performer to have appeared on the pages of Polish *Playboy* magazine. Her best-known song is "Bierz co chcesz" (Take what you want). Other prominent groups in this vein are Bayer Full, Boys, and Akcent.

Długosz, Jan (1415–1480). Outstanding late-medieval chronicler and historian of Poland from its earliest times to 1480, the year of his death. Długosz used modern historical methods, including careful research and reliance on sources, and is himself the source for many otherwise unknown events. His history of Poland, *Annales seu cronicae incliti Regni Poloniae* (Annals or chronicles of the famous Kingdom of Poland), written in 1455–1480, was published only in 1711–1712. Długosz was a Catholic priest, secretary to Kraków bishop and *szara eminencja* (gray eminence) Zbigniew Oleśnicki during the reign of Władysław II Jagiełło, and an active diplomat under King Kazimierz IV Jagiellończyk. The fact that Polish scholars like Długosz wrote their treatises in Latin well into the sixteenth century ensured that they belonged to the European intellectual mainstream. The downside is that examples of secular writing in Polish before the sixteenth century are largely lacking.

Dmowski, Roman (1864–1939). Next to Józef Piłsudski, his nemesis, Dmowski was the most important politician of the *dwudziestolecie międzywojenne* (interwar period). He was a pursuer of a nationalistic agenda under the Stronnictwo Narodowo-Demokratyczne (see *endecja*), which he cofounded. A scientist by training, as a politician Dmowski was a social Darwinist and believed in the survival of the strongest nations. Since Poland after World War I was foreseen to be weak, he sided with tsarist Russia against

Germany, hoping that Poland would be united with its Prussian and Austrian territories under a Russian umbrella. Dmowski was inimical to the interests of the national minorities (Jews, Ukrainians, Belarusians, Lithuanians), whom he considered to be at a lower level of national consciousness and a potential threat to the Polish spirit. He was an effective spokesman for Polish interests at the konferencja wersalska (Versailles Conference; see *traktat wersalski*) in 1919, helping Poland to obtain a mostly favorable outcome. Dmowski and Piłsudski were able to momentarily set aside their differences to form a functioning Polish state, an achievement in which **Ignacy Paderewski** was instrumental.

dni wolne od pracy (days free from work, i.e., state holidays). Under Polish law, thirteen days in the calendar year are officially free from work: Nowy Rok (New Year's Day); **Święto Trzech Króli** (Three Kings' Day, January 6); **Wielkanoc** (both Easter Sunday and Monday); Pierwszy Maja (May 1), once Święto Pracy (labor day), now an unnamed *święto państwowe* (state holiday); Dzień Konstytucji Trzeciego maja (Constitution Day, May 3); **Zielone Świątki** (Green Holidays), liturgically Zesłanie Ducha Świętego (the Descent of the Holy Spirit; that is, Pentecost, held on Sunday forty-eight days after Easter); **Boże Ciało** (Corpus Christi, a mobile holiday); Wniebowzięcie Najświętszej Maryi Panny (the Ascension of the Virgin Mary; that is, Feast of the Assumption), the same day as Święto Wojska Polskiego (Polish Armed Forces Day, August 15); **Dzień Wszystkich Świętych** (All Saints' Day, November 1); Dzień Niepodległości (Independence Day, November 11); **Boże Narodzenie** (Christmas and the day after, December 25–26). See also: **wolne soboty**.

Doda. The stage nickname of Dorota Rabczewska (b. 1984), a pop rock singing star of the new millennium. Rabczewska, the self-proclaimed queen of Polish pop, is a celebrity in the Lady Gaga mode, and her public and private doings are a constant topic of the pulp press. Doda's latest album is *Siedem pokus głównych* (Seven cardinal temptations). Her rival as to voice and number of appearances on magazine covers and in men's magazines is Edyta Górniak, who was in 1994 the second place winner in the Eurovision song contest (Poland's best finish ever).

dożynki (harvest festival). One of many rites handed down by the pre-Christian Balts and Slavs, *dożynki* are usually held on the last day of summer and celebrate the end of the year's harvest. Elaborate *wieńce dożynkowe* (harvest wreaths) are made from a stand of grain that has been intentionally left unharvested. Traditionally the wreaths were presented by peasants to the landowner. Nowadays they can be presented to local town officials or the local church. The wreaths are kept until the following spring, and their seeds are mixed into the next year's sowing. Dożynki are often accompanied by folk festivals and a general celebration of the rural way of life. Under Communism they were co-opted and used as a paean to socialism. See also: Siwiec, Ryszard. *A dożynki wreath from Kobierzyce near Wrocław.*

Druga Rzeczpospolita Polska (Second Polish Republic). The term describes what at the time was also called Polska Odrodzona (reborn Poland), the interwar Polish state from 1918–1939 (*dwudziestolecie międzywojenne,* interwar period). The name emphasized continuity with the pre-1795 Rzeczpospolita Obojga Narodów (Polish-Lithuanian Commonwealth). Its official name was Rzeczpospolita Polska, and its most important leader was Józef Piłsudski. Some consider that the Second Republic did not end in 1939 but lasted until 1990 as the *rząd na uchodźstwie* (government in exile) in London. At first the Second Polish Republic was a parliamentary democracy, but it later turned into a largely authoritarian regime under the *sanacja* (return to health) camp of Józef Piłsudski.

druga wojna światowa (World War II). World War II began, for Poland and the rest of the world, on September 1, 1939, with the attack first on Wieluń in central Poland, and then on the Westerplatte garrison near Gdańsk, followed by the pincer attack by the Soviet Union from the east on September 17, in accordance with the secret pakt Ribbentrop-Mołotow (Molotov-Ribbentrop Pact). Despite their treaty obligations, England and France took no immediate action in defense of Poland. The war ended in Europe on May 7–9, 1945, with the capitulation of German forces in all theaters. Due to military action, emigration, and the change of borders, during the war Poland lost almost one-third of its population (from 35 million down to 24 million people), including almost all of its Jews. A large percentage of prewar Polish *inteligencja* had been murdered, the country's major national monuments had been destroyed, and its museums and churches systematically ransacked. In actual mortality, Poland lost around one-sixth of its prewar population, the largest proportion of any country. See also: druga wojna światowa: muzea; druga wojna światowa: wojna bez zwycięstwa

druga wojna światowa: muzea (World War II museums). Under Communism, Poles were not allowed to commemorate their greatest wartime tragedies, including the Katyń massacre, the powstanie warszawskie (Warsaw Uprising), and the Holocaust as a specifically Jewish catastrophe (it was taboo to break down the wartime dead into Polish vs. Jewish). Excellent museums now deal with two of these subjects, the multimedia Muzeum Powstania Warszawskiego (Museum of the Warsaw Uprising) in Warsaw, and the permanent exhibit *Kraków: Czas Okupacji 1939–1945* (Kraków under the Occupation, 1939–1945), located in the building of the former Oskar Schindler enamelware factory in Kraków. Schindler, a German from Bohemia, saved by clever ruse some 1,300 of his workers from extermination at Auschwitz. Steven Spielberg's 1993 film *Schindler's List*, devoted to his story, won seven Oscars. The museum in Schindler's building gives eloquent testimony and homage to the fate of Kraków's prewar Jewish population. Several other World War II museums are presently in the planning and design stage.

druga wojna światowa: wojna bez zwycięstwa (war without victory). World War II for Poland was not a "good war," as it is sometimes called in the West, by any stretch of the imagination. It was primarily waged between Nazi Germany and Soviet Russia on the Polish and Russian "bloodlands," to use Timothy Snyder's term from the title of his 2010 book on the subject. Poles are only too aware that they did not win the war, but lost it, despite the unparalleled heroism of the civilian population, against whom in practice the war was largely waged. After 1945 terrorism did not cease but shifted into the hands of the Soviets, whose troops left Poland only in 1991–1993, nearly fifty years later. With the country having lost some 5.5 million people in wartime casualties (only 240,000 of them military), including almost all of its Jews (3 million out of 3.5), one can more easily appreciate why many Poles, while understanding the tragedy of the Jewish Holocaust, at the same time view it as part of a larger picture of their own national catastrophe and the struggle for survival not only of Poland but of its entire people. Western historians, with notable exceptions, have been slow to appreciate that the war told primarily from the perspective of the Western Allies gives a highly skewed picture of its reality for those most affected by it.

---

drukarstwo (printing). Poland was the ninth country in Europe to implement the technology of movable type, invented in Mainz, Germany, in 1455 by Johannes Gutenberg. The Polish center of printing was Kraków, and most printers were German immigrants. The oldest Polish print is the *Almanach cracoviense ad annum 1474* by Kasper Straube, qualifying as an *incunabulum* (print work from before 1501). It is a kind of farmer's almanac made to be hung on a wall and describes, among other things, the best time to let your blood. It is preserved at the Uniwersytet Jagielloński. The earliest printed work in the Polish language to be preserved (until World War II) was *Raj duszny* (Paradise of the soul), a reworking by Biernat of Lublin of *Hortulus Animae* (Little garden of the soul), printed in 1513 by Florian Ungler in Kraków. In the sixteenth century, Polish printeries were among the most ideologically liberal in Europe, with different centers associated with different religious offshoots. Of these, Brześć and Pińczów were important for Calvinist works, Raków for Arian, Królewiec for Lutheran, Wilno for Orthodox, and Lublin for Hebrew. See also: religie w Polsce.

Drużbacka, Elżbieta (ca. 1695–1765). One of the first Polish woman writers, popular in the time of the late *barok* (baroque) and early *oświecenie* (Enlightenment). A skilled rhymester, she wrote long spiritual verse, rhymed adventure tales, and social satires, for which she can be viewed as the first Polish feminist. Her most widely read work was *Opisanie czterech części roku* (Description of the four times of year), which goes on and on.

Dulska, dulszczyzna. The title character in the 1906 play *Moralność pani Dulskiej* (The morality of Mrs. Dulska) by Gabriela Zapolska (1857–1921, pictured), a play that was racy for its time and gave rise to the term *dulszczyzna*, meaning crass upper-middle-class hypocrisy hidden behind a mask of outer morality. A 1930 film based on the play was Poland's first talking movie. Zapolska herself, besides writing plays and satirical short stories, was a working actress, appearing in more than two hundred productions. She is buried in Lwów's Łyczakowski cemetery.

dwa nagie miecze (two bared swords). Presented in an act of arrogance by Ulrich von Jungingen, grand master of the Krzyżacy (Teutonic Knights) to Władysław II Jagiełło in 1410 before the bitwa pod Grunwaldem (Battle of Grunwald) as a sign to stop stalling, that combat between the two should commence. The Poles had been calmly resting in the shade while the Germans in their armor were parading and overheating in the sun. Once back in the royal treasury in Kraków after the resounding Polish victory (and Ulrich's death), the swords began to be treated as insignia of Polish royal power. Following the fall of the powstanie listopadowe (November Uprising, 1830–1831), they were hidden in a small parish church from the Russians until 1853, when they were accidentally discovered and confiscated by tsarist police. Their whereabouts today are unknown. *Dwa nagie miecze monument in Skarżysko-Kamienna, Góry Świętokrzyskie.*

dwór szlachecki, dworek szlachecki (manse, manor house). In the sixteenth and seventeenth centuries Poland developed a distinctive type of manor house in which landowners resided. The style lasted into the twentieth century and is often copied today in single-family dwellings. The typical *dwór* or *dworek* was one-storied and symmetrical, with entry through a peak-roofed porch supported on pillars, with rooms to one side and the other. The orientation was at 11:00 into the sun, so that all rooms were illuminated during the course of the day. An excellent description of such a dwór/dworek appears in book I of Adam Mickiewicz's Pan Tadeusz. When farm property was confiscated from the landowning class after World War II, most Polish manor houses were handed over to public use. It is estimated that 80 percent of Polish former manor houses are presently in a state of utter ruin, presenting a real challenge for movie directors trying to find rural locations for filming the interwar period. *Dwór in Żelazowa Wola,* Chopin's birthplace.

dwudziestolecie międzywojenne (interwar period, 1918–1939). The twenty years between the two world wars witnessed a vigorous flowering of Polish culture. The main centers were Warszawa (Warsaw), Kraków, Lwów, and Wilno. In the literary arena, see under *Skamander*. In the political arena, after defending itself from an invasion by Soviet Russia in 1919–1920, and following the assassination of the republic's first president, Gabriel Narutowicz, in 1922, Poland's political situation was unstable. The 1926 *przewrót majowy* (May coup d'état) put Józef Piłsudski in charge under the so-called *sanacja* (return to health) camp, increasingly autocratic after Piłsudski's death in 1935. Poland, left dangling by France and England despite their treaty obligations, was in no condition to withstand the pincer attack of Europe's two biggest armies — Germany from the west and the Soviet Union from the east in 1939. France, aided by England, did not last any longer in 1940 against a German-only attack for which it should have been well prepared.

Dymitr Samozwaniec (first "False Dimitry," ca. 1581–1606). Claiming to be the son of the Russian tsar Ivan IV (the Terrible, who had killed his son with his own hand), Dymitr enlisted the help of certain Polish magnates (*magnateria*) and Don Cossacks to install himself briefly on the Russian throne during the Russian "Time of Troubles." He had the new and old tsars' family murdered, except for Princess Xenia, whom he fancied and kept as a sex slave. A surprisingly liberal tsar, although with a certain reputation for licentiousness, and apparently not disliked by the Russian people, Dymitr was resented by the boyars for his Catholicism and Polish ways and retinue. Along with five hundred Polish retainers, he was killed in a rebellion within a year, incinerated, and his ashes were shot by cannon toward Poland. Whereas many countries celebrate their liberation from Russia, Russia celebrates its liberation from Poland on November 4 (National Unity Day). Poles soon found a second Dimitry pretender, leading to a protracted Polish-Russian conflict in 1608–1613.

Dymna, Anna (b. 1951). Polish film and theater actress, with many film and theater credits to her name. In her earlier work she was known for her cinematic undressing scenes, but Dymna is better known today for her multifaceted charity work and television specials on behalf of the disabled, disadvantaged, and handicapped, in the name of her organization Mimo wszystko (Despite Everything). Poland has been slow to recognize the needs of the disabled but is now making strides to remedy the situation, in part because of activists like Dymna.

Dyzma, Kariera Nikodema Dyzmy (The career of Nikodem Dyzma). A 1932 satirical social and political novel by Tadeusz Dołęga-Mostowicz (1898–1939), in which a down-on-his-luck provincial comes to Warsaw looking for a job as a gigolo and, through a series of accidents and misunderstandings, ends up making a meteoric political career. The character of Dyzma has become the symbol of the boorish social upstart, achieving success by pretending to be someone he is not. The novel was turned into a popular 1980 television costume drama by Jan Rybkowski and Marek Nowicki, and the idea of the novel was turned into a 2002 film, set in modern times by Jacek Bromski. The plot may have been lifted by Jerzy Kosiński for his novel *Being There*, although Kosiński dubiously claimed not to have read it. It is still considered a good read (or a good listen, as there is an audiobook version).

Dziady (Forefathers' Eve). Some people translate the word as "Halloween," but that is misleading. It is a pre-Christian Slavic and Baltic festival for making contact with and honoring the dead, brought to literary life by Adam Mickiewicz in his Romantic drama by the same name (see *Dziady* [Romantic play]). Gifts of food, especially *miód* (honey), *kasza* (cooked grain), *kutia* (a dish of grain and sweetmeats), and eggs, were left on graves. Candles were lighted to show dead souls the way to eternal rest. In Christian times the holiday more or less merged with Dzień Zaduszny or Zaduszki (All Souls' Day), held one day after Dzień Wszystkich Świętych (All

Saints' Day). On both of these days alms were and are given to the poor.

Dziady (Romantic play). A Romantic drama by Adam Mickiewicz, mixing folk elements, mystical occurrences, and patriotic themes. It consists of parts II, III, and IV, and a fragmentary part I. Part II describes the conjuring up of spirits during the folk rites of Dziady (Forefathers' Eve). Part IV refers to Mickiewicz's personal unhappy love for Maryla Wereszczakówna. Part III, infused with *mesjanizm polski* (Polish national messianism), takes place among imprisoned conspirators of the unsuccessful powstanie listopadowe (November Uprising, 1830–1831), waiting to be transported to Siberia. A 1968 performance of *Dziady* in Warsaw was cut short through the intervention of the Soviet embassy when the audience clapped too enthusiastically at the anti-Russian lines, a tinderbox that set off the *wydarzenia marcowe* (March events). A 1989 film version of the play, titled *Lawa* (Lava), was made by Tadeusz Konwicki.

działka (garden plot). To maintain "contact with the land" many Polish apartment-bound city-dwellers own or lease garden plots within a town or on its fringes. *Rodzinne Ogrody Działkowe* (RODs, family garden plots) are little gated communities, membership in which is open to the general public. They are organized under the Polski Związek Działkowców (Polish Plot-Gardeners' Union). Most *działki* are large enough for a little cottage (pictured), which will have electricity and running water for the intensive cultivation of flowers, decorative plants, shrubs, fruits, and vegetables. Smaller *działki* may have only a sheltering lean-to or gazebo. More prosperous city dwellers aspire to the ownership of a *domek letniskowy* (summer cottage) far out in the country. A favorite activity in either instance is sitting outside in a chair doing nothing, followed in the evening by putting meat or *kiełbasy* (sausages) on a grill.

dzień dobry, do widzenia (hello, goodbye). One "greets" in Poland noticeably more often than, for example, in the United States. One automatically greets a small store owner with *dzień dobry* (hello) upon entering his or her establishment, and says *do widzenia* (goodbye) upon leaving. The greeting obligation falls upon the one entering or leaving, and saying hello and goodbye can even occur in elevators with total strangers. Poles liberally sprinkle *proszę* (please, you're welcome) and *dziękuję* (thank you) into their everyday dealings. One says *smacznego* (bon appétit) before a meal and *dziękuję* when getting up from table. See also: całowanie w policzek, podanie ręki; całowanie w rękę.

Dzień Kobiet (International Women's Day, March 8). The first Women's Day was celebrated on February 29, 1910, in New York City. Later, Vladimir Lenin declared March 8 to be International Women's Day, in commemoration of a pre-Revolutionary 1913 Russian women's rights demonstration. The holiday in the PRL (communist Poland) was a postwar transplant from the Soviet Union. Women were given as presents such "deficit" (hard to obtain) products as nylon stockings, soap, and cosmetics. Women's Day is one holdover from the communist era that many Polish women (and women throughout the former Soviet Bloc) are reluctant to part with. On this day, now devoid of the pomp and speeches of former times, men give the women in their lives and work environments candy, flowers (traditionally, carnations or tulips), or small presents. The day is also used for feminist equal-rights demonstrations such as Manifa.

KALEIDOSCOPE OF POLAND   47

Dzień Wszystkich Świętych (All Saints' Day, November 1). In the Catholic Church, this day is set aside for honoring all those who have lived saintly lives, whether officially recognized or not. Beyond this, All Saints' Day is a Polish national holiday for honoring the dead in general, accompanied by the visiting of cemeteries (see *cmentarz*), the lighting of votive candles, and sometimes by the placing of food on graves. Cemeteries across the country are ablaze with candles. The day is followed by Dzień Zaduszny (Zaduszki), or All Souls' Day, for all those who have achieved salvation. Zaduszki are a successor to the pre-Christian ceremony of *Dziady* (Forefathers' Eve), honoring ancestors. Cemeteries use the occasion as an opportunity to collect money for the upkeep of older monuments, many of which are falling to ruin. *All Saints' Day in a cemetery in Boronów.*

Dzierżyński, Feliks (1877–1926). Known as "Bloody Felix," Dzierżyński was a Polish-born Soviet Communist revolutionary responsible for creating under Vladimir Lenin the ruthless state security terror apparatus known as the Cheka, forerunner of the NKVD and its successor, the KGB. During the Russian Civil War of 1917–1922, tens of thousands of opponents to the Bolshevik regime were executed by members of the Cheka without trial. Dzierżyński was venerated as a communist "saint" throughout the Soviet period. As a constant affront to Poles in the PRL (communist Poland), a major square in Warsaw bore his name, and a statue of his likeness. The hands of the statue were regularly painted red by "hooligans." Dzierżyński's statue was one of the first to be dismantled in the waning days of the PRL, and the square was returned to its prewar name, Plac Bankowy (Bank Square).

dzwon Zygmunta (Zygmunt's Bell). Cast in Kraków in 1520 at the behest of King Zygmunt I Stary (Zygmunt the Old), the bell hangs in a tower in Wawel Cathedral in Kraków. It weighs twelve tons, and until recently it was the largest bell in Poland (it has been displaced in size by the bell in Licheń). For good luck, visitors to the bell touch its tongue, itself weighing 365 kilograms. The bell is rung only on rare occasions, for example on September 1, 1939, when Germany invaded Poland, or after the April 10, 2010 *katastrofa pod Smoleńskiem* (Smolensk air disaster), when president Lech Kaczyński, his wife, most of the Polish military command, and many ordinary citizens lost their lives.

E

Edelman, Marek (1919 or 1922–2009). The last surviving leader of the powstanie w getcie warszawskim (Warsaw Ghetto Uprising, 1943), Edelman was one of the organizers of the resistance group Żydowska Organizacja Bojowa (Jewish Fighting Organization). During the uprising he took over from Mordechaj Anielewicz when the latter committed suicide to avoid capture. Edelman escaped the ghetto through the sewers and lived to fight alongside the Armia Krajowa (Home Army) in the powstanie warszawskie (Warsaw Uprising, 1944). After the war he completed a medical degree in Łódź and became a renowned cardiologist. His story is told in Hanna Krall's *Zdążyć przed Panem Bogiem* (Arriving before God). Always active in progressive politics, he was a consultant on health matters at the rozmowy Okrągłego Stołu (Round Table Discussions, 1989). Until his death Edelman was elder statesman and spokesman on behalf of Jews and other national minorities. He was awarded, belatedly, the Order Orła Białego (Order of the White Eagle) in 1998.

---

edukacja (educational system). *Szkoła podstawowa* "*podstawówka*" (grade school) begins at age six and lasts six years. *Gimnazjum* (middle school) begins at age twelve and lasts three years. Competency exams after gimnazjum largely determine whether a pupil will enter a two- or three-year *szkoła zawodowa* "*zawodówka*" (vocational school) or four-year *technikum* (technical high school) or *liceum* (liberal arts school) — in American terms, both "high school." *Technikum* and *liceum* are both capped by the *matura* (high school achievement examination), successful performance on which entitles one to apply for acceptance at a *szkoła wyższa* (higher school, usually *uniwersytet*, "university"), of which there are commonly three degrees: three years for a *licencjat* (BA), two additional years for a *magisterium* (MA), and usually at least four additional years of study and writing for a *doktorat* (doctorate). Some programs, like medical school, can last longer. Grade school grades range from one (lowest) to six (highest), university grades from two to five, entered in the student's green *indeks* (grade book). Despite being the object of constant local criticism, the Polish pre-university educational system has attracted favorable international attention of late for demonstrated improvements in outcomes.

Eichelbaum, Aaron, Szmul, Hirsz, i Itzhak (Warner Brothers). Jewish emigration in the nineteenth century was more of a general Eastern European phenomenon than specifically Polish (Poland in any case did not exist until 1918), and it is therefore not part of the Polish national narrative. Nevertheless, it is still worth remarking on a few noteworthy examples of Polish Jews who made spectacular careers in the Hollywood film industry. The first three Eichelbaum brothers, Jews from Mazowsze, emigrated to North America in 1903, changing their names from Aaron, Szmul, and Hirsz Eichelbaum to Albert, Sam, and Harry Warner. A fourth brother, Itzhak (Jack), was born in Canada. The brothers transformed a Newcastle, Pennsylvania, nickelodeon into a movie theater business, and by the 1920s had established a film production company in Hollywood (Warner Bros.), which today is part of Time-Warner, one of the largest media conglomerates in the world. See also: Faktorowicz, Maksymilian; Gelbfisz, Szmuel.

---

emigracja polska (Polish emigration). A word redolent with connotations of failed uprisings, political repression, hardship, and privation. Emigration in the early nineteenth century was to escape the repercussions of the failed uprisings of 1830 (the Wielka Emigracja, "Great Emigration," mainly to France) and of 1863 (mainly to Brazil). The greatest works of Chopin, Krasiński, Mickiewicz, Słowacki, and Norwid were produced in emigration. The emigration of Poles to the United States around the turn of the nineteenth to twentieth century, especially from Galicja (Galicia) in the southeast, was to escape dire poverty. The cataclysm of World War II dispersed additional Poles, and the political situation during the communist years also produced a steady stream of dissident emigration, especially after 1968, to Israel, and after 1981, during *stan wojenny* (martial law), to the United States. Today Polish emigration has a different face, as Poles, free to travel and work around the European Union, have, for example, flooded the hotel, nursing, and building trades in the British Isles while at the same time remaining in close touch with friends and family and coming home for the holidays. See also: hydraulik polski.

---

empik. A large commercial outlet for books, press, music, videos, and computer software, with stores throughout Poland and Ukraine. It also has a thriving internet business and operates a well-regarded chain of foreign language schools. Empik has grown into an institution; people routinely "umówić się przed empikiem" (meet in front of empik) as a place of orientation. It is popular with foreigners, as it has a good selection of international press. The company is the privatized successor to the communist-era Klub Międzynarodowy Prasy i Książki (International Press and Book Club, MPiK), first established as a network of press clubs in 1948.

Enigma (Enigma Machine). The name for the German military cipher machine for encoding secret messages (pictured). Polish mathematicians Marian Rejewski, Jerzy Różycki, and Henryk Zygalski broke the code as early as 1932, and their decryption techniques were passed to the French and British before the war started. British experts at top secret Bletchley Park, including computer legend Alan Turing, relying on the Polish intelligence, were able to decipher

German secret messages through much of World War II, making a critical contribution to the Allied victory. The story of the Enigma machine and the Polish contribution to its deciphering was not revealed until the 1970s. The utterly fictional 2001 film *The Enigma Machine* starring Kate Winslet, with screenplay by Tom Stoppard, and coproduced by Mick Jagger, shamefully does not mention the Polish contribution nor, for that matter, even Turing, and preposterously features a Polish villain willing to betray Bletchley Park's secrets to the Nazis.

epoki (okresy) literackie (literary periods). Because of their differing underlying ideologies, Polish literary works from the Middle Ages through the middle of the twentieth century are commonly divided into the periods *średniowiecze* (Late Middle Ages, fourteenth to fifteenth centuries), *renesans* or *odrodzenie* (Renaissance, sixteenth century), *barok* (baroque, seventeenth century), *oświecenie* (the Enlightenment, eighteenth century), *romantyzm* (Romanticism, early nineteenth century), *pozytywizm* (Positivism, late nineteenth century), *modernizm*/**Młoda Polska** (Modernism, Symbolism, Young Poland, early twentieth century), and the *dwudziestolecie międzywojenne* (interwar period, Parnassism, 1918–1939). From the period of *romantyzm* on, these periods in Poland have an increasingly specific national flavor. Discounting the brief period of *socrealizm* (socialist realism), it is sometimes said that after World War II *literatura współczesna* (contemporary literature in general) finds itself in the period of *postmodernizm* (postmodernism), too self-aware to take any ideology seriously.

Euro 2012 (Mistrzostwa Europy w Piłce Nożnej) (European Soccer Championships). Cosponsored by Poland and Ukraine in the summer of 2012, and hyped as the "greatest event in the history of Polish sports," the event was preceded by years of frantic efforts to build or renovate stadiums, hotels, public toilets, train stations and, especially, highways to handle the expected gigantic influx of fans. For months in advance there was hardly a newspaper or news program that did not carry increasingly panic-stricken segments devoted to the preparations, paying special attention to road projects, many of which never were completed on time. Still, the games took place without major incident and with credit to the two sponsoring countries. In the championship match, held in Kiev, Spain routed Italy 4–0. Poland fell out in the first round of play. See also: **Deyna, Kazimierz; piłka nożna**.

Europa Środkowa, Europa Wschodnia (the "Other" Europe). During the period 1945–1990, the West used the term Europa Wschodnia (Eastern Europe) to refer loosely to the *demoludy*, countries on the other side of the so-called *żelazna kurtyna* (Iron Curtain). The peoples of these countries themselves found irksome the idea of being labeled as being in the Soviet *obóz* (bloc or camp). The reintroduced term Europa Środkowa (Central Europe) now is used to refer to the Czech Republic, Hungary, Poland, and Slovakia, plus sometimes Germany, Austria, and Slovenia. "Eastern Europe," then, consists of the Baltic states (Latvia, Lithuania, and Estonia), Belarus, Bosnia and Herzegovina, Bulgaria, Croatia, Moldova, Romania, Serbia, and Ukraine. Europa Środkowo-Wschodnia (East-Central Europe) has become the all-inclusive term. These terms can still irk residents of these countries, who consider that they are being labeled as peripheral and unimportant. Indeed, Western historians and politicians often treat them as just that.

F

Faktorowicz, Maksymilian (Max Factor, 1875 or 1877–1938). A Łódź-born Jewish cosmetologist, hair stylist, wig-maker, and pioneer of the modern cosmetics industry, credited with coining the word *makeup*. After serving for a while as cosmetics expert to the Russian royal family, in 1904 he emigrated to the United States, changed his name to Max Factor, and ended up in Los Angeles where he developed theatrical greasepaint specifically adapted to the needs of the emerging film industry. He became known as cosmetician to the stars, including the actresses Gloria Swanson, Mary Pickford, and Jean Harlow, among many others. Factor received an honorary Oscar in 1929 for his contributions to the film industry, and he has a star on the Hollywood Walk of Fame. His cosmetics are still among the most popular in the industry. *Max Factor applying his product to Renée Adorée.*

festiwale filmowe (film festivals). Three film festivals many Poles follow are the Festiwal Polskich Filmów Fabularnych (Festival of Polish Feature-Length Films), held in September in Gdynia (formerly in Gdańsk), which awards the Złoty Lew (Golden Lion) to the best Polish films,

52

actors, directors, and so on; the Nowe Horyzonty festival, in Wrocław since 2006 (formerly in Sanok and Cieszyn), which provides a yearly venue in July for the latest in world experimental cinema; and the Camerimage festival (first in Toruń, then Łódź, now Bydgoszcz), awarding the gold, silver, and bronze Żaba (frog, pictured) for the best in international camerawork.

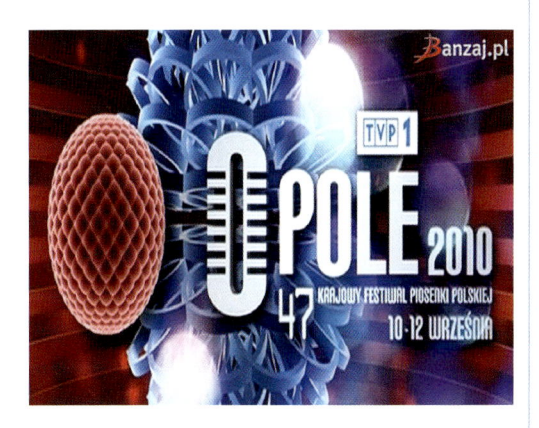

festiwale muzyczne (popular music festivals). The grandfather of Polish music festivals is the Krajowy Festiwal Piosenki Polskiej (National Festival of Polish Song) in Opole (see poster), at which virtually all Polish singers of any note have appeared. The Międzynarodowy Festiwal Piosenki (International Festival of Song) in Sopot has had a long history (since 1961), but its future is shaky. The former festival of Soviet song in Zielona Góra continues as a festival of Russian song, and the former festival of army song in Kołobrzeg lives on as the Arsenał Artystyczny (Artistic Arsenal) in Gdynia. Among newer entries in this crowded field are the legendary rock festival in Jarocin, big in the 1980s but recently fallen in popularity; the Open'er festival in Gdynia; the summer's-end Coke Live Music Festival in Kraków; and the Off Music Festival in Katowice.

Fiat 125p, duży Fiat (large Fiat). A midsized passenger car produced at first on an Italian license and then independently, from 1967–1991, at the Żerań factory in Warsaw. It replaced the Warszawa, produced from 1951–1973 in the same factory. Known as the *duży Fiat* (large Fiat) to distinguish it from the *mały Fiat* (small Fiat, or Fiat 126p), the 125p featured both pickup and station wagon models, in addition to a sedan. It was unusual among Polish automobiles in having a fairly successful export career. In all, 1,445,689 were made. The Fiat 125p was eventually replaced by the Polonez (1978–2002).

Fiat 126p, mały Fiat (little Fiat). Known colloquially and affectionately as *maluch* (tiny), a name that was eventually adopted officially. Produced originally in Italy and later, from 1973, in Poland, the little Fiat was responsible for introducing many Polish families to the ownership of *cztery koła* (four wheels), in connection with the drive toward the *motoryzacja* (motorization) of the country during the Gierek years. In all, 4,671,586 vehicles were produced in the years 1973–2000. The *mały Fiat* joined its larger brother, the *duży Fiat* (large Fiat), or Fiat 125p.

KALEIDOSCOPE OF POLAND 53

filmy kultowe (cult films). If it refers to cinematic works appealing mainly to narrow fringes of film cognoscenti, then the term can be misleading in the instance of some of the members of the pantheon of Polish "cult films." Many of them scored at the box office and are appreciated by more than just a narrow public, although not necessarily outside the country. Among those of the last forty to sixty years, one may cite *Rękopis znaleziony w Saragossie* (Manuscript found in Saragossa) by Wojciech Jerzy Has, 1965; *Rejs* (River trip) by Marek Piwowski, 1975; *Miś* (Teddy bear) by Stanisław Bareja, 1980; *Seksmisja* (Sex-mission) by Juliusz Machulski, 1984; *Psy* (Pigs) by Władysław Pasikowski, 1992; and *Dzień świra* (Day of the wacko) by Marek Koterski, 2002. One could name many more. Except for the escapist *Rękopis*, set in Spain sometime before the Napoleonic Wars, these are mostly dark comedies capturing Polish society at important junctures in its sociopolitical development. *Zbigniew Cybulski and Iga Cembrzyńska-Kondratiuk in* Rękopis znaleziony w Saragossie.

---

filomaci i filareci (Philomaths and Philarets). Secret patriotic and self-help societies modeled after the Freemasons, at the University of **Wilno** at the beginning of the nineteenth century. Among the founding members of the Philomaths was **Adam Mickiewicz**. Tsarist authorities clamped down on both organizations and sent many members, including Mickiewicz, into exile in the depths of Russia, an event that finds reflection in his play *Dziady* (Forefathers' eve), part III. Polish university *korporacje akademickie* (fraternities) of the nineteenth and twentieth centuries often modeled themselves after these organizations. The first lines of the "Pieśń filaretów" (Song of the Philarets) are:

> Precz, precz od nas smutek wszelki!
> Zapal fajki, staw butelki!

> Away, away from us all sadness!
> Light the pipes and set up the bottles!

---

flaga (flag of the Republic of Poland). The Polish national colors are, and have been since the end of the eighteenth century, *biało-czerwony* (red and white), the red being at one time more crimson (purple-tinged) than now. A movement is afoot to change it back to its original hue. The flag is divided horizontally into two equal stripes, white on top and red on the bottom. The *Orzeł Biały* (white eagle) insignia may be placed in the white area; that version of the flag is flown at foreign missions. Sports broadcasters refer to the members of a national representative team as the *biało-czerwoni* (red-and-whites).

---

flisak (raftsman). The ancient trade of raftsman, plying lumber and other goods on *tratwy* (rafts) down the **Wisła** to the **Bałtyk** (Baltic Sea), has been romanticized in Polish literature as far back as Sebastian Klonowic's 1595 narrative poem *Flis* (Rafting). Over time raftsmen earned for themselves status as a craft, rights for which were granted by the king. In **Kraków** raftsmen were called *włóczkowie*. They had their own dress and insignia and, according to legend, helped defend Kraków from a Tatar onslaught in 1287, in memory of which the *lajkonik* festival is held each year. Rafting along the Wisła as a trade has fallen off, but a popular tourist attraction is *spływ Dunajcem*, floating by raft down the Dunajec River through the Pieniny Mountains. *A modern re-creation of a lumber raft, here on the San River. Photograph by Darek Delmanowicz.*

Fogg, Mieczysław (1901–1990). The stage name of Mieczysław Fogiel, of Swedish extraction, one of Poland's most popular singers and recording artists of the twentieth century, both before and after World War II. His sweet baritone voice lent credence to the romantic lyrics of his songs, best remembered of which are "Ostatnia niedziela" (The last Sunday) and "Tango Milonga." His career stretched an incredible sixty years. During the powstanie warszawskie (Warsaw Uprising, 1944), Fogg gave more than one hundred concerts on the barricades, in hospitals, and in bomb shelters. In 1989 Yad Vashem in Jerusalem honored him with the designation "Righteous among Nations" for his saving the lives of the bandleader Iwo Wesby and his family. *Mieczysław Fogg on board SS* Batory.

Frank, Jakub (ca. 1726–1791). Charismatic self-proclaimed messiah and leader of the Frankists, who were an influential Jewish breakaway group in late eighteenth-century eastern Poland and Podole (Podolia, Ukrainian Podilia). The Frankists were in many ways similar to the Hasids, but more radical — for one thing, by accepting the New Testament. Having a Manichean streak, they believed in fighting evil by being evil. Their practice of ecstatic dance and orgiastic ritual outraged mainstream rabbis, and they were excommunicated as Jews. A goodly number converted to Catholicism as an expression, for them, of ultimate debasement on the path to salvation. Frank himself was baptized in Warsaw, with King August III as his godfather, but was later imprisoned by the Church for his radical teachings, spending thirteen years confined in the Częstochowa monastery. On Frank's death (in Germany), many Frankists became active in the Freemasonry movement and eventually merged with Polish upper society. See also: Żydzi w Polsce.

KALEIDOSCOPE OF POLAND   55

Fredro, Aleksander (1793–1876). A late-Romantic comic playwright, diarist, and poet, Fredro came from old Polish nobility in the *kresy*, and remained outside the concerns of mainstream Polish literature of his time, being considered something of a fossil by the Romantics. He distinguished himself in Napoleon's Russian campaign of 1812–1814 and was politically active through most of his life. Fredro is best remembered for his comedies *Pan Jowialski* (Mr. Jovial), *Śluby panieńskie* (A maiden's vows), and *Zemsta* (Revenge). He is credited by some for writing an otherwise anonymous and incredibly bawdy sequel, book XIII, to **Adam Mickiewicz**'s *Pan Tadeusz*, titled *Noc poślubna Tadeusza i Zosi* (Tadeusz's and Zofia's wedding night). Two of Fredro's plays have recently been adapted to the screen: *Zemsta* (Revenge) in 2002 by **Andrzej Wajda**, and *Śluby panieńskie* (A maiden's vows, 2010), by Filip Bajon. After World War II Fredro's monument was moved from **Lwów** (now Ukrainian L'viv), where he died, to **Wrocław**.

Funk, Kazimierz (1884–1967). Warsaw-born biochemist who formulated the concept of vitamins and gave them their name by combining *vita-* (from *vital*) and *amine*, incorrectly surmising at the time that all vitamins contain organic compounds called amines. The founder of a research institute in the United States, he also conducted significant research into hormones, diabetes, ulcers, and cancer. Funk, who vehemently claimed not to be Jewish, is listed in a book by Michael Shapiro (*The Jewish 100*, 2012) as number sixty among the most influential Jews of history, one position ahead of the American composer George Gershwin.

G

Galicja (Galicia, Ukrainian: Halychyna). The designation for the *zabór austriacki* (Austrian partition), the lands occupied by Austria as the result of the *pierwszy i trzeci rozbiory* (first and third partitions) in 1772 and 1795. From 1741 it was a crown kingdom under Austria-Hungary, and included the large towns of **Kraków** (at least at the beginning), **Rzeszów**, **Przemyśl**, **Lwów** (today's L'viv) and Stanisławów (today's Ivano-Frankivsk). The population was more Polish in the west and more Ukrainian in the east, with Jews comprising roughly a third of the urban population everywhere. More or less from 1860 to the end of World War I the Habsburg monarchy granted Galicia increasing local autonomy, allowing Polish to be used in the schools, state offices, and the courts (often to the detriment of Ukrainian and Ukrainians). Symbols of Polish patriotism (such as the *Panorama Racławicka*) were not forbidden as they were in Prussian and Russian Poland. Galicia was riven with friction among its various political, ethnic, and religious factions. Among vying Christian denominations Roman Catholicism and Greek Catholicism predominated.

Gall Anonim (Gallus Anonymus, the anonymous Gaul). An anonymous historian who, working in the court of King **Bolesław III Krzywousty** (Bolesław the Wrymouth) in the years 1112–1116, wrote *Gesta principum Polonorum* (Deeds of the Princes of the Poles), Poland's first history and the source for many early Polish legends, for example, the story of King **Popiel** being eaten by mice. Long considered to have been a Frenchman (that is, from Gaul), the author's sophisticated style, knowledge of the South Slavs and of sailing, along with his craving in Poland for fresh fish — not salted — incline current scholarly opinion toward his being a monk from Venice, driven out of the city by flooding at the beginning of the twelfth century.

Gałczyński, Konstanty Ildefons (1905–1953). Poet of the *dwudziestolecie międzywojenne* (interwar period) with whom romantic themes predominated. After the war he became widely known for his short absurdist pseudodramas in the series Teatrzyk "Zielona Gęś" (The green goose theater), published in the popular weekly *Przekrój* (Cross-section). A large number of his poems have been set to music and recorded by well-known artists such as **Marek Grechuta** and **Maryla Rodowicz**. Gałczyński became notorious for his ideological rootlessness, including writing a paean to the Easter Resurrection, followed by fascist-leaning verse in the 1930s, matched by a panegyric on the death of Joseph Stalin in 1953. His "Ukochany kraj!" (Beloved country), set to music, was a popular choir piece in the **PRL** (communist Poland). Gałczyński's best-known poem, the semi-lyrical, semi-jocular "Zaczarowana dorożka" (Enchanted cab), was inspired by an actual hansom cab in **Kraków**, used there until 1985, when, ironically, it collided with a German Wartburg automobile and was withdrawn from service. *Drawing by Henryk Hermanowicz.*

"Gaude, mater Polonia" (Rejoice, O Mother Poland). A 760-year-old medieval Latin hymn, the first piece of Polish music and verse for which the author is known: the Dominican priest Wincenty of Kielcza. Wincenty is thought to have written the hymn to honor the canonization of **Święty Stanisław ze Szczepanowa** (Saint Stanisław) in 1253. The popular Latin hymn was sung by Polish knights after victories in battle, including in 1683 by the victorious troops of **Jan III Sobieski** after the **odsiecz wiedeńska** (Relief of Vienna), and at the coronation of kings. Today, alongside "Gaudeamus igitur," it is sung at the opening ceremonies of major Polish universities, and during important military commemorations. Its first lines:

> Gaude, mater Polonia
> Prole fecunda nobili.
> Summi regis magnalia
> Laude frequenta vigili.

> Rejoice, O Mother Poland
> Rich in noble offspring.
> Mighty works of the greatest king
> Worship with incessant praise.

---

gaz łupkowy (shale gas). Traditionally energy-dependent, Poland has been discovered to have possibly the largest reserves of shale gas in all of Europe, the most sizable deposits of which are in the Baltic basin, with more in Silesia and around **Lublin** and **Podlasie**. The extraction process depends on the tricky technology of hydraulic fracturing. If estimates are correct, which is far from certain, Poland would have gas reserves of more than two hundred times its annual consumption, and more than 750 times its current annual production, lessening the importance of gas imports from Russia and making Poland relatively energy-independent. Together with this discovery come all the concerns that shale-gas extraction raises; for example, that the international conglomerates involved are going to despoil the landscape, poison the environment, and take their profits out of the country. The verdict is still out, so Poles should not collectively hold their breath until it becomes clear whether shale gas is a curse, a cash cow, or a mirage. Most European countries are holding off development of shale gas until the risks become clearer.

Gazeta Wyborcza (Electoral gazette). Originally an organ of the independent trade union **Solidarność** (Solidarity), this newspaper was one of the outcomes of the **rozmowy Okrągłego Stołu** (Roundtable Discussions) of 1989. Its editor from the beginning has been Adam Michnik, who severed ties with Solidarność in 1990. It is now a national-circulation liberal newspaper appearing in twenty-two regional editions, often with entertaining and informative inserts, the best of which is "Wysokie Obcasy" (High heels), aimed primarily at women. *Gazeta Wyborcza* (GW) has prosecuted a number of high-profile exposés, such as the *afera Rywin* (Rywin affair) and the *łowcy skór* (skin hunters) scandal in Łódź, and it also sponsors occasional social actions such as "Rodzić po ludzku" (Giving birth humanely), a national campaign to improve obstetric care. Because of its large circulation and liberal political agenda, GW is a lightning rod drawing the ire of rival news outlets and the religious right.

gazety (newspaper). Important Polish dailies with a national reach include: *Gazeta Wyborcza* (Electoral gazette, circ. 319,800), a liberal paper aimed at a general readership; *Rzeczpospolita* (The republic, circ. 141,200), with news, commentary, and special coverage of business and administrative news; *Nasz Dziennik* (Our daily, circ. 150,000), with a conservative Catholic profile; *Polska* (Poland, circ. 417,600), a general-purpose newspaper published in cooperation with the London *Times* (circulation numbers from around 2010). *Trybuna* (The tribune), the left-leaning continuation of the former communist *Trybuna Ludu* (Tribune of the people), finally went out of business in 2009. In addition to "serious" newspapers, there are a number of mass-circulation *brukowce* (tabloids), such as *Fakt* (Fact) or *Super Express*, with circulations in the hundreds of thousands. The Polish public is clearly a reading one, as *tygodniki* (weeklies), *dwutygodniki* (biweeklies), and *miesięczniki* (monthlies) are in abundance.

Gdańsk (German: Danzig). Poland's main seaport on the Bałtyk (Baltic Sea). Its history — German and Polish — goes back more than a thousand years. Because of its trade connections (it was a member of the Hanseatic League of northern German and Baltic merchant associations), it has always been prosperous. In the sixteenth through seventeenth centuries it was the main center for the export of Polish grain (see Polska spichlerzem Europy). At 455,800 inhabitants, it is the country's sixth most populous city, although the entire Trójmiasto (Tri-City) area, along with Gdynia, Sopot, and surrounding towns, numbers around 1,235,000. During the *dwudziestolecie międzywojenne* (interwar period) the town was the Wolne Miasto Gdańsk (Free City of Gdańsk), under the jurisdiction of the Liga Narodów (League of Nations). The *Stare Miasto* (old town) section of Gdańsk has been painstakingly restored after massive wartime damage. The attack on the Polish garrison at Westerplatte on the Zatoka Gdańska (Gdańsk Bay) is generally taken as the beginning of World War II; see also Obrona Poczty Polskiej w Gdańsku. The 1617 Neptune Statue and Fountain in Gdańsk (pictured) is one of the town's trademarks, as is the late medieval grain elevator in the port.

Gdynia. Gdynia belongs to the Trójmiasto (Tri-City) of Gdańsk, Gdynia, and Sopot, all of them on the Bałtyk (Baltic Sea). By itself it numbers not quite 250,000 inhabitants and is Poland's twelfth-largest city. As a response to Poland's uncertain access to the Baltic through the Wolne Miasto Gdańsk (Free City of Gdańsk) during the *dwudziestolecie międzywojenne* (interwar period), Gdynia changed from a sleepy fishing village into a major seaport and shipbuilding center, an important accomplishment of the interwar period. A yearly major cultural event in the city is the Open'er (Open Air) music festival held at the beginning of July, one of Europe's largest. Gdynia also currently hosts the yearly "Polish Oscars," the Festiwal Polskich Filmów Fabularnych (Polish Feature Film Festival). Current talk concerns the inarguably ugly new Sea Towers trade center, pictured, marring the Gdynia skyline.

Gelbfisz, Szmuel (Samuel Goldwyn, 1879–1974). The founder of the Hollywood film company that would become Metro-Goldwyn-Mayer (emerged from bankruptcy in 2010), with the trademark roaring lion. Samuel Goldwyn was born Szmuel Gelbfisz in Warsaw during the Kongresówka or Królestwo Kongresowe (Congress Kingdom, then in the Russian Empire) to a Polish Hasidic Jewish family. He changed his name to Goldfish upon emigrating to England. Later, in America, he went into business with the Selwyn brothers and changed his name to match the resulting company's hybrid name, Goldwyn. A colorful and irascible character, Goldwyn was forced out of the company bearing his name and set himself up independently, producing many films that are still remembered. He had a number of Oscar nominations, and his *The Best Years of Our Life* won the Oscar for best film of 1946. His last film was *Porgy and Bess* in 1959. See also: Faktorowicz, Maksymilian; Eichelbaum, Aaron, Szmul, Hirsz, i Itzhak.

Generalne Gubernatorstwo (General Government; German: General-Gouvernement, GG). In World War II, the GG was the part of Poland occupied by Germany but not directly annexed to the Reich. It included Warsaw, Kraków, Lublin, and all of Galicja (Galicia). In it, all Polish secondary and higher education was banned; the official language was German. Adolf Hitler had no desire to set up a puppet government in Poland. His declared aim was to deport or exterminate the entire Polish population of twelve million and replace it with five to six million German settlers. He began with the Jews, and six death camps were established in the GG, in which some four million Jews from all over Europe were killed. The GG was centered in Kraków under the command of the notoriously vicious Hans Frank, who was put on trial at the War Crimes Tribunal in Norymberga (Nuremberg). Found guilty, he was hanged in 1946.

German, Anna (1936–1982). Singer, songwriter, and actress of German/Dutch ancestry, born in Soviet Uzbekistan. Her father was executed for "treason" by the NKVD (security services) in 1937. Her mother then married an **Armia Ludowa** (People's Army) officer, and in 1949 the family moved to **Wrocław**, where Anna studied geology and simultaneously became involved in musical theater. Her haunting, crystal-clear voice and wholesome personality won her numerous festival honors in Poland and internationally. Especially popular in Russia and with Poles abroad, German recorded songs beautifully in seven different languages. She died of cancer in the prime of her career. Among her most popular songs were "Tańczące Eurydyki" (Dancing Eurydices), with which she won the 1964 **Opole** festival of song, and "Greckie wino" (Grecian wine).

getta żydowskie (Jewish ghettos). During World War II Jewish ghettos were set up by the Germans in the poorer parts of larger Polish towns; the biggest were in Warsaw, **Łódź**, **Kraków**, **Lwów**, **Białystok**, and **Wilno**. Jews from outlying towns and villages were herded into them under increasingly squalid conditions. Poles were subject to the death penalty for attempting to bring aid, and so-called *szmalcownicy* (from *szmalec*, "lard," figuratively "dough," i.e., money) lurked everywhere, ready to blackmail Jews or denounce them to the Germans. Nevertheless, the Polish underground relief organization **Żegota** succeeded in smuggling out a sizable number of Jewish children (see **Sendlerowa, Irena**). Day-to-day order in the ghettos was maintained by a Jewish police force, who hoped to survive through collaboration but who later shared the fate of the rest. As the Germans began to formulate the Final Solution to the "Jewish question," residents of smaller ghettos were transported to larger ones, and the overall population began to be transported to *obozy zagłady* (extermination camps), a chilling scene of which is depicted in **Roman Polański**'s *Pianista* (*The Pianist*, 2002); see **Umschlagplatz**. Very few Jews from the ghettos survived the war. *The Monument to the Heroes of the Jewish ghetto uprising of 1943.*

Gierek, Edward (1913–2001). Polish communist politician, first secretary of the Central Committee of the **Polska Zjednoczona Partia Robotnicza** (Polish United Workers' Party; that is, the communist party) from 1970 to 1980. Gierek, from the coal-mining region of **Śląsk** (Silesia), rose to power on waves of unrest following the brutal suppression of the **Gdańsk** shipyard strikes of 1970 (*grudzień 1970*). His regime was greeted with great expectations as it opened economically to the West, and shelves temporarily swelled with consumer goods. The motto of the day was "budujemy drugą Polskę" (We're building a second Poland), but those words took on hollow meaning as mushrooming national debt led to consumer goods shortages, food rationing, a political crisis, and the rise of the **Solidarność** (Solidarity) independent trade union. Scapegoated, thrown out of the party, and even interned under *stan wojenny* (martial law) for his supposed abuse of power, Gierek lived in seclusion until his death, reportedly able to afford only the tiny Fiat 126p with which he had "motorized" the country. A legacy of the Gierek years (for which some still harbor a nostalgic longing) is the *gierkówka*, a highway linking Warsaw with his native Katowice. A motto from the times is Gierek's rhetorical "Pomożecie?" (Will you help?), to which the thundering crowds replied "Pomożemy!" (We will!).

Gierymski, Ignacy Aleksander (1850–1901). Like Piotr Michałowski before him, Gierymski was unappreciated during his lifetime but is now considered one of the best Polish painters. Faced with economic hardship, he left Poland in 1888 and spent the rest of his life in Germany, France, and Italy, painting mainly landscapes and nighttime cityscapes. Before doing so he left a lasting legacy of Polish-themed work, especially genre paintings depicting Warsaw's Jewry and the poor, including *Pomarańczarka* (The orange-seller, pictured). That particular painting was plundered from the National Museum of Art in Warsaw during the war, to reappear in 2010 at an auction near Hamburg. After the intervention of the Polish government it was returned to Poland in 2011. Ignacy Gierymski's older brother Maksymilian Gierymski (1846–1874) also had a successful career as an artist in Germany, and died of tuberculosis at the age of twenty-eight.

Gniezno. A town of nearly seventy thousand situated in northwest Poland. According to legend Gniezno was founded by the prince Lech (see Lech, Czech, Rus), who decided to build his seat of power on the site of an eagle's nest (*gniazdo*) he encountered. Historically, Gniezno was the center of the Polanian state and the site of the first Polish cathedral, built by Mieszko I following his baptism in 966 (see *chrzest Polski*). It is considered to be the first Polish capital. Gniezno is especially known for the *drzwi gnieźnieńskie* (Gniezno Cathedral doors), a set of cast bronze doors in the Gniezno Cathedral, commissioned by Mieszko III Stary (Mieszko the Old), a unique example in the world of Romanesque art and craft. The doors depict scenes from the life of Święty Wojciech (Saint Adalbert). *A fragment of the Gniezno Door.*

gołębie (pigeons and pigeon fancying). Pigeons clutter and foul statues and public squares in Poland as anywhere else. Beyond that, *gołębiarstwo* (the raising of exotic or sports pigeons) is a big hobby, with an estimated forty-three thousand pigeon-fanciers nationwide. Polish pigeon breeding developed in the nineteenth century, and it was especially popular in Galicja (Galicia) and Śląsk (Silesia), where every farmhouse had an obligatory dovecote in the yard. Pigeons were raised as a hobby, for sport racing, and for eating as "squab." Pigeon raising was forbidden under the German occupation, since pigeons could carry messages. On January 28, 2006, a large exhibition hall on the outskirts of Katowice collapsed under a heavy snow cover during an international exhibition of carrier pigeons, killing sixty-five people and hospitalizing more than 170, in Poland's worst postwar civilian disaster. *A high-altitude thoroughbred racing pigeon on exhibit in Toruń.*

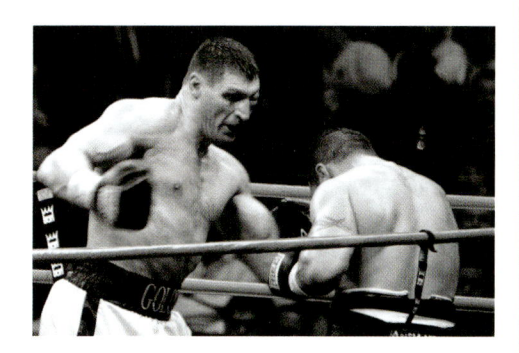

Gołota, Andrzej (b. 1968, active 1992–2009). Polish professional heavyweight boxer and Olympic bronze medalist (Seoul 1988), known more for brawn than for finesse. Gołota had an overwhelmingly winning career but lost in four separate bouts for the heavyweight championship of the world, to a large extent because of his tendency to hit below the belt. The phrase "pięść Gołoty" (fist of Gołota) became synonymous with a low blow, delivered powerfully. Gołota fared poorly in 2010 when he appeared on Polish television's version of *Dancing with the Stars*. Other Polish boxers making the world stage have been Dariusz "Tiger" Michalczewski and Tomasz "Góral" Adamek. *Andrzej Gołota vs. Mike Mollo, 2008.*

Gombrowicz, Witold (1904–1969). A Polish experimental novelist and playwright whose works often bordered on the absurd. Gombrowicz published his first novel — and one of his best — *Ferdydurke*, in 1937, about a grownup who finds himself transformed into a schoolboy — because everyone treats him that way. Gombrowicz found himself outside Poland at the beginning of World War II en route to Argentina, where he stayed and worked as a bank clerk, writing his semiautobiographical novel *Trans-Atlantyk* (1953), concerned with rootlessness and national identity. After 1963 he settled in France. Gombrowicz's best-known novel is *Pornografia* (Pornography, 1966), made into a not entirely successful film in 2003 by Jan Jakub Kolski. His best-regarded play is *Ślub* (The wedding, 1953). Fascinated by the themes of (im)maturity, the strictures of social form, and in general with taking ideas to extremes with no sense of shame, he received many international prizes toward the end of his life, and he had a significant influence on modern Polish and world literature. One of his enduring contributions is the "duel of grimaces," from *Ferdydurke*, consisting of two schoolboy antagonists making increasingly disturbing faces at each other.

Gomułka, Władysław (1905–1982). An old-time Polish communist activist from the 1930s, Gomułka assisted in the takeover of Poland after World War II, only to be denounced in 1948 as a right-wing reactionary, expelled from the party, and in 1951 placed under detention. Released during a brief period of liberalization in the aftermath of riots in **Poznań** in 1956 (see **czerwiec 1956, wypadki czerwcowe**), the supposedly liberal Gomułka took over as first secretary of the Komitet Centralny (Central Committee) of the Party. He at first enjoyed popular goodwill as he tried to carve out a *polska droga do socjalizmu* (Polish road to socialism), but he soon engaged in backtracking, repression, and clumsy maneuvering, while the economy steadily deteriorated. His incompetence was largely responsible for precipitating *marzec 1968* (the March 1968 events), which led to the mass emigration (around twenty thousand in all) of intellectuals and Jews. Toward the end of his tenure he was broadly disliked, including by people in his own party. His not learning from the mistakes of 1956 that had brought him to power led to the tragic *wydarzenia grudniowe* (December events) of 1970, which spelled the end of his term in office.

---

gościnność (Polish hospitality). A frequent Polish saying is "Gość w dom, Bóg w dom" (A guest in the house is like God in the house). Still, Poles can be less "hospitable" than they imagine themselves as a people to be. Outside the *rodzina* (family) — which in Polish means extended family, including grandparents, aunts, uncles, and cousins — and close friends (see *przyjaciel, przyjaciółka*) — Poles often seem to have little interest in cultivating a broader circle of acquaintances, and to be cool toward, or at least uninterested in, outsiders. Within the narrow circle of family and close friends, however, and in the instance of official foreign guests, Poles can be generous and hospitable to the point of exaggeration, according to the old principle "Zastaw się, a postaw" (Go into hock if you must, but put on a good show). This principle is best put on display at the traditional Polish *wesele* (wedding party), which, at least in the countryside, lasts three days and nights and can involve hundreds of "guests" (who may or may not have been issued an invitation).

---

góral (mountaineer). An ethnically and dialectally diverse group of people native to the Carpathian Mountains (**Karpaty**), not all of whom are ethnically Polish, the *górale* are usually associated by Poles with people living in the **Podhale** area around **Zakopane** south of **Kraków**, one of the few places where the dialect feature of *mazurzenie* is still common, and where *strój ludowy* (folk dress) is regularly encountered. Toward the east, górale become Ukrainian/Carpatho-Rusyn (**Łemko**, Bojko, Hucuł). Podhale górale are by tradition knowledgeable on the weather, a kind of living *Farmers' Almanac*, and they are often interviewed by TV stations for their views on the upcoming season. They are known for their bravery, honor, and piety, but also for their stubbornness, craftiness, and skill at turning a quick buck with *cepry* (their term for lowland tourists). See also: baca. *Fiddle player from Podhale.*

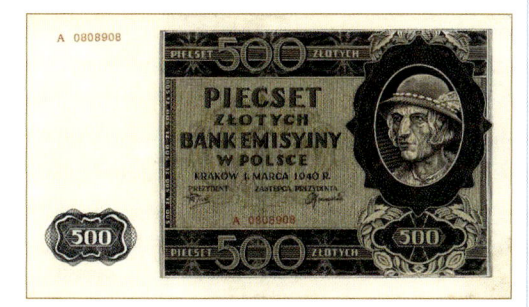

Góral, akcja (Operation Mountaineer). A daring 1943 bank robbery under the German occupation that netted the Armia Krajowa (underground Polish Home Army) 105 million złotys (around one million dollars) in cash. The money was to be used for resistance activities — especially the purchase of weapons. The operation was named after the 500-złoty note (pictured), which featured a *góral* (mountaineer). Totally illogically — *górale* employed swastikas in their woodcarvings — the Nazis considered them to belong to a separate "Aryan" race, hence their appearance on German-issued Polish currency. The operation, involving the hijacking of a bank delivery vehicle, was fourteen months in the planning and two minutes in the execution. Several people on both sides were killed; numbers of casualties are inexact. The robbers were never caught, but after that the Germans were more careful about guarding their money transports. A somewhat similar caper, the subject of a 2011 film by Waldemar Krzystek, was perpetrated in 1981 by activists from Solidarność (Solidarity), who managed to withdraw some eighty million złotys from the union's account before the government managed to declare *stan wojenny* (martial law).

"Góralu, czy ci nie żal?" (Mountaineer, do you not regret?). The first words to a late-night drinking song that everyone knows and which usually evokes a tear or two, telling of a *góral* (mountaineer) who has to leave his native mountain parts *za chlebem* (for bread; that is, to make a living). The song became ennobled while Pope Jan Paweł II (John Paul II) was alive, as his family came from such mountain regions, and he liked to trek and ski across them. People wished he would "return," in the words of the song, instead of going back to Rome. The first verse is:

> Góralu, czy ci nie żal
> Odchodzić od stron ojczystych?
> Z świerkowych lasów i hal,
> I tych potoków srebrzystych?

> Mountaineer, do you not regret
> To be leaving your native haunts
> The spruce forests and valleys,
> And those silvery streams?

In fact, many latter-day *górale* emigrants did return to the region to build nice houses and live on their US social security checks.

Górecki, Henryk (1933–2010). Composer of serious music from Silesia who first came to attention through performances at Warszawska Jesień (Warsaw Autumn new music festival) beginning in 1958. His breakthrough piece was his III Symfonia (Third symphony), also known as *Symfonia pieśni żałosnych* (Symphony of sorrowful songs), combining orchestral and vocal

KALEIDOSCOPE OF POLAND 65

elements, as many of his pieces do, which became a worldwide crossover classical and popular hit. Górecki was not afraid of tonality and simple melodies, often reprising folk themes.

dinosaur fossils. In the Middle Ages they were mined for copper and iron. The highest peak is Łysica (Baldy) at 612 meters above sea level, and the second-highest is Łysa Góra (Bald Mountain) at 594 meters. A cloister on Łysa Góra, pictured, holds a relic of the Holy Cross, giving name to the entire range. Notwithstanding, each year covens of witches and sorceresses congregate on Łysa Góra to celebrate Czarna Sobota (Black Sabbath). The largest town in the area is **Kielce** (population 234,800).

górnictwo (mining). The **Śląsk** (Silesia) area of Poland has extensive coal mines, both hard and soft, whose intensive development dates to the second half of the eighteenth century. Poland is one of the world's largest coal exporters, although its mines have often lagged behind in safety, productivity, and minimizing effects on the environment. Some two hundred miners have lost their lives over the last thirty years or so, the worst being in the Halemba disaster of 2006, in which twenty-three miners perished. Polish *górnicy* (miners), who are relatively well paid in exchange for following a grimy and dangerous line of work, are a political constituency to be reckoned with. Like miners in Wales, they have their own special traditions, folk tales, festivals, parade dress, orchestras, and choirs. The patron saint of miners is Święta Barbara (Saint Barbara), in whose honor the yearly festival and pageant Barbórka is held (pictured).

Góry Świętokrzyskie (Holy Cross Mountains). A not very high, but geologically quite old, range of mountains in the south-central part of the country. The mountains have yielded important

granatowa policja (navy-blue police). Officially, the Policja Polska Generalnego Gubernatorstwa (Polish Police of the Generalgouvernement) in World War II. Polish collaboration with the German occupant was minimal, a partial exception being the navy-blue police, mostly consisting of

66 KALEIDOSCOPE OF POLAND

prewar Polish policemen forcibly conscripted into a wartime force under the command of the Nazi authorities (although some were infiltrators from the Polish underground). They retained their prewar uniforms, hence the nickname. The navy-blue police were minimally armed, used as traffic police and as Polish–German interpreters, and placed in charge of routine criminal matters. They occasionally assisted the Germans in *łapanki* (roundups) for forced labor camps, and looked after the security of the Jewish ghettos from the outside. Inside the ghettos the similarly conscripted Jewish police were nominally in charge; see *getta żydowskie*. The navy-blue police were not placed in charge of major reprisal or pacification operations, as they were considered by the Nazis to be too unreliable. They were viewed with deep contempt by the Polish population at large.

Grechuta, Marek (1945–2006, active from the late 1960s). Singer, songwriter, poet, and painter, associated with Kabaret Piwnica pod Baranami (see *kabaret*) in Kraków, winner of numerous festival awards (including a grand prize for the entirety of his work in Opole in 2006). Equally well suited to the large stage as to the cabaret, Grechuta was known for tasteful progressive jazz recordings of his own poems and of classical works of Polish poetry, sung to his own music. He is buried in Rakowicki cemetery in Kraków, in the Aleja Zasłużonych (Boulevard of the Meritorious). Most Poles would be able to hum bars from his classic songs, including "Będziesz moją panią" (You will be my lady), "Nie dokazuj" (Don't misbehave), "Niepewność" (Uncertainty), and "Dni, których jeszcze nie znamy" (The days we don't know yet).

GROM (Polish special services force). An acronym meaning "thunder," formed from the awkward phrase "Grupa Reagowania Operacyjno-Manewrowego" (Group for Operational-Maneuver Reactions). Founded in 1990, GROM is an elite quick-reaction military force along the lines of the American Delta Force, trained to respond to emergency situations at home and abroad, especially hostage and terrorist situations. GROM has operated under NATO in Iraq and Afghanistan.

Gross, Jan Tomasz (b. 1947). Thoroughly crushed, demoralized, terrorized, and powerless under German occupation, Poland arguably has less to apologize for in regard to the Holocaust than some, even most, other European countries. Nevertheless, as the historian and sociologist Jan Gross has demonstrated with his 2001 book *Sąsiedzi* (*Neighbors*) on the Jedwabne massacre; in his *Strach: Antysemityzm w Polsce po Auschwitz* (Fear: Anti-Semitism in Poland after Auschwitz, 2008); and recently in *Złote żniwa* (Golden harvest, 2011), there are blots on the record that do not always support Poland's national myths. Gross's books have stirred up a hornets' nest of protest, but facts are facts, even if Gross sometimes stretches (some say distorts) them. For example, his oft-cited number of 1,600 victims of the Jedwabne massacre compares to around 340 actual verified remains. The Church, government, media, schools — and the ordinary citizen — could do more to confront Poland's past and the ongoing present on this issue. Anti-Semitic slurs and street graffiti, frequently encountered throughout the country, are, first, ignorant and, second, do nothing but besmirch the reputation of the country and make it easier for non-Poles to form or maintain their own prejudices about Poland.

Grotowski, Jerzy (1933–1999). A theater director, experimentalist, and developer of an acting method, Grotowski was one of the most significant reforming forces in twentieth-century theater both in Poland and abroad. He developed his acting and directing method, and his notion of the *teatr ubogi* (poor theater), in Opole beginning in 1959 in his Teatr 13 Rzędów (Theater of Thirteen Rows), but his international fame spread from his Teatr Laboratorium (Laboratory Theater) in Wrocław beginning in 1965. Under Grotowski's meticulously rehearsed approach (productions could take years in the making), theater-specific elements, including costumes, are reduced to the possible minimum, and attention is focused on the actor and his ability to project out of himself. UNESCO proclaimed 2009 the Year of Grotowski.

Grottger, Artur (1837–1867). A prodigiously talented late-Romantic artist whose life was cut short at the age of thirty by tuberculosis. Born in eastern Galicja (Galicia), Grottger studied painting in Lwów, Kraków, and Vienna. During his brief life he produced a voluminous body of work, including charcoal drawings, allegories, portraits, genre scenes, and highly expressive historical battle scenes. Grottger is probably best known to the broad public for his poignant paintings and drawings depicting the 1863 powstanie styczniowe (January Uprising) and its aftermath, including pictures of dead or crippled soldiers, women on the home front, the starvation of dispossessed landowners, and prisoners being marched to Siberia. Some of his Romantically imbued illustrations remind one of the roughly contemporaneous Pre-Raphaelite school in England. Grottger died in France but is buried in Lwów's Łyczakowski cemetery. *Pictured:* Przejście przez granicę (Crossing the border, *1865*).

Grób Nieznanego Żołnierza (Tomb of the Unknown Soldier). In Warsaw, on the edge of the immense Plac Piłsudskiego (Piłsudski Square, until 1990 Plac Zwycięstwa, "Victory Square"), a three-arcade remnant of the Pałac Saski (Saxon

Palace) dynamited by the Germans in World War II serves as the Tomb of the Unknown Soldier, commemorating the numerous anonymous Polish war dead lost in World Wars I and II and in other conflicts. Within the monument burns an eternal flame, and it is guarded around the clock by an honor guard. It is the location of solemn yearly ceremonies and of visits of homage paid by foreign dignitaries.

---

grudzień 1970, wydarzenia grudniowe (December 1970, the December events). In December 1970 protest strikes broke out across the *wybrzeże Bałtyckie* (Baltic seacoast) region, especially in Gdańsk and Gdynia, in response to a sharp rise in food prices. Workers at the Stocznia Gdańska (Gdańsk Shipyards) went on strike and were joined by students and workers from other factories. Street demonstrations grew increasingly strident and violent. On Thursday, December 17, orders were given for the army to open live fire on demonstrators. More than five hundred tanks, five thousand policemen, and twenty-seven thousand soldiers were brought in to deal with the situation. Some forty to eighty civilians were killed across the region, including Zbigniew Godlewski, whose death gave rise to the "Ballada o Janku Wiśniewskim" (Ballad of Janek Wiśniewski). A consequence of the December events was the replacement of Party secretary Władysław Gomułka with Edward Gierek. Food prices were rolled back. A decent film version of the December events, *Czarny czwartek: Janek Wiśniewski padł* (Black Thursday: Janek Wiśniewski has fallen), directed by Antoni Krauze, came out in 2011.

Grunwald, bitwa pod Grunwaldem (Battle of Grunwald; German: Tannenberg, July 15, 1410). In one of the largest pitched medieval battles ever fought, combined Polish-Lithuanian forces, led by King Władysław II Jagiełło, overwhelmed the army of the Krzyżacy (Teutonic Knights), leading to the death of the Teutonic Knights' leader Ulrich von Jungingen (see *dwa nagie miecze*), and the capture of over fifty division banners. Along with the year 966 (*chrzest Polski*, the baptism of Poland) and 1683 (*odsiecz wiedeńska*, the Relief of Vienna), the year 1410 is of the same order as 1492, 1620, or 1776 in America; almost every schoolchild knows it. The battle had its six-hundredth anniversary in 2010. Reenactment battles, in which "combatants" adhere strictly to the dress and armament codes of the time (no sneakers), are popular and draw participants from all over the world. See also: operacja Tannenberg.

---

gry podwórkowe (playground games). Before the advent of video games, children spent more time playing outside in an apartment building's *podwórko* (courtyard). Girls jumped rope while boys played soccer. A typical Polish girls' game is, or used to be, *gra w gumę* (elastic band jumping). A giant elastic band, usually made of old underwear waistbands tied together, would be set up around two girls' legs, creating parallel lines calf-high or, later in the game, knee-high. A third girl jumps in, around, and across the bands, performing various figures in sequence. The figures and sequences vary from region to region. Another game was *hacele* (horseshoe studs), regionally *sztule*, like American jacks but without the ball. It uses five horseshoe studs (otherwise used for winter horse traction), one of which is thrown up in the air while various combinations of the other studs are picked off the ground before the tossed stud is caught. The bat game *kiczki*, "tip-cat," once popular with boys in the *kresy*, has gone so far out of popularity that hardly anyone remembers it.

grzybobranie (mushroom gathering). Mushroom picking in Poland is a national mania. In the fall the edges of forests are lined with the cars of bent-over mushroom pickers carrying baskets and trowels in search of edible fungi. The number of deaths from poisonous mushrooms is negligible, as Poles instinctively can tell edible ones from the deadly varieties. At least they only make the mistake once. A classic scene of *grzybobranie* is in Adam Mickiewicz's *Pan Tadeusz*, book III. Mushroom exporting from Poland is strictly controlled, as though one were dealing with a national treasure. Poland is Europe's largest mushroom exporter (and greatest source of smuggled mushrooms). It is worth noting that the word for mushroom, *grzyb*, is treated by the Polish language as an animate noun. Colloquially, *grzybobranie* can refer to the practice of frequenting low-cost prostitutes, with the probability of contracting an STD. Franciszek Kostrzewski, "Grzybobranie," an illustration to Pan Tadeusz.

---

grzyby (mushrooms, fungi). For those to whom "mushroom" means the common *pieczarka* (button or portobello; *Agaricus bisporus*), the world of Polish mushrooms is an education. The most sought-after varieties are the *prawdziwki* or *borowiki* (varieties of *Boletus*, pictured), *kurki* (chanterelles), *maślaki* (*Suillus*), *podgrzybki* (*Xerocomus*), *kanie* (*Macrolepiota*), *koźlarze* (*Leccinum*), and *rydze* (*Lactarius*, saffron milk cup). If a person is in the pink of health, in Polish he is "zdrowy jak rydz" (healthy as a saffron milk cup). The *smardz* (sponge morel) is a protected species under Polish law: it cannot be picked, exported, or even imported. There are thousands of species, varieties, and subvarieties, and the folk nomenclature is not always precise. Among poisonous mushrooms the *muchomor* (flybane toadstool) has the worst reputation. Fatalities can occur from mistaking the young of the poisonous *muchomor sromotnikowy* (*Amanita phalloides*) for the edible *gąska zielona* (*Tricholoma equestre*). After washing, mushrooms are eaten fresh, sautéed in butter and cream, cooked in myriad dishes, sliced and hung on threads to dry, or marinated. A favorite is *jajecznica z kurkami* (chanterelle omelet).

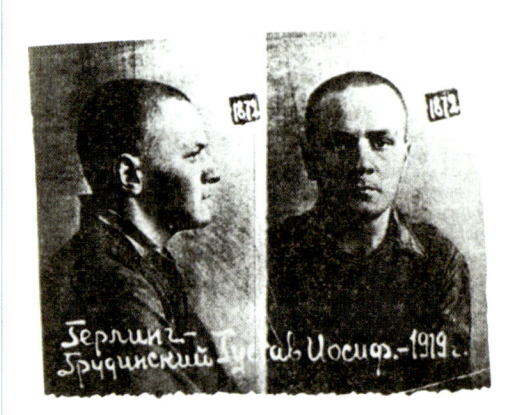

Gułag, łagry (Gulag, prison camps). At its height the Gulag (the Soviet system of *łagry*, or forced labor camps in the far Russian northeast) consisted of several thousand camps holding some ten to twelve million people. Overall, an estimated forty million people perished in them. They were dissolved only in 1960. Many Poles were sent to the Gulag in 1939–1941 for no other reason than being Polish. One of the earliest and best accounts of Gulag life was that of Polish émigré author Gustaw Herling-Grudziński (1919–2000); his prison photograph is pictured. His experiences are recounted in *Inny świat* (A world apart), published in London in 1951 but not in Poland until 1989. Like thousands of other Poles, Herling-Grudziński was released from Soviet prison in 1942 after the *układ Sikorski-Majski* (Sikorski-Majski Pact), joined General **Władysław Anders**'s army, survived the war, and stayed abroad afterward, helping to found the Polish émigré press. Besides Herling-Grudziński, the Gulag is known in the West from the works of Aleksander Solzhenitsyn, Robert Conquest, Martin Amis, and Anne Applebaum.

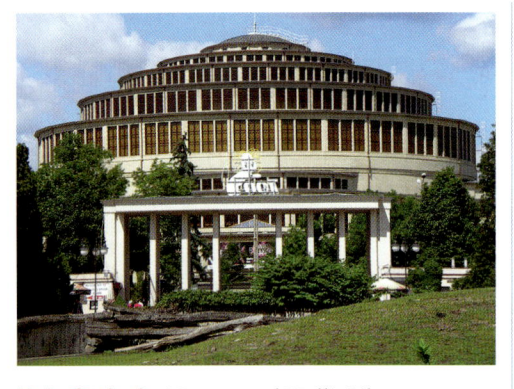

Hala Stulecia (Centennial Hall). This immense multipurpose recreation and exhibition facility was erected in 1911–1913 by the expressionist architect Max Berg in **Wrocław** (at the time, German Breslau) in commemoration of the one-hundredth anniversary of the Prussian defeat of Napoleon at Leipzig in 1813. It encompasses fourteen thousand square meters of space. When Poland took control of the city from Germany after World War II, the name was changed to Hala Ludowa (People's Hall), but the name has now reverted to the Polish version of the German *Jahrhunderthalle*. The structure, one of the most interesting examples of German modernist architecture, was one of the first to show the potential of reinforced concrete construction. As such it has been placed on the list of UNESCO's world heritage sites — one of thirteen such sites in Poland.

Halik, Tony (Mieczysław Sędzimir Antoni Halik, 1921–1998). Larger-than-life fighter pilot, adventurer, explorer, journalist, filmmaker, and author. In World War II Halik served in the **Polskie Siły Powietrzne** (Polish air force), and was shot down over France twice. During one such occasion he met his first wife. Later he worked as photographer for the Argentine dictator Juan Peron, then became a professional explorer, investigating remote reaches of the Amazon, jeeping from the bottom of South America to Alaska, and other adventures too numerous to mention. Around 1953 he began a thirty-year career as a Latin American correspondent for NBC. In 1976 he helped rediscover the long-lost historic Peruvian capital of the Incas, Vilcabamba, destroyed by the Spanish in 1572. Over the last twenty years of his life, Halik wrote thirteen books and, together with his second wife Elżbieta Dzikowska (pictured here with him), produced over three hundred travel documentaries for Polish television. His series *Pieprz i wanilia* (Pepper and vanilla) gave Polish viewers of the time a rare look at the outside world.

---

halny (southern mountain wind). The *halny* is caused by a high-pressure buildup on the southern side of the Tatry Mountains combined with low pressure on the northern side. The resulting winds are dry, warm, gusty, and come rushing down with considerable destructive force into the plains below, reaching as far as Kraków. The main season for the halny is October–November. They are blamed for mood swings, suicides, headaches, heart palpitations, and other maladies. The suicide rate in the Podhale is, in fact, nearly twice that of the rest of Poland.

Hanuszkiewicz, Adam (1924–2011). A stage and television director and actor. Like many other notables of postwar Polish culture, Hanuszkiewicz was born and raised in Lwów. As a theater director Hanuszkiewicz was an ambitious, productive, and controversial figure, specializing in placing the classical repertoire of Polish and world theater in modern settings. He raised eyebrows when in 1968 he took over the Teatr Narodowy (National Theater) from Kazimierz Deymek, who was removed from that position for political reasons. Nevertheless, Hanuszkiewicz's innovative productions led to a revival of that theater. Still talked about is his 1974 adaptation of Juliusz Słowacki's *Balladyna* (1834), originally set in Polish prehistory, in which the heroine enters the stage on a ramp over the audience on a Honda motorcycle. He neglected few major Polish theatrical works. He also produced notable stage versions of originally nontheatrical works, such as Dostoyevsky's *Crime and Punishment*. Some consider that his adaptations were popularizing and shallow, but they were almost always successful at the box office.

---

hejnał mariacki (Mariacki bugle call). An interrupted bugle call that is played every hour on the hour, four times in four different directions, from a tower of the kościół Mariacki (Marian Church) in Kraków. A signature Kraków tourist attraction, the bugle call is said to commemorate the appearance of Tatar troops at Kraków's gates ca. 1241, when the trumpeter was shot through the throat by an arrow while trying to warn the city with his call. The *hejnał* is played over Polish Radio I throughout the country at noon. During the Euro 2012 (European Soccer Championships), the British team, stationed in Kraków, complained that the trumpeter was preventing them from getting a good night's sleep. *Trumpeter playing the hejnał mariacki with the Sukiennice (Cloth Hall) in the background.*

Hel, Półwysep Helski (Hel and the Hel Peninsula). A very thin line of land — a giant sand bar, really — juts out into the Bałtyk (Baltic Sea) from Władysławowo, creating the Zatoka Pucka (Puck Bay), with the town of Hel at its end. The peninsula ranges from around two hundred to three hundred meters across at its narrowest to three kilometers across at Hel. The town was an important defense outpost in the two world wars. Three 405-millimeter so-called Adolf cannons were mounted on it in World War II, capable of firing a shell weighing 1,026 kilograms (more than a ton). With its beaches, Hel today is a popular summer tourist destination. Its mascot is the gray Baltic seal, once hunted close to extinction, but now protected and making a modest comeback. Rising ocean levels threaten to turn Hel into a series of sandy islands, which at one time it was — not good news for owners of some of Poland's most expensive real estate.

Henryk I Walezy (later Henri III de Valois of France, ruled Poland 1573–1575). Heir to the French throne from the Valois dynasty, Henryk was brought to Kraków from France as a foppish twenty-two-year-old to be the Polish-Lithuanian Commonwealth's first elected king. Used to having his way, before coming to Poland he reluctantly signed the *artykuły henrykowskie* (Henrician Articles) drawn up by the Polish nobles, considerably restricting his royal power (see *złota polska wolność*). The Henrician Articles amounted to Poland's first constitution. Another condition, noted in an addendum (*pacta conventa*), which he kept putting off fulfilling, was his marriage to Anna Jagiellonka (1523–1596), thirty years his senior and sister of Zygmunt II August, the last Jagiellonian king. Upon hearing that his brother had died, opening up the throne in France, Henryk left Kraków in disguise under cover of night. He never officially renounced the Polish crown, but Stefan Batory (who did marry Anna Jagiellonka) was soon elected to replace him. Henryk, an unpopular king in France, was assassinated in 1589.

Herbert, Zbigniew (1924–1998). A poet, dramatist, and essayist of international repute, and recipient of many prizes (short of the Nobel, for which he had been shortlisted). Herbert was born in Lwów, now Ukrainian L'viv, but along with much of the town's Polish population, he relocated to Poland ahead of the advancing Soviet army in 1944. His sense of uprootedness became an important theme in his poetry. Herbert produced most of his work after the 1956 *odwilż* (thaw) and the ensuing *mała stabilizacja* (slight stabilization), a term coined by fellow poet and dramatist Tadeusz Różewicz. Herbert's poetry can be characterized as historico-philosophical, without following any particular ideology other than being antitotalitarian. His most admired collection of poems sees the world through the eyes of the persona of Pan Cogito (Mr. Cogito), who tries, not always successfully, to use his intelligence in order to make sense of the world immediately around him.

herby polskie (Polish coats of arms). Polish coats of arms arose in the fourteenth century, not long after their counterparts in Western Europe. They flourished especially during the old **Rzeczpospolita Obojga Narodów** (Polish-Lithuanian Commonwealth). Polish coats of arms differed from Western ones in their tying together families of many different last names into clans, rather like Scottish tartans. The frequent use of rune-like symbols also set them apart from Western heraldic tradition; see the pictured Odyniec coat of arms. At first *oznaki godności* (signs of rank), drawn in pictures above or around the *herb*, were missing, reflecting the equality of the Polish gentry. Polish towns, too, have their coats of arms, adopted upon town incorporation.

Hermaszewski, Mirosław (b. 1941). The first and so far the only Polish astronaut. In 1978 Hermaszewski was carried into space aboard the Russian *Soyuz 30* spacecraft and spent nearly eight days on the *Salyut 6* space station. Upon his return he was granted the title of Hero of the Soviet Union. He was later a member of Wojskowa Rada Ocalenia Narodowego during *stan wojenny* (martial law) — to which he was apparently appointed without his knowledge — and retired with the rank of general in the Polish air force. In 2003 he was awarded the Commander's Cross of the Order of the Rebirth of Poland (pictured).

hetman. The name for the commander-in-chief of the armed forces in the old **Rzeczpospolita Obojga Narodów** (Polish-Lithuanian Commonwealth), before the *rozbiory* (partitions) of the eighteenth century. Poland and Lithuania had two hetmans each, one the *hetman wielki koronny* (Grand Hetman of the Crown), his Lithuanian counterpart being the *hetman wielki litewski* (Grand Hetman of Lithuania). They were mainly in administrative command of their respective armies. The hetman in charge of field operations (reconnaissance, espionage, and battle) was the *hetman polny* (field hetman), both *koronny* and *litewski*.

Heweliusz, Jan (German Johannes Hevelius, 1611–1687). Jan Heweliusz was a **Gdańsk** brewer,

KALEIDOSCOPE OF POLAND   75

mayor, and astronomer of international renown, and a member of the Royal Society of London. The Sejm RP (parliament) proclaimed 2011 the four-hundredth anniversary of his birth, to be "rok Jana Heweliusza" (Jan Heweliusz Year). Heweliusz founded the discipline of lunar topography, and described ten new constellations, of which seven are still recognized. Poland's first satellite, designed by students of the Warsaw Polytechnical University and launched in February 2012, was named after Heweliusz. In Poland's worst peacetime maritime disaster in history, on January 14, 1993, a ferry named for Heweliusz carrying trucks and freight cars capsized on the Bałtyk (Baltic Sea) in heavy seas. The accident claimed the lives of twenty seamen and thirty-five passengers. Only nine were rescued. An equally famous rough contemporary of Heweliusz from Gdańsk was Daniel Gabriel Fahrenheit (1686–1736), who developed the alcohol and mercury thermometers and the Fahrenheit temperature scale, still used in Belize, the Cayman Islands, and the United States. Fahrenheit's zero degrees was supposedly based on the temperature at which the brackish water in Gdańsk Bay freezes; and one hundred degrees was set at the body temperature of his seemingly warmer-than-average wife (although this may be an urban legend).

---

hip-hop (Polish hip-hop). Improbably, the metrical quality of the Polish language is well suited to rap music and the hip-hop musical style, and the accompanying breakdancing has not only caught on in Poland but achieved considerable heights and has a big following. A pioneering if still inchoate at the time moment was the 1995 gangsta-style rap album *Alboom* by Liroy z Kielc (Leroy of Kielce), selling half a million CDs. It was followed by the more sophisticated *Księga Tajemnicza: Prolog* (The secret volume: Prologue) by Kaliber 44 (with Magik, Joka, and AbradAb), representing so-called hardcore psycho rap. Despite their spectacular success, Magik (Piotr Łuszcz) split and formed the group Paktofonika with Rahim and Fokus, whose successes were cut short by Magik's suicide in 2000. Rappers such as O.S.T.R., Peja, and Mezo have stepped forward to fill the vacuum left by Paktofonika, each in his own way.

Hłasko, Marek (1934–1969). Short-form fiction writer, the most promising prose talent in the 1950–1960s, aided in his career by his working-class background. Hłasko as a writer was largely self-taught. As a person he was a rabble-rouser, playing out the Polish version of Britain's "angry young man." The collection *Pierwszy krok w chmurach* (First step in the clouds, 1956) broke definitively with the aesthetics of *socrealizm* (socialist realism), showing the seamy side of working-class existence. *Ósmy dzień tygodnia* (Eighth day of the week), about the clumsiness of first sexual encounters, was turned into a 1957 film by Aleksander Ford. Seven other stories underwent screen adaptation. From 1958 Hłasko lived outside Poland. He died in Germany of an apparently accidental drug and alcohol overdose. In 1975 his remains were brought to Poland and interred in Warsaw's Powązki Cemetery.

Holland, Agnieszka (b. 1948). Film director, script writer, and occasional actress, living and working mostly abroad since 1981, Holland has collaborated as screenwriter with many of Poland's best directors, including Kieślowski, Wajda, and Zanussi. She has had three Oscar nominations, one for directing *Gorzkie żniwa*

(Bitter harvests, 1985), one for the script to *Europa, Europa* (Europe, Europe, 1990), and one for directing *W ciemności* (In darkness, 2012), about the Holocaust in Lwów (L'viv), Poland's submission that year for the Oscars, filmed largely in semidarkness in sewers.

Holoubek, Gustaw (1923–2008). Legendary actor of the stage, screen, and television; performer of many of the major male roles of the Polish national repertoire. His filmography comes close to one hundred items, including many of the classics of Polish cinema; for example, Wojciech Jerzy Has's 1957 *Pętla* (The noose). In 1968 Holoubek was portraying Gustaw/Konrad in Kazimierz Dejmek's production of Adam Mickiewicz's *Dziady* (Forefather's eve) when its cancellation by the authorities provoked the March events (see *marzec 1968, wydarzenia marcowe*). Among his lighter roles was as Professor Tutka in Polish television's 1960s adaptation of Jerzy Szaniawski's whimsical stories featuring the professor whose academic subject could never exactly be ascertained, but who had a story to tell on any subject. Holoubek also had an on-again, off-again political career in the Polish Sejm RP (parliament). He was married to the much younger actress Magdalena Zawadzka, who recently published a biography about him.

---

honor (Polish honor). Minister of Foreign Affairs Józef Beck's response on the eve of World War II to the demand of Adolf Hitler that Poland renounce the Gdańsk Corridor: "We in Poland do not know the concept of peace at any price. Only one thing in the life of people, nations, and states is priceless, and that thing is honor." Probably no other representative of any other nation would have put the matter in this way — not that putting it another way would have had any effect on Hitler's actions. Beck, playing an impossible balancing act between Germany and the Soviet Union, elicited with this declaration a combination of worldwide admiration and incredulity. The last major European work on regulating affairs of honor, *Polski kodeks honorowy* (Polish codex of honor, 1919, cover pictured), was written by a Pole, Captain Władysław Boziewicz. The motto Bóg, Honor, Ojczyzna (God, honor, fatherland) appears on Polish army standards.

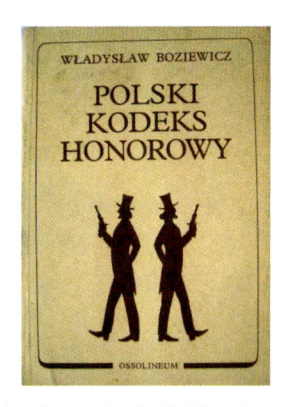

Hubal (Major Hubal). Hubal was the pseudonym of major Henryk Dobrzański (1897–1940) who, after the overrunning of Poland by the German army in World War II, formed a uniformed band of partisan horse cavalry under the name Oddział Wydzielony Wojska Polskiego (Detached Division of the Polish Army) which, active in central Poland, initially had success inflicting losses on German troops. Hubal lost his life and his band came to an end when it was caught in a trap, leading to a final pitched battle against vastly superior German forces (approximately eight thousand Germans vs. three hundred Poles) armed with tanks and heavy artillery. Hubal's body was incinerated by the Germans and buried in an unmarked grave, never located. His story was told in the 1973 film *Hubal* by Bohdan Poręba.

---

husaria (Polish hussars). Modeled on the Hungarian and Serbian cavalries, Polish hussars were a heavily armed lightning-strike horseback force in the sixteenth through seventeenth centuries, said to be the best of its kind in Europe. They were formed under King **Stefan Batory**. Their trademark (at least in nineteenth-century romanticized portraiture) was one or two intimidating flying *skrzydła* (wings) behind the rider, attached either to the shoulderpieces of the armor or to the saddle after mounting. In practice the wings, possibly originally designed to foil Turkish *arkany* (lassos), were mainly used in parades. A hussar would carry a light wooden steel-tipped *kopia* (lance) for one time use; a *koncerz* (a long stabbing and armor-piercing sword); and possibly a *łuk* (bow) and a *czekan* (small battle-ax). The weapon of choice for close fighting after an initial charge was the Polish curved *szabla*, a refinement of the Hungarian saber, to become the standard of European and even the American cavalry into the nineteenth century. *Wacław Pawliszak*, Straż Hetmańska *(Hetman's guard)*.

---

hydraulik polski (Polish plumber). Following the accession of Poland and several other countries of the former Communist Bloc into the European Union in 2004, fear of cheap labor (like plumbers) from the East driving out traditional trades in the West was successfully exploited by rightist parties in France to defeat in that country the 2005 referendum approving the EU constitution. In tongue-in-cheek retaliation, the Polska Organizacja Turystyczna (Polish Tourist Organization) launched an ad campaign featuring a buff Polish plumber (actually, a professional model) who announced that he was staying put, but you could visit him in Poland if you wanted. His appeal was glaringly bisexual, an additional wink at the French. The campaign not only won an advertising award but seemingly contributed to a major increase in tourism to Poland from France. A companion poster featuring a seductive-looking Polish nurse (another major Polish export to the West), appealing to the French heterosexual male, soon followed, with the message "Je t'attends" (I'm waiting for you).

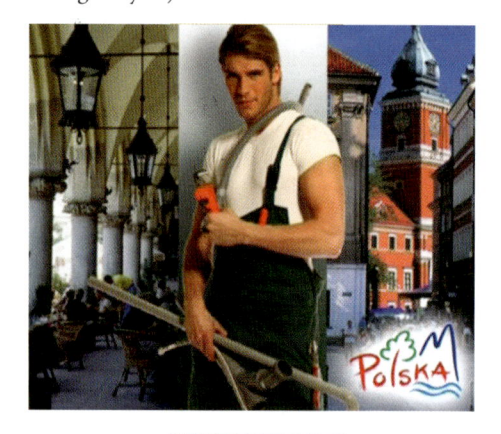

KALEIDOSCOPE OF POLAND

Ida. Ten Polish films have been selected for Hollywood's Academy of Motion Picture Arts and Sciences award (an Oscar), beginning with Roman Polański's 1963 "Nóż w wodzie" (Knife in the water), but it was not until Paweł Pawlikowski's 2015 *Ida* that a Polish film was selected as the winner in the category of Best Foreign Film. Beautifully filmed in black and white, it is the story of a novitiate in a convent who is sent into the secular world for several days before making her final decision to become a nun. In the process she learns that her family was Jewish and murdered for their property by a Polish family during World War II. Of Polish directors, Andrzej Wajda won a special lifetime achievement award in 1999. Many Polish directors, including Wajda (four times), have been nominated for the Oscar for Best Director, but only one, Roman Polański in 2002 for *The Pianist,* has won. Similarly, many Polish cameramen have been nominated for the Oscar for Best Cinematographer, but only Janusz Kamiński has won, in 1993 for *Schindler's List* and in 1998 for *Saving Private Ryan*. Polish cameramen, mostly products of the Łódź film school (see Łódzka Szkoła Filmowa), have broadly infiltrated the Hollywood film industry.

---

imieniny, urodziny (name day, birthday). Some Poles lay greater store by their *imieniny* (name day, the day of the saint after whom one is named), others by their *urodziny* (birthday). If you are named Ringo or Tiffany, where corresponding saints are missing, then of necessity you have only your birthday. Many Poles hold open house on their imieniny, and guests drop by (even without being specifically invited) and bring flowers and small gifts (or something to eat or drink). One's most important birthday is when one celebrates one's *osiemnastka* (eighteenth birthday), having attained *pełnoletniość* (legal maturity); see wiek (age). On either occasion, but especially on one's birthday, the song "Sto lat" (One hundred years) is called for.

---

imiona staropolskie (old Polish first names). Pre-Christian Polish first names, many of which are currently in vogue, were usually composed of two parts, and were intended to confer upon the person certain attributes. A few examples: Bogdan, "God's gift"; Kazimierz, "peace-breaker"; Mieczysław, "sword-glory"; Mścisław, "revenge-glory"; Sędzimir, "judge-peace"; Włodzisław/Władysław, "power-glory." Such double names were princely, not generally used by the common people. Female versions were formed by adding the feminine ending –*a*: Bogdana, Kazimiera, and so on. Upon conversion to Christianity, Poland added to its inventory the names of Christian saints; for example, the men's names Bartłomiej, Jan, Łukasz, Marek, Mateusz, Mikołaj, and Paweł, or women's names Anna, Barbara, Elżbieta, Ewa, Katarzyna, Maria, Zofia, and so on. It is most convenient for a child if his or her name appears on the Polish saints' calendar, but Poles are not averse to borrowing names from international popular culture, like Dzesika (Jessica) or Elwis (Elvis). See also: nazwiska polskic.

Inka. May refer to: (1) The most popular Polish brand of *kawa zbożowa* (ersatz coffee, a delicious instant grain beverage), good hot or cold. (2) The pseudonym of Danuta Siedzikówna, a nurse in the partisan Armia Krajowa (Home Army) who was arrested, tortured, convicted on false charges, sentenced to death, and executed in 1946 at the age of eighteen by the new communist government under president Bolesław Bierut, who personally upheld her sentence. She was buried in an unmarked grave, never discovered. (3) The pseudonym of Halina G., involved one way or another in the 2001 contract killing of former minister of sport Jacek Dębski for reasons that were never fully explained. That particular "Inka" received eight years in prison (and has since been released), while two other people involved in the murder allegedly committed suicide while awaiting trial.

---

inni (others). A major trend in contemporary Polish literature is a preoccupation with re-creating the vanished memory and never-recorded stories of the "inni," non-Poles who historically occupied the space of today's country: Germans and Kashubians in the north; Germans around Wrocław; Jews in Warsaw, Kraków, Łódź, and elsewhere; and Ukrainians in the southeast. Before 1989, because of governmental hypersensitivity on the subject, many such themes were taboo. A prominent author in this vein is Paweł Huelle (b. 1957), whose stories are set in the historical landscape of Gdańsk and elsewhere in Pomorze (Pomerania) among Germans, Kaszubi (Kashubians; see Kaszuby, *język kaszubski*), and Olendrzy – Mennonite settlers from Holland in the sixteenth and seventeenth centuries. The lore of prewar Gdańsk and Kashubia is well known to Western readers from the works of Gdańsk-born Nobel Prize–winning German-Kashubian author Günter Grass. Another notable Gdańsk author dealing with German themes is Stefan Chwin.

---

insurekcja kościuszkowska (Kościuszko Insurrection). A revolt of Polish citizens in response to the *drugi rozbiór* (second partition, 1793; see rozbiory) of Poland among Russia and Prussia. Led by Tadeusz Kościuszko, the rebellion lasted from the spring to the fall of 1794. A major initial success was the revolt of the army and the citizenry of Warsaw against the Russian occupation army in the *insurekcja warszawska*

(Warsaw Insurrection) on March 17–18, 1794. The insurrection's most important battles were at Racławice and Maciejowice. The Kościuszko Insurrection was eventually brutally suppressed by Russia, especially in the *rzeź Pragi* (massacre of civilians in the Praga district of Warsaw on November 4, 1794), and led to the third and final partition of Poland in 1795.

---

inteligencja (intelligentsia, intellectual elite). A term seemingly coined by Polish social philosopher Karol Libelt (1807–1875), but entering world vocabulary through Russian. The term refers to the socially progressive but alienated intellectual, professional, and artistic elite living in the autocratically ruled countries of Eastern Europe, especially in the second half of the nineteenth century. Their sense of alienation came from their inability to influence, other than indirectly (through their art and writing, subject to censorship), the political, social, and economic order of their countries so as to bring them closer to what they viewed to be more progressive models. In Poland the intelligentsia often came from the impoverished gentry, a good example being the journalist and positivist writer Bolesław Prus.

Iwaszkiewicz, Jarosław (1894–1980). One of the best and most multifaceted twentieth-century European writers the world outside Poland has barely heard about. A poet, novelist, music critic, and, especially, the author of psychologically profound short stories, known for his political ideological rootlessness and opportunism, Iwaszkiewicz began his career in the *dwudziestolecie międzywojenne* (interwar period). As a poet he was associated with the *Skamander* group. During the communist period Iwaszkiewicz was active in literature and its politics (he was a longtime president of the Polish writers' union) until his death. Several of his stories were put to film, including *Matka Joanna od Aniołów* (Mother Joanna of the angels, by Jerzy Kawalerowicz, 1960), *Brzezina* (Birchwood, 1970), *Panny z Wilka* (Girls of Wilko, 1979), and *Tatarak* (Sweet rush, 2009) by Andrzej Wajda. A museum for Iwaszkiewicz is maintained in his and his wife Anna's former villa, Stawisko, in the forested suburb of Podkowa Leśna, near Warsaw.

J

Jadwiga, królowa (Queen Jadwiga of Anjou, ca. 1373–1399). Hungarian-born queen of Poland from 1384, crowned when she was only eleven years old. Unlike most other queens of Poland, who were merely the wives of kings, Jadwiga was a ruler in her own right, a status secured by her father, King Ludwik Węgierski (Ludwik the Hungarian) with the *przywilej koszycki* (Koszyce privilege), which lowered fivefold the tax paid on grain by the rich nobility in exchange for the concession. From 1386 Jadwiga was the wife of and co-ruler with **Władysław II Jagiełło**. Active in promoting culture and education, she funded with her jewels the restoration of the Akademia Krakowska (Kraków Academy), later renamed **Uniwersytet Jagielloński** (Jagiellonian University). Canonized only in 1997, she is the patron saint of queens. Her beautiful sarcophagus, carved in white marble in 1902, lies — without her in it — in the **Wawel** Cathedral. In 2010 part of her relics were transferred to the Franciscan church in **Wilno** (Lithuanian: Vilnius). *Wincenty de Lesseur,* Saint Jadwiga.

Jagiellonowie (Jagiellonian dynasty). A dynasty of Lithuanian origin, members of which at one time or another were rulers in Lithuania, Belarus, Poland, Ukraine, Latvia, Estonia, parts of Russia, Bohemia, and Slovakia in the fourteenth through sixteenth centuries. The Polish dynasty was initiated by **Władysław II Jagiełło**

(1362–1434), succeeding the Piast dynasty (see *Piastowie, dynastia*). As rulers of the Polish-Lithuanian Commonwealth from 1386 to 1572 the Jagiellons were militarily successful and expanded the country's territory to the east until it was one of the largest in Europe, additionally overseeing a general flowering of culture and multiculturalism. The last Polish Jagiellonian king was **Zygmunt II August** (1520–1572), whose death set off a brief interregnum followed by the importation from France of **Henryk I Walezy** as Poland's first elected king.

Jagiełło, Władysław II (ca. 1362–1434, ruled from 1386). Lithuanian Grand Prince and king of Poland from 1386, founder of the *dynastia* Jagiellonów (Jagiellonian dynasty; see **Jagiellonowie**), which was to last until 1572. As Lithuanian Grand Prince Jagiełło survived many skirmishes with his uncle Kiejstut and with the **Krzyżacy** (Teutonic Knights), who persistently attacked and laid waste to Lithuanian lands. He was invited by Polish lords to become husband of and co-ruler with the eleven-year-old Queen **Jadwiga**, establishing a dynastic union between Poland and Lithuania. On becoming king he converted to Roman Catholicism and pursued the Christianization of Lithuania. He was the leader of the victorious Polish-Lithuanian troops at the *bitwa pod Grunwaldem* (Battle of Grunwald, 1410). According to legend he died from hypothermia after hearing a nightingale sing. He is buried in a grand sarcophagus in the **Wawel** Cathedral crypts.

Jałta, konferencja (Yalta Conference, February 4–11, 1945). A resort town in the Crimea on the Black Sea, Yalta is where Joseph Stalin, Franklin D. Roosevelt, and Winston Churchill carved out respective spheres of influence in post–World War II Europe for the Soviet Union, the United States, and Great Britain. Poland and most of the countries of central Europe were relegated (most Poles would say "betrayed") to the Soviet sphere. With Soviet troops already on the ground, one may question what Roosevelt and Churchill could have done to achieve a different outcome. Poland lost the *kresy wschodnie* (eastern territories) to the Soviet Union. At the Potsdam Conference held later that year, Poland received by way of reparation formerly German lands in the west — the so-called *ziemie odzyskane* (recovered territories), along with **Gdańsk** and most of East Prussia. The German population in those lands was for the most part forcibly "repatriated" to Germany, the lands then being repopulated with people displaced from the kresy.

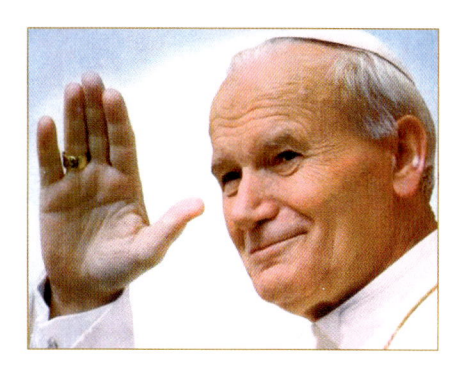

Jan Paweł II (papież) (Pope John Paul II, 1920–2005). Born Karol Józef Wojtyła in **Wadowice**, he became a Polish priest, spiritual leader, archbishop of **Kraków**, later cardinal, and, from 1978–2005, leader of the world Roman Catholic Church, the first non-Italian pontiff since 1523. A charismatic, popular, and much-traveled Church leader (104 pilgrimages around the world), Pope John Paul II's reign led to a revival in Polish national pride, improved the image of the Church worldwide, led to better Catholic-Jewish relations, and is believed to have been a factor in the breakup of the Communist Bloc, especially after his first pilgrimage to Poland in June 1979 was met with such an ecstatically enthusiastic reception. Young people growing up during his papacy were said by the Polish media to belong to the *pokolenie JP2* (JP2 generation). After his death one had the sense of being surrounded everywhere by Jan Paweł II memorials: streets, squares, schools, organizations, even soccer stadiums. Pope John Paul II was beatified on May 1, 2011, and was elevated to sainthood on April 27, 2014, along with Pope John XXIII. See also: Kościół rzymskokatolicki.

Janda, Krystyna (b. 1952). Film and dramatic actress, singer, theater director, writer of satirical sketches, selected in a national plebiscite as the best Polish actress of the twentieth century. Winner of the Golden Palm in Cannes and the Silver Conch in San Sebastian, she is a favorite actress of director Andrzej Wajda. She got her film start in Wajda's *Człowiek z marmuru* (Man of marble, 1976) as a young journalist investigating what became of a famous *przodownik pracy* (hero of labor) of the 1950s, whose son she ends up marrying. Her role as an unfaithful wife contemplating an abortion in Krzysztof Kieślowski's *Dekalog II* is also well remembered. In 2010 she founded her own theater in Warsaw, the Och-Teatr in Ochota.

Jankiel. The revered Jewish tavern proprietor in Adam Mickiewicz's mock epic poem *Pan Tadeusz* (1832–1834), known for his honesty, flawless Polish, patriotism, and skill on the *cymbały* (hammered dulcimer). Jankiel and the mysterious Byronic figure of Father Robak confabulate on conspiratorial matters in his tavern late at night. At the heroine Zosia's betrothal to Tadeusz, Jankiel plays a grand polonaise re-creating in sound the history of the *rozbiory* (partitions) of the old Rzeczpospolita Obojga Narodów (Polish-Lithuanian Commonwealth), simultaneously providing the main characters one last time to parade before the reader — or the viewer, in Andrzej Wajda's 1999 film version, with Wacław Kowalski in Jankiel's role.

Janosik, Juraj (1688–1713) was a Slovak mountain *harnaś* (chieftain) of a band of Tatra Mountain brigands whom the Poles have adopted as their own semi-national hero. In both countries he is widely admired as a "gentleman robber," who reputedly avoided harming his victims and who, like Robin Hood, gave much of his plunder to the poor. He was captured and hanged (or, some say, executed in an even more gruesome manner) in 1713. Many stories have grown up around his exploits. In Poland he has been the subject of comic books, a television series (with Marek Perepeczko creating the definitive role), and movies, the most recent being Agnieszka Holland's 2009 *Janosik: Prawdziwa historia* (Janosik: The real story). So-called *janosikowe*, named after the brigand, are payback levies exacted on richer counties to subsidize the welfare budgets of poorer ones.

Jantar, Anna (1950–1980). The most popular Polish vocalist of the 1970s, Jantar died in a Polish airplane crash on the outskirts of Warsaw while returning from New York, a crash in which most of the US national boxing team also perished. Among Jantar's most popular songs were, fittingly, "Nic nie może wiecznie trwać" (Nothing can last forever) and "Tyle słońca w całym mieście" (So much sun in the whole town). Many of Jantar's songs were composed by her husband, Jarosław Kukulski, who later wrote songs for their daughter, Natalia Kukulska, also a singer.

Jarmark Europa (Europa Bazaar). In 1989 the deteriorating **Stadion Dziesięciolecia** (Tenth Anniversary Stadium) in Warsaw – formally the country's national stadium – was leased to a company that established on its upper ridge the largest flea market in the Eastern Bloc, and one of the largest in Europe (pictured). The Jarmark became a notorious center for illicit trade of all sorts: guns, drugs, cigarettes, alcohol, prostitution, pirated CDs, and computer software. The statistics of illegal CD sales alone are mind-boggling: some ten million were confiscated. A number of criminal films and novels are situated in and around the Jarmark. The site was demolished and turned into a new national sports complex in time for the **Euro 2012** (European Soccer Championships).

Jarocin, festiwal w Jarocinie (Jarocin rock festival). Jarocin is a town of around twenty-six thousand in west-central Poland. With its origins as far back as the 1970s, in the 1980s the Jarocin rock festival was the largest outdoor rock festival in the entire Soviet Bloc. It was dubbed the "Polish Woodstock," and attendance at it carried the flavor of political protest. Suspended in 1994–2005, it is trying to regain its former prestige. The Jarocin festival was the launching pad for the careers of such contemporary groups as Dżem (Jam), Dezerter (Deserter), and Hej (Hey). Nowadays the roving festival Przystanek Woodstock (Woodstock Stop), organized by Jerzy Owsiak and the **Wielka Orkiestra Świątecznej Pomocy** (Great Orchestra of Christmas Charity), lays claim to the title of the "Polish Woodstock."

Jaroszewicz, Piotr (1909–1992). Polish communist army general, member of the Biuro Polityczne KC **PZPR** (Political Office of the Central Committee of the Polish United Workers' Party, the Politbiuro) in 1964–1980, vice premier 1952–1970, and premier 1970–1980. Jaroszewicz was implicated in the price changes that precipitated the June 1976 "events" in Warsaw and Radom (see *czerwiec 1976, wydarzenia czerwcowe*), and was scapegoated in 1980 for failing to quell worker unrest on the seacoast. He was subsequently expelled from the party. He and his wife were murdered in 1992 in their villa near Warsaw, and the manuscript of his memoirs was stolen, in one of Poland's most famous unsolved crimes.

Jaruzelski, Wojciech (1923–2014). A Polish general and politician. The minister of national defense from 1968 to 1983, the pro-Soviet Jaruzelski came to prominence after the March events (*marzec 1968, wydarzenia marcowe*). He organized the brutal suppression of striking workers in the "December events" (*grudzień 1970, wydarzenia grudniowe*). Later he consolidated power as both prime minister and first Party secretary. As head of the ad hoc Wojskowa Rada Ocalenia Narodowego (WRON, Military Council for National Salvation), he outlawed the independent trade union **Solidarność** (Solidarity) and proclaimed *stan wojenny* (martial law), lasting from December 13, 1981, until July 22, 1983. In 1989 Jaruzelski was elected (by just one

KALEIDOSCOPE OF POLAND 85

vote) the last president of Polska Rzeczpospolita Ludowa (PRL, People's Republic of Poland), and served for one year as the president of postcommunist Poland. As a credit to the relative civility of postcommunist Polish politics, Jaruzelski was not subjected to demotion in rank, imprisonment, or other kinds of revanchism for his roles in the PRL, although some politicians demanded it. The Jaruzelski daughter Monika, a fashion editor, in 2013–2014 wrote a humanizing two-volume autobiographical portrait of her family.

Jasiński, Jakub (1759–1794). A Polish-Lithuanian military engineer and general who was active in support of the insurekcja kościuszkowska (Kościuszko Insurrection, 1794). He was also a major poet of the Polish Enlightenment whose better-known verse proclaimed the radical ideas of the French revolution. Jasiński effectively led partisan troops in Lithuania, defeating Russian garrisons in Wilno and elsewhere, but he worried the leaders of the insurrection with his Jacobite politics and pronouncements. He perished in the defense of Warsaw.

Jasna Góra (Bright Mountain Monastery). A Pauline monastery complex on a hill in Częstochowa, a center of the *kult maryjny* (cult of the Virgin Mary), and a frequent destination of *pielgrzymki* (pilgrimages), including the largest Polish pilgrimage, the *warszawska pielgrzymka* (Warsaw pilgrimage), which has covered the 243-kilometer (150-mile) trek over the same course almost every year since 1771. Thousands of people take part in it (8,500 in 2005, but as many as two hundred thousand in the 1980s). The Jasna Góra monastery, sometimes referred to as *serce Polski* (Poland's heart), has seen several major military engagements, most famously in 1655, when the monastery's prior, Father Augustyn Kordecki, refused on four separate occasions to surrender to a Swedish siege during the potop szwedzki (Swedish Deluge). The siege was eventually lifted, due to, it is said, the intervention of the monastery's miracle-working icon, the age-darkened Matka Boska Częstochowska (Mother of God of Częstochowa), otherwise known as the Czarna Madonna (Black Madonna).

---

jedenastego (11) listopada (November 11). This national holiday, the Narodowe Święto Niepodległości (National Independence Day), celebrates the recovery of sovereignty after 123 years of partition under Prussia, Russia, and Austria, and the beginning of modern Poland. On this day Józef Piłsudski assumed supreme military command of the country. During the PRL (communist Poland), the holiday was dropped from the calendar; its functional correspondent was 22 *lipca* (July 22), the date of the Manifest Lipcowy (July 22 Proclamation). The holiday was reintroduced in 1989. It is a day free from work (see *dni wolne od pracy*). Commemorative ceremonies are held at the Grób Nieznanego Żołnierza (Tomb of the Unknown Soldier) on Piłsudski Square in Warsaw.

Jedwabne, pogrom w Jedwabnem (Jedwabne Pogrom of 1941). Jedwabne is a small town in northeastern Poland. On July 10, 1941, during the German occupation, members of the Polish population massacred several hundred Jews from the town, burning some alive in a barn. Exact details and numbers are not known, and are to an extent still being investigated. The event was made prominent in Poland and the world by the publication of the book *Sąsiedzi* (*Neighbors*), by Jan Gross, devoted to the event. Some people in Jedwabne were tried and convicted for the crime following the war, but they received light sentences. The story of Jedwabne reverberated around Poland and the world, and shook the national orthodoxy that Poles uniformly sheltered the Jews in World War II. Tadeusz Słobodzianek's 2008 play *Nasza klasa* (Our class), based on the Jedwabne massacre (without mentioning the town by name), won the 2010 **Nike** prize for literature, the first play to be so honored. The 2012 film *Pokłosie* (Aftermath), by Władysław Pasikowski, treats a similar theme, as does the 2008 novel *Pingpongista* (The ping-pong player), by Józef Hen.

Jeziorański, Zdzisław (1914–2005). A courier for the underground **Armia Krajowa** (Home Army) during World War II. On the eve of the collapse of the **powstanie warszawskie** (Warsaw Uprising, 1944), using false documents under the name Jan Nowak, Jeziorański smuggled out of Poland hundreds of documents and photographs to the *rząd na uchodźstwie* (government in exile) in London. After the war (1952–1976) Jeziorański was in charge of the Polish section of **Radio Wolna Europa** (Radio Free Europe) and was a frequent consultant in Washington on the Polish and East European political situation. In 1978 he published his wartime reminiscences — also under the name Nowak — in the well-received *Kurier z Warszawy* (Courier from Warsaw). Once communism fell he was active in promoting the acceptance of Poland and Lithuania into NATO. See also: **Karski, Jan**. *Photograph from 1989.*

Jeż Jerzy (George the Hedgehog). The creation of Rafał Skarżycki and Tomasz Lew Leśniak, Jerzy evolved from a comic strip character in the children's magazine *Świerszczyk* into an iconoclastic counterculture figure, a punk skateboarding hedgehog with backwards baseball cap, vulgar language, and satirical swipes at just about everyone and everything in contemporary politics, culture, and subculture, Polish or otherwise. A special foe of political correctness, Jerzy drinks, smokes pot, prolifically beds women (some of whom find him strangely attractive), and carries on feuds with local skinheads and various underworld types. A particularly raunchy eponymous 2011 full-length animated film brought Jeż Jerzy to international attention, one of Poland's more dubious contributions to world culture.

język polski, języki słowiańskie (Polish language, Slavic languages). Polish is one of the *języki słowiańskie* (Slavic languages). Along with *czeski* (Czech), *słowacki* (Slovak), *łużycki* (Sorbian), and *kaszubski* (Kashubian; see **Kaszuby, język kaszubski**), Polish is a member of the west Slavic branch of languages, related to the east Slavic languages *rosyjski* (Russian), *ukraiński* (Ukrainian), and *białoruski* (Belarusian), and to the south Slavic languages *bułgarski* (Bulgarian), *macedoński* (Macedonian), *bośniacki* (Bosnian), *chorwacki* (Croatian), *serbski* (Serbian), and *słoweński* (Slovene). By and large, predominantly Catholic Slavic countries use the Latin alphabet, while Orthodox countries use the Cyrillic alphabet. Polish retains the Common Slavic inflectional system of *przypadki gramatyczne* (grammatical cases) and the distinction between *aspekt dokonany i niedokonany* (perfective and imperfective verbal aspect). It is the only Slavic language to retain the Common Slavic *nosówki* (nasal vowels), ę and ą. Polish is spoken not only in Poland but also in parts of Lithuania, Belarus, and Ukraine and in major centers of Polish settlement around the world; see *emigracja polska*.

Judym, Tomasz. The main character in Stefan Żeromski's 1899 novel *Ludzie bezdomni* (Homeless people), the action of which is placed at the end of the nineteenth century and beginning of the twentieth century, Dr. Judym is an idealistic physician who wants to cure the world's ills but is his own worst enemy, the embodiment of disinterested self-sacrifice for the good of humanity combined with an introverted, conflicted, and self-destructive personality that undermines his chances at success. The novel was adapted into a 1975 film by Włodzimierz Haupe. Another term from Żeromski that has entered the national idiom is "Siłaczka," after his story by that name, referring to a woman who devotes herself to a higher calling, usually teaching, at the expense of a family life and personal happiness.

juwenalia (Latin *iuvenalia*, university student holiday). A holiday going back to fifteenth-century Kraków, *juwenalia* are held anywhere from the middle of May to the beginning of June (in any case, before examinations) and last for three or more days. Classes are canceled and students "own the city." Juwenalia start off with a parade of costumed students from the university to the city center, where the mayor hands them the city's key. University campuses turn into one huge tailgate party (sans tailgates). Juwenalia are accompanied by concerts, sporting and other events, and a certain amount of letting off steam with the help of alcohol. City monuments are sometimes dressed in funny costumes. Most universities have their own way of dubbing the holiday. In Gdańsk they are called Neptunalia, in Opole Piastonalia, at the medical academy Medykalia, and so on. *Juwenalia participants from Wrocław dressed as little green men.*

K

kabaret (cabaret). Specializing in stand-up comedy, variety acts, and topically satirical songs and sketches, cabarets are a venerable Polish institution with a continuing popularity unmatched almost anywhere else. They remind one of the American television show *Saturday Night Live*, except for the incomparably better quality of the *kabaret*, as the best literary and musical talent goes into them. Under communism, cabarets functioned as a social safety valve and barometer of the public mood by offering less-censored fare than other cultural outlets. Each larger Polish town has its legendary ones, such as **Kraków**'s Kabaret pod Baranami (Cellar under the Rams, from 1956) and Warsaw's historic Qui pro Quo.

Currently roving cabarets include Kabaret pod Egidą (Kabaret under the Auspices) and Kabaret Moralnego Niepokoju (Cabaret of Moral Anxiety); the latter troupe is pictured. A special category is the television cabaret, the classic being *Kabaret Starszych Panów* (Cabaret of old gentlemen, 1958–1966), with debonair performers Jeremi Przybora and Jerzy Wasowski.

Kaczmarski, Jacek (1957–2004). Poet, singer, and songwriter. Although his talent was wide-ranging, Kaczmarski is inevitably associated with the image of a guitar-playing singer of protest songs from the period of **Solidarność** (Solidarity) and *stan wojenny* (martial law). His best-known songs are "Mury" (Walls), adapted from a Spanish anti-Franco song, "Obława" (Roundup), "Nasza klasa" (Our high school class), and "Rejtan, czyli raport ambasadora" (Rejtan, or the ambassador's report). The refrain from "Mury":

> Wyrwij murom zęby krat
> Zerwij kajdany, połam bat
> A mury runą runą runą
> I pogrzebią stary świat!

> Rip out the walls' bars of teeth
> Tear apart the shackles, break the whip
> And the walls come tumbling down
> And they will bury the old world!

Kaczyński, Jarosław (b. 1949). A prominent conservative Polish politician, representative to the **Sejm** (parliament), and Prezes Rady Ministrów (Chairman of the Council of Ministers, i.e., premier) in 2006–2007, at the same time his twin brother **Lech Kaczyński** was president. Jarosław and his brother first came to public attention as child actors in the 1962 film *O dwóch takich, co ukradli księżyc* (Two boys who stole the moon). In the 1980s Jarosław Kaczyński was a lawyer and activist in the **Solidarność** (Solidarity) trade union movement; his relations with union leader **Lech Wałęsa** later became strained. A cofounder, with his brother, of the political party Prawo i Sprawiedliwość (PiS, Law and Justice), in 2010 he lost a presidential election to **Bronisław Komorowski**. Kaczyński's campaign motto was "Polska jest najważniejsza" (Poland is most important). He continues to play an oppositionist role as a member of the PiS party. Kaczyński, a bachelor, is known for his love of cats. His favorite, Alik, recently passed on to cat heaven.

Kaczyński, Lech (1949–2010). By profession a lawyer and law professor, Lech Kaczyński was a legal adviser to the **Solidarność** (Solidarity) trade union movement and participated in the **rozmowy Okrągłego Stołu** of 1989. With his twin brother **Jarosław Kaczyński** he cofounded the politically conservative Prawo i Sprawiedliwość (PiS, Law and Justice) political party, under whose anticorruption banner he was elected *prezydent* (mayor) of Warsaw, serving 2002–2005. A popular mayor, he successfully pushed for the foundation of the Muzeum Powstania Warszawskiego (Museum of the Warsaw Uprising). In 2005 he was elected president of Poland, serving until his death in 2010 in the **katastrofa pod Smoleńskiem** (Smolensk air disaster). He is buried in the crypts of **Wawel** Cathedral in **Kraków**.

Kadłubek, Wincenty (1161–1223). An important medieval chronicler of Polish history, and arguably the first Polish writer (if one assumes that the earlier historian **Gall Anonim** was not a Pole). Kadłubek's work was in Latin: *Chronica seu originale regum et principum Poloniae* (Chronicle of the kings and princes of Poland). In four volumes, it covered Polish history from its beginnings to the year 1202. An establishment figure, Kadłubek was the bishop of Kraków, a participant in the Fourth Lateran Council of 1215, and beatified by the church in 1764. He was the first to use, in reference to Poland, the phrase "res publicae" (republic). One owes to Kadłubek such legends as those of the founding of Kraków by Krak, the *smok wawelski* (Wawel dragon), the drowning of Wanda, and the battle of Psie Pole.

Kalisz. A city in west-central Poland with a population of around 170,000. Historically it was an important trading town located along the *szlak bursztynowy* (amber road; see *bursztyn*). It was possibly the first Polish place name to enter history, the strikingly similar name Calisia mentioned in the second century AD by Ptolemy of Alexandria. The *statut kaliski* (Kalisz statute, 1264), issued in Kalisz by Bolesław Pobożny (Bolesław the Pious) granted legal status to Jewish courts as well as to Jews in Polish courts, and guaranteed personal safety and protection to Jews in travel, trade, and religion. The statute was subsequently ratified by Kazimierz III Wielki in 1334, Kazimierz IV Jagiellończyk in 1453, and Zygmunt I Stary (Zygmunt the Old) in 1539. There is little in present-day Kalisz to testify to its ancient history.

kalwaria (calvary). A complex of chapels or churches replicating more or less faithfully in distance and topography the stations of the cross and the hill on which Jesus was crucified. There are more than a dozen major calvaries in Poland, and some sixty in all, serving as places of worship and destinations of *pielgrzymki* (pilgrimages). Ethnologists consider that Polish pilgrims "live through" the process of going through the stations of the cross much more deeply than is the case in other countries. The best known and most geographically propitiously situated is Kalwaria Zebrzydowska (pictured), a town of around 4,500 inhabitants in the south of Poland containing a large monastery and related buildings established in 1602 by Michał Zebrzydowski, *wojewoda* (governor) of Kraków. It is significant enough architecturally to have been placed on the UNESCO list of World Heritage Sites, one of thirteen such sites in Poland. The town itself survives through tourism and its upholstered furniture and leather-goods industries.

kamienica (nineteenth-century apartment house). A *kamienica* can refer to a medieval or Renaissance townhouse with decorated facades, located on or near the *rynek* (market square) of an older town. Here, however, we are talking about the classic nineteenth-century kamienica. It is built of stuccoed brick or stone and consists of from two to five floors above a *parter* (ground floor) built around a *podwórko* (courtyard), entered through a locked and often imposing *brama* (gate), and guarded by a *dozorca* (groundskeeper or caretaker) who is responsible for the routine upkeep of the building. These days security is more often provided by a *firma ochroniarska* (security company; see *ochrona*). The courtyard will usually have a *trzepak* (rug-beating rack), serving alternatively as a children's jungle gym, and off to one side a *śmietnik* (garbage bin). Spacious individual apartments are accessed from within the courtyard through locked *klatki schodowe* (stairwells). An apartment will usually have allocated to it a locked compartment in the *piwnica* (basement) for storage. *Kamienica pod żabami in Bielsko-Biała.*

Kamieniec Podolski. A town of 93,300 in the picturesque Podole province (once Polish, now Ukrainian Podilia). Kamieniec was one of the linchpins of *Polska przedmurzem chrześcijaństwa* (Poland the bulwark of Christianity), protecting the southeast of Poland from Turkish invasion. This it did successfully, repulsing many onslaughts, until 1672, when the Kamieniec fortress (pictured) succumbed to the overwhelming might of the Turkish army. According to a legend, a despondent artillery officer named Hejking lit a fuse to a keg of gunpowder in the munitions tower, blowing it, himself, and his commanding officer to smithereens, a scene immortalized in Henryk Sienkiewicz's *Pan Wołodyjowski* (Colonel Wołodyjowski). The fall of Kamieniec sent shock waves around the Rzeczpospolita Obojga Narodów (Polish-Lithuanian Commonwealth).

Kamińska, Ida (1899–1980). Grande dame of the Polish Yiddish theater during and after World War II and founder of the Teatr Żydowski (Jewish/Yiddish Theater) in Warsaw that today is named after her and her mother, who was also an actress in it. The Teatr Żydowski is one of the few world theaters devoted to preserving the Yiddish theatrical repertoire. Kamińska was nominated for an Oscar as best actress for her role as the shopkeeper in the 1965 Czechoslovak film *Little House on Main Street* (pictured). She emigrated from Poland after the March events (*marzec 1968, wydarzenia marcowe*), and died and is buried in New York.

kampania wrześniowa (September campaign, 1939). World War II began at 4:45 on *pierwszego września* — September 1, 1939 — with the bombardment of the military depot at Westerplatte on the Baltic sea (but see Wieluń). The campaign came to an end with the occupation of western Poland by Germany and the invasion and occupation of the eastern part by the Soviet Union on September 17, in accordance with the secret pakt Ribbentrop-Mołotow (Molotov-Ribbentrop Pact). The campaign took Germany much longer and exacted many more casualties than they had expected, significantly delaying its invasion of the Soviet Union. Decisive battles were on the Bzura River outside Łódź, at the Modlin fortress north of Warsaw, and the defense of Warsaw itself. In the September campaign some 66,300 soldiers died and 420,000 were taken captive. In the east, some 250,000 Polish troops were placed in internment camps by the Soviets, many thousands of whom were later executed without cause or charge at Katyń and other camps. Others were allowed to proceed south to Romania under General Władysław Anders. Each year in remembrance of the invasion on that day air-raid sirens are sounded all across Poland; traffic comes to a halt, and pedestrians stop in their tracks.

Kanał Augustowski (Augustów Canal). A 101-kilometer-long canal through verdant countryside connecting the Wisła and the Niemen rivers. Built in 1824–1839, its aim was to skirt the Prussian chokehold on Polish exports via the Wisła through Gdańsk. It is named after the town of Augustów, along its route. A marvel of early nineteenth-century engineering, the canal has eighteen locks and is still operative today, with all its antique mechanisms. It finds increasingly intensive recreational use by pleasure cruises, kayakers, and sailboaters, and is in line for inclusion as a UNESCO World Heritage Site. The canal exits into the Niemen River in Belarus, from which point water traffic enters the Bałtyk through Lithuania.

Kanał Elbląski (Elbląg Canal). An antique canal and monument of technology in former East Prussia, between Elbląg and Ostróda. Built beginning in 1844, it links seven lakes by means of four locks and — where rises in elevation are too steep to allow locks — five ingenious inclined planes on which specially engineered carriages (pictured) carry overland boats of up to fifty tons. In all, the canal rises one hundred meters along its 84.2-kilometer path. Its minimum width is seven meters. The canal today is fully functional and is used largely by pleasure and tourist craft. In 2007 the canal was a surprise fifth-place winner in a plebiscite run by the newspaper *Rzeczpospolita* to select the "seven wonders of Poland," the others being the Wieliczka salt mine, Toruń's old town and panorama, Malbork castle (see Krzyżacy), Wawel castle and cathedral, the renaissance town of Zamość, and the main market square and old town of Kraków.

---

kanapki (small open-face sandwiches). The word *kanapka* can refer to any old sandwich, usually open-face, but the art of making appetizing-looking decorative party canapés, including the artistic slicing of cucumbers, radishes, and other vegetables, is a carefully maintained tradition among Polish women. Magazine

KALEIDOSCOPE OF POLAND   93

articles and entire websites are devoted to the subject. A favorite kanapka spread is flavored *smalec* (lard), preferably containing bits of fried *boczek* (bacon) called *skwarki*. *Archetypical Polish kanapki waiting to be consumed at a cocktail party.*

Kantor, Tadeusz (1915–1990) An internationally known **Kraków**-based avant-garde theater producer, actor, painter, sculptor, set and costume designer, theoretician, and stager of happenings, Kantor is known for his unorthodox stagings of the Romantic-poetic works of **Juliusz Słowacki** and **Stanisław Wyspiański** as well as the absurdist-cubist works of Jean Cocteau and Stanisław Ignacy Witkiewicz (**"Witkacy"**). His theater was the self-founded Cricot 2, which operated until his death. His most famous work was *Umarła klasa* (Dead class, 1975), filmed by **Andrzej Wajda** as it was staged in 1976. In it, a schoolroom of the dead sit alongside mannequins representing their former selves as they sat in class. The Cricoteka museum in Kraków is devoted to preserving Kantor's legacy through archives and exhibitions.

Kapitan Kloss (Captain Hans Kloss). The pop culture icon of a 1967–1968 television serial *Stawka większa niż życie* (A stake more important than life), still in reruns, about a Polish double agent working for Soviet intelligence, known to his superiors as J23, who infiltrates the German Gestapo in World War II. After the serial finished Captain Kloss lived on, and still does, in spin-off books and comic book series. *Stanisław Mikulski, the creator of Kapitan Kloss.*

Kapitan Żbik (Captain Żbik, "Wildcat"). Something of a Polish Dick Tracy, Kapitan Żbik appeared as the hero of one of the most popular comic book series of the **PRL** (communist Poland) in 1967–1982, depicting the adventures and derring-do of a member of the Polish police force — at that time called the **Milicja Obywatelska** (Citizens' Militia). It has its continuation in today's adventures of Komisarz Żbik (Commissioner Żbik), the original's grandson. When Kapitan Żbik waxes nostalgic with his grandson over the **Fiat 125p** squad car he used to drive, his grandson rolls his eyes. Old issues are big sellers on the used comic book market.

kapliczka przydrożna (roadside shrine). There is scarcely a crossroads in the Polish countryside that does not have a roadside devotional shrine of one form or another placed next to it, and the placement is not limited to crossroads. Usually the shrine is devoted to the Virgin Mary or some other saint. The practice of placing shrines at crossroads goes back to pagan times (the **Światowid** may have been a crossroads monument). *Kapliczki* range from carved wooden or brick posts, to glass cases with holy images in them nailed to trees, to more elaborately constructed chapels. They often contain holy icons and *świątki* (carved wooden figurines),

94   KALEIDOSCOPE OF POLAND

although theft these days can be a problem. *S. Czachorowski, Crossroads shrine in Warmia.*

Kapuściński, Ryszard (1932–2007). A journalist and foreign correspondent born in Pińsk (now in Belarus) known for the quality of his writing and for continually putting himself in harm's way with his embedded reporting from revolutions and danger spots around the world. Among his best works are *Cesarz* (1978, published in English as *The Emperor: Downfall of an Autocrat*), about Ethiopia; and *Imperium* (1993), about the last days of the Soviet Union. One of Poland's most frequently translated authors, Kapuściński was at one point raised as a possible candidate for the Nobel Prize in Literature, which would have been appropriate, as his work was often described as "literary reportage" rather than journalism narrowly speaking, and the author was not above occasionally embellishing the truth. His reputed role as an informer for the Polish security services in 1965–1972 may have impeded his selection.

karczma (village tavern). While also providing lodging for travelers, *karczmy* were more important as the village venue for music, dancing, and the sale of alcoholic beverages. They were leased by the local landowners to the tavernkeepers — often Jews who could do business on Sunday — and they functioned under the right of *propinacja* (propination), giving landowners exclusivity in the sale of beer, mead, and — mainly — vodka. Propination in the Russian part of Poland was discontinued only toward the end of the nineteenth century. The karczma (alternatively *gospoda*, *oberża*, *zajazd*) was usually built in a square or T-shape with a two-stage *dach polski* (Polish roof). Only a few examples of traditional taverns still survive, one of them in Jeleśnia near Żywiec, pictured, but the tradition is kept alive by the sprouting up everywhere of country dining facilities built in the style of the old karczma.

karp, akcja żywy karp (carp, live carp campaign). Carp served one way or another is as much a part of the **Wigilia** (Christmas Eve) meal as the turkey is for American Thanksgiving. A tradition beginning in the **PRL** (communist Poland) due to the lack of fresh fish of any other variety, large containers seething with carp turn up at supermarkets for customers to point out to the shop assistant, buy, and take home in a bucket. The carp is kept in the family bathtub until killed, typically with a blow to the head

KALEIDOSCOPE OF POLAND

with a meat-tenderizing hammer (which every family has, because it is used to make Poland's favorite meat dish, *kotlet schabowy* [veal cutlet]). It is illegal to carry a live fish out of a store in a shopping bag, but it happens. An animal rights campaign known as "żywy karp" (live carp) attracts increasingly more attention by urging stores to give carp more breathing room, and people to buy fish frozen, as fish-processing plants supposedly kill them more humanely. One of the group's slogans is the punning "Lud lubi karpia, a karp lubi lód" (People love carp, and carp love ice): the words *lud*, "people," and *lód*, "ice," are pronounced the same. The tradition is described sarcastically by Olga Tokarczuk in her vignette "Gość" (Guest), in which the hallowed Christmas "guest" is the carp.

Karpaty (Carpathian Mountains). A large and long central European mountain range arcing in a curve across the Czech Republic, Poland, Slovakia, Hungary, Ukraine, Romania, and Serbia. Its highest peak is Gerlach (pictured) in Slovakia, visible from Poland, at 2,655 meters. In all countries the Carpathians tend to be inhabited by people of particular ethnic character and interest; see *górale*. In Poland the Karpaty are subdivided into the Tatry (Tatras), Beskidy (Beskids), Bieszczady (Bieszczads), and Pieniny.

Karski, Jan (1914–2000). Sometimes called "the person who tried to stop the Holocaust," Karski was a Polish resistance fighter and courier for the underground Armia Krajowa (Home Army) in World War II. Later he was a popular professor of history at Georgetown University. During the war he communicated between Warsaw, Paris, and London, informing especially on the ongoing extermination of the Jews in the Warsaw ghetto and in concentration camps — one of the earliest people to bring the murder of Europe's Jews to the attention of world leaders (who broadly dismissed his reports as being too fantastic to be believed). In 2012 he was posthumously awarded the US Medal of Freedom by President Barack Obama, whose use of the phrase "Polish death camps" at the award ceremony caused an international incident (see "polskie obozy koncentracyjne"). It is worth noting that Poland is by far first among forty-five nations in the number of persons recognized by Yad Vashem, the Israeli Holocaust remembrance authority, as "righteous among nations" for saving Jews in World War II. See also: Jeziorański, Zdzisław.

Karta Polaka (Certificate of Polish Nationality). The law establishing the legal status of Polish identity for persons of Polish background living on the territories of the former Soviet Union was passed in 2007. To obtain the certificate one must demonstrate Polish ancestry, proficiency in Polish, and knowledge of Polish history and customs, and declare that one considers oneself to be Polish. The purpose of the certificate is to tighten the bonds between Poland and those Poles who, through no fault of their own, found themselves east of the Polish border after World War II. The certificate does not confer citizenship or the right to settle permanently in Poland, but it does provide certain benefits to cardholders while in the country; for example, study opportunities, reduced rates for train travel, free museum entrance, and emergency medical care. The Karta Polaka has been virulently attacked by the government of Białoruś (Belarus) for supposedly violating its national sovereignty.

kasza, kutia (kasha, groats, kutia). In essence, *kasza* is simply cooked grain, possibly lightly roasted and cracked beforehand, a staple of the Polish diet since the Middle Ages. The most popular type is *kasza gryczana* (buckwheat groats). Other types are *jęczmienna* (barley), *jaglana* (millet), and *manna* (processed from wheat). Within each type there are several subtypes. *Kutia* is a specialty of Ukraine, Belarus, Lithuania, and hence of the Polish *kresy*. It is a dish of kasza (in this case, boiled wheat) mixed with sweetmeats (raisins, nuts, dried fruit) and honey, and is one of the traditional dishes served at Wigilia (Christmas Eve Supper), especially in the east. Kutia is mentioned in the earliest Slavic writings.

Kaszuby, język kaszubski (Kashubia, Kashubian language). Kashubia is a region of southern Pomorze (Pomerania) to the north of Kujawy with a corridor running north to the Zatoka Gdańska (Gdańsk Bay) in which a substantial number of inhabitants speak Kashubian, a West Slavic dialect close to Polish, but since 2005 accorded the status of a separate language. The Kashubians have a strong sense of ethnic separateness. There are Kashubian books, periodicals, regional television programs, a Kashubian Wikipedia, and it is even possible to take one's *matura* (high school achievement examinations) in Kashubian. The Polish prime minister (and, subsequently, president of the European Council), Donald Tusk, is ethnically Kashubian. Here are the names of the months in Polish and Kashubian:

	Polish	Kashubian
January	styczeń	stëcznik
February	luty	gromicznik
March	marzec	strumiannik
April	kwiecień	łżëkwiôt
May	maj	môj
June	czerwiec	czerwińc
July	lipiec	lëpińc
August	sierpień	zélnik
September	wrzesień	séwnik
October	październik	rujan
November	listopad	smùtan
December	grudzień	gòdnik

Katowice. Situated in Górny Śląsk (Upper Silesia) in the south of Poland, in a large multi-urban complex of heavy industry and mining, Katowice numbers around 308,720 inhabitants and is the tenth-largest city in Poland. Following the death

KALEIDOSCOPE OF POLAND 97

of the Soviet leader Joseph Stalin in 1953, it was called Stalinogród, a name that lasted three years. Katowice's railway station, built in 1972, was known for being the ugliest in the country, or at least the most out of character with its older architectural surroundings. It is being replaced by a modern combined travel and business center, despite the loud protests of "architecture lovers" who consider the old building to be a world-class monument of ugliness (in engineering and design), representing the so-called brutalism movement. More popular is Katowice's modernistic Spodek (saucer), a sports and entertainment facility built in 1964–1971. *Greater Katowice-Chorzów.*

Katyń, zbrodnia katyńska (Katyń, Katyń massacre). Katyń is a village and nearby forest in Western Russia and site of the mass execution of interned Polish army officers in 1940 by the Soviet NKVD, or security forces. In Katyń, Kozielsk, Ostashkov, and other localities across Ukraine and Russia, more than twenty-two thousand officers were murdered on the orders of Joseph Stalin and the Soviet Politburo, an atrocity that for many years the Soviet government attributed to the Nazis. The British and American governments colluded with the Soviets in concealing the truth for fear of offending their wartime ally. The subject was taboo in the PRL (communist Poland); see Józef Mackiewicz. The Katyń murders were chillingly recaptured in Andrzej Wajda's film *Katyń* (2007). Hardline revisionists in Russia continue to claim against all evidence that the event never took place. However, the Russian Duma has issued a declaration laying the blame squarely with the Soviet government. As if to compound the tragedy, in 2010, on the way to the commemoration of the seventieth anniversary of the Katyń massacre, the Polish president Lech Kaczyński, his wife, and ninety-four other people perished in the *katastrofa pod Smoleńskiem* (Smolensk air disaster). See also: Operacja Polska NKWD.

---

kawiarnia (coffee house, café). Poles may have acquired their taste for *kawa* (coffee), and for nursing a cup of it in a *kawiarnia*, from the Turks following the odsiecz wiedeńska (Relief of Vienna) of 1683. Be that as it may, the first Warsaw coffee shop opened nearly one hundred years later, in 1763. Ever since, the kawiarnia, especially in Warsaw and Kraków, is the place where great ideas are hatched and endlessly discussed. A development in the PRL (communist Poland) was the government-financed seeding of so-called *klubokawiarnie* (café clubs) by the thousands in rural Poland, with the doomed-to-fail aim of bringing big-city culture to the countryside. Despite the cultural status of kawa, in a Polish household one is more than likely to be offered tea (*herbata*). In a traditional Polish home, coffee and tea are served in a *szklanka* (glass), not a *filiżanka* (cup) or a *kubek* (mug), a tradition that is slowly dying out. *Art nouveau interior of Kraków's Jama Michalika.*

Kazania świętokrzyskie (Holy Cross sermons). The oldest example of original Polish prose, thought to be a thirteenth- or fourteenth-century copy of an earlier work. Written on parchment, they were discovered in 1890 by the distinguished philologist Aleksander Brückner in Saint Petersburg, Russia, cut into strips to strengthen the binding of another codex. It contains one complete sermon for Saint Catherine's

Day (November 25) and parts of five additional ones, written in a sophisticated rhetorical style. Another important collection of sermons is the *Kazania gnieźnieńskie* (Gniezno sermons, early fifteenth century), written later and in a much more natural style.

Kazimierz. A city district in Kraków on the eastern side of the Stare Miasto (old town). It was founded by Kazimierz III Wielki (Kazimierz the Great) in 1335. Jews were encouraged by King Jan I Olbracht to locate there, and for centuries the town existed separately from Kraków as a major center of Jewish life and culture in Poland and Europe. The Synagoga Stara (Old Synagogue) is today a museum of Judaica. The Jewish cemetery and the large Kościół Bożego Ciała (Corpus Christi Church) are prominent landmarks. Kazimierz today is a seedily attractive district consisting of *kawiarnie* (coffee houses), pubs, a flea market, and *zapiekanka* stalls, and it is gaining popularity as a bohemian artists' district. A yearly Festiwal Kultury Żydowskiej (Jewish Culture Festival) draws increasingly greater notice and international participation. *Kazimierz town hall, fifteenth century.*

Kazimierz Dolny. A picturesque small town (fewer than five thousand inhabitants) on the Wisła in east-central Poland, preserving the appearance of a prosperous market town of the fifteenth through sixteenth centuries so well that it is often used as a movie set. The town was laid to waste in the Swedish wars of the seventeenth century, and it never regained its former prominence. *Market Square, Kazimierz Dolny.*

Kazimierz III Wielki (Kazimierz the Great, 1310–1370, ruled from 1333). The son of Władysław I Łokietek (Władysław the Short), Kazimierz was the last member of the *dynastia Piastów* (Piast dynasty). An effective king, he fortified Poland in the west, normalized relations with the Czechs and the Krzyżacy (Teutonic Knights), enlarged territory in the east, and strongly allied himself with Węgry (Hungary). He was succeeded on the throne by his Hungarian nephew Ludwik Węgierski (Ludwig the Hungarian, ruled 1370–1382), and then by Ludwik's daughter Jadwiga. A major diplomatic success, and the first high-level meeting of its kind in Europe, was the *uczta u Wierzynka* (feast at Wierzynek's, 1364), gathering rulers from around Europe. Kazimierz helped to codify laws

KALEIDOSCOPE OF POLAND   99

and develop cities, especially around Kraków, where he established the Akademia Krakowska, the first higher educational institution in Poland and the second in northern Europe. It is said that he "zastał Polskę drewnianą, a zostawił murowaną" (found Poland in wood and left it in stone).

"Kiedy ranne wstają zorze" (When the morning dawn arises). A popular singable religious hymn almost everybody knows, by Franciszek Karpiński (1741–1825). The first verse:

> Kiedy ranne wstają zorze,
> Tobie ziemia, Tobie morze,
> Tobie śpiewa żywioł wszelki,
> Bądź pochwalon, Boże wielki!

> When the morning dawn arises,
> To You to earth, to You the sea,
> To You sings all creation,
> May you be praised, almighty God!

Karpiński is also the author of "Bóg się rodzi, moc truchleje" (God is born, powers tremble), a hymn sung in church at the ringing of a bell at midnight on Christmas Eve, and at Christmastime generally.

Kielce. Kielce is a city of nearly 205,000 inhabitants situated in the middle of the Góry Świętokrzyskie (Holy Cross Mountains) in central Poland. It is the capital of the Świętokrzyskie voivodeship in an area that has been inhabited since the fifth century BC. The area is rich in copper, iron, and lead ore, and Kielce has long been associated with metallurgy. Like many Polish towns, the etymology of its name is up for grabs. One legend names the town after its founder from the noble family of Kiełcz, while another claims that it stems from the Kelts who inhabited the town before the Slavs. Other theories abound, one being that the word is related to kieł (tusk), after the discovery of huge white tusks near the site — not that crazy, since the region has yielded dinosaur fossils. Kielce was the first Polish city to be liberated from Russian rule by Józef Piłsudski's legions in 1914.

Kielce, pogrom kielecki (Kielce pogrom). In 1946 thirty-seven Jews from Kielce who had survived the Holocaust were preposterously accused of planning the ritual murder of a child to make matzo, and were murdered by an angry Polish mob. The incident mobilized public opinion against Poland around the world and contributed to the emigration of most of the remaining Jews who had survived the war. Twelve people were arrested and tried in a show trial, of whom nine were executed. Conspiracy theories are rife, including the notion that the pogrom was orchestrated to distract attention from communist brutality against the Poles, but there is no question as to its occurrence, and the enduring blot it left on postwar Polish history.

kiełbasa (sausage). There are dozens of varieties of kiełbasa, including regional. Most are made of pork, and most are smoked, both for the taste and to help in preservation. Poles tend not to go in for the extremely dry varieties of sausage like salami. The typical U-shaped kiełbasa wiejska/swojska (country/homemade sausage), known in the United States as "Polish sausage," is flavored with marjoram and garlic and is especially good grilled. Kabanosy are thin air-dried sausages traditionally made of horsemeat but these days more often of turkey, often eaten cold. They have just been awarded the status of a regional specialty within the EU. Kiełbasa krakowska is a thick straight sausage flavored with pepper and garlic; biała kiełbasa (white sausage) is fresh,

100   KALEIDOSCOPE OF POLAND

unsmoked, and cooked by boiling. *Kaszanka* (blood sausage) is made primarily from buckwheat or barley groats, to which subcuts of meat (liver, lungs, skin, fat) are added. *Biała, wiejska, and kabanosy.*

Kiepura, Jan (1902–1966). An internationally recognized Polish opera singer and film actor of the *dwudziestolecie międzywojenne* (interwar period), Kiepura sang in the famous opera halls of Europe, including La Scala in Milan. In film, not surprisingly, he specialized in musicals. Half Jewish, he fled Europe for the United States before the war but, according to his wishes, he was buried in Powązki Cemetery in Warsaw. A yearly festival of European song is held in his honor in Krynica-Zdrój, where he built a large resort hotel in the 1920s.

Kieślowski, Krzysztof (1941–1996). The most prominent of the directors of the Polish *kino moralnego niepokoju* (cinema of moral anxiety) of the 1980s, Kieślowski got his start in documentary filmmaking. Early films were *Amator* (Camera buff, 1979) and *Przypadek* (Blind chance, 1981). His ten-hour-long, made-for-television series *Dekalog I-X* (1988), modern stories illustrating moral dilemmas related to those posed by the Ten Commandments, is widely considered one of the outstanding achievements of twentieth-century cinema. Kieślowski went on to make several notable French-Polish coproductions: *Podwójne życie Weroniki* (*The Double Life of Véronique*, 1991), about two women, one Polish and one French, who live similar lives and face similar choices unbeknownst to each other; and the tricolor trilogy *Niebieski* (*Blue*, 1993, winner of the Golden Lion at the Venetian Film Festival), *Biały* (*White*, 1994), and *Czerwony* (*Red*, 1994, nominated for an Oscar).

Kilar, Wojciech (1932–2013). A **Lwów**-born composer of serious music, at first avant-garde, but with time more conventional, Kilar was a first-rate and prolific composer of more than 130 film scores, including for many of the classics of Polish cinema. He has worked with most major Polish directors, and he was a special favorite of **Krzysztof Zanussi**, who made a 1991 documentary about him. Kilar did the music to **Andrzej Wajda**'s *Pan Tadeusz* (Master Thaddeus, 1999) and *Zemsta* (Revenge, 2002). For **Roman Polański** he did the scores for *Death and the Maiden* (1994), *The Ninth Gate* (1999), and *The Pianist*

(2002). Americans may be most familiar with his ominous soundtrack for Francis Ford Coppola's *Dracula* (1992).

Kiliński, Jan (1760–1819). A Warsaw shoemaker who rose to political prominence in late eighteenth-century Warsaw, elected three times to the Warsaw city council. In the Warsaw Uprising of 1794, during the **insurekcja kościuszkowska** (Kościuszko Insurrection), Kiliński formed a national militia that eventually numbered twenty thousand men. He later joined forces with the regular army under **Tadeusz Kościuszko** and was promoted to the rank of colonel. After years of arrest and exile in Russia following the insurrection's collapse, Kiliński returned to Warsaw and wrote his memoirs. He is buried in the Powązki Cemetery church. His prominent statue (pictured) stands on Warsaw's Podwale Street.

kino studyjne (studio or art cinema). The *Sieć Kin Studyjnych* (network of studio cinemas), partially supported by the government and the Polski Instytut Sztuki Filmowej (Polish Institute of Film Art), celebrated its fiftieth anniversary in 2009. The network helps to supply larger Polish towns with a rich selection of the best in foreign and, especially, Polish movies. Unlike in multiplexes, films are shown commercial-free. In 2009 **Kraków**'s Kino Pod Baranami (Cinema under the Rams) received an award from Europa Cinemas for being, according to its repertoire, the best studio cinema in Europe. The Kino Pionier (Pioneer Cinema, pictured), located in **Szczecin** and founded in 1909 as the Helios-Welt-Kino, is listed in the Guinness Book of Records as the world's oldest continuously existing cinema. In one of its auditoria one sits behind tables, as if in a *kawiarnia* (café).

kiosk (newsstand-plus). The *kiosk* is a mini variety store. Its customer base is provided by the people waiting for buses and trolleys at the stops where kiosks are located. Besides offering trolley and bus tickets, kiosks are the place to turn for newspapers and magazines and cigarettes, but also such things as postcards, maps, cheap cosmetics, laundry products, writing supplies, batteries, phone cards, cheap toys, chewing gum and candy bars, sometimes lottery tickets, and whatever else the kiosk owner thinks people will buy. Recently kiosks have begun to sell bottled water and other drinks from a remote-controlled refrigerated display case located alongside. If you buy at a kiosk, be prepared to have the right change or to have the proprietor say "Nie mam wydać" (I don't have the change); see **money, banknoty**.

---

kirkuty (Jewish cemeteries). Few Jewish places of worship survived the Holocaust, and the small number that remained were often not returned to religious use – for lack of worshippers. Some have become museums. Although many Jewish cemeteries, or *kirkuty*, were destroyed or built over, or their *macewy* (grave markers) were used for building material, many remain, testimony to a once vibrant culture that has been lost. Often the kirkuty sites are untended, tumbledown, overgrown with weeds, and all but forgotten. However, a large number have been partially or fully restored, often with outside help. A website devoted to Polish kirkuty lists over six hundred. The largest are in Warsaw, **Łódź**, **Kraków**, and **Częstochowa**, but ones in smaller towns in the east can be just as poignantly memorable to visit. *Macewy in the Old Jewish Cemetery in Sanok.*

---

klimat, pory roku (climate, seasons). In Poland moist Atlantic air collides with the drier air of the inner continent, resulting in a constantly changing weather mix. Poles constantly complain about changes in *ciśnienie* (atmospheric pressure) and its effect on one's *samopoczucie* (well-being). In Polish one speaks of six or seven seasons, not only four: *zima* (winter), *przedwiośnie* (the first month of spring), *wiosna* (the last two months), and *lato* (summer). *Jesień* (autumn) is the most variegated, with *babie lato* (Indian summer) falling in the middle, and *przedzimie* (late autumn) at the end. The north and west tend to be more moderate, the south and east more variable and extreme. Except for the occasional *halny* (mountain wind), the daily weather report almost always predicts *wiatry słabe i umiarkowane* (weak to moderate winds). The hottest temperature ever recorded in Poland was 40.2°C/104.36°F in 1921 near **Opole**, the lowest, −41°C/−41.8°F in 1940 in Siedlce.

Kmicic, Andrzej. A swashbuckling fictional character based on the historical figure of Samuel Kmicic, in **Henryk Sienkiewicz**'s historical novel *Potop*, about the seventeenth-century **potop szwedzki** (Swedish Deluge). During the course of the novel the former rabble-rousing nobleman becomes transformed into a fervent Polish patriot. He takes part in the siege of **Jasna Góra** monastery, later saves King Jan Kazimierz's life, and still later leads a division of Crimean Tatars bringing aid to the Poles. In Jerzy Hoffman's 1974, Oscar-nominated film version of the novel, in which he is played by **Daniel Olbrychski** (pictured), he at one point loses a duel with

KALEIDOSCOPE OF POLAND   103

sabers in a driving rain to the novel's main hero, Sir Michał Wołodyjowski, played by Tadeusz Łomnicki, in one of world cinema's most memorable swordfights.

kobiety w polityce (women in politics). In post-communist Poland, in accord with a general East European trend, the participation of women in politics has fallen, to about 20 percent in the Sejm RP and 8 percent in the Senat. Against this background, certain exceptions stand out. Hanna Suchocka (b. 1946) served as Poland's first woman prime minister in 1992–1993. She has been serving as Poland's representative to the Holy See since 2001. Ewa Kopacz (b. 1956), Minister of Health under Donald Tusk, in 2011 was elected Marszałek (marshal, or speaker) of the Sejm RP by an overwhelming majority, placing her second in line to the presidency, arguably a higher office than has been achieved by any woman so far in the United States. At present, she is Poland's premier, having replaced Donald Tusk. Another prominent woman politician is Hanna Gronkiewicz-Waltz (b. 1952), twice elected *prezydent* (mayor) of Warsaw. See also: Pierwsza Dama.

Kochanowski, Jan (1530–1584). Polish court secretary under King Zygmunt II August, Kochanowski was the major poet of the Polish *odrodzenie* (Renaissance), and the first Slavic literary figure of international prominence (a fact of which he himself was quite aware). Kochanowski set the standard for the important literary genres of the time with his lyrics, psalms, dramas, narrative verse, and *fraszki* (epigrams, many of which are quite readable and racy; Kochanowski established the genre in Polish). His translation of the Psalms (*Psałterz Dawidów*) can also still be read with pleasure. His most enduring work is Treny (Threnodies, or laments), a cycle of nineteen poems on the death of his daughter Urszula. Kochanowski's estate Czarnolas (Blackwood), with its sheltering *lipa czarnoleska* (Czarnolas linden tree), has become symbolic of the contemplative bucolic life. As a gruesome footnote, Kochanowski's skull was removed from his grave by a collector in 1791 and eventually ended up in the Czartoryski Museum in Kraków.

Kolbe, ojciec Maksymilian Maria (Saint Maximillian Maria Kolbe, 1894–1941). A prominent conservative Catholic priest, publicist, and activist before World War II, Father Kolbe founded monasteries in Poland and in Japan, as well as a seminary, a radio station, and other organizations and publications — a sort of early Father Rydzyk. During the war he was arrested, held in Pawiak prison, and sent to the Oświęcim (Auschwitz) concentration and extermination camp. Bargaining with his captors, he selected death by starvation to save the life of another prisoner, Franciszek Gajowniczek, who had a

104 KALEIDOSCOPE OF POLAND

wife and children. Rather than be allowed to die a martyr's death, after two weeks in a cell without food or water and in the final stages of starvation, Kolbe was killed by lethal injection and his body was incinerated. He was beatified in 1971 and canonized as a Roman Catholic saint in 1982. Gajowniczek survived the war (although his children did not), and lived to attend the canonization ceremony. Father Kolbe is the patron saint of drug addicts, political prisoners, families, journalists, and the pro-life movement. The film *Życie za życie* (A life for a life, 1991), by **Krzysztof Zanussi**, portrays his life and end.

Kolberg, Henryk Oskar (1814–1890). Poland's pioneer and preeminent folklorist. A rough age-mate and neighbor of **Fryderyk Chopin** in Warsaw, Kolberg had ambitions of becoming a composer, but his life course was changed by his interest in folk music. He began collecting folk melodies in and around Warsaw, something he was able to do by ear, and soon he had more than six hundred melodies, many of which he adapted for piano and choral singing — to the disapproval of folklore purists. However, his *Pieśni ludu polskiego* (Songs of the Polish people) of 1856–1857, containing four hundred folk melodies in unembellished form, established his reputation as Poland's foremost ethnomusicologist. At a time when Polish folk customs in much of the country were being lost, little by little he broadened his interests to collecting Polish folklore generally. The first volume of his series *Lud: Jego zwyczaje, sposób życia, mowa, podania, przysłowia, obrzędy, gusła, zabawy, pieśni, muzyka i tańce* (The Folk: Their customs, ways, dialects, traditions, sayings, ceremonies, witchcraft, past times, songs, music, and dances) appeared in 1856, and thirty-three volumes would appear before his death. He left behind material for another seventy volumes at least.

kolejka, kultura kolejkowa (standing in line). Waiting in line became a metaphor for life in the **PRL** (communist Poland), a theme exemplified in **Tadeusz Konwicki**'s 1977 novel *Kompleks polski* (The Polish complex). Often people would stand in line outside a shop without even knowing what was on offer, sometimes on the mere rumor of a shipment, just to buy something to hoard or to trade with. Sometimes a person in line was put in charge of a *lista kolejkowa* (line list), so that people could leave to take care of other business. Older people would offer their services as *stacze* (line-standers) for people who had better things to do than stand in line. Invalids, mothers with babes in arms, and certain other categories of people had special line privileges. A board game called Kolejka was recently published by the Instytut Pamięci Narodowej (Institute for National Memory). Appropriately, people stood in long lines to buy it, and it sold out immediately.

kolędnicy (carolers). Poland has a rich tradition of *kolędy* (Christmas carols) and *kolędnicy* (carolers) who traipse from house to house singing Christmas carols while being treated to food and drink in return (these days, people mostly expect money). Traditionally a village custom, caroling is making inroads into the city. Caroling season is anywhere from Christmas day to **Święto Trzech Króli** (Three Kings Day, or Epiphany, January 6), although carol singing itself continues until Ofiarowanie Pańskie (Presentation of Jesus at the Temple, February 2). In a tradition mostly practiced in the countryside, in Poland carolers are costumed as scary characters, favorites being, besides the now politically incorrect *Żyd* (Jew) and *Cyganka* (Gypsy woman), the *dziad* (old man), *śmierć* (death), *diabeł* (the devil), *kobyłka* (horse and Turkish rider), *Herod* (King Herod), and — everybody's favorite — the *turoń* (a ramlike figure). A default character is one of the three kings. One person among the group holds aloft a bright star of Bethlehem or carries a *szopka* (crèche).

kolumna Zygmunta (King Zygmunt's column, Warsaw). The impressive column in front of the **Zamek Królewski** (royal palace) in Warsaw, at the entrance to **Starówka** (old town), was erected in 1643–1644 to honor King Zygmunt III Waza, who had moved the capital from **Kraków** to Warsaw, by his son, Władysław IV. On it, Zygmunt III carries a cross and a sword. It is the oldest non-church monument in Warsaw, and one of the oldest in northern Europe. The column was knocked down in 1944 by a German tank shell; it was repaired and erected again in 1949. The remnants of the original marble column knocked down by the Germans are displayed next to the royal palace.

Kołakowski, Leszek (1927–2009). Eminent philosopher of history and cocreator of the Polish school of the history of ideas at the University of Warsaw. An early Marxist and Communist Party member, Kołakowski spent the first part of his career pursuing the idea of Marxism with a human face, only to abandon the whole enterprise later in life, calling Marxism the biggest hoax of the twentieth century. His widely read essay "Kapłan i błazen" (The priest and the jester) analyzes the antipodes of the intelligentsia's engagement with socialism, ranging from the true believer to the irreverent skeptic. After the March events *(marzec 1968, wydarzenia marcowe)*, for his anti-government statements in lectures Kołakowski was fired from his university post without the right to publish or hold any other academic position, and was thus forced into the emigration, after which he taught at Berkeley, Yale, Chicago, and Oxford. He is buried in the Powązki Cemetery in Warsaw.

Komeda, Krzysztof (1931–1969). Born Krzysztof Trzciński, Komeda was an important jazz pianist and composer of film scores, especially for **Roman Polański**. His score for Polański's 1968 *Rosemary's Baby*, including the creepy lullaby, is especially remembered. He died from complications from a head injury following a fall involving horseplay with **Marek Hłasko** in California. Komeda was one of the foremost representatives of what became known in Europe as the *polska szkoła jazzu* (Polish jazz school), which emerged from its mostly underground existence to become a fully developed movement following the 1956 *odwilż* (thaw). For a while, until reissues appeared, Polish jazz records commanded astronomical prices abroad. The Polish school was characterized by a high level of professionalism in performance, as many of its representatives had classical musical training; for example, the pianist Andrzej Trzaskowski (1933–1998) or the violinist Zbigniew Seifert (1946–1979). *Commemorative plaque for Komeda in Poznań.*

Komisja Edukacji Narodowej (KEN, Commission of National Education). Established in 1773 at the instigation of King **Stanisław II August Poniatowski**, the commission was Europe's first national ministry of education. A response to the suspension (1773–1814) of the Jesuit teaching order by Pope Clement XIV, it led to the reorganization, secularization, and relative uniformity of educational instruction on all levels throughout the country. Two figures of importance are Hugo Kołłątaj, who undertook the reform of the Akademia Krakowska (Kraków Academy, later **Uniwersytet Jagielloński**), and Ignacy Potocki, who chaired the commission in charge of creating elementary-level textbooks in all subjects. The Potocki commission established the basic vocabulary for the natural and exact sciences that is still largely in use today. The KEN ended its activities in 1794.

Komitet Obrony Robotników (KOR) (Workers' Defense Committee). KOR was established by a group of prominent Polish intellectuals and political oppositionists, originally to help fired and imprisoned workers following the strikes and protests in the *wydarzenia czerwcowe* (June 1976 events in Warsaw and Radom). It first consisted of fourteen prominent people who signed a public *apel* (appeal) demanding the immediate release and reinstatement of all workers. Among its founding members were Antoni Macierewicz, Piotr Naimski, **Jerzy Andrzejewski**, **Stanisław Barańczak**, and **Jacek Kuroń**. When the workers were granted amnesty one month later, in 1977 KOR transformed itself into an ongoing opposition group under the name Komitet Samoobrony Społecznej "KOR" (The KOR Committee for Social Self-Defense). Its members were subject to the constant harassment of the authorities. In Kraków in 1977, a student member of KOR, Stanisław Pyjas, was beaten to death in a downtown stairwell, an unsolved crime most attributed to the secret police.

Komorowska, Maja (b. 1937). One of Poland's most highly regarded stage and screen actresses. Komorowska received her theatrical training in **Jerzy Grotowski**'s Teatr Laboratorium in Wrocław, where she worked until 1968. Since then she has belonged to the company of the Teatr Współczesny (Contemporary Theater) in Warsaw. She got her start in film with **Krzysztof Zanussi**, under whose direction she starred in more than half a dozen of his best-known film works. She has also appeared in major works by **Andrzej Wajda** and **Krzysztof Kieślowski**, among others. Komorowska in Teatr Współczesny's Quartet *by Ronald Harwood*.

Komorowski, Bronisław (b. 1952). A prominent dissident in the late 1970s and 1980s, Komorowski was interned under *stan wojenny* (martial law) in 1981. In the so-called **Trzecia Rzeczpospolita** (Third Republic) he served as vice minister of defense under several prime ministers, and was later full minister of defense under the government of **Jerzy Buzek**. Komorowski was elected Marszałek (speaker) of the **Sejm RP** (parliament) in 2007, and became acting Polish president when President **Lech Kaczyński** perished in the *katastrofa pod Smoleńskiem* (Smolensk air disaster). Komorowski won the election for the presidency over Lech's brother **Jarosław Kaczyński** in an election held in July 2010.

Komorowski, Tadeusz (1895–1966), nicknamed "Bór" (pine forest). From 1943, commander of the Polish **Armia Krajowa** (Home Army) and leader of the valiant but failed **powstanie warszawskie** (August 1–October 2, 1944), raised on orders of the *rząd na uchodźtwie* (government in exile) in London. Komorowski engineered the honorable surrender of the Warsaw insurgents, whom the Germans — exceptionally for them — treated as legitimate prisoners of war. After World War II Komorowski served as prime minister in the rząd na uchodźtwie. See also: **"Nil," Generał**.

komunizm (communism). Because of its negative connotations for most Poles, the word *komunizm* was euphemistically avoided by the Polish press in referring to the governmental situation during the **PRL** (communist Poland). Poland supposedly had *socjalizm*, not komunizm, and the party in power was called the **Polska Zjednoczona Partia Robotnicza** (PZPR, Polish United Workers' Party). This gave Poles ready-made words (*komunistyczny*, "communist"; *komuna*, "communism" [pejorative]; and *komuch*, "commie") for referring contemptuously to their country's government and its leaders. Today's politicians who continue the traditions of the PZPR, mostly under the banner of the Sojusz Lewicy Demokratycznej (SLD, Left Democratic Alliance), are referred to in the contemporary press as *postkomuniści* (postcommunists).

konfederacja, rokosz, zajazd. Differently nuanced names for armed insurrections. The first, *konfederacja* (confederation), is a label for a

108   KALEIDOSCOPE OF POLAND

virtually institutionalized system of armed noble revolt within the Polish Rzeczpospolita Obojga Narodów (Polish-Lithuanian Commonwealth), the aim being to pressure the king on some political issue. The most famous of the confederations were the konfederacja barska (Bar Confederacy, 1768–1772), raised against the rising influence of Russia in Polish affairs, and the konfederacja targowicka (Targowica Confederacy, 1792–1793), raised by wealthy magnates against the reforms of the Konstytucja 3 maja (May 3 Constitution). A *rokosz* (rebellion) had less legal status. The rokosz Zebrzydowskiego (Zebrzydowski Revolt, 1606–1609) occurred in response to King Zygmunt III Waza's plans to restore a hereditary monarchy and limit the rights of the nobility and the Sejm (parliament). A *zajazd* (foray) was sort of like a "posse," organized locally to enforce legal rulings, although forays were also sometimes organized extrajudicially, as in Adam Mickiewicz's *Pan Tadeusz*, the subtitle of which translates to "The last foray in Lithuania."

konfederacja barska (Bar Confederacy, 1768–1772). An armed alliance of Polish noblemen against the Russian tsarina Catherine the Great and against the Russian-installed king Stanisław August Poniatowski, in defense of Polish independence, the privileges of the magnates, and of the special position of the Catholic faith in Poland. Its leaders were Adam Krasiński, Kazimierz Puławski, and Michał Krasiński. Named after the town and fortress in Podole in which its articles were formulated, the Bar Confederacy is considered by some to be the first Polish national uprising. It was eventually suppressed, leading to the exile or forced impressment into the Russian army of thousands of Poles. It was a major factor leading to the first partition of Poland in 1772 (see *rozbiory*). Józef Chełmoński, Kazimierz Pułaski near Częstochowa.

konfederacja targowicka (Targowica Confederacy, 1792–1793). A reactionary conspiracy of Polish and Lithuanian magnates in response to the Konstytucja 3 maja (May 3 Constitution, 1791) which abridged their powers. It is named after a small town in Ukraine where the pact was supposedly concluded, although in reality it was concocted by a Russian general in Saint Petersburg in collusion with Stanisław Szczęsny Potocki, Franciszek Ksawery Branicki, Seweryn Rzewuski, and others whose names are still today synonymous with treachery. The confederacy served as a pretext for the armed intervention of Russia and helped lead to the second and third partitions of Poland in 1793 and 1795 (see *rozbiory*). The leaders of Targowica were sentenced to death in absentia during the insurekcja kościuszkowska (Kościuszko Insurrection). As the sentences could not be carried out, the conspirators were instead hanged in effigy, as depicted in Jan Piotr Norblin's 1794 painting, pictured.

Konrad. The ideal Romantic hero in Adam Mickiewicz's drama *Dziady*, *część III* (Forefather's Eve, part III), written in Dresden, Germany, after the fall of the powstanie listopadowe (November Uprising, 1830–1831). In it, the

KALEIDOSCOPE OF POLAND

maudlin individualist Gustaw, finding himself in a prison in Wilno awaiting exile for anti-tsarist activity, becomes transformed into the committed poet-patriot activist Konrad in the course of a monologue known as the "Wielka Improwizacja" (great improvisation). In his improvisation, Konrad outlines the conception of **mesjanizm polski** (Polish national messianism), in his mind rising above others and committing the blasphemy of comparing the Russian tsar to God.

Konstytucja 3 maja (May 3 Constitution, 1791). The second modern national constitution after the US Constitution of 1787, the culmination of the raucous Sejm Czteroletni (Four-Year Sejm), held with the encouragement of King Stanisław August Poniatowski, incorporating progressive ideas of the *oświecenie* (Enlightenment). Its ultimately unsuccessful aim, given the de facto Russian control over Polish politics of the time, was to rescue the Polish-Lithuanian Commonwealth from its virtually paralytic state that was due to the privileges enjoyed by the nobility, especially their veto power (*liberum veto*) over all legislation. Short-lived, the constitution led to a revolt of the nobles under the **konfederacja targowicka** (Targowica Confederacy, 1792–1793); to the intervention of Russia and Prussia in the *drugi* and *trzeci rozbiory* (second and third partitions, of 1793 and 1795 respectively); and to the loss of Polish statehood. In effect, as two of its authors, Hugo Kołłątaj and Ignacy Potocki proclaimed, the constitution amounted to the old republic's last will and testament. May 3, Constitution Day, is now a major Polish national holiday (see *dni wolne od pracy*).

kontusz (Polish split-sleeved coat). Of possibly Hungarian or Turkish inspiration, and also used among the East Slavs (the picture is Ukrainian), the *kontusz* was the trademark outergarment worn by the Polish male nobility in the seventeenth and eighteenth centuries, emblematic of the *sarmacki* (Sarmatian) style of dress; see *sarmatyzm*. Loose and cut like a bathrobe, it was closed with a *pas słucki*, a broad oriental-style cloth belt named after the Belarusian town, Słuck, that specialized in its manufacture. The sleeves were cut from the armpit to the sleeve so as to hang loose or even to be tossed to the back. The kontusz was often imitated in Polish folk dress. It was worn over a *żupan*.

Konwicki, Tadeusz (1926–2015). Novelist, literary critic, screenwriter, and film director, Konwicki is one of the most important Polish literary figures of the second half of the twentieth century. Following the war he collaborated with the communist regime, but later broke with it and became a vocal spokesman for the political opposition, publishing mostly abroad. His novels explore both national and universal themes seen through a moral perspective commonly described as existential. Many of his works are miscellanies, consisting of loosely connected passages dancing around a particular theme. Representative novels are *Sennik współczesny* (A dreambook for our time, 1963), *Wniebowstąpienie* (Ascension to heaven, 1967), *Kompleks polski* (The polish complex, 1977), and *Mała Apokalipsa* (A minor apocalypse, 1979). As a filmmaker Konwicki is one of the outstanding representatives of the *polska szkoła filmowa* (Polish film school). His *Ostatni dzień lata* (Last day of summer) won the prize for experimental film at the 1958 Venice Film Festival.

Kopaliński, Władysław (1907–2007). A prolific popularizing lexicographer, encyclopedist, translator, essayist, and chronicler of myths, legends, folklore, symbols, cultural icons, word origins, and foreign expressions. His best-known work is the 1967 *Słownik wyrazów obcych i zwrotów obcojęzycznych* (Dictionary of foreign and foreign-language expressions, 1967). The answer to almost any cultural or literary question could be found "*u Kopalińskiego*" (in Kopaliński), that is, in one or another of the nearly two dozen dictionaries and encyclopedias he authored. These days, of course, Poles, like everyone else, tend to look things up on Wikipedia.

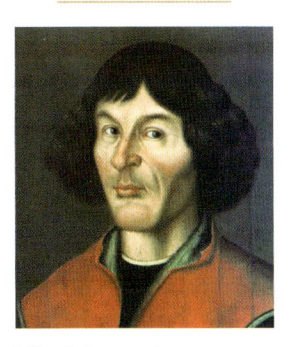

Kopernik, Mikołaj (Nicolaus Copernicus, 1473–1543). Astronomer and mathematician of mixed German-Polish background from Toruń, Copernicus was educated in Kraków and Padua, and worked and died in Frombork in Warmia. In his *De revolutionibus orbium coelestium* (*On the Revolutions of the Heavenly Spheres*, 1543), published in the year of his death, he formulated the heliocentric theory of the solar system. Because it seemed to contradict scripture, it was put on the Vatican's list of proscribed books for many years. Copernicus's work led to a seismic shift in scientific thought often referred to as the *przewrót kopernikowski* (Copernican revolution). His body was recently exhumed in Frombork, its identity confirmed, and more prominently buried. A computer program was used to reconstruct his appearance at the age of seventy, looking rather like an older version of his picture here. Major monuments to Copernicus are in Warsaw in front of the building of the Polska Akademia Nauk (Polish Academy of Sciences) and in Toruń. The radioactive chemical element with the atomic number 112, discovered in Germany in 1996, was named Copernicium, after him.

kopiec (memorial mound). Memorial mounds, or hills built in honor of a dead person by piling up dirt higher and higher, are a relic of pre-Christian and pre-Slavic (probably Celtic) societies. In the Kraków area there are two notable prehistoric *kopce* (mounds), *kopiec Wandy* (the mound of Wanda, daughter of legendary King Krak), and the mound of Krak himself. Other prehistoric mounds can be found, especially in the Polish southeast. The tradition has carried over into modern times in Kraków with the erection in 1820–1823 of the kopiec Kościuszki (Kościuszko Mound) and in 1934–1937 of the *kopiec Piłsudskiego* (Piłsudski mound), both in the hilly Zwierzyniec (zoo) district. A mound in honor of Jan Paweł II (Pope John Paul II) is being planned for the grounds of the Sanktuarium Bożego Miłosierdzia (Sanctuary of Divine Mercy) in Kraków's Łagiewniki district. *The Kościuszko mound, lighted at night.*

KOR. See **Komitet Obrony Robotników (KOR)**.

Korczak, Janusz (1878–1942). Born under the name Henryk Goldszmit, Korczak was a renowned doctor, children's rights activist, and pioneer in the social rehabilitation of the young. He was also a well-known publicist, radio commentator, and author of a still-read children's book, *Król Maciuś Pierwszy* (*King Matt the First*, 1922), and its sequel. *Król Maciuś Pierwszy* has seen a number of film and cartoon adaptations, as well as a children's opera based on it. Before and into World War II, Korczak ran an orphanage for Jewish children, on Warsaw's Krochmalna Street, which became incorporated into the Warsaw ghetto. He voluntarily accompanied the children in his care in cattle cars to the gas chambers to his and their deaths in **Treblinka** when the decision was made to liquidate the ghetto. A film of Korczak's life was made in 1990 by **Andrzej Wajda**. A large bronze memorial is devoted to Korczak in Israel's Yad Vashem.

Korona Królestwa Polskiego (Latin: *Corona Regni Poloniae*, Crown of the Polish Kingdom). The name of the late medieval Polish state. The designation was first applied under **Kazimierz III Wielki** (Kazimierz the Great, 1333–1370) and was meant to emphasize the stability of the state and its independence above and beyond the ruler or dynasty of the moment. By implication, the *korona* also claimed suzerainty over lands that were ethnically Polish but were not, at the time, part of the kingdom. During the **Rzeczpospolita Obojga Narodów** (Polish-Lithuanian Commonwealth, 1569–1795), the term *Korona* was used to refer to the Polish part of the union, as contrasted to the Wielkie Księstwo Litewskie (Grand Duchy of Lithuania). Ukraine belonged to the Korona.

korporacje akademickie (university fraternities). University fraternities in Poland were modeled on similar institutions at German universities, and also drew on the tradition of Polish secret patriotic fraternities at the University of Wilno (the *filomaci* and *filareci*) in the early nineteenth century. Fraternities flowered in the *dwudziestolecie międzywojenne* (interwar period), when they were elite organizations with their own uniforms, swagger sticks, secret words, and codes of conduct (including dueling), not to mention a mostly nationalistic and anti-Semitic ideology, although Jewish students also had their own *korporacje*. They were outlawed under communism, but their members often continued to meet privately. Some were reactivated after 1989, especially in Warsaw, **Poznań**, and **Toruń**. There are about a dozen or so, but at the moment they play a minor role in university life. A well-known prewar fraternity was Arkonia, taking its name from the pagan Slavic temple Arkona, the remains of which can be found on the German island of Rügen on the **Bałtyk** (Baltic Sea). *Old and new members of Korporacja Sarmatia.*

Korzeniowski, Robert (b. 1968). One of the world's best speedwalkers ever, the first to win successive gold medals at different Olympics

(Atlanta, Sydney, and Athens in the 50 km), and the first to win gold in both the 20 km and 50 km events (Sydney, 2000). In all, he won seven gold medals in the Olympics or world championships. At present he sponsors running and walking events across Poland.

Kosiński, Jerzy (1933–1991). Born Józef Lewinkopf to an upper-middle-class Jewish family in Łódź, Kosiński was a writer in English about whom it is difficult to distinguish fact from fiction. He left Poland in 1957 — according to him, by awarding himself a fellowship to study in New York. He achieved renown and joined the jet set with his novel about the Holocaust, *The Painted Bird* (*Malowany ptak*, 1965), a purportedly autobiographical novel crammed with shocking scenes of sex and violence. In fact, Kosiński spent the war relatively peacefully in Poland with his family, sheltered by non-Jews. His novel *Steps* (*Kroki*, 1968) won the National Book Award. Some suspected him of using ghostwriters. He died by suicide. His last days were described in a book by Janusz Głowacki, another (and probably better) Polish author who also "made it" in New York literary circles. A room is devoted to Kosiński in the Łódź city museum.

Kossak, Wojciech (1857–1942). Prolific realistic painter known for his depictions of historic battle and cavalry scenes. Almost no picture of his did not have a horse in it. Kossak was one of the creators of the *Panorama Racławicka* (*Racławice Panorama*). Another panorama of his, *Berezyna*, depicting Napoleon's retreat, was later cut up into individual paintings. Kossak inherited his talent for military scenes from his painter father Juliusz Kossak (1824–1899), and he passed it on to his own son Jerzy Kossak (1886–1955). His two daughters also made famous artistic careers: the writer Magdalena Samozwaniec (1894–1972) and the prominent interwar poet Maria Pawlikowska-Jasnorzewska (1891–1945). *Wojciech Kossak,* Piłsudski on Horseback, *1928.*

Kostka, Święty Stanisław (Saint Stanislaw Kostka, 1550–1568). Patron saint of novitiates, students, and children, and also one of Poland's patron saints, Saint Stanisław Kostka was a particularly pious youth and model seminarian of fragile health who fled his family in north-central Poland, near Przasnysz, to study in Vienna. He later joined the Jesuit order in Rome. He died of a fever at the age of eighteen, as he himself had predicted, in the midst of visions in which he conversed with God, the saints, and the Virgin Mary. He was canonized in 1726.

kościół Mariacki (Marian Church or Basilica, Kraków). An eye-catching Gothic church adjoining the *Rynek Główny* (main square) in Kraków, of which the church is one of the most recognizable symbols. Built in the thirteenth through fifteenth centuries on the foundations of an earlier church, it is the second-most important Kraków church, after the Katedra Wawelska (**Wawel** Cathedral). It houses the renowned triptych of the medieval wood sculptor **Wit Stwosz**, as well as other notable artwork; for example, the polychromies of **Jan Matejko** and **Stanisław Wyspiański**. On the hour an interrupted *hejnał* (bugle call) is played live from the taller of the two church towers, commemorating, according to legend, an invasion of Kraków by Tatars. The two uneven towers were built by competing brothers, the younger of whom killed the older when he saw that the other's tower was rising faster. At least, that is the story that local tour guides tell.

Kościół rzymskokatolicki (Roman Catholic Church). The Roman Catholic Church in Poland traces its origin to the beginnings of the Polish state, when Polanian prince **Mieszko I** accepted Christianity in 966 (see **chrzest Polski**). Although officially church and state are separate in Poland, the agendas and rhetoric of some politicians and members of the clergy suggest otherwise. The head of the church is the bishop of Rome, i.e., the *papież* (pope). Its smallest unit is the *parafia* (parish), several of which go together to form a *diecezja* (diocese) with a *katedra* (cathedral), at the head of which stands a *biskup* (bishop). *Arcybiskupi* (archbishops) are placed over larger regions (archdioceses), and over all of Poland is placed the Prymas Polski (Polish Primate), currently Archbishop Józef Kowalczyk, who is simultaneously archbishop of **Gniezno**. One feature distinguishing the Roman Catholic priesthood from other Christian faiths is *celibat* (the vow of celibacy) on the part of priests and nuns.

Kościuszko, Tadeusz (1746–1817). Polish general, leader of the celebrated but unsuccessful 1794 *insurekcja kościuszkowska* (Kościuszko Insurrection) against Russian occupation. Earlier he had fought in the American Revolutionary War and was a close friend of Thomas Jefferson. Trained as a military engineer, he designed the fortifications at West Point, where a prominent monument stands in his honor. On March 24, 1794, Kościuszko preceded his uprising with his *przysięga* (oath) to the Polish nation. Later that spring, on May 7, he delivered the *uniwersał połaniecki* (Połaniec Manifesto), granting civil liberties to the peasantry. In addition to reflecting his beliefs, the document helped attract the peasant class to his cause. Kościuszko's insurrection is associated with two major battles, one victorious at **Racławice**, and the other at Maciejowice, at which he was wounded and he and his men were defeated, captured, and taken to Russia. He was later pardoned by the Russian tsar Paul I, along with twenty thousand soldiers (contrast with **Katyń** under the Soviets). Most Polish towns have a street named for Kościuszko. Between 1820 and 1823, the people of **Kraków** erected the *kopiec* Kościuszki (Kościuszko mound) to his memory.

Kotański, Marek (1942–2002). A psychotherapist and untiring nationwide activist and organizer of causes, methods, and institutions designed to aid the disadvantaged of whatever kind: those racked with debilitating diseases like AIDS and Alzheimer's, people with drug and alcohol dependency or with mental or physical handicaps, the homeless, and the list runs on. His work was all the more impressive given that in the PRL (communist Poland), in which he largely worked, such afflictions tended to be ignored or denied. He died from injuries sustained in a car accident. Many of the nongovernmental organizations he founded still continue his work, among them Markot (bringing aid to the homeless) and Monar (aiding the homeless and those suffering from drug addiction and AIDS).

"Kotki dwa" (Two kittens). A lullaby known to most children and mothers, attributed by some to Zofia Rogoszówna. There are various versions, one being:

> Aaa, kotki dwa,
> Szarobure obydwa,
> Jeden duży, drugi mały
> Oba mi się spodobały.
>
> A-a, kittens two
> Gray-brown both of them,
> One big, the other small
> I've come to like both of them.

Kowalczyk, Justyna (b. 1983). Five-time Olympic medalist in cross-country skiing, Kowalczyk twice won gold in world championships, as well as the overall 2008–2009 Cross-Country Skiing World Cup. Her latest Olympic success was in the 10 km mass start classic at the 2014 Winter Olympics in Sochi. Kowalczyk is known for being vocally critical of other skiers' use of performance-enhancing substances. She is the first and only woman to win more than 2,000 points in one World Cup series. She is also the only cross-country skier in history to have won all the "Big Crowns": Olympic Games (2010, Vancouver, 30 km), World Championship (2009, Liberec, 15 km pursuit and 30 km), World Cup (2008–2009, 2009–2010, 2010–2011), and Tour de Ski (2009–2010, 2010–2011, 2011–2012).

Kowalska, siostra Maria Faustyna (Saint Faustina, 1905–1938). The first Roman Catholic saint of the twenty-first century, a member of the order of the Sisters of Our Lady of Mercy. Sister Maria Faustyna was simple and virtually unschooled. Having had a vision of Christ in Purgatory, she commissioned a painting, *Christ of Divine Mercy*, with the motto "Jezu ufam Tobie" (Jesus, I put my trust in you), which became an object of general veneration. Her diary of everyday travails and conversations with Christ and the Virgin Mary, controversially including direct quotations, was published after her death and was temporarily put on the Vatican's index of banned books. Pope Jan Paweł II (John Paul II) commissioned a reexamination of her work and person, leading to her beatification in 1993 and her canonization in 2000. Her relics are in the Sanktuarium Bożego Miłosierdzia (Sanctuary of Divine Mercy), part of an immense ongoing project in Saint Faustyna's honor in Kraków's Łagiewniki district.

Kozacy, powstania kozackie (Cossacks, the Cossack uprisings). The Cossacks were a

KALEIDOSCOPE OF POLAND   115

much-romanticized Ukrainian-Ruthenian group of warlike people, who often enlisted runaway serfs or criminals fleeing the law and lived in the steppes on the fringes of the **Rzeczpospolita Obojga Narodów** (Polish-Lithuanian Commonwealth) in the sixteenth through seventeenth centuries. A series of revolts by the Cossacks of Ukraine broke out against feudal conditions in the Polish-Lithuanian Republic and Imperial Russia in the years 1591 into the 1770s. The largest and best known of the revolts was that led by Bogdan Chmielnicki (Ukrainian: Bohdan Khmelnytsky), which lasted from 1648 to around 1655 and is considered to be the beginning of the dissolution of the old Rzeczpospolita. In a gambit to gain Ukrainian independence from Poland, in 1654 Chmielnicki made an alliance with Russia, an ill-timed move that ended up placing eastern Ukraine under Russian rule for the next 350 years. *Juliusz Kossak,* Don Cossacks.

Kozakiewicz, Władysław (b. 1953). A Polish pole vaulter who broke the world record three times and was Olympic champion in the 1980 summer games in Moscow, where he defeated Soviet vaulter Konstantin Volkov to the jeers of the partisan crowd. His obscene gesture to the crowd upon winning the gold medal became known as the *gest Kozakiewicza* (Kozakiewicz's gesture). The Soviets demanded that he be stripped of his medal for unsportsmanlike conduct, while the official Polish response described it as an involuntary muscle spasm, an interpretation somewhat undermined by Kozakiewicz's reprising the gesture years later in an Ultrafastin pain gel commercial. After the Olympics Kozakiewicz emigrated to West Germany, where he won the national title twice.

Koziołek Matołek (Matołek the billy goat). A 1933–1938 children's cartoon in verse by Kornel Makuszyński and Marian Walentynowicz that was published in four books, still popular today. It later became a film. All storylines, of which there are hundreds, center around a not very bright goat's quest to find the town of Pacanów where, it is rumored, they make goat shoes, taking him to the far corners of the earth. His search is based on his misreading of the ambiguous saying "W Pacanowie kozy kują" (In Pacanów they shoe goats), which can also be interpreted as "the Kozas are at work in their smithy." The signature rhyme:

> W sławnym mieście Pacanowie,
> Tacy sprytni są kowale,
> Że umieją podkuć kozy,
> By chodziły w pełnej chwale.

> In the famous town of Pacanów,
> The blacksmiths are so clever,
> That they know how to shoe goats,
> So that they might walk in full glory.

Two postage stamps were issued in commemoration of the goat with a mission.

kółeczko, trójkącik (little circle, triangle). This means of designating women's and men's toilets, respectively, in public places was invented somewhere in central Europe, and has not especially caught on elsewhere. The signs often confuse visitors to Poland, where they appear to be most often used. Whether or not these signs symbolize something, and what, is a matter of conjecture. Let us say that the triangle, point down, symbolizes a male torso, and the circle the roundness of a female body. Public *toalety* (toilets) in Poland can be few and far between. They are often guarded by a *babcia klozetowa* (toilet lady), who takes a small fee for supposedly keeping the lavatory clean. In an emergency, one can often go into a *kawiarnia* (café) and use theirs — again, for a fee. Since Poland joined the European Union, a great cultural leveler, the *kółeczko* and *trójkącik* are more and more being replaced by icons representing men and women.

---

krakowiak. The *krakowiak* (cracovienne) is a lively Polish folk dance from the environs of Kraków, set for several couples. Its meter is a syncopated 2/4 and said to imitate the movement of horses. The krakowiak rhythm was adopted by various composers, both serious and popular. It is often danced to a song sung by the lead male dancer and the jingling of metal disks on the men's belts. The word itself means "resident of Kraków," where the regional folk costume is the nation's most recognized. Dolls in Krakowiak outfits are a big seller in Cepelia stores. *The folk dance troupe Mazowsze in a krakowiak.*

Kraków (Cracow). Poland's second-largest city at around 758,400 residents, Kraków is located in the south of Poland and is said to date back to the seventh century. It is the capital of Małopolska (Lesser Poland). Wawel castle, on a promontory along the Wisła River, was the royal residence until the capital was shifted to Warsaw in the late sixteenth century. Kraków's Uniwersytet Jagielloński (Jagiellonian University, founded 1364) is central Europe's second-oldest, after Charles University in Prague. The town has one of the largest and best-preserved medieval marketplaces in Europe, its centerpiece being the enormous Sukiennice (Cloth Hall, pictured), redone in Renaissance style in the sixteenth century. It is flanked by the kościół Mariacki (Saint Mary's Basilica) and by many grand kamienice (townhouses), once belonging to rich merchants and magnates. Kraków is a living museum, and was the first Polish location to be placed on UNESCO's list of World Heritage Sites.

Krasicki, Ignacy (1735–1801). Bishop of Warmia, Polish encyclopedist, and the major literary figure of the Polish *oświecenie* (Enlightenment), called at the time the "Prince of Polish Poets." Krasicki was the author of fables, satires, mock epics, and the first Polish novel *Mikołaja Doświadczyńskiego przypadki* (The adventures of Mikołaj Doświadczyński, 1776). His remarkably concise fables are the source of many sayings still quoted today. The following fable was obliquely descriptive of Poland's political situation:

> Zawsze znajdzie przyczynę, kto zdobyczy pragnie.
> Dwóch wilków jedno w lesie nadybali jagnię.

Już go mieli rozerwać; rzekło: "Jakim prawem?"
"Smacznyś, słaby i w lesie." . . . Zjedli niebawem.

If one desires something, one will always find a justification for it.
Two wolves spotted a lamb alone in the forest.
They were about to tear him apart when he spoke up: "By what right?"
"You're tasty, weak, and in the forest." . . .
And they forthwith gobbled him up.

Krasiński, Zygmunt (1812–1859). One of the triumvirate of distinguished Polish Romantic writers, alongside the better-known and today more appreciated Adam Mickiewicz and Juliusz Słowacki. Krasiński came from an aristocratic family and published much of his work anonymously to avoid his property being confiscated by the Russian authorities. A dramatist, poet, and prose-writer, Krasiński's best-known work is his prescient drama about the "coming revolution," *Nieboska komedia* (*The Undivine Comedy*, 1833). The revolution did come, of course, but not until 1917. His nearly daily correspondence with his soulmate, the aristocratic divorcée Delfina Potocka, eventually amounted to over six thousand letters.

Kraszewski, Józef Ignacy (1812–1887). Kraszewski is sometimes called the "father of the Polish novel." Besides novels, he was a writer of well-loved fairy tales and many other things besides. Kraszewski is by far Poland's most prolific author, with some six hundred to seven hundred volumes of writings to his name, including 232 novels, ninety-nine of them the historical novels for which he is best known. His best-known works are probably *Bruhl* (1875) and *Hrabina Cosel* (Countess Cosel, 1874), both about *saskie czasy* (Saxon times). *Hrabina Cosel* was adapted to a 1968 film by Jerzy Antczak. Kraszewski's *Stara baśń* (An ancient tale, 1876), about Polish prehistory (embarrassingly translated into English as *The Old Fairy*), was turned into a fairly dreadful 2003 film by Jerzy Hoffman.

kresy wschodnie (eastern territories, or borderlands). A vast and emotion-laden subject that cannot be successfully condensed in a brief article. The name *kresy* designates the eastern territories (large parts of today's Lithuania, Belarus, and Ukraine) once belonging to the **Rzeczpospolita Obojga Narodów** (Polish-Lithuanian Commonwealth). These territories, lost to Russia under the eighteenth-century *rozbiory* (partitions), were partially regained after the *wojna polsko-bolszewicka* (Polish-Bolshevik War) of 1920, to be lost again after World War II according to the determinations of the *konferencja jałtańska* (Yalta Conference) of 1945. A disproportionately large number of Polish writers, artists, scientists, statesmen, politicians, and military leaders have historically come from the kresy, as did many favorite Polish dishes; for example, *chłodnik* (cold beet-leaf soup), *kartacze* (potato/meat dumplings), *sękacz* (cake cooked on a spit), *kulebiak* (meat or salmon pie), *kołduny* (in essence, fried pierogi), and *kutia* (*kasza* with sweetmeats). While most Poles show political maturity in coming to terms with historical reality, they remain justifiably sensitive on the subject of the treatment of the Polish minority still living in the former kresy.

Królestwo Kongresowe, "Kongresówka" (Congress Kingdom). Names for what was officially called the Królestwo Polskie (Kingdom of Poland), referring to the Russian-held part of Poland as set in 1815 at the *kongres wiedeński* (Congress of Vienna). It was formed out of parts of the **Księstwo Warszawskie** (Duchy of Warsaw) and roughly corresponded to today's **Kalisz** region and the **Lublin**, **Łódź**, **Mazowsze**, and Świętokrzyskie voivodeships. The Kongresówka, as it was informally called, had a separate **Sejm** (parliament), army, and currency. The Russian tsar was the titular Polish king, represented in Warsaw by his *namiestnik* (viceroy), at first Józef Zajączek, later the tsar's brother, the duke Constantine, followed in 1832 by the unsavory General Ivan Paskevich, who had put down the **powstanie listopadowe** (November Uprising). Following the failed **powstanie styczniowe** (January Uprising, 1863) the pretense of a constitutional monarchy was dropped, civil liberties were abolished, and the lands of the Kongresówka were demoted to the status of a Russian province, the so-called Privislanskii Krai (Vistula Territory).

krówki (cow-candy). A Polish candy specialty is the *krówka*, a milk caramel that, instead of being chewy, melts in one's mouth (and hence doesn't pull out one's fillings). It was developed by a **Poznań** confectioner in the early twentieth century and gets its name "little cow" from the picture of a cow on the paper wrapper — which, half of the time, sticks to the candy when one tries to unwrap it. It is always socially appropriate to bring someone a bag of krówki, because everybody likes them. Krówki are bought by the ton by the Polish Ministry of Defense for consumption by its armed forces. Avoid any other flavor besides the traditional caramel one.

Krzyżacy, zakon krzyżacki (Order of the Teutonic Knights). A Germanic Roman Catholic knightly order arising out of the crusades of the twelfth century in what would later become

KALEIDOSCOPE OF POLAND 119

East Prussia (lands along the Baltic seacoast) and the territory of contemporary Latvia and Estonia. They were given land around Chełmno by the Mazovian princes with the mission of conquering the pagan Baltic Prussians. They succeeded beyond expectations, establishing one of the strongest states in that part of Europe, threatening not only Mazovia but all of Poland, which had been reunited in the early fourteenth century. Their seat was the enormous castle in Malbork (German: Marienburg, pictured), now a UNESCO World Heritage Site. Their coat of arms was a black cross on a white shield. The Order was temporarily and famously defeated by Poland-Lithuania at the *bitwa pod Grunwaldem* (Battle of Grunwald, 1410), and it became a Polish fief in 1525 (the *hołd pruski*, "Prussian fealty"), but then regained independence in 1657 during the potop szwedzki (Swedish Deluge). Its later alliance with the Brandenburgian Hohenzollerns gave rise to the modern Prussian state. The Knights of the Teutonic Order exist to the present day as a charitable organization headquartered in Vienna.

Książ, Zamek Książ (Książ Castle, German: Schloss Fürstenstein). Of various German baronial castles left to Poland after the "adjustment of borders" following World War II, the humongous Książ Castle takes first prize, being third in size of Polish castles only after Wawel and Malbork. It is situated on a hill outside Wałbrzych in Lower Silesia. The Hochberg family owned the castle until 1941. In 1943–1945, on Hitler's orders, slave labor was used to dig a vast network of underground tunnels beneath the castle and into the nearby Sowie Góry (Owl Mountains), absorbing a huge amount of men and materiel just as the German war machine could no longer afford it. This immensely ambitious *Riese* (Giant) project, largely unfinished, aimed to place German munitions production underground and out of reach of Allied bombing. The castle was captured and thoroughly looted by the advancing Soviet army in 1945. Some of the underground complexes are open to visitors. Some are still unexplored. Książ Castle and its environs formed the backdrop for the 2013 Nike prize-winning novel *Ciemno, prawie noc* (Dark, almost night), by Joanna Bator.

książka skarg i wniosków, książka życzeń i zażaleń (book of wishes, complaints, and suggestions). Such a book was located with the administration of most stores and service outlets during the PRL (communist Poland). In it customers would inscribe complaints about goods or services received (or not), next to which the administration would place a response, one way or another absolving itself of responsibility. Here is an example from the *stan wojenny* (martial law) period:

> Complaint: Even though I do not have coupons registered in this store, I request to be sold 30 dekagrams of Kraków sausage.
>
> Response: Request cannot be granted in view of the zero state of sausage.

Księstwo Warszawskie (Duchy of Warsaw, 1807–1813). A puppet state under Napoleonic

120 KALEIDOSCOPE OF POLAND

France, created in 1807 by the *pokój tylżycki* (Treaty of Tilsit) signed between Napoleon Bonaparte of France and Alexander I of Russia. It first consisted of territory taken from the second and third Prussian *rozbiory* (partitions). After Prince Józef Poniatowski's brief, successful war with Austria in 1809, the Księstwo expanded to include Kraków and Lwów. Hopes for its becoming truly independent came to naught in the wake of Napoleon's disastrous Russian campaign of 1812. The 1815 *kongres wiedeński* (Congress of Vienna) apportioned Poland once again among Russia, Prussia, and Austria. The bulk of the Księstwo was transformed into the Królestwo Polskie (Kingdom of Poland, the so-called Królestwo Kongresowe, "Kongresówka," or Congress Kingdom) under Russia. Kraków became a city-state (Wolne Miasto Kraków, "Free City of Kraków") under the three powers until its annexation by Austria following the failed *powstanie krakowskie* (Kraków Uprising) of 1846.

—**Kto ty jesteś? —Polak mały.** (Who are you? A young Pole). Part of a naïve patriotic rhyme by Władysław Bełza (1847–1913). The first lines are known by most Poles:

> –Kto ty jesteś? –Polak mały.
> –Jaki znak twój? –Orzeł biały.
> –Gdzie ty mieszkasz? –Między swemi.
> –W jakim kraju? –W polskiej ziemi.
>
> –Who are you? –A young Pole.
> –What's your sign? –A white eagle.
> –Where do you live? –Among my people.
> –In what country?
> –In the Polish land.

Kujawy. An ethnic region in the north-central part of Poland, northwest of Mazowsze, east of Wielkopolska, south of Pomorze, and west of the Wisła. Control over the territory was often contested between the Krzyżacy (Teutonic Knights) and the Korona Królestwa Polskiego (Polish Crown). Its landscape is gently undulating, and the land is among Poland's most fertile and productive. Large towns in the Kujawy region are Bydgoszcz, Inowrocław, and Włocawek. A major body of water there is Lake Gopło, figuring in early legends of the Polanie and Goplanie tribes, and of Queen Goplana. It was in the town of Kruszwica, on the north shore of Lake Gopło, that King Popiel is said to have been devoured by hungry mice. The *kujawiak*, a slow, minor-key, pensive 3/4 or 3/8 folk dance rhythm, is said to reflect the Kujawy landscape and the temperament of the people: expansive and somber.

Kukliński, Ryszard (1930–2004). High-ranking Polish army officer who passed a huge amount of information to the CIA about the Polish and Soviet armies and the Układ Warszawski (Warsaw Pact) over the period 1971–1981, after which he defected to the West. Sentenced to death in absentia in 1984, Kukliński was rehabilitated in 1997. He visited Poland in 1998 but did not settle there, and died in Tampa, Florida. Conspiracy theorists, with whom Poland is always rife, claimed that Kukliński passed word of the pending imposition of *stan wojenny* (martial law) to the CIA, which nevertheless did not act on the information so as to provoke an international outcry against the Polish communist government. Kukliński's story has been told on film by Władysław Pasikowski in the 2014 thriller *Jack Strong*.

Kukuczka, Jerzy (1948–1989). One of the twentieth century's best high-altitude climbers in winter ascents, Kukuczka set a still-standing record of conquering all fourteen 8,000-meter mountains in the world in eight years, all but Mount Everest without the aid of supplemental oxygen. He conquered most peaks along previously unclimbed routes. Inevitably, Kukuczka died from a fall, attempting a climb up the unscaled south face of Lhtose in Nepal. A widely circulated documentary film about his life was made, and a memorial mass-participation marathon was held in **Katowice** on the twentieth anniversary of his death. The Fundacja Wspierania Alpinizmu Polskiego (Foundation for the Support of Polish Mountain Climbing), supporting the training of Polish alpinists, is named after him. Another famous Polish alpinist was Wanda Rutkiewicz, who disappeared in 1992 while attempting a climb up Kangchenjunga in the Himalayas, trying to complete a trifecta of the world's three highest peaks. In 1989 five Polish alpinists perished in an avalanche on the slopes of Mount Everest, including Zygmunt Andrzej Heinrich, who took this picture of Jerzy Kukuczka (left) and Andrzej Czok on their 1980 ascent.

kulig (sleigh ride). A traditional winter entertainment of the Polish gentry, especially during *karnawał* (carnival), was to form a caravan of horse-drawn sleighs, often at night with lighted torches, and chase over hill and dale to the accompaniment of song and drink, visiting one another's manses and picking up more sleighs full of merrymakers along the way. These days the *kulig* mostly continues as a winter tourist attraction around **Zakopane**. Elsewhere it has degenerated into what looks a lot like the American hayride: a hay wagon full of teenagers pulled by a tractor to the accompaniment of canoodling and campfire songs. *Kulig in Gorce.*

kult maryjny (Marian cult). The special veneration accorded in Poland to the Virgin Mary as the Mother of God goes back to early medieval times and is visible at almost every turn: in icons (**Matka Boska Częstochowska**), sculpture (*Madonna z Krużlowej*), prayers (**Apel Jasnogórski**), roadside shrines (*kapliczka przydrożna*), church names (**Kościół Mariacki**), radio stations (**Radio Maryja**); in short, nearly universally. The Marian order of priests is responsible for the postwar development of **Licheń** as a pilgrimage destination for having the largest of things religious (bell, organ, church).

Kuroń, Jacek (1934–2004). A historian deprived of his right to teach for his political views, Kuroń, born in **Lwów**, was a tireless activist and spokesman for human rights and national

122 KALEIDOSCOPE OF POLAND

independence in the **PRL** (communist Poland), during which time he was repeatedly arrested, interned, and imprisoned. A signatory of the *list 59*, an adviser to **Solidarność** (Solidarity), cofounder of **KOR** (Workers' Defense Committee), and a participant in the 1989 **rozmowy Okrągłego Stołu** (Round Table Discussions), Kuroń constantly put his personal welfare on the line for what he believed. He was later given broad recognition for his role in helping to bring down the communist government, and was four times elected *poseł* (representative) to the **Sejm** (parliament). As the minister of labor and social services in the early 1990s, Kuroń personally handed out free meals, or *kuroniówki*, to the needy of Warsaw. The word still exists as a general name for handouts to the poor.

Kurpie. An ethnic subregion of **Mazowsze** in the north-central part of Poland, a traditionally poor region consisting of sandy soil, swamps, and forests, but abundant in wildlife and boasting a rich folk heritage, to be seen in regional dress, architecture, a characteristic style of *wycinanka* (paper cutout), elaborate *palmy wielkanocne* (Easter palms), and a distinct regional dialect. *Kurpie-style paper cutout.*

Kusociński, Janusz (1907–1940). Long-distance runner of the *dwudziestolecie międzywojenne* (interwar period). Kusociński's distances were the 1,500, 3,000, 5,000, and 10,000 meters. He set the world record in the 3,000 meters, and won the 10,000 meters in the 1932 Olympics in Los Angeles. During World War II Kusociński worked for the underground while holding a day job as a waiter. He was arrested by the Gestapo in 1940, imprisoned in the Mokotów prison, and was executed in Palmiry, possibly because his name was on a Nazi list of Polish cultural icons to be purged; see also **Pawiak**; **operacja Tannenberg**. An annual memorial track meet has been held in his honor since 1954.

Kwaśniewski, Aleksander (b. 1954). A Polish left-wing politician, who got his start in communist youth organizations and publications. In 1989 he was a member of the **rozmowy Okrągłego Stołu** (Round Table Discussions). As a member of the postcommunist Sojusz Lewicy-Demokratycznej (SLD, Left Democratic Alliance), which he helped found, Kwaśniewski was twice elected president of Poland, serving from 1995–2005. His presidency is overall considered to have been successful and professionally run. During his presidency, Poland joined NATO in 1999 and the Unia Europejska (European Union) in 2004. One of Kwaśniewski's important achievements was succeeding in passing a new Polish constitution to replace the one still in use from the **PRL** (communist Poland). His presidency was not without controversy, as the *afera Rywin* (Rywin affair) and *afera Orlenu* (Orlen affair) both occurred on his watch, and he may have been complicit in the "rendering" of American prisoners of war to Polish detention centers.

Kwaśniewskie, Jolanta i Aleksandra. As Poland's **Pierwsza Dama** (First Lady), Jolanta Kwaśniewska (b. 1955) was in stylish contrast to presidential wives both before and after her. She was a successful businesswoman in her own right, and for a while even considered running for the presidency. Instead, she became a television personality, advising viewers on matters of style and etiquette, including how to eat a meringue (with a spoon, of course), a question that famously stumped a contestant on the Polish version of *Who Wants to Be a Millionaire?* The recently married Kwaśniewski daughter, Aleksandra ("Ola," b. 1981), an erstwhile television journalist, film actress, and contestant on *Taniec z Gwiazdami* (Dancing with the stars) — in which she placed second — lost her job as a television commentator for tearfully defending her father on her program. Kwaśniewski had been mocked for his public bouts of *choroba filipińska*, a tropical disease supposedly contracted in the Philippines, broadly interpreted as simply having too much to drink.

Kwiecień, Mariusz (b. 1972). An opera singer broadly recognized as one of the world's leading baritones, Kwiecień appears in companies around the world, including New York's Metropolitan Opera, London's Covent Garden, Paris Opera, Vienna State Opera, the Lyric Opera of Chicago, and the Bavarian State Opera. Renowned for his clear voice and dramatic presence, he is in special demand for his portrayals of the title roles in *Don Giovanni* and *Eugene Onegin*. Kwiecień is only one of several Polish opera stars currently prominent on the world stage, another being coloratura soprano Aleksandra Kurzak (b. 1977).

L

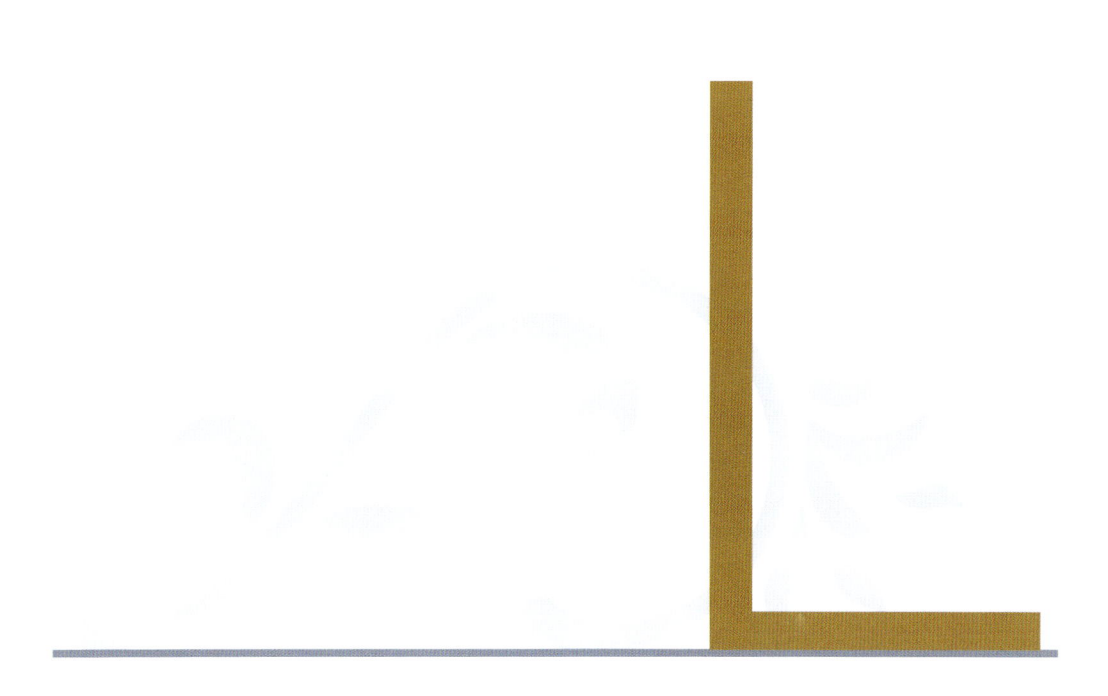

lajkonik. In a unique **Kraków** folk tradition held the Thursday after **Boże Ciało** (Corpus Christi), the *lajkonik*, a bearded person dressed in Turkish or Tatar garb with a hobbyhorse attached to his waist, dancingly leads a colorful retinue from the Zwierzyniec (zoo) district to the *Rynek Główny* (main square) to the accompaniment of musicians playing folk instruments. Along the way he collects "tribute" from street vendors and attempts to capture a banner held by a *włóczek* (raftsman). At the main square, the lajkonik accepts tribute from the city fathers and then heads to a restaurant for dinner. The event has its origins either in medieval guild ceremonies or in an actual Tatar attack on Kraków, successfully repelled by raftsmen in 1287, after which one of them paraded in the garb of a captured Tatar leader. The present-day lajkonik outfit was designed in 1904 by the artist-writer **Stanisław Wyspiański**.

lampa naftowa (kerosene lamp). The kerosene lamp, which lighted nineteenth-century and early twentieth-century houses and even streets before gaslights were available, and often until the electric light bulb and the availability of electricity, was invented in 1853 by Ignacy Łukasiewicz (1822–1882), a pharmacist who was born in **Rzeszów** and practiced in **Lwów**, who first used it to light hospitals. He also, in 1852, developed the methods for refining kerosene from raw petroleum, and built the first oil well in Poland in 1854, preceding Edwin Drake's well in Titusville, Pennsylvania, by four years. As such, he

the first to record Bach's Goldberg Variations for the instrument for which it had been originally intended, inspiring an entire movement of historically aware performers. *Photograph from 1945.*

can be considered to be the father of the modern petroleum industry (although he is virtually unknown outside Poland). A claim for priority in developing the method for distilling kerosene was filed in 1853 by Łukasiewicz's colleague, Jan Zeh (1817–1897). As a tragic-ironic footnote, in 1858 Zeh's twenty-one-year-old wife and her seventeen-year-old sister perished in a kerosene-fueled shop fire. *A kerosene street lamp in Gorlice.*

Landowska, Wanda (1879–1959). A harpsichordist of Jewish background born in Warsaw who lived first in Paris and later in the United States. As a performer, teacher, and prolific recording artist of Renaissance and baroque music composed for the harpsichord, Landowska more or less singlehandedly brought the use of this instrument into the modern era. She was

Lany Poniedziałek, Śmigus-dyngus (Easter Monday). The relic of a pre-Christian fertility ritual observed around Eastern Europe. On Lany Poniedziałek boys traditionally sprayed girls with water or dumped them in ponds or water troughs. If a girl didn't get soaked, it meant she wasn't worth courting. Originally a village tradition in which village boys hid near wells waiting for girls to draw water, by the eighteenth century the custom was in full swing in cities, where it deteriorated into a holiday of water terrorism in which girls and grown women also took part. Today it can include tossing water balloons from balconies and the drive-by spraying of random pedestrians. In some parts of the country, farmers symbolically pour on their fields water that has been blessed. Sometimes people play elaborate pranks, similar to American Halloween. In **Kraków**, Easter Monday is accompanied by a church carnival called Emaus. The day after Easter is a Polish national holiday; otherwise people would come to work wet.

Lech, Czech, Rus. The three brothers who, according to legend, founded the respective states of Lechia (Poland), Czechia, and Old Rus. Lech founded the town of **Gniezno** on the spot where the three encountered a white eagle, which became the Polish state symbol (see ***Orzeł Biały***). The name Gniezno is etymologically related to the word *gniazdo* (nest) — figuratively appropriate, as the town became the birthplace of the fledgling Polish state. The name *liakhy*, related to Lech, was the original East Slavic designation for Poles, appearing in the twelfth-century Old Rus Primary Chronicle as a more general term than *poliane*, who were considered to be one of the *liakh* tribes. The word *liakh* continues to be used in contemporary Ukrainian as a derogatory word for "Pole."

Legiony Polskie 1914–1918 (Polish Legions, World War I). Polish divisions within the Austro-Hungarian army during World War I, 1914–1918, fighting for Polish independence in the Russian-held part of Poland, organized and led until 1917 by **Józef Piłsudski**. Their existence referred back to the late eighteenth- to early nineteenth-century **Legiony Polskie we Włoszech** (Polish Legions in Italy) under General **Jan Henryk Dąbrowski**. Piłsudski was a brilliant military strategist, and his legions' effectiveness and his resulting popularity helped place him in a position of power after the war. There were three brigades in all. The hymn of the first one, "Pierwsza Brygada" (First brigade) was at one time proposed as a national anthem. Its well-known refrain:

> My, pierwsza brygada,
> Strzelecka gromada,
> Na stos rzuciliśmy
> Nasz życia los: na stos, na stos!

> We, the first brigade,
> The riflemen's corps,
> Have tossed onto the pyre
> The fate of our lives, onto the pyre!

Legiony Polskie we Włoszech (Polish Legions in Italy). Following the loss of Polish statehood after the *trzeci rozbiór* (third partition, 1795; see *rozbiory*) and the unsuccessful **insurekcja kościuszkowska** (Kościuszko Insurrection, 1794), General **Jan Henryk Dąbrowski** and other officers organized several Polish divisions from among Polish émigrés and Austrian army deserters. They fought under Napoleon in Italy and elsewhere — as far afield as Haiti — the ultimate aim being to liberate Poland. Their motto was "Ludzie wolni są braćmi" (free people are brothers). Only a few of the original legionnaires lived to participate in Napoleon's disastrous 1812 campaign in Russia. One of the Polish generals, Józef Wybicki, wrote the **"Mazurek Dąbrowskiego"** (Dąbrowski mazurka), which, in the twentieth century, became Poland's national anthem. The Polish Legions were used cynically by Napoleon to suppress other nations' similar aspirations for independence, notably in Haiti in 1797–1807. *Juliusz Kossak,* Jan Henryk Dąbrowski.

lektura szkolna, lektura obowiązkowa (required school readings). A list published for the nation's schools by the Ministerstwo Edukacji Narodowej (Ministry of National Education), the *lektura* consists of literary works, both Polish and foreign, whether required or supplementary, to be read for each grade in school, the idea being to establish universal standards of educational achievement across the nation. For the most part these are so-called classics of Polish and world literature. Reputedly, appearance on the list of required readings guarantees that the enjoyment of the work will be forever ruined for the schoolchild. In the age of the Internet, websites like sciaga.pl, zgapa.pl, and others, providing plot summaries and *bryki* (interpretive crib sheets) have proliferated, reducing what should be reading pleasure to the dry accumulation of facts and standard interpretations.

Lelewel, Joachim (1786–1861). A historian and political activist educated in Wilno whose lectures on Polish history at Warsaw University led to his removal by the Russian authorities. Lelewel made major contributions to Polish and medieval European history, to world geography (a specialty of his was meticulously engraving plates for his own works), and to numismatics. His totalistic approach to history had a major effect on subsequent Polish historiography. Living modestly in exile in Paris and Belgium after the failed powstanie listopadowe (November Uprising) of 1830–1831, he headed the Towarzystwo Demokratyczne Polskie (Polish Democratic Society), a rival group to the Hôtel Lambert faction in Paris (see Wielka Emigracja), working tirelessly — if unsuccessfully — to organize Polish émigrés around his revolutionary program. Together with Karl Marx and Friedrich Engels, he was a founding member of the influential Brussels-based Democratic Society for the Unity and Brotherhood of All Peoples.

Lem, Stanisław (1921–2006). Polish science fiction writer and futurologist, currently one of the most widely translated Polish authors. Lem's works, many of which are satirical, but all of which raise penetrating philosophical questions about man and technology, and about the limits of the knowability of the universe, have had a major influence on science fiction writing worldwide. His most popular works have been *Solaris* (1961), *Cyberiada* (1967), and *Kongres futurologiczny* (*The Futurological Congress*, 1971). *Solaris* has been adapted to film twice, in 1972 and 2002, the most recent starring the American actor George Clooney. Lem was known for being a devastating critic of American science fiction writing and writers, for which opinion in 1976 he was drummed out of the Science Fiction and Fantasy Writers of America. In general, Polish science fiction writers are numerous — too numerous to list — and of high quality.

Licheń. A village of barely one thousand inhabitants in west-central Poland that is the site of the immense Bazylika Matki Boskiej Licheńskiej (Basilica of the Mother of God of Licheń, pictured), Poland's largest church, housing Poland's largest pipe organ and a renowned icon representing Matka Boża Bolesna Królowa Polski (Mother of God, Queen of Poland of Sorrows). Instead of bearing the Christ child, the Virgin cradles a Polish *Orzeł Biały* (white eagle) on her breast. The Licheń Church and sanctuary was built after World War II by the Marian order of priests and is visited by one and a half million visitors a year. In 1999 Poland's largest bell — at nineteen tons together with its yoke, surpassing even Wawel Cathedral's dzwon Zygmunta — was consecrated there. It is rung every day just before noon.

liczebniki polskie (Polish numerals). The Polish system of counting is one of the most complex in the world, and can take years of study for the foreigner to master. For only one example, there are five different ways to say "two students," depending on whether they are: (a) both male (*dwaj studenci*), (b) both female (*dwie studentki*), (c) specifically one male and one female (*dwoje studentów*), (d) ambiguous as to male or female (*dwóch studentów*), or (e) acting as a unit (*dwójka studentów*). And this does not even address questions of declension and grammatical government, nor such things as ordinal numerals, fractional numerals, indefinite numerals, replicative numerals, and yet other kinds. See also: przypadki gramatyczne; aspekt dokonany i niedokonany.

Linde, Samuel Bogumił (1771–1847). Linde was a Polonist of German and Swedish extraction from Toruń who worked in the spirit of the eighteenth-century encyclopedists. Over the years 1807–1815, with the support of count Józef Maksymilian Ossoliński (founder of the famed Ossolineum library), Linde researched, wrote, and published a monumental six-volume dictionary of the Polish language of the sixteenth through eighteenth centuries, accomplishing singlehandedly work that today would be undertaken by an entire computerized research institute. Linde's is the first modern Polish dictionary, and it is still used by scholars today. His word descriptions are exhaustive and richly documented with references to sources and translations into other languages, and they stand up well even when judged by contemporary lexicographical standards. Today it is available at one's fingertips in digitized format.

linia Curzona (Curzon Line). The line that was proposed on the eve of the Bolshevik Russian invasion of Poland in 1920 by the British foreign secretary George Curzon as the demarcation line between the newly arisen Polish state and what would become the Soviet Union. Curzon attempted to follow ethnic boundaries to the extent possible but the Curzon Line was accepted by neither side, and the outcome of the resulting *wojna polsko-bolszewicka* (Polish-Soviet War, 1919–1921) was such that the eventual border ended up around two hundred kilometers farther east. In World War II, the secret protocol of the pakt Ribbentrop-Mołotow (Molotov-Ribbentrop Pact) ceded control of the territory east of the Curzon Line to Soviet Russia. The current border of Poland with Lithuania, Belarus, and Ukraine roughly follows that line.

list 34 (letter of the 34, 1964). A letter sent to Premier Józef Cyrankiewicz, signed by

KALEIDOSCOPE OF POLAND   129

thirty-four Polish intellectuals, protesting the cultural policies of the government. In particular, the letter demanded the easing of censorship, access to reliable information, the right to free and open critical discussions, and, on a more practical level, an increase in the amount of paper allocated to the printing of books. The letter served mainly to get the signatories in various kinds of hot water, with some deprived of the right to publish or to travel abroad. Under such pressure, ten signatories later repudiated the claim that there was political repression in Poland in a letter sent to the *Times* of London.

---

list 59, Memoriał 59 (memorandum of the 59, 1975). An open letter signed by fifty-nine well-known Polish intellectuals objecting to proposed changes in the constitution of the **PRL** (communist Poland) that would incorporate the leading role of the **PZPR** (communist party) and the "eternal bond of friendship" with the Związek Radziecki (Soviet Union). Eventually the list of signatories grew to sixty-six, and included such notables as **Stanisław Barańczak, Zbigniew Herbert, Jacek Kuroń, Leszek Kołakowski, Adam Michnik**, and **Wisława Szymborska**. The government went ahead with its plans anyway, only slightly modifying the initially proposed wording. However, the memorandum had established the existence of a clear rift between the communist government on one side and the majority of the country's intellectuals on the other. With the fall of communism and of the Soviet Union, the constitutional issue became moot.

---

lista Wildsteina (Wildstein's list). A list stolen from the Instytut Pamięci Narodowej (IPN, Institute of National Memory) in 2005 by the journalist Bronisław Wildstein (pictured), which was then placed on the internet. The IPN is responsible for *lustracja* (cleansing the civil service ranks of former communist agents). The list was said to provide the names of informers to the secret police in the **PRL** (communist Poland). However, the list also included the names of people who were merely under consideration for recruitment, and it was impossible to distinguish who was who. The list instantly became the most-searched-for heading on the Polish internet, but in the end there were few concrete repercussions, except that Wildstein was fired from his job. He rebounded, and now has his own TV interview program. Lustracja has not made much headway in Poland, in part because some of the relevant files were destroyed or sent to the Soviet Union in the last days of communism, and in part out of a lack of political will.

LOT, Polskie Linie Lotnicze LOT (LOT, Polish National Airlines). Established in 1928, Poland's "flagship carrier," LOT (the word *lot* means "flight") is one of the world's oldest airlines still in existence. It is two-thirds government-owned and has connections to Europe, North America, the Middle East and, recently, to Asia. In the

United States it has connections to Chicago, Newark, and New York. LOT has a reputation as a safe and well-run airline. Its worst crash, and the worst disaster in the history of Polish aviation, was in the *las kabacki* (Kabacki forest) near Warsaw in 1987, in which 183 people lost their lives. On November 2, 2011, the pilot Tadeusz Wrona became a national hero for saving the lives of 231 passengers and crew when he soft-landed his Boeing 767 on a flight from Newark to Warsaw after it failed to deploy its landing gear.

lotto. The lottery run by the state monopoly Totalizator Sportowy (Sports Lottery) began in 1957. Its drawings, held three times a week, are based on picking six numbers from 1 to 49. The former name, Toto-Lotek, is still used by die-hards. Part of the earnings from the lottery goes to support the Ministry of Sport and the Ministry of Culture. If the six numbers are not picked, the amount is rolled over to the next drawing, and winnings can sometimes be huge, drawing in people who normally wouldn't consider playing. One winner in 2010 received over 24.5 million złotys (more than $9 million).

Lublin. The largest Polish town east of the **Wisła**, Lublin is in the southeast on the Bystrzyca River on a major historic east–west trade route. The town today has around 350,460 inhabitants, making it the ninth-largest Polish city. Its rich history goes back to the early Middle Ages. In 1569 the town witnessed the signing of the *unia lubelska* (Union of Lublin), formalizing the union between Poland and Lithuania in the **Rzeczpospolita Obojga Narodów** (Polish-Lithuanian Commonwealth). During the Reformation it was an important center of Protestantism, as well as a major center of Talmudic and Kabala study, known throughout Europe. Under communism the Katolicki Uniwersytet Lubelski (KUL, Catholic University of Lublin), founded in the interwar period, continued to train Catholic priests, albeit under the constant invigilation of the authorities. Lublin's economy has been stagnant of late, but the town stands to gain from European Union funds being directed toward Poland, especially the east. Maybe the recent discovery of *gaz łupkowy* (shale gas) in the region will have a positive effect. *Lublin's royal castle, which has its origins in the twelfth century.*

Lubomirscy, rodzina Lubomirskich (Lubomirski family). A magnate family from **Małopolska** (Lesser Poland) whose money and noble status ultimately derived from salt mines. Among the Lubomirski family were several prominent military leaders in the seventeenth century, including Stanisław, victorious at the *bitwa pod Chocimiem* (Battle of Chocim, 1621), and Hieronim, leader of mercenary troops in the *bitwa pod Wiedniem* (Battle of Vienna, 1683). In 1739 their *latyfundia* (landholdings) included five towns and nine hundred villages in nine different voivodeships. Descendants of the Lubomirski family were active in early "speed sports" (automobiles and aircraft) in the first half of the twentieth century. *Lubomirski coat of arms.*

Lutosławski, Witold (1913–1994). One of Europe's prominent twentieth-century composers, considered by many to be Poland's greatest composer of symphonic music. Early in his career, to avoid political pressure and the strictures of *socrealizm* (socialist realism), he composed anonymous popular vocal and film music. His early work was influenced by Polish folk music. Later he was associated, from its inception, with the *Warszawska Jesień* (Warsaw Autumn) new music festival as an exponent of novel tonalities and compositional techniques, including "aleatoric" music, in which certain compositional elements are left to chance or the discretion of the performer. He was also a prominent conductor, usually of his own music.

Lwów (L'viv). A town of 762,000 residents in Western Ukraine. Until 1939 Lwów belonged to Poland, was mostly Polish in population (60 percent Polish, 30 percent Jewish, 10 percent Ukrainian), and, besides being one of its most populous cities, was one of the country's most important centers of science, education, and culture. It is still treated by Poles as belonging to their cultural heritage, mute testimony to which are the large, not terribly well tended cemeteries containing the graves of Polish notables and war dead — most prominently, the Cmentarz Łyczakowski (pictured) and the neighboring Cmentarz Orląt Lwowskich (Cemetery of the Lwów Eaglets). The "Eaglets" were child and youth soldiers who perished mainly in the *wojna polsko-ukraińska* (Polish-Ukrainian War of 1918–1919). During World War II Lwów was the scene of shocking atrocities committed against Poles and Jews, including the Germans' mass arrest and murder of Polish professors, in some instances along with their entire families, in 1941. Almost no Jews in Lwów survived the war. Lwów continues to be the most important center of Polish activity in Ukraine, although, according to a recent estimate, only around nineteen thousand persons of Polish nationality live in the Lwów region, out of a total of some 144,000 Poles in Ukraine as a whole. Most were forcibly repatriated after the war to the so-called *ziemie odzyskane* (recovered territories).

Lwów, pogrom lwowski (Lwów pogrom, November 21–23, 1918). Following the breaking of the Ukrainian army siege of *Lwów* (German: Lemberg; Ukrainian: L'viv) during the *wojna polsko-ukraińska* (Polish-Ukrainian War), elements of the Polish army, joined by local thugs, acting on the bogus pretext that Jews were closet supporters of Ukrainan independence, ransacked Jewish-owned businesses and murdered from fifty to 150 Jews and as many as 270 Ukrainians, prompting an international outcry and an official investigation initiated by US president Woodrow Wilson. The pogrom lasted two days and was accompanied by the conspicuous lack of intervention by the Polish authorities, although eventually over one thousand people were arrested in connection with it. The Lwów pogrom was only the most prominent of several at the time, some perpetrated by Poles, others by Ukrainians, the basically neutral Jews being caught in the middle between the two warring factions.

Łańcut, zamek w Łańcucie (Łańcut Castle). Łańcut is a town of less than twenty thousand in the Podkarpacie region in southeast Poland and is the site of the imposing Łańcut castle that once belonged to the Lubomirski family. Later, and up through the end of World War II, the castle was owned by the Potocki family. It was not damaged during the war and is now a museum and cultural center. The carriage house contains a large collection of antique horse-drawn conveyances.

Łaski, Jan (1499–1560). A Polish Protestant reformer with an international reputation, acquired first in Frisia (northern Holland) and then in England, where he espoused the ideas of Calvinism. Returning to Poland in 1553 he settled in Pińczów, where he established a school and vainly attempted to organize Protestant sects into a single force, simultaneously trying — unsuccessfully — to persuade King Zygmunt II August to establish state control over the Catholic Church, as England had done. His evangelical work is said to have increased the number of Protestant congregations in Poland threefold.

Łazienki Królewskie, Park Łazienkowski (Royal "Baths" in Warsaw). A park and royal palace complex within the city of Warsaw, built during the reign of King Stanisław August Poniatowski. The palace itself (pictured) is built on an island in a small lake on which swans swim. Peacocks roam the surrounding park, displaying their feathers and looking for handouts. The buildings are well preserved and are intensively used today for all manner of cultural events. The park itself is used for leisurely Sunday strolling. At the west side of Łazienki is the Belweder palace, and not far to the north of it is the pomnik Chopina (Chopin monument).

KALEIDOSCOPE OF POLAND   133

Łemkowie, mniejszość karpatorusińska (Lemkos, the Carpatho-Rusyn ethnic minority). The *Łemkowie* (Lemkos) traditionally inhabited the lower Beskid Mountains (see **Beskidy**) in southeast Poland. They are related to the Bojkowie (Boykos), Huculowie (Huculs), and, on the other side of the Carpathian Mountains in Slovakia, to the Rusyny/Rusnaky (Rusyns) — ethnic names also used by the Łemkowie. Their language is close to Ukrainian, but the Lemkos have a strong sense of ethnic separateness. After the *unia brzeska* (Union of Brześć, 1596) most Lemkos became Greek Catholic. About half today have reconverted to Russian Orthodoxy. A large number emigrated to the United States or Canada around the turn of the nineteenth to the twentieth century. Only some six thousand Lemkos live today on their ancestral lands, most having been deported under the *akcja Wisła* (Operation Vistula) of 1947. An international Lemko festival, Łemkowska Watra (Lemko Watchfire), is held each year in Zdynia. Lemkos use the Cyrillic alphabet, a fact connected to their Orthodox heritage; see the village sign, pictured.

Łempicka, Tamara de (née Maria Górska, 1895 or 1898–1980). Judging from her presence in the world's art galleries, possibly Poland's most-collected modern artist, who iconically captured the fast life of the roaring 1920s and '30s. Her crisp, direct style is late Art Deco/early Cubist. Born into a wealthy bourgeois family from Warsaw, she spent most of her extravagant life after the age of fifteen abroad, eventually divorcing her aristocratic Polish husband Łempicki but keeping his last name and adding *de* in front of it. By that time she was a glamorous international personality and painter of homoerotic, often muscular, female nudes (she herself was lithe and svelte) or of aristocrats able to afford her work. On the eve of World War II she settled temporarily in Hollywood and immediately joined the crowd there. After the war she moved her studio to Paris. Łempicka died in Cuernavaca, Mexico, and her ashes were scattered over the Popocatapetl volcano. *Self-Portrait in Green Bugatti.* © 2015, Tamara Art Heritage. Licensed by www.MuseumMasters.com

Łomnicki, Tadeusz (1927–1992). Outstanding actor of stage, screen, and television. On the stage he largely specialized in classical roles, but

for the public he is best remembered for playing the swashbuckling Michał Wołodyjowski in Jerzy Hoffman's film versions of **Henryk Sienkiewicz**'s novels *Pan Wołodyjowski* (Colonel Wołodyjowski) and *Potop* (The deluge). He acted for most of the well-known Polish film directors. Many never forgave him for his open collaboration with the communist regime, although he resigned from the party in 1981 after the declaration of *stan wojenny* (martial law). He died during a dress rehearsal for *King Lear,* in which he was to play the title role and, he hoped, recapture his former reputation.

łowcy skór (skin hunters). The "skin-hunters affair" was a grisly scandal exposed by investigative journalists at *Gazeta Wyborcza* (Electoral gazette). In a series of trials beginning in 2002, members of an ambulance service in **Łódź**, including two doctors, were convicted of giving lethal injections to accident victims in exchange for kickbacks from funeral parlors. The exact number of victims is not known; the main perpetrator confessed to being responsible for at least fifty "assisted deaths." He was sentenced to life imprisonment, while another received twenty-five years. The events served as the basis of the 2003 film *Łowcy skór*, by Rafał Lipski.

Łowicz. A town with a population of nearly thirty thousand located between **Łódź** and Warsaw, in nearly the center of Poland and the **Mazowsze** region, an area often characterized as archetypical of traditional Polish village life. It was near here that **Władysław Reymont** placed the action of his Nobel Prize–winning novel *Chłopi* (The peasants). Here one may still encounter authentic lived-in Polish *chałupy* (peasant cottages), and on Sunday a few people in folk dress. The Łowicz region is known for its distinctive style of *wycinanki* (paper cutouts) and colorful orange and green striped wool fabric used for men's Sunday trousers and women's dress aprons. It has a major **Boże Ciało** (Corpus Christi) celebration each year, attracting tourists from all over. The town itself has an excellent folk museum. Nearby is Nieborów, the palace of the **Radziwiłł** family, with its romantic garden park Arkadia. Łowicz-brand fruit preserves are nationally recognized. *Łowicz-style paper cutout.*

Łódzka Szkoła Filmowa (Łódź Film School). Its official name is *Państwowa Wyższa Szkoła Filmowa, Telewizyjna i Teatralna imienia Leona Schillera* (Leon Schiller State Higher School of Cinema, Television and Theater). Nicknamed the "Filmówka" (its logo is pictured), it was founded in 1948 as the center of the postwar Polish film industry because **Łódź** was a large relatively intact city close to bombed-out Warsaw. Although present-day film production has mostly moved to Warsaw and **Kraków**, the school still exists as the main Polish formal training ground for film directors and camera operators. Even under communism it established a worldwide reputation for the solid quality of its technical training, especially of cameramen, and it drew students from around the world. Among Polish directors who attended the school are **Andrzej Wajda**, **Roman Polański**, **Krzysztof Zanussi**, and **Krzysztof Kieślowski**. Recently the school has expanded its offerings to encompass audiovisual media in general as well as acting.

Łódź. The third-largest Polish town as to population (744,541 inhabitants in 2009), Łódź is located in almost the exact center of Poland. Having lost its predominance in the textile industry, for which it was known in the nineteenth and early twentieth centuries, Łódź remains an important educational and cultural center. Its main tourist attraction is its elegant shopping and bar-hopping district, lined up along its main street, **ulica Piotrkowska**. For many Poles, the town is forever associated with **Władysław Reymont**'s novel of robber-baron capitalism, *Ziemia obiecana* (The promised land). In 1974 the town's still-remaining workers' slums, (which have recently been turned into upscale housing) and pretentious baronial mansions provided a natural setting for **Andrzej Wajda**'s film version of the novel. After World War II Łódź became Poland's filmmaking capital, or "HollyŁódź," with the creation there of the **Łódzka Szkoła Filmowa** (Łódź Film School). The origin of the town name, meaning "boat," has never been satisfactorily explained, but a boat has been part of the Łódź coat of arms since the beginning. *The palace of nineteenth-century textile magnate Izrael Poznański, now the Łódź city museum.*

M

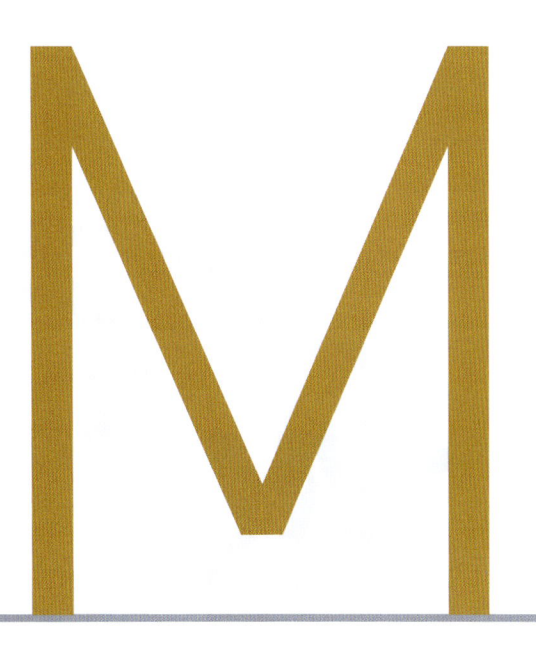

Maanam i Kora. As judged by albums sold, one of the most popular Polish rock bands over the past forty years, formed in 1975 by Marek Jackowski and Milo Kurtis and joined a year later by Olga Jackowska (Kora, pictured), with other musicians passing in and out of the group. At first operating in a punk band mode with a heavy guitar and featuring Kora's rough lyrics and vocal gymnastics, the band later subsequently developed a subtler and more tuneful sound. Their "Się ściemnia" (It's getting dark, 1984) was the first Polish music video to be aired on MTV International. Other memorable hits were "Boskie Buenos" (Heavenly Buenos) and "Nocny patrol" (Night patrol). Kora appeared on the cover of and inside Polish *Playboy* in April 1999. Maanam suspended performing in 2008, with Jackowski and Kora going their separate ways in music, as they already had done years earlier in their personal lives. Jackowski was residing in Italy when he died of a heart attack in 2013.

Mackiewicz, Józef (1902–1985). A Polish émigré author who was reduced in the PRL (communist Poland) to the status of an un-person, forbidden even to be discussed because of his staunch opposition to communism and, especially, because of his lifelong mission of bringing the Soviet-perpetrated *zbrodnia katyńska* (Katyń massacre) to world awareness. He eked out a meager existence in Paris, London and, eventually, Munich, living on royalties from his books published in the *wydawnictwa drugiego obiegu* (Polish underground press). Mackiewicz grew up in Wilno where he was witness in 1941 to the Ponary massacre of one hundred thousand Jews, Poles, and Russians by German and Lithuanian death squads, later described in his documentary short story "Ponary-Baza" (Base Ponary), almost impossible to read for its raw, shattering detail. His best-known novel, *Droga do nikąd* (*Road to Nowhere*, 1955), describes the brutal Soviet takeover of Lithuania in 1940–1941. Mackiewicz's voluminous oeuvre is finally receiving the critical attention it deserves.

Madonna z Krużlowej (Krużlowa Madonna). A remarkably realistic, exquisitely executed 119-centimeter-tall late medieval (early fifteenth century) wood sculpture whose creator is unknown, originally from the town of Krużlowa Wyżna, eighty-three kilometers southeast of Kraków. Attention was directed to it in 1889 by Stanisław Wyspiański, and the work was subsequently acquired by the National Museum in Kraków. The richly garbed and unabashedly pretty Mary belongs to the "standing" and so-called beautiful Madonna iconographic traditions. The apple held by the Christ child alludes to the tradition of Mary as the "second Eve," sent to redeem the world from the sin introduced into the world by the first. The sculpture was requisitioned in 1940 for the office of German Governor General Hans Frank in Wawel castle. Since 2007 it has been on view in the museum of early art in the Pałac Biskupa Ciołka in Kraków, where it is listed as its most prized holding.

mafia pruszkowska, wołomińska, łódzka (Pruszków, Wołomin, and Łódź mafias). Poland has had three major centers of organized crime, two in the Warsaw suburbs of Pruszków and Wołomin, the other in Łódź. Supposedly they were broken up by the police by the end of the 1990s. The Warsaw groups specialized in illegal alcohol sales, extortion, and drug sales and manufacture. The Łódź group, dubbed the *łódzka ośmiornica* (Łódź octopus) added to the list kidnapping for ransom and contract killing. Gang members are by now mostly dead, in jail, or in hiding abroad. A famous unsolved crime from the heyday of the three organizations is the apparent contract killing in Warsaw of former Polish police chief Marek Papała outside his apartment in June 1998.

magnateria (aristocracy, magnates). The name for the rich (extravagantly so) nobility in the Rzeczpospolita Obojga Narodów (Polish-Lithuanian Commonwealth). In principle all Polish *szlachta* (nobility or gentry) were equal before the law, according to the saying "szlachcic na zagrodzie równy wojewodzie" (a squire on his plot is equal to a palatine). In practice, some nobles acquired enormous wealth and were not

138 KALEIDOSCOPE OF POLAND

afraid to use it for political ends. Magnates could own vast lands, multiple palaces, tributary villages (so-called *latyfundia*), and even personal armies. The accumulation of wealth was aided by the principle of *ordynacja*, inheritance by primogeniture along the male line. No more than sixty families ever deserved the name, most notable of them being the Czartoryski, Kalinowski, Koniecpolski, Lubomirski, Potocki, Wiśniowiecki, Zamoyski, Radziwiłł, and Sapieha families. Most Polish magnates held land in the east; many were from Lithuania, and most used the title of *książę* (prince or duke). *Jan Matejko,* Polska magnateria, *1576–1586.*

Majdanek. A German *obóz koncentracyjny i zagłady* (concentration and extermination camp) built in 1941 on the edge of the town of Lublin. Estimates vary widely, but at least eighty thousand persons, three-quarters of whom were Jewish, were executed there by firing squad or in *komory gazowe* (gas chambers). Majdanek was liberated in 1944 by the Soviet army but was maintained by the Soviet NKVD (security forces) as a detention camp for soldiers of the Polish Armia Krajowa (Home Army). The well-preserved camp is now a museum, and it is one of the easiest to visit since it is off the main road for most tourists, hence rarely crowded.

---

mak (poppy). Bright red fields of poppies carpet the Polish countryside. As in other countries, poppy-red is often used to symbolize blood spilled in defense of the *ojczyzna* (fatherland), and the bright red of the Polish flag carries out the theme. Polish poppy varieties can be of the narcotic variety, but their most frequent use is in baking, to decorate bread and to make *makowiec* (poppyseed rolls). The refrain of the song "Czerwone maki na Monte Cassino" (Red poppies on Monte Cassino) commemorating the valiant Polish charge up to the Monte Cassino fortress under General Władysław Anders in World War II is known to most Poles:

> Czerwone maki na Monte Cassino,
> Zamiast rosy piły polską krew . . .
> Po tych makach szedł żołnierz i ginął,
> Lecz od śmierci silniejszy był gniew!

> The red poppies on Monte Cassino
> Instead of dew drank Polish blood . . .
> Over these poppies the soldier trod and died
> But stronger than death was his wrath!

Makowski, Tadeusz (1882–1932). A much-reproduced Polish painter who, mid-career, left for and remained in Paris, where he developed a signature style that combined elements of cubism, primitivism, and folk romanticism. He is best known for his paintings of rural children with spiked hats, which he produced in great number. *Tadeusz Makowski,* Under the Road Sign.

---

malarstwo na szkle (glass painting). A folk craft originating in the Karpaty (Carpathian Mountains). Designed for display in a cottage,

KALEIDOSCOPE OF POLAND

images of the Virgin Mary, saints, or folk heroes (e.g., Janosik), are painted on glass in reverse and from the inside out (with foreground figures painted first) so as to show through correctly from behind the glass pane. Colors are bright and contrasting, and the border areas are often decorated with flowers or other motifs. *Glass painting by Marta Walczak-Stasiowska.*

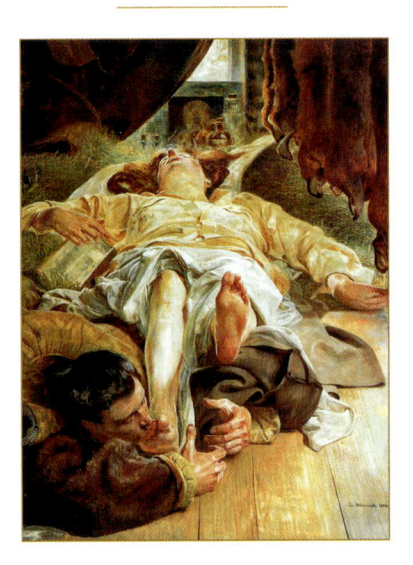

Malczewski, Jacek (1854–1929). Polish symbolist painter active around the turn of the nineteenth to the twentieth century. His favorite themes were patriotic martyrology, evanescence and death, and the process of artistic creation. Malczewski's paintings, executed with striking realism, often placed real people together with figures from folklore and legend. He was a skilled portraitist, and he left behind many likenesses of himself. A work that cemented his reputation was *Śmierć Ellenai* (1906–1907, pictured), inspired by a female character in Juliusz Słowacki's poem in prose, "Anhelli." Ellenai dies from the rigors of exile in Siberia. Other iconic paintings were *Błędne koło* (*Vicious Circle*, 1895–1897) and *Melancholia* (*Melancholy*, 1890–1894). A museum dedicated to Malczewski is in Radom, where he was born.

Malinowski, Bronisław (1884–1942). Pioneer anthropologist and ethnologist, one of the first to elaborate the principles of serious fieldwork in the investigation of societies called "primitive," principles that are still followed today. He founded what became known as the "functionalist" school of anthropology, breaking away from anthropology's former evolutionary focus. His research on the beliefs and religions of the people of the South Seas debunked Sigmund Freud's theory as to the universality of such concepts as the "Oedipus complex." Malinowski came to prominence with his published work on the sex lives of the Trobriand Islanders in Melanesia (in which he may have taken part, according to his method of "participatory observation"). His later academic life was spent in Great Britain and America. He received an honorary doctorate from Harvard

University in 1936 and was associated with Yale University until his death at age fifty-eight.

Małopolska (Lesser Poland). Historically, the southeast part of Poland, including the lands around Kraków, Zakopane, Rzeszów, Sandomierz, and Lublin, as contrasted with Wielkopolska (Greater Poland) in the northwest, centered in Gniezno and Poznań. The terrain of Małopolska ranges from undulating to mountainous. Its historical capital, and the capital of the current administrative unit, *województwo małopolskie* (Lesser Poland Voivodeship), is Kraków.

Małysz, Adam (b. 1977). One of Poland's most internationally successful sportsmen in history, and the Olympic Games' most decorated ski-jumper. The list of his successes includes four World Cup wins. Małysz's unprepossessing demeanor made him a favorite with the public, and the national interest in ski-jumping in Poland skyrocketed to such unprecedented proportions during his career that it acquired the name *małyszomania* (Małysz mania). His favorite pre-event snack, *bułka z bananem* (roll with banana), became a general good-luck totem. Małysz was awarded two different degrees of the Order Odrodzenia Polski (Order of Reborn Poland), one of Poland's highest civilian decorations, and his fans designed and officially registered for him a coat of arms in the Polish heraldic registry. In 2001 a postage stamp featuring his likeness was issued. Małysz announced his retirement as of the 2011 season, and made his final jump off Zakopane's Wielka Krokiew (Great Rafter) on March 26, 2011. Unable to remain inactive, he now trains for car rallies. His ski-jumping mantle has lately been assumed by Kamil Stoch, who won two gold medals in the 2014 Sochi Olympics.

Manifest Lipcowy (July Manifesto). Nominally issued from Chełm on July 22, 1944, but actually approved by Joseph Stalin in Moscow two days earlier, the July Manifesto was addressed to the Polish nation. Among other things it proclaimed the Polish *rząd na uchodźstwie* (government in exile) to be illegitimate, declared a close union with the Soviet Union, and promised the distribution of land to the peasants. At the same time, it designated the Polski Komitet Wyzwolenia Narodowego (PKWN, Polish Committee for National Liberation), formed in Moscow, as the only legitimate power in postwar Poland. In commemoration of the Manifest, July 22 was the main national holiday during the PRL (communist Poland).

Marszałkowska Dzielnica Mieszkaniowa (MDM) (Marszałkowska Housing Complex). A much-ballyhooed monumental socialist-realist housing and shopping complex built on the ruins of former apartment houses along Marszałkowska Street in the center of Warsaw in the years 1950–1952. Only about one-eighth of the original project was realized, and its construction

KALEIDOSCOPE OF POLAND 141

destroyed many of the few Warsaw buildings still left standing after the war. Its appearance has grown mellower with age and no longer offends the eye as it once did. A well-known song in the spirit of *socrealizm* (socialist realism) accompanied its construction, the last verse of which went:

> I tak jak sen, wspaniały sen
> Wstaje nowa MDM . . .
> Bo MDM, bo MDM
> Rośnie nocą, rośnie dniem!

> And like a dream, a marvelous dream
> Arises the new MDM . . .
> For the MDM, the MDM
> Is growing by day and by night!

Parade of youth in front of the MDM, 1952.

Marzanna, topienie Marzanny (Marzanna, drowning of Marzanna). Marzanna was a Slavic pagan goddess of winter and death. In a folk ritual surviving to the present day, women (today, mostly schoolgirls) set on fire a straw effigy of Marzanna. They then set it afloat and let it drown, to signify the end of winter and the start of spring. The holiday, sometimes called Jare Święto (early-spring holiday), takes place on March 21.

marzec 1968, wydarzenia marcowe (March 1968, the March events). A political crisis in the regime of **Władysław Gomułka** brought on by student protests, especially in Warsaw, **Gdańsk**, **Poznań**, and **Wrocław**, sparked by the shutting down of a performance of **Adam Mickiewicz**'s *Dziady* at the National Theater. Demonstrations were violently suppressed with water tanks and police truncheons by detachments of the **Ochotnicza Rezerwa Milicji Obywatelskiej** (ORMO, Voluntary Reserve of the Citizens Militia). The government crackdown eventually took on anti-Semitic overtones and led to the firing and emigration of people and entire families of Jewish background, as well as many non-Jewish intellectuals. As many as twenty thousand emigrated, most of them to Israel and the United States. A film about the events to watch is *Różyczka* (Rosie, 2010), by Jan Kidawa-Błoński.

Masłowska, Dorota (b. 1983). A precocious literary sensation known first for her 2002 best-selling novel told from the point of view of a drug-wasted *dresiarz* ("sweatpants bum"), published when she was only nineteen. The novel, *Wojna polsko-ruska pod flagą biało-czerwoną* (Polish-Russian War under the red and white flag, published in the United States as *Snow White and Russian Red*), was nominated for the **Nike** award, but Masłowska had to wait until 2006 to win the Nike for her next novel, *Paw królowej* (The queen's puke). The title is ambiguous, for *paw* literally means "peacock." She has published two plays, sings, and wrote the screenplay for the well-received 2009 film version of *Wojna polsko-ruska*, directed by Xavery Żuławski, in which she also acted, playing herself. Her plays, one of which has been performed in New York, seem destined to bring her to international attention. *Photo by Mariusz Kubik.*

Matejko, Jan (1838–1893). A prolific Polish painter of panoramic historical and battle scenes as well as a portraitist, Matejko is especially known for his charcoal series *Poczet królów i książąt polskich* (Gallery of Polish kings and princes), representing Polish rulers from the Polanian prince Piast to King **Stanisław August Poniatowski**. Especially admired in France, his paintings won two gold medals at Paris international exhibitions. Matejko was present at the opening of the tomb of **Kazimierz III Wielki** (Kazimierz the Great) in 1869, and his drawings of the regalia, still intact, were used to make museum copies. His polychromies in **Kraków's kościół Mariacki** (Marian Church) are also greatly admired. Matejko's large *kamienica* (townhouse) in Kraków just off the *Rynek Główny* was willed to the city as a museum devoted to his work, although his most important canvases are to be found in the country's national museums. Some of his best-known images are *Stańczyk*, *Kazanie Skargi* (Skarga's sermon), *Rejtan*, and *Bitwa pod Grunwaldem* (Battle of Grunwald). *Jan Matejko, Self-Portrait.*

Matka Boska Częstochowska, Czarna Madonna (Mother of God of Częstochowa; the Black Madonna). An age-darkened icon in the **Jasna Góra** monastery in **Częstochowa**, representing the Virgin Mary and Christ child. Its origins are obscure, and it has been painted over several times. Although the icon comes out of the Byzantine iconic tradition, it is one of the most widely recognized symbols of the Roman Catholic Church in Poland. It bears scars from 1430, when it was temporarily stolen by Hussites. Many miracle-working legends attach to the icon. It is supposed to ward off injury in battle, and it was said to have discouraged the Swedes in their siege of the Jasna Góra monastery in 1655. Images of the icon are often carried into battle by Polish soldiers. From 1957 to 1980, to the consternation of the communist authorities, a likeness of the icon was hand-carried in a continuous procession to all the parishes in Poland.

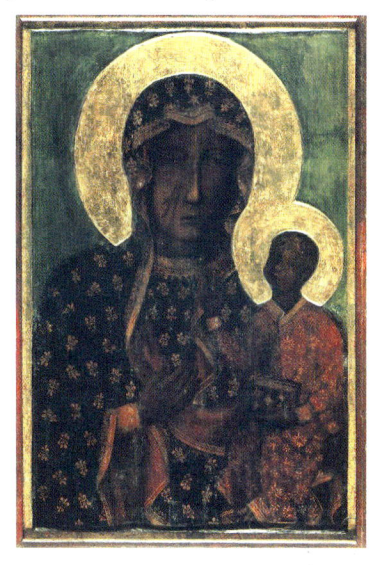

Matka Polka (Mother Pole). The image of the proverbially fertile, self-sacrificing, patriotic, and religious "Polish Mother" takes its name from a pessimistic poem of that title by **Adam Mickiewicz**, written in 1830 under the influence of the **powstanie listopadowe** (November Uprising). In latter times the name is often used

KALEIDOSCOPE OF POLAND   143

sarcastically to refer to women slaving away in heroic and unrecognized self-sacrifice to support their families. Poland's largest gynecological and pediatric medical facility in Łódź (its symbol is pictured) is named after the Matka Polka. Although in Poland one speaks of the country as the *ojczyzna* (fatherland, although the noun itself is of feminine gender), the personified symbols of the country are female as, for example, the Nike monument in Warsaw, dedicated to the heroes of Warsaw, 1939–1945. The name for the country itself, *Polska*, is feminine, but then so are the Polish names for most countries.

---

matura (high school achievement examinations). The *matura* functions as the ticket of admission to institutes of higher learning. It occurs in May, and so is associated with the flowering of chestnut trees. There is both a written and an oral portion, with some subjects being obligatory and others optional. In order to make a good impression on the oral examination board, students often come dressed formally, in dark suits and white shirts or blouses. For good luck, girls may wear the same red underwear they wore to the *studniówka* (high school prom) and practice other good-luck rituals; for example, bringing a good-luck stuffed animal and entering the room with one's right foot but choosing questions with one's left hand. A wealth of study guides and private tutors and schools exists to help students prepare for the matura, whose questions and answers are published afterward and are the subject of national discussion and critique. *Students in Szczecin ready to take the written portion of their matura.*

Mazowsze (Mazovia). A historical region in the north-central Polish heartland along the Wisła; its traditional capital was Płock (now it is Warsaw). In the early tenth century the Mazowsze region found itself within the sphere of influence of the Piasts of Wielkopolska (Greater Poland, that is, the Polanian princes of Gniezno). Beginning in the thirteenth century until 1529, Mazowsze was a fief of the Polish crown ruled by a series of Piast dukes or princes (see *dynastia Piastów*). After that it became incorporated into the Korona Królestwa Polskiego (Polish Crown), with its seat in Kraków. The Mazovian region is often taken as representative of the archetypical Polish countryside and landscape. Mazowsze is also the name of Poland's best-known professional folk song and dance troupe, Zespół Ludowy Pieśni i Tańca "Mazowsze," founded in 1948 by Tadeusz Sygietyński.

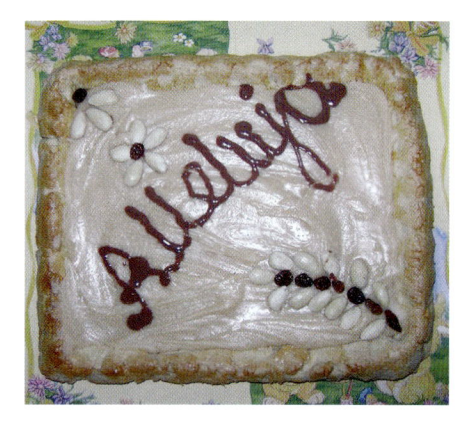

---

mazur, mazurek (mazurka). A lively Polish folk dance in three-quarter time, with stress on the second beat. Originally associated with the Mazury region, the mazurka was adopted by the seventeenth-century Polish court and nobility and also by many Polish composers, including Fryderyk Chopin. It is a demanding dance, requiring physical strength from the man and grace from the woman. The Polish national anthem, "Mazurek Dąbrowskiego" (Dąbrowski mazurka) is called a mazurek, but it is too slow to qualify as a genuine example. Various unconvincing explanations have been proposed for why the European name for the dance is *mazurka* and not *mazurek*; the word entered international vocabulary through French *mazourka*. In Poland, the word *mazurek* also refers to a rich iced and decorated Easter cake layered with jam and marmalade (pictured).

***

"Mazurek Dąbrowskiego" (Dąbrowski mazurka). The Polish *hymn narodowy* (national anthem) since 1927. Based on a folk rhythm, the lyrics were written in 1797 by Józef Wybicki (1747–1822) for the **Legiony Polskie** (Polish Legions) fighting for Napoleon in Italy, which Wybicki helped to raise along with General **Jan Henryk Dąbrowski**. The motive of the song was to counteract **Tadeusz Kościuszko**'s reputed declaration after his defeat at Maciejowice, "Finis Poloniae!" (Poland is finished). The first lines of the song as it is sung today are:

> Jeszcze Polska nie zginęła
> Kiedy my żyjemy . . .
> Co nam obca przemoc wzięła
> Szablą odbierzemy!

> Poland has not yet perished
> As long as we are alive . . .
> What foreign force has taken from us
> We will take back with the saber!

***

Mazury, Pojezierze Mazurskie (Mazurian Lake District). The Mazury are a historical region in northeast Poland, richly forested and blessed by an abundance of wildlife. Historically, the Mazury were a part of **Warmia** in Prusy Wschodnie (East Prussia), and were under the rule of the **Krzyżacy** (Teutonic Knights) until 1525. The Mazury were settled by Poles from **Mazowsze** who were, however, subjected to strong German cultural pressure up through World War II, after which most of the German population was expelled (the film on the subject to watch is *Róża* by Wojciech Smarzowski, 2011). The Mazury encompass the Pojezierze Mazurskie (Mazurian Lake District), sometimes referred to as the *kraina tysiąca jezior* (land of a thousand lakes). In fact there are many more lakes than that, many of them interconnected. *Śniardwy, the largest of the Mazurian lakes.*

***

Medaliony (*Medallions*, 1946). The respected writer Zofia Nałkowska (1884–1954) was a member of an international commission investigating German crimes against Poles in World War II, and she converted a number of her notes into brief, chilling sketches published in a slim volume under this title (which also means "death notices"), which was for many years required reading in Polish schools (see *lektura obowiązkowa*). Among the most notorious of her cases was that of Dr. Rudolf Spanner, the German head of the Gdańsk Anatomical Institute during World War II, whose contribution to the war effort was to render the fat of corpses from the nearby Stutthoff concentration camp and the local **Gdańsk** prison into soap. The matter was eventually referred to the Nuremberg War Crimes Tribunal. It was never determined exactly how large Professor Spanner's operation was, but the fact of its existence is not in dispute. In the end the professor was not prosecuted. The motto of Nałkowska's book, "Ludzie ludziom zgotowali ten los," roughly translates as "People devised this fate for people."

***

Mehoffer, Józef (1869–1946). Next to **Stanisław Wyspiański**, Mehoffer was the most prominent painter of the **Młoda Polska** (Young Poland) period. Like Wyspiański, Mehoffer had been a student of **Jan Matejko** in **Kraków**, and the three of them worked together on the frescoes of Kraków's **kościół Mariacki** (Marian Church). Mehoffer went on to study in Vienna and Paris and, like many artists of Young Poland, developed an interest in the decorative arts, including posters and stained glass windows executed in the flowing style of the *secesja* (Art Nouveau). Representative works are *Dziwny ogród* (Strange garden, 1903) and *Słońce majowe* (May sun, 1907), both of which hang in the Muzeum Narodowe (National Museum) in Warsaw. His home in Kraków — coincidentally the same house in which Wyspiański was born in the same year that Mehoffer was born elsewhere, 1869 — is now the Mehoffer Museum.

mesjanizm polski (Polish national messianism). A romantic/mystical view of the special position of Poland as the "Christ of nations," destined to be sacrificed to redeem other nations. The concept traces back to seventeenth-century *sarmatyzm* (Sarmatism) and its concept of *Polska przedmurzem chrześcijaństwa* (Poland the bulwark of Christianity) or, even earlier, to the *Kazania sejmowe* (Sermons to the **Sejm**) of 1597, by **Piotr Skarga**. Polish messianism reached its zenith in the early nineteenth century in the teachings of Andrzej Towiański (1799–1878, pictured), who especially influenced **Adam Mickiewicz**. Polish messianism was interpreted differently by each of the three great Polish Romantic poets — by **Adam Mickiewicz**

in his *Księgi narodu polskiego i pielgrzymstwa polskiego* (Books of the Polish nation and the Polish pilgrimage, 1832), by **Juliusz Słowacki** in his *Król Duch* (King Spirit, 1847), and by **Zygmunt Krasiński**, who (as would be expected) emphasized its Roman Catholic nature and the leading role of the aristocracy.

metal, muzyka metalowa (heavy metal music). Heavy metal rock music arose in England and the United States at the beginning of the 1970s, and in Poland some ten years later, where it developed a sizable following. Without going into its subvarieties, it is characterized by deafening guitar and drum solos; reference in its lyrics to occultism, Satanism, catastrophism, and/or nihilism (although some bands are, instead, Christian in profile); and fans called *metalowcy* (metalheads), who, in imitation of band members, wear long hair and almost obligatory black leather jackets, black T-shirts, and black denim trousers. The rock festival in **Jarocin** was an early launching pad, and, later, Metalmania at **Katowice**'s **Spodek**. The best-known groups come not from the heartland but from the west and north of Poland, such as Behemot, from **Gdańsk**; KAT, from Katowice (the word *kat* by itself means "executioner"); TSA, from **Opole**; Turbo, from **Poznań**; and Vader, from Olsztyn. *Behemot.*

miasto i wieś (town and country). A dichotomy etched in the respective Polish adjectives: *miejski*, *wiejski* (urban, rural). The division between those living in cities and in the country has traditionally been sharp, amplified sometimes by differences in dialect, and with one group mistrusting and looking down on the other. It was not too long ago that as much as half of the Polish population was rural; the figure is now around 40 percent, with 15 percent engaged in agriculture (as compared to 20 percent and 1 percent, respectively, in the United States). The communists tried to treat farmers and industrial workers as belonging to the equivalent *klasa chłopska i klasa robotnicza* (peasant and workers' classes), but the two did not and still do not see eye-to-eye on many issues. The existence of the traditional small Polish farm is under dual pressure: from the younger generation, who have been leaving the country for the city or abroad in droves; and from large concerns converting smaller farms into economically more competitive operations. The structure of the contemporary Polish GDP breaks down as follows: agriculture, 5 percent; industry, 31 percent; services, 65 percent — not too far out of line with the EU average as a whole.

Michałowski, Piotr (1800–1855). Underestimated in his day, Michałowski is now recognized as the most talented Polish painter of the Romantic period (the first half of the nineteenth century), a view aided by Pablo Picasso's picking him out as a "true artist" on a visit to the national gallery in Warsaw in 1948. He specialized in peasant genre portraits and equestrian and battle pieces. Many of his works have a Rembrandt-like quality. A room devoted to Michałowski's work and influence is in the National Gallery of Art in **Krakow**'s Sukiennice. Głowa Konia, *1846*.

Michnik, Adam (b. 1946). A political activist, public intellectual, and one of Poland's most influential media figures. A history student at Warsaw University in 1968, Michnik was imprisoned following the *wydarzenia marcowe* (March 1968 student protests). Released under a general amnesty in 1969, he completed studies in **Poznań** and, in the late 1970s, became active in the oppositionist Workers' Defense Committee (see **Komitet Obrony Robotników, KOR**), an adviser to the **Solidarność** (Solidarity) independent trade union, and an editor of underground publications. Arrested under *stan wojenny* (martial law) in 1981, he was not released until 1984. Michnik helped organize and participated in the 1989 **rozmowy Okrągłego Stołu** (Round Table Discussions) and emerged from them as chief editor of the independent newspaper *Gazeta Wyborcza* (GW, Electoral gazette), a position he still holds as of 2014. He eventually broke with Solidarność and built GW into what is arguably Poland's most influential daily under the Agora Corporation. He received the Order Orła Białego (Order of the White Eagle) in 2010.

Mickiewicz, Adam (1798–1855). Born on Christmas Eve in Nowogródek, in what he called Lithuania, now part of Belarus, Mickiewicz was a Polish poet, political/cultural activist, a lecturer on Slavic literature at the Sorbonne, and the most renowned of a triumvirate of distinguished Polish Romantic poets (along with Zygmunt Krasiński and Juliusz Słowacki). He is best known for his early Romantic folk-inspired *ballady* (ballads), sonnets (of which he is the unrivaled Polish master), narrative poems, his Romantic drama *Dziady* (Forefathers' Eve), and above all else his nostalgic novel in verse *Pan Tadeusz* (Master Thaddeus, 1834), which is often called the Polish national epic (even if it is written in mock-epic style). The powstanie listopadowe (November Uprising) of 1830 caught Mickiewicz outside the country, where he remained for the rest of his life as part of the Wielka Emigracja (Great Emigration). His later works took up the cause of *mesjanizm polski* (Polish national messianism). He contracted cholera and died while trying to raise a Jewish legion in Constantinople to fight the Russians in the Crimean war. Mickiewicz's lifelong Judeophilism, especially visible in his portrayal of Jankiel in *Pan Tadeusz*, led some to speculate on his possible Jewish origins. His mother may have been descended from a follower of Jakub Frank, but on his father's side he was descended from a long line of Lithuanian gentry. His body is interred in the crypts of Wawel Cathedral. See the many cross-references from Mickiewicz in the index.

---

miesiące, nazwy miesięcy (names of the months). Polish month names relate to the weather or agriculture. *Styczeń* (January) was once *sieczeń*, related to *siec* (chop), this being the time to fell forests. It was reassociated with *styk* (joint), as if joining together the old and new year. *Luty* (February) is an old word meaning "fierce." *Kwiecień* (April) is related to *kwiecić się* (blossom); *czerwiec* (June) to *czerw*, a larva whose pupae were dried to make crimson dye; *lipiec* (July) to the *lipa* (linden tree), which flowers at this time; *sierpień* (August) to *sierp* (sickle), used to harvest grain; *wrzesień* (September) to *wrzosy* (heather), whose purple flowers bloom at this time. *Październik* (October) comes from *paździerz*, a stalky by-product of linen manufacture. *Listopad* (November) is when *liście opadają* (leaves fall); and *grudzień* (December) is related to *gruda*, "clod," the uneven state of frozen ground in winter. *Marzec* (March) and *maj* (May) are taken from Latin.

---

mieszkania (apartments). Apartments in Poland have long been a deficit commodity for which new families sometimes wait years. In the PRL (communist Poland) parents would often open a *książeczka mieszkaniowa* (apartment savings book) for a child at its birth, and pay into it with the expectation of receiving an apartment allotment upon the child's maturity at the age of eighteen. In 2005–2007, after Poland joined the EU, there was a housing boom and prices skyrocketed. People would sometimes put down cash on little more than holes in the ground to make sure they had something. The housing situation has alleviated in recent years, but apartments are still expensive compared to income. In Warsaw a square meter of living space currently costs around 10,000 PLN (new Polish złotys), or $3,600. The government sponsors a program to help young couples buy apartments, called *Rodzina na swoim* (a family in its own place), but the red tape involved is formidable, and the program will soon come to an end. Habitat for Humanity Polska is available for the truly destitute working poor. See also: **mieszkania: rodzaje**; **mieszkanie M1, M2, M3**.

mieszkania: rodzaje (apartment types). Without going into detail on a complex subject, Polish apartments may be *własnościowe* (owned), *spółdzielcze* (cooperative), *służbowe* (provided by the workplace), *komunalne* (publicly supported, low-rent), or simply *wynajmowane* (rented). These days, apartment house complexes (*osiedla*) are mostly put up by *deweloperzy* (developers); see also *osiedle strzeżone*. Cooperative apartments are like condominiums, in that one has shares in the entire complex rather than merely owning an individual apartment. Affairs of the cooperative are run by an elective board. *Projected new apartment complex in Szczecin.*

mieszkanie M1, M2, M3 (M1, M2, M3 apartments). In the **PRL** (communist Poland) there were six different classifications for apartments depending on size and number of rooms, the numbers designating the number of people for which the apartment was designed: M1, 25–28 square meters; M2, 30–35 square meters; M3, 44–48 square meters; M4, 56–61 square meters; M5, 65–70 square meters; M6, 75–85 square meters. An M1 apartment might contain as little as a single multi-use room, a kitchen nook, and a bathroom. An M3 might contain a hall, a *duży pokój* (large or common room), and two small bedrooms. Certain professions, such as teachers, were allowed to have extra space for a home office. These designations are still used, especially in sales ads, although in newer construction the old limits are often ignored. To economize on space, many apartments have multi-use rooms with a *tapczan* or, fancier, a *wersalka*, converting each night from a cot or sofa to a bed.

Mieszko I (ca. 930–992). A Polish prince of the *dynastia* Piastów (Piast dynasty), the first historical ruler of the Polanie, and considered to be the founder of the Polish state, Mieszko I ruled from 960 and was, according to chroniclers, the great-grandson of Piast and the son of Siemomysł. He was the father of **Bolesław I Chrobry** (Bolesław the Brave), the first Polish king. It was Mieszko who accepted Christianity (see *chrzest Polski*) in 966 by marrying the Czech princess Dobrawa (Dąbrówka). According to legend, Mieszko was blind from birth but regained his sight upon undergoing the ceremony of *postrzyżyny* (having his hair cut) at the age of seven.

Międzyrzecki Rejon Umocniony (MRU, Międzyrzecz Fortified Region; German: Ost-

KALEIDOSCOPE OF POLAND   149

wall). Built by Nazi Germany between the Warta and the Odra (Oder) rivers in 1934–1938 on what was then German territory as a defense along its eastern frontier, the MRU consisted of a network of tunnel-connected above- and belowground bunkers, barracks, and workshops, and it was the most technologically advanced and elaborate such system of the time. It was overrun in a matter of days by the advancing Soviet army in January 1945. Today the MRU is Europe's largest bat sanctuary, with some thirty-two thousand individuals representing twelve species. Parts of the MRU are open to tourists. *MRU aboveground machine-gun emplacement.*

---

mikołajki (Saint Nicholas's Eve, December 6). An evening upon which Święty Mikołaj (Saint Nicholas) visits children, questions them on their behavior, and gives good children presents. The Polish Mikołaj (regionally, "Gwiazdor" or "Aniołek") is not a merry old elf but a stern bishop. He hands out either *prezenty* (presents) or, alternatively, *rózgi* (switches), depending on behavior. Święty Mikołaj often comes in secret on *mikołajki* and leaves small presents or sweets in children's shoes or stockings or on the windowsill, but he can also bring bigger presents and leave them under the bed or the *choinka* (Christmas tree). These days he is just as apt to pay a visit on Wigilia (Christmas Eve). A recent newspaper article documents how Święty Mikołaj runs afoul of at least half a dozen Polish laws by stealing people's personal information, breaking into their houses, and providing the means for the illegal corporal punishment of children.

Milicja Obywatelska (MO, Citizens' Militia). The euphemism for the police in the PRL (communist Poland). The MO having been created in 1944 primarily out of members of the communist-led wartime Armia Ludowa (People's Army), the name stood in opposition to the prewar designation *policja* (police), and was misleadingly intended to suggest a voluntary force composed of ordinary citizens. Analogous designations were used throughout the Soviet Bloc. Besides combating routine criminality, the MO was actively engaged in putting down manifestations of political opposition. Particularly toward the end of the PRL, members of the MO were the constant butt of jokes and the object of social ostracism. In 1990 the MO was renamed the *policja* (police). *The standard MO Nysa paddy wagon.*

Miłosz, Czesław (1911–2004). Polish poet, essayist, translator, literary historian, and scholar. Like many other Polish writers, Miłosz was from the *kresy* (eastern borderlands) — in his case from around Kowno (Kaunas) in Lithuania. His book *Zniewolony umysł* (*The Captive Mind*, 1953), a classic of the *zimna wojna* (Cold War), portrayed selected Polish writers in their adaptation to authoritarianism. Miłosz emigrated from Poland and lived in France and the United States in 1951–1989, teaching at Berkeley and Harvard, but he later returned to Poland and lived in Kraków in a government-provided apartment. He was a recipient of the Nobel Prize for literature in 1980, after which the ban on his works in Poland was lifted, and his novel *Dolina Issy* (The Issa river valley, 1955) was made into a well-received film by Tadeusz Konwicki in 1982. He is buried in the Krypta Zasłużonych (Crypt of the Meritorious) in Skałka. In Poland, 2011 was declared to be *rok Miłosza* (the year of Miłosz).

miód, miód pitny (honey, mead). The early Poles were reputed to be master beekeepers, and honey and beeswax, alongside amber and slaves, were among the items most frequently traded with the Roman Empire. A special Polish honey is *miód spadziowy* (dew honey), which bees make from tiny droplets that form on linden leaves or conifer needles. Fermented honey and water, or mead, was mentioned by medieval chroniclers as a Polish specialty, a substitute for having no native wine. Being expensive, it was reserved for festive occasions. Polish mead is registered with the European Union as a Guaranteed Traditional Specialty. Sculpting beehives in the shape of religious and other figures was a traditional folk craft. A living beehive museum may be found in Swarzędz near Poznań, where this beehive in the image of a *Łowiczanka* (Łowicz woman) may be found.

Miss Polonia. The oldest Polish beauty pageant, having been founded, improbably, in 1929 by the literary critic Tadeusz Boy-Żeleński. Winners of the pageant feed into international beauty pageants such as Miss World, Miss Europe, Miss Universe, Miss Earth, and so on. The Polish pageant is older than all of these except for Miss Europe. The 1989 winner, Aneta Kręglicka (pictured here in 2010 at age forty-five), went on to win the Miss World contest, the only Pole thus far to have done so.

Mitoraj, Igor (b. 1944). A graphic artist and largely self-taught sculptor with an international reputation, who has lived and worked in France and Italy since 1968, Mitoraj is known for his large bronze or marble heads, posed lying on their side as if they were the remains of some still more monumental piece of classical antiquity, now lost. He has created outdoor-park pieces for cities across Europe, the United States, and Japan. In Poland his work may be seen in Kraków in front of the opera and on the *Rynek Główny* (main square), where a head entitled *Eros spętany*

(Eros in fetters, pictured) has children constantly crawling inside and looking out through the eye cavities.

Młoda Polska (Young Poland). The term refers to the simultaneously decadentist, modernist, neo-Romanticist, individualist, and nativist trend in Polish art, music, and literature that flourished more or less in the years 1890–1918. The movement was strongest in the south, especially around Kraków and Zakopane, where many authors and painters moved to be closer to nature and the "peasant" way of life, an excessive variant of which was called *chłopomania* (peasant mania). The most prominent figure of the movement in both painting and literature was Stanisław Wyspiański, who himself married a peasant woman. Other major painters were Jacek Malczewski, Józef Mehoffer, and Leon Wyczółkowski. In music, best-known was the composer Karol Szymanowski. Literary figures were mostly poets and dramatists, of whom Jan Kasprowicz (1860–1926), Leopold Staff (1878–1957), and Kazimierz Przerwa-Tetmajer (1865–1940) stood out. Major novelists were Władysław Stanisław Reymont and Stanisław Przybyszewski.

mniejszości narodowe i etniczne (national and ethnic minorities). Due to the Holocaust, the redrawing of borders after World War II, the forcible resettlement of Germans out of the so-called *ziemie odzyskane* (recovered territories) in the west, and the repatriation of ethnic Poles out of the *kresy* (eastern territories), Poland has the lowest percentage of national minorities of any European country. They do not play a significant role in national politics as they once did. Among national minorities are (in alphabetical order): Armenian, Belarusian, Czech, German, Jewish, Lithuanian, Russian, Slovak, and Ukrainian. An incredibly small number of Americans live in Poland — estimated at 1,504 in 2002, of whom most had Polish citizenship. Ethnic minorities (minorities not identified with an external territory of their own) include: Karaim (a Crimean offshoot of Judaism), Kaszub (Kashubian), Łemko (Carpatho-Rusyn/Ukrainian), Rom (Roma), Śląsk (Silesian), and Tatar.

Modlin, twierdza Modlin (Modlin Fortress). A complex of defensive fortifications, barracks, and ammunition depots built near where the Narew River joins the Wisła about thirty kilometers north of Warsaw. It was originally built on the orders of Napoleon in 1806. Under the Russian-controlled Królestwo Polskie (Kingdom of Poland), it became one of the mightiest fortresses of the Russian Empire until 1915, when it fell to the German army. It became Polish after World War I. During the *kampania wrześniowa* (September Campaign) of 1939 the Modlin Fortress defended itself and Warsaw valiantly, and was among the last emplacements to lay down its arms, on September 29. Under German occupation in World War II parts of it were used as a concentration camp where upwards of twenty thousand Poles died. Since the war, Modlin has been largely unused and allowed to deteriorate. Like the Cytadela warszawska (Warsaw Citadel), it is waiting for a person or organization to revitalize it as a tourist attraction.

Modrzejewska, Helena (1840–1909). A celebrated actress first on the Polish and then on the international stage, specializing in tragic Shakespearean roles. Modrzejewska emigrated to the United States in 1876, mastered English, and

152   KALEIDOSCOPE OF POLAND

spent most of her subsequent career playing to sold-out houses in the United States and Britain under the name Modjeska. Throughout her life Modrzejewska actively promoted Polish causes, women's rights, and various charities. The Narodowy Stary Teatr (National Old Theater) in **Kraków** is officially named after her. *Portrait by Tadeusz Ajdukiewicz, 1880.*

Modrzewski, Andrzej Frycz (1503–1572). A Polish Renaissance political philosopher and court secretary under King **Zygmunt I Stary** (Zygmunt the Old), Modrzewski's best-known work was his utopian — before the term existed — *De Republica emendanda* (On Reforming the Republic, 1551–1554), which was read around Europe in either the Latin original or the German translation. It expressed such radical views on the Church that it was placed on the Catholic index of banned books, along with **Kopernik**'s (Copernicus's) work on heavenly bodies. Much ahead of his time, Modrzewski advocated, among other things, universal education, social welfare, and the equality of all social classes before the law. He is named as the patron of the recently opened Akademia Krakowska (Kraków Academy, founded in 2000) — appropriately, since the academy's focus is on administration and political science. *Jan Matejko,* Andrzej Frycz Modrzewski.

monety, banknoty (coins, bills). An unchanging aspect of life in Poland over the years is the perpetual shortage of coins. It is almost impossible to offer a bill of any size in a store, not to mention a *kiosk*, without being asked by the cashier, "Proszę drobne" (Small change, please), or being informed "Nie mam wydać" (I don't have the change). It is common to see a cashier sorting through a customer's change for anything she or he can use. A problem with Polish coins is that they are so small and in so many different

KALEIDOSCOPE OF POLAND   153

sizes: 1 grosz; 2 grosze; 5, 10, 20, and 50 groszy; 1 złoty; 2 złote; and 5 złotych. Bills, featuring Polish rulers beginning with Mieszko I, come in denominations of 10, 20, 50, 100, and 200 zł. Poland is obliged to adopt the euro as soon as certain economic criteria are met. *The 50-złoty note features Kazimierz III Wielki.*

Monitor. The first regularly appearing Polish periodical — first a weekly and later a semi-weekly — founded by Ignacy Krasicki and Franciszek Bohomolec (pictured) at the instigation of King Stanisław August Poniatowski. It appeared in the years 1765–1785. Modeled on the British *Spectator*, the *Monitor* featured news, opinion pieces, and letters to the editor, and it became an organ for progressive social and political change in the waning years of the Rzeczpospolita Obojga Narodów (Polish-Lithuanian Commonwealth). The contemporary *Monitor Polski* is the name for the official gazette of the Polish Republic, in which government announcements are made.

Moniuszko, Stanisław (1819–1872). Poland's best-known composer of operas, Moniuszko also composed accompaniment to many famous poems and the music for ballets. He is best remembered for two operas: *Halka* (complete four-act version in 1858), Poland's first important national opera, about a village girl seduced and jilted by a young gentleman; and *Straszny dwór* (The haunted manor, 1865), about soldier brothers who vow celibacy but become entranced by the daughters of the owner of the titular manor. The opera's emblem is a famously haunted grandfather clock. Both operas belong to the permanent Polish operatic repertoire, but they are largely unknown outside the country.

Monte Cassino, bitwa pod Monte Cassino (Battle of Monte Cassino, 1944). Monte Cassino was a mountaintop monastery heavily fortified by the Germans in World War II that blocked the march of Allied forces from Anzio northward to Rome. Three successive attacks by American, British, French, New Zealand, and Indian troops were repulsed with huge loss of life. The fourth attack, with the aid of Polish troops of the II Korpus (Second Corps) under General Władysław Anders, finally overcame the German resistance, and the Polish flag was the first to be planted on the captured fortress. The role of the Polish army in the Battle of Monte Cassino was downplayed by the Polish communist government. The well-known song commemorating the battle, "Czerwone maki na Monte Cassino" (Red poppies at Monte Cassino; see *mak*), sung while standing at attention, became a virtual hymn of passive anti-communist resistance in the early postwar years. See also: Wojtek, niedźwiedź Wojtek.

Morskie Oko (Eye-of-the-Sea Lake). A large (nearly one million cubic meters), deep (up to fifty meters), and clear (visibility up to twelve meters) lake, situated in the Wysokie **Tatry** (High Tatra) Mountains with stunning views in all directions, including of Rysy, the highest peak in the Polish Tatras. Reachable by a two-hour walk from the nearest motorway or by horse-drawn wagon, Morskie Oko is one of the Tatras's most-visited tourist spots, and it has been the inspiration for many artists, including **Leon Wyczółkowski**. According to legend it is connected to the Adriatic Sea and hence does not have a bottom.

Mrożek, Sławomir (1930–2013). A writer of satirical plays, short stories, and novels, and also a cartoonist in a primitivist vein, Mrożek was one of the better-known and most widely translated Polish writers during the 1960s–1970s. He earned an international reputation with his absurdist short stories, especially the collection *Słoń* (*The Elephant*; see *ogrody zoologiczne*); various politically satirical short plays suitable for student performance: *Policja* (The police), *Na pełnym morzu* (On the open sea), and *Striptease*; and the longer and more philosophical **Gombrowicz**-inspired play *Tango* (1964). Something of a recluse and eccentric, Mrożek left Poland in 1963 and lived variously in France, Germany, Italy, the United States, and Mexico. He returned to Poland in 1996 but, after suffering and recovering from a debilitating stroke in 2002, he re-emigrated in 2008 and died in Nice, France, five years later. He is buried in **Kraków**. Mrożek's autobiography, *Baltazar*, was published in 2006, and the last of his diaries in 2010–2013.

KALEIDOSCOPE OF POLAND

N

Narew. A boggy meandering river originating in Belarus. Four hundred forty-eight kilometers of the Narew are in Poland, where it flows southeast into the **Wisła** after first merging with the **Bug**. The Narew is Europe's primary example of a so-called braided river, flowing along much of its length through twisted channels, making it not well-suited to extended river traffic. The Narew is the fifth-longest Polish river. *The braided Narew near Strękowa Góra.*

Narodowa Demokracja, endecja (National Democratic Movement). A radical nationalistic political movement with an element of anti-Semitism that originated at the end of the nineteenth century under the leadership of **Roman Dmowski** and operated under various party names throughout the *dwudziestolecie międzywojenne* (interwar period). The *endecja* was vehemently opposed to **Gabriel Narutowicz**'s election as president, which occurred with the help of the national minorities in 1922; one of its members was responsible for his assassination soon thereafter. The party was held in check by the *sanacja* (Return to Health) government of **Józef Piłsudski**. During World War II the endecja formed its own partisan fighting units, not known for their sympathy toward Jews in hiding; see **Narodowe Siły Zbrojne** (NSZ, National Armed Forces). The ideology of the endecja survives in the platforms of certain contemporary Polish political parties.

Narodowe Siły Zbrojne (NSZ) (National Armed Forces). A paramilitary partisan army in competition with the larger **Armia Krajowa** (AK, Home Army) in World War II, numbering at its height some seventy thousand soldiers. The NSZ was nationalist, pro-Catholic, and virulently anticommunist. It sometimes had trouble distinguishing between Jews and communists. The NSZ mostly successfully resisted efforts to have its operations incorporated into those of the AK. It was opposed to the **powstanie warszawskie** (Warsaw Uprising of 1944) but, when it broke out, supported it. Toward the end of the war, the NSZ tried to negotiate with the Nazis against the Soviets. Some NSZ partisans continued operations after the official cessation of military operations, and many thousands were exiled or executed after the war as so-called **żołnierze wyklęci** (excommunicated soldiers).

Narutowicz, Gabriel (1865–1922). A prominent Lithuanian-born hydroelectric engineer, Narutowicz returned from Switzerland to Poland upon its regaining independence, and served in 1920–1922 as minister of public works and then as minister of foreign affairs. A fairly unwilling candidate for president in the 1922 elections, he won after several ballots as a compromise candidate with the support of the *mniejszości narodowe* (national minorities) and the peasant parties. Several days after his inauguration, while attending an exhibition at the **Zachęta** gallery, he was assassinated by a fanatic of the **Narodowa Demokracja** (National Democrats). The times and the event are portrayed in Jerzy Kawalerowicz's film *Śmierć prezydenta* (Death of a president, 1977).

Nasza Klasa (Our Class). Poland's most popular homegrown social networking site, developed in 2006 in **Wrocław**, based on the idea of getting in touch with one's classmates. The name alludes to the bitter song of the same title by **Jacek Kaczmarski**. The site's phenomenal growth was credited for getting older people involved with the internet for the first time. Despite increasing competition from Facebook, it is continually developing and adding new features, including a Skype-like feature allowing for real-time conversations and the ability to create personal blogs. Nasza Klasa claims to have over thirteen million active users. The title *Nasza Klasa* was also given to a play about the **Jedwabne** massacre of 1941 by Tadeusz Słobodzianek, which won the 2010 **Nike** prize for the best Polish book of the previous year.

Nawojka. Nawojka was a fifteen-year-old girl from **Gniezno** who, in the early 1400s, masqueraded as a boy and enrolled for studies at the Kraków Academy at a time when higher education was for males only. She was unmasked just before she was to take her baccalaureate exams — according to one story, by a fellow student from Gniezno who recognized her. Excused from disciplinary action because of her exemplary record, she joined a convent as a teacher and later became its mother superior. The first women's dormitory at **Uniwersytet Jagielloński** (Jagiellonian University) in **Kraków**, built in 1929, is named after her, as is a street in Kraków. Uniwersytet Jagielloński did not allow women to study until 1897, nor to hold academic positions until 1906.

nazwiska polskie (Polish surnames). Polish surnames that end in *-ski* are male, and those that end in *-ska* are female: pan Kowalski (Mr. Kowalski), pani Kowalska (Ms. Kowalski). The male + female plural suffix is *-scy*: państwo Kowalscy (Mr. and Mrs. Kowalski). Last names ending in consonants (like Nowak) have theoretical forms for "Mrs." (Nowakowa) and "Miss" (Nowakówna), but these are rarely encountered nowadays. For the most part women use the unsuffixed form: pani Nowak (Ms. Nowak). The plural ends in *-owie*: państwo Nowakowie (Mr. and Mrs. Nowak). Polish children typically take the last name of the father, while wives either adopt the name of their husbands or, increasingly among professional women, keep their own last name or use a hyphenated one, as in Anna Kowalska-Nowak. See also: **nazwiska polskie: pochodzenie**.

---

nazwiska polskie: pochodzenie (Polish surnames: origins). Last names were first adopted by the gentry and were only slowly adopted by other classes. Originally, noble surnames consisted of the first name plus the place of origin; for example, Jan z Tęczyna, "Jan of Tęczyn." Later the suffix *-ski* was used: Jan Tęczyński. Laws requiring surnames arose in the late eighteenth century. Surnames often designate place of origin or ethnic affiliation: Podolski (from Podole), Mazur/Mazurski (from **Mazury**). Names in *-owicz* or *-ik* can be patronymic, such as Dawidowicz or Adamik. Others refer to trades: Kowal (smith), Krawiec (tailor); and yet others arose from nicknames or names of plants and animals: Nochal (big nose), Grzyb (mushroom), Zając (hare). The suffix *-ski* was often added to make a name sound more gentrified; for example, Kowalski from Kowal. Polish has lots of last names of foreign or unknown origin. The two most common Polish surnames, not to anyone's surprise, are Nowak and Kowalski. See also: **nazwiska polskie**.

Negri, Pola (1897–1987). The stage name of Barbara Apolonia Chałupiec, a sexy Polish film actress, later an international silent movie star in the United States and Germany. She was one of the richest Hollywood actresses of her day, and her name is inscribed on Hollywood's Walk of Fame. She named herself after the Italian poet Ada Negri. Pola Negri was linked romantically with Charlie Chaplin and Rudolph Valentino, and she caused a sensation in 1926 by repeatedly throwing herself on Valentino's coffin. Because of her strong Polish accent she had a difficult transition into talking movies, but still her last film role was in 1965.

"Nie chcem, ale muszem" (I don't want to, but I must). **Lech Wałęsa**'s explanation, written this way (*chcem, muszem* instead of the standard *chcę, muszę*) to convey his working-class accent, for why he was entering the 1990 presidential race, which the Nobel Prize–winning labor unionist later won. The statement is often reprised in Polish political commentary, most recently in describing **Jarosław Kaczyński**'s bid for the presidency in 2010. Another of Wałęsa's endearing quotations (similar to George Bushisms) was "Jestem za, a nawet przeciw" (I'm in favor of it, and even against it).

"Niech będzie pochwalony Jezus Chrystus!" (May Jesus Christ be praised!). An old phrase of greeting, now heard mostly among older people in the countryside or, mainly, in addressing or being addressed by priests, especially on a formal visit. The response is "Na wieki wieków! Amen" (World without end! Amen). Another religious greeting is "Szczęść Boże!" (Godspeed, or, May God favor your endeavors), addressed to persons in religious garb and, at least traditionally, also to a layperson who is performing honest work, to which the reply is "Daj Boże" (God willing), "Bóg zapłać" (May God reward you), or simply "Szczęść Boże" again. "Bóg zapłać" is also an appropriate response to a person who has made a contribution to the welfare of the church or a needy individual. "Z Bogiem" (Go with God) is a phrase of parting favored by some older people. The internet is full of lamentations about how these religiously tinged phrases are going out of use.

Niemczyk, Leon (1923–2006). One of Poland's and the world's most prolific film and television actors. He reputedly never turned down a role. During his nearly fifty-year career, he played in over four hundred Polish films and one hundred fifty foreign ones. Two of Niemczyk's most famous roles were as the passenger Jerzy in Jerzy Kawalerowicz's *Pociąg* (Night train, 1959), and as the overbearing journalist husband Andrzej in **Roman Polański**'s *Nóż w wodzie* (Knife in the water). During World War II Niemczyk served in the American army under General Patton. *Leon Niemczyk with Lucyna Winnicka in* Pociąg *(1959).*

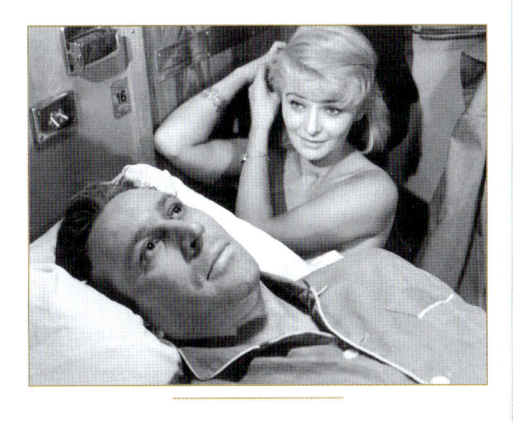

Niemen, Czesław (1939–2004). A vocalist and songwriter from the 1960s until his death from cancer at age sixty-five, Niemen is said to be Poland's most popular singer of all time. Born Czesław Wydrzycki, he took his stage name from the Niemen River in Belarus, near where he was born. Also an erstwhile painter, Niemen started out as a large-voiced rock singer and gradually transformed himself into a keyboard artist and singer of progressive jazz-rock, often putting poetry to music sung with his inimitable penetrating voice. Among his most popular songs were the 1960s-style protest song "Dziwny jest ten świat" (It's a strange world) and the country-and-western-style ballad "Czy mnie jeszcze pamiętasz?" (Do you still remember me?). Niemen sang the role of the *chochoł* (straw mulch) in **Andrzej Wajda**'s film *Wesele* (The wedding, 1972). *Czesław Niemen statue in Opole.*

Nike (Warsaw monument; book-of-the-year award). The Nike victory monument and statue (pictured) stands along the major Warsaw artery Trasa W-Z (W-Z Roadway). Erected in 1964 in a different location, it commemorates the heroes of Warsaw, 1939–1945. The annual Nike book award is funded and promoted by the newspaper *Gazeta Wyborcza* and its owner, the Agora Foundation, and is followed with great interest in the national press. Its aim is to select, in a three-

KALEIDOSCOPE OF POLAND 159

stage process, the best work of fiction from the previous year, with priority given to novels. The award has been in existence since 1997. Among its recipients have been Stanisław Barańczak, Dorota Masłowska, Czesław Miłosz, Jerzy Pilch, Tadeusz Różewicz, Tadeusz Słobodzianek, Olga Tokarczuk, and Joanna Bator.

Nikifor (1895–1968). An illiterate Łemko naïve painter from Krynica-Zdrój whose huge body of work (over forty thousand works in watercolor or colored chalk), featuring self-portraits, religious paintings, and buildings and life from around Krynica, Nikifor, born Epifaniusz Drowniak, became appreciated only over time. Deported from Krynica in 1947 in the course of *akcja Wisła*, he returned on his own and was allowed to stay after the third attempt. Living in abject poverty, he made a meager income by selling his paintings on the street to spa visitors. The painter Marian Włosiński, among others, helped to preserve Nikifor's heritage and to organize his triumphant exhibition in 1967 at the Zachęta art gallery in Warsaw. Many of Nikifor's works are preserved in museums in Nowy Sącz and Krynica. The film *Mój Nikifor* (My Nikifor, 2004) by Krzysztof Krauze, with the actress Krystyna Feldman brilliantly playing the title role, created a stir and brought the artist to broad public attention.

"Nil," Generał (General "Nile," Emil August Fieldorf, 1895–1953). A brigadier general and deputy commander of the Armia Krajowa (AK, Home Army) during the powstanie warszawskie (Warsaw Uprising), "Nile" began his military career as a corporal in the First Brigade (Pierwsza Brygada) under Józef Piłudski in World War II and later participated in the *wojna polsko-bolszewicka* (Polish-Bolshevik War) of 1919–1920. After the defeat of the Polish army in World War II, he escaped to France, was promoted to colonel, and was smuggled back into Poland as an emissary of the *rząd na uchodźstwie* (government in exile), taking the pseudonym "Nile" from the Egyptian river across which his roundabout journey led him. Following the end of the war he was living under an assumed name in Łódź when he was naïve enough to turn himself over to the communist authorities, who had proclaimed a fake amnesty for former members of the AK in 1948 (see *żołnierze wyklęci*). Imprisoned and tortured for five years before being executed in 1953 on preposterously trumped-up charges of collaborating with the Nazis, his sentence was upheld on appeal to Bolesław Bierut. His grave has never been discovered; see also Inka. The film *Generał Nil*, based on his life, appeared in 2009 and was directed by Ryszard Bugajski.

Nivea krem (Nivea Creme). One of the first cosmetic products to be marketed worldwide, and probably still the world's most widely recognized and used cosmetic, Nivea Creme was formulated by the Beiersdorf Company in Gliwice in 1911, and its formula has barely changed since. After World War II it was produced in Poland by Pollena-Lechia, and Poles would tell you that only its Nivea Creme was any good. This statement is less persuasive now that the Poznań-based company operates as a branch of the still-existing Bcicrsdorf Company, now headquartered in Hamburg, Germany.

Niżyński, Wacław (Vaslav Nijinsky, 1889 or 1890–1950). Few know that the legendary Russian ballet dancer and choreographer, born in Kyiv, Ukraine, was of Polish descent. His parents both graduated from Warsaw's ballet school, and he considered himself to be Polish, although most of the world knew him as Russian. Even though he spoke Polish poorly, he reportedly prayed only in that language. The most agile male dancer of his time, Niżyński toured in Sergey Diaghilev's renowned Ballets Russes and was famed for his leaps in the performance of *Le Spectre de la Rose*, in which he seemed to pause in midair. His sister Bronisława was a first-rate choreographer, also for Ballets Russes. Niżyński's career was cut short in 1919 by the onset of schizophrenia.

---

noc świętojańska (Saint John's Eve). Also *sobótka* (short Saturday) or *noc kupały* or *kupałnocka*. Celebrated on the shortest night of the year (the summer solstice), around June 24, the holiday is a relic of a pre-Christian fertility or premarriage rite subsequently taken over by the Christian Church and associated with John the Baptist. It was (and is) a way for young couples to get together. Bonfires are lit and jumped across. Unmarried women weave *wianki* (wreaths) as headdresses and later set them ablaze and floating down a river. People go into the woods in search of the legendary *kwiat paproci* (fern flower), said to bloom only on that night — or at least that is what they say they are doing. A fine literary rendition of the tradition is **Jan Kochanowski**'s long poem "Pieśń świętojańska o sobótce." Today larger Polish cities sponsor outdoor wianki festivals featuring concerts and fireworks. *Henryk Siemiradzki,* Noc Kupały *(ca. 1880).*

---

nomenklatura (high-ranking party officials). In the **PRL** (communist Poland), leadership positions in all branches of government and the economy, including education and culture, were held by Communist Party members who were "named" to these positions centrally from within the party. The word *nomenklatura* referred to the system of naming people to positions of leadership, and was later applied to the people themselves taken as an aggregate, especially the very top-ranking people. Those with high standing within the nomenklatura had access to special stores, clinics, and travel opportunities. Party members adopted from the Soviet Union the frequently mocked custom of addressing each other with the titles *towarzysz* (comrade), while addressing others as *obywatel* (citizen).

Norwid, Cyprian Kamil (1821–1883). An artist, sculptor, and post-Romantic poet. Misunderstood and unappreciated in his lifetime, Norwid was discovered by the poets and critics of **Młoda Polska** (Young Poland). He is considered the last of the great poets of Polish Romanticism, although thematically he stands outside that stream. He spent most of his life abroad and in poverty, and his last years in Paris as part of the **Wielka Emigracja** (Great Emigration). Besides lyric poetry, Norwid wrote longer narrative poems, dramas, and short stories. His most prodigious work, *Vade-mecum*, a compendium of nearly one hundred poems, was written between 1858 and 1865 and was only published in full nearly a hundred years after his death. Norwid was buried in a common pauper's grave in Paris. In 2001 an urn containing soil from that grave was placed in the Krypta wieszczów narodowych (Crypt of the National Bards) in Wawel Cathedral. *Norwid's statue in Lublin.*

Nowa Huta. A large-scale experiment in socially engineered housing in eastern Kraków built primarily in the years 1953–1956 next to a gigantic steel combine, at first named after Vladimir Lenin. Nowa Huta was conceived as a workers' paradise, built to rival nearby cosmopolitan Kraków with a combination of neo-Renaissance and modernistic styles, with ample space devoted to parks and entertainment centers. Its symmetrically radiating boulevards converged on a central plaza containing a statue of Lenin. The communist authorities had not planned for churches here, but they were ultimately unsuccessful in resisting popular sentiment. The modernistic church Arka Pana (the Lord's Ark, pictured), was finally dedicated in 1977, with Cardinal Karol Wojtyła, the future Pope Jan Paweł II, officiating. The district is now considered a monument worth restoring and maintaining in its own right, and it is gaining a reputation as a tourist attraction.

O

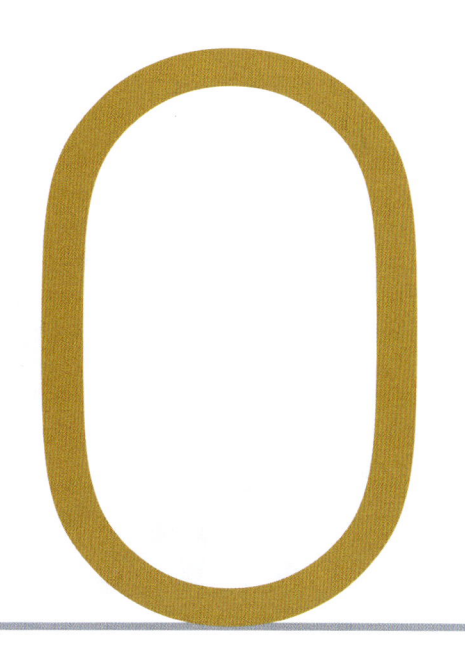

Obrona Poczty Polskiej w Gdańsku (Defense of the Gdańsk Post Office, 1939). In the early morning of September 1, 1939, as part of the opening German offensive on Poland, police and paramilitary units of the **Wolne Miasto Gdańsk** (Free City of Gdańsk) opened fire on the militarily insignificant Poczta Polska (Polish post office), demanding that the one hundred or so postal workers and guards leave. Instead, the guards and postal workers stubbornly proceeded to defend it with what few paltry weapons they had. The Germans brought in heavy artillery, explosives, and flame throwers, and by night the defenders had surrendered. Eight people died at the scene, and six more in excruciating pain from burn wounds over the next few days. Most of the rest were tried on trumped-up charges, convicted, executed, and buried in secret. Their mass grave was discovered by accident in 1991. *The building today.*

obwarzanek (Kraków bread ring). *Obwarzanki* come in four basic varieties: plain, salted, with poppy seeds, and with sesame seeds. A symbol of **Kraków** since the late Middle Ages, they are

163

mentioned as early as 1394 in the account books of King **Władysław II Jagiełło**. An edict of King Jan I Olbracht in 1496 granted Kraków bakers the exclusive right to produce and sell them. Today they are still made and sold primarily in Kraków by individual vendors from mobile stalls (pictured), which in Kraków are ubiquitous. About two hundred thousand are sold daily. Obwarzanki are bagel-shaped, and in fact the bagel (*bajgiel*) developed in parallel with the obwarzanek. In 2010 obwarzanki were declared a regional specialty by the European Union.

Ochotnicza Rezerwa Milicji Obywatelskiej (ORMO) (Volunteer Reserve of the Citizens' Militia). In the **PRL** (communist Poland) the police were called the **Milicja Obywatelska** (MO, citizens' militia) to avoid connection with the prewar *policja*. ORMO was a supposedly volunteer paramilitary reserve unit of the MO used for putting down riots with water cannons, tear gas, and truncheons. It was under the direct control of the Komitet Centralny (Central Committee) of the Communist Party but in fact had no legal standing when it violently intervened in student protests at Warsaw University in *marzec 1968* (the "March events"). After that, a statute was rapidly passed to legalize ORMO. A parallel organization to ORMO was **Zmotoryzowane Odwody Milicji Obywatelskiej (ZOMO)**, under the control of the Polish premier. ORMO helmets (pictured), notable for their primitive lettering, are now a prized camp fashion accessory, occasionally appearing at flea markets and militaria stores and on websites.

ochrona, agencja ochrony, firma ochroniarska (security service). A growth industry in Poland, suggesting that burglary and theft, too, are on the rise, even if statistics suggest otherwise. More than twelve thousand companies in Poland offer security services for protecting home, person, and property, and the sight of uniformed security personnel in stores and on the street with "ochrona" (security) written across their backs is universal, as are the signs announcing that a given property is *pod ochroną*, "protected." Some security services in remote areas have the reputation of being protection rackets: either you sign up with them or your house gets burglarized. *Sign of the Pogoń (Knight in Chase) security service.*

oczepiny (capping ceremony). In a wedding custom mostly gone out of practice, the *wesele* (wedding party) would start out at the cottage of the *panna młoda* (bride). Around midnight the bride would be taken by the married women into a side room to have her wreath removed and her maidenly *warkocze* (braids) shorn. An elaborately embroidered *czepiec* (cap) would be pinned to her shortened hair, a sign of her married status. The ceremony was accompanied by mostly humorous *przyśpiewki* (ditties) appropriate to the occasion, often with a sexual subtext, sung by the women. The custom today is for the bride to toss her veil or wedding bouquet, and the groom his tie, to the eligible women and men of the party respectively, a ceremony sometimes preceded by silly games and competitions.

Odra (German: Oder). A river in west Poland with its source in the Czech Republic. The second-longest Polish river (counting its Czech part) at 854.3 kilometers, it flows through **Opole** and **Wrocław** and enters the **Bałtyk** near **Szczecin**. The destructive Odra floods of 1997, which inundated entire towns and villages, are still remembered. The Oder-Neisse Line, formed primarily by the Odra and Nysa Łużycka (Lusatian Nysa) rivers, demarcates today's boundary between Poland and Germany, as demanded by Joseph Stalin at the Potsdam Conference of 1945. It was not recognized by East Germany until 1950, and not by the West German government at all, although German chancellor Willi Brandt, in accordance with his *Ostpolitik*, gave it lip service in 1970. Following the reunification of East and West Germany in 1990, Poland and Germany signed a treaty finalizing the Oder-Neisse Line as the border between them.

---

odsiecz wiedeńska (Relief of Vienna). In one of Poland's most glorious military victories, on September 11, 1683 (the "other" 9/11) King **Jan III Sobieski** came to the relief of Vienna, which had been under siege by the Turkish army under Pasha Kara Mustafa for two months. Sobieski stood at the head of an army of some seventy to eighty thousand Polish, Austrian, and German troops. The victorious battle included the largest cavalry charge in history, and it marked the end of the Ottoman Empire's westward expansion, at the same time giving impetus to the rise of the Habsburg monarchy. A major Polish-Italian cinematic coproduction, *September 11, 1683*, with Jerzy Skolimowski in the role of Jan III Sobieski, was released in September 2012, but was broadly panned.

---

odwilż gomułkowska, październik 1956 (Gomułka Thaw, October 1956). The "October events," often referred to simply as *październik* (October), refers to the liberalization of government policies following the death of Joseph Stalin in the Soviet Union in 1953 and, especially, following the June 1956 events in **Poznań** (*czerwiec 1956, wypadki czerwcowe*); that is, vast workers' strikes and street protests giving vent to increasing frustration over the economic situation. The most immediate outcome of the October events was the election of the supposedly liberal **Władysław "Wiesław" Gomułka** as first Party secretary, replacing Edward Ochab, who briefly held the role following the mysterious death of **Bolesław Bierut** in the Soviet Union. Momentarily, there was a relaxation of censorship, and many political prisoners were released from prison. The notorious Jakub Berman, de facto head of the Stalinist secret police, was removed from his position on the Politbiuro, and his entire ministry was disbanded and reorganized.

---

odzież na wagę (clothes by weight). A loosely connected network of stores in Poland that deals in inexpensive clothing primarily imported from Western Europe and the United States, whether *odzież używana* (used — but clean — clothing) or discontinued or overstock styles, and sells it by the kilogram. One picks through piles of clothing, chooses what one wants, and pays according to how much the selection weighs. If one is patient enough, one can find real bargains in such stores, along with a lot of junk. Going treasure-hunting at various kinds of cheap or secondhand outlets is referred to as *chodzenie na ciuchy* (going rag-picking), whence the slang word for referring to such stores, *ciucholand* (ragland), originated. They became popular among the poor in the 1990s but show no sign of losing popularity as Poland prospers. On the contrary, they are increasingly frequented by students and the "artsy" crowd.

---

ogrody zoologiczne (zoos). Poland boasts some fourteen major zoos. An intimation of the Polish fascination with zoos can be gleaned from **Sławomir Mrożek**'s short story "Słoń" (The elephant), in which an ambitious zoo director decides to economize by constructing an inflatable elephant, only to see it fly away. The **Poznań** zoo has Europe's largest elephant house, while **Wrocław**'s has around six hundred species of vertebrates, more than practically any other zoo in the world. The lives of the Wrocław animals were recounted for over thirty years by Hanna and Antoni Gucwiński in their TV program *Z kamerą wśród zwierząt* (Camera among the animals). During World War II the more desirable Warsaw zoo animals were transported to Germany, while the rest were "executed" by German soldiers in a shooting spree on New Year's Eve, 1939. The zoo director Jan Żabiński and his wife Antonina remained in place and provided shelter on zoo property to some three hundred Jews in hiding, for which action they received, in 1965, the title of Righteous among Nations. Their story was told in Diane Ackerman's bestselling book *The Zookeeper's Wife* (2007).

---

ogród jordanowski, park jordanowski (Jordan park, children's urban park and playground). The brainchild of gynecologist and social activist Henryk Jordan (1847–1907) of **Krakow**. In the spirit of late *pozytywizm* Jordan founded and propagated the idea of large forested urban play and exercise areas for promoting the physical culture and health of inner-city youth, a concept unique in Europe at the time. The original Jordan park from 1889 is in Kraków, but they spread to other cities throughout Galicia and elsewhere. They caught on especially well in Warsaw, where essentially every *dzielnica* (town district) has what are called *ogrody jordanowskie*, even if most are reduced in size and resemble conventional playgrounds.

Okrągły Stół, rozmowy Okrągłego Stołu (Round Table Discussions, 1989). A wave of strikes in February–April 1988, and then later that summer, persuaded the Polish government to hold "round table" discussions in Warsaw with leaders of the political opposition and the trade union **Solidarność** (Solidarity), in order to hammer out mechanisms for introducing political reform. Participants included the leading politicians and activists of the day, along with observers from the Church. Talks were literally held around a large round table (pictured). As a result of the discussions, a bicameral legislature and the office of president were created (actually, reintroduced). It became easier to register non-governmental organizations (including Solidarność), and the opposition was guaranteed access to the media, including the right to establish its own newspaper, *Gazeta Wyborcza* (Electoral gazette).

Olbrychski, Daniel (b. 1945). Since 1963, one of Poland's most prolific stage and, especially, film actors, with over one hundred film credits to his name, usually in leading roles. He came to broad public attention for his portrayal of Hamlet in **Adam Hanuszkiewicz**'s 1970 production. Olbrychski is a skilled fencer and horseman, and played most of his own stunt scenes in his many swashbuckling roles; see **Kmicic, Andrzej**. On November 17, 2000, he reprised his swordfighting talents when he slipped a saber past a guard at the **Zachęta** art gallery and slashed his own photographic likeness portraying a Nazi army officer. He is a particular favorite of **Andrzej Wajda** and has appeared in around a dozen of his films. He has played in a number of foreign films, recently as a Russian spymaster opposite Angelina Jolie in *Salt* (2010). He plays **Józef Piłsudski** in Jerzy Hoffman's 2011 film *Bitwa Warszawska 1920* (Battle of Warsaw 1920). Olbrychski has received the French Legion of Honor (1986) and the Stanislavski Award at the Moscow International Film Festival (2007) for his lifetime devotion to the principles of the Stanislavskian acting method.

Olewnik, Krzysztof. The kidnapping and murder of Krzysztof Olewnik is a case that will not die, even though its namesake did. On the night of October 26, 2001, Olewnik, the son of a **Płock** industrialist, was kidnapped, and a $300,000 ransom was demanded. Later, reflecting the weakening dollar, the demand was changed to 300,000 euros. Despite the ransom having been paid, Olewnik was murdered on September 5, 2003. In a saga playing out ever since then, kept alive by the persistence of the Olewnik family, three people implicated in the crime have died in prison, officially by their own hand, giving rise to various conspiracy theories, continually rekindled in the press because of events such as the theft of police records and computer files, new witnesses, the discovery of previously unnoticed blood stains, and so on. Because of the shoddiness of the official investigation and the incompetence of various penal institutions, the minister of justice Zbigniew Ćwiąkalski was forced to resign.

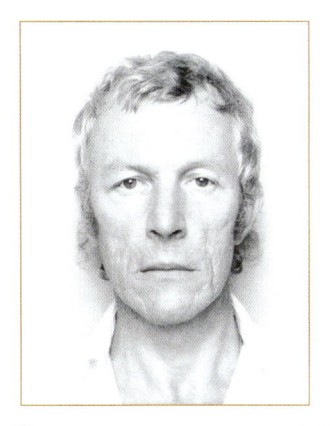

Opałka, Roman (1931–2011). A French-born conceptual artist of Polish parentage whose family returned to Poland in 1935 only to be deported by the Nazis. After the war he returned to Poland and studied art in **Łódź** and Warsaw, where, in 1965, he began his life's project: meticulously painting with a tiny brush numbers in serial from 1 to a projected infinity, on 4′ × 6′ canvases. Opałka continued his project in France, speaking each number in Polish into a recorder upon painting it, and taking his snapshot against the background of each successively completed canvas. His numbers were in white, painted on a background that, with each canvas, turned a successively lighter shade of gray. He estimated that he would be painting totally white on white (possibly signifying his personal oblivion) by the number 7777777 (he eschewed punctuation) and he had passed 5500000 at the time of this death. Just months before, he had received the Cavalier's Cross of the Order of the Rebirth of Poland (Order Odrodzenia Polski) from President **Bronisław Komorowski**.

Operacja Polska NKWD (Operation Poland NKVD, 1937–1938). In an ethnic-cleansing action little known in the West, as part of Joseph Stalin's Great Terror, in 1937 the NKVD (Soviet "security" services) received the order to murder, imprison, or deport essentially every person of Polish nationality, of whatever age, denomination, profession, or political persuasion, living in Belarus or Soviet Russia. Having a Polish surname condemned a person to death, as the NKVD calmly leafed through telephone books in order to identify victims. Polish prisoners of war remaining from the *wojna polsko-bolszewicka* of 1920–1921 were summarily shot. In the end, over one hundred thousand Poles were murdered; thirty thousand were sent to the **Gułag** (itself a kind of death sentence), and another hundred thousand were exiled, mainly to Kazakhstan and Siberia. Operacja Polska, a clear-cut instance of genocide, took more than ten times the number of lives than did the better-remembered, equally cold-blooded **Katyń** massacre of Polish army officers by the NKVD in 1940.

Opole. The historical capital of Górny Śląsk (Upper Silesia), and presently the capital of the *województwo opolskie*, Poland's smallest voivodeship. Located on the **Odra** (Oder) River, Opole has nearly 126,000 inhabitants and the highest density of ethnic Germans in Poland, one of the reasons why the voivodeship has not been merged into neighboring ones. Its earliest mention is in the ninth century, but archaeological records trace its beginnings to the eighth century. Over the centuries the territory around Opole has alternately been Polish, Czech, or German. It remained in Germany following World War I, but was ceded to Poland in 1945 at the Potsdam Conference. The Polish and German populations were so intermixed here that Germans were not routinely expelled after the war, as happened in Dolny Śląsk (Lower Silesia). Recently, bilingual toponymical signs in Polish and German have appeared. Opole's Krajowy Festiwal Piosenki Polskiej (National Festival of Polish Song), one aim of which was to put a stamp of Polishness on the town, has run since 1963.

Order Uśmiechu (Order of the Smile). An international medal that originated in Poland in 1968, presented to people who have made a significant positive contribution to children's well-being. The Chapter of the Order of the Smile is an independent, nonsectarian, nongovernmental organization with headquarters in Świdnica. Two awards are given per year. Among the recipients have been Pope **Jan Paweł II**, Mother Teresa, the Dalai Lama, Sarah Ferguson, Oprah Winfrey, Nelson Mandela, and **Irena Sendlerowa**.

Order Virtuti Militari (Order of Military Merit, pictured). Poland's highest strictly military honor, awarded for bravery in battle. Established in 1792 by King **Stanisław August Poniatowski**, it is the world's oldest military decoration still in use today. Other important Polish orders are the Order Orła Białego (Order of the White Eagle, 1705), awarded for service to the state, and the Order Odrodzenia Polski (Order of the Rebirth of Poland, 1921), awarded to outstanding members of the arts, sciences, culture, and sport.

Ordon, Julian (1810–1887). An officer in the **powstanie listopadowe** (November Uprising) of 1830–1831, immortalized in a poem by **Adam Mickiewicz** for ordering his artillery battery to blow up his redoubt rather than surrender it to the Russians. Mickiewicz has Ordon's redoubt parting the waves of enemy soldiers "jak głaz bodzący morze" (as a boulder butts apart the sea), a metaphor for blind steadfast resistance that has made it into common parlance. Mickiewicz assumed that Ordon blew himself up as well, but in fact he emigrated to Scotland and later participated in various military conflicts across Europe, eventually taking his own life in Florence in 1887. Mickiewicz's lofty poem should be read in combination with **Sławomir Mrożek**'s parodical re-creation of the event in the short play *Śmierć porucznika* (Death of a lieutenant). Mickiewicz himself, having been outside the country, never witnessed the November Uprising personally.

Ordonówna, Hanka (1902–1950). Stage name of Maria Anna Tyszkiewicz (née Petruszyńska), nicknamed Ordonka. Hanka Ordonówna was a cabaret singer and movie actress in the 1920s–1930s with an unforgettable Mae West vamp style. During World War II, along with many Poles who found themselves in the *kresy* (eastern borderlands), she was deported to the Soviet Union, where she worked on behalf of Polish war orphans. She ended up leaving Russia with General **Władysław Anders**'s army and found herself after the war in Lebanon, where she died of tuberculosis. Her remains were transferred to Warsaw's Powązki Cemetery. Ordonówna's signature song was "Miłość ci wszystko wybaczy" (Love will forgive everything), from the movie *Szpieg w masce* (Spy in the mask, 1933). Its key lines: "Miłość ci wszystko wybaczy / Bo miłość, mój miły, to ja!" (Love will forgive you everything / Because love, my dear, is I!). Among traditional songs she sang that are still remembered are "O mój rozmarynie" (Oh, my rosemary), "Rozkwitały pęki białych róż" (Bunches of white roses bloomed), and "Ułani, ułani" (Ulans).

ordynacja (landed property entailed to a given family line). A principle established in the late sixteenth century by King **Stefan Batory** as a means of maintaining the integrity of large landed estates in the **Rzeczpospolita Obojga**

Narodów (Polish-Lithuanian Commonwealth). Under *ordynacja*, landed property could only be passed down to a single male heir according to the principle of primogeniture (that is, to the eldest male offspring). Property under ordynacja could not be mortgaged or sold. Ordynacja was the basis of the accumulation of wealth of many members of the Polish-Lithuanian *magnateria* (magnates), including the **Radziwiłł**, **Zamoyski**, **Czartoryski**, **Potocki** and **Lubomirski** families. The issue of ordynacja was at the heart of the plot of the potboiler novel *Trędowata* (The leper, 1909), by Helena Mniszkówna.

organy w Oliwie (Oliwa organ). An immense one-off baroque organ with moving figures, one of the most valuable organs in Europe. It was completed in 1763–1788 by Johann Wilhelm Wulff, a Cistercian monk, for the basilica in Oliwa (next to **Gdańsk**). With some 5,100 pipes (the longest one at ten meters), ninety-six registers, and five keyboards, it puts out a monumental sound as twenty-nine of its forty carved figures move and pretend to be playing instruments, while the sun shines and stars twinkle overhead. For all that, the Oliwa organ is not Poland's largest — that would be in social-climbing **Licheń**. The Oliwa organ was renovated in 1966–1968 to be concertworthy, and it can be heard among other times during the Oliwa Cathedral's long-running International Festival of Organ Music.

Orle Gniazda (Eagles' Nests). A line of twenty-five medieval castles erected on rocky promontories (like nests of eagles) running between **Kraków** and **Częstochowa** along the western border of the Królestwo Polskie (Polish Kingdom) by **Kazimierz III Wielki** (Kazimierz the Great) to guard against the Czechs and, farther north, the Germans. They run in a curving line from **Wawel** castle in Kraków as far as Olsztyn near Częstochowa in the north. Today, except for Pieskowa Skała (Dog's Rock), which is near Kraków and was remodeled in the sixteenth century as a Renaissance-style residence, they consist of picturesque ruins. The largest, most picturesque, and most visitable of Polish medieval castle ruins is Ogrodzieniec (pictured), located halfway between Kraków and Częstochowa. It was the backdrop for **Andrzej Wajda**'s film *Zemsta* (Revenge, 2002). A bicycle and hiking trail connecting the castles — in need of much better signage — runs for 188 kilometers.

Orlen, afera Orlenu (Orlen Affair). Orlen — the full name of which is Polski Koncern Naftowy SA (Polish Petroleum Concern, Inc.) — is a Polish oil refiner and retailer with headquarters in **Płock** and is central Europe's largest publicly-traded commercial entity. The name Orlen is a fusion of the word *orli* (eagle's) and the segment *en* (for *energia*, energy). The biggest political corruption scandal in recent Polish history was the *afera Orlenu* (Orlen affair), sometimes called Orlengate, which broke in 2004 out of the reporting of the newspaper *Gazeta Wyborcza*. It concerned allegations of interference and back-room dealing on the part of members of the postcommunist administration of President **Aleksander Kwaśniewski** and Premier Leszek Miller in the running of the Orlen oil company. As the affair widened, a year long special investigatory committee of the Polish **Sejm RP** was convened, but eventually fizzled out without proving anything.

ORMO. See **Ochotnicza Rezerwa Milicji Obywatelskiej** (**ORMO**).

Orzeł Biały (white eagle). The Polish national coat of arms (pictured) consists of a left-facing white crowned eagle on a red shield background. Tradition traces it to **Lech**, the legendary founder of the Polanian state. During the **PRL** (communist Poland) the eagle did not have a crown. The crown returned in 1989. The Order Orła Białego (Order of the White Eagle), established in 1705 during the reign of August II Mocny (August the Strong), is Poland's oldest and highest state honor.

Orzeszkowa, Eliza (1841–1910). A late nineteenth-century novelist and short story writer, one of the "triumvirate of Polish Positivists," along with **Bolesław Prus** and **Henryk Sienkiewicz**. Orzeszkowa was a finalist for the 1905 Nobel Prize in Literature alongside the eventual winner, Sienkiewicz. Her novels take the side of the socially downtrodden, disadvantaged, and discarded of humanity. She championed the cause of sympathy and equal rights for the Jews, and she campaigned tirelessly for the emancipation of women. Throughout her life she was an activist in many charitable and philanthropic causes. The novel for which she is best remembered is *Nad Niemnem* (On the Niemen), concerning the failed **powstanie styczniowe** (January Uprising of 1863) and its aftermath on a family of country petty gentry. A film version of the novel was directed by Zbigniew Kuźmiński in 1986.

oscypek, oszczypek. A symbol of the Polish **Podhale** (High Tatra) region, *oscypki* (in Góral dialect) are spindle-shaped smoked cheeses usually made of salted sheep's milk, to which a small amount of cow's milk may be added. They

KALEIDOSCOPE OF POLAND 171

are formed in molds with geometrical patterns and sold throughout Poland, but especially in the south, mainly at outdoor stalls. The cheese lends itself to frying or grilling. In former times oscypki were used as a kind of currency. They are registered with the European Union as a regional specialty and may be produced only in designated localities from specified ingredients using particular methods.

Osiecka, Agnieszka (1936–1997). One of the most versatile talents on the Polish postwar cultural scene, Osiecka was a poet, playwright, children's author, journalist, world traveler, essayist, television and stage director, and more. She is best remembered by the public at large as the author of over two thousand popular songs sung by a wide range of artists, including **Marek Grechuta**, **Maryla Rodowicz**, and Kora of **Maanam i Kora**. At different stages in her career she was romantically involved with the writer **Marek Hłasko**, the entertainer Jeremi Przybora, and the journalist Daniel Passent. A book of her correspondence with Przybora was published recently. Her daughter Agata Passent established the Okularnicy (People Who Wear Glasses) Foundation, named after one of Osiecka's songs, to help conserve her legacy. As a footnote to her multifaceted career, in 1972 Osiecka won a contest for coming up with a catchy Polish version of the slogan "Coke is it!": "Coca-Cola — to jest to!"

---

osiedla strzeżone (guarded or gated communities). Individual houses in Poland are almost always surrounded by a sturdy fence, with a locked gate, often a snarling dog behind it, and a display sign from a *firma ochroniarska* (security service; see ***ochrona***). A phenomenon of the last twenty years has been the rise in and around larger cities of entire communities of "luxury homes" — whether self-standing, duplexes, or townhouses — accessed through a guarded gate and inhabited by the comparatively well-to-do. When placed in the middle of a city, such communities pose major problems for getting from one place to another, especially for pedestrians. Rules outlawing such pastimes as outdoor barbecuing or playing noisy street games can make life pleasant for adults seeking a peaceful haven in an urban setting, but miserable for youngsters whose natural urge is to run around and make noise.

---

osobliwości przyrodnicze (curiosities of nature). On anyone's short list of natural curiosities in Poland are: the Maczuga Herkulesa (Hercules' Cudgel), a striking rock formation in the shape of a gigantic club in Ojców National Park above **Kraków**; Jaskinia Niedźwiedzia (Bear's Cavern), Poland's largest natural visitable cave, located in the **Sudety** (Sudeten Mountains), discovered only in 1966; the Krzywy Las (crooked forest), a stand of some four hundred pine trees in western Pomerania growing with big bends in their trunks (pictured), presumably planted and trained that way by some unknown forester in the 1930s (although some do not preclude a natural explanation); and the Pustynia Błędowska

172 KALEIDOSCOPE OF POLAND

(Błędów Desert), a sizable (32 sq km) patch of shifting sands up to seventy meters deep, located in Upper Silesia. Known as the "Polish Sahara," the *pustynia* was used by Germany in World War II as a training ground to prepare for the North African Campaign.

Ossolineum, Zakład Narodowy imienia Ossolińskich (Ossoliński National Institute). A major Polish scientific and cultural center founded in 1817 by Józef Maksymilian Ossoliński in Lwów (now Ukrainian L'viv). Its immense holdings were second in Poland only to those of the Uniwersytet Jagielloński in Kraków. Many of its most priceless collections were saved from Soviet confiscation by being confiscated and evacuated by the retreating Germans in World War II. A large portion of what remained, including the most complete collection of the Polish press of the nineteenth and twentieth centuries, was kept in Ukraine and was either intentionally destroyed in a campaign to eradicate traces of Polish presence in the area or remains there. In 1947 the Ossolineum was reconstituted as a library and publishing house in Wrocław, much of the prewar population of Lwów having been resettled to Wrocław after the war. The prestigious Ossolineum press specializes in the humanities and natural sciences. *Headquarters of the Ossolineum in Wrocław.*

ostatki (Shrovetide, Carnival). *Ostatki* are the last days of *karnawał* (Carnival, formerly *zapusty*), a traditional time for feasts, parties, and masked balls, lasting from *tłusty czwartek* (Fat Thursday) to the following Tuesday, which in Poland is called *śledzik* (herring day). Tłusty czwartek is associated with eating *pączki* (jelly- or crème-filled doughnuts, pictured) and *chrusty/chruściki/faworki*, a pastry made from fried dough. Pączki-eating contests and prizes for the best pączki are held. After ostatki falls the somber *Środa Popielcowa* or *Popielec* (Ash Wednesday), on which one goes to church to have one's forehead sprinkled with ashes as a sign of penance, followed by *Wielki Post* (Lent) and the forty-day wait for Wielkanoc (Easter).

Ostra Brama (Sharp Gate). The old city gate of Wilno (now Lithuanian Vilnius), next to which stands the Kaplica Ostrobramska (Ostra Brama Chapel), containing the richly decorated icon of the Matka Boska Ostrobramska (Mother of God of Ostra Brama, pictured), according to legend modeled after the future Polish queen Barbara Radziwiłłówna (ca. 1523–1551), a renowned beauty. The icon is said to be more private and approachable than the Matka Boska Częstochowska (Mother of God of Częstochowa), because with the latter icon the baby Jesus, carried in his mother's arms, can eavesdrop. **Adam Mickiewicz** alludes to the healing powers of the icon in the opening stanzas of *Pan Tadeusz* (Master Thaddeus):

> Jak mnie dziecko do zdrowia powróciłaś cudem, . . .
> Tak nas powrócisz cudem na Ojczyzny łono
>
> As you returned me as a child to health with a miracle, . . .
> So also, with a miracle, you will return us to the bosom of our Fatherland.

---

oświecenie (Enlightenment). The Enlightenment arrived later in Poland than elsewhere, and lasted longer, into the 1820s. In art and architecture it followed classical models. Unlike the French Enlightenment's anticlericalism, leading Polish exponents were precisely the clergy, foremost being the archbishop poet **Ignacy Krasicki**. The Polish Enlightenment was utilitarian, concerned with political and educational reform, and was supported by the monarch **Stanisław II August Poniatowski**. The political trend bore fruit in the **Konstytucja 3 maja** (May 3, 1791, Constitution), with leading supporters being the Jesuit priests Stanisław Staszic, Franciszek Bohomolec, and Hugo Kołłątaj (pictured). The educational trend led to the creation of the **Komisja Edukacji Narodowej** (Commission of National Education, 1773). The first Polish newspaper, the *Monitor*, began publishing in 1765, and a national theater was developed under Wojciech Bogusławski. At Wilno University, the Śniadecki brothers, Jan (in astronomy, mathematics, and philosophy) and Jędrzej (in chemistry), helped advance these fields while developing a Polish scientific vocabulary.

Oświęcim (German: Auschwitz). A town in southern Poland numbering around 40,200 inhabitants, Oświęcim is located at the point where the Soła River joins the **Wisła**, about fifty kilometers west of **Kraków**. It traces its history to the twelfth century. During World War II Oświęcim was the site of the infamous complex of German Nazi *obozy koncentracyjne* (concentration camps) and *obozy zagłady* (extermination camps) known as Auschwitz-Birkenau, at which more than a million people died, most of them in *komory gazowe* (gas chambers), others from medical experiments, beatings, or executions. Ninety percent were Jews. The camp, notorious among other things for the proclamation above the entrance, "Arbeit macht frei" (Work makes one free, pictured), was liberated by the Soviet army in 1945. Today it houses a museum visited by nearly one million people yearly, the heavy tourist traffic contributing to the site's slow deterioration. It is a UNESCO World Heritage Site.

owczarek podhalański (**Podhale** sheepdog). If there is a national dog in Poland, it is this large winterized breed of mountain sheepdog, registered with the Federation Cynologique Internationale (FCI, International Canine Association). Other registered breeds are the *polski owczarek nizinny* (Polish lowland sheepdog, a breed also registered with the American Kennel Club); the *ogar polski* (Polish hound), *chart polski* (Polish greyhound), and the *gończy polski* (Polish hunting dog). By reputation the Podhale sheepdog is smart, docile, and protective. It is in danger of being overbred. One finds its pups for sale in boxes on the streets of **Zakopane**.

P

paczki żywnościowe (food packages). Following World War II, the United States government and the relief organization CARE (Cooperative for Assistance and Relief Everywhere) organized a massive food-relief effort for Europe. Some other countries did the same, sending food, clothing, and other necessities. The effort was not merely symbolic, as communist propaganda held, but of genuine material assistance. Poles abroad continued to send *paczki żywnościowe* to relatives in Poland through the 1980s. Nowadays commercial enterprises in Poland arrange for Polish paczki żywnościowe to be sent to relatives outside the country as a reminder of what real food is like. The Catholic charitable organization Caritas distributes paczki żywnościowe to the Polish needy. Since 2001 the Wiosna (Spring) organization, under the banner Szlachetna Paczka (Noble Package, logo pictured), has raised money and identified needy families in order to send them packages for the holidays.

Paderewski, Ignacy Jan (1860–1941). A composer and concert pianist on the international stage in the latter nineteenth century and

early twentieth century, Paderewski traveled extensively in the United States and took up residence there for a while. He composed the music for the opera *Manru*, based on a novel by **Józef Ignacy Kraszewski**, the only Polish opera thus far to have been performed at New York's Metropolitan Opera. Paderewski also played an important role as a national politician and international spokesman for Poland. He was the Polish premier in 1919 and one of Poland's two representatives (alongside **Roman Dmowski**) at the konferencja wersalska (Versailles Conference; see *traktat wersalski*) in 1919–1920. Twenty years later he took a leading role in the *rząd na uchodźstwie* (government in exile) in London.

———

pakt Ribbentrop-Mołotow (Molotov-Ribbentrop Nonaggression Pact). A nonaggression treaty signed on August 23, 1939, between Germany and the Soviet Union (just prior to Germany's invasion of Poland), a *tajny protokół* (secret protocol) that divided Eastern Europe into spheres of influence between the two countries. Sometimes referred to as the "fourth partition of Poland," the pact in effect gave Germany the go-ahead to attack and occupy Poland, at first as far as the **Wisła** but eventually up to a line renegotiated to match more or less the current border in the east with Lithuania, Belarus, and Ukraine (in general outline, the **linia Curzona**, or Curzon Line), while the eastern Polish territories, the so-called *kresy wschodnie*, were "ceded" by Germany to the Soviet Union, which invaded them on September 17. The pact was modified on September 28 in a document specifying borders and proclaiming mutual friendship — not that that friendship lasted very long.

———

palenie papierosów (cigarette smoking). Government statistics say it all. It is estimated that 33.5 percent of men and 21 percent of women in Poland are daily smokers of *tytoń* (tobacco). Around eight to nine million Poles smoke between fifteen and twenty cigarettes per day. Minors under the age of eighteen alone are said to consume three to four billion cigarettes yearly. Around one hundred thousand deaths per year can be directly attributed to smoking. Average life expectancy in Poland is currently 72.3 years for men and 80.4 for women. Compared to this, 40 percent of habitual smokers die before the age of sixty-five. Strange statistics for a country whose unofficial motto is "Zdrowie jest najważniejsze" (Health is the most important). As elsewhere, today's cigarette packs carry dire health warnings such as "Palacze umierają młodziej" (Smokers die younger). Since 2010 it is not permitted to smoke in offices, restaurants, and other public indoor places.

———

palma wielkanocna (Easter palm). Easter palms, carried in procession on Niedziela Palmowa (Palm Sunday) the week before **Wielkanoc** (Easter), can be quite elaborate. They are woven not from palm leaves but from willow or other sprigs, cut on Środa Popielcowa (Ash Wednesday) and kept in water so as to bud on Palm Sunday. Native grasses and paper flowers are added to the mixture. The weaving of elaborate Easter palms is a living folk tradition in many parts of Poland, where some believe them to have curative powers. Sometimes after their use they are returned to the church, burned, and their ashes used for the following year's Ash Wednesday. Some villages hold contests for the tallest and prettiest "palms."

———

Pałac Kultury i Nauki w Warszawie (PKiN, Palace of Culture and Science in Warsaw). Originally named after Soviet leader Joseph Stalin, it is the tallest building in Poland at forty-two stories and 231 meters high. An observation point on the thirtieth floor provides a fine view of the city. The PKiN was built on the cleared-out ruins of bombed-out downtown Warsaw in 1952–1955 by Soviet architects and some 3,500 Russian laborers, the "gift of the Soviet people" to the people of Poland. It is an example of the Soviet Gothic style (reaching for the sky), and its exterior boasts monumental examples of socialist-realist sculpture. The building houses theaters, cinemas, restaurants, bookstores, public institutions, a museum of technology, and many private offices. The enormous Sala Kongresowa (Congress Hall) holds up to three thousand people. Older Poles resent the building as a reminder of past Soviet oppression, while it finds more acceptance among the younger generation who grew up with it.

pan, pani, państwo (sir, madam, ladies and gentlemen). In addressing an adult with whom one is not familiar, one automatically uses the titles *pan* (mister, sir) and *pani* (madam, lady). Upon greater familiarity, one may use *pan* and *pani* with one's *imię* (first name): pan Wacław, pani Zofia. Use of *pan* and *pani* with the **nazwisko** (surname) is stiff and formal. The customs and justification for going over to a first-name basis, or *mówienie po imieniu*, with a person, not using any title and using the first name and the intimate pronoun *ty*, are extremely subtle, and cannot be described in a brief article; see *bruderszaft*. It is best to leave the choice to a Pole steeped in the culture, and even they may have hesitation. The title *państwo* is the plural of *pan* and *pani*, and it also means "Mr. and Mrs." Using *panna* (miss) to refer to an unmarried woman has all but gone out of use; *pani* is used instead. See also: **tytułowanie**.

Pan Tadeusz (Master Thaddeus). The title and title character of **Adam Mickiewicz**'s light epic poem in thirteen-syllable verse (Polish Alexandrine), published in 1834 and justifiably referred to as the "Polish national epic." In it, two families in "Lithuania," the Horeszkowie and Soplicowie, battle over the ownership of a tumbledown castle but are reconciled when the respective female and male heirs fall in love. Action takes place against a background of preparations for Napoleon's invasion of Russia in 1812. It is a shame that this work of true genius can be properly appreciated only in Polish. A largely successful film version of the novel was made in 1999 by **Andrzej Wajda**. Polish schoolchildren learn the *inwokacja* (invocation) to *Pan Tadeusz* by heart, beginning: "Litwo! Ojczyzno moja! ty jesteś jak zdrowie. / Ile cię trzeba cenić, ten tylko się dowie, Kto cię stracił" (Lithuania! My fatherland! You are like health. / Only one who has lost you will learn how much you should be valued). For Mickiewicz, Litwa (Lithuania) was a historical region, the land of his childhood, rather than a linguistic or political entity.

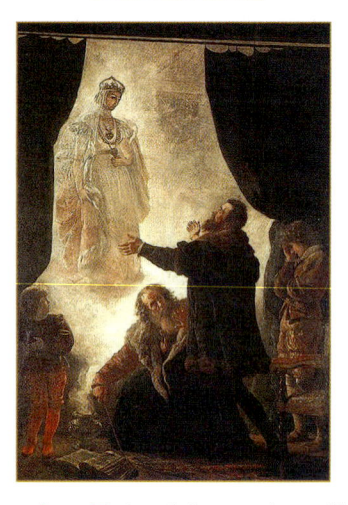

Pan Twardowski. A Polish Faust legend based on the real figure of a sixteenth-century alche-

178 KALEIDOSCOPE OF POLAND

mist, Jan Twardowski, attached to the court of King Zygmunt II August. Twardowski used a magic mirror to call up the king's dead wife, Barbara Radziwiłłówna. According to legend he had signed a pact with the devil in exchange for his magical powers, agreeing to hand over his soul in Rome, where he had no intention of going. However, one day the devil caught up with him carousing at a local *karczma* (tavern) named Rzym (Rome). According to Adam Mickiewicz's version, Twardowski had included in the pact a stipulation that the devil first had to spend a year with Twardowski's wife. When reminded of this clause, the devil quietly slipped away. Twardowski himself escaped on a rooster to the moon, from where he sends down a spider (actually, a friend of his whom he turned into a spider) on long strands to listen in on people's gossip. With a friend like Twardowski, who needs enemies? *Wojciech Gerson,* Barbara Radziwiłłówna's Ghost.

Panorama Racławicka (*Racławice Panorama*). A monumental (114 meters long by 15 meters high) panorama (a circular painting with an eerie 3D effect) re-creating the *bitwa pod Racławicami* (Battle of Racławice, 1794; see Racławice) during the insurekcja kościuszkowska (Kościuszko Insurrection). Painted in Lwów (L'viv) in 1893–1894, the panorama was the communal work of a number of artists, including Jan Styka and Wojciech Kossak. It was transported to Wrocław after World War II. Since the battle had been fought against Russia, the panorama was politically sensitive in communist Poland, and it was only under constant civic pressure that a special building (pictured) was constructed for its maximally effective exhibition. Opened in 1985, it quickly became the town's most visited tourist attraction.

Państwowe Gospodarstwo Rolne (PGR) (state collective farm). Modeled after Russian collective farms, PGRs were created in 1949, most often out of the expropriated farms of larger landowners. The drive to collectivize farming in Poland was by and large unsuccessful, as the better farmers clung stubbornly to their land. The low productivity of the PGRs, despite substantial government subsidies and preferential treatment in the allocation of fertilizer and farm machinery, was a poorly concealed national joke. PGRs were liquidated in 1991, causing economic hardship for their workers, who had become dependent on them for almost everything. To the extent possible, the PGRs and their property were sold to private individuals and entities (see *prywatyzacja*). *PGR in Szczyrzyc, not far from Kraków.*

Parkoszowic, Jakub (d. ca. 1455). A rector of the Akademia Krakowska (Kraków Academy) and an early Polish linguist, Parkoszowic was the first to address the question of how many sounds the Polish language had and to suggest an orthography for them. Parkoszowic recognized the need to have separate ways to write long and short vowels (a distinction that has since been lost in Polish), and the need to distinguish hard and soft consonants (a distinction still existing). His orthographic principles were ungainly, not well disseminated, and never caught on — not that modern Polish orthography is a work of particular genius either.

Parowozownia Wolsztyn (Wolsztyn steam locomotive barn and museum). The town of Wolsztyn, in west-central Poland, boasts the only active roundhouse for steam locomotives in all of Europe, with a stable of over a dozen different models, ranging from relatively recent to antique. Many are still-working locomotives that operate along a regularly scheduled route linking Wolsztyn, Poznań, and Leszno. The pride of the Wolsztyn barn is the last remaining Pm36, nicknamed Piękna Helena (Beautiful Helen), manufactured in Chrzanów in 1936 and capable of speeds of up to 120 km/h (80 mph). Each year a locomotive parade is held along the Wolsztyn line, featuring selected models from the collection. *The Wolsztyn roundhouse in action.*

---

partie polityczne (political parties). At present there are seventy to eighty registered political parties in Poland. Only half a dozen or so are represented in the Sejm RP (parliament), the most important at the moment being the centrist Platforma Obywatelska (PO, Civic Platform); the right-of-center populist Prawo i Sprawiedliwość (PiS, Law and Justice); the conservative agrarian Polskie Stronnictwo Ludowe (PSL, Polish People's Faction); and the left-leaning postcommunist Sojusz Lewicy Demokratycznej (SLD, Left Democratic Alliance). The upstart Ruch Palikota (Palikot Movement) scored well in the 2011 elections, placing third (see *wybory 2011*), but the jury is still out on how long it will last. The premier comes from the party with the largest representation; lacking an absolute majority, the party must form a *koalicja* (coalition) with one or more other parties in order to govern. Political parties spring up, change names, merge, and disappear with dizzying frequency (as the Polska Partia Przyjaciół Piwa, PPPP, "Polish Party of Friends of Beer," 1990–1993). The Polish press rarely resolves party abbreviations. One simply has to know what they stand for. The logo of the PO is in the shape of Poland with a big smile in the middle.

Pasek, Jan Chryzostom (ca. 1636–1701). Often cited as representative of seventeenth-century *sarmatyzm* mentality, Pasek led a boisterous life as a Polish cavalryman under *hetman* Stefan Czarniecki in wars across Denmark, Poland, and Russia, to settle down in his later years as a quarrelsome country farmer, all of which is colorfully recounted in his *Pamiętniki* (Memoirs), discovered in the nineteenth century and published only in 1936. The *Pamiętniki* have served as source material for numerous subsequent Polish authors, especially Henryk Sienkiewicz in his historical *trylogia* (trilogy). Adam Mickiewicz rated his work highly in his lectures on Slavic literature at the Sorbonne. High-schoolers know the story of Jan Pasek's pet otter Robak (Worm), who died as the result of King **Jan III Sobieski**'s carelessness, allowing Robak to run off-leash to then be killed by a passing soldier. *Juliusz Kossak, Jan Pasek at the Battle of Lachowicze.*

Pawiak (Pawiak prison). So nicknamed after ulica Pawia (Peacock Street) in Warsaw, on which it was located, Pawiak prison was built by the Russians in the 1830s and saw heavy use as an interrogation center for political prisoners during the **powstanie styczniowe** (January Uprising) of 1863, which was the start of its infamous reputation. During World War II Pawiak was under the control of the German Gestapo (state secret police). It is estimated that some ninety thousand Polish prisoners were processed through Pawiak in the years 1939–1945, of which thirty-seven thousand lost their lives during the course of interrogation, by execution, or in prison cells from disease or the aftereffects of interrogation. Many were taken for execution outside Warsaw to the village of Palmiry, where a large cemetery (pictured) and monuments now stand; see **Kusociński, Janusz**. Following the **powstanie warszawskie** (Warsaw Uprising, 1944), the Germans shot all remaining prisoners and destroyed the prison. Its remaining fragments function today as a memorial and museum.

Pawłowski, Jerzy (1932–2005). A wiry 5′ 9″, Pawłowski was Poland's and one of the world's best fencers ever, with five Olympic medals to his credit (gold in 1968) and eighteen world championship medals, including seven gold. With Pawłowski as team captain the Polish team defeated perennial world champion Hungary in 1959, 1961, 1962, and 1963, leading to a national craze for fencing. Suave, well-educated, and cosmopolitan, Pawłowski tarnished his reputation and is rarely mentioned today for his being an informer for the Urząd Bezpieczeństwa (UB) and **Służba Bezpieczeństwa** (**SB**), and later, as a double agent, for the American CIA. Arrested for the latter in 1974 and tried by Polish courts, he was sentenced to twenty-five years in prison, of which he served ten, after which he lived out his life as a faith healer and painter, avocations he acquired while in prison.

Penderecki, Krzysztof (b. 1933). A major twentieth-century composer and conductor of symphonic music and operas, Penderecki debuted in 1959 at the **Warszawska Jesień** (Warsaw Autumn) new music festival. He is currently Poland's greatest living composer. His avant-garde "Ofiarom Hiroszimy – tren" (Threnody to the Victims of Hiroshima, 1960), for fifty-two-piece string orchestra, brought him to international attention, followed by acclaim for his choral piece "Pasja według świętego Łukasza" (Saint Luke's Passion). Penderecki evolved from a representative of the atonal avant-garde to more classical tonalities beginning in the 1980s. He is known for his religiously themed pieces, for constantly expanding on already-performed works of his own, and for subcontracting compositional work to assistants while remaining in charge of a piece's overall conception.

Perun, Pierun. The Slavic pagan god of thunder and war, analogous to Scandinavia's Thor, and one of the major pre-Christian Slavic deities; in conflict with Żmij, the deity of chaos, and also no friend of Weles, the cattle god. Other Slavic gods included Swaróg, god of heaven, sun, and fire; his son Dadźbóg, god of plenty; also Mokosz, goddess of rain. Pagan gods left little trace on Polish cultural memory. The early historian **Jan Długosz** tried to make more out of them than was probably justified by concocting Polish correspondents to the Greek deities; for example, Dziewanna, supposedly goddess of forests, similar to the Greek Diana. The regionally used oath *do pieruna!* (by thunder!), once a serious swearword, today substitutes for saying something stronger. To be sure, various pagan rituals survive into the modern era as Polish folk customs, including *pisanki* (Easter eggs), **Dziady** (Forefathers' Eve), **Śmigus-Dyngus** (Easter Monday), *topienie Marzanny* (the drowning of Marzanna, goddess of winter), and others.

Peweks (Pewex stores). An abbreviation of the oxymoron Państwowe Przedsiębiorstwo Eksportu Wewnętrznego (State Enterprise for Internal Export). Pewex stores existed in the **PRL** (communist Poland) in the 1970s and 1980s as a way of attracting foreign currency held by Polish citizens into national coffers. The złoty at that time was not an exchangeable "hard" currency. Pewex stores sold "luxury" goods, both foreign and domestic, generally unavailable in regular stores for Polish money. Instead of money for change, customers were given *bony towarowe* (trade coupons) that could be used for future Pewex purchases. Outside the Pewex stores lurked *cinkciarze* (money changers), who would approach hard-currency shoppers with the invitation "cincz many?" (change money?). The Pewex stores went out of business once Poland established a free-market economy. The Baltona hard-currency stores, with an even older history, survive today as a network of duty-free stores at sea- and airports.

Piastowie, dynastia Piastów (Piast dynasty). The first historical dynasty of Polish rulers, reigning from 960–1370. The semilegendary progenitor was Piast Kołodziej (Piast the Wheelwright) of **Gniezno**. The name Piast itself means something like "caregiver." Piast's son Siemowit was prince of the **Polanie** in the ninth century, having deposed **Popiel**. Siemowit was followed by his brother Lestek, then by his son Ziemomysł, and finally by the first truly historical Piast ruler, **Mieszko I** (d. 992), Siemowit's grandson. Mieszko accepted Christianity (*chrzest Polski*) in 996, marking the beginning of Polish statehood. During the period of *rozbicie dzielnicowe* (division into districts, 1128–1320), the dynasty was divided into several princely lines. The last Piast ruler was King **Kazimierz III Wielki** (Kazimierz the Great), d. 1370.

Piątek (village of Piątek, "Friday"). A small village of around 2,100 residents, situated slightly north of **Łódź**, which claims to be the geometric center of Poland and has an unattractive monument (pictured) to prove it. If one would balance a paper cutout map of Poland on a pin, the pin would presumably stick out at Piątek, at 52°04′09″N, 19°28′50″E. The geometric center of Europe was once calculated (by a Pole, in 1775) to fall somewhere around Białystok, but later and better estimates place it near Wilno in Lithuania.

pielgrzymki (pilgrimages). Visits to holy places as a gesture of penance or thanksgiving, usually on foot and with the singing of hymns along the way, *pielgrzymki* are typically organized by churches. However, some travel agencies specialize in group excursions to the Holy Land, Lourdes, the Fatima shrine in Portugal, and other places, also called *pielgrzymki*. Touristic pilgrimages often visit other, nonreligious places along the way. In Poland popular pilgrimage sites are the Jasna Góra monastery in Częstochowa, Kalwaria Zebrzydowska (southeast of Kraków; see *kalwaria*), Licheń, Wadowice (near Kraków, birthplace of Jan Paweł II), the Sanktuarium Bożego Miłosierdzia (Sanctuary of God's Mercy, shrine of Saint Faustyna (see Kowalska, siostra Maria Faustyna) in Kraków, the Święta Lipka (Holy Linden) basilica in Warmia in the north, and Góra Świętej Anny (Saint Anne's Mountain, near Opole). Trips to holy sites in the *kresy* (Ukraine, Belarus, Lithuania) are currently popular. *Pilgrims to the Jasna Góra monastery in the pielgrzymka warszawka (Warsaw Pilgrimage, Poland's largest).*

Pieniny. The Pieniny Mountains are part of the western Karpaty (Carpathian) Mountains in far south Poland and northern Slovakia, to the east of the Tatry. Its best-known peak is Trzy Korony (Three Crowns), which stands at 982 meters. The Pieniny are the second-most-popular mountain tourist destination after the Tatry. The Dunajec River spectacularly flows through a gorge in the range, and raft trips along the river (pictured) are a popular tourist draw.

pierniki toruńskie (Toruń ginger cookies). History records the baking of a special honey and ginger *ciastko* (cookie) in Toruń as early as the fourteenth century. Being located on an important east–west trade route, Toruń would have been a logical place to develop a spice cookie. The recipe for *pierniki* was a secret closely guarded by Toruń bakers. Today the cookies tend to be made in the shape of a heart and are one of the most generally recognizable Polish food items. Toruń celebrates a yearly Festiwal Piernika (Piernik Festival) organized by the Fabryka Cukiernicza "Kopernik" (Copernicus Confectionery Factory), and even boasts a piernik museum.

KALEIDOSCOPE OF POLAND 183

pierogi. Poland's main contribution to international cuisine. Although also made in Ukraine and Russia, the Polish version has made the biggest imprint abroad, wherever Poles have settled. *Pierogi* are cheap, nutritious, and delicious, if somewhat labor-intensive. Polish pierogi are boiled, not necessarily baked, typically served in butter with browned onions, and possibly topped with sour cream or *skwarki* (bacon bits). They may be lightly fried after boiling. An egg dough is rolled out and cut into circles with a glass tumbler. Filling is placed on the dough circle, which is folded over and crimped shut by hand. Most popular are *pierogi ruskie* (Ruthenian pierogi), which are stuffed with potato, *twaróg* (farmer's cheese), and onion. Pierogi may be stuffed with almost anything: mushrooms, ground meat, eggs, cabbage, lentils, *kasza*, skwarki, and so on. There are also dessert pierogi, stuffed with sweetmeats, currants, strawberries, or other fruit, sprinkled with sugar, and topped with cream.

Pierwsza Dama (First Ladies of Poland). After the creation of the office of president in 1989, the role of president's wife took on the prominence it has in other democracies. The president's children also sometimes make the news. Danuta Wałęsa had eight children (four sons followed by four daughters) with her husband Lech (term 1990–1995), and she is remembered for accepting the Nobel Peace Prize in his name in 1983. Her memoirs of those times, published in 2012, caused a sensation for its discussion of marital problems with her husband at all stages of their life together. Maria Kaczyńska, who died alongside her husband Lech (term 2005–2010) in the *katastrofa pod Smoleńskiem* (Smolensk air disaster), was active in charities, in recognition of which a Dutch grower named a newly developed tulip variety (pictured) after her. By far the flashiest of the presidential wives and their children were and are the **Kwaśniewskie, Jolanta** and **Aleksandra**, the wife and daughter, respectively, of Aleksander (term 1995–2005). Anna Komorowska, the current First Lady at the time of this writing, has emerged as a champion of adoption.

Pierwsza Komunia (First Communion). A Roman Catholic ceremony, usually held around the age of eight or nine, signifying that a child is old enough to understand the meaning of *grzech* (sin), *spowiedź* (confession), *pokuta* (penance), and the transubstantiation of bread and wine into the body and blood of Christ. In Poland communicants receive the *Hostia* (consecrated

184 KALEIDOSCOPE OF POLAND

bread), wine usually taken only by the priest. Pierwsza Komunia is preceded by months of catechism lessons. In the ceremony, the child recites religious passages and prayers and sings hymns he or she has learned. Despite efforts in some parishes to keep expenses down, boys often purchase new suits for the day, over which they wear a white cassock, while girls wear white communion dresses and wreaths on their heads. Family and close friends come from near and far, bringing presents. Traditionally, one grandfather would give a watch and the other a bicycle, although these days they are just as apt to give electronic toys, computers, or smartphones. The ceremony in church is often followed by a fancy dinner held in a restaurant. *First Communion class in Saint George's Parish, Sopot, 2006.*

pijalnia piwa (beer drinkery). A trip down memory lane. Not too long ago in the summer one could belly up alongside one's fellow workers after work (or during lunch hour) against an outdoor counter whose sole purpose was to offer generic beer in large glass mugs (*kufle*), cursorily washed between thirsty customers. Even more iconic of the **PRL** (communist Poland) was the street vendor of *woda sodowa* (soda water) from a *saturator* (a pushcart with a single glass, sprayed between uses, serving all customers, pictured). A dollop of fruit syrup cost extra. Somehow no one ever caught a dread disease. Besides sporadic bottled beer, helpfully labeled *piwo*, grocery stores also occasionally stocked something called *wino* (wine), laughingly called *wino marki "wino"* (wine-brand wine) made from apples, strawberries, and other fruit, guaranteed to give an instant headache and drunk mainly by students and winos. Along with large glass Groucho Marx–style seltzer-water siphons bought from and returnable to the local food store, these and many other features helping to make Poland excitingly different for the foreigner have largely disappeared. And just try to find a shop today that will repair a rip in your stockings (*podnoszenie oczek*) or replenish the fluid and flint in your disposable lighter.

piłka nożna (football, soccer). Soccer is Poland's largest participant and spectator sport. League play is divided into an Ekstraklasa (the best) as well as first-, second-, third-, and fourth-tier leagues. The sixteen Ekstraklasa teams in 2014–2015 (this changes from year to year) are Cracovia Kraków, GKS Bełchatów, Górnik Łęczna, Górnik Zabrze, Jagiellonia Białystok, Korona Kielce, Lech Poznań (insignia pictured), Lechia Gdańsk, Legia Warszawa, Piast Gliwice, Podbeskidzie Bielsko-Biała, Pogoń Szczecin, Ruch

KALEIDOSCOPE OF POLAND

Chorzów, Śląsk Wrocław, Wisła Kraków, and Zawisza Bydgoszcz. The glory days of Polish soccer were the early 1970s, when Poland, coached by legend Kazimierz Górski (1921–2006) and Poland's all-time top scorer Włodzimierz Lubański, regularly competed at the highest international level, winning an Olympic gold (1972) and silver (1976), and a bronze in the 1974 world championships. Poland did not make it into the 2014 World Cup in Brazil. Poland and Ukraine jointly hosted **Euro 2012** (the 2012 European championships), in connection with which many improvements in national infrastructure were made – without, however, affecting the quality of the soccer team. However, in October 2014 the Polish national team defeated Germany, defending world champions, for the first time ever, so perhaps things are looking up. See also: **Deyna, Kazimierz**.

Piłsudski, Józef (1867–1935). Hailing from historically Lithuanian lands, Piłsudski was an oft-arrested anti-Russian conspirator before World War I. In 1914 he formed the **Legiony Polskie** (Polish Legions) in Austro-Hungary to fight for Polish independence in the *zabór rosyjski* (Russian partition). Appointed Polish commander-in-chief after the war, Piłsudski arrived in Warsaw in November 1918, and it fell to him to oversee the forging of the new Polish state (see **Polska Odrodzona**). In 1920 he soundly defeated a Soviet invasion, which had threatened to engulf the entire country, before it reached the outskirts of Warsaw in the *wojna polsko-bolszewicka* (Polish-Bolshevik War), the so-called Cud nad Wisłą (Miracle on the Vistula). He was the major Polish military leader and statesman during the *dwudziestolecie międzywojenne* (interwar period), taking over the government after the *przewrót majowy* (May coup d'état) of 1926 and assuming the title of *marszałek* (marshal). Piłsudski, often pictured astride his favorite mount Kasztanka (Chestnut), built a cult following during his lifetime that is still alive today, even if his figure is not entirely free of controversy. His funeral in 1935 turned into a huge national patriotic manifestation and gesture of respect. He is buried in **Wawel** Cathedral. His museum is in **Belweder**.

piosenki biesiadne (party songs). It is difficult to choose among the songs Poles most like to sing at parties, but everyone knows "Szła dzieweczka do laseczka" (The lass walked into the woods), the provenance of which seems to be Silesian. Its first lines: "Szła dzieweczka do laseczka, do zielonego, do zielonego, do zielonego . . . / Napotkała myśliweczka bardzo szwarnego, bardzo szwarnego, bardzo szwarnego" (The girl walked into the forest, a green one, a green one, a green one . . . / She encountered a hunter, very handsome, very handsome, very handsome). The refrain is borrowed from a Russian/Yiddish song: "Gdzie jest ta ulica, gdzie jest ten dom, gdzie jest ta dziewczyna, co kocham ją? / Znalazem ulicę, znalazłem dom, znalazłem dziewczynę, co kocham ją!" (Where is that street, where is that house, where is that girl that I love? / I found the street, I found the house, I found the girl that I love!). See also: "*Góralu, czy ci nie żal?*"

Piotrkowska, ulica (Piotrkowska Street). The longest (4.2 km) and straightest street in Poland going by the same name the whole way. It is the main commercial street of **Łódź**, occupied by stores, hotels, restaurants, and the exotically themed pubs for which Łódź is known. Much of the street is a showcase for Łódź-specific mid-nineteenth-century eclectic architecture. Traditionally the street performed the function of what in older towns was filled by the town square. Recently this role has been co-opted by the nearby immense Manufaktura shopping center, creatively constructed in and around the renovated former Poznański textile factory. Along Piotrkowska Street may be found Łódź's answer to Hollywood's Walk of Fame, a sidewalk with stars for the most famous Polish actors and actresses, along with bronze statues of Łódź cultural notables such as the poet **Julian Tuwim**, the novelist **Władysław Reymont**, and the pianist **Artur Rubinstein**. Motorized traffic is prohibited along most of the route, turning the street into a gigantic sidewalk teeming with pedestrians and the bicycle rickshaws for which the city is also known.

pisanki (Easter eggs). The veneration and decoration of eggs as a sign of the rebirth of spring has its origins in pagan times. The tradition was adopted by the Christian Church, which added to the symbolism the belief, expressed in the celebration of **Wielkanoc** (Easter), in the Zmartwychwstanie (Resurrection) of Christ. In Poland eggs are usually decorated by drawing patterns on them in wax and then dipping the egg in vegetable dye, leaving the wax-marked portion undyed. Different regions have their own favorite patterns. Eggs that have been merely dyed, not patterned, are called *kraszanki*; those made by scratching a pattern through the dye are *drapanki*. Easter eggs are an obligatory part of the Easter feast. They are cut and distributed to those at table, and good wishes are exchanged, as at **Wigilia** (Christmas Eve) with the *opłatek* (wafer).

piwo (beer). Only a few years ago in the **PRL** (communist Poland), beer was limited to a couple of brands, if one could find them. Presently the beer industry is one of the fastest-growing sectors in the Polish economy. Poland currently ranks fourth worldwide in per-capita beer consumption. About forty-six large breweries and seventeen microbreweries produce and market beer under some 750 different brands, threatening the status of *wódka* (vodka) as the national beverage. Many brands questionably claim origin going back as far back as the sixteenth century or even earlier. Eighty percent are in the hands of a few multinational concerns. Major brands include Żywiec, Tyskie, Lech, Żubr, Harnaś, Łomża, Perła, Warka. Ordinary *piwo jasne* (light beer or lager) contains about 6.2 percent alcohol, while so-called *piwo mocne* (strong beer) contains twice as much. *Piwo ciemne* (dark beer) comes in at 9 percent. *Lane piwo* (draft beer) is served in either 0.3-liter (*małe piwo*, "small beer") or 0.5-liter (*duże piwo*, "large beer") glasses. *Małe piwo* is also Polish for "small potatoes," i.e., no big deal. In bars and pubs, women often drink beer through straws, especially when it has been flavored with a dollop of raspberry *sirop*, something "real men" wouldn't be caught dead doing. *Łomża beer, produced in the northeast.*

PKP, PKS, MZK. Three abbreviations for means of transportation that are rarely resolved by the press. They stand for Polskie Koleje Państwowe (Polish State Railways), Przedsiębiorstwo Komunikacji Samochodowej (Automotive Transportation Enterprise, the intercity bus lines), and Miejskie Zakłady Komunikacyjne (Urban Transportation Companies, the trolley and inner-city bus lines). The last name is not as recognizable nationwide as the first two, but may vary from town to town. As for the railways, they are divided into intercity, regional, and cargo subdivisions. Once a mighty and respected institution, the Polish train system today faces problems that nearly everyone talks about, because nearly everyone has to use it at one time or another. It suffers from poorly maintained roadbeds, outdated rolling stock, high ticket prices, and the lack of coordinated scheduling among its several passenger branches, to name only the most important of the problems.

plakaty (posters). Polish posters advertising cultural events such as the circus, plays, concerts, and especially films — both Polish and foreign — began to attract attention and to be collected and exhibited internationally in the 1960s, to the extent that the term *polska szkoła plakatu* (the Polish school of poster art) came into use. As distinct from the psychedelic drug-inspired posters of the San Francisco school that arose at about the same time, the Polish school is distinguished by intellectualism, irony, surprise visual juxtapositions, and finding ways to weave the shape of the letters into the theme of the poster. Many representatives of the school live and work outside the country, especially in New York City. One of the world's few poster museums is located in **Wilanów**, near Warsaw, and sponsors a biannual international poster exhibition. A museum of Polish film posters is located in **Łódź**.

Plater, Emilia (1806–1831). A **Wilno**-born countess with an early predilection for horsemanship and marksmanship, Plater became caught up in the fervor of the **powstanie listopadowe** (November Uprising) of 1830, and helped bring the uprising to Lithuania by raising a detachment of 280 artillery, several hundred peasant *kosynierzy* (scythe-soldiers, armed with scythes beaten into bayonets), and sixty horse cavalry, which she herself commanded, cutting off her hair and donning an army uniform. In several victorious encounters with the Russian army, she demonstrated bravery and leadership, and was promoted to the rank of captain. When the revolt began to falter in Lithuania, she decided to break through to Warsaw, but fell ill and died before managing to do so. Plater became one of the enduring legends of the November Uprising, owing much to **Adam Mickiewicz**'s poem "Śmierć Pułkownika" (The captain's death), in which the dying Emilia asks to bid farewell to her horse, her arms, and her uniform. *Jan Rosen,* Emilia Plater Conducting her Scythemen.

Płock. Attractively situated on high banks over the Wisła, Płock is an important river port with a population of 127,000 people and is the center of the Orlen petroleum corporation. The historical capital of Mazowsze and the actual capital of Poland in 1079–1138, Płock almost became the permanent Polish capital, instead of Warsaw. It certainly had a more illustrious history than Warsaw before the sixteenth century. It was capital of a diocese as early as 1075. A sarcophagus containing the remains of King Władysław I Herman and his son King Bolesław III Krzywousty (Bolesław the Wrymouth) lies in the royal chapel of the Płock basilica of 1144. Płock is not often seen by tourists but it is worth a visit for its attractive location, well-preserved *Stare Miasto* (old town), and various museums and architectural monuments. *Płock castle and cathedral.*

Podhale. The southernmost mountain region of Poland in the higher foothills of the Tatry (Tatra) range of the Karpaty (Carpathian) Mountains. It is often called Poland's highlands, and the people who live in it, *górale,* "highlanders" or "mountaineers," exist to a large extent as sheepherders. The word's root, *hala,* means "high mountain meadow" or "pastureland." The region is rich in folklore and *architektura drewniana* (wooden architecture), especially old churches, and it is a major winter sports, resort, and mountain-climbing area. Its largest towns are Zakopane and Nowy Targ.

Podkarpacie (Sub-Carpathia). Geographically, a very large area of Eastern Europe extending as far south as Hungary. In the Polish context the term refers to the southeastern part of Poland with Rzeszów at its center, the capital of the *województwo podkarpackie* (Sub-Carpathian Voivodeship). Podkarpacie is the southeastern tip of Małopolska (Lesser Poland). It is an area that gently rises up into the Karpaty (Carpathian) Mountains the farther one goes south. Other larger towns in the Podkarpacie are Przemyśl, Krosno, Leżajsk, Łańcut, and Tarnobrzeg.

Podlasie, Polesie. Podlasie is a northeastern region just below Suwalszczyzna and north of Polesie, located at the confluence of Polish, Belarusian, Ukrainian, and Lithuanian ethnicities, and extending much farther east into present-day Lithuania and Belarus. Additionally, it is the center of the small Polish Tatar ethnic minority. Located within Podlasie is the immense

KALEIDOSCOPE OF POLAND   189

forest and nature preserve **Puszcza Białowieska** (Białowieża wilderness). Its largest town is **Białystok**. To the south of Podlasie, Polesie is a vast, marshy, thinly populated historical region in the east of Poland north of **Lublin**, a haven for storks. Most of it extends farther east into present Ukraine and Belarus, where the largest town, now in Belarus, is Brześć (Brest).

pogoń (knight in chase). An image incorporated into the coat of arms of the Wielkie Księstwo Litewskie (Grand Duchy of Lithuania), the Lithuanian part of the **Rzeczpospolita Obojga Narodów** (Polish-Lithuanian Commonwealth), and by various families of Lithuanian and Belarusian origin, including the **Czartoryski** family. For a while, independent Belarus used the *pogoń* sign in its coat of arms as well. The pogoń is used as a commercial trademark by a *firma ochroniarska* (security service; see *ochrona*), but it is mainly a name associated with sports clubs, most famously Pogoń Szczecin, which takes its name from a pre–World War II club of that name in **Lwów**. For a picture, see **Czartoryscy, rodzina; ochrona**.

"Polacy nie gęsi" (Poles are not geese). This self-conscious assertion comes from **Mikołaj Rej**'s *Zwierzyniec* (Bestiary, 1562), and it continues "iż swój język mają" (they have their own language). The quotation shows Rej's awareness that he was opening new territory by writing in Polish instead of Latin. The grammar of the saying is contested by scholars, some of whom claim it means "Poles don't have a goose language, but their own," with the adjective *gęsi*, "anserine," pejoratively referring to Latin, alluding to the legend that Rome was saved from Gallic invasion by geese cackling in the night. Whatever the case, the sentence in either interpretation makes sense, and is used in humorous nonsense coinages of the sort "Poles are not geese, and also make good sausage." See also: **przysłowia o Polsce i Polakach**.

Polanie (Polanians). The semihistorical north-central tribe inhabiting the **Warta** River basin, emerging in the ninth century to organize the rudiments of the first Polish state with its center in **Gniezno**. The Polanie gave rise to the first Polish rulers, the *dynastia* **Piastów** (Piast dynasty) and, some say, to the name of the future country. Other proto-Polish tribes referred to in early writings were the Wiślanie, Goplanie, Lędzianie, Mazowszanie, and Pomorzanie. To the East Slavs, the Polish tribes were collectively known as the *liakhy*; see **Lech, Czech, Rus**.

Polański, Roman (b. 1933). The best-known Polish-born film director outside Poland; also a talented actor. He is known for his flamboyant lifestyle, for his family tragedy (his pregnant wife, Sharon Tate, was murdered by the Manson "family"), and for his ongoing arrest warrant for statutory rape in Los Angeles. He first received attention for his student short *Dwaj ludzie z szafą* (Two men with wardrobe, 1958), and he hit the international big time with *Nóż w wodzie* (Knife in the Water, 1961). Among his better-known films in the West are *Rosemary's Baby* (1968), *Chinatown* (1974), and *Tess* (1979). Polański received both the Golden Palm award in Cannes and an Oscar in 2002 for *Pianista* (The Pianist), based on the story of Władysław Szpilman, a Jewish concert pianist who survived the war hiding in the rubble of bombed-out Warsaw and who later went on to a distinguished musical career in postwar Poland; see *Robinsonowie warszawscy*. Polański, himself of Jewish background, escaped from the Kraków ghetto in 1943 at the age of ten and survived the war living with village families. His mother died in Auschwitz. Polański remains vigorous as a director, coming out with *Ghost Writer* (*Autor widmo*) in 2010. His *Carnage* (*Rzeź*) opened the Venice Film Festival in 2011.

polka (polka). Not the Polish national dance, which would have to be the *polonez* (polonaise), but a dance rhythm associated with the oom-pah bands of southern Germany, Bohemia, Slovakia, and Slovenia. It was a dance craze in nineteenth-century Europe that spread as far as Ireland, where it entered Irish folk culture. The name possibly comes from the Czech word *půlka*, which means "little half," referring to the lively 2/4 beat. From the beginning, however, the dance has been associated with the word *Polka* (Polish woman), especially since the dance was enthusiastically adopted by Poles living in the United States, with polka bands galore. By contrast, one finds few polka enthusiasts in Poland (although any Pole can readily dance one).

Polonez (automobile). A midsize passenger car produced in Warsaw from 1978–2002, in two- and four-door models, and in a hatchback and station wagon model. The brainchild of party secretary Edward Gierek, it was designed to replace the Fiat 125p, on whose frame it was first constructed, although that car, too, continued to be produced until 1991. The Polonez was judged to be quite safe in crash tests, and a certain number were exported to China, Great Britain, and France. In Poland it was widely used as a taxicab, police car, and official government vehicle. In all, 1,061,807 vehicles were produced, and many are still on the road today, especially in the countryside.

polonez (polonaise). Considered the Polish national dance, the *polonez* has its origins in folk dance but was adopted early by the court and nobility as a showy means of opening balls. It is still used on ceremonial occasions such as *studniówki* (high school formals, pictured), where it is virtually obligatory, and other gala events. It depends for its effectiveness on one's ability to make seemingly simple movements gracefully. Another name for it is the *chodzony* (walked dance). The polonez is played to a stately 3/4 rhythm. The polonez scene in Andrzej Wajda's film *Pan Tadeusz* (1999) nicely encapsulates the stateliness of the dance, as does the music of Fryderyk Chopin's well-known Polonaise in A-flat major, Op. 53, "Polonaise Héroïque."

Polonia (Poles abroad). The term has been used since the second half of the nineteenth century to refer to the Polish diaspora, that is, Poles living outside Poland for whatever reason — political, economic, or by plain free choice — and who still maintain a Polish consciousness and interest in Poland, even if they may not be citizens, or speak the language. Many members of Polonia belong

KALEIDOSCOPE OF POLAND 191

to Polish-related fraternal, social, and sports organizations, and group adhesion is furthered by Polish-associated church organizations and local radio and television stations. It is estimated that the ranks of Polonia number twelve to fifteen million worldwide, of which by far the largest group is in the United States (more than eight million), with the largest settlements in Chicago and Greenpoint, New York. Other major Polish settlements are in Germany, France, Brazil, Canada, Great Britain, and Argentina. External Polish state radio and television offer services specifically geared to Polonia audiences.

Polska (Poland). Officially Rzeczpospolita Polska (the Republic of Poland), Poland is situated in **Europa środkowa** (Central Europe) south of the **Bałtyk** (Baltic Sea). It borders Niemcy (Germany) on the west, Czechy (Czech Republic), Słowacja (Slovakia) in the south, Ukraina (Ukraine) in the southeast, Białoruś (Belarus) in the east, and Litwa (Lithuania) and a part of Rosja (Russia) in the northwest. With 312,683 square kilometers, it is the ninth-largest country in Europe and the world's thirty-fourth-most populated country with around thirty-eight million people. The capital is **Warszawa** (Warsaw). Poland is a parliamentary democracy with legislative power vested in the **Sejm RP** (parliament) and Senat (senate) and executive power in the Prezydent (president), together with the Rada Ministrów (Council of Ministers, some eighteen in all) and its chairman, the premier. The currency is the złoty, currently worth around ⅓ US dollar. Poland is a member of the Unia Europejska (European Union) and of NATO.

Polska A i B (Poland A and Poland B). Poland is cut roughly in two from top to bottom into the more industrialized region of the west (Poland A) and the more rural and agricultural region of the east (Poland B). The regions to an extent reflect the historically more economically developed *zabór pruski* (Prussian partition) in the west and the less efficiently run *zabór rosyjski* and *zabór austriacki* (Russian and Austrian partitions) in the east. The division is clearly visible on a map of Polish railroads (denser in the west, sparser in the east) and in the voting preferences of people in national elections (people in the east are more conservative and nationalistic in their voting patterns). The situation is slowly changing as investments are naturally attracted to the underdeveloped east. A recent series of ads running in the British *Economist* asks, "What will you say when your father-in-law asks, 'Why didn't you invest in Eastern Poland?'"

Polska Kronika Filmowa (PKF) (Polish Weekly Newsreel). A weekly short newsreel covering current events and featuring stories about Poland and the world, preceding the feature film in Polish cinemas from 1944–1994. Although often used for propaganda purposes, its quality was high, and occasionally important social problems, such as the plight of working women, were highlighted in brief documentaries. During its last years it was included in weekly television programming, to be eventually rendered irrelevant by television's faster news turnaround.

Polska Odrodzona (Reborn Poland, 1918). Five different currencies and sixty-six different kinds of rails were in use in the territories that became Poland after World War I. That Poland came together after 1918 into a cohesive, economically progressive country after 124 years of territorial nonexistence under three different countries was something of a miracle, to an extent a testimony to the iron will of its most important leader, **Józef Piłsudski**. Despite the incredibly fractious politics of the day, Piłsudski was able to meld together different legal and monetary systems, bureaucracies, legislative bodies, and states of economic development — all this and raise a fighting force capable of resisting the Bolshevik march on Western Europe; see *wojna polsko-bolszewicka* (Polish-Bolshevik War). Interwar Poland made tremendous strides in building a centralized industrial infrastructure while cultural life blossomed (see *dwudziestolecie międzywojenne; Skamander*). The flaw in the shape of Poland as many saw it was its limited access to the **Bałtyk** (Baltic Sea) via the narrow and vulnerable so-called *korytarz polski* (Polish Corridor) past the **Wolne Miasto Gdańsk** (Free City of Gdańsk).

Polska przedmurzem chrześcijaństwa (Latin *antemurale christianitatis*, bulwark of Christianity). The term describes how the Polish state viewed itself in the seventeenth century, as it was besieged on all sides by non-Catholics — especially Muslim Turkey in the southeast, but also Protestant Sweden and Germany in the north and west, and Orthodox Russia in the east. The concept was amplified and solidified by **Jan III Sobieski**'s resounding trouncing of the Turks in the **odsiecz wiedeńska** (Relief of Vienna) in 1683, an occurrence that not only Poles viewed as decisive in stemming the Turkish flood westward.

Polska Rzeczpospolita Ludowa (PRL, "pe-e-rel") (People's Republic of Poland). The official name of Poland as part of the Communist Bloc from 1952–1989, replacing the name Rzeczpospolita Polska, used from 1918–1952. Informally the name was Polska Ludowa (communist Poland). The word *ludowa* (people's) was dropped from the country's name in 1989, and the name reverted to Rzeczpospolita Polska. Excellent popularizing works have been written describing what life was like in the PRL, but some say the comedic films of director Stanisław Bareja (1929–1987) capture it best (his best-remembered film is *Miś*, "Teddy bear," 1980). The insignia of the PRL (pictured) lacked the crown over the eagle (see **Orzeł Biały**). See also: **PRL, nostalgia za PRL-em**.

Polska spichlerzem Europy (Poland the granary of Europe). A term that goes hand in hand with the foregoing *Polska przedmurzem chrześcijaństwa*. Both were part of the seventeenth-century *ideologia sarmacka* (Sarmatian ideology; see *sarmatyzm*) ascribing to Poland a special place in the European scheme of things. Poland's role was to keep the rest of Europe well fed, an ideology that justified the accumulation of enormous wealth and property by Polish magnates (*magnateria*) in the eastern part of the Polish-Lithuanian **Rzeczpospolita Obojga Narodów** (Commonwealth) by keeping the territory agrarian through specializing in the export of grain. Today it would be more accurate to say "Poland the appliance store of Europe," as the country is the European Union's largest producer of household appliances. For tourists, Poland is the *spichlerz* of good *piwo* (beer), strong *wódka* (vodka), and cheap *papierosy* (cigarettes).

polska szkoła filmowa (Polish film school). The name given by French film critics to the direction taken by Polish cinema in the period 1955–1965. Production was centered in **Łódź**. Its films were characterized by a mixture of realism and symbolism and a concern with coming to terms with national myths and the effects of World War II. Outstanding representatives of the genre were **Andrzej Wajda**'s *trylogia* (trilogy): *Pokolenie* (1954), *Kanał* (Sewer, 1957), and *Popiół i diament* (Ashes and diamonds, 1958); Andrzej Munk's *Eroica*, 1957; Wojciech Jerzy Has's *Jak być kochaną* (How to be loved, 1963); and Tadeusz Konwicki's *Salto* (Somersault, 1965). The Polish school enlisted as screenwriters some of the most prominent writers of the day, including **Jerzy Andrzejewski**, **Tadeusz Konwicki**, Stanisław Dygat, and **Marek Hłasko**.

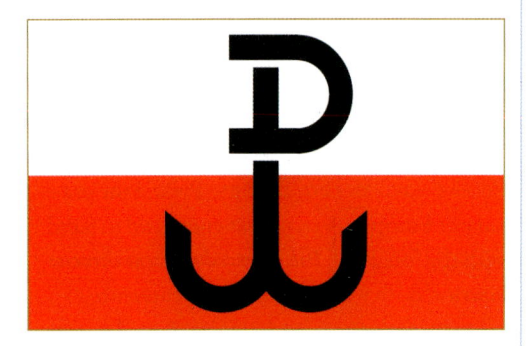

Polska Walcząca (Fighting Poland). The motto of the **Armia Krajowa** (Home Army), the Polish underground army, embedded in the *kotwica* (anchor, the name for the *P* over *W* symbol) on the flag of the resistance, and painted as graffiti on walls beginning in 1942 and throughout World War II. The letters also connote *Wojsko Polskie* (Polish army), *wolna Polska* (free Poland), and **powstanie warszawskie** (Warsaw Uprising). Reference was made to the phrase on a recent cover of the news weekly *Polityka* (Politics), with the headline "Polska Warcząca" (Poland snarling), alluding to the contentious state of contemporary Polish politics.

Polska Zjednoczona Partia Robotnicza (PZPR) (Polish United Workers' Party). Founded in 1948 as a union of former communists, the Polska Partia Socjalistyczna (Polish Socialist Party), and the Polska Partia Robotnicza (Polish Workers' Party), the PZPR was the name for the communist party ruling Poland and its economy from 1948–1989. Its governing body was the Komitet Centralny (KC, Central Committee), headed by a *sekretarz* (secretary). Its official organ was the communist newspaper *Trybuna Ludu* (Tribune of the people) with the international call "Proletariusze wszystkich krajów, łączcie się!" (Proletarians of the world, unite!) as its motto. As happens in centralized command economies, the Polish system was extremely bureaucratized and unwieldy, and eventually began to implode of its own accord. The PZPR was disbanded in 1990, its main continuant being the Socjaldemokracja Rzeczypospolitej Polskiej (Social Democracy of the Polish Republic), which in 1999 merged with what is today's Sojusz Lewicy Demokratycznej (SLD, Left Democratic Alliance).

"polskie obozy koncentracyjne" ("Polish concentration camps"). Poland did not build, administer, or staff concentration or death camps during World War II. Rather, Poles died by the millions both inside and outside them. To the extent that the camps were staffed by non-Germans, these were recruits from Ukraine, Belarus, and the Baltic states: Latvia, Lithuania, and Estonia. This point has been made so often that the use of the term "Polish concentration camps" or "Polish death camps" in the international media, as happens surprisingly often, amounts to complicity in perpetuating an anti-Polish slur born of willful ignorance. There is, in the end, a difference between saying "concentration camps in Poland" and "Polish concentration camps," the latter implying direct responsibility, a distinction anyone should be able to understand. The *New York Times* and the *Wall Street Journal*, after years of prodding, have finally settled on "concentration camps in German-occupied Poland." In 2012, US President Barack Obama chose an incredibly inept time to reiterate this falsehood in a ceremony awarding **Jan Karski** with the US Medal of Freedom.

polskie regalia królewskie (Polish royal regalia). Considering Poland's turbulent history, a fair amount of royal regalia has been preserved, including the reproduction of the *włócznia świętego Maurycego* (spear of Saint Maurice) presented to **Bolesław I Chrobry** by Otto III at the **zjazd gnieźnieński** in the year 1000, and the thirteenth-century coronation sword known as the **Szczerbiec** (Old Nick), both in the treasury of **Wawel** castle. Besides a *korona* (crown), Polish kings usually received as part of their insignia a *berło* (scepter), *jabłko* (orb), and a *miecz* (sword). These often were not passed down from one king to the next but were buried with the king and made anew for each coronation. *Contemporary reproductions of the Polish coronation insignia.*

Polskie Siły Powietrzne w drugiej wojnie światowej (Polish air force in World War II). As Polish pilots and other soldiers gradually found their way first to France and, after the fall of France, to England during the war, sixteen Polish fighter and bomber divisions were eventually created there under an independent Polish command. The most famous was Dywizjon 303 (303rd Kościuszko Fighter Division, insignia pictured). The British were slow to appreciate that the Polish pilots, already battle-hardened, often had more skill than they did. The Polish air force played a major role in the defense of Britain and in missions all over Europe. It is estimated that as many as 970 enemy aircraft and 190 V1 flying bombs were downed or destroyed on the ground by Polish air action. Most Polish air force officers, not eager to return to a communist Poland, stayed in Britain after the war.

Polskie Towarzystwo Turystyczno-Krajoznawcze (PTTK) (Polish Tourist and Sightseeing Society). One of the oldest tourist societies in Europe, reformed in 1950 out of the Polskie Towarzystwo Tatrzańskie (Polish Tatra Society, 1873) and the Polskie Towarzystwo Krajoznawcze (Polish Sightseeing Society, 1906). It promotes tourism and sightseeing, is active in environmental protection, and helps to maintain bicycle, horse, pedestrian, and river trails throughout Poland. It also has a network of tourist accommodations, including hostels, museums, libraries, and mountain *schroniska* (shelters). Members are eligible to earn any of twelve dif-

KALEIDOSCOPE OF POLAND   195

ferent *odznaki* (badges) testifying to proficiency in various aspects of Polish tourism (climbing, hiking, skiing, sailing, cycling, and so forth).

---

pomnik Chopina w Warszawie (Chopin Monument). One of Warsaw's most recognizable monuments is the statue in the *styl secesyjny* (secessionist or Art Nouveau style) depicting **Fryderyk Chopin** beneath a willow tree quavering in the wind. It was unveiled in Warsaw's **Łazienki** park in 1926. During World War II, as part of their campaign of Polish cultural extermination, the Germans dynamited the statue, cut it into pieces, and melted it down. They additionally attempted to hunt down and destroy all of the statue's copies. The best copy was found in Warsaw after the war, in the rubble of the house of the statue's designer, Wacław Szymanowski, upon which the present statue, unveiled in 1958, was modeled. Benches surround the monument, and in summer evenings Chopin concerts are held around it.

Pomnik Grunwaldzki (Grunwald Monument). A large monument to King **Władysław II Jagiełło** on **Kraków**'s **Matejko** Square, unveiled in 1910 on the five hundredth anniversary of the Polish-Lithuanian victory over the **Krzyżacy** (Teutonic Knights, 1410) — see **Grunwald, bitwa pod Grunwaldem**. The project of Antoni Wiwulski, it was funded by the musician and statesman **Ignacy Paderewski**. The monument was dynamited and dismantled in 1939–1940 by the Germans, and its metal fragments were transported to Germany. As early as 1945 the decision was made to rebuild it, but the project was brought to fruition only in 1976. The lifting by military helicopter of the equestrian statue of Jagiełło to its place atop the monument's base was broadcast nationally via live television. Like the **pomnik Mickiewicza** (Mickiewicz monument) in Kraków's *Rynek Główny* (main square), the Grunwald monument is public-friendly and encourages sitting and picture taking on its edges. It is bestrewn with flowers on major national holidays.

pomnik Mickiewicza w Krakowie (Mickiewicz monument in Kraków). Known locally as "Adaś," the Adam Mickiewicz Monument, dedicated to Poland's nineteenth-century poet, is one of Kraków's most photographed objects. It is a popular meeting place on Kraków's *Rynek Główny* (main square) and the site of various happenings. On its four sides sit figures representing *ojczyzna* (fatherland), *nauka* (science), *męstwo* (bravery), and *poezja* (poetry). The monument was unveiled in 1898 on the one hundredth anniversary of the poet's birth. It was dismantled in 1940 by the Germans and its fragments taken to a scrapyard in Hamburg, Germany, where they were discovered in 1946. The resurrected monument was unveiled in 1955, on the one hundredth anniversary of Mickiewicz's death. Mickiewicz himself was never in Kraków until his remains were transported there from Paris in 1890 to the crypts of the Katedra Wawelska (Wawel Cathedral). On Christmas Eve (Mickiewicz's birthday) Kraków's flower-sellers bedeck the monument with flowers.

Pomorze (Pomerania). A large region of Poland and, in part, Germany, abutting the Bałtyk (Baltic Sea) and extending a considerable distance inland. It is divided into Pomorze Gdańskie (Gdańsk or Eastern Pomerania) and Pomorze Szczecińskie (Szczecin or Western Pomerania). Major Polish towns are Gdańsk, Szczecin, Gdynia, Chojnice, Toruń, Koszalin, Słupsk, Grudziądz, and Stargard Szczeciński. For most of its history Pomorze was under the control of the Krzyżacy (Teutonic Knights). After the first and second *rozbiory* (1772, 1793), some of Pomorze belonged to Prusy Zachodnie (West Prussia).

Poniatowski, Józef (1763–1813). The nephew of King Stanisław II August Poniatowski, Prince Józef Poniatowski served first in the Austrian army and later against Austria in the army of the Księstwo Warszawskie (Duchy of Warsaw), helping to enlarge its territory to include Kraków and Lwów. He accompanied Napoleon at the head of Polish troops in Napoleon's failed campaign against Russia in 1812. Poniatowski was put in charge of the French retreat from Russia with the rank of Marshal of France, a role he pursued with exemplary bravery and resourcefulness. He died plunging into the Weisse Elster

River near Leipzig, repeatedly wounded, shouting "Bóg mi powierzył honor Polaków, Bogu go tylko oddam" (God entrusted to me the honor of the Poles, and I will yield it only to Him). His remains are interred in the crypts of Wawel Cathedral, and his imposing equestrian statue stands before the Pałac Namiestnikowski (Presidential Palace) on Krakowskie Przedmieście in Warsaw. *Józef Grassi,* Count Józef Poniatowski.

Poniatowski, Stanisław II August (King Stanisław August Poniatowski, 1732–1798, ruled 1764–1795). The last king of the Polish-Lithuanian state, handpicked by Catherine the Great of Russia — Poniatowski was one of her numerous lovers. Born Count Stanisław Antoni Poniatowski, he adopted the name Stanisław II August upon ascending to the throne. Despite being in effect a Russian puppet, he was a comparatively progressive ruler who introduced political and social reforms and reigned during rapid growth in the cultural life of the country. He was known for his *obiady czwartkowe* (Thursday dinners, 1770–1777), over which he presided and to which he invited people prominent in literature and the arts. Poniatowski was king during the *rozbiory* (partitions) of Poland in 1772, 1793, and 1795. After Poland ceased to exist, he lived out the rest of his life in Russia. *Marcello Bacciarelli, Stanisław August Poniatowski in his coronation regalia.*

Popiel. Legendary ninth-century ruler of the Polanie or Goplanie in Gniezno. According to legend Popiel was a cruel, vengeful, and incompetent despot who poisoned twenty uncles plotting to depose him. Commoners overthrew Popiel and his wife, and chased him to a tower near Lake Gopło where he took refuge, only to be nibbled to death by the mice that had been feeding on the corpses of his uncles. The legend is included in the early Polish histories of Gall Anonim (Gallus Anonymous) and Wincenty Kadłubek.

Popiełuszko, Jerzy (1947–1984). An uncompromising anticommunist activist priest in Warsaw during *stan wojenny* (martial law), known for his motto "Zło dobrem zwyciężaj" (Conquer evil with good) and as the chaplain of Warsaw's section of the trade union Solidarność

(Solidarity). In 1983 he presided at the funeral of nineteen-year-old Grzegorz Przemyk, who was beaten to death by the police for no apparent reason other than for celebrating the end of high school. The funeral turned into a huge antigovernment manifestation. Popiełuszko was himself abducted, tortured, and murdered on October 19, 1984, by officers of the Polish Ministerstwo Spraw Wewnętrznych (Ministry of Internal Affairs, i.e., the secret police), who detained him in a fake traffic stop as he was returning to Warsaw from a meeting in **Bydgoszcz**, beat him to death, and threw his stone-weighted body into a **Wisła** reservoir. His burial turned into a much huger antigovernment demonstration than Przemyk's, with more than 250,000 in attendance. Popiełuszko was beatified by the Roman Catholic Church in 2010, his one-hundred-year-old mother attending the ceremony. His story was told on film by **Agnieszka Holland** in *Zabić księdza* (To kill a priest, 1988), and later by Rafał Wieczyński in *Popiełuszko: wolność jest w nas* (Popiełuszko: freedom is within us, 2009).

portret trumienny (coffin portrait). Coffin portraits were popular in ancient Egypt and Rome, and also during the period of **sarmatyzm** (Sarmatian baroque) in seventeenth- through eighteenth-century Poland. The likeness of the deceased was painted on a tin sheet and affixed to the head of the coffin, which was faced toward the congregation during the funeral, giving the deceased a chance to participate in the ceremony. An epitaph was placed at the opposite end, and the coat of arms on the side. *Coffin portrait of Stanisław Woysza.*

posiłki (meals). Polish meals follow a time-honored routine, often a mystification to foreigners. Although modern life disrupts the pattern for many, ideally *śniadanie* (breakfast) consists of rolls, butter, and jam, coffee or tea, and possibly also cheese and cold cuts. It is followed by *drugie śniadanie* (second breakfast) around 11:00, with modest **kanapki** (open-face sandwiches). The main Polish meal is midafternoon *obiad* (dinner), an obligatorily hot meal consisting of *pierwsze danie* (first course, i.e., soup) and *drugie danie* (second, or meat course, pictured, almost always with potatoes and *surówka*: grated cabbage, cucumbers, carrots, or other raw vegetables). Poles get their liquid from soup and, possibly, from a glass of *kompot* (thin stewed fruit), water not normally being served. Sweets are also not normally part of *obiad*, but around 6:00 p.m. *podwieczorek* is held, at which cookies, sweets, or pastries and coffee or tea are on offer. The last meal of the day is *kolacja* (supper), typically consisting of kanapki, served around 8:00 p.m. Later, sweets, wine, and liqueurs may be brought out before retiring for the night. The American tradition of midday *lancz* (lunch) instead of *obiad* (dinner) is catching on, especially in the city.

postrzyżyny (ritual first haircut). An old Slavic custom according to which a son was given his first haircut by his father and elevated to adulthood around the age of seven. A male child was given a new name and passed into the care of the father, who with this act formally recognized his paternity. According to the chronicler Gall Anonim, Piast Kołodziej, a modest tiller of the soil, was celebrating his son Siemowit's *postrzyżyny* when his household was visited by two traveling strangers, whom he and his wife Rzepicha treated hospitably. After their visit Piast's larder was never empty. The strangers predicted future greatness for Piast and his son, as came to pass. Piast came to sit on the throne in Kruszwica, and Siemowit in Gniezno. Thus was born the *dynastia Piastów* (Piast dynasty), which emerged into history in the person of Mieszko I, whose *postrzyżyny* are pictured here.

Potocka, Delfina (1807–1877). An unhappily married countess of celebrated beauty and talent who became the romantic interest of both Fryderyk Chopin and the poet Zygmunt Krasiński, both of whom dedicated works to her. In Chopin's case, this was his Waltz in D-flat major, Op. 64 — the famous "Minute Waltz." Krasiński, who wrote to her almost daily between 1839 and 1848, left behind several volumes of correspondence with her — some six thousand letters in all — published in the 1930s.

Potocki, Jan (1761–1815). Aristocratic engineer, ethnologist, orientalist, pioneer balloonist, and adventurer, Potocki is remembered today chiefly as the author of the gothic-picaresque novel *Rękopis znaleziony w Saragossie* (*Manuscript Found in Saragossa*, 1805–1815), written in a box-in-a-box structure reminiscent of the Arabic *Thousand and One Nights*. Potocki wrote in French, but the French version was lost, and the "original" work exists today only in a Polish translation of the now lost truly original version, appearing as late as 1847. In 1965 the novel was turned into a cult film (see *filmy kultowe*) starring Zbigniew Cybulski, directed by Wojciech Jerzy Has.

Potocki, rodzina Potockich (Potocki family). A numerous and many-branched family of Polish aristocracy, including some of the wealthiest *magnateria* of the Rzeczpospolita (Commonwealth), as well as some of the most modestly situated. In the nineteenth century they allied themselves with the Habsburgs. A distant female member of the family, Maria Potocka (d. 1764), was, according to legend, abducted by Tatars and ended up in the harem of the khan, where she became his favorite, inspiring Adam Mickiewicz's Crimean sonnet "Grób Potockiej" (Potocka's grave). A Potocka by marriage, Zofia (1760–1822), was a Greek-born courtesan renowned across Europe for her many high-placed lovers. See also Potocka, Delfina, and Potocki, Jan. The Potockis were one of several families appearing under the Pilawa *herb* (coat of arms). The southeast of Poland is dotted with magnificent palaces built by members of the family. One of the most elegant is the Beaux-Arts palace in Lwów (now Ukrainian L'viv), now appropriated as one of the residences of the Ukrainian president.

---

potop szwedzki (Swedish Deluge). The informal name for the invasion and devastation of a large swathe of Polish territory by Swedish forces in 1655–1660, revealing the weakness and disorganization of the Polish state. The rulers of the time were Poland's Jan II Kazimierz and Karol X Gustaw of Sweden. Poland's *hetman wielki koronny* (Hetman of the Crown, i.e., commander-in-chief) was the future King Jan III Sobieski. A turning point in the *potop* was in 1655 at Jasna Góra monastery near Częstochowa, where a two-month Swedish siege of the monastery was called off after the claimed intercession of the Virgin Mary, said to be working through the icon Matka Boska Częstochowska (Mother of God of Częstochowa). The potop ended with the *pokój oliwski* (Peace of Oliwa) in 1660. The times of the potop are known to Poles mostly through the novel of that name by Henryk Sienkiewicz and its 1974 film version by Jerzy Hoffman.

---

powstania śląskie (Silesia uprisings). Three separate uprisings in 1919, 1920, and 1921, arising out of the unstable territorial situation in Górny Śląsk (Upper Silesia) following the German defeat in World War I. They were sparked when German security guards opened fire on Polish miners and their families as they protested long waits in line to receive pay. The ultimate result, decided by a bitterly contested and disputed plebiscite, was that most of Górny Śląsk, including heavily industrialized Katowice, came under Polish control and helped contribute to the rapid industrial development of interwar Poland. Polish Silesians remaining under German control, including those living in Gliwice and parts west, became subject to Germany and to harsh reprisals and restrictions on the use of Polish.

---

powstanie listopadowe (November Uprising). A national uprising against Russian rule that engaged large numbers of rank-and-file Warsaw citizenry, lasting from the night of November 29, 1830 (*noc listopadowa*, November night), until October 21, 1831. The uprising attacked the Belweder palace but was unsuccessful in an attempt to assassinate the Russian Archduke Constantine. Next it overcame the Warsaw

Arsenał (armory). One of the bloodiest battles was near Grochów, a stalemate that left some seven thousand Polish and ten thousand Russian soldiers dead. The ultimate failure of the insurrection led to severe cultural repression, deportations, conscription into the Russian army, and emigration, especially to France, in what became known as the Wielka Emigracja (Great Emigration). Freedoms within the Królestwo Polskie (Polish Kingdom) were severely curtailed, and the Polish army was disbanded. The uprising's slogan, "Za naszą i waszą wolność" (For your and our freedom), expresses sympathy also for the Russian Decembrists. The slogan outlived the insurrection, and continues to surface today in political speeches.

---

powstanie styczniowe (January Uprising). The bloodiest Polish national uprising, against Russian rule in the *zabór rosyjski* (Russian-occupied Poland), broke out in January 1863 and lasted until the fall of 1864. Its final leader, sometimes called its *dyktator* (dictator), was Romuald Traugutt, who was apprehended, incarcerated in the Cytadela, convicted, and hanged by the Russian authorities. The uprising's failure led to mass emigration, deportations to Siberia, confiscation of property (some four thousand Polish estates were confiscated for being in sympathy with the insurgency), and to the even harsher cultural repression of things Polish in Russian-occupied Poland. The Kongresówka (Congress Kingdom) was demoted to the status of a Russian province (Privislanskii Krai, "Vistula Land"). Women in the zabór rosyjski wore everyday black dresses to express solidarity with the uprising, as in Artur Grottger's *Pożegnanie powstańca* (The insurgent's farewell, 1866).

---

powstanie w getcie warszawskim (Jewish Ghetto Uprising, Warsaw, April–May 1943). The first civilian uprising in World War II against German occupation anywhere broke out on April 19, 1943. The Jewish rebellion was a desperate act of heroism sparked by the German plan to liquidate the ghetto and deport its remaining inhabitants (fifty to seventy thousand) to the death camp at Treblinka. Poorly armed and barely supported from the outside by the Polish underground working through the Żegota organization, the uprising was doomed to failure but lasted a surprising month. The commanders of the Żydowska Organizacja Bojowa (Jewish Fighting Organization), who mainly conducted the operation, were Mordechaj Anielewicz and Marek Edelman, the latter of whom escaped and survived the war. He worked as a medical doctor and prominent Jewish spokesperson in Łódź until his death in 2008. On Hitler's orders, the territory of the former Jewish ghetto in Warsaw was leveled to the ground. In 2013, on the anniversary of the uprising's outbreak, Polish President Bronisław Komorowski opened in Warsaw the Muzeum Historii Żydów Polskich (Museum of the History of Polish Jews). See also: Żydowski Związek Wojskowy. *Internationally famous photograph showing German soldiers rounding up Jewish "insurgents."*

---

powstanie warszawskie (Warsaw Uprising, August 1, 1944–October 3, 1944). An insurrection against the German occupation led by General Tadeusz Komorowski of the Armia Krajowa (Home Army); see also Generał Nil. It turned into a general uprising of the entire Warsaw population. Its aim was to place the country in Polish hands before the Soviets arrived, bringing with them certain occupation. It began at 5:00 p.m. (*Godzina "W.,"* or *Wybuch*, outbreak hour). The Soviet army, on the other side of the Wisła, did not assist or allow Allied air forces to lend assistance themselves. After sixty-three days the uprising was crushed with heavy loss of life, much of it meted out as indiscriminate retaliation on the civilian population by the Nazis; see *rzeź Woli*. As many as two hundred thousand people perished in the uprising, three-quarters of them civilian. Whatever important buildings or cultural monuments were left standing were systematically dynamited or burned by the retreating German army, leaving 85 percent of the city in ruins. The book to read is *Rising '44: The Battle for Warsaw*, by Norman Davies. An interesting cinematic re-creation of the uprising, based on bringing to life archival footage and still photographs, appeared in 2014. *The German "Brennkommando" setting fire to Warsaw.*

powstanie wielkopolskie (Greater Poland Uprising, 1918–1919). An insurrection by Polish citizens and troops across Wielkopolska (Greater Poland) at the conclusion of World War I, demanding the repatriation to Poland of lands taken by Prussia in the eighteenth-century rozbiory (partitions), including the territory around the Wielkopolska capital, Poznań. Armed conflict between German and Polish armies was sparked by the arrival of the musician and statesman Ignacy Paderewski to Poznań in 1918. The Polish leader was at first Captain Stanisław Taczak and then, later, General Józef Dowbor-Muśnicki. The aims of the uprising were largely achieved. Poland's new borders in the west were secured internationally by the *traktat wersalski* (Treaty of Versailles), making this one of Poland's few successful armed insurrections in its history out of many unsuccessful ones.

Poznań. The fifth-largest Polish city with a population of over 580,000. Poznań was one of the capitals of the Piast princes (see *Piastowie, dynastia*) in the ninth through tenth centuries. Located on the Warta River, it is a major commercial, industrial, and academic center. The enormous collections of the Biblioteka Raczyńskich (Raczyński Library) were almost completely destroyed in World War II. Workers' demonstrations in 1956 (see *czerwiec 1956, wypadki czerwcowe*) helped precipitate liberalization within the Polish communist party. To the outside world, Poznań is best known for its Międzynarodowe Targi Poznańskie (Poznań International Trade Fairs), by far the largest organizer of commercial fairs in the country. Because of its western location, good transportation connections, and trade reputation, the city attracts considerable foreign investment. The Poznań mechanical goats (*koziołki*) on the town hall clock (pictured) have become the town's symbol, and gave their name to the local American football team, Kozły Poznań (Poznań Goats).

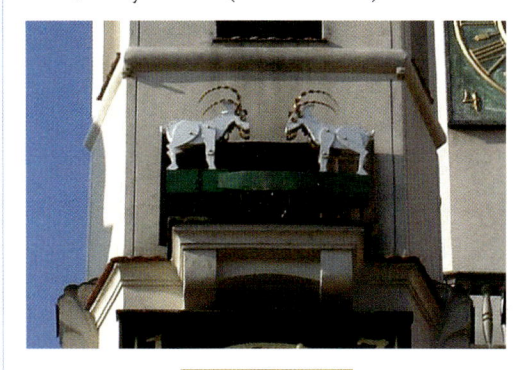

pozytywizm (positivism). A trend in late nineteenth-century literature popular in Poland in the approximate years 1864–1894 based on the philosophy of the Frenchman August Comte (1798–1857), who advocated applying scientific thinking to social problems. In Poland its prophet was Aleksander Świętochowski (1849–1938). Under positivism, prose forms (novels and short stories) predominated, and writers took a curative approach to social ills, believing that people are basically good and that man can improve his lot and that of society through rationality, the spread of education, and *praca u podstaw* (grassroots social work). Not surprisingly, this literary movement constantly ran the danger of being too naïve and openly didactic. Among its major themes were the education of the peasants, the emancipation of women, and the assimilation of Jews into the rest of society. Major Polish positivist authors were Bolesław Prus (1847–1912), Eliza Orzeszkowa (1841–1910), Maria Konopnicka (1842–1910) and, with certain reservations, Henryk Sienkiewicz (1846–1916) and Stefan Żeromski (1864–1925). See also: Antek.

prawo magdeburskie (Magdeburg Law). Also known as *prawo niemieckie* (German law). Most medieval towns in Poland (from the thirteenth century on) were granted town privileges (in modern terms, incorporated) by the king according to so-called Magdeburg or German law, which defined the town layout and set down the principles of its government, as well as the town's rights and obligations under the king. Part of the reason for implementing German law was to set internationally recognizable town standards that would encourage immigration into Poland. There were many variations, but a typical town under Magdeburg law had *mury obronne* (defensive walls), a *ratusz* (town hall), a *sukiennice* (trade hall) in the *rynek* (market square), with *rzemieślnicy* (craftsmen) belonging to given *rzemiosła* (crafts) located along streets radiating from the rynek. The kamienice (townhouses) of rich merchants and nobles lined the town square. An excellent example of such a town is Kraków, with its central Sukiennice and radiating streets, some named after crafts, such as ulica Szewska (Cobbler Street). Central Wrocław (pictured) was also clearly laid out under Magdeburg law.

Preisner, Zbigniew (b. 1955). A self-taught pianist, guitarist, and composer, Preisner (born Kowalski) has grown from a creator of cabaret music into one of the world's best-known and admired composers of film music. He came to the world's attention largely through his soundtracks for the films of Krzysztof Kieślowski, including all four of his Polish-French coproductions. His style could be called neo-Romantic. In Kieślowski's films his work is sometimes attributed to the fictional Dutch composer Van den Budenmayer. Preisner's "Requiem dla mojego przyjaciela" (Requiem for my friend, 1998) was dedicated to Kieślowski's memory.

PRL. See Polska Rzeczpospolita Ludowa (PRL).

PRL, nostalgia za PRL-em (nostalgia for communist Poland). The well-known longing for the good old days that were not really that good has been embraced by Polish popular culture in regard to the years of the PRL. Costume dramas set in the PRL are all the rage in contemporary Polish cinema, as are photographic exhibits, television retrospectives, recent books, and scholarly conferences devoted to the phenomenon of how it is possible to idealize in retrospect long lines, food ration cards, empty shelves, lack of spare parts, bad cigarettes, rude waiters and service staff, vacuum cleaners that made the appropriate noise but didn't vacuum, stores where one could pay only with dollars (themselves barely legal), an official press that insulted one's intelligence at every turn, and the list goes on. Not to mention the secret police, phone bugging, and the violent suppression of dissent. On the other hand, life was simpler then, not so much ruled by the pursuit of money as nowadays, and one felt better taken care of by the state's social safety net.

proszę (please). *Proszę* literally means "I ask," or "I beg," and reminds one a bit of Shakespearean English "prithee." One uses the word a hundred times a day at least, in all manner of situations. Depending on context it can mean "please," "you're welcome," "here you are," "help yourself," "after you," "please come in," "if you please," "by all means." A store owner will say *proszę* to mean "may I help you?" and *proszę* is the polite way to say "I beg your pardon?" when one has not understood something. One may also use *proszę?* when answering the telephone instead of *słucham?* or *halo?* The form *proszę* (or *poproszę*) is also used to ask for things in restaurants, kiosks, and stores: *Poproszę/proszę dwa bilety tramwajowe* (I'd like two trolley tickets, please).

prowokacja gliwicka (Gliwice Provocation, 1939). One of several provocations planned in secrecy by Hitler and staged on the eve of the German invasion of Poland. On August 31, 1939, a band of Germans disguised as Polish saboteurs, aided by a band of soldiers in fake uniforms pretending to be Polish, staged an attack on a German radio station in Silesian Gliwice, ten kilometers inside the German border. Hitler effectively used the event as international propaganda for justifying his already elaborately prepared invasion the following day. The details of the operation become known only after the war, coming out at the Nuremberg War Crimes Tribunal.

Prus, Bolesław (1847–1912). The pen name of Aleksander Głowacki. A journalist, novelist, and short-story writer, Prus was the exemplar of the socially committed positivist writer (see *pozytywizm*), and is widely considered to have been the best Polish novelist of the nineteenth century. His best-known novel is the two-volume *Lalka* (*The Doll*, 1890), about a wealthy department store owner named Stanisław Wokulski whose money cannot buy him the love of a woman above his social station. *Faraon* (*Pharaoh*, 1897), a historical novel about power politics, set in ancient Egypt, is also well regarded. Both have been made into feature-length films: *Faraon* in 1966 by Jerzy Kawalerowicz and *Lalka* by Wojciech Jerzy Has in 1968. Prus's short stories "Antek," "Kamizelka" (The waistcoat), and "Katarynka" (The organ-grinder) are known to most Polish schoolchildren, and all have been made into television movies.

Prusy (Prussians). The original Prussians were a Baltic tribe whose language, related to Lithuanian and Latvian, died out in the eighteenth century. Their territory across the north of present-day Poland was occupied by German colonists spearheaded by the *Krzyżacy* (Teutonic Knights), who either converted or annihilated the Prussian tribes and, from the thirteenth century on, established rule in what eventually became known as Prusy Wschodnie (East Prussia). Prusy Zachodnie (West Prussia) came into existence after the *pierwszy rozbiór Polski* (first partition of Poland, 1772; see *rozbiory*). Both East and West Prussia became joined in the province of Prussia (German Preussen) in the unified German state after 1871. Most of East Prussia and all of West Prussia were ceded to Poland as one of the outcomes of World War II. Part of East Prussia went to the Soviet Union, including land around the former East Prussian capital Königsberg (Królewiec), now Russian Kaliningrad.

prywatyzacja (privatization). As an outcome of the *rozmowy Okrągłego Stołu* (Round Table Discussions), the privatization of formerly state-owned enterprises began in 1989 under finance minister *Leszek Balcerowicz*. In all, 512 firms — covering manufacturing, telecommunications, petroleum, mining, and banking — were placed in the Narodowe Fundusze Inwestycyjne (National Investment Fund), shares in which were made available to every Polish adult in the form of a negotiable Powszechne Świadectwo Udziałowe (General Share Certificate, pictured). At the beginning corruption was rife, as members of the *nomenklatura* had the inside track on many private acquisitions and made quick fortunes. Most firms ended up in foreign hands. Privatization often resulted in worker layoffs, as foreign owners instituted more efficient means of production. On the whole, however, the process was realized with benefit to the Polish economy and worker, and with a lower component of corruption than in some of the other former Soviet Bloc countries.

Przemyśl. One of the oldest towns in Poland, with its earliest mention in 981 in the Rus Primary Chronicle, and the oldest Polish town with records of Jewish settlement (early eleventh century), Przemyśl is located in the southeast on the San River, a tributary to the *Wisła*, close to the Ukrainian border. It has around sixty-six thousand inhabitants. Historically, Przemyśl was contested between the Kievan and Polish princes. After the *pierwszy rozbiór Polski* (first partition of Poland, 1772; see *rozbiory*), Przemyśl belonged to Austria. Twierdza Przemyśl (Przemyśl Fortress) was one of Austro-Hungary's largest outposts, and it was twice besieged by the Russian army in World War I. Before World War II the population was approximately one-third Polish, one-third Ukrainian, and one-third Jewish. Przemyśl was and still is a town of many different Christian denominations: Roman Catholic, Eastern Orthodox, Greek Catholic (Uniate), and Protestant (Methodists, Seventh-Day Adventists, Baptists, and Jehovah's Witnesses).

przesądy i uprzedzenia (superstitions). Most superstitions Poles think are uniquely theirs — such as not sitting in a draft or unmarried girls not sitting at the corner of a table — are shared throughout Central Europe. They cannot possibly all be catalogued here, but some that Czesław Miłosz remembered from his childhood in Polish Lithuania are: redheaded women are unfaithful, taking a bath is bad for your health, and drinking milk with certain foods causes intestinal blockage. Never spit into a fire, turn a loaf of bread upside down, or throw bread away (see also *chleb i sól*). Don't walk backwards, for that means you're measuring your mother's grave. The widespread superstition about not lighting three cigarettes on a match possibly comes out of World War I, when that gave a sniper enough time to draw a bead on you.

Przesmycki, Zenon (1861–1944), pen name Miriam. Poet, translator, and literary critic of the Młoda Polska (Young Poland) period. A proponent of art for art's sake, between 1901 and 1908 Przesmycki published the sumptuously designed and edited literary journal *Chimera*. He was the discoverer for the broader public of the poetry of Cyprian Kamil Norwid, who by that time had been almost forgotten, and he was also a gifted translator into Polish of the poetry of the French symbolists (Verlaine, Baudelaire, Rimbaud) and the American Edgar Allan Poe. His version of Poe's *The Raven* (*Kruk*) is especially deserving of admiration.

Przygoda na Mariensztacie (An adventure in Mariensztat, 1954). A Hollywood-type musical film directed by Leonard Buczkowski (1900–1967), this was the first Polish feature-length film in color, and an artistically successful example of cinematic *socrealizm* (socialist realism). The plot (boy meets girl, boy and girl lose each other, boy and girl find each other again) plays out against the reconstruction of the war-destroyed Mariensztat district near Warsaw's Starówka (old town), where the boy is a *przodownik pracy* (hero of labor) bricklayer, and the girl is a performer in a folk troupe (played here by the Mazowsze folk ensemble) who takes up the bricklaying trade. The girl's singing voice is dubbed by Irena Santor. The film, which introduced the popular song "Jak przygoda, to tylko w Warszawie" (An adventure as only in Warsaw), may still be viewed with pleasure.

---

przyjaciel, przyjaciółka. Using a Polish social networking service (in practice, Facebook or Nasza Klasa) draws one's attention to the relative indiscriminate use of *friend* in English. In Poland one typically has from three to six people whom one considers a "friend" (*przyjaciel*-m., *przyjaciółka*-f.). To acquire a new one sometimes means getting rid of an old one, for, after *rodzina* (one's extended family), there is only so much room in one's life for true friends. Others are either "acquaintances" (*znajomy*-m., *znajoma*-f.) or, if one knows them from work or school, "colleagues" or "mates" (*kolega*-m., *koleżanka*-f.). To "friend" someone in Facebook is "dodać znajomego" (add an acquaintance), while the brutal English "to unfriend" is "usunąć użytkownika z grona znajomych" (remove a user from the group of one's acquaintances). To speak of the *przyjaciel* of one's wife is to refer genteelly to her lover; *przyjaciółka* has a similar, if less frequent, use for referring to a husband's mistress.

KALEIDOSCOPE OF POLAND

przypadki gramatyczne (grammatical case). Learning to speak Polish gives one an idea about what it was like to speak one of the highly inflected languages of classical antiquity — ancient Greek, Latin, or Sanskrit. Like them, Polish has a well-developed system of grammatical cases (expressed by endings attached to nouns) and relatively free word order. The names of the cases and their main function are as follows: *mianownik* (nominative, subject of sentence), *dopełniacz* (genitive, possession), *celownik* (dative, indirect object), *biernik* (accusative, direct object), *narzędnik* (instrumental, means by which), *miejscownik* (locative, location), *wołacz* (vocative, direct address). There is the potential for as many as fourteen different forms for a noun, although in practice it comes to fewer than this. Here is the declension of *pies* (dog):

	Singular	Plural
Nom.	pies	psy
Gen.	psa	psów
Dat.	psu	psom
Acc.	psa	psy
Inst.	psem	psami
Loc.	psie	psach
Voc.	psie	psy

See also: **aspekt dokonany i niedokonany**; **język polski, języki słowiańskie**.

---

przysięga Kościuszki (Kościuszko's Oath to the Polish Nation). On March 24, 1794, in the *Rynek Główny* (main market square) in **Kraków**, on a spot marked today by a commemorative stone slab, **Tadeusz Kościuszko** proclaimed an armed insurrection against tsarist Russian rule, giving his oath to the Polish nation that he would not use his military power for any personal gain but only to defend the territorial integrity of Poland. He thereby assumed the position of the sole leader of the rebellion. The vow is reen-acted yearly by the Polish military as part of the celebration of Święto Wojska Polskiego (Polish Armed Forces Day, August 15). *Wojciech Kossak*, Przysięga Kościuszki.

przysłowia o Polsce i Polakach (national proverbs). A self-conscious proverb about Poles was **Mikołaj Rej**'s sixteenth-century **"Polacy nie gęsi, iż swój język mają"** (Poles are not geese; they have their own language). A more biting one is "mądry Polak po szkodzie" (a Pole is wise after the fact), like the English "shutting the stable door after the horse is gone," but taking a swipe at the national character as having a propensity for rushing into something without giving it due thought only to regret it later, but not necessarily profiting from the experience. "Polska nierządem stoi" (Poland stands in anarchy) comes from the seventeenth-century Saxon period (see *saskie czasy, noc saska*) and has been used off and on by politicians ever since. "Polak potrafi" (a Pole can do it) was a slogan dreamed up in the 1970s (the Gierek years) to buck up national pride, but nowadays it is just as often spoken sarcastically, as in the sense "if there's a way to get around the spirit of a regulation, a Pole will find it." It is also the saying of choice for referring to something preposterously jerry-rigged, as with the pictured station wagon converted into a trailer. The saying "słoń a sprawa polska" (the elephant and the Polish question), originating among participants at the Versailles Peace Conference of 1919, refers to the Poles' ability to inject Poland into any discussion. See also: Teraz Polska.

Psie Pole, bitwa (Battle on Dog's Field). A military engagement in the vicinity of Wrocław in 1109 in which Bolesław III Krzywousty (Bolesław the Wrymouth) was victorious over invading Germans — or maybe not. The field was described by medieval chronicler Wincenty Kadłubek as being overrun with dogs feeding off the corpses of the fallen Germans, hence the name, which survives as a district of Wrocław. Kadłubek wrote one hundred years after the fact, and no other historical attestation of the battle exists. Consequently, historians are divided over who fought with whom, and as to whether the battle even took place. This has not prevented painters from depicting the event, comic books from telling the tale, historical reenactments from taking place, and a local committee from forming to erect a monument to it.

Psy (Pigs). The title (literally, "dogs") is a vulgar name for the police, and the title of a breakout film by Władysław Pasikowski about organized crime, drugs, violence, and corruption in the Polish police force in the years following the fall of communism. Made in 1992, after the lifting of censorship, the film went after a new and younger audience raised on the sex and violence of Western cinema, and it introduced topics and used language not seen before on the Polish screen. It featured a pleiad of male stars of the time, including Bogusław Linda, Marek Kondrat, Janusz Gajos, Cezary Pazura, and Olaf Lubaszenko; and it was followed by the inevitable sequel, *Psy II: Ostatnia krew* (Dogs II: last blood, 1994).

PTTK. See Polskie Towarzystwo Turystyczno-Krajoznawcze (PTTK).

Pudzianowski, Mariusz (b. 1977). Nicknamed Pudzian, Pudzianowski is a Polish strongman and mixed martial arts competitor. He has won the World's Strongest Man title five times (he was second twice), more than any other person. He is a four-time winner of the Strongman Super Series, and two-time winner of the World Strongman Cup. During the 2000 and 2001 seasons he was incarcerated for assault, and thus unable to compete. According to his website he has 56 cm biceps, a 148 cm chest, and a personal best of pressing 290 kilograms (638 lb.) from a supine position.

Pułaski, Kazimierz (1745 or 1747–1779). One of the leaders of the konfederacja barska (Bar Confederacy) of 1768–1772. Implicated in an attempt to kidnap the king, Pułaski had to emigrate. George Washington made him a general in the American revolutionary army. Sometimes called the "father of the American cavalry," Pułaski died from wounds suffered at the Battle of

Savannah. In the United States, Pułaski Day (March 4) is celebrated mainly in Chicago, which has a day off from school. Federally, Pułaski Day (October 11) is a so-called holiday by presidential proclamation, renewed each year. On November 6, 2009, President Barack Obama signed a joint resolution of the US Senate and House of Representatives making Pułaski an American citizen, 230 years after his death.

PZPR. See Polska Zjednoczona Partia Robotnicza (PZPR).

Q

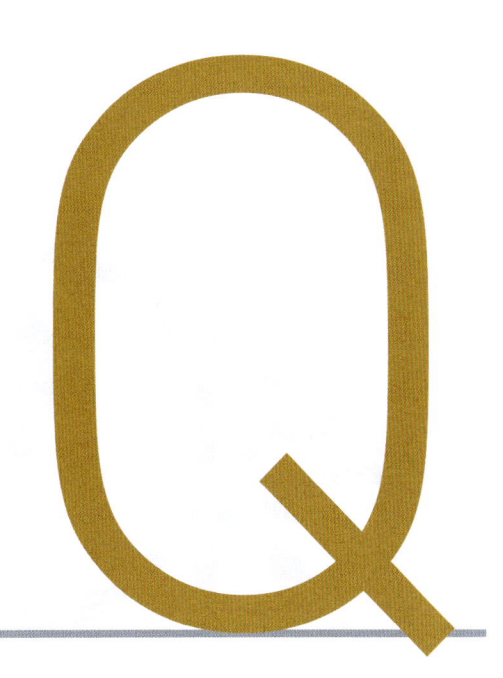

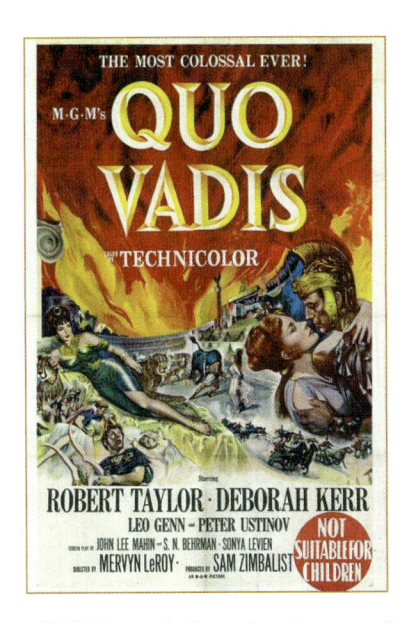

Quo vadis? Alongside **Stanisław Reymont's Chłopi** (The peasants), **Henryk Sienkiewicz**'s novel, published in 1896, is one of few Polish novels to have become an international best seller. It has been translated into more than fifty languages. The content is decidedly not Polish, but is set in the time of the early Christians under Nero, allowing Sienkiewicz to indulge his taste for graphic violence. According to an apocryphal story, as Peter was leaving Rome to escape the persecution of the Christians, he encountered Jesus going in the opposite direction. To the question "Quo vadis, domine?" (Where are you going, master?), Jesus replied, "To Rome, to be crucified a second time." Peter returned to Rome and was himself crucified, upside down. One of the few possible allusions to Poland in the novel is the maiden Lygia, a barbarian ruler's captive daughter who has converted to Christianity. Sienkiewicz won the 1905 Nobel Prize in Literature for his life's work, but really primarily for this novel. *Quo vadis?* was made into a Hollywood-type extravaganza by Mervyn LeRoy (see poster) in 1951, superior by almost anyone's evaluation to Jerzy Kawalerowicz's 2001 Polish rendition.

rabacja galicyjska (alternatively, *rzeź galicyjska*, the Galician jacquerie). Egged on and monetarily encouraged by the Austrian authorities in Galicja, who were trying to put down insurrectionist activities in Kraków and across Galicia, a peasant uprising against Polish landowners over the course of several days in 1846 resulted in the slaughter of up to three thousand landowners and their families, along with town officials and priests, in the counties around Sanok, Tarnów, and Jasło. The uprising, led by Jakub Szela, was pursued with particular bloodthirstiness, with people being cut in half with saws while still alive. The Austrians rewarded Szela with a distinguished service medal and a farm in Bukowina, Ukraine. Szela appears as a ghost from the past in Stanisław Wyspiański's symbolist drama *Wesele* (1901). A bitter irony of the "affair" was that Edward Dembowski (1822–1846), one of the Kraków insurgency's leaders, had as an aim precisely the freeing of the peasants. For their part, the peasants did not want Polish intellectuals to get credit for anything.

Racławice. A village in southern Poland on the Racławka River that was the site of a victory of Polish insurgents under Tadeusz Kościuszko over the Russian army in 1794, during the insurekcja kościuszkowska (Kościuszko Insurrection). Kościuszko's forces included peasants called *kosynierzy* (scythe-soldiers), whose main weapon was a scythe beaten into a bayonet on a long pole, a surprisingly effective weapon. One peasant soldier who distinguished himself at the battle was Wojciech Bartosz Głowacki, who disarmed and captured a Russian cannon by first snuffing out its wick with his cap, becoming thereby a symbol of a newly born Polish peasant patriotism. The battle is the subject of the famous *Panorama Racławicka* in Wrocław.

Rada Wzajemnej Pomocy Gospodarczej (RWPG) (Council for Mutual Economic Assistance, COMECON, 1949–1991). The Communist Bloc's response to the West's Organization for European Economic Cooperation, which was established in 1948 to help administer the

Marshall Plan for the reconstruction of Europe after World War II. Having the hidden aim of binding the economies of its states to that of the Soviet Union, the RWPG was an economic parallel to the defense-oriented Układ Warszawski (Warsaw Pact), with more or less the same members — although membership was eventually extended to communist countries outside Europe. The RWPG, in which the Soviet Union dependably looked after its own interests and had the power to enforce them, was signally unsuccessful in promoting the economic integration of the increasingly lagging economies of its members, few of whom really felt like cooperating in the first place. Most agreements ended up being bilateral and based on barter, one result of which was that Polish consumers, in even the drabbest of times, had occasional access to Cuban cigars, rum, and oranges; Hungarian and Bulgarian wines; and Soviet champagne and cameras.

Radio Maryja. A radio station with a national reach projecting a conservative nationalist-Catholic point of view on matters of religion, society, and national and international politics. Founded by the controversial Father Tadeusz Rydzyk in 1991, it is headquartered in Toruń. Supported by private donations, it is run by the Zgromadzenie Najświętszego Odkupiciela (Congregation of the Most Holy Redeemer). Radio Maryja is often criticized for engaging excessively on the side of particular political candidates in the Narodowa Demokracja (National Democratic) tradition, and for airing the occasionally bigoted opinions of its commentators and listenership. The latter are predominantly older, rural, and female, sarcastically referred to as the league of the *moherowe berety* (mohair berets), named after the kind of headgear they seem to prefer. Radio Maryja broadcasts a daily Holy Mass and catechism classes, and adopts a negative stance on Poland's being in the European Union. Its motto reads, "A Catholic voice in your home." The cable TV wing of Radio Maryja, Trwam (I persist), has recently been denied a digital broadcasting license, causing more controversy. See also: Kościół rzymskokatolicki.

Radio Wolna Europa (RWE), Rozgłośnia Polska (Radio Free Europe, Polish Service). RWE was a Cold War broadcast service to Russia and the countries of the Soviet Bloc, in the languages of those countries, funded by the American government. RWE was a reliable source of international and national news. It began in 1950, and its signals were jammed (not always successfully) in Poland until 1988. It played a particularly useful role during times of political turmoil, such as *październik 1956* (the October 1956 events in Poznań; see *odwilż gomułkowska*), *marzec 1968* (the March 1968 events in Warsaw), or the *grudzień 1970* (December 1970 events on the seacoast). The director of the Polish Section from 1952 to 1976 was Zdzisław Jeziorański. Zdzisław Najder, the director from 1982 to 1987, was sentenced to death in absentia for "collaborating with American intelligence." After Poland regained its independence, RFE Poland was moved to Warsaw in 1990 and was disbanded in 1994.

Radom. The fifteenth-largest Polish town, with a population of 223,400, Radom is located in east-central Poland, and has been the site of many important historical events, including the selection of eleven-year-old Jadwiga, daughter of Ludwik Węgierski (Ludwik of Hungary), as queen of Poland in 1384. The *wydarzenia radomskie* (massive workers' demonstrations) in

1976 and its aftermath of repression (see *czerwiec 1976*) helped to unite Polish labor and intellectuals in their opposition to the communist government, leading to the formation of the Workers' Defense Committee, **KOR**. Radom's Łucznik (Archer) firearms factory produces assault rifles and other state-of-the-art military hardware. *Radom city hall.*

Radziwiłłowie, rodzina (Radziwiłł family). A magnate family of Lithuanian origin (see *magnateria*), now into its seventeenth generation and counting. The Radziwiłłowie held (and hold) the title of *książęta* (princes) of the Holy Roman Empire, confirmed in articles of the *unia lubelska* (Union of Lublin) of 1569. Barbara Radziwiłłówna, the second wife of King **Zygmunt II August**, was crowned queen of Poland-Lithuania in 1550. In the United States the name is familiar as the name by marriage of Jacqueline Kennedy's younger sister Lee Radziwill. *Radziwiłł coat of arms.*

Rakowski, Mieczysław (1926–2008). A key figure in communist Poland from the late 1950s until its end in 1990. By profession a journalist, Rakowski cofounded the reformist (within the party) weekly *Polityka* and was its editor-in-chief from 1958 to 1982. He was a member of the party's central committee from 1964, and was deputy prime minister when *stan wojenny* (martial law) was declared in 1981, of which he was a staunch supporter, alienating those who had taken him for a real reformer. Rakowski's most prominent political role was as communist Poland's last prime minister in 1988–1989, when he presided over the **rozmowy Okrągłego Stołu** (Round Table Discussions, 1989) which led to the legalization of the **Solidarność** (Solidarity) trade union and to the eventual dissolution of the communist party and to Polish independence.

Rawicz, Sławomir (1915–2004). In 1941 six prisoners escaped from the Soviet **Gułag** near the Arctic Circle in midwinter and completed the most arduous journey on foot ever recorded — or maybe they didn't. In his best seller *The Long Walk*, published in English in 1956 and in Polish in 1993, Rawicz narrates how he organized the escape and made the six-thousand-kilometer trek unaided across the Siberian taiga, the Gobi Desert, Tibet, and the Himalayas, to arrive in India along with two other survivors a year later. Soviet archives contradict Rawicz's story, but he could have been telling the story of another Pole, Witold Gliński. British army records indicate that three people did arrive out of the Himalayas and were debriefed in India, but the trace ends there. The story was retold in the film *The Way Back* (in Polish, *Niepokonani*, The unconquered, 2011) by Australian director Peter Weir. See also: **Robinsonowie warszawscy**.

reakcja pogańska (pagan reaction). Following the reign of Mieszko II (ruled 1025–1034), a mass pagan revolt against the Piast princes (see **Piastowie, *dynastia***) and the authority of the Church laid waste to churches and monasteries throughout **Wielkopolska** (Greater Poland) and encouraged a devastating Czech invasion from the south. Besides religious issues, the common folk had had enough of financially supporting the wars of **Bolesław I Chrobry** and Mieszko II, and of paying tribute for the expansion of churches and monasteries. Mieszko II's son Kazimierz I Odnowiciel (Kazimierz the Restorer, ruled 1034–1058) succeeded in quelling the pagan revolt and negotiating a favorable peace with the Czechs. However, Wielkopolska had been so plundered and weakened that the capital was moved from Gniezno to Kraków in Małopolska.

reformacja (Reformation in Poland). In Poland the Protestant Reformation of the Christian Church was vigorous in the sixteenth through the seventeenth centuries, shielded by the konfederacja warszawska (Warsaw Confederation) of 1573, guaranteeing freedom of religious belief throughout the Rzeczpospolita Obojga Narodów (Polish-Lithuanian Commonwealth). The Reformation was almost exclusively a gentry phenomenon, never significantly affecting the peasantry. In some areas more than half of the nobility converted to one of the three main branches of Protestantism in Poland: *luteranizm* (Lutheranism, popular among urban merchants), *kalwinizm* (Calvinism), and *arianizm* (Arianism), including the *bracia polscy* (Polish Brethren; see arianie). The Reformation contributed to the development of a national literature and to education in the provinces. That it died out as quickly as it did, becoming practically a nonissue by the eighteenth century, was due to the apathy of the peasantry, the effective Counter-Reformation activism of the *jezuici* (Jesuit order; see Skarga, Piotr), and the fact that during the potop szwedzki (Swedish Deluge), Protestantism had become identified with the enemies of the Commonwealth.

Rej, Mikołaj z Nagłowic (1505–1569). A Polish Renaissance writer, sometimes called the "father of Polish literature," although Biernat z Lublina (Biernat of Lublin) also competes for the honor with his *Raj duszny* (Paradise of the soul, 1513). Rej (alternatively spelled Rey) was prolific and is exceptional in earlier Polish literature for being a Protestant. Both a prose writer and a poet, albeit of unoriginal rhymed couplets, Rej's works tend to be didactic but they are linguistically robust and visually evocative. His best-known works are *Żywot człowieka poczciwego* (Life of a virtuous man, 1558) and *Krótka rozprawa między trzema osobami: Panem, wójtem a plebanem* (A short discourse between three persons: A lord, a mayor, and a pastor, 1543). See also: "Polacy nie gęsi."

Rejtan, Tadeusz (1742–1780). A participant in the konfederacja barska (Bar Confederacy) and representative to the Sejm (parliament) from Nowogródek, famous for his 1773 bodily protest in the Sejm at the first partition of Poland of 1772. He is said to have declared, after baring his chest, "Zabijcie mnie, ale nie zabijajcie ojczyzny!" (Kill me, but not the fatherland!). By tradition, Rejtan was so dismayed by the downfall of Poland that he withdrew to his estate in Lithuania, went mad, and committed suicide. That event and Jan Matejko's controversial award-winning (in Paris) painting *The Fall of Poland*, fragment pictured, showing Rejtan's protest, were the inspirations for Jacek Kaczmarski's protest song of the 1980s, "Rejtan, czyli raport ambasadora" (Rejtan, or the ambassador's report), recounting the Russian ambassador Repnin's report on the success of the first partition to Empress Catherine the Great.

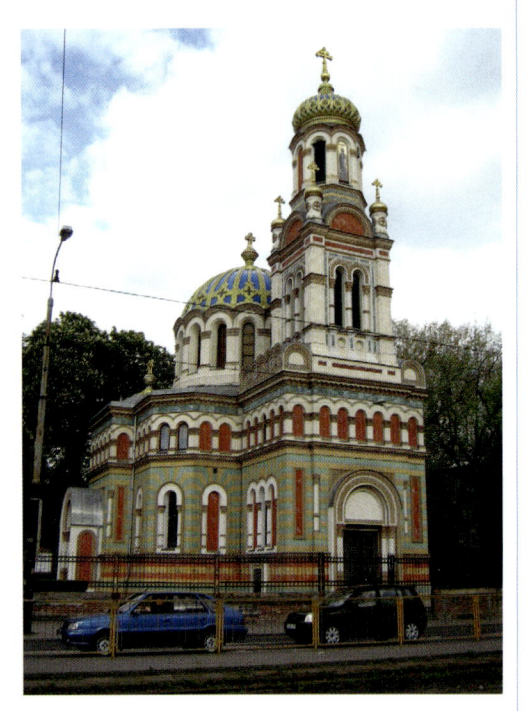

religie (religions in Poland). At one time fairly religiously diverse, Poland today is overwhelmingly Roman Catholic (see Kościół rzymskokatolicki), with around 95 percent of the population baptized as such and around 60 percent regularly attending church, a larger percentage than in any other European country. Other Christian denominations with a sizable number of followers in Poland include Prawosławny (Eastern Orthodox, 506,000); Ewangelicko-Augsburski (Lutheran, 100,000); Greckokatolicki, Unicki (Greek Catholic or Uniate, 53,000); Starokatolicki Mariawitów (Mariavite, 23,000); Zielonoświątkowy (Pentecostal, 23,000); Kościół Polskokatolicki (Polish National Catholic Church — a transplant from America — 20,000); and Adwentyści Dnia Siódmego (Seventh-Day Adventists, 9,600). Active in door-to-door proselytizing are the Świadkowie Jehowy (Jehovah's Witnesses, 123,000). Historically Poland bordered the Ottoman Empire, and there are, in fact, around five thousand followers of Islam in Poland. Despite a long historical tradition, and many remaining synagogues, there are today probably fewer than five thousand practitioners of Judaizm (Judaism; see also Żydzi w Polsce). *The Alexander Nevskii Eastern Orthodox Church in Łódź.*

rewolucja roku 1905 (1905 Revolution). The 1905 Revolution in Russia, a prelude to the Russian Revolution of 1917, was accompanied in Russian-occupied Poland by spontaneous massive strikes and worker demonstrations, especially in Warsaw and Łódź, during which hundreds of demonstrators were killed by police. Students at Polish schools and universities went on strike for more than two years over the issue of the language of instruction, Polish versus Russian. The 1905 Revolution actually won some concessions for Polish lands under Russian control, including the right to form Polish organizations and the right to use Polish in local government offices.

Reymont, Władysław Stanisław (1867–1925). A Polish writer and representative of the Młoda Polska (Young Poland) movement in prose fiction, Reymont's writing style was highly ornate and often imitated folk dialect. Reymont received the Nobel Prize for Literature in 1924 for his four-volume epic novel *Chłopi* (The peasants), in which the traditional rural life plays out against a family tragedy of Grecian proportions. Reymont is also remembered for his grim novel of the textile industry in Łódź, *Ziemia obiecana* (The promised land, 1899). Both works have been turned into films, *Chłopi* in 1973 by Jan Rybkowski and *Ziemia obiecana* in 1974 by Andrzej Wajda. An operatic version of *Chłopi*, with music by Witold Rudziński, appeared in 1972. *Władysław Stanisław Reymont by Jacek Malczewski.*

Robinsonowie warszawscy (Warsaw Robinson Crusoes). Several hundred people, mostly Jews, survived in the rubble of bombed-out Warsaw between the end of the powstanie warszawskie (Warsaw Uprising) on October 2, 1944, and its liberation in January, 1945, living on remaining scraps of food and, mainly, starving. The two most famous were Marek Edelman, a leader of the powstanie w getcie warszawskim (Warsaw Ghetto Uprising) and a prominent cardiologist and Jewish spokesman after the war, and the concert pianist and composer Władysław Szpilman, who later became head of the music section of Polish Radio and the subject of Roman Polański's Oscar-winning film *The Pianist* (2002). Another and even more amazing Polish Robinson Crusoe story, although not of Warsaw, is that of Marek Głowacki, the only survivor of a shipwreck in the Pacific Ocean in 1917. Głowacki lived for nineteen years on an island that was little more than a rock, surviving on nothing but fish and writing a sporadic diary in his own blood with a pen fashioned from sea urchin spines. His remains were discovered in 1945 by an American navy patrol boat. See also: Rawicz, Sławomir.

Rodowicz, Maryla (b. 1945). A Polish popular singer in the pop rock and folk rock vein who got her start in the 1960s. Winner of many awards and widely traveled, Rodowicz was especially popular in the Soviet Union. She even tried her hand at American country music — without, however, making a dent in that market. She has recorded more than two thousand songs and is still going strong in 2015. Among her biggest hits are "Sing, sing," "Małgośka," "Wsiąść do pociągu" (Hop on the train), "Ale to już było" (But that already happened), "Kolorowe jarmarki" (Colored fairs), and Agnieszka Osiecka's "Niech żyje bal" (Long live the ball), some of the lyrics from which are:

> Niech żyje bal!
> Bo to życie to bal jest nad bale!
> Niech żyje bal!
> Drugi raz nie zaproszą nas wcale!

> Long live the ball!
> For life is the ball of all balls!
> Long live the ball!
> Next time they won't invite us at all!

---

rodzaj męskoosobowy (masculine-personal gender). The Polish language is unique among European languages in distinguishing the so-called virile, or masculine-personal gender, used to refer to any group of people or objects at least one of whose members is a male person. Any other group (for example, a woman and her cats, or tables and chairs) usually count as non-masculine personal, although Poles themselves are often unsure. The distinction is expressed with different noun, numeral, adjective, and past-tense verb endings. See the contrast between "Ci dwaj młodzi mężczyźni czekali" (male), and "Te dwie młode kobiety czekały" (female): "Those two young men/women were

KALEIDOSCOPE OF POLAND 217

waiting." The distinction strikes many foreigners as male chauvinistic, but it does not seem to bother women in Poland too much. See also: **aspekt dokonany i niedokonany; język polski, języki słowiańskie; przypadki gramatyczne**.

rogal świętomarciński (Saint Martin croissant). Baked in the shape of a bull's head, *rogale świętomarcińskie* are a white poppy-seed roll specialty of the **Poznań** area rolled out especially for November 11, Saint Martin's Day. They are dubiously said to have served in pagan times as a surrogate for offering a bull to the gods. Later the Church equally dubiously strained to associate them with Saint Martin, whose horse had lost a shoe of that shape. Poznań bakers revived the custom toward the end of the nineteenth century, with a certain number being given to the poor. Permission to produce them commercially is strictly controlled, and they are a regional specialty recognized by the European Union. Some 250 tons of the pastry are produced around November 11, and a total of some five hundred tons during the course of the year.

Rokossowski, Konstanty (1896–1968). A Warsaw-born Soviet army officer with the rank of marshal, of unquestioned military brilliance and bravery during World War II, two times Hero of the Soviet Union. His name in Poland is forever connected to the Soviet takeover of the country, in which Rokossowski, as a Polish citizen but representing the Soviet presence (and speaking Polish with a pronounced and often parodied Russian accent), held many high-ranking offices, including Minister of National Defense (1949–1956). As such he authorized the use of the army against workers in **Poznań** (see *czerwiec 1956, wypadki czerwcowe*). After **Władysław Gomułka** took over as party secretary in 1956, Rokossowski returned to Russia and changed his citizenship. He is buried in Red Square in Moscow. Rokossowski's daughter Ariadna is a prominent journalist today in Russia.

"Rota Marii Konopnickiej" (Maria Konopnicka's credo). A poem and hymn by positivist writer Maria Konopnicka (1842–1910) that was a response to forced Germanization in the part of Poland under the *zabór pruski* (Prussian partition); see **Września**. Published in 1908 with music by Feliks Nowowiejski, it was a candidate for the Polish national anthem following World War I, but did not win — fortunately, for it is far too defensively nationalistic in tone for today's tastes. It was sung at the unveiling of the **Pomnik Grunwaldzki** (Grunwald Monument) in **Kraków** in 1910. Its first lines are:

> Nie rzucim ziemi skąd nasz ród!
> Nie damy pogrześć mowy
> Polski my naród, polski lud
> Królewski szczep piastowy.

> We'll not abandon the country of our birth!
> We'll not allow our tongue to be buried,
> We're the Polish nation, Polish people,
> Of royal Piast lineage.

rozbicie dzielnicowe (division into districts). A period of Polish history lasting from the death of **Bolesław III Krzywousty** (Bolesław the Wrymouth) in 1138 to the coronation of **Władysław I Łokietek** (Władysław the Short) in 1320. In his *testament* (will), Krzywousty established the principle of dividing the Polish kingdom up among his sons according to seniority. Accordingly, during this time Poland was ruled by a series of regional princes, chief among them being the ruler of **Małopolska** (Lesser Poland) in **Kraków**. The system led ipso facto to the weakening of central authority. As a plus, certain provincial towns acquired prominence. As a negative, Poland's hold over **Śląsk** (Silesia) and **Pomorze** (Pomerania) was lost for the next six hundred years, the former to Bohemia and the latter to the **Krzyżacy** (Teutonic Knights).

rozbiory (partitions of Poland: 1772, 1793, 1795). Three successive divisions of Poland among Russia, Prussia, and (except for the second partition) Austria, eventually leading to the total incorporation of Polish territory into the lands of its neighbors. The partitions testified to the weakness of the Polish state and the inadequacy of its semidemocratic form of government in the face of the powerful monarchies by which it was surrounded. The individual partitions were referred to as *zabory*, as in *zabór pruski*, *rosyjski*, *austriacki* (the Prussian, Russian, and Austrian partitions). Poland emerged again as an independent country only following World War I, in 1918.

Różewicz, Tadeusz (1921–2014). A major figure in postwar poetry and drama. He has been called an anti-poet, as he shuns meter, rhyme, and often logical connections. His plays are termed absurdist. In them, people occupy the morally barren landscape between the Holocaust of the past war and the nuclear holocaust yet to come. One of his signature pieces is the two-person recitation "Świadkowie, albo nasza mała stabilizacja" (The witnesses, or our little stabilization, 1962), whose coined phrase described the situation in post-1956 Poland, but more generally speaking in today's world, in which people engage in trivial activities and occupations and pursue empty relationships, all the while being careful not to step out of line and endanger the small semblance of normality they think they enjoy. A major play of his was *Kartoteka* (The card index, 1961). Różewicz won the 2000 **Nike** prize for his *Matka odchodzi* (Mother leaves), an autobiographical collage consisting of thoughts, verse, reminiscences, and photographs.

Rubinstein, Artur (1887–1982). A **Łódź**-born concert pianist of international renown, widely considered to be one of the best pianists of the twentieth century, specializing among others in the works of Polish composers **Chopin** and **Szymanowski**. He made his debut with the Berlin Philharmonic in 1900 at the age of thirteen, and at New York's Carnegie Hall in 1906, at nineteen. Fluent in eight languages, he could hold entire concerts in his head. Fearing for his life in Europe as a Jew, Rubinstein emigrated in 1939, and became a US citizen in 1946. He never played in Germany afterward. Rubinstein retired only at the age of eighty-nine. He retained an affection for Poland, and visited the country in 1960 as honorary chairman of judges in the **Konkurs Chopinowski** (International Chopin Piano Competition). Several Polish musical institutions are officially named after him, including the Łódź Philharmonic. His recordings come to more than 107 hours. The Arthur Rubinstein International Piano Master Competition is held in Łódź, and a bronze statue of him playing the piano (with a coin-operated music selection until Sony Corporation threatened a copyright infringement lawsuit) is located along Łódź's Piotrkowska street in front of his former apartment. *Cast of Rubinstein's hands in the Łódź city museum.*

Ruch Palikota (Palikot Movement). Janusz Palikot (b. 1964) is a controversial politician given to outré statements and stunts that got him tossed out of the mainstream Platforma Obywatelska (PO) party. Palikot formed his own party with an anticlerical and liberal agenda, among other things favoring the legalization of marijuana under the slogan "Sadzić, palić, zalegalizować" (Plant, smoke, legalize). The fact that 10 percent of the electorate voted for his candidates in the 2011 parliamentary elections (see *wybory 2011*), making them the number-three political bloc, was a shock to many. It points to either an opening up of voters to liberal ideas and candidates, or merely to their disenchantment with the political establishment.

---

rusałka. In Slavic folk mythology, *rusałki* (alternatively *boginki*) are the spirits of young maidens who have died and have been reincarnated in the form of forest, field, or, especially, water nymphs. Their typical role is to appear scantily clad to young men and lure them to their death, as in Jacek Malczewski's picture *Rusałki* (pictured). An eastern cousin of the rusałka is the *świtezianka*, limited to Lake Świteź in present-day Belarus. A slightly different kind of female spirit is the *południca*, a girl who has died just before or during her wedding. She lies in wait for people foolish enough to come out into the noonday sun, gives them riddles, maims them, and steals their children. Who can blame her? A rusałka is also a kind of butterfly, *Inachis io* (in English, the peacock butterfly).

RWPG. See Rada Wzajemnej Pomocy Gospodarczej (**RWPG**).

Rydzyk, Tadeusz (b. 1945). A charismatic, conservative, outspoken, and controversial Roman Catholic priest, head of a national Catholic media empire unique in the world. Rydzyk, who is a member of the order of the Most Holy Redeemer, the Redemptorists, founded the Catholic radio station Radio Maryja (Radio Maria, 1991), the conservative nationalist newspaper *Nasz Dziennik* (Our journal, 1998), the Catholic television network Trwam (I persist, 2003), and even a Catholic cell phone network. He is also the founder and president of the Wyższa Szkoła Kultury Społecznej i Medialnej (Higher School of Social and Media Culture) in Toruń, one mission of which is to train journalists. His political line has been described as xenophobic and anti-Semitic, and his activities are not warmly welcomed by the Church in Rome, which considers that he meddles too much in politics and strays too far from the main line and mission of the Church. See also: Kościół rzymskokatolicki.

Rywin, afera (Lew Rywin affair). A political and media scandal in which a free press flexed its wings and tried to expose corruption in the government of leftist premier Leszek Miller. Lew Rywin was a film producer, chairman of television's Canal+, and a would-be power broker in the early days of postcommunist Poland who, in 2002, supposedly demanded a huge bribe from the group that owned *Gazeta Wyborcza* in order to influence a new law governing media ownership. The moment was captured on tape by Adam Michnik, the CEO of *Gazeta Wyborcza*.

Despite years of exposés and lengthy televised special-committee investigations, whether Rywin was acting on his own or on the behalf of a clique within the government (or whether he ever even made the offer) was never definitively established. Rywin himself was sentenced to two years of imprisonment. The Rywin affair quieted down when it was overshadowed in 2004 by the even more sensational *afera Orlenu* (Orlen affair).

rząd na uchodźstwie (Polish government in exile, 1939–1990). The *rząd londyński* (London government) continued that of the so-called Druga Rzeczpospolita Polska (Second Republic), forced to abandon the country after the German and Soviet invasions of 1939. It continued to conduct international diplomacy on Poland's behalf throughout the war. Its first premier was Władysław Sikorski, followed by Stanisław Mikołajczyk. The *układ Sikorski-Majski* (Sikorski-Majski Pact) of July 30, 1941, restored relations with the USSR and laid the basis for the formation of a Polish army in Russia under General Władysław Anders. The government in exile ended in 1990, when Lech Wałęsa was sworn in as president and accepted the symbols of power (the presidential banner, seals, sashes, and the original text of the 1935 Constitution) from the last president of the *rząd na uchodźstwie*, Ryszard Kaczorowski (pictured). Kaczorowski was one of the victims of the *katastrofa pod Smoleńskiem* (Smoleńsk air disaster) of 2010.

Rzeczpospolita Obojga Narodów (Polish-Lithuanian Commonwealth). The name Rzeczpospolita translates the Latin *res publica*. The First (or *szlachecka*, "nobles'") Republic dates from the 1569 *unia lubelska* (Union of Lublin) and the formalization of the combined Polish-Lithuanian state. The resulting entity is often referred to as the Rzeczpospolita Obojga Narodów (Republic of Two Nations), its two parts being the Korona Królestwa Polskiego (Crown of the Polish Kingdom), or simply the Korona, and the Wielkie Księstwo Litewskie (Grand Duchy of Lithuania). Its coat of arms (pictured) combined the Polish *Orzeł Biały* (white eagle) and the Lithuanian *pogoń* (knight in chase). It was the largest and most populous country of sixteenth- and seventeenth-century Europe, with some four hundred thousand square miles (1,000,000 sq km) and a multiethnic population of eleven million at its peak in the early seventeenth century. The Commonwealth lasted until the *trzeci rozbiór* (third partition of Poland; see *rozbiory*) in 1795. The modern designation Pierwsza Rzeczpospolita (First Republic) contrasts it to the Druga Rzeczpospolita (Second Republic) of interwar Poland and the Trzecia Rzeczpospolita (Third Republic) of postcommunist Poland.

KALEIDOSCOPE OF POLAND 221

rzeki (rivers, waterways). The Polish river network is dense, and it is further enhanced by important canals. Almost all of Poland's rivers are ultimate tributaries of either the **Wisła** (1,047 km) or the **Odra** (742 km in Poland), both of which empty into the **Bałtyk** (Baltic Sea). Among the Wisła's major tributaries are the **Bug** (pictured near Włodawa, 587 km in Poland) which flows into the **Narew** (448 km), the San (443 km), the Pilica (319 km), and the Wieprz (303 km). The Odra's major tributaries are the **Warta** (803 km) and the Warta's tributary, the Noteć (388 km). The Wisła is connected via the 101-kilometer **Kanał Augustowski** to the Belarus-Lithuanian Niemen (937 km) and from there to the Bałtyk. The Wisła is connected to the Odra via the Noteć, the Warta, and the twenty-five-kilometer Kanał Bydgoski (**Bydgoszcz** canal). Some smaller rivers (streams, really) in the southeast of Poland flow into Ukraine and eventually into the Black Sea. See also: **Kanał Elbląski**.

Rzeszów. The largest town in southeast Poland at 173,000 inhabitants, and the capital of the *województwo podkarpackie* (Sub-Carpathian Voivodeship), Rzeszów is located on the Wisłok River and along historically important north–south and east–west trade routes. Rzeszów is approximately one hundred kilometers from Ukraine toward the east and Slovakia toward the south. It was once a possession of the **Lubomirski** family. The current Lubomirski castle (pictured) was built in 1902–1906 on the site of a former castle for use as a courthouse and jail. A unique Rzeszów attraction is a museum housing a large, formerly private collection of communist-era *dobranocki* ("nighty-night" TV shows) and associated memorabilia. To the northeast of Rzeszów begins the Roztocze, a pleasant range of low hills and mountains that stretches into Ukraine. Toward the south, gently rise the **Karpaty** (Carpathians).

---

rzeź Woli (Wola massacre). In an attempt to quell the **powstanie warszawskie** (Warsaw Uprising) of 1944, German armed forces systematically rounded up and executed on the spot all Warsaw civilians — men, women, and children — found in the **Wola** and Ochota districts of Warsaw. This included the summary execution of all hospital patients. In all, some 59,400 civilians lost their lives on August 5–7, 1944. The massacre only served to stiffen the Polish resistance. No one was ever held responsible for the Wola massacre, which falls under anyone's definition of a war crime.

---

rzeź wołyńska (Wołyń massacres, 1942–1944). The ethnic cleansing of non-Ukrainian minorities initiated by the Organization of Ukrainian Nationalists (Organizatsiya Ukrainskikh Natsionalistiv, OUN) and implemented by the Ukrainian Insurgent Army (Ukrain'ska Povstan'ska Armiya, UPA) on the territory of German-occupied Wołyń province. While the murder of more than 150,000 Jews was carried out by German forces using Ukrainian auxiliaries, the roundup and murder of forty to sixty thousand Poles during the same period was carried out semi-independently by the UPA, which aimed at the extermination of the entire non-Ukrainian population. On the night of July 11, 1943, more than one hundred villages were torched and their inhabitants murdered. The UPA continued as a partisan force in the forests and villages of western Ukraine and southeastern Poland as late as 1946–1947, one of the factors cited by the postwar government for initiating *akcja Wisła*, i.e., the resettlement of the Ukrainian population of southeast Poland to the so-called *ziemie odzyskane* (recovered lands) in the west. To this day certain nationalist groups in Ukraine advocate taking back what they consider to be "greater Ukraine"; that is, much of the Polish southeast.

S

Sabała (1809–1894). A singer of tales in a tradition more often associated with Ukraine and the Balkans, Jan Krzeptowski, known as "Sabała," was a self-proclaimed former mountain brigand and an unparalleled repository of tales, legends, and songs of the Polish **Podhale** (Highlands). He was discovered when he was already in his sixties and was lionized by the artists of **Młoda Polska** (Young Poland). Called the "Homer of the Tatras," Sabała accompanied his stories on the native stringed instrument *gęśle* or *złóbcoki*. Sabała's son, also named Jan, was recorded in 1904 singing wedding and other songs in the earliest extant Polish sound recording. Sabałowe Bajania (Sabała Tale-Telling) — a competition among folk singers, storytellers, folk instrumentalists, and givers of wedding speeches — is held yearly in August in Bukowina. Sabała is buried alongside other notables of Młoda Polska in **Zakopane**'s Pęksowy Brzyzek Cemetery. *Stanisław Witkiewicz,* Sabała.

---

salon (salon). Foreigners are often struck by the unpretentious names of Polish stores. For example, a lamp store may simply proclaim *lampy* (lamps), or a bicycle store *rowery* (bicycles). A trendy word is *salon*, as in *salon elektroniki* (electronics), *salon psów* (dog grooming), *salon meblowy* (furniture, pictured), *salon samochodowy* (automobiles), *salon ślubny* (wedding supplies), *salon urody* (beauty parlor), and so on. *Studio* is expanding, as in *studio paznokci* (nail studio).

224

Another expanding store name is *świat* (world), as in *świat alkoholi* (alcohol world), *świat bagażników* (luggage rack world), *świat kostki* (paving-stone world), *świat łazienek* (bathroom world), *świat wikliny* (wicker world), and so on. Yet another fashionable word is *galeria* (gallery), referring to a fancy shopping mall, whence the term *galerianki* (gallery-girls), referring to underage prostitutes hanging out at galerie, emerged. Some service outlets are called *biura* (offices), such as *biuro matrymonialne* (dating service), *biuro podróży* (travel bureau), and others. See also: sklep.

Sandomierz. An important fifteenth- and sixteenth-century trade town attractively situated on hills overlooking the Wisła, and an important stop on the *szlak cysterski* (trail of Cistercian monasteries). Like Kazimierz Dolny, it never regained its economic importance after the potop szwedzki (the Deluge, or seventeenth-century Swedish wars). Sandomierz preserves many examples of Renaissance and later architecture, and it is a deservedly popular tourist destination. It numbers today around twenty-five thousand inhabitants.

sarmatyzm (Sarmatism). A cultural pattern original to the Polish *szlachta* (nobility) from the late sixteenth century to the middle of the eighteenth century, the name of which derives from the fantastic myth that the nobility were descended from the Sarmatians, an ancient tribe inhabiting the lower Volga River. The period is sometimes referred to as the Polish or Sarmatian baroque. *Sarmatyzm* exhibited itself in extravagant eastern-based clothes, customs, weaponry, funerary customs (see *portret trumienny*, coffin portraits), male hair styles (long mustaches being de rigueur), and in Polish "exceptionalism," glorifying government institutions (see *złota polska wolność*) and the nobles' way of life. Sarmatian political philosophy was originally democratic, multicultural, and tolerant, but during the course of the potop szwedzki (Swedish Deluge) it turned more xenophobic and pro-Catholic, Jan Pasek being a good illustrative example. The Sarmatian period had genuine achievements in art, architecture (the style of the *dwór szlachecki*, "manor house," was developed during this time), and, especially, poetry (see barok). *Polish nobleman in Sarmatian dress.*

saskie czasy, noc saska (Saxon period, the Saxon night). Ruinous wars on all fronts in the seventeenth century left Poland in a state of near anarchy without a clear successor to the throne. The saying of the day was "Polska nierządem stoi" (Poland stands in anarchy), and foreign armies felt themselves free to march across it with impunity. In 1697 August II Mocny (August the Strong) of Saxony was elected king, initiating the Saxon period in Polish history, or the "Saxon night," as it is sometimes called, which lasted until 1763. Although recent historians evaluate the period more positively — especially in consideration of the lively eyewitness description of Polish social practices under the Saxon reign by the priest Jędrzej Kitowicz (1728–1804) — the Saxon kings took little interest in Poland; the **Sejm** (parliament) rarely met or accomplished anything; the nobility divided into rival factions; and the level of culture and national cohesion sank to an unprecedented low. How unlike the present day. A rhymed saying from Saxon times is "Za króla Sasa jedz, pij i popuszczaj pasa" (Under the Saxon king, eat, drink, and let out your belt).

Sasnal, Wilhelm (b. 1972). Born in Tarnów and educated at **Kraków**'s Fine Arts Academy, Sasnal is one of postcommunist Poland's most internationally exhibited artists, with some fifty solo exhibitions to his name. His work hangs in major museums throughout Europe and America. Arguably overhyped and overpriced, and more popular abroad than in his native country, Sasnal received the Vincent van Gogh Biennial Award for Contemporary Art in 2006. His work is at times reminiscent of Andy Warhol's in its graphic reductivity and stark photographic quality, but beyond that he is difficult to pigeonhole, as his topics and style rarely repeat. However, his girl smoking a cigarette, pictured, has appeared in several versions. Whatever he paints, his image attains an iconic quality, even if it is difficult to say of what. Western commentators sometimes say that it is the afterimage of a communist iconography that has faded and lost its meaning, but that interpretation is wearing thin. *Anka, 2001, oil on canvas, 17⅓ x 19¾ in. Copyright © the artist, courtesy of the Sadie Coles HQ, London.*

sądownictwo (judiciary). As in most continental European countries, the Polish *wymiar sprawiedliwości* (system of justice) derives from Roman or so-called statute law and does not rely to a significant degree on reference to legal precedent, as in the Anglo-Saxon tradition. Cases and verdicts in civil, criminal, administrative, or military law are decided by one or more professional judges applying the law as they see it; i.e., there is no right to a "jury of one's peers." Courts may be district or regional. The highest court of appeals is the Sąd Najwyższy (Supreme Court, building face pictured). The Trybunał Konstytucyjny (Constitutional Tribunal), to which judges are appointed for a term of nine years, rules on the constitutionality of rulings, laws, and treaties. A Trybunał Stanu (State Tribunal) adjudicates cases involving high-ranking persons in government. Poles are famous for their litigiousness, and have a higher proportion of judges and lawyers to population than in almost any other European country.

SB. See **Służba Bezpieczeństwa (SB)**.

Schiller, Leon (Leon Schiller de Schildenfeld, 1887–1954). Born in **Kraków**, Austro-Hungary, to a family of Austrian origin, Schiller was the most prominent dramatic theorist and stage director of the 1930s in Poland. He was known especially for his monumental productions of the classics of Polish *romantyzm* (especially works by **Mickiewicz** and **Słowacki**), which were said to have been waiting nearly a hundred years for their proper realization according to his vision. After World War II (which he narrowly survived, being for a while imprisoned in Auschwitz) he was rector of the State School of Drama in **Łódź**, now named after him, and editor-in-chief of the periodical *Teatr* (Theater). *Leon Schiller monument off Piotrkowska Street in Łódź.*

Schulz, Bruno (1892–1942). A Polish translator, illustrator, and writer of Jewish extraction, Schulz was one of the most promising authors of his generation until his murder on the streets of his native Drohobycz (now in Ukraine) by a German policeman. Calling him the "Polish Kafka" (the two are often mentioned in the same breath) does not do him justice. Schulz left two slim volumes of stories that have gained him increasing recognition as a major figure of twentieth-century European literature. His often surreal stories, teeming with metaphors, deal with the fears, distorted understandings, and erotic repressions of childhood maturation, themes that also find outlet in his illustrations (self-portrait pictured). Schulz's two volumes were *Sklepy cynamonowe* (Cinnamon stores, 1934) and *Sanatorium pod klepsydrą* (Sanatorium under the sign of the hourglass, 1937), the latter of which was turned into a film by Wojciech Jerzy Has in 1973, winner of the Jury Prize at the Cannes Film Festival.

Secesja (secessionist art). In Poland this term is used to describe what is referred to in French and English as art nouveau, a modernist trend in art and architecture prominent between 1890 and 1918, hence largely congruent with the period of **Młoda Polska** (Young Poland), especially popular in and around **Kraków**. In Poland the influence and the term came mainly from Vienna, where a group of artists had "seceded"

from mainstream art. The secessionist style is associated with impressionism in painting and with flowing and sinuous shapes in the decorative and applied arts, including stained glass, signs, posters, hardware, and furniture. The style is still very much in vogue today, as a visit to home decoration stores will attest. A good museum of secessionist art may be found in **Płock**.
Angel door knocker in the secessionist style.

Sejm (Polish diet, or parliament). The word *sejm* originally meant "convocation" or "get-together." The power of biannual gatherings of nobles to vote on matters of state gained momentum toward the end of the fifteenth century. Certain important towns also had representatives to the Sejm. After the *unia lubelska* (Union of Lublin, 1569) and the establishment of the **Rzeczpospolita Obojga Narodów** (Polish-Lithuanian Commonwealth), the sejm's powers increased, and royal rule over the Commonwealth became elective, a unique system in Europe of the time. Perniciously, the principle became established whereby an entire session's resolutions required unanimity to pass — the so-called principle of *liberum veto* (in Latin, "I freely forbid"; see *złota polska wolność*) — a power that became exploited toward the end of the eighteenth century by nobles who had their own interests at heart more than those of the Commonwealth. The Polish state became paralytic, and the reforms of the short-lived **Konstytucja 3 maja** (May 3 Constitution, 1791) came too late to rescue Poland from partition among its neighbors.

Sejm RP (Sejm of the Republic of Poland). In the contemporary Polish parliament, the Sejm, consisting of 460 *posłowie* (representatives) and chaired by the Marszałek Sejmu (speaker, who also takes over as head of government when the president is incapacitated), is Poland's main legislative body. It operates alongside the Senat, consisting of one hundred members. Both *izby* (chambers) of the Polish parliament are elective, with four-year *kadencje* (terms of office). Its meetings are public and are broadcast over radio and television. The Sejm RP (whose building is pictured) traces its origins to the end of the fifteenth century (see **Sejm**), when it represented only members of the *szlachta* (nobility). To be sure, the nobility in Poland represented a much larger proportion of the population — up to 8 percent — than in Western countries of the time.

Seksmisja (Sex-mission). A 1983 hit film by Juliusz Machulski, starring Olgierd Łukaszewicz and **Jerzy Stuhr** playing Albert and Maks, two men who wake up after a war and find that the world is now populated exclusively by gorgeous women, some of them of a decidedly dominatrix profile. Although tame by today's standards, the topless nudity of the voluptuous actresses, some of whom were chosen in a national "talent" contest, was considered racy at the time. The movie pokes fun at contemporaneous politics and is a cult classic. It has left behind such sayings as "Copernicus was a woman!"

Sendlerowa, Irena (née Krzyżanowska, 1910–2008). Under the organization Żegota in World War II, Sendlerowa saved some 2,500 children from the Warsaw ghetto, placing them with Polish church missions and families. Arrested, tortured, and sentenced to death by the Nazis, she was saved when bribed German guards released her, and she continued to work saving Jewish children until the end of the war. In 1965 she was recognized by Israel's Yad Vashem as Righteous among Nations, and in 2003 she received Poland's highest civilian award, the Order Orła Białego (Order of the White Eagle). Sendlerowa's story was largely unknown in Poland until a group of US high school students in Kansas in 1999 wrote and performed a play about her entitled *Life in a Jar*, referring to the buried jars in which she preserved data about each rescued child's family. Her story was further told in a feature film, *The Courageous Heart of Irena Sendler* (2009), and the documentary *Irena Sendler: In the Name of Their Mothers*, broadcast on PBS in 2011.

SHL. Out of a handful of motorcycles produced in postwar Poland, the SHL, originally designed in 1938 on an engine licensed from England and manufactured in Kielce up through 1970, attained cult status, with collectors' clubs and websites devoted to it. No one has ever succeeded in resolving the meaning of the initials, unlike the WFM (Warszawska Fabryka Motocykli, "Warsaw Motorcycle Factory," 1948–1965), or the last motorcycle to be produced in Poland, the WSK (Wytwórnia Sprzętu Komunikacyjnego, "Manufactory of Transportation Equipment," 1954–1985). Also the victim of global market forces is the array of *motorowery* (mopeds) that were produced in Poland in the 1950s–1980s, polluting the air with their smoky two-cylinder engines, including the Ryś (Lynx), Żak (Schoolboy), and Komar (Mosquito).

Sienkiewicz, Henryk (1846–1916). One of the most popular Polish writers, primarily of historical fiction, in the second half of the nineteenth century. Sienkiewicz received the Nobel Prize for Literature in 1905 for his life's work. While he is known in the West for his novel *Quo vadis?* (1896), about Christianity in the time of Nero, in Poland he is better known for his historical novels set in Poland, written "ku pokrzepieniu serc" (to buck up the heart) during a time of foreign occupation. His *trylogia* (trilogy) describes the wars of the seventeenth century: *Ogniem i mieczem* (By fire and sword, 1884), *Potop* (The deluge, 1886), and *Pan Wołodyjowski* (Colonel Wołodyjowski, 1888). *Krzyżacy* (The Teutonic Knights, 1900) is set in the fifteenth century and depicts among other events the Polish victory over the Krzyżacy at Grunwald. Largely because of Sienkiewicz's novels, Polish children traditionally played Poles and Teutonic Knights more than cowboys and Indians. These days, of course, they sit around watching television and playing video games.

Sikorski, Władysław (1881–1943). Named commander-in-chief of the Polish armed forces in World War II after General Edward Śmigły-Rydz was interned in Romania, Sikorski was premier of the *rząd na uchodźstwie* (government in exile) in London and was a vigorous spokesman for the Polish cause internationally. In 1941 he signed the *układ Sikorski-Majski* (Sikorski-Majski Pact), temporarily normalizing relations between Poland and the Soviet Union after Germany's invasion of the latter. In 1943 he caused a definitive rift with the Soviet Union by demanding an International Red Cross investigation into the *zbrodnia katyńska* (Katyń massacre). Sikorski died in an airplane crash while taking off from Gibraltar after an inspection of Polish troops. He was buried in Nottingham, England, but in 1993 his remains were transferred to Poland and now rest in a crypt in the Katedra Wawelska (Wawel Cathedral). Because of conspiracy theories surrounding his death, his remains were disinterred in 2008 and subjected to a detailed autopsy, which did not reveal any findings inconsistent with death in an airplane accident.

Siły Zbrojne RP (Armed Forces of the Republic of Poland). The Polish Armed Forces are currently being transformed into a modern professional fighting force rather than a conscripted army. They consist of the Wojsko Polskie (army, 60,000), Marynarka Wojenna (navy, 14,000), Siły Powietrzne (air force, 26,000), Wojska Specjalne (special services), and Żandarmeria Wojskowa (military police), all under the Ministerstwo Obrony Narodowej (Ministry of National Defense). Army ranks are *marszałek* (marshal of Poland, not currently filled), *generał* (general), *pułkownik* (colonel), *major* (major), *kapitan* (captain), *porucznik* (lieutenant), *chorąży* (warrant officer), *sierżant* (sergeant), *kapral* (corporal), *szeregowy* (private). Poland is the only world military organization to use a two-fingered salute (pictured). Poland is a member of the United Nations and NATO and has participated in peacekeeping operations in Bosnia, Iraq, and Afghanistan.

Singer, Isaac Bashevis (1902–1991). Born Icek-Hersz Zynger, the writer was the son of a Hasidic rabbi. His brother Joshua and sister Esther also were writers. He grew up in Warsaw on Krochmalna (Starch) Street in the poor Jewish quarter of town, the life of which he later immortalized in his writing. In 1917–1923 he lived with his mother and younger brother in Biłgoraj, a traditional Jewish shtetl in the southeast, absorbing its traditions and folklore. In 1935 he emigrated to the United States. Not particularly religious, Singer nevertheless felt

230 KALEIDOSCOPE OF POLAND

comfortable mainly among Jews, and, while natively fluent in Polish, published only in Yiddish, being one of the leading figures in that literary movement. Singer wrote some eighteen novels but is best known for his short stories, many written for children, typically situated in a generalized version of the shtetl of his youth, suffused in a slightly magical light born of nostalgia for things lost. Singer received the Nobel Prize for Literature in 1978.

Siwiec, Ryszard (1909–1968). A fifty-nine-year-old accountant and father of five from Przemyśl who committed suicide by self-immolation in front of a crowd of a hundred thousand spectators at the 1968 national *dożynki* festival at the **Stadion Dziesięciolecia** (Decadal Stadium) in Warsaw to protest the invasion of Czechoslovakia by the armies of the **Układ Warszawski** (Warsaw Pact) and, especially, Poland's participation in it. The act was the first of its kind in Eastern Europe. News of Siwiec's action was suppressed, but it became widely known through the broadcasts of **Radio Wolna Europa** (Radio Free Europe). Siwiec was posthumously awarded the Order of Polonia Restituta in 2003, as well as similar awards by the Czech and Slovak governments in 2001 and 2006. He became the subject of the documentary *Usłyszcie mój krzyk* (Hear my cry, 1991) by Maciej Drygas, which won the European Film Award for best documentary of that year. A monument in Siwiec's honor was unveiled in 2012 at the new National Stadium, built on the site of the former Stadion Dziesięciolecia.

Skałka (Crag). The colloquial designation for the church, Pauline monastery, and sanctuary built on the site of the martyrdom of **Święty Stanisław ze Szczepanowa** (Saint Stanisław) on a promontory on the **Wisła** in **Kraków** not far downstream from **Wawel** castle. Skałka contains in its Krypta Zasłużonych (Crypt of the Meritorious) the remains of major Polish cultural and political figures, including **Jan Długosz**, **Józef Ignacy Kraszewski**, **Jacek Malczewski**, **Czesław Miłosz**, **Karol Szymanowski**, and **Stanisław Wyspiański**.

Skamander. A Warsaw literary monthly (cover pictured) and group, founded by the best Warsaw poets of the *dwudziestolecie międzywojenne* (interwar period), including **Julian Tuwim** (1894–1953), Jan Lechoń (1899–1956), **Jarosław Iwaszkiewicz** (1894–1980), Antoni Słonimski (1895–1976), Kazimierz Wierzyński (1894–1969), and, loosely, Maria Pawlikowska-Jasnorzewska (1891–1945). Their meeting place was the *kawiarnia* (café) Pod Picadorem (Under the Sign of the Picador). The Skamandryci (Scamandrites) adhered to classical poetic forms, into which they introduced themes of everyday life and social awareness. Their style was described as Parnassian. The group stood in loose opposition to the so-called *awangarda krakowska* (Kraków avant-garde) existing at more or less the same time, which was more futuristic, iconoclastic, and experimental, although in the end there was much cross-fertilization between the two groups.

---

skansen. A *skansen* is an open-air ethnographical museum in which examples of usually wooden folk architecture relating to a particular region are displayed. The name is taken from the first such museum, opened in Sweden in 1891. Often traditional crafts, customs, and technology will be highlighted. There are some forty-five registered skansens in Poland, most of them well worth visiting, often interestingly narrated by knowledgeable costumed docents. The name has also come to be used for a railroad car museum, of which there are several in Poland, especially the Parowozownia Wolsztyn, but also one in downtown Warsaw near the main train station. *A peasant cottage in the skansen in Sanok.*

Skarbek, Krystyna (1908–1952). The glamorous heroine of the Polish World War II resistance, known for her daring ski exploits over the Tatra Mountains in covert missions in and out of Nazi-occupied Poland. She was born into an old Warsaw family (her father was a count, her mother an heiress of Jewish background), and raised to an outdoor life. The outbreak of war caught her with her husband in Kenya, from where she made her way to England and volunteered for action in the British secret service under the assumed name Christine Granville. Skarbek became one of the agency's longest-serving and most-decorated female special agents. Being fluent in French, in 1944 she parachuted into France, where she also completed many dangerous missions for the French resistance, for which she received the Croix de Guerre. Said to have been irresistible to men, Skarbek was reportedly the prototype for one or more of Ian Flemings's "Bond girls." Let go without support by the British government after the war, she died penniless at the hands of a rejected suitor in a cheap London hotel.

Skarga, Piotr (1536–1612). Jesuit priest, theologian, and orator, born under the name Powęski. Through his establishment of Jesuit colleges throughout the Rzeczpospolita Obojga Narodów (Polish-Lithuanian Commonwealth), Skarga was the principal player in the successful Polish Counter-Reformation. He was the first rector of Wilno University and later court chaplain under King Zygmunt III Waza. His *Żywoty świętych* (Lives of the saints) was popular reading. His still-readable *Kazania sejmowe* (Sermons to the Sejm) castigate the nobility for its blindness to national priorities, and cast Poland in the role of *Chrystus narodów* (Christ of nations), a theme taken up later by *mesjanizm polski* (Polish national messianism) of the early nineteenth-century Polish Romantics. In another famous prophetic image of his, Poland was like a sinking ship.

sklep (store or shop). The main kind of *sklep* is a *sklep spożywczy* (food store). There is perhaps a greater density of them in Poland than anywhere else in Europe, although lately smaller private stores are dropping like flies. Not uncommonly two food stores will inexplicably stand side-by-side in a small village. During the PRL (communist Poland), alcoholic beverages were primarily sold in so-called *sklepy monopolowe* (monopoly stores, i.e., package or liquor stores). Although the alcohol monopoly system no longer exists, the name has stuck for stores that mainly engage in the sale of alcoholic beverages. A similar anachronistic holdover is the term *sklep kolonialny* (colonial products store), referring to a store selling coffee, tea, chocolate, and spices or, more broadly, anything imported from far abroad. Poland never had overseas colonies (its colonies were contiguous and to its east). A *sklep wielobranżowy* (multibranch store) is a variety store, possibly including food, but mainly *artykuły przemysłowe* (literally, industrial products): cleansers, polishes, light bulbs, cheap dishes and cutlery, and other household items. See also: sklep: rodzaje sklepów.

sklep: rodzaje sklepów (kinds of stores). Here is a partial list of kinds of Polish stores: *sklep AGD* (*artykuły gospodarstwa domowego*, "household goods," i.e., appliances), *antykwariat* (used book store), *apteka* (pharmacy), *sklep bławatny/tekstylny* (fabric shop), *butik* (boutique), *cepelia* (folk art), *cukiernia* (confectionery), *delikatesy* (specialty food items), *desa* (antiques), *drogeria* (cosmetics, etc.), *skład galanteryjny* (haberdashery), kiosk (newsstand and small items), *księgarnia* (bookstore), *kwiaciarnia* (florist), *sklep mięsny* (butcher's), *sklep ogrodniczy* (garden supplies), *sklep papierniczy* (stationery supplies), *pasmanteria* (sewing supplies, notions), *sklep przemysłowy* (durable goods), *sklep RTV* (radio and TV store), *sam* (*sklep samoobsługowy*, self-service grocery), *sklep spożywczy* (grocery), *sklep ślubny* (bridal shop), *trafika/sklep tytoniowy* (tobacconist), *sklep warzywny* (greengrocer), *tysiąc i jeden drobiazgów* (1,001 sundries, variety store), *zielarnia* (herbal medicine). An insidious addition is the *sklep dyskont* (discount store), driving smaller specialty stores out of business (one popular discount chain is the Portuguese-owned Biedronka, "ladybird"). Service stores can go by the name of salon, *biuro* (office), or by the name of what they do, such as *szewc* (cobbler's) or *krawiec* (tailor's).

Juljusz Słowacki
ur. 1809 † 1849.

Słowacki, Juliusz (1809–1849). A Romantic poet and dramatist born in Krzemieniec, a city now in Ukraine. Alongside Adam Mickiewicz and Zygmunt Krasiński, Słowacki is one of three distinguished Polish Romantic poets and, like the others, he was part of the Wielka Emigracja. Despite living for only forty years, he was quite prolific. Słowacki is known for long narrative poems with an oriental or Byronic flavor, for elegies and odes, and for mystical-philosophic narratives written in poetic prose. His Romantic dramas *Balladyna* (1835), *Kordian* (1834), and *Mazepa* (1840) are classics of the Polish theater. An English version of *Mazepa* had a career as

KALEIDOSCOPE OF POLAND 233

a melodrama on stages of the American Wild West. Słowacki's phrase "Nie czas żałować róż, gdy płoną lasy" (No time for pitying the roses when the forests are burning), from *Lilla Weneda*, has entered the common idiom. Słowacki is interred in the Katedra Wawelska (Wawel Cathedral) in Kraków.

Służba Bezpieczeństwa (SB) (Polish secret police). Placed under the Ministerstwo Spraw Wewnętrznych (Ministry of Internal Affairs) in the PRL (communist Poland), the SB's mission was to infiltrate and monitor the activities of people, the church, and organizations thought to pose a threat to communist rule. It existed from 1956–1990. As late as 1989 it employed 24,300 workers monitoring some ninety thousand informants, some of them made public in 2005 on *lista Wildsteina* (Wildstein's list). The SB's predecessor was the even larger and more sinister Urząd Bezpieczeństwa (UB, Office of Security) of the Ministerstwo Bezpieczeństwa Publicznego (Ministry of Public Security), under the *szara eminencja* (gray eminence) Jakub Berman. Berman was removed, and the UB was reorganized into the SB, after a high-ranking UB official, Józef Światło, defected to the West in 1953 and in 1955 broadcast over Radio Wolna Europa (Radio Free Europe) everything he knew about the UB's workings — which was a lot, including the torturing of political prisoners.

smok wawelski, smocza jama (Wawel dragon, dragon's cave). A series of natural caverns can be found beneath Wawel castle in Kraków, the former residence of the *smok wawelski* (Wawel dragon), who had an insatiable appetite for Kraków damsels (who wouldn't?), and destroyed savior knights one after another. According to one legend, he was defeated by an enterprising cobbler named Szewczyk Dratewka, who fed the dragon a sheepskin stuffed with sulfur, resulting in the dragon's enormous thirst. The dragon leaped into the Wisła and drank himself to the point of explosion. The dragon's former cavern is now a popular tourist attraction, as is the dragon's nearby statue (pictured), which belches fire every few minutes and is a town symbol. Each year an increasingly elaborate *parada smoków* (dragon parade) is held on the streets of Kraków — also lately as a nighttime lights show on the Wisła. Compare *bazyliszek*.

Smoleńsk, katastrofa pod Smoleńskiem (Smolensk air disaster). On April 10, 2010, ninety-six people died in an airplane crash at Smolensk airport, including the Polish president Lech Kaczyński, his wife, and ninety-four other individuals, including almost the entire general staff of the Polish military. Among the victims were Ryszard Kaczorowski, the last president of the *rząd na uchodźstwie* (government in exile); parliament members of all political parties; and the original Solidarność (Solidarity) activist Anna Walentynowicz. The flight was en route to commemorate the seventieth anniversary of the *zbrodnia katyńska* (Katyń massacre). Although conspiracy theories abound and the event is still being interminably investigated, no definitive evidence has emerged to contradict the notion that the crash was the result of bad weather and pilot and air traffic controller error.

Sobibór. A Nazi-run *obóz koncentracyjny i zagłady* (concentration and extermination camp) built in 1942 in east present-day Poland about four kilometers from a village by the same name. In it some 250,000 Jews from Poland and Europe perished. The camp was destroyed by the Nazis after a prisoner breakout in 1943 in which about three hundred prisoners managed to escape, of whom all but forty-nine were recaptured. In the United States, Sobibór was in the news in recent years in connection with John Demjaniuk, a retired Ukrainian automobile worker accused of being a guard there (not for any specific actions of his). Deported to Germany, Demjanjuk was convicted at the age of ninety-one on May 12, 2011, as an accessory to the murder of 27,900 Jews and sentenced to five years in prison. He died in 2012 while his case was under appeal.

Sobieski, Jan III (1629–1696, ruled from 1674). A well-educated, popular, and militarily successful Polish king. Sobieski had been *hetman wielki koronny* (Hetman of the Crown, i.e., commander-in-chief) during the **potop szwedzki** (Swedish Deluge). Known as the Defender of the Faith, he led the Polish forces that came to the rescue of Vienna in the **odsiecz wiedeńska** (Relief of Vienna) when it was besieged by the Turks in 1683. He married the French princess Maria Kazimiera d'Arquien de la Grange, known to him affectionately as Marysieńka, with whom he carried on a famous romantic correspondence while on campaign.

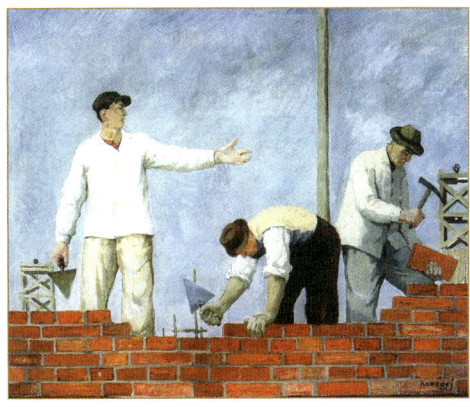

socrealizm (socialist realism). Art in the service of the communist party, showing a positive view of life, uncomplicated characters, and the leading role of the party and the working class in creating a better world. This Soviet-concocted doctrine was imposed on Polish creative artists and journalists from 1949 to 1956 both through professional unions and by universal *cenzura* (censorship), resulting in extremely bland fare that was radically at odds with reality. In painting and sculpture, heroic images of leaders and of working-class figures predominated. The doctrine was relaxed following the *odwilż* (thaw) in 1956. However, work even obliquely critical of the government or communist party remained illegal until the end of the **PRL** (communist Poland) in 1989. Many monumental works of early *socrealizm* painting and sculpture are now on display in a former palace of the **Zamoyski** family in Kozłówka near **Lublin**. Aleksander Kobzdej's iconic picture in this style, *Podaj cegłę* (*Pass a Brick*, 1950, pictured), provides the name for contemporary Poland's largest internet building-material supply portal.

Solidarność (Solidarity). The full name is Niezależny Samorządny Związek Zawodowy "Solidarność" (Independent Self-Governing Trade Union "Solidarity"). Solidarność came into existence in 1980 as the result of workers'

KALEIDOSCOPE OF POLAND   235

strikes at the Gdańsk shipyards (see Stocznia Gdańska) over price rises, the so-called August events (*wydarzenia sierpniowe*) led by Lech Wałęsa. The strike was sparked by the firing of union activist Anna Walentynowicz, whose name became a rallying cry. Another woman, trolley driver Henryka Krzywonos, similarly became famous by stopping her vehicle and declaring, "Ten tramwaj dalej nie jedzie" (This tram won't go any farther) — taken up by the political opposition as a protest metaphor. The right to organize was one of the *dwadzieścia jeden postulatów* (twenty-one demands) put forth by the workers. Solidarność soon grew into a nationwide antigovernment movement numbering nine to ten million members. It was outlawed in 1981 and its leaders were interned under *stan wojenny* (martial law), but it emerged again to force the government to negotiate at the rozmowy Okrągłego Stołu (Round Table Discussions) of 1989. It weakened as a political force as Poland entered the 1990s as a democratic country. The Solidarność emblem (pictured) is widely recognized around the world.

Somosierra, bitwa (Battle of Somosierra, 1808). In a famous battle up a Spanish mountain gorge, Polish light cavalry troops in Napoleon's army under Jan Kozietulski charged up seemingly impossibly steep slopes and, with heavy loss of life, in the course of eight minutes overran three successive Spanish defensive emplacements, allowing Napoleon to surmount the pass and soon afterward capture Madrid in his drive to enforce a blockade on Britain. Kozietulski was one of eighteen Poles to be awarded the French Legion of Honor after the battle. He was later credited for saving Napoleon's life in the Russian campaign of 1812 by coming between him and a charge of Cossacks. His lance-pierced and blood-stained uniform is preserved in Warsaw's Polish Army Museum. *January Suchodolski,* The Charge up Somosierra, *1860.*

Sonderaktion Krakau (Special Action Kraków). On November 6, 1939, in a chilling prelude of things to come during the German occupation, the German authorities commanded the entire professorial body, more than 180 in all, of the Uniwersytet Jagielloński (Jagiellonian University), along with professors of other institutions, to assemble in a lecture hall. Here they were informed that since they had attempted to begin fall classes without permission, they were under arrest; anyone attempting to speak would be shot on the spot. Three women professors were released. The remaining professors were at first imprisoned at the Montelupi prison in Kraków and then sent to concentration camps in Sachenhausen and Dachau, Germany, where a number of them died due to the harsh conditions. They were released following the personal intervention with Adolf Hitler of scholars around the world and of Italy's Benito Mussolini.

Sopot (German: Zoppot). A resort town of 38,500 people on the Zatoka Gdańska (Gdańsk Bay) between Gdańsk and Gdynia, the three of them comprising the Baltic Trójmiasto (Tri-City). A long wooden *molo* (quay) juts out into the Bałtyk (Baltic Sea), the longest such in

236 KALEIDOSCOPE OF POLAND

Europe at 511 meters. Sopot traditionally hosted Poland's largest international song festival, but its future is uncertain. *The quay in Sopot.*

Spodek w Katowicach (Katowice Saucer). An architecturally innovative multi-use sports and entertainment facility in Katowice, often used in the city's own advertisements of itself, built in 1964–1971. So named because of its resemblance to a flying saucer, it can accommodate events of ten thousand people or more. Despite being in some sense a symbol of the past, the Spodek evokes positive resonances because of its association with many of Poland's great rock concerts. The list of foreign groups that have performed here reads like an international who's who: Elton John, Eric Clapton, Joe Cocker, Jethro Tull, Sting, Tina Turner, and many more. This being Śląsk (Silesia), while excavating the foundations the workers were digging as much through coal as through soil. Polish rock music events held here include Festiwal Rawa Blues and Metalmania.

sport w Polsce (sports in Poland). Poles are not among the most enthusiastic sports participants, even though specialized sports schools still exist as a holdover from communist times. Television campaigns and the achievements of individual athletes may be slowly changing the situation. Poles as a nation closely follow the career of anyone currently making it big on the international level, no matter what the discipline. One can mention here Otylia Jędrzejczak in *pływanie* (swimming), Adam Małysz and Kamil Stoch in *skoki narciarskie* (ski jumping), Tomasz Gollob in *żużel* (cinder track motorbike racing), Justyna Kowalczyk in *biegi narciarskie* (cross-country skiing), the 2012 Wimbledon finalist Agnieszka Radwańska in *tenis* (tennis), Andrzej Gołota in *boks* (boxing), Marcin "The Hammer" Gortat (pictured here in his Phoenix Suns uniform) in *koszykówka* (basketball), Robert Kubica in *wyścigi samochodowe* (automobile racing), and Michał Kwiatkowski in *kolarstwo* (cycling). The men's and women's teams in *siatkówka* (volleyball, both regular and beach) are currently internationally competitive and have an enthusiastic following. The men's volleyball team were world champions in 2014. Poles take pride in the many Polish-surname athletes representing other countries, such as Lukas Podolski on the German national soccer team, and Denmark's Caroline Wozniacki and Germany's Sabine Lisicki, both currently big on the international tennis circuit. See also: piłka nożna.

Stachura, Edward (1937–1979). A promising but mentally troubled poet and short story and novel writer of the 1960s–1970s. Sort of a Jack Kerouac type, he was a perpetual wanderer and "seeker after truth." He also wrote songs and occasionally performed them. His short story collection *Się* (One) was noteworthy for being told entirely in impersonal voice. Stachura is also remembered for his novel *Siekierezada, albo Zima leśnych ludzi* (Axeriade, or the winter of the forest people, 1971). The title is based on a pun associating the Polish word for ax (*siekiera*) with Scheherezade. Over time becoming more and more the victim of mental illness, he committed suicide at the age of forty-one.

Stadion Dziesięciolecia (Tenth Anniversary Stadium in Warsaw). An immense national soccer and track stadium built in the early 1950s to commemorate the tenth anniversary of the **Manifest Lipcowy** (July Manifesto). After 1989 its name was changed to the Stadion Narodowy (National Stadium). Built on the top of refuse from the ruins of war-destroyed Warsaw, the stadium deteriorated to such an extent that from 1989 to 2008 it was leased out as an immense outdoor bazaar known as **Jarmark Europa**. The stadium has since been demolished, and a grand new national multisports facility was built in its place in time for the **Euro 2012** (European Soccer Championships), which Poland hosted in conjunction with Ukraine. To some minds the old stadium will forever be connected with the self-immolation of **Ryszard Siwiec** in protest of the invasion of Czechoslovakia in 1968. *The sorry state of the Stadion Dziesięciolecia in 2006.*

Staff, Leopold (1878–1957). One of the outstanding Polish poets of the twentieth century, Staff's work spanned three different literary epochs: **Młoda Polska** (Young Poland), the *dwudziestolecie międzywojenne* (interwar period), and the immediate postwar. He accommodated himself appropriately to the requirements of each period. The main body of his poetic work was done in what is called the Parnassian mode, calm and contemplative and striving for classical perfection, while at the same time celebrating life and the joy of existence. Staff was much admired by the poets of the Warsaw *Skamander* group to which, being from **Lwów**, he did not actively belong. He was also one of Poland's leading translators into Polish.

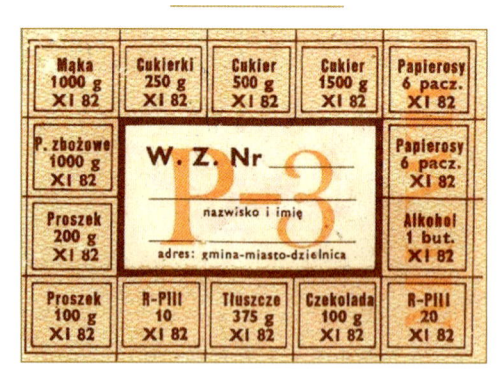

stan wojenny (martial law). In view of the rapidly spreading independent union movement **Solidarność** (Solidarity) and the danger of its turning into a call for true national democracy, in order to keep Poland in the Communist Bloc martial law was proclaimed on December 13,

1981, by the newly formed Wojskowa Rada Ocalenia Narodowego (WRON, Military Council for National Salvation) under General **Wojciech Jaruzelski**, who was at the time also the premier and first secretary of the communist party. Jaruzelski's justification was that he was trying to spare Poland the bloody experiences of Hungary in 1956 and Czechoslovakia in 1968. Union activists were interned (some ten thousand, including most union leaders), various organizations were disbanded (including independent labor unions), the ruling communist party clique was scapegoated, a *godzina policyjna* (curfew) was imposed, and the military took control of the mass media, with uniformed officers reading the nightly television news. The martial law period was characterized by *kartki żywnościowe* (food ration cards) and long lines for an increasingly smaller assortment of goods and products of all sorts. Martial law was lifted on July 22, 1983. *Ration card for flour, sugar, cigarettes, alcohol, and other commodities.*

Stanisław ze Szczepanowa, Święty (Saint Stanisław or Stanislaus of Szczepanów, ca. 1030–1079). Stanisław was the bishop of **Kraków** when he was assassinated by King **Bolesław II Śmiały** (Bolesław the Bold) for criticizing royal actions or, as some believed, for plotting the king's overthrow. According to legend he was attacked from behind by the king while celebrating mass at the **Skałka** monastery. Stanisław was then dismembered, but after three days his body miraculously reconstituted itself. His dismembered body was taken by many as symbolic of the divided Polish kingdom under the *rozbicie dzielnicowe* (division into districts), and its reconstitution as predictive of the kingdom's eventual restoration as a united whole. Stanisław's relics reside in the **Wawel** Cathedral. Canonized in 1253, he is one of the main patron saints of Poland alongside **Święty Wojciech** (Saint Wojciech or Adalbert). A yearly procession carries his relics from Wawel to the sanctuary at Skałka near where he was murdered, a ritual practiced since the year of his canonization.

Stańczyk (ca. 1480–1560). The legendary *błazen* (jester) at the courts of the kings Aleksander Jagiellończyk, **Zygmunt I Stary**, and **Zygmunt II August** onto whom posterity projected the gift of foreseeing Poland's political future. **Jan Matejko**'s portrait of himself as Stańczyk (1862, pictured) projects his own concern over Poland's fate — prophetically, as it turned out, on the eve of the disastrous **powstanie styczniowe** (January Uprising) of 1863. Stańczyk appears as a character in **Stanisław Wyspiański**'s 1901 play *Wesele*. The Stańczycy, named after him, were a conservative political group in **Kraków** in the latter part of the nineteenth century who advocated cooperation with the Austrian occupier, condemned the country's national uprisings as foolhardy, and blamed Poland's misfortunes on the anarchistic tendencies of its people.

Stare Miasto (old town). Any town that was built up in the fifteenth through sixteenth centuries and organized under **prawo magdeburskie** (Magdeburg Law) will likely have an old town, once the walled and protected part of the city, oriented around a central *rynek* (market square) surrounded by narrow three- or four-story-high *kamienice* (townhouses) once belonging to the city's burghers and nobility. The architecture will be late Renaissance. The periphery of the *Stare Miasto* would have once been surrounded by thick defensive walls and possibly a moat, generally taken down and filled in when they ceased to perform a function. Some towns have replaced the defensive perimeter with a pleasant strip park surrounding the Stare Miasto, the best example being **Kraków**'s Planty. Towns take great pains to keep their old town sections looking smart, for they are a natural tourist draw.

Starówka. Warsaw's *Stare Miasto* (old town) seems surprisingly cramped standing next to the large **Zamek Królewski** (Royal Castle). Its tiny square is literally that: a nearly perfect square. The Starówka, as the Warsaw old town is affectionately known, was 90 percent destroyed in the **powstanie warszawskie** (Warsaw Uprising, 1944). Only two buildings, barely, were left standing. The decision to rebuild the Starówka was made even before the decision was made to return the capital to Warsaw, and it was done carefully, with love, and with much volunteer work. Every effort was made to rebuild it and Warsaw's main business street, Krakowskie Przedmieście, leading up to the Starówka, ending at the **kolumna Zygmunta** (Zygmunt's Column), as historically accurately as possible, using a well-trained force of committed art historians, architects, and conservationists, guided in many instances by the eighteenth-century paintings of **Canaletto**.

"**Stary niedźwiedź mocno śpi**" (The old bear is sound asleep). A preschoolers' game, where one child is the sleeping bear and the other children walk around in a circle chanting "Stary niedźwiedź mocno śpi, stary niedźwiedź mocno śpi, / My się go boimy, na palcach chodzimy, / Jak się zbudzi to nas zje, jak się zbudzi, to nas zje!" (The old bear is sound asleep, we're afraid of him, we walk on tiptoes, then if he wakes up, then he'll eat us! . . . if he wakes up, then he'll eat us!) At the words "to nas zje!" (then he'll eat us!) the bear wakes up and chases and grabs the nearest child, who becomes the next "sleeping bear."

Stary Wiarus (faithful old soldier). The image of a simple, stalwart, uncomplaining, battle-worn old soldier occurs in Polish literature throughout the nineteenth century. The stereotype was made especially popular by a character in **Stanisław Wyspiański**'s play *Warszawianka* (Varsovienne, 1898) about the **powstanie listopadowe** (November Uprising) of 1830–1831. In the play the *Stary Wiarus* symbolizes what true unquestioning commitment to the cause of national liberation means, as opposed to how people talk about it in the salons. The character, which is easily parodied, became inextricably linked to the actor Ludwik Solski (1855–1954), who went on to a distinguished career in acting and directing (the Kraków Academy for the Dramatic Arts is named after him), but who was still reprising the role of Stary Wiarus well into the 1950s and his nineties.

"Sto lat," życzenia (one hundred years, greetings). The Polish equivalent of "For he's a jolly good fellow," sung obligatorily at birthdays, name days, and other similar celebrations, whether formal or informal. The words are:

> Sto lat, sto lat, niech żyje, żyje nam! (2×)
> Jeszcze raz, jeszcze raz, niech żyje, żyje nam!
> Niech żyje nam!
>
> One hundred years, one hundred years, may (s)he live for us!
> Once more, once more, may (s)he live for us,
> May (s)he live for us!

One may also say "Sto lat!" when someone sneezes, as an alternative to "Na zdrowie!" (To your health). A good all-purpose greeting is "Wszystkiego najlepszego!" (All the best). "Wesołych Świąt!" (Happy Holidays) is used for Christmas and Easter, although the Easter card greeting is "Wesołego alleluja!" Most greetings tend to be in the genitive case as if after the verb "to wish." Other examples: *pomyślności* (success), *szczęścia* (happiness), *powodzenia* (good luck); and others.

Stocznia Gdańska (Gdańsk Shipyards). One of Poland's largest shipyards, originally named after Lenin (whose connection with shipbuilding was tenuous). In the 1960s the Gdańsk shipyards primarily produced ships for export to the Soviet Union (at below cost, people suspected). In December 1970 workers went on strike over an increase in food prices. Increasingly violent street protests (the so-called December events; see *grudzień 1970, wydarzenia grudniowe*) broke out across northern Poland and were put down by the army with considerable loss of life. Ten years later an occupational strike over deteriorating living conditions and the firing of worker Anna Walentynowicz — the so-called *wydarzenia sierpniowe* (August events) led, in September 1980, to the signing (with a gigantic red and white pen) of the *porozumienie* (Gdańsk Accord) between the government and Lech Wałęsa, granting to Solidarność (Solidarity) the right to register as a legal nationwide independent trade union.

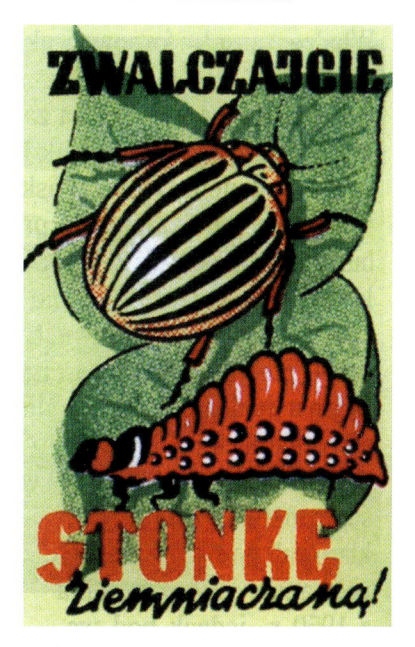

stonka ziemniaczana (Colorado potato beetle). Introduced by accident from America to Europe in the early twentieth century, this harmful pest, dubbed the *pasiasty dywersant* (striped infiltrator) by Polish communist propaganda, reached Poland in the 1940s and by the 1950s began to do serious damage to the potato crop. At first lacking chemical insecticides, the government organized quixotic mass beetle- and larva-picking actions. Bad harvests of all sorts were laid at the doorstep of the potato beetle, whose appearance in Poland was characterized by the official press as a deliberate act of economic sabotage. A headline of the time in the communist party organ *Trybuna*

Ludu (Tribune of the people) read "Niesłychana zbrodnia imperialistów amerykańskich" (Unprecedented crime of the American imperialists). A joke of the day went:

–The Americans are dropping potato beetles onto our fields.

–Good, now maybe they'll drop some potatoes to go with them.

---

strój ludowy (Polish folk dress). Polish folk dress was systematized in the latter part of the nineteenth century; it varied by region. Often modeled on the dress of the nobility of older times, it was used mainly on Sundays and special occasions. Today folk dress in regular use can be found in the Podhale part of the Carpathian Mountains and in the Łowicz area of central Poland. Elsewhere it is mostly worn for special occasions (like weddings) or for show at folk festivals. Probably the most easily recognizable Polish folk costume is that of the Kraków region, with its *sukmana* (peasant coat), peacock-feathered cap and, for women, a sequined vest and coral necklaces. *Folk dress from the Żywiec highlands.*

---

strzygoń, strzyga (Polish vampire). A special type of Polish "undead" creature, said to arise from a stillborn child, or one that dies before being baptized. Alternatively, a *strzygoń* (masculine) or *strzyga* (feminine) can be a naturally born person-within-a-person, with a separate heart and set of teeth, who comes to life upon the death of the carrier. In either case a strzyga/strzygoń tends to hide out in forests and prey on nighttime travelers, eating their insides (they have to live somehow). Less admirably, *strzygonie* tempt married women to betray their husbands. Burying the head separately from the body of the strzyga corpse helps prevent their coming back. The word is related to the Latin *strix strigis*, "screech owl, vampire."

---

studniówka (high school formal dance). Held one hundred days before the *matura* (high school achievement examinations, hence the name), the *studniówka* is an occasion for storing up psychic energy for the matura. Girls, and sometimes boys, wear red underwear, and wear the same pair again at the matura. The event obligatorily opens with a *polonez* (polonaise) and often features the presentation of humorous sketches from school life, and pranks done to teachers. One does not cut one's hair between the studniówka and the matura (because that is where one's accumulated knowledge resides). Following the matura, the *komers* (end-of-school party) will be held, a custom that was originally a frat party but is now spreading even to elementary and middle schools. The *półmetek* (halfway party) is a party held at the midpoint of one's high school studies.

Stuhr, Jerzy (b. 1947). Versatile film and stage actor who played chiefly, but not only, comic roles. Stuhr is also a theater and film director, screenwriter, professor, and past rector of Kraków's national drama school. In 2006 he received the prestigious Laur Krakowa (Kraków Laurel) for outstanding contributions to the city's science, culture, and business. In 2008 he was selected in a national plebiscite as Poland's best comedic actor of the past century. He has worked with most of Poland's best directors, including Krzysztof Kieślowski, Agnieszka Holland, Andrzej Wajda, and Krzysztof Zanussi. His most memorable roles were in *Wodzirej* (Top dog, 1978), *Amator* (Camera buff), *Seksmisja* (Sex-mission, 1984), and as the voice of Osioł (Donkey) in the Polish versions of the *Shrek* movies (2001, 2004, 2007). He is the father of the similarly talented actor Maciej Stuhr and of Marianna, a painter. His well-reviewed book *Stuhrowie – historie rodzinne* (The Stuhrs – family stories, 2008) traces the Stuhr family's history in Kraków (the Stuhrs originally came from Austria) since the middle of the nineteenth century. Jerzy Stuhr was recently diagnosed with throat cancer, presently in remission, and has been exceptional in discussing it publicly.

Stwosz, Wit (Veit Stoss, ca. 1447–1533). A Bavarian sculptor in wood and a distinguished representative of the late Gothic style, Stwosz is the creator, in 1477–1489, of the renowned and strikingly realistically executed folding *ołtarz* (altarpiece) in the kościół Mariacki (Marian Church) in Kraków, showing scenes from the life of Mary, most importantly her dormition, ascension, and coronation. It is the world's largest Gothic altarpiece, and a Polish national treasure. The figures were modeled on Kraków burghers of the time. The folds on the clothing are often singled out for special praise. The altarpiece was removed by the Germans in 1940 and hidden in the Nuremberg castle, where it was discovered in 1945. Painstakingly restored, it was returned to church display in 1957.

Sudety (Sudeten Mountains). A chain of not-very-tall mountains in the southwest shared by Poland and the Czech Republic. The highest peak is Śnieżka (Snowy, pictured), at 1,602 meters, in the Karkonosze range. Like that one, the peaks of the Sudetens are rounded and their slopes relatively gentle, making for good mountain bike riding. The largest town in the mountains is Jelenia Góra, population 86,300. The Sudetens are separated from the western Karpaty (Carpathians) by the Brama Morawska (Moravian Gate). Nearby Chojnik Castle is associated with the legend of Kunegunda, a princess who set as the condition of her hand in marriage that the prospective knight should ride around the castle walls on their edge. Many died in the attempt, until one day a handsome knight turned up, and Kunegunda, captivated by him, retracted her condition. However, the knight proceeded to ride successfully around the walls and then rode off in disdain. Kunegunda leaped to her death in despair.

Suwalszczyzna. A small, pretty, sparsely populated, and, in the winter, frigid region in far northeast Poland, the only place in the country where permafrost may be found. Its largest town is Suwałki, at 69,300 in population. Hardly a Polish weathercast takes place without commenting on the weather in Suwalszczyzna, which in addition to low temperatures also has perpetually strong winds. Historically the area was inhabited by the warlike Baltic tribe of Jaćwingowie (Jatwingians) who died out in the sixteenth century, being no match for the even more warlike Krzyżacy (Teutonic Knights). Dotted with lakes, bogs, and swamps, geographically the region extends far into present-day Lithuania, into which its streams drain via the Niemen River. Poland's deepest lake, Hańcza, at 106.1 meters, is located in Suwalszczyzna; the Kanał Augustowski (Augustow Canal) flows through it; and the Via Baltica highway, connecting Warsaw with Estonia, passes across it. The pristine Rospuda River valley (pictured) is threatened by the construction of a vociferously protested bypass on the Via Baltica around Augustów.

---

swaty, zaręczyny (matchmakers, engagements). Even in older times matchmaking was mostly a formality, as feelers would already have been sent out to determine whether a match was acceptable to a young woman and her family. The suitor would take two men, one a family member, on a visit to the young woman's family, who would pretend to be surprised to see them. Little by little the action would move to the family room, where *wódka* brought by the *swaty* would be opened, and a deal struck. Often the purpose of the visit would not even be discussed. Although it rarely happened, if a suit was turned down by the girl's family the visitors would be served *czarna polewka*, or *czarnina* (duck's blood soup), as happens in Adam Mickiewicz's *Pan Tadeusz*. The *zaręczyny* (engagement party) was held later at the bride's house, an opportunity for the two families to get better acquainted. *Włodzimierz Tetmajer,* Zaręczyny.

Sybir, Sybiracy (Siberia, Siberian exiles). Exile (*zesłanie*) to Siberia (located in the far northeast of Russia) was used in Russia beginning in the sixteenth century as a way of dealing with criminals and dissidents. It could involve the relocation of entire families and even villages. Often the punishment was combined with *katorga*, or forced labor under inhuman conditions. The mortality rate was high. Tens of thousands of Poles living in the *zabór rosyjski* (Russian partition) were sent to Siberia after the failed uprisings of 1830–1831 (powstanie listopadowe) and 1863 (powstanie styczniowe). As recently as World War II, it is often forgotten, hundreds of thousands of Poles and other ethnicities from the kresy (eastern Poland) were deported to Siberia and Kazakhstan, often to be interned in *łagry* (prison labor camps) in the Soviet Gułag system, more or less the equivalent of a death sentence.

In 2003 the order of the Krzyż Zesłańców Sybiru (Cross of Siberian Exiles) was created to honor those exiled during the Soviet period. See also: **Operacja Polska NKWD**. *Artur Grottger, Pochód na Sybir* (March to Siberia, *1866*).

sylwester, noc sylwestrowa (New Year's Eve). Celebrated in Poland as elsewhere, if not more so, with both public and private partying. Larger towns organize downtown concerts and fireworks, and the president's New Year's *orędzie* (proclamation) is broadcast. Some people put a fish scale in their billfold as a guarantee of prosperity in the coming year. After midnight unmarried women listen attentively and with trepidation to male names, as the first name heard will be that of their future husband. The usual greeting is "Szczęśliwego Nowego Roku!" (Happy New Year) or, in archaic Polish, "Do siego roku!" (To this year). Originally the last phrase referred to the year just past, but now it is taken to refer to the upcoming one.

Syrena (automobile). Known affectionately as the *syrenka*, this was a two-cylinder, two-stroke, small (very small) passenger car produced first in Warsaw and later in Bielsko-Biała. It was the first postwar automobile of exclusively Polish manufacture, and many Polish families owned one. Ranging from model 100 through 105, in all 521,311 vehicles were produced between 1957 and 1983. A pickup and a sports car model were also produced. One of its nicknames was *skarpeta*, "the big sock," since fitting into it was so tight. Another name that stuck was *kurołap* (chicken-catcher), after the forward-opening doors of the original model, which could be used to scoop up your neighbor's chickens as they walked unsuspectingly along the road.

Syrena warszawska (Warsaw mermaid). Known more commonly and affectionately as "Syrenka." Some creature resembling a half-woman, half-creature has appeared on the Warsaw coat of arms since the late fourteenth century. Gradually the image has been reinterpreted as a mermaid, and the one whose statue stands next to the Wisła in Warsaw (pictured) is said by tour guides to be sister to the one in Copenhagen. She swam upriver from Gdańsk, got out to rest near Warsaw, and she liked the town so much she decided to stay. For a brief while she was captured and displayed at fairs, but the townsfolk rescued her. In gratitude, she stands ready with her sword to defend the city against invaders. Another version has her figuring in the legend of Wars i Sawa.

szalikowcy (hooligan sports fans). The name comes from the scarves (*szaliki*) that fans wear bearing team colors. Poland has become plagued by the same phenomenon as some other countries have (most notoriously in South America), where *pseudokibice* or *kibole* (pseudo–sports fans) go to matches drunk and carrying knives, brass knuckles, and baseball bats, insulting and picking fights with fans of the opposing team. It is worse when they come from rival towns or from different parts of the same town. Notable sports rivalries are ŁKS (Łódzki Klub Sportowy, "Łódź Sports Club") vs. Widzew Łódź, Wisła Kraków vs. Cracovia, and Górnik Zabrze vs. Ruch Chorzów. There have been a number of fatalities. Sports fan rabidity is exacerbated by discussion boards on websites that do not bother to edit the content of their often ignorant, bigoted, and foulmouthed visitors.

Szał uniesień (*Frenzy of Exultations*). An iconic and much-copied (and parodied) painting of the Młoda Polska (Young Poland) period by Władysław Podkowiński (1866–1895) who, exceptionally for the time, came from Warsaw rather than Kraków. The wall-sized painting, featuring a horse symbolizing "unbridled passion" carrying a naked lady into an abyss, caused scandal when it was exhibited by itself at the Zachęta gallery in 1894. An additional sensation occurred when the distraught, lovesick artist brought a knife to the gallery and slashed the painting to shreds, claiming to be dissatisfied with its quality. It was restored after the artist's early death from tuberculosis and is today displayed in the museum over Kraków's Sukiennice. The ice cream concoction by the same name in the Sukiennice museum café fails to live up to expectations.

szara eminencja (gray eminence, eminence grise). The term refers to a sinister person who wields the strings of power from behind the scenes, an example being the dreaded Jakub Berman, called Joseph Stalin's *prawa ręka* (right-hand man) in Poland, and the chief of the repressive Polish secret police between 1944 and 1956. See also: odwilż gomułkowska, październik 1956 and Służba Bezpieczeństwa. Berman finished out his career in a publishing house as an editor of encyclopedias. Another gray eminence would be General Mieczysław Moczar, the minister of the interior in 1964–1968 and head of the nationalist Związek Bojowników o Wolność i Demokrację (ZBoWiD, League of Fighters for Freedom and Democracy). As part of a factional struggle within the communist party, Moczar instigated the vicious crackdown on student protests of *marzec 1968* (March 1968) and played the anti-Semitic card as a power ploy to eliminate Jewish-connected members of the communist government. The ploy worked to the extent that even party chief Władysław Gomułka, whose wife was Jewish, joined the campaign in order to save his political skin. The "anti-Zionist" campaign got badly out of hand and led to the firing and emigration of thousands of Polish Jews. In the end Moczar was gradually shunted aside.

Aleksander Kamiński, re-created on film in 2014 by Robert Gliński, and with Warsaw's Pomnik Małego Powstańca (Monument of the Little Insurgent), pictured.

Szczecin. The town was Polish in the tenth century and is now again, but before World War II it was German Stettin. Szczecin lies on the Odra River near the present Polish-German border on the Bałtyk (Baltic Sea). It is the historical capital of Pomorze Zachodnie (Western Pomerania) and, at 406,000 inhabitants, it is the seventh-largest city in Poland as well as its largest seaport. Its industries have traditionally been fishing and shipbuilding.

Szare Szeregi (Gray Legions). The name encompassing the conspiratorial activities of the Polish *harcerstwo* (scouting) organizations during World War II, so called because they did most of their work at dusk. The Szare Szeregi were active in sabotage operations throughout Poland, where their motto was the rhyming "Tylko świnie siedzą w kinie" (Only swine sit in the cinema). They were especially effective during the powstanie warszawskie (Warsaw Uprising), in which their battalions, named Parasol (Umbrella), Zośka, and Wigry, distinguished themselves with their bravery, suffering heavy losses and entering into legend. The scouts helped deliver conspiratorial messages through its Harcerska Poczta Powstańcza (Scouts' Insurrectionist Mail). Their deeds were commemorated in the widely read young adult novel *Kamienie na szaniec* (Stones onto the rampart) by

Szczerbiec (Old Nick). The coronation sword used in coronation ceremonies of most Polish kings from 1320 (Władysław I Łokietek) to 1764

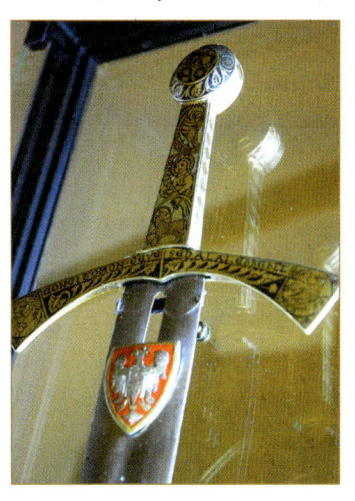

KALEIDOSCOPE OF POLAND   247

(**Stanisław II August Poniatowski**), the most valuable of the preserved Polish royal regalia, and the only piece directly related to the **Piastowie** (Piast dynasty). Despite its name, its blade has smooth edges, and the tradition linking it to **Bolesław I Chrobry**'s Kievan exploits is some three centuries off. Looted by Prussian troops in 1795, it was purchased in 1884 for the Hermitage Museum in Russia. The Soviet Union returned it to Poland in 1928. During World War II it was secreted to Canada, and was returned only in 1959. It is preserved in the treasury in **Wawel** castle in **Kraków**.

Szewińska, Irena Kirszenstein (b. 1946). The best Polish woman sprinter ever, Szewińska had seven Olympic medals (three gold) over four Olympics from 1964 to 1976 and ten medals in the European Track Championships (five gold). In 1974 she was ranked number one in the world in the 100-meter, 200-meter, and 400-meter races, in all of which she set world records at one time or another. Being Jewish, even she was subject to attack in the aftermath of the events of *marzec 1968* (March 1968), despite her fame. A 1998 plebiscite run by *Przegląd Sportowy* (The sporting review) voted her Poland's leading sports figure of the twentieth century. Szewińska was the chair of the Polish Track and Field Union from 1997 to 2009 and is currently a member of the International Olympic Committee.

szklane domy (glass houses). An image taken from a vision about the future presented in **Stefan Żeromski**'s 1924 novel *Przedwiośnie* (Early spring), in which the main character Seweryn Baryka tries to convince his son Cezary that futuristic, self-cleaning, and virtually self-building glass houses are to arise across Poland. The image symbolizes the unrealizable vision of prosperity and justice for Poland, one's sense of disappointment born of the confrontation of one's dreams against the reality of what is possible, and the impractical naïvety of Poland's social idealists at the beginning of the twentieth century.

szkoła lwowsko-warszawska logiki matematycznej (Lwów-Warsaw school of mathematical logic). The most important movement in the history of Polish philosophy. Originating in the last part of the nineteenth century at the University of **Lwów** under Kazimierz Twardowski and his disciples, the Polish school of philosophy during the interwar years rivaled in prestige the British school of analytical logic and the Viennese school of logical positivism. Its most important representatives were Kazimierz Ajdukiewicz, Tadeusz Kotarbiński, Stanisław Leśniewski, Jan Łukasiewicz, Alfred Tarski, and Władysław Tatarkiewicz. Łukasiewicz invented the parenthesis-free system of logical and mathematical notation known as "Polish notation," still used in computer science today. The school was re-established at the University of Warsaw after the war, but under Marxism it could no longer flourish, even if its traditions of rigorous thought helped maintain the high standards of Polish philosophy during the postwar period.

szlachta polska (Polish nobility/gentry). Deriving from the medieval state of *rycerstwo* (knighthood), by the sixteenth century the title of Polish nobleman amounted to possessing land and a *herb* (coat of arms; see *herby polskie*), and consequently a vote in *sejmy* and *sejmiki* (national and regional parliaments). In Poland the nobility were legally equal among themselves, the divisions such as they existed being based on wealth. Their primary duty was military service. The poor *szlachta zagrodowa*, or *szlachta zaściankowa* (petty gentry), were an especially large class, comprising in places as much as 20 percent of the population. At the opposite end were the incredibly rich magnateria (magnates). During the *zabory* (partitions; see rozbiory), their status depended on that of the nobility in the partitioning powers. Poles claim that the Polish noble tradition lives on in contemporary culture in social relationships, the use of titles and in manners in general, and in the occasional touchiness of Poles on what they perceive to be questions of honor (points of honor). The legal status of the nobility was curtailed only by the constitution of March 1921. *Rembrandt van Rijn,* Szlachcic polski.

szopka krakowska (Kraków crèche). The craft of making elaborate multitowered miniature crèches (tableaux depicting the birth of Jesus) out of wood and cardboard, decorated with colorful foil taken from candy wrappers, alluding in their architecture to the historical monuments of Kraków, is unique to that area. It originated in the nineteenth century among workers in the construction trades with idle hands in the winter. The craft is kept alive by yearly contests, exhibitions, and workshops, and the practice has spread to Polish communities abroad. *Szopka in the Kraków Historical Museum.*

Szucha, Aleja (Szucha Boulevard in Warsaw). During World War II major Nazi administrative offices were located along this street, named after the architect Jan Chrystian Szuch. It was one of the few parts of Warsaw not taken over

KALEIDOSCOPE OF POLAND   249

by insurgents in the powstanie warszawskie (Warsaw Uprising) of 1944. As a result, it is one of the few places in Warsaw where one may today view buildings as they appeared before the war, including luxury apartment houses. The infamous Gestapo prison, noted for the cruelty of its interrogations, was located at 25 Szucha Boulevard, now the headquarters of both the Ministry of Education and the Mauzoleum Walki i Męczeństwa 1939–1945 (Mausoleum of Struggle and Martyrdom, 1939–1945). The name Aleja Szucha is still synonymous with sadism, torture, beatings, and death. *A cell in the Gestapo prison in the museum.*

Sanskrit), which today houses a museum devoted to his life and work. Among his lasting pieces are his études for piano, two string quartets, a sonata for voice and piano, and the choral masterpiece *Stabat Mater*. Szymanowski died in Switzerland after a long bout with tuberculosis and is interred in Kraków at Skałka in the Krypta Zasłużonych (Crypt of the Meritorious).

Szymanowski, Karol Fryderyk (1882–1937). A concert pianist and, next to Fryderyk Chopin, Poland's most widely acclaimed composer. His music, which includes vocal as well as orchestral music, is characterized by the impressionistic neo-romanticism of the Młoda Polska (Young Poland) movement. He was not averse to introducing folk elements from the Podhale (Polish Highlands) into his pieces. Openly gay, he wrote a number of erotic poems in French devoted to a fifteen-year-old French boy, as well as a novel on Greek love. Szymanowski maintained a residence in Zakopane in the *styl zakopiański* (Zakopane style), named Atma ("peace of mind" in

Szymborska, Wisława (1923–2012). A major voice of postwar Polish poetry and winner of the Nobel Prize for Literature in 2006, having lived down an early period in which she wrote fawning verse admiring communism and the Soviet dictator Joseph Stalin. Szymborska lived most of her life in Kraków. Her poems are often whimsical, adopting unusual points of view, either toward inanimate objects (like a rock), or that of a cat bereft of its owner. Like her contemporary Zbigniew Herbert, Szymborska was an "anti-Platonist" in that she tried to build up her own world around her from scratch, using as building blocks the material of everyday reality. The following verse was turned into a rock song:

> Nic dwa razy się nie zdarza
> I nie zdarzy. Z tej przyczyny
> Zrodziliśmy się bez wprawy
> I pomrzemy bez rutyny.

Nothing ever happens twice
Or ever will, because
We've been born without the know-how
And we'll die without ever working it out.

Ściegienny, Piotr (1801–1890). Catholic priest, political organizer, pamphleteer, and peasant rights activist in the **Lublin** and **Kielce** regions in the years between the **powstanie listopadowe** (November Uprising of 1830) and the **powstanie styczniowe** (January Uprising of 1863). He was said to be the author of a fake papal bull calling on Polish peasants to revolt (Pope Gregory XVI was actually vehemently opposed to revolutionary movements). For his political activism Father Ściegienny was sentenced to death by the tsarist government, a sentence later commuted to perpetual hard labor in Siberia. After twenty-five years he returned to Poland and continued his work, living to a ripe old age. Ściegienny became a symbol of endurance and of the socially committed activist priest with which many priests identified during the **Solidarność** (Solidarity) period of the 1980s.

Śląsk (Silesia; German: Schlesien; Czech: Slezsko). A part of southwestern Poland overlapping in places with Germany and the Czech Republic. Over the centuries borders between the three countries have shifted back and forth, and the region is practically synonymous with German-Polish ethnic tension. Major parts of today's Śląsk belonged to Germany before World War II and after the war much of the German-speaking population was "repatriated" to Germany. Rich in coal, Śląsk has its own distinctive dialects, traditions and, prominently, cuisine. It is divided into Dolny Śląsk (Lower Silesia) to the northwest and Górny Śląsk (Upper Silesia) to the southeast. The terms "Upper" and "Lower" refer to elevation above sea level, not to the positions north and south on the map. Its capital, **Wrocław**, has had a long and checkered history, now under Czechs, now Germans, now Poles. Other major towns in the region are **Katowice**, Gliwice, Zabrze, Bytom, Bielsko-Biała, and **Opole**. Śląsk is also the name for Poland's second-best-known (after **Mazowsze**) folk song and dance ensemble.

śledź (herring). The herring is the unofficial Polish national fish. Historically, pickling was a good way to preserve fish for long-distance transport, and herring are usually eaten marinated, especially in the form of *rolmopsy* (herring fillets wrapped around a pickle or olive, pictured) — said to be good for a hangover. In Poland herring are closely associated with the last day of *karnawał* (carnival), Shrove Tuesday, which, in fact, is called *śledzik* (herring day). Herring continue to be eaten throughout the Easter fast, and can be found on one's plate both on Wielki Piątek (Good Friday) and **Wigilia** (Christmas Eve). It is an especially good "fasting" food, as it is rich in vitamins D, E, B2, and B6, calcium, and phosphorus.

Śmigły-Rydz, Edward (1886–1941). Appointed by President Ignacy Mościcki as inspector-general of the Polish armed forces in 1935, Śmigły-Rydz was promoted to *marszałek* (commander-in-chief) as war broke out on September 1, 1939. In view of the rapidly collapsing Polish defenses coupled with the Soviet invasion of the *kresy* on September 17, he retreated to Romania on September 18 and returned to Poland in 1941 under an assumed name in order to join the underground. He died shortly afterward under unclear circumstances, probably from a heart attack. Fairly or not, Śmigły-Rydz is treated unkindly by most historians for failing to assess adequately the combined threat from Germany and the Soviet Union, for inadequate military preparations, for poor strategic decisions during the defense of Poland, and for leaving the country for Romania before Warsaw had actually fallen.

Śpiący Rycerze (slumbering knights). Seen from a certain angle, the peak of Giewont Mountain in the high Tatras reminds some of the profile of a reclining knight in armor (see the picture). That would make sense, as within its hidden grottoes lies a fully armed regiment of Polish knights, sleeping there since the time of Bolesław I Chrobry (Bolesław the Brave, 967–1025), Poland's first king. They await the signal that "już nadszedł czas" (the time has finally come) for them to awake, mount their steeds, and rescue the *ojczyzna* (fatherland) from impending danger. Considering Polish history since 1025, one has to wonder what it would take to rouse them. A recent short story by Jacek Dehnel sees the knights arise to the threat of a third world war sparked by a military coup in North Korea. Unfortunately they instantly fall asleep again just outside their cavern and all attempts to reawaken them prove fruitless.

Światowid ze Zbrucza. A tall (2.6 meters), intriguing, and virtually unique limestone four-faced idol. It may have been a crossroads marker, with one face for each compass direction. It was extricated in 1848 from the river Zbrucz in Podole (Podolia), now Ukrainian Podilia. The Światowid is judged to come from the ninth or tenth century AD and is said by some to represent four Slavic pagan gods, or possibly one god (Perun?) with four heads. Others interpret the idol to be of Turkish or Iranian origin. Its phallic shape (in some people's minds) has been speculated to represent fertility but, in the end, the idol's sense, purpose, and origin are anyone's guess. The name Światowid was applied to the idol, probably in error, after the Polabian god Świętowit, with the root *święt-* (holy); folk etymology has reinterpreted the name as related to *świat* (world) and *wid-* (see), as though it is looking out over the world. The idol is on display in the Kraków Archaeological Museum.

świątki (carved wooden saint figurines). These are a traditional and much-collected variety of Polish folk sculpture. *Świątki* usually, but not always, represent religious figures, and were often carved for placement in a *kapliczka przydrożna* (roadside shrine). These days they are mostly produced in mass numbers for the tourist trade by craftsmen working for Cepelia. Świątki often have disproportionately large heads. Being designed for frontal display, they are often not finished in back. Besides religious figures, they can also depict folk musicians, craftsmen, mountaineers, rabbis, animals, and so on.

Świątynia Opatrzności Bożej (Temple of Divine Providence). Part of a huge new religious complex, the Centrum Opatrzności Bożej (Center of Divine Providence) is being developed in Warsaw's Wilanów area. It is intended to be a temple of national remembrance and thanksgiving, stressing Poland's tradition as a Christian (Roman Catholic) nation, the realization of a two-hundred-year-old plan originally intended to commemorate the passage of the Konstytucja 3 maja (May 3 Constitution, 1791). Besides a church, the complex includes museums devoted to Pope Jan Paweł II and Cardinal Stefan Wyszyński, and a Panteon Wielkich Polaków (Pantheon of Great Poles) — which is to say, crypts. The project has generated controversy and has had trouble raising money, with people questioning its point, need, cost, and scale, and rejecting its implicit ideology that "Polak to Katolik" (to be a Pole is to be a Catholic).

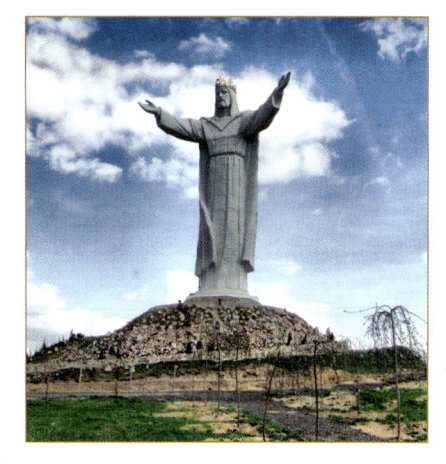

Świebodzin, pomnik Chrystusa Króla (monument of Christ the King in Świebodzin). Following in the footsteps of the village of Licheń, which built Poland's largest basilica and organ, and commissioned its largest bell, the local parish in twenty-two-thousand-strong Świebodzin in western Poland decided to erect the world's tallest statue of Jesus Christ. Weighing in at 440 tons, the statue is modeled on the Christ the Redeemer statue in Rio de Janeiro, Brazil, but slightly taller: fifty-two meters in all, including the base. The statue itself is thirty-three meters tall, corresponding to the number of years of Jesus's life. The town hopes the statue will become a destination of *pielgrzymki* (pilgrimages), as has happened with Licheń. The sense of the project and its final form has drawn decidedly mixed reviews. See also: Częstochowa.

KALEIDOSCOPE OF POLAND   253

Świerszczyk (Cricket). One of the few cultural constants in postwar Poland alongside the general-interest weekly *Przekrój* (Cross-section), the grade-school children's magazine *Świerszczyk* (the name "Cricket" intended to connote hearth and home) has been published uninterruptedly since 1945, enlisting the best of children's authors and illustrators. It is currently a biweekly that schools often subscribe to, containing poems, fairy tales, stories, popular science and general interest articles, games and puzzles. Colloquially and jocularly the word *świerszczyk* is used to refer to a so-called gentleman's magazine (of which there is no lack in Poland).

Święto Trzech Króli (Holiday of the Three Wise Men, January 6). One of the oldest Christian holidays, conflated with Objawienie Pańskie (Epiphany), obligatorily celebrated by Roman Catholics. Beginning in 2011 it became a national holiday. Święto Trzech Króli commemorates the visit of the three magi to the Christ child. In Poland it is celebrated, among other ways, by having a piece of chalk blessed in church, with which either the priest or the apartment owner will write the letters "K M B" on one's door during a New Year's pastoral visit, called a *kolęda*. The letters stand for the names of the wise men (Kacper, Melchior, Baltazar) and for the phrase *Christus mansioni benedicat* (May Christ bless this home). The holiday is dedicated to missionaries abroad.

Świnoujście (German: Swinemünde). Historically a German sea resort at the outlet of the Świna River into the **Bałtyk** (Baltic Sea), Świnoujście is today Poland's westernmost seaport and a major ferry terminal, with connections to Sweden and Denmark. It numbers around forty-one thousand inhabitants. Built on three large islands and numerous smaller ones, Świnoujście has a broad ten-mile-long beach and the tallest lighthouse on the Baltic at sixty-eight meters. The lighthouse (pictured) has become the town symbol. Świnoujście was carpet-bombed by the British Royal Air Force in the closing days of World War II, heavily damaging the city and killing around twenty-three thousand of its German residents.

T

tajne komplety (underground studies). Both under the *zabory* (partitions, see *rozbiory*) in the nineteenth century and during World War II, Poles proved adept at organizing secret courses of study on all academic levels and in all fields. In the **Generalne Gubernatorstwo** (General-Gouvernment, German-occupied Poland in World War II), study beyond the fourth grade was banned; even there, reading was not taught. Schoolteachers and university instructors continued to work throughout the war as part of an elaborate network of clandestine studies under the Towarzystwo Oświaty Niepodległościowej (Society for Independent Education), without parallel elsewhere in wartime Europe. Classes were typically held in private apartments at the risk of the lives of all concerned: teachers, students, apartment building owners, and other residents. Through the *tajne komplety* thousands of Polish students were able to earn a *matura konspiracyjna* (conspiratorial high-school certificate) or a university degree in the humanities or sciences. See also: **Uniwersytet Latający**.

tak-tak (yes-yes). Foreigners visiting Poland feel bombarded on all sides by the word *tak* (yes), often repeated in multiples of two, three, or more, but especially two: *tak-tak*. The word is staccato and fun to say, and learning it is the first step toward fluency in the language. It's not surprising, then, that Tak-Tak is the name of a popular prepaid mobile phone service. One can download as a cell phone ringtone a chorus from the group Republika's popular song based on looking into a mirror, titled "Tak-tak, to ja!" (Yes-yes, that's me!), the final chorus of which goes "tak tak tak tak tak tak tak tak tak tak tak taaaaaak!" As in English, the single word all by itself can carry a variety of readily understandable inflections. Are Poles as a nation then positively disposed toward life? The answer to this and almost any other sociopolitical question may be obtained, for a fee (after sixty days, for free), from Ośrodek Badania Opinii Publicznej (OBOP, Public Opinion Research Center). The best correspondent to English "yeah" is *no*, which, disconcertingly for English speakers, means anything other than "no," and probably has even more meaningful inflections than tak.

"Tango"; animacja polska ("Tango"; Polish animated films). "Tango" is not only the title of Sławomir Mrożek's best-known play but also the title of an ingenious animated film by Zygmunt Rybczyński, in which an increasing number of characters repeatedly enter and leave a small room while eating, dressing, undressing, making love, and generally going about their business without taking any notice of one another. Produced in Łódź by the Se-ma-for studio, it won an Oscar in 1983 for best animated short film. Se-ma-for won a second Oscar in 2008 for an animated version of *Peter and the Wolf*. Many of the classic Polish *dobranocki* ("nighty-night" cartoons) were produced either in Se-ma-for or in Bielsko-Biała's Studio Filmów Rysunkowych (Cartoon Film Studio). In the area of computer animation Tomasz Bagiński has had several successes, most notably with the multiple prize–winning shorts "Katedra" (Cathedral) and "Sztuka spadania" (Art of falling). Bagiński has also created animation for the Wiedźmin (Witcher) video game.

Tannenberg, operacja (Operation Tannenberg; German: Unternehmen Tannenberg). In advance of the invasion of Poland in 1939 the Nazis systematically drew up a list of some sixty thousand culturally significant and active Polish people: writers, teachers, scholars, journalists, sportsmen, cultural activists — in short, most of the Polish *inteligencja* (intelligentsia) and other people with a public face — who were to be exterminated upon occupation. Within the first two months of the invasion, some twenty thousand Poles on this list had been murdered. In choosing the name Tannenberg (the German name for Grunwald), the Nazis were expressing their desire for revenge for the defeat of the Krzyżacy (Teutonic Knights) at the hands of the Polish-Lithuanian army more than five hundred years earlier.

tańce ludowe (folk dances). Authorities distinguish five main Polish folk dances, differentiated by region, rhythm, syncopation, and tempo. The king of Polish national dances is the stately "walked" *polonez* (polonaise) with a 3/4 time signature and accent on the first beat. The *krakowiak*, from the Kraków region, is a lively dance with a syncopated 2/4 rhythm. The *mazur* or *mazurek* (mazurka), from the Mazury region, has a lively 3/4 or 3/8 measure, also with syncopation. Similar to but faster than the mazur is the *oberek* or *obertas*, a dance with twirling couples that is characteristic of the village *karczma* (tavern). Finally there is the *kujawiak*, a somber dance associated with the Kujawy region, also in 3/4 or 3/8 measure. Polish composers have often looked to Polish folk rhythms for inspiration, and the dances themselves have migrated to contemporary pair-dancing contests. Missing here is the *polka*, scornfully disowned by Poles as being German or Czech.

targ, hala targowa (market hall). The legitimate continuant of the medieval trade hall. *Targi* (product and produce markets) may be open-air, semi-enclosed, or completely indoor areas containing stalls with sellers of almost anything, a lot of it cheap clothing imports but mostly farm products. Many Poles buy ordinary groceries at a grocery store, but would not think of buying fresh fruits and vegetables, eggs, or dairy products like *twaróg* (farmer's cheese) anywhere other than from a small private vendor. Probably gone are the days when one could buy at a city market a live chicken, ready to slaughter and pluck, with its squawking head sticking out of a bag. *The immense hala targowa in Wrocław, built in Breslau before World War II.*

tarpan. A Eurasian wild horse with distinctive shape and coloration, memorialized in Cro-Magnon cave paintings. Hunted for their succulent flesh, the last died out in Russia around 1890, to be semi-resurrected by 1930s German experiments in back-breeding on horses descended from the Polish *konik* (wild horse), aimed at re-creating the "Aryan horse." Despite their unsavory origin, herds of *tarpan*-like horses, said to thrive on bad weather and impoverished food, are preserved in Poland's Białowieża forest, along with the more famous *żubr* (European bison). Tarpan is also the name of a Polish army light utility vehicle, similar to a Jeep or Hummer. The Asian Przewalski's horse, the only other true wild (and not simply feral) horse, is not claimed by Poland, as its discoverer, the naturalist Nikolai Przewalski (1839–1888), despite his Polish surname, was a strong proponent of Russian imperialism. After almost being declared extinct, the Przewalski's horse lives a subsistence life in zoos and, having been reintroduced there, in the wilds of Mongolia.

Tatry (Tatra Mountains). An approximately eighty-kilometer stretch of the Karpaty (Carpathian Mountains) along the border between Poland and Slovakia. Slovakia has the tallest peak, Gerlach, at 2,655 meters. The tallest peak on the Polish side of the Tatras, and in Poland generally, is Rysy at 2,499 meters. The tallest peak of the western Tatras is Giewont at 1,894 meters, topped by a distinct-looking metal-frame cross. The unofficial capital of the Polish Tatras is Zakopane, whose nearby peak is Gubałówka at 1,126 meters, connected to town by a cable railway, a tourist favorite. In general the Tatras are a popular tourist area; the area around Kasprowy Wierch (pictured), also reachable by cable railway, was developed as a ski destination as early as the 1930s. The Tatrzańskie Ochotnicze Pogotowie Ratunkowe (Tatra Volunteer Rescue Service) is kept busy year-round rescuing mountain climbers and avalanche victims. The Tatras are inhabited by animal species not encountered elsewhere in Poland, such as the *nornik śnieżny* (snowy vole), the *świstak* (groundhog/marmot), and the *kozica* (chamois) — a kind of half deer, half mountain goat.

telenowela (daily serialized television drama). The name comes from Portuguese and Spanish, as the earliest ones shown on Polish television in the 1980s originated in Latin America. More than mere "soap operas," the Polish *telenowela* is characterized by a high level of writing, acting, and realism, even if it does tend toward the melodramatic. In Poland actors often move freely between the big and small screens. The variety, longevity, and topicality of telenowela situations are remarkable. The pioneering Polish telenowela was *W labiryncie* (1988–1990), about life in a Warsaw pharmaceutical institute, which appeared at a time when politically sensitive topics could be discussed more freely than previously. The currently longest-running serial, by the same director, Paweł Karpiński, is *Klan* (Clan), about the Lubicz/Chojnicki family in Warsaw (pictured here at **Wigilia**). It has broadcast over two thousand installments since beginning in 1997. Others worth mentioning are *M jak miłość* (M is for love), *Złotopolscy* (The Złotopolski family), and *Barwy szczęścia* (Colors of happiness). Telenovelas imported from Mexico and South America continue to be popular.

Telimena. The name of the pretentious and flirty "older woman" in **Adam Mickiewicz**'s novel-in-verse *Pan Tadeusz* (Master Thaddeus), a word still used to describe a woman of that type; i.e., a woman slightly past her prime but versed in the art of style and makeup so as not to betray her true age. In *Pan Tadeusz* she is the legal guardian of the novel's female protagonist, and Tadeusz's romantic interest, Zosia, whose name has become synonymous with youthful natural grace and charm. Grażyna Szapołowska was excellently cast in the role of Telimena in **Andrzej Wajda**'s film version (1999, pictured).

Telewizja Polska, **TVP** (state-owned Polish television). The first attempts at television broadcasting in Poland go back to 1938, and the first regular broadcasts began in 1952, with color broadcasting from 1971. Current channels include the most popular TVP1 (Jedynka) and TVP2 (Dwójka), along with TVP Kultura (Culture), TVP Historia (History), TVP Info, TVP Seriale, TVP Sport, and TVP HD. There are ten channels in all, of which TVP1 and TVP2 reach up to 97 percent of the population. TVP Polonia is aimed at Poles living abroad, and TVP Belsat is for those living in Belarus. Poles supposedly spend an average of four hours daily sitting in front of the tube, watching news programs like *Wiadomości* and *Teleexpress*, **telenowele** (soap operas), and entertainment programs, many of which are Polish adaptations of programs developed elsewhere, like *Jaka to melodia?* (Name that tune), *Familiada* (Family feud), and *Szansa na sukces* (Chance for success).

Teraz Polska (Now Poland). A competitive label awarded in recognition of high quality in selected goods or services produced in Poland or promoting Poland outside the country, a kind of "seal of approval" awarded by the Fundacja Polskiego Godła Promocyjnego (Polish Promotional Emblem Foundation). It originated in 1993. The badge is also used to endorse noteworthy local initiatives undertaken in promotion of Poland. To younger Poles the term "Teraz Polska" more often signifies a mixed drink consisting of raspberry syrup on the bottom and vodka on the top, the result looking like the Teraz Polska emblem, pictured. Be sure to pour the vodka first, then the raspberry juice, which will sink to the bottom. Otherwise, the proper effect will be not be achieved. See also: **przysłowia o Polsce i Polakach**.

Tokarczuk, Olga (b. 1962). A major contemporary literary figure specializing in short literary forms but also a novelist and poet. She is a psychologist by training but now is a full-time writer. Tokarczuk won the 2008 **Nike** prize for *Bieguni* (Runners), a novel interweaving various stories united by travel. She lives in Dolny Śląsk (Lower Silesia) and, besides traveling and giving readings, leads creative writing seminars at the university in **Opole**. Her most popular work to date is *Prawiek i inne czasy*, published in English as *Primeval and Other Times* (1996), which documents eighty years of life, beginning in 1914, in a fictional village in the heart of Poland.

Tomek, agent (Agent Tomek). The code name of Tomasz Kaczmarek, the suave secret agent of the Centralne Biuro Antykorupcyjne (Central Anticorruption Office), who specialized in masquerading as a rich businessman with all the accoutrements (brand-name suits, gold watches, Porsche sports car) and seducing politically or socially prominent women and inducing them to commit financial crimes. His most famous operation was taking down the member of parliament Beata Sawicka, who was caught red-handed accepting a bribe in connection with a real estate concession on **Hel** peninsula. Arrested in 2007, her case dragged on until 2012, when she was convicted and sentenced to three years' imprisonment. Agent Tomek and the mystery of his identity was a staple of the tabloid press until his outing, after which (of course) he wrote a book and became a media personality. In 2011 he was elected to parliament from the **Kielce** district.

Toruń (German: Thorn). A town of 205,700 on the **Wisła** River between Warsaw and **Gdańsk**, the sixteenth-largest in Poland. Toruń was established as an outpost of the **Krzyżacy** (Teutonic Knights) in the thirteenth century, and it was a member of the medieval trade union Hansa (Hanseatic League). The nicely preserved fourteenth- and fifteenth-century center of Toruń is listed as a UNESCO World Heritage Site. Its silhouette from across the river was voted one of Poland's "seven wonders." In 1466, following a thirteen-year-long war between Poland and the Krzyżacy, the town was joined to the Polish **Korona Królestwa Polskiego** (crown), but it remained a bastion of Lutheranism. A conflict between Protestants and Catholics in 1724 provoked the intervention of King August II Mocny, who scandalized world opinion by allowing the decision of a Catholic court to stand, resulting in the beheading of Protestant leaders and the town's mayor. Toruń is forever associated with *pierniki toruńskie* (Toruń gingerbread cookies) and the sixteenth-century astronomer Mikołaj Kopernik (Copernicus) — who, however, though born in Toruń, did much of his work in Frombork in Warmia. *Photogenetic Toruń spread out along the Wisła.*

---

traktat ateński (Athens Accord, April 16, 2003). The five-thousand-page document describing the conditions under which Poland, along with nine other countries, would be accepted into the Unia Europejska (European Union, EU), following a *referendum akcesyjne* (accession referendum). On the referendum, 77.45 percent of Polish voters responded yes, and 22.55 percent voted no. Poland had already joined NATO (the North Atlantic Treaty Organization) in 1999, along with Hungary and the Czech Republic. Poland officially became a member of the EU at midnight May 1, 2004, as President Aleksander Kwaśniewski raised the EU flag over the Grób Nieznanego Żołnierza (Tomb of the Unknown Soldier) on Piłsudski Square. Poland is the sixth-largest EU country in size and population.

---

traktat wersalski (Treaty of Versailles). Also known as the *pokój paryski* (Paris Peace), the *traktat wersalski* was the treaty drawn up in 1919–1920 by the victorious countries of the so-called *ententa* (entente) following World War I at the konferencja wersalska (Versailles Conference). The treaty legitimized the new and independent Polish state, the so-called Druga Rzeczpospolita (Second Republic) or Polska Odrodzona (Reborn Poland) and helped facilitate the cession, via plebiscite or revolt, to Poland of some former German lands in Wielkopolska (Greater Poland) and Prusy Zachodnie (West Prussia) — lands taken from Poland by Prussia in the *rozbiory* (partitions) of 1772, 1793, 1795 — and in Górny Śląsk (Upper Silesia). The treaty also set up the entity of the Wolne Miasto Gdańsk (Free City of Gdańsk). Poland was represented at the conference by Ignacy Paderewski and Roman Dmowski. Of Woodrow Wilson's famous Fourteen Points, the thirteenth stipulated Polish independence with access to the sea.

Treblinka. Two *obozy koncentracyjne* (concentration camps), one a so-called *obóz pracy* (work camp), the other an *obóz zagłady* (extermination camp), built by the Germans in the forest next to the Bug River in the east, near the village of Poniatowo. Despite its fairly short existence from 1942 to 1943, some eight hundred thousand Jews, more than 310,000 from the Warsaw ghetto, were put to death here in *komory gazowe* (gas chambers), second in number only to Auschwitz-Birkenau. The camp was destroyed by the Germans ahead of the advancing Soviet army. The Austrian commander at Treblinka, Franz Stangl, worked in Brazil under his own identity until 1961, when he was extradited to West Germany and put on trial for the deaths of nine hundred thousand people. He admitted to the deaths but pleaded not guilty by reason of following orders. He died in prison in 1971 of heart failure. An eyewitness account of life in Treblinka was written by Jankiel Wiernik, who escaped the camp in an uprising in 1943. See also: "polskie obozy koncentracyjne."

Treny (Threnodies, or Laments, 1580). The Threnodies are regarded as the greatest literary achievement of the sixteenth century, of the

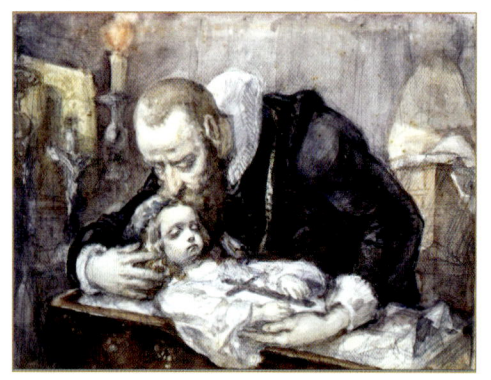

260 KALEIDOSCOPE OF POLAND

Polish poet Jan Kochanowski, and of the Polish Renaissance generally. The genesis of this cycle of nineteen poems lay in the early death of Kochanowski's young daughter Urszula. The Threnodies are a mixed genre, ranging from epigram to elegy, from epitaph to song, and conclude with a lengthy didactic verse narrative. They mix together classical and religious themes, folk motifs, and references to ancient philosophers. As a whole the Threnodies represent a literary form unknown to classical or Renaissance authors. They are often taken as a forerunner of the baroque style that was characteristic of literature of the following seventeenth century. Several highly inadequate attempts have been made to translate them into English. *Jan Matejko,* Kochanowski over the Casket of Urszula.

Trędowata (The leper, 1909). A melodramatic two-volume potboiler novel by Helena Mniszkówna about how true love between Waldemar Michorowski, the scion of a noble family, and Stefania Rudecka, a governess in his aunt's house from an impoverished noble family, becomes the victim of social prejudice. Virtue is about to win out in the end when the heroine catches her death of cold and dies on her wedding day. The novel was ridiculed by critics but was destined to become the best-selling novel of the *dwudziestolecie międzywojenne* (interwar period), and it led to the best-selling sequel *Ordynat Michorowski* (Squire Michorowski). Three film versions of the novel have been made, the latest and best of which was lushly filmed in 1976 by Jerzy Hoffman. Magdalena Samozwaniec's recently republished *Na ustach grzechu* (In the mouth of sin, 1920) parodies the book.

Trzecia Rzeczpospolita Polska (III RP) (Third Polish Republic). A term used by Lech Wałęsa at his presidential inauguration in 1990, and later formally enshrined in the preamble to the 1997 constitution. The Third Polish Republic, that is, postcommunist Poland, is usually dated from 1989, when the term *Ludowa* (People's) was dropped from the name of the country and the constitution. The official name then became Rzeczpospolita Polska, the name that was used in the so-called Druga Rzeczpospolita (Second Republic), interwar Poland. Both refer back to the name of the old Polish-Lithuanian Commonwealth, the "first" republic (see Rzeczpospolita Obojga Narodów). Lech Kaczyński in his presidential campaign used the term "Czwarta Rzeczpospolita Polska" (Fourth Polish Republic), a future and somehow purified version of the present, third one.

---

trzy razy tak, 3 × TAK (three times yes). A phony plebiscite forced through by the Soviet-backed communists in June 1946, depending on voting yes to three vague and innocuous-sounding questions (such as accepting the postwar borders with Germany). The covert aim was to create the appearance of broad democratic support for the communists in advance of the *wybory 1947* (1947 elections to the Sejm). The results, blatantly forged, showed 68 percent of voters voting yes on all three ballots. According to documents released after 1989, the actual results were closer to 27 percent in favor — even though the army and security services had been counted as yes votes en masse.

---

tur (aurochs). The aurochs, wild cattle of medieval legend, once ranged fearsomely over most of Europe, and had their last stand in the forests of Poland and Lithuania, the last one dying in 1627 in the Jaktorów Wilderness in central Poland. By that time hunting them had become the prerogative of kings. The Polish royal efforts to save the last remaining specimens have been called the world's first, albeit unsuccessful, effort to prevent species extinction. The Polska Fundacja Odtworzenia Tura (Polish Foundation for Resurrecting the Aurochs) has been working since 2006 to unlock the aurochs' genetic secrets, with the aim of bringing them back to life through cloning and then introducing them to the Puszcza Białowieska (Białowieża wilderness) — where they will compete for space alongside the *żubr* (bison) and *tarpan* (wild horse).

turoń. A mythological figure and masquerade character in Christmas carol singing (see **kolędnicy**). A primitive horned creature with shaggy hair, he scares the children in the houses carolers visit and keeps time to the *kolędy* (carols) by swaying and clacking his jaws. Sometimes he faints and has to be revived. The figure of the *turoń* seems to be based on the mighty bisonlike *tur*, which once roamed northern Europe but became extinct in the seventeenth century.

Tusk, Donald (b. 1957). Centrist politician, cofounder in 2001 of the Platforma Obywatelska (Civic Platform) political party, and Polish prime minister since from 2007 to 2014. He was deputy speaker of the Senat in 1997–2001, deputy speaker of the **Sejm RP** in 2001–2005, and leader of the opposition in 2003–2007. In 2011 Platforma Obywatelska once again placed first in the general elections, and he retained his position, the first postcommunist Polish premier to win two terms in office. As prime minister he worked to improve relations with Germany and Russia. More recently he sounded practically American, promising to cut taxes, close loopholes, and reform entitlements (although his actual achievements in these areas can be questioned). Tusk became president of the European Council in December 2014. Fluent in German, Tusk comes from **Gdańsk** and has a Kashubian background (see *Kaszuby, język kaszubski*).

Tuwim, Julian (1894–1953). Prominent poet of Jewish background from **Łódź**, later Warsaw, Tuwim cofounded the *Skamander* group of poets along with Antoni Słonimski and **Jarosław Iwaszkiewicz**. The author of ebullient urban poetry in the *Skamander* vein, Tuwim also wrote biting satirical verse and song lyrics for the prominent cabarets of his day, including for **Hanka Ordonówna**. He is also known for his children's verse, his onomatopoietic "Lokomotywa" (The steam locomotive) being a perennial favorite for declamation. In exile in New York during the war, he wrote a long epic poem, *Kwiaty polskie* (Polish flowers), full of nostalgic reminiscences about his childhood in Łódź. A leftist in his politics, Tuwim returned to Poland

262 KALEIDOSCOPE OF POLAND

in 1946. One can sit next to his statue on a bench and strike up a conversation with him on Łódź's Piotrkowska Street. Tuwim left behind many sardonic aphorisms; for example, "The difference between a camel and a man is that a camel can work all week without drinking; a man is just the opposite."

Tygodnik Powszechny (TP) (Universal weekly). A lay Catholic weekly founded in 1945, suspended 1953–1956, and afterward published until today, devoted to social and cultural issues. *TP* counted under communism as liberal press, as it was allowed to express opinions at variance with official doctrine — up to a point. Its single editor-in-chief until 1999 was Jerzy Turowicz. After 1956 *TP* officially became the organ of Znak (Signpost), one of the few noncommunist organizations in the PRL (communist Poland) allowed to hold seats in the Sejm (parliament). Many prominent authors either worked at or published in *TP*, including the religious poet Father Jan Twardowski, writer and publicist Stefan Kisielewski, philosopher Leszek Kołakowski, writers Stanisław Lem, Zbigniew Herbert, and, after 1982, poet Czesław Miłosz, whose death in 2004 was front-page news. Karol Wojtyła contributed to it both before and after becoming Pope Jan Paweł II. *TP*'s aim is the reconciliation of humanistic philosophy with Roman Catholic doctrine. It is sometimes criticized by conservative Catholics for being too liberal.

tygodniki (weeklies). The quality of Polish newsweeklies is exceptionally high. The most important among many are: *Polityka* (Politics), a liberal-left newsweekly; *Newsweek Polska* (Newsweek Poland), independent from and of much higher quality than its troubled American namesake, now reduced to an online version; *Wprost* (Straight on), which sees itself as a liberal business magazine but comes out on both sides of the political spectrum; *Przekrój* (Cross-section), a general-interest and light humor magazine published since 1945; *Przegląd* (Review), with a leftist agenda; *Tygodnik Powszechny* (Universal weekly), a Catholic newsweekly since 1945, not as influential as it once was. A new entry in this crowded field is the slightly right-wing *Uważam, Rze* (I consider), launched in 2011, with numbers rivaling those of the more established publications. *Dwutygodniki* (biweeklies) and *miesięczniki* (monthlies) also appear in great number, especially women's magazines, too many to list, but including *Twój Styl* (Your style), *Gala*, *Claudia*, *Elle Polska* (*Elle*, Polish edition), and *Zwierciadło* (Looking-glass).

Tyniec. A village located a few kilometers upriver from Kraków and now administratively incorporated into the city, Tyniec is known for its Benedictine monastery (pictured). Founded in 1044 and imposingly situated on a promontory overlooking the river, it is one of the oldest and richest in Poland. The abbey has been devastated by war numerous times, each time to be rebuilt. Today in addition to its strictly religious functions it runs a publishing house and sells a line of Benedictine foodstuffs. Its current prior is the media-savvy Leon Knabit, known for his sense of humor and good contact with young people. The abbey in Tyniec initiated the project of the Biblia Tysiąclecia (Bible of the millennium, 1965), the first new Catholic translation of the Bible into Polish in more than 350 years (see Biblia).

tytoń, papierosy (tobacco, cigarettes). Poland is one of Europe's larger tobacco producers, and Poles are prodigious consumers of *papierosy* (cigarettes). The highly regulated industry is concentrated in the southeast, and produces

KALEIDOSCOPE OF POLAND

around twenty to twenty-five thousand tons of tobacco per year, putting Poland in the contradictory position of both promoting the health of its citizens and subsidizing the cultivation of tobacco. The literature of the PRL (communist Poland) is difficult to fully understand without appreciating the social gradations of the many no-longer-produced cigarette brands people are described as smoking, including the filterless and rough-smoking Sporty or Popularne; the somewhat more refined Klubowe, Ekstra Mocne, Giewonty, and Piasty (with filters); women's Carmeny; menthol Zefiry; and top-of-the-line Caro, made from American tobacco. Polish cigarette companies were privatized and internationalized in the 1990s, the largest company being Philip Morris Polska SA of Kraków. Polish cigarettes are relatively cheap and are bought by the armload by smoke-happy tourists.

---

tytułowanie (titling people). Poles combine the titles of formal address *pan* (Mr.) and *pani* (Ms.) with a person's professional title to form combinations such as *pan dyrektor* (Mr. Director), *pani dyrektor* (Madam Director); *pan profesor* (Mr. Professor), *pani profesor* (Madam Professor); and so on. In direct address to men, vocative forms such as *panie dyrektorze* and *panie profesorze* are obligatory (the feminine terms remain the same). One more or less obligatorily titles ministers, directors, judges, parliamentary representatives, and so on, at the beginning of a conversation. As the conversation proceeds, the title is dropped. Titling at every opportunity, and extending its use to persons with doctoral or even master's degrees, is called *tytułomania* (titlemania), and can sound pretentious. It is somewhat more prevalent in the former *zabór austriacki* (Austrian partition), including Kraków, than elsewhere. See also: pan, pani, państwo.

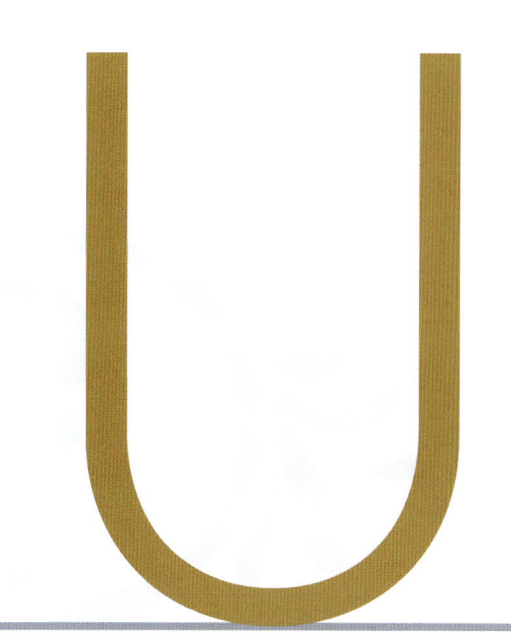

uczta u Wierzynka (feast at Wierzynek's). In 1364, during the reign of Kazimierz III Wielki (Kazimierz the Great), the Kraków city council, including the wealthy local merchant and banker Mikołaj Wierzynek, organized a twenty-one-day "feast" attended by most of the major Central European rulers. The ostensive purpose was to celebrate the marriage of Kazimierz's granddaughter Elżbieta to the Czech King Karol IV, but a further aim was to work out an international policy for dealing with the Turkish menace in the east. The feast was judged to be a triumph of Polish diplomacy. It is referred to in the name of Kraków's reputedly most elegant restaurant, the Wierzynek on the *Rynek Główny* (main square), which tries to trace its origins to 1364.

Układ Warszawski (Warsaw Pact). A military alliance of countries in the Soviet Bloc created to counter the "military threat" of the West's NATO (North Atlantic Treaty Organization). It was ratified in Warsaw in 1955 under the official title Układ o Przyjaźni, Współpracy i Pomocy Wzajemnej (Pact of Friendship, Cooperation, and Mutual Assistance). Its members were Albania (until 1968), Bulgaria, Czechoslovakia, East Germany, Poland, Romania, Hungary, and the Soviet Union. Its operations came under the command of the commander-in-chief of the Soviet armed forces, and Soviet forces were stationed in the member countries. The Warsaw Pact undertook only one military operation, the invasion of Czechoslovakia in 1968, carried out with surgical precision under the Soviet Union's Leonid Brezhnev's doctrine of coming to the "assistance" of member states in danger of straying from the "socialist path." The Czech invasion seriously damaged Poland's self-image as a defender of freedom, and prompted the self-immolation of Ryszard Siwiec. The pact ceased to exist in 1991. See also: Rada Wzajemnej Pomocy Gospodarczej.

---

ułan (Polish lancer). Modeled after Turkish cavalry, the *ułani* continued the traditions of the *hu-*

265

saria (hussars) of earlier centuries. The ułan was a light cavalry officer armed with a *kopia* (lance), a *szabla* (saber), and a light firearm or two. A trademark of dress was the *furażka* (peaked cap). Ułan divisions were part of the Polish army from the late eighteenth century through World War II, romanticized especially for their role in the insurekcja kościuszkowska (Kościuszko Insurrection, 1794–1795); in Dąbrowski's Italian legions; and in Napoleon's invasion of Russia in 1812. They were widely imitated throughout Europe. Their finest hour was possibly in the wojna polsko-bolszewicka (Polish-Bolshevik War, 1919–1921), where they repulsed two divisions of the elite Russian *Konarmiia* (horse cavalry) under the famed Soviet general Semen Budennyi. Their swan song was in World War II, by which time the horseback soldier had become too vulnerable to modern techniques of mechanized warfare to be an effective fighting force; see Hubal. *January Suchodolski,* Ułani polscy.

Umschlagplatz (Transfer Square). The infamous train junction in Warsaw in World War II, formerly a center of the Jewish wholesale trade, from where some three hundred thousand Jews rounded up from the Warsaw Ghetto were "transferred" by the Nazis to the Treblinka death camp, the largest mass murder in all of World War II, according to some. A stone monument in the shape of an open freight car is today all that marks the former site in what has become a nondescript residential neighborhood near downtown Warsaw. The Umschlagplatz is depicted in Roman Polański's Oscar-winning *The Pianist*, and its name is the title of the bestselling novel by Jarosław Marek Rymkiewicz, a pastiche of recollections and fiction. For Rymkiewicz the Umschlagplatz is a transcendent symbol weighing on the national conscience.

---

unia brzeska (Union of Brześć, 1596). Through this union, concluded in the town of Brześć (now Brest in Belarus), the Eastern Orthodox Church on the territory of the Polish-Lithuanian Commonwealth became united with the Roman Catholic Church (Kościół rzymskokatolicki) while maintaining the Orthodox liturgy (and the right of priests to marry). The union split the Eastern Church into the *unici* (Uniates, or *grekokatolicy,* "Greek Catholics"), and the *ortodoksyjni/dyzunici* (Eastern Orthodox/dis-Uniates), a division that still exists, although in Ukraine many Greek Catholic churches reverted to Russian Orthodoxy, partly under pressure from the authorities. Even though both are under Rome and live side by side in southeast Poland, the rzymskokatolicy and the grekokatolicy do not especially get along. The Greek Catholic Church remains vital in the United States and Canada, including among the Ukrainian diaspora, and among the remaining Łemkowie (Lemkos) of the Polish Podkarpacie (Sub-Carpathia).

---

unia lubelska (Union of Lublin, 1569). The act signed in Lublin formalizing the combined Polish-Lithuanian Commonwealth, the Rzeczpospolita Obojga Narodów (Commonwealth of Two Nations), divided into the Korona Królestwa Polskiego (Crown of the Polish Kingdom) and the Wielkie Księstwo Litewskie (Grand Duchy of Lithuania). Formerly the two states had been united merely dynastically under the Jagiellonowie (Jagiellons). The commonwealth had a common monarch, insignia, parliament, currency, and foreign policy, but maintained separate treasuries, titles, armies, and judicial systems. The union was formed during the reign of Zygmunt II August. It came to an end with the three *rozbiory* (partitions) of 1772, 1793, and 1795. *Jan Matejko,* Unia lubelska.

Uniwersytet Jagielloński (Jagiellonian University). The oldest Polish higher educational establishment and one of the oldest universities in northern Europe. Founded in 1364 by Kazimierz III Wielki (Kazimierz the Great) as the Akademia Krakowska (Kraków Academy), it was renovated and expanded in 1400 by King Władysław II Jagiełło following the *testament* (will) of his coruler Jadwiga Andegaweńska, who donated her jewelry for its upkeep. Among the university's first chairs were those in liberal arts, medicine, canon law, Roman law, mathematics, and astronomy. Among its students have been the astronomer Mikołaj Kopernik, the future king Jan III Sobieski, and the future Pope Jan Paweł II. The present name dates from 1817. It was recently ranked by the *Times* "Higher Education Supplement" as Poland's top university. It has a student body of nearly forty-four thousand studying in fifty-one different majors, and one of Poland's most important academic libraries. *Collegium Novum of the Jagiellonian University.*

Uniwersytet Latający (Flying, or Floating, University). In recent history the term refers to informal courses in the humanities and social sciences, operating outside official censorship, organized in private homes during the late 1970s by academic members of the political opposition in collaboration with KOR (Workers' Defense Committee). The term harked back to secret courses organized in the 1880s in Warsaw under Russian occupation, mainly for women. During the twenty or so years of its existence the earlier Uniwersytet Latający educated around five thousand women, including the future Nobel Prize–winner Maria Skłodowska-Curie.

---

uniwersytety (universities). Although all state-supported universities in all major cities in Poland are of good quality, the traditional "prestige" universities in Poland are the Uniwersytet Jagielloński in Kraków, the formerly Polish universities in Wilno (Lithuanian Vilnius) and Lwów (Ukrainian L'viv), the Uniwersytet Warszawski in Warsaw, and Poznań's Uniwersytet im. Adama Mickiewicza (Adam Mickiewicz University). Under communism, the private Katolicki Uniwersytet Lubelski (KUL, Catholic University of Lublin), since 2005 named after Pope Jan Paweł II, was the only Catholic university operating in the entire Soviet Bloc, subject to the constant harassment of the government. Nowadays, as in the rest of the world, universities — including private ones — are sprouting like mushrooms, as higher education becomes increasingly perceived as necessary for achieving success on the job market. Private universities

KALEIDOSCOPE OF POLAND

tend to specialize in business, management, and technology, and, in order to attract international students, to have parallel offerings in Polish and English.

Urban, Jerzy (b. 1933). Contrarian and, some would say, unprincipled journalist and political commentator. Urban was banned from publishing under the Gomułka regime (1956–1970) for his critical opinion pieces in the weekly *Po prostu* (Straight talk). Known for his large ears, and nicknamed "uszaty" (big ears), he was broadly loathed by the public for his role as press spokesman and apologist for the Polish government in 1981–1989. Currently he is owner and editor-in-chief of the anticlerical and semipornographic weekly *Nie!* (No!).

---

urlop, wakacje (leave, holiday). The right to a vacation is guaranteed by the Polish constitution. For up to ten years of employment, workers receive twenty days of paid vacation per year — after that, twenty-six days, four of which may be *na żądanie* (on demand), at any time of the year for any reason. New mothers are entitled to twenty weeks of *urlop macierzyński* (maternity leave), plus two weeks for each additional child born at the same time. A mandated *urlop ojcowski* (paternal leave) is considerably less. One "requests" an urlop, but "spends" a *wakacje* (summer vacation, normally in July or August). Often wakacje take the form of *wczasy*, where one travels to a resort location with meals provided. Winter two-week school holidays are called *ferie*. Poles are clever about combining requested leaves and state holidays to form *długie weekendy* (long weekends), lasting in effect for an entire week. Despite having the Bałtyk (Baltic Sea) at their doorstep, Poles increasingly travel to countries of the Mediterranean for sunny seaside relaxation.

V

Villas, Violetta (1938–2011). A colorful coloratura soprano, with improbably long curly hair, a range of four octaves, and a predilection for over-the-top ball gowns. Villas, born Czesława Cieślak in Belgium, forsook an opera career and flamboyant notoriety in Poland to become a cabaret star in Las Vegas, performing alongside such luminaries as Frank Sinatra, Barbra Streisand, Paul Anka, and others. She took a stage name on the advice of Władysław Szpilman, who debuted her on Polish radio and predicted a famous world career for her. In 1970 she returned to Poland. Her passport was revoked by the authorities, and it was only in 1987 that she was able to attempt a comeback in the United States, beginning with a triumphant performance at Carnegie Hall in New York City. In her later years she lived in seclusion in southwest Poland, running an overcrowded animal shelter and making increasingly less successful comeback bids, the last in Kielce in February 2011.

Volksdeutsche (Polish spelling *folksdojcz*; ethnic Germans in Poland). This historical term referred to people of German ancestry, but not German citizens, living outside the borders of Germany in the nineteenth century and in the twentieth century leading up to World War II.

In occupied Poland during the war the Volksdeutsche were encouraged to register with the authorities and to declare German allegiance, in return for which they received special privileges, often including property confiscated from Poles and Jews. Many ethnic Poles also registered as Volksdeutsche in order to avoid persecution, especially in Śląsk (Silesia) and Pomorze (Pomerania). The Volksdeutsche were viewed by the Polish population at large as a traitorous fifth column, and were in fact the only significant segment of the population to collaborate with the German authorities during the war.

W

Wadowice. A town of around twenty thousand located fifty kilometers east of Kraków, close to Kalwaria Zebrzydowska (see *kalwaria*), and a destination of personal and group *pielgrzymki* (pilgrimages) for reason of its being the birthplace of Karol Wojtyła, the future Saint Jan Paweł II (Pope John Paul II). The two-room apartment with kitchen where the Wojtyła family lived, and where Karol was born and took his first steps, are on display in the Dom Rodzinny Jana Pawła II (John Paul II Family Home) museum along with memorabilia from his life, including his skis, for he was an avid hiker and skier. The local *ciastkarnie* (pastry shops) specialize in the sale of the *kremówki* (cream puffs) of which young Karol was said to be fond.

Wajda, Andrzej (b. 1926). A Polish film and theater director, Wajda was one of the creators of the *polska szkoła filmowa* (Polish film school). A creator of auteur films with rich symbolism and carefully composed shots, Wajda has made a specialty of adapting classics of Polish literature

271

to film. He made his mark internationally with an adaptation of Jerzy Andrzejewski's *Popiół i diament* (Ashes and diamonds, 1958). Wajda received the Golden Palm of Cannes in 1981 for his *Człowiek z żelaza* (Man of iron, 1981). Four of his films have been nominated for an Academy Award, including his 2007 film *Katyń*, about the zbrodnia katyńska (Katyń massacre). It could easily have won, except that in 2000 he had already received an Oscar for his life's work. His film *Pan Tadeusz* (1999), wildly popular in Poland, probably did as much to instill appreciation for Mickiewicz's classic among rank-and-file Polish viewers as the Polish national school system. Wajda released a film on the life of Lech Wałęsa in 2013, selected to be Poland's nominee for best foreign film at the 2014 Oscars.

Walewska, Maria (1786–1817). Napoleon's Polish lover. Walewska, born Łączyńska, was married under duress at eighteen to a titled nobleman fifty years her senior, with whom, from the legal point of view at least, she had a son. She met Napoleon in Warsaw in 1807 and soon became his mistress, bearing him a son (also legitimized by Count Walewski) and proving to Napoleon that Josephine, not he, was the reason for his not having produced an heir. Napoleon divorced Josephine and married Princess Maria Ludwika (Marie-Louise) of Austria, but set up Walewska in Paris and gave their son the title of count. In 1816 she married Napoleon's cousin Philip d'Ornano, with whom she had a third son, but she died shortly afterward at the age of thirty-one. Pani Walewska has been the subject of books and films (including Leonard Buczkowski's 1966 *Marysia i Napoleon*, with Beata Tyszkiewicz and Gustaw Holoubek in the main roles), and a perfume and a richly layered torte have been named after her. Descendants of her second and third sons have been and still are active in French politics and business.

Wałęsa, Lech (b. 1943). Polish politician and trade union activist, an electrician by training, and cofounder of Solidarność (Solidarity) in 1980, the first legal independent trade union in the Communist Bloc. Wałęsa was selected as *Time* magazine's Person of the Year in 1981, and received the Nobel Peace Prize in 1983, the only Pole to have been so honored individually (not counting the emigré nuclear physicist Józef Rotblat in 1995, who shared the prize with others). In 1981–1982 Wałęsa was interned along with other Solidarity leaders under stan wojenny (martial law). He was prominent in the

272 KALEIDOSCOPE OF POLAND

1989 rozmowy Okrągłego Stołu (Round Table Discussions), which led to power-sharing between the communists and the opposition. In 1990 he won the election for president and served 1990–1995. Wałęsa's presidency oversaw the beginning of the privatization (*prywatyzacja*) of state property and the conversion to a market economy under plan Balcerowicza (the Balcerowicz Plan). Although within Poland he is no longer especially popular, he is Poland's most internationally recognizable elder statesman, and gives talks and represents Poland at various ceremonial functions. A feature-length film on his life by Andrzej Wajda, with script by Janusz Głowacki, appeared in the fall of 2013. See also: Pierwsza Dama.

Wanda. A name apparently original to Poland, possibly thought up by the twelfth-century chronicler Wincenty Kadłubek, according to whom Wanda was the daughter and heir of the legendary King Krak of Kraków. Some relate the name to the East Germanic Vandals, several of whose rulers carried the name Vandalarius. In Kadłubek's legend, Wanda drowned herself in the Wisła rather than marry a German. Her story is reflected in various songs and works of literature, and suggests among other things how far back Polish mistrust of Germans goes. The name has caught on in other countries besides Poland, especially in the United States, reaching the peak of its popularity in the 1930s. A *kopiec* (memorial mound), said to have been erected to Wanda in the seventh or eighth century, is located in Nowa Huta, while Krak's mound is located across the river in the Podgórze district of Kraków. *Maksymilian Piotrowski,* The Death of Wanda, *1859.*

Warmia (German: Ermland). A comparatively small but historically important land in northeast Poland. Long under the control of the Krzyżacy (Teutonic Knights), after 1466 Warmia was part of Prusy Królewskie (Royal Prussia), a Polish province. An important bishopric was in Fromborku, where Kopernik (Copernicus) lived, did much of his scientific work, and died. Copernicus and his entire family were Warmian patriots, staunchly supporting the Polish king against the Krzyżacy. Warmia was incorporated into Poland after 1945. It is still characterized by a sizable Protestant population. Warmia's largest town and historical capital is Olsztyn (German: Allenstein), which is capital of today's *województwo warmińsko-mazurskie* (Warmia-Mazurian Voivodeship). *Frombork Cathedral.*

Wars i Sawa (Wars and Sawa). In one of several mutually contradictory legends about the origin of the name Warszawa (Warsaw), Wars and Sawa were twin sons of a fisherman along the Wisła, where Warsaw later arose, for whom King Kazimierz I Odnowiciel (Kazimierz the Restorer) became godfather when he was hospitably welcomed by the fisherman's family while traveling

KALEIDOSCOPE OF POLAND   273

between Kraków and Gniezno. According to another version, Wars was a fisherman who fell hopelessly in love with a mermaid named Sawa, whom he caught in his net. Sawa begged to be let go, in exchange for which she would sing to him each evening and protect his family, becoming the future Syrena warszawska. In yet another version, Sawa grows legs and she and Wars marry, have normal children, and live happily ever after. The Warsaw store Wars & Sawa, which sells clothing for the entire family, seemingly opted for the last version of the legend.

Warszawa (automobile). Officially FSO Warszawa, colloquially warszawka or garbuska (female hunchback). The Warszawa was the first postwar Polish passenger car, produced from 1951 to 1973 in the Żerań factory in Warsaw on a license from Soviet Pobeda. If the car looked suspiciously like an early 1940s Plymouth, that was because the Soviet car was produced on a prewar license from the American company. In all, 254,471 cars were made. The Warszawa enjoyed heavy use as a taxi, and it provided the frame for the main delivery vans of the time, the Żuk and the Nysa. It was replaced by the Fiat 125p, produced on an Italian license. A few are still in use as ceremonial cars for hire; for example, for carrying a wedding couple to and from church.

Warszawa (city). Located in the east center of Poland on the Wisła River, Warsaw is the capital of Poland and its most populous city (some 1,712,000 inhabitants) as well as its governmental, political, scientific, banking, commercial, communications, and media center (Kraków claims to the be country's "cultural capital"). Warsaw is home to the country's largest university, Uniwersytet Warszawski, and its largest library, Biblioteka Narodowa (National Library). The town arose in the thirteenth through the fourteenth century and became Poland's capital only in 1596, when King Zygmunt III Waza moved his court permanently to the Warsaw castle, in part to be closer to his native Sweden. Over the centuries Warsaw has seen its share of wartime devastation, especially in World War II, when the departing German army systematically leveled the city to the ground after the powstanie warszawskie (Warsaw Uprising). See also: Warszawa, bitwy. *Warsaw skyline.*

Warszawa, bitwy (Battles of Warsaw). Many wars fought on Polish soil have a "Battle of (or near) Warsaw." Here are the main ones: (1) During the potop (Swedish Deluge), on July 28–30, 1656, Polish-Lithuanian soldiers lost a nondecisive battle against Swedish forces. (2) On July 31, 1705, Polish-Lithuanian-Saxon forces lost to a Swedish army that had been brought to Poland by a conspiracy of Warsaw nobles to defend the coronation of Stanisław Leszczyński, who had usurped the throne of August II Mocny. (3) On November 4, 1794, in the *rzeź Pragi* (Praga massacre), Russian troops dealt a final blow to the insurekcja kościuszkowka (Kościuszko Insurrection) when they began slaughtering civilians on the right side of the Wisła. (4) To most, "bitwa warszawska" (Battle of Warsaw) means the repulsion of Soviet forces before Warsaw on August 13–25, 1920, in the *Cud nad Wisłą* (Miracle on the Vistula) during the *wojna polsko-bolszewicka*, sometimes described (mainly by Poles) as one of the most important battles in the history of Western civilization. (5) German and Soviet forces pounded each other for over two months in the late summer of 1944 on the outskirts of Warsaw, until the Soviet offensive was called off due to the outbreak of the powstanie warszawskie (Warsaw Uprising).

"Warszawianka" (La Varsovienne). A patriotic march and song originally composed in France and in French by Casimir François Delavigne to celebrate the powstanie listopadowe (November Uprising) of 1830. It was translated into Polish by Karol Sienkiewicz, a great-uncle of Henryk Sienkiewicz. The song had been all but forgotten when it was resurrected by Stanisław Wyspiański in his 1898 play of the same name, in which Helena Modrzejewska starred; see also Stary Wiarus. Another song by the same name was written in the late nineteenth century and became associated with workers' demonstrations in sympathy with the rewolucja roku 1905 (1905 Revolution) in tsarist Russia. The earlier march is played on ceremonial military occasions. Its first two lines are: "Oto dziś dzień krwi i chwały, / Oby dniem wskrzeszenia był!" (The day of blood and glory is upon us, / May it also be the day of revival!).

Warszawska Jesień (Warsaw Autumn new music festival). Its full name is Międzynarodowy Festiwal Muzyki Współczesnej "Warszawska Jesień," and it is organized by the Związek Kompozytorów Polskich (Union of Polish Composers). Held in September since 1956, having its beginning in the liberalization following the *odwilż* (thaw) of that year, it is devoted to contemporary and "new" music. This was the only such festival in the Soviet Bloc. It served as an exposition of new music from Eastern Europe, and a number of prominent Polish composers first came to the public eye through it, including Henryk Górecki, Krzysztof Penderecki, and Witold Lutosławski. Recent years have narrowed the festival's focus to certain world areas or trends. See also: festiwale muzyczne.

Warta. The third-longest Polish river (808 km), flowing south-central to north in west Poland through Częstochowa, Warta, and Poznań, emptying into the Odra River at Kostrzyn. The Warta is listed alongside the Wisła in the Polish *hymn narodowy* (national anthem), in the line "Przejdziem Wisłę, przejdziem Wartę, będziem Polakami!" (We'll cross the Vistula and the Warta and be Poles once more). Most Poles would also associate the name Warta with one of the country's oldest and largest insurance and indemnity companies (the word *warta* in Polish means "watch" or "guard'). *The Warta flows under Poznań's Saint Rocha Bridge.*

Waryński, Ludwik (1856–1889). A Polish underground activist and martyr for the socialist cause under Russian tsarist rule. In 1882 he founded the first Polish workers' party, Proletariat. Waryński was arrested by the tsarist police and sentenced to sixteen years in the prison in the Shlisselburg fortress near Saint Petersburg, but he died of tuberculosis and the rigors of life there at the age of thirty-three. In the PRL (communist Poland) his likeness appeared on the 100-złoty note (pictured), and schoolchildren learned by heart Władysław Broniewski's gruesome "Elegia o śmierci Ludwika Waryńskiego" (Elegy on the death of Ludwik Waryński), in which Waryński coughs up his last blood and dies, and his spirit flies from his prison back to his Polish homeland, where, he says, "tam na mnie czekają" (they are waiting for me there).

Wawel. Built in Kraków on a promontory overlooking the Wisła on the site of a seventh- to eighth-century fortified settlement, Wawel castle was the royal seat in the twelfth through sixteenth centuries. It is one of Poland's most popular tourist sites, where the Szczerbiec (coronation sword of the Piasts), one of Poland's most valuable historical relics, is on view. The castle's construction reflects its various historical periods: Romanesque, Gothic, Renaissance, and baroque, with the arcaded Renaissance-style inner courtyard being particularly noteworthy; see architektura. Especially valuable are the arrasy wawelskie (Belgian tapestries) depicting biblical and hunting scenes. Also popular is the Sala Poselska (Deputies' Hall), in which the carved wooden heads of Kraków's sixteenth-century burghers are affixed to the ceiling. The Wawel Cathedral's beautiful Kaplica Zygmuntowska (Zygmunt's Chapel), one of nineteen chapels in the cathedral, contains the sarcophagi of selected Polish kings. The remains of other rulers and Polish notables lie in the cathedral's crypts. According to Hindu tradition (or, mainly, Wawel tour guides), one of the world's seven *chakras* (spiritual energy centers) is located at Wawel.

Wazowie, dynastia (Vasa dynasty). A dynasty of Swedish kings with a branch in Poland initiated with the election of Zygmunt III Waza as Polish king in 1587. The Polish line was Catholic and the Swedish Protestant, and they were at constant war with each other, with negative consequences for Poland's development; see *saskie czasy*. The Vasas were elective kings who unsuccessfully tried to return the Polish monarchy to a hereditary one. The Polish line died out in 1672 with Jan II Kazimierz (pictured), who had already abdicated the throne in 1668. The dynastic name comes from Swedish *vasa*, "sheaf of grain."

Wedel, Fabryka E. (E. Wedel Chocolate Factory). The firm was founded in Warsaw in 1851 by Karol Wedel, a polonized German. It is named after Emil Wedel, who took it over in 1876. Its confectionery products, particularly its *torcik wedlowski* (chocolate-covered layer wafer cakes) and *mieszanka wedlowska* (chocolate assortment), are known throughout Poland. During the PRL (communist Poland) the company was nationalized and renamed the 22 Lipca (July 22) factory, after the Manifest Lipcowy, while maintaining the Wedel trademark on its wrappings. The factory was sold to the PepsiCo corporation in the wild early days of privatization (*prywatyzacja*) without regard for Wedel family heirs. Today the factory is owned by the Japanese Lotte Group. Another old Warsaw firm with a similar history and national reach is A. Blikle, a fancy sweets and pastries manufacturer established in 1869 — in which, however, the Blikle family still has managed to retain a financial interest. Kraków's Krakowski Kredens (Krakow Cupboard), a purveyor of fancy jams, jellies, pastries, coffees, and teas, is also acquiring national brand recognition. A specialty is their *piszingier*, a cake made from thin wafers interlayered with caramel or chocolate icing.

Wernyhora. A legendary eighteenth-century Ukrainian Cossack bard with the prophetic gift who foretold the demise and dismemberment of the old Republic (Rzeczpospolita Obojga Narodów) as well as its later reconstitution. He appears in works of Polish Romanticism, notably in Juliusz Słowacki's *Beniowski* and *Sen srebrny Salomei* (Silver dream of Salome). He later shows up in Stanisław Wyspiański's *Wesele* (1901), in which he offers his host a *złoty róg* (golden horn) to be blown in a call for a national uprising in the name of liberation from Russia and the peaceful harmony and equality of the Polish and Ukrainian people. Needless to say, the horn is never blown.

Wesele (The wedding). A symbolist play by Stanisław Wyspiański, the most important literary work of Młoda Polska (Young Poland), first performed in 1901. The action takes place at a wedding party in the village of Bronowice near Kraków. Based on a real wedding between the poet Lucjan Rydel and a peasant girl, it mixes real people together with historical and legendary figures. Among its symbols that have found a place in the national memory are: the *chochoł* (straw mulch stack), which leads a dance of national indolence; the *złoty róg* (golden horn), waiting to call people to action (which is never blown); and the *czapka z piór* (peacock feathered hat), symbolizing the gentry's placing of individual vanity over the good of the country. *Wesele* was made into a successful film by Andrzej Wajda in 1972. The house where the historical wedding took place, Rydlówka, now within Kraków city limits, is a museum. *Playbill from the first performance.*

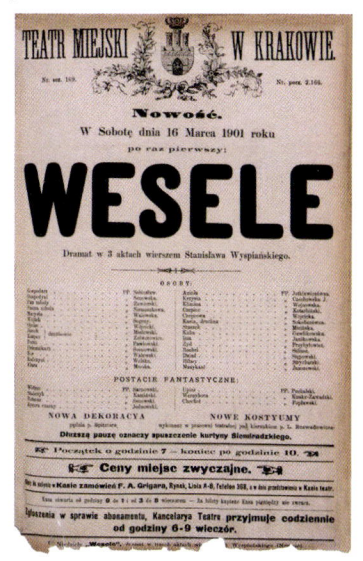

Westerplatte. A Polish military supply depot on the Gdańsk peninsula that became symbolic of fierce Polish resistance to German occupation when it was attacked by the battleship

KALEIDOSCOPE OF POLAND 277

Schleswig-Holstein at 4:48 a.m. on September 1, 1939, initiating World War II. The Germans estimated that the resistance would last several hours, but the heavily outmanned and unaided Polish garrison bravely held out until September 7. Their daily radio communiqué, "Westerplatte jeszcze się broni" (Westerplatte is still holding out), kept up the spirits of the rest of the Polish resistance. *The Heroes of Westerplatte Memorial on the spot of the Polish garrison.*

Węgry (Hungary). Poles like to recite the rhyme "Polak, Węgier — dwa bratanki, i do szabli i do szklanki" (A Hungarian and a Pole are like brothers, ready for a fight or a drink). Poland has a history of getting along with Hungary and Hungarians (unlike with some other neighboring countries). After Kazimierz III Wielki (Kazimierz the Great), the Polish kingship passed to Ludwik Węgierski (Ludwik the Hungarian) in 1370, and then to his Hungarian-born daughter Jadwiga in 1384. King Stefan Batory, another Hungarian, was one of Poland's favorite rulers. Poland's flagship passenger liner (1936 postcard pictured) in its two instantiations (1936–1969 and 1969–2000) was named after him until its service was discontinued. In 1956 during the Hungarian revolution against Russian occupation, Poles lined up to give blood as a sign of solidarity with the fallen Hungarian insurgents.

wiatrak (windmill). The wooden windmill, picturesquely looming up against the horizon across the Polish countryside, exists now more in people's memories and imagination than in actuality, although some skeletons still stand along the Wisła south of Warsaw and elsewhere. Constructed so that the entire body was on a movable axis (so-called *koźlaki*, "kids"), so that it could be shifted to face the wind, both the windmill and the watermill were in wide use for grinding grain in Poland well into the twentieth century. Now there are just a few of them operating as curiosities. Most of those that are not

278   KALEIDOSCOPE OF POLAND

in ruins have been moved to *skanseny* (outdoor antique building museums). A *wiatrak* looming across the Wisła was what inspired Antek to seek his fortune outside his village. *A Polish windmill of the "Hollander" type.*

---

wiedźmin (witcher). A male fantasy figure, the name of which by etymology is formed from *wiedźma*, "witch," although it is not simply a witch's male counterpart. A *wiedźmin* hires himself out to destroy monsters threatening humanity. Drawing on the *strzygoń* (Polish vampire) tradition, a wiedźmin is created out of a cast-off or unwanted baby subjected to special training and potions until he possesses superhuman strength and powers. His training leaves him infertile and often disfigured. A wiedźmin appears in stories and novels created by Andrzej Sapkowski (b. 1948), Poland's most prolific author of the fantastic. The best-known wiedźmin is Geralt of Rivia, the main figure in the series of novels. Besides novels, two volumes of short stories, comic books, and several role-playing video games, the wiedźmin has spun off a film of the same name starring the actor Michał Żebrowski, as well as a television series. Most of the *Witcher* stories and games are available in English translation. US President Barack Obama was presented with English copies of the *Witcher* books and video games by the Polish government during his official visit to the country in May 2011.

---

wiek (age). In Poland the voting age and age of full legal responsibility, including for crimes committed, is eighteen, as is the age at which one must possess a *dowód osobisty* (personal identification), may obtain a driver's license, get married without the consent of one's parents, or purchase alcoholic beverages and tobacco products. There are no age limits regulating drinking or smoking per se. One may be elected to the Sejm RP (parliament) at the age of twenty-one, and at thirty-five one may run for the presidency. The current retirement age for both men and women has recently jumped to sixty-seven. The age of consent (for engaging freely in sexual activity) is fifteen. Men register for the *pobór* (draft) at the age of eighteen, although the draft itself has not been implemented since 2008. Poland is converting to a volunteer professional army.

Wieliczka. A town of around twenty thousand, now mostly a bedroom community, near Kraków. Wieliczka is the site of a unique underground *żupa*, or *kopalnia soli* (salt mine), active since the Middle Ages, that draws over a million visitors a year. A special attraction is the halls containing sculptures made out of salt. Part of the underground caverns functions as a medical facility for treating respiratory diseases. Wieliczka has an aboveground salt-mining museum and is a UNESCO World Heritage Site. According to legend, Saint Kinga, the Hungarian wife of the Kraków prince Bolesław V Wstydliwy (Bolesław the Chaste, reigned 1243–1279), pointed out where to dig the mine's first shaft. Alongside the first salt encountered was the same ring Kinga had thrown into a salt mine shaft in Hungary. An even older functioning salt mine, in Bochnia, dating to 1248, counts as the oldest in Europe. *Rock salt statue of Pope John Paul II in Wieliczka.*

Wielka Emigracja (Great Emigration). Following the collapse of the 1830–1831 **powstanie listopadowe** (November Uprising), many politicians, soldiers, and cultural figures either emigrated from Poland or remained abroad, eight thousand to nine thousand in all. Eventually most settled in Paris, where the center for their activities was Hôtel Lambert (pictured), a mansion owned at the time by Prince Adam Czartoryski. Czartoryski also founded in Paris the Biblioteka Polska, the first Polish cultural center outside the country, with the aim of preserving historically important archives, documents, memoirs, and maps. It is still in existence. The group assembled around Hôtel Lambert included **Fryderyk Chopin**, Zygmunt Krasiński, **Adam Mickiewicz**, **Juliusz Słowacki**, and **Józef Bem**, among others. Opposed to the diplomatic inclinations of that group was the Towarzystwo Demokratyczne Polskie (Polish Democratic Society) under **Joachim Lelewel**, which plotted how to regain Polish independence through force.

Wielka Orkiestra Świątecznej Pomocy (WOŚP) (Great Orchestra of Christmas Charity). Founded by entertainer-impresario Jerzy Owsiak and others, this yearly charity concert held since 1993 raises large amounts of money for specific purposes, usually related to children's medical care. Leading up to the finale, donations are taken on the street, like America's Salvation Army, and *serduszka* (little hearts, pictured) are given out to donors in recognition. In the final event entertainers volunteer their service for free. In 2012 WOŚP raised over forty-seven million zlotys (around $14 million) for treating premature births and for insulin pumps for pregnant women with diabetes. WOŚP is Poland's second largest charity, after the Catholic-run Caritas.

Wielkanoc, Wielki Tydzień (Easter, Holy Week). Beginning with Niedziela Palmowa (Palm Sunday), Holy Week commemorates the days leading up to the death and resurrection of Jesus Christ on Wielkanoc (Easter), the most important day on the Christian calendar. Wielka Środa (Holy Wednesday) commemorates the betrayal of Jesus by Judas Iscariot; Wielki Czwartek (Holy Thursday) recalls the Ostatnia Wieczerza (Last Supper), at which the Sacraments were established; and Wielki Piątek recalls the day of crucifixion. On Wielka Sobota (Holy Saturday) the *święconka* (representative food for the Easter table, in Easter baskets, pictured) are blessed. The Easter meal, on Sunday, is multicourse and sumptuous. Easter eggs are cut and pieces are distributed, and good wishes are exchanged. The formal Easter greeting is "Wesołego Alleluja!" The figure of a *baranek* (lamb), usually made of iced cake or sugar, is placed on the table to remind one of the religious nature of the holiday, and eaten afterward.

Wielkopolska (Greater Poland). The term originally referred to the lands of the Polanie around Gniezno and Poznań in the western part of Poland, as distinct from Małopolska (Lesser Poland) in the southeast. Today it is used loosely to describe the lands around Poznań, Kalisz, Konin, Piła, Ostrów Wielkopolski, Gniezno, and Leszno. Under the *zabory* (partitions), Wielkopolska belonged to Prussia and was returned to Poland in the aftermath of World War I and the powstanie wielkopolskie (Greater Poland Uprising). The capital of the present administrative unit *województwo wielkopolskie* (Great Poland Voivodeship) is Poznań.

Wieluń. According to some, World War II began for Poland at 4:40 a.m. on September 1, 1939, with the indiscriminate German bombing of the small town of Wieluń in central Poland, of no military or industrial significance. An estimated 1,300 civilians were killed, and 90 percent of the downtown center was destroyed. Some surmise that the town was used by the Luftwaffe as an experiment in carpet bombing, to see what it would look like in practice without having to worry about the nuisance of antiaircraft defenses. Others claim that the damage to the town was due to poor visibility on that morning, and that a Polish army garrison was stationed nearby. Whatever the case, this action was followed eight minutes later by the attack of the German battleship Schleswig-Holstein on the military garrison at Westerplatte on the Bałtyk, traditionally considered to be the start of the war.

Wieniawski, Henryk (1835–1880). A virtuoso violinist and composer of technically difficult pieces, including some of the most challenging works in the violin repertoire. Wieniawski's L'École Moderne, 10 Études-Caprices is de rigeur for aspiring violinists. He toured extensively around the world, including in the United States in 1872 with the Russian pianist, composer, and conductor Anton Rubinstein, and died at an early age of a heart attack in Moscow. He is buried in Warsaw's Powązki Cemetery. An international Wieniawski violin competition is held every five years in Poznań.

wieszcz narodowy (prophet-poet of the nation). The meaning of *wieszcz* is difficult to convey in another language. "Bard" or "seer" does not do it justice. A handful of Polish poets have written with such inspiration as to have entered an elite pantheon of prophet-spokesmen for the nation. The sixteenth century poet Jan Kochanowski, the *wieszcz z Czarnolasu* (seer of Czarnolas) has been characterized as such, although he was not exactly in the mold. The three greatest poets of the Romantic era, Adam Mickiewicz, Juliusz Słowacki, and Zygmunt Krasiński became known as the *trójca* (triumvirate) of seers. The term was also applied to Cyprian Kamil Norwid, although he would probably have objected, since the concept involves the poet's accepting and wearing the mantle. The last poet to have had the term seriously applied to him was the neo-Romanticist and symbolist Stanisław Wyspiański.

Wigilia (Christmas Eve and Supper). Wigilia begins when the first star (*gwiazdka*) appears. The name refers to the evening and the meal. An empty place is left at table in readiness for an unexpected visitor. *Siano* (hay) is placed under the tablecloth, sometimes obtained from a holiday insertion in the local newspaper; the *opłatek* (Christmas Eve communion wafer) is shared around the company as well-wishes are given. The dinner is multicourse (twelve by tradition, each of which must be tasted). It is meatless, with *karp* (carp) being nearly obligatory, as well as *barszcz* (beet soup) with *uszka* (ear-shaped dumplings). Although few are around to hear it, animals in the barn speak in human tongue. Toward midnight the family heads for the *pasterka* (midnight mass). One does not quarrel or cry on Wigilia, for that sets the tone for the entire year to follow. *Table set for Wigilia.*

Wilanów. Wilanów lies to the south of Warsaw but has been incorporated into its borders. Here, overlooking the Wisła, stands a magnificent baroque-style palace, the pałac w Wilanowie, built by King Jan III Sobieski in 1677–1696 as a summer residence — his "villa nova," as he called it. At different times, Wilanów was in the possession of the Czartoryski, Lubomirski, Potocki and Branicki families. The palace is surrounded by large gardens and is one of Poland's most valuable architectural treasures. Wilanów also houses the world's first poster museum, and one of its largest, presently with more than fifty-four thousand holdings.

Wilczy Szaniec (German: Wolfsschanze; Wolf's Lair). Adolf Hitler's expansive, heavily fortified, camouflaged, and mosquito-infested command headquarters during the years 1941–1944, a complex of bombproof concrete bunkers, barracks, airstrips, and other facilities located in the heart of the Mazury (Mazurian Lake District) near Kętrzyn. It accommodated over two thousand people, including Hitler's closest advisers, concentrated on Germany's war effort in the east. Here on July 20, 1944, Claus von Stauffenberg and Werner von Haeften committed an unsuccessful attempt on Hitler's life. The Germans blew up the facility ahead of the Russian advance in 1945. It took nearly ten years, until 1955, for Polish sappers to finish disarming approximately fifty-four thousand mines laid on the Lair's perimeter. Long neglected, an attempt is being made to turn the facility, at present consisting of little more than immense piles of reinforced concrete rubble (making it an excellent bat sanctuary), into a tourist destination with a restaurant, informative markers, and a hotel (for those wanting to spend their honeymoon in Hitler's bunker). See also Międzyrzecki Rejon Umocniony; Książ.

Wilno (Vilnius). Located on the Wilia River, Wilno is Lithuania's largest city, with a population of 547,000. It was the capital of the Wielkie Księstwo Litewskie (Grand Duchy of Lithuania) when it was joined with the Korona Królestwa Polskiego (Crown of the Polish Kingdom) in the Rzeczpospolita Obojga Narodów (Polish-Lithuanian Commonwealth, 1569–1795). Before 1939 it was the capital of the Polish *województwo wileńskie* (Wilno Voivodeship). Wilno's large and thriving Jewish community was almost completely exterminated in World War II. Following the war Wilno was the capital of the Lithuanian Soviet Socialist Republic, and it continues as the capital of the Republika Litewska (Lietuvos Respublika; Republic of Lithuania), which gained its independence in 1991. It has the largest Polish heritage and presence of any city in Lithuania, and it is the birthplace of many famous Poles. Wilno University, founded in 1579 by King Stefan Batory, was one of the country's outstanding higher educational institutions, the alma mater of many outstanding Poles. A Polish-language Uniwersytet Polski w Wilnie (Polish University in Wilno, founded in 1998), working in cooperation with the university in Białystok, is trying to establish legitimacy. *Saint Anne's Church, the Benedictine monastery church, and the Adam Mickiewicz monument in Wilno.*

Wisła (Vistula). Poland's lifeline throughout its history, and still its most important waterway, the Wisła is the longest Polish river (1,047 km) and the largest river flowing into the Bałtyk (Baltic Sea). With its source in the Silesian Beskidy (Beskid Mountains) near the Czech border, it flows the entire length of the country through Oświęcim, Kraków, Tarnobrzeg, Sandomierz, Puławy, Dęblin, Warszawa, Płock, Włocławek, Toruń, Chełmno, Świecie, Grudziądz, Tczew, and enters the Bałtyk through the Zatoka Gdańska (Gdańsk Bay). At the source of the Wisła River lies a resort town of the same name, the only Polish town where Lutherans outnumber Catholics, the birthplace of the Olympic and world champion ski jumper Adam Małysz and of the writer Jerzy Pilch. Wisła is also the name of a Kraków soccer team founded in 1906, twelve-time national champions in the years 1927–2009. *The Narew flows into the Wisła near the Modlin fortress.*

Wisła, akcja (Operation Vistula). The name refers to the 1947 forcible resettlement of people of Ukrainian and Carpatho-Rusyn (mainly, Łemko) extraction from southeast Poland after World War II, with the declared aim of breaking the power of Ukrainian nationalist terrorist groups such as the Ukrain'ska Powstan'ska Armiya (UPA, Ukrainian Insurgent Army),

KALEIDOSCOPE OF POLAND

which continued to operate after the war; see *rzeź wołyńska*. The action was carried out by the Polish army with the assistance of the police, border patrol, and paramilitary groups. For the most part these people were resettled to the so-called *ziemie odzyskane* (recovered territories), territory "ceded" by Germany to Poland. Akcja Wisła affected around 140,000 people and left large swaths of territory in the southeast virtually unpopulated. In 2007 a joint communiqué by the Polish president Lech Kaczyński and the Ukrainian president Viktor Yushchenko condemned the action as having been contrary to the rights of man.

Wiśniowiecki, Michał Korybut (1640–1673, reigned 1669–1673). Scion of an illustrious Ruthenian magnate family, Wiśniowiecki was elected king with the support of the rank-and-file gentry, fed up with foreign monarchs in the wake of the potop (Deluge), but also in the hope that he would be a do-nothing king and not endanger their *złota polska wolność* (golden Polish freedoms). Their hopes were largely fulfilled, as Wiśniowiecki was ineffective as a ruler, military leader, or statesman. What plans he tried to implement were frustrated by the *magnateria* (wealthy magnates), most of whom deeply resented his being on the throne in the first place. He was succeeded by his bitter rival, the much more effective Jan III Sobieski. He is buried in the Wawel crypts.

Witkacy (Stanisław Ignacy Witkiewicz, 1885–1939). A colorful nonconformist painter, novelist, playwright, and philosopher of art during the *dwudziestolecie międzywojenne* (interwar period), when he articulated his complex theory of *Czysta Forma* (pure form). His absurdist and catastrophist plays such as *Matka* (The mother, 1924) and *Szewcy* (The shoemakers, 1931–1934) were revived after the war by Tadeusz Kantor. *Wariat i zakonnica* (The madman and the nun), a jibe at Freudian psychoanalysis, remains popular among student theatrical groups. An experimenter with the effects of drugs on artistic creativity, his diabolic paintings (see his self-portrait, pictured), which he turned out by the hundreds, became appreciated mainly after World War II. Witkiewicz committed suicide in Ukraine shortly after the outbreak of World War II. A body thought to be his was transferred to and ceremoniously buried in Zakopane in 1988. The coffin that was exhumed in 1994 contained the body of an unknown young woman.

Witos, Wincenty (1874–1945). An important politician of peasant background, first in the *zabór austriacki* (Austrian partition) and later in the *dwudziestolecie międzywojenne* (interwar period), when he was three times the Polish premier. His government was overthrown by the *przewrót majowy* (May coup d'état) of 1926 and the subsequent *sanacja* (return to health) regime under Józef Piłsudski, which imprisoned him for a time as one of the leaders of the opposition. Witos declined an offer by the Nazis to form a collaborative Polish puppet government in World War II, and later rejected a similar offer to serve as vice premier in the postwar communist government. He served briefly, until his death, as chairman of the newly formed Polskie Stronnictwo Ludowe (PSL, Polish Peasant Party), the main opposition party to the communists in the immediate postwar period.

---

wizy do USA (visas to the United States). A topic roiling Polish-American diplomatic relations for the last twenty years or so. Poland requires no visas from US citizens, and expects the same courtesy for Polish citizens traveling to the United States, all the more so given that Poland supports US foreign policy more than most European countries. The United States sets a threshold of a no more than a 10 percent visa application rejection rate before a country may apply for a visa exemption. Poland has never even come close to meeting this threshold. Visas are expensive: a Polish tourist visa to the United States costs around $150, or around one-tenth of an average Pole's monthly salary. Just to talk to the American consulate costs $1.50 per minute. Most often applications are rejected from persons whose aim, in the opinion of consular officials, is to work or settle permanently in the United States rather than travel for business or pleasure, or to visit relatives, as stated. The subject has become a topic for humorous sketches in cabarets (see *cabaret*), as though an American visa were an unobtainable dream. The problem remains unresolved as of 2015.

"Wlazł kotek na płotek" (The cat climbed up onto the fence). The first lines to a children's song most people know, and typically the first tune children learn to pick out on a keyboard (sort of like "Twinkle, twinkle, little star" in English). The words were written down by the early nineteenth-century ethnographer Oskar Kolberg (1814–1890). Stanisław Moniuszko composed a three-part harmony to the extremely simple melody. Its first lines are:

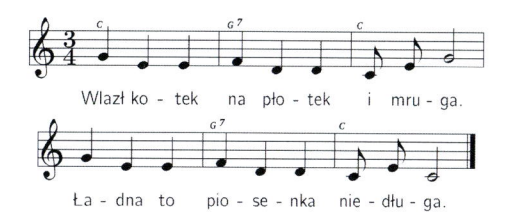

> Wlazł kotek na płotek i mruga
> Ładna to piosenka niedługa
> Niedługa, niekrótka, lecz w sam raz
> Zaśpiewaj koteczku jeszcze raz!

> The cat climbed up onto the fence and winked
> This is a pretty song, not too long.
> Not too long, not too short, just right
> Sing it, kitty, one more time.

Władysław I Łokietek (Władysław the Short, or Elbow-High, 1260–1333, reigned 1320–1333). A continuer of the *dynastia* Piastów (Piast dynasty), Łokietek's turbulent reign was aimed at uniting the Korona Królestwa Polskiego (Polish Crown) under a single throne in Kraków after the period of *rozbicie dzielnicowe* (division into districts) established by Bolesław III Krzywousty (Bolesław the Wrymouth). A major tactical

KALEIDOSCOPE OF POLAND   285

blunder was to lose Pomorze (Pomerania) and Kujawy to the Krzyżacy (Teutonic Knights), with whom he had formed an alliance against the marauding Brandenburg Germans, only to see the Krzyżacy become even more firmly established and continue plundering Poland and Lithuania. His main battle against the Krzyżacy near the village Płowce in Kujawy ended in a stalemate but established Poland as a military power to be reckoned with. Under his reign the Polish kingdom began to develop the administrative infrastructure that would be developed more fully by his son Kazimierz III Wielki (Kazimierz the Great).

Władysław III Warneńczyk (1424–1444). He ascended to the Polish throne as the third Jagiellonian king at the age of ten under the regency of Kraków bishop Zbigniew Oleśnicki. Władysław III became king of Hungary in 1440 at the age of sixteen, the aim of the offer being to enlist Poland's help against the Turkish menace. After an initial victory against Turkey in 1443, he led an ill-conceived campaign against Turkey the following year and was killed in a battle at Warna on the Black Sea. For the Turks, this battle was a stepping stone on the way to capturing Constantinople in 1453. Władysław's body and armor were not recovered. According to legend his head was cut off by a janissary as a war trophy and given to the Turkish pasha, who kept it preserved in a jar of honey. Another legend has him surviving as an anonymous penitent knight on Madeira. *Aleksander Lesser,* Władysław III Warneńczyk.

Wojciech, Święty (Saint Wojciech; Czech: Vojtech; known in English as Saint Adalbert of Prague, ca. 956–997). Wojciech adopted the name Adalbert after his mentor Adalbert of Magdeburg. Deposed as Bishop of Prague, he first went to help baptize Hungary and then was sent to Poland as a missionary. He was martyred and beheaded while chopping down a sacred oak in an effort to convert the Bałtowie (Baltic Prussians) to Christianity. His remains were ransomed by Bolesław I Chrobry for Wojciech's weight in gold and placed in Gniezno. He was canonized in 998 or 999. One of the main patron saints of Poland alongside Święty Stanisław, his remains lie in a silver reliquary (pictured) in the cathedral in Gniezno, the oldest of all destinations of Polish *pielgrzymki* (pilgrimages).

województwo (voivodeship). A Polish administrative unit in existence since the days of the Rzeczpospolita Obojga Narodów (Polish-Lithuanian Commonwealth). In the years 1975–1998 Poland had forty-nine voivodeships, roughly corresponding to states or provinces. In 1999 the number was reduced to sixteen. Voivodeships are divided into *powiaty* (counties) subdivided into *gminy* (townships). A *miasto* is either a town or a city. A *wieś* is a village, typically laid out along both sides of a main road. The head official in a wieś is a *sołtys*; in a gmina, a *wójt*; of a powiat, a *starosta*; of a województwo, a *wojewoda*; of a small town, a *burmistrz*; of a large town or city, a *prezydent miasta* (town president). All of these are elected except the wojewoda. He is appointed centrally, by the Prezes Rady Ministrów (Chairman of the Council of Ministers), i.e., the premier (prime minister).

---

wojna polsko-bolszewicka (Polish-Bolshevik War, 1920). A war following World War I between recently reborn Poland and recently arisen Bolshevik Russia, in which the latter attempted to bring communism to Germany and the entire European continent — still reeling from the war — over the body of Poland. The Armia Czerwona (Red Army) under the ruthless Marshal Mikhail Tukhachevsky had initial successes and advanced as far as Warsaw. Despite the expectations of the rest of the world, Polish forces under the command of the brilliant strategist **Józef Piłsudski** routed the Soviet forces in the so-called Cud nad Wisłą (Miracle on the **Wisła**, Warsaw, August 13–25, 1920), and drove them far to the east. The Polish victory gave Poland control over much of the **kresy** (eastern territories), at least until 1939. The Cud nad Wisłą is celebrated on August 15 as Święto Wojska Polskiego (Polish Army Day). It is sometimes compared to the Poles' driving back the Turkish armies from the gates of Vienna in 1683 (see **Sobieski, Jan III**). A 3D superproduction, *1920 Bitwa Warszawska* (Battle of Warsaw, 1920), by Jerzy Hoffman appeared in 2011, with **Daniel Olbrychski** in the role of Piłsudski.

---

wojna polsko-ukraińska (Polish-Ukrainian War, 1918–1919). A prelude to the *wojna polsko-bolszewicka* (Polish-Bolshevik War, 1920). Political disarray in Galicja following the collapse of the Austro-Hungarian Empire encouraged the rise of a long-simmering Ukrainian independence movement with the aim of taking eastern Galicja for its own and establishing a new Ukrainian state, with **Lwów** (German: Lemberg; Ukrainian: L'viv) as its capital. The movement took the nascent Polish state by surprise. Emergency militias were formed from school-age youth, the so-called Lwowskie Orlęta (Lwów Eaglets), who suffered heavy losses while successfully resisting the Ukrainian siege of the town. Over the course of the next half year the more skillfully led and better-supplied Polish army slowly regained control over territory considered theirs. The Poles did not cover themselves exclusively with glory. An estimated twenty-five thousand Ukrainian prisoners died from typhus and dysentery in the squalid detention camps set up to hold them. See also: **Lwów, pogrom lwowski**.

Wojtek, niedźwiedź (Wojtek the Bear). A five-hundred-pound Persian bear nurtured from a young cub in 1942 by men under General **Władysław Anders** as they assembled in Iraq and later marched through Syria, Palestine, Egypt, and Italy. Weaned on condensed milk and beer, Wojtek became not only a mascot but an official enlistee with the rank of *szeregowy* (private). The first component of his name, *woj-*, comes from old Slavic for "soldier." In the allied assault on **Monte Cassino** he hauled ammunition up the steep slopes to help achieve victory. Along with many of Anders's troops, Wojtek was demobilized and settled in Scotland after the war. In his twilight years he lived in the Edinburgh Zoo, reportedly responding to speech only in Polish. His death in 1963 made headlines across the United Kingdom — not in communist Poland, where Anders's army was non grata. Several memorials in animal-loving Great Britain commemorate his valorous career. A Facebook page for him is maintained, and his seventieth birthday party was held in 2012.

wola (freeland). Many village names (there are over 1,500 of them) incorporate *wola* as a second component; for example, Fryderyk Chopin's birthplace Żelazowa Wola. In use since at least the thirteenth century, the word designates land given by a landowner to settlers for their rent-free utilization for a set number of years. Wola is also the name of a large, western, traditionally working-class district of Warsaw, in which a horrendous Nazi pacification campaign (*rzeź Woli*, the Wola massacre) took place during the powstanie warszawskie (Warsaw Uprising) in 1944.

Wolne Miasto Gdańsk (WMG) (German: Freie Stadt Danzig; Free City of Gdańsk). The *traktat wersalski* (Versailles Treaty, 1920) created a duty-free and self-governing zone containing the city of Gdańsk under the jurisdiction of the Liga Narodów (League of Nations). About 10 percent of the population was Polish or Kashubian (see Kaszuby, *język kaszubski*), the rest German. Poland and Germany maintained separate postal and telecommunications services. Poland was guaranteed access to the Bałtyk (Baltic Sea) by land, rail, and water (via the Wisła), as well as the right to station in its port ships of the Polish navy — rights that were disputed by Germany, which concocted the term "the Polish Corridor" (*korytarz polski*) for referring to Poland's access, as if it were something whose privileges could be abrogated at any time. The WMG's government was largely German and inimical to Polish interests. Germany's cutting off the "corridor" and annexing the WMG, with simultaneous attacks on the garrison at Westerplatte and the Poczta Polska (Polish Post Office) in Gdańsk, set off World War II. Following the war Gdańsk became Polish. *Twenty-gulden bill from the WMG.*

wolne soboty (free Saturdays). Until 1972 the Polish work-and school week lasted five and a half days, with Saturday afternoon and Sunday off. After that, Saturdays as *dni wolne od pracy* (days completely off work) were introduced gradually — at first one a year, but soon twelve, one for each month. By 1981, thanks to Solidarność trade union efforts, every other Saturday was free, creating chaos, as smaller stores would close down on Saturdays according to unfathomable schedules. The twenty-first of the *dwadzieścia jeden postulatów* (twenty-one demands) of the Solidarity strike in 1980 (see Solidarność) called for the reduction of the work week from six to five days. By the end of the PRL (communist Poland) most workplaces recognized all Saturdays as "free," as they are under contemporary Polish law.

wódka (vodka). Poland falls within the so-called *pas wódczany* (vodka belt) of northern Europe where vodka is the main alcoholic beverage consumed. The original Polish word was *gorzałka*. The first lexical attestation of *wódka* is 1405, whence the word migrated into Russia and, ultimately, into world vocabulary as *vodka*. Jokingly referred to as *eau de Pologne*, the substance has been distilled in Poland since the thirteenth century, and it is one of the most recognizable Polish products abroad, the brands Wyborowa, Żytnia, Luksusowa, Chopin, Sobieski, and Belweder being most popular. There are close to one hundred contemporary Polish brands, almost all indistinguishable from one another and at the 80-proof (40 percent) level. Polish wódka is produced from potatoes, sugar beets, or rye. It is traditionally served in fifty- or one hundred–milliliter glasses and is usually drunk cold, neat, and all at once (*duszkiem*). Flavored vodkas, including Wódka Żołądkowa Gorzka (a digestif), are popular. *Starka* is a vodka aged in oak casks for at least ten years. Home-produced, non-purified vodka is called *bimber* (moonshine). One hundred-percent grain alcohol, used more in cooking than for drinking (one hopes), is *spirytus*. *Nalewki* (liqueurs) are generally made from spirytus poured over fruits, nuts, or other ingredients and allowed to steep. See also: żubrówka. *Sobieski wódka, named after Król Jan III Sobieski.*

wóz Drzymały (Drzymała's wagon). At the turn of the nineteenth to the twentieth century, Michał Drzymała (1857–1937), a Polish peasant, became a symbol of grassroots Polish resistance to anti-Polish policies in *zabór pruski* (Prussian-occupied Poland). Not being permitted by the Prussian authorities to construct a house on the parcel of land he had bought in a village near Poznań, Drzymała bought a circus wagon to live in (reconstruction pictured) and made sure to move it every day so that it did not count as a permanent structure. Eventually the Prussian authorities confiscated it as an attempt to "undermine the spirit of the law." After that, Drzymała lived in a hole he excavated in the ground.

Wrocław (Breslau). A city with an ancient history going back to the early tenth century, Wrocław is Poland's fourth-largest city, with some 633,000 inhabitants. Over the centuries, the city has been Polish, Czech, Austrian, Prussian, German, and again Polish. Located on the Odra River in the southwest of the country, it is the historical capital of Dolny Śląsk (Lower Silesia). It has always been a major scientific, educational, and cultural center, especially renowned for its theatrical and musical life, among which the international oratorio festival Wratislavia Cantans is especially well known. It is also the reputed Polish center of *krasnoludki* (gnomes). During the 1980s, political oppositionists in Wrocław representing the so-called Pomarańczowa Alternatywa (Orange Alternative) puckishly drew pictures of gnomes over paint spots covering up antigovernment graffiti. Wrocław has Poland's oldest and largest zoo (from 1865), containing more species than almost any zoo in the world. The city has been proclaimed the European Capital of Culture for the year 2016. *Wrocław's ratusz (city hall) built in "brick Gothic" style.*

Września. A Polish town of around twenty-nine thousand located fifty kilometers east of **Poznań**. In 1901 it became a symbol of Polish resistance to the forced Germanization of Polish children in the *zabór pruski* (Prussian-occupied Poland), after 118 schoolchildren went on strike when a German teacher meted out harsh physical punishment to Polish children for not giving answers in German in religious classes. Some children from Września are pictured here. Protesting Polish parents feared that religious instruction in German was one step away from being indoctrinated in Protestantism. The Prussian authorities responded to the strike by jailing the parents, fining them, and threatening to remove their parental rights. Some received jail sentences of up to two and a half years. Strikes in sympathy with the children of Września gained strength until, by 1906, more than seventy-five thousand children in eight hundred schools in Prussian Poland were on strike. Events such as those in Września inspired Maria Konopnicka to write her **"Rota"** (credo).

Wujek, kopalnia (Wujek coal mine). The Wujek coal mine has been operating in **Katowice** since 1900. A workers' strike there in 1980 led to the improvement of pay and working conditions, increasing the prestige of the **Solidarność** (Solidarity) independent trade union. An occupational strike in 1981, protesting the imposition of *stan wojenny* (martial law), was viciously put down by the army and detachments of the **Zmotoryzowane Odwody Milicji Obywatelskiej,** (ZOMO, Motorized Detachments of the Citizens' Militia), who killed nine workers and hospitalized some twenty others. After a long-running series of trials stretching over twenty-eight years, the first of which began ten years after the event, in April 2009 the courts upheld guilty verdicts in the instances of seventeen ZOMO officers for their role in the massacre. In 2009 a methane explosion in the Wujek mine caused the death of twenty miners.

wybory 1947 (1947 elections to the Sejm). With the communists in power, free democratic elections to the **Sejm** (parliament) in accordance with the provisions of the *konferencja jałtańska* (Yalta Conference) posed a problem, inasmuch as a 1946 referendum, before its results were falsified, had indicated that the vast majority of the population was opposed to the communists; see *trzy razy tak*. Enlisting the help of Soviet "experts," **Bolesław Bierut** went ahead with the elections after unleashing security forces on members of the main opposition party, the Polskie Stronnictwo Ludowe (PSL, Polish People's Faction), arresting thousands and murdering some two to three hundred. The elections themselves were falsified in every conceivable way, including the disqualification of over four hundred thousand voters. According to the official results, the communist parties had won 80 percent of the vote, the PSL 10 percent, and all others 10 percent. The leader of the PSL, Stanisław Mikołajczyk, who had come to Poland from London to join a provisional coalition government pending the outcome of the election, resigned his post and left (fled) the country.

wybory 1989 (June 4 and 18, 1989, parliamentary elections). In 2014 Poland celebrated twenty-five years of postcommunist rule, in ceremonies attended by Western leaders, including US President Barack Obama. Commonly referred to as the "partially free," or *czerwcowe* (June) elections to a newly created bicameral legislature, the *wybory 1989* are viewed by Poles as marking the beginning of democratic rule not only in their country but in Eastern Europe generally. Under conditions set at the **rozmowy Okrągłego Stołu** (Round Table Discussions) of April of that year, 65 percent of the seats in the lower house were set aside for parties supportive of the regime. The elections themselves were run openly, and resulted in a stunning victory for candidates put forward by Solidarity (**Solidarność**), which won all seats available to them in the **Sejm** and ninety-nine out of one hundred seats in the Senat. In the aftermath, the Sejm elected communist party secretary **Wojciech Jaruzelski** president — by just one vote, with Solidarity's Tadeusz Mazowiecki being named prime minister in a coalition government. The 1989 elections paved the way for the fully free presidential elections of 1990, in which **Lech Wałęsa** was elected president in two rounds of voting, over Canadian businessman Stanisław Tymiński.

wybory 2011 (2011 election results). Whether the 2011 parliamentary election results point to a growing openness in Polish society or merely to disenchantment, especially among the young, with mainstream politics, is a matter of debate. Whatever the case, in them Robert Biedroń of **Ruch Palikota** was elected parliament's first openly gay deputy, and Anna Grodzka of the same party became the first transgender MP in any European parliament. Running under Platforma Obywatelska, John Godson joined fellow party member Killion Munyama to give Poland one more black representative than the French parliament had at the time (and France, unlike Poland, has a sizable African population).

Wybrzeże Bałtyckie (Baltic seacoast). Poland's Baltic seacoast compares favorably with beaches anywhere in the world. It is a popular and seasonally jam-packed destination for Poles who opt for a beach vacation. The sands are lush and wide and stretch for miles, edged by scrub forest on the land side. The air, if not the water itself, is clean and healthy, with a high iodine content. The main drawback is the cold water temperature. The **Bałtyk** (Baltic Sea) is swimmable in the summer, but just barely. Popular resort spots are Międzyzdroje, **Świnoujście**, Ustka, and Władysławowo — but, actually, any of the two dozen or so towns along the Bałtyk.

wycinanki (paper cutouts). The folk tradition of decorating the inside of one's cottage with elaborate cuttings of paper with either representational or abstract designs, especially at holiday times, is most commonly practiced in central Poland (in the **Kurpie** and the **Łowicz** areas), and in the **Podkarpacie** in the southeast. Each area has its own distinctive patterns and style.

KALEIDOSCOPE OF POLAND

Polish architects modeled the distinctive Polish pavilion for Shanghai's international exposition Expo 2010 after a folded piece of paper with lace-patterned cutouts (pictured). A good wycinanki collection is at the *skansen* and Muzeum Wsi Mazowieckiej (Museum of the Mazowsze Countryside) in Sierpc.

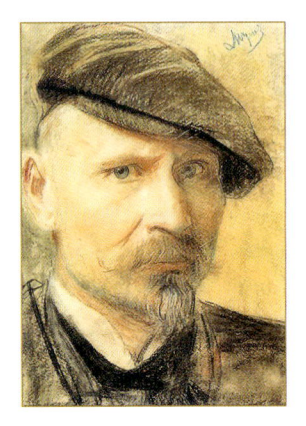

Wyczółkowski, Leon (1852–1936). A realistic, though tending toward impressionistic, painter of the Młoda Polska (Young Poland) school. As a portraitist, he captured the likenesses of most of Kraków's artistic community of the early twentieth century, but he is also known for his still lifes, landscapes, and genre paintings. At times his works border on the moody and phantasmagoric. One cycle of works features national relics from the Wawel treasury. Although Wyczółkowski was associated with Kraków, his widow donated over seven hundred of his works to the regional museum in Bydgoszcz, which now bears his name and many of his paintings. *Leon Wyczółkowski, self-portrait.*

wydawnictwa drugiego obiegu (secondary or underground publication outlets). The term refers to the publication through foreign or illegal Polish outlets of works unpublishable through regular channels because of *cenzura* (censorship) in the PRL (communist Poland). The best-known foreign publisher of Polish works was the monthly journal *Kultura* in Paris (pictured), under the longtime editorship of Jerzy Giedroyc/Giedroyć (1906–2000), in which authors such as Witold Gombrowicz, Zbigniew Herbert, Marek Hłasko, Leszek Kołakowski, Tadeusz Konwicki, and Czesław Miłosz published. It concluded its operations in 2000.

wyliczanki (counting rhymes). While American counting rhymes used to choose or eliminate participants in children's games pretty much all begin with "Eenie meenie miney moe," Polish ones are numerous and are regionally differentiated; there is no single standard. An amusing one from the 1960s–1970s, featuring Hanna-Barbera cartoon characters (still in rerun on Polish TV) and the PRL (communist Poland) laundry detergent icon ixi 65, goes as follows:

> Raz, dwa, trzy, cztery
> idzie sobie Hackelbery
> za nim idzie misio Jogi
> co ma strasznie krótkie nogi
> a za nimi Pixi-Dixi
> co się kapią w proszku ixi

> One, two, three, four
> Here comes Huckleberry Hound
> And after him comes Yogi Bear
> Who has terribly short legs
> And after them come Pixie and Dixie
> Who bathe in ixi [laundry detergent]!

As for ixi 65, legends circulating about it were such that one might not have wanted to bathe

292   KALEIDOSCOPE OF POLAND

in it, but visiting dignitaries from the *demoludy* (Soviet Bloc) were said to fill extra space in their suitcases with it before returning home.

Wyspiański, Stanisław (1869–1907). A dramatist, poet, painter, and overall the most prominent and artistically versatile figure of the **Młoda Polska** (Young Poland) period, hailing from **Kraków**. As a painter he was a master of both monumental works and intimate portraits of family and friends, and his talent extended to graphic art, murals, polychromies, and stained glass. His stained-glass rendition of Bóg Ojciec (God the Father) in Kraków's Franciscan church is especially well known. As a dramatist he was concerned with themes of the past, present, and future of the Polish nation. In addition to writing, he designed stage settings and costumes (including the costume for the *lajkonik*). His most famous play is the symbolic drama *Wesele* (The wedding, 1901). Wyspiański has been called the last *wieszcz narodowy* (national prophet-poet). He is buried in the Krypta Zasłużonych (Crypt of the Meritorious) in the **Skałka** monastery in Kraków. *Stanisław Wyspiański, self-portrait.*

Wyszyński, Stefan (1901–1981). The archbishop and primate of Poland from 1948, and cardinal from 1953, called the Prymas Tysiąclecia (Primate of the Millennium), the millennial celebration of the *chrzest Polski* (baptism of Poland) falling in 1966. Through Wyszyński's diplomacy, the Church maintained the Catholic University of **Lublin** and religious instruction in schools — unique situations in the Soviet Bloc. Under house arrest between 1953–1956, he wrote the *Jasnogórskie śluby narodu polskiego* (Jasna Góra Vows of the Polish Nation) addressed to the Virgin Mary, delivered in his name to a throng at the **Jasna Góra** monastery in 1956. That event was a turning point in church-state relations, and Wyszyński was released later that year. In 1957 he initiated a multiyear pilgrimage carrying on foot a copy of the **Matka Boska Częstochowska** (Mother of God of Częstochowa) to every Polish parish. Wyszyński preached a policy of accommodation with the authorities without compromising principles.

Wyścig Pokoju (Berlin–Warsaw–Prague Bicycle Peace Race). A bicycle stage race organized first in 1948 and sponsored by the communist daily newspapers in East Germany, Poland, and Czechoslovakia. The Peace Race was one of the hardest amateur cycling events in the world, and it was usually won by representatives (amateurs in name only) from the Communist Bloc who were familiar with the often atrocious roads and weather conditions. The first Polish winner was Stanisław Królak in 1956. Each year the race had a different start and finish point. Winners were national heroes. The glory years for Poland were the early 1970s, when Ryszard Szurkowski won four times. Stanisław Szozda won in 1974, Lech Piasecki in 1985, and Piotr Wadecki in 2000. After the amateur pretext was dropped, the race became a second-tier professional event in search of sponsors. It has not been held since 2007 for lack of financial backing. Poland's oldest bicycle stage race is the Tour de Pologne, originating in 1928 and still going. *Stage six of the final, 2006 Peace Race, in Dippoldiswalde, Germany.*

Z

Zachęta (National Gallery of Contemporary Art in Warsaw). The Zachęta's imposing building (pictured) was erected in 1900 by the Towarzystwo Zachęty Sztuk Pięknych (Society for the Encouragement of Fine Arts), founded in 1860. The gallery's traditional profile came to an end with the looting of most of its works in 1940 by the German occupation. Its current mission is to promote the contemporary arts. Its exhibits attempt to be trendsetting and controversial, and they often are — as, for example, Julita Wójcik's live installation *Obieranie ziemniaków* (*Potato Peeling*, 2001), in which the artist comments on women's lot by sitting in an apron and peeling fifty-five kilograms of potatoes (or perhaps she was commenting on the poetry of everyday life). Katarzyna Kozyra's video installations *Łaźnia kobieca* (*Women's Bathhouse*, 1997) and *Łaźnia męska* (*Men's Bathhouse*, 1999), received attention for using hidden cameras, violating privacy, in order to capture the goings-on inside Budapest men's and women's public baths. The Zachęta is forever linked to the assassination there in 1922 of Gabriel Narutowicz, first president of Reborn Poland (see Polska Odrodzona).

Zagajewski, Adam (b. 1945). One of contemporary Poland's most often translated poets, because of the universality of his themes. Zagajewski was at one time an émigré in Paris but now lives in Kraków. He has taught at the Universities of Houston and Chicago. His contemplative poetry ranges over many topics, including the meaning of contemporary existence torn between simultaneous allegiance to a locale and to a broader European culture.

295

Zagajewski was one of the signatories of the *list 59* (memorandum of the 59). Along with **Stanisław Barańczak** and others, Zagajewski is counted among the Nowa Fala (New Wave) of Polish poets coming into their own in the late 1960s. His most recent volume is *Niewidzialna ręka* (*Invisible Hand*, 2009, published in English in 2011). He was shortlisted for the Nobel Prize for Literature in 2010.

Zagłoba, **Jan Onufry**. A colorful secondary character in **Henryk Sienkiewicz**'s historical *trylogia* (trilogy), exaggeratedly embodying the stereotypical characteristics of a seventeenth-century Polish nobleman: quick to drink, quick to fight, a braggart and coward on the one hand, on the other a patriot, faithful friend, and, when put to the test, a brave and resourceful soldier, especially full of clever stratagems. He is said to be partly modeled on the historical figure **Jan Pasek**. *Mieczysław Pawlikowski as Zagłoba in Jerzy Hoffman's* Pan Wołodyjowski, *1969.*

zakazane piosenki (forbidden songs). Highly catchy war songs composed, prohibited, and severely punished under German occupation in World War II. Many were flippant, sarcastic, and satirical in tone. The phrase was turned into an idiom by the 1946 film of the same name by Leonard Buczkowski, the first Polish postwar film to be widely distributed, in which a loosely strung-together plot serves as an excuse for singing Polish wartime songs known to everyone. Here is a refrain from one, sung to a fast waltz and the melody of the Mexican song "Cielito Lindo":

> Teraz jest wojna, kto handluje ten żyje . . .
> Jak sprzedam rąbankę, słoninę, kaszankę
> To bimbru się też napiję.
>
> Now it's war, who engages in trade survives . . .
> If I sell some chopped meat, pork fat, blood sausage
> I can have a drink of homebrew as well.

The *zakazane piosenki*, along with other urban folk songs, belong to the repertoire of the postwar Warsaw *orkiestra uliczna* (street orchestra, pictured), originally largely composed of disabled war veterans.

Zakopane. A town of around twenty-five thousand in the high **Tatra** Mountains in the **Podhale** region. Traditionally an artist's colony and, more recently, a major winter sports center billing itself as the *zimowa stolica Polski* (winter capital of Poland), Zakopane is visited by some two to three million tourists a year, at all hours crowding the main street Krupówki (pictured), full of souvenir shops and people selling oscypki (molded sheep's milk cheese), *kierpce* (leather moccasins), and *owczarek podhalański* puppies by the boxload. In the winter mulled wine and hot beer with raspberry syrup are specialties. The *styl zakopiański* (Zakopane style) of wooden architecture, used by Polish summer home builders everywhere, was popularized by the architect Stanisław Witkiewicz, father of the writer Witkacy. Zakopane is the site of Poland's tallest ski jump, the Wielka Krokiew (Great Rafter). The town is reached via the perpetually jam-packed Zakopianka highway, at a virtual standstill on sylwester (New Year's Eve). Despite the crowds, one is likely to find a *wolny pokój* (available room) at any time of the year.

Zakopane: styl zakopiański (Zakopane style). A style of architecture achieved by grafting elements of the *secesja* (secessionist or Art Nouveau style) onto native Podhale (high Carpathian) wooden house construction, with an admixture of the Austrian chalet. The result is accommodations suitable for modern living but fitting into native architecture and landscape. Roofs are steeply and severally gabled, and natural wood is used inside and out. The style was developed by Stanisław Witkiewicz (1851–1915), father of the artist/playwright of the same name (a.k.a. Witkacy), and its development more or less ceased with his death, although the style is copied to this day in villas and country houses throughout Poland. The first significant house of this style was the villa Koliba, now housing the museum of the *styl zakopiański*. It and most prominent examples of the style, including its largest example, the villa Pod Jedlami ("beneath the firs," pictured), are to be found in Zakopane.

Zamek Królewski w Warszawie (royal castle in Warsaw). The official residence of Polish kings from the end of the sixteenth century until the fall of the Rzeczpospolita Obojga Narodów in 1795. In 1926–1939 the castle was the residence of the president of Polska Odrodzona (Reborn Poland). It was bombed and looted by the Germans at the outbreak of World War II. They further systematically dynamited it to the ground as they were leaving Warsaw in 1944. The structure today is a painstakingly executed reconstruction of the prewar castle, built beginning in 1971, at first financed largely from private donations, using fragments of the former castle when available. It is now a museum, with important paintings by Canaletto and Bacciarelli. It is one of Warsaw's most frequently visited tourist attractions.

Zamenhof, Ludwik (1859–1917). By profession a doctor from Białystok, Zamenhof was the creator of the world's most successful attempt at an artificial common world language, Esperanto. Built primarily out of components of the Romance languages with an admixture of Germanic and Slavic, Esperanto is still used to an extent by an estimated two million people worldwide. The name means "hopeful," and Zamenhof's aim was to create an easy-to-learn and politically neutral language to help further world peace and understanding. By some estimates, Esperanto can be learned in from one-fifth to one-twentieth of the time required for another language. Because Zamenhof was Jewish, the Nazis viewed Esperanto as part of a world Jewish conspiracy and persecuted its use and Zamenhof's family. Zamenhof also published an Esperanto textbook and dictionary. He was a candidate for the Nobel Peace Prize in 1913.

Zamość. A town of 66,500 inhabitants in southeast Poland, Zamość calls itself the *perła renesansu* (pearl of the Renaissance) for its excellently preserved sixteenth-century architecture and town square. Its Stare Miasto (old town area) is a listed UNESCO World Heritage Site, and it was selected in a national plebiscite conducted by the newspaper *Rzeczpospolita* (The republic) ahead of Kraków as one of the "seven wonders of Poland." Planned as both a town and a fortress, in the seventeenth century Zamość withstood attacks by Swedes and Turks. The city attracted Jews from around Europe beginning from its date of founding in 1580, when they were granted the right to settle in the town by its founder and *hetman* wielki koronny Jan Zamoyski. Its Jews were subject to almost complete extermination under the German occupation, most of them in the nearby Bełżec concentration camp. *Zamość town hall and the so-called Armenian tenements.*

Zamoyscy, rodzina (Zamoyski family). A Polish noble family distinguished both militarily and politically, now in its sixteenth generation. Its historical center is Zamość, which was once a family possession. Family members have taken part in every Polish national uprising through the powstanie warszawskie (Warsaw Uprising, 1944), and they are intermarried with most other old Polish former magnate families (see *magnateria*). The Zamoyscy profited immensely from the system of *ordynacja* (male primogeniture), the first family *ordynat* (scion) being Jan Zamoyski. At the end of World War I the Zamoyski landholdings were the largest in Poland. They were expropriated after World War II. The sixteenth and last Zamoyski *ordynat*, Jan Tomasz (1912–2002), was imprisoned by the communists for eight years for no particular reason. His son Marcin is currently mayor of Zamość. The former Zamoyski palace in Kozłówka near Lublin now houses the Zamoyski family museum as well as a museum of *socrealizm*, socialist realist art.

Zamoyski, Jan (1542–1605). A politically astute and influential politician, military leader, and kingmaker in sixteenth-century Poland, Zamoyski was a close adviser to the kings Zygmunt II August and Stefan Batory (the latter of whom he helped install on the throne). Under Batory he was grand chancellor and *hetman wielki koronny* (Hetman of the Crown, commander-in-chief of the army). In 1580 he founded the town of Zamość and within it, in 1585, the Zamość Academy. Rising from petty nobility and for much of his career defending them from the power of the magnates (*magnateria*), Zamoyski himself became extremely wealthy, at one point possessing twenty-four towns and 816 villages extending over 6,400 square kilometers, as well as a standing army of four thousand infantry and two thousand cavalry.

Zanussi, Krzysztof (b. 1939). Film theorist and writer, and director of more than twenty-five feature-length films as well as many movies made for television. A physicist and philosopher by training, Zanussi is one of Poland's best-known directors abroad, virtually unique in his putting difficult questions in a moral light refracted through the point of view of Roman Catholicism. He is a professor of film studies at Uniwersytet Śląski (Silesian University) in Katowice. Among some of his important films are *Struktura Kryształu* (The structure of crystals, 1969), *Iluminca* (Illumination, 1972), *Barwy ochronne* (Protective coloration, 1976), *Constans* (Constant factor, 1980), *Rok spokojnego słońca* (Year of the quiet sun, 1984), and *Persona non grata* (2004).

zapiekanka. A popular kind of Polish street food, the Polish answer to the pizza, but not

KALEIDOSCOPE OF POLAND

likely to take over the world any time soon. Bet instead on *pierogi*. The *zapiekanka* consists of half a baguette topped with cheese, mushrooms, and other toppings (including corn, peas, and bean sprouts). It is baked in an oven until the cheese is melted and the bread is crisp, and it is often topped with ketchup and chives. It is not as good as it looks. Speaking of ketchup, Poles will sometimes pour it on top of a pizza, horrifying pizza lovers everywhere.

Zawacka, Elżbieta (1909–2009). A brigadier general and underground courier in the **Armia Krajowa** (AK, Home Army) during World War II. At first a women's paramilitary organizer, she later worked carrying messages between the AK and the **rząd na uchodźstwie** (government in exile) in London. The only woman in the elite special forces unit Cichociemni, (The dark and quiet ones), in 1943 she parachuted into Poland, participated in the **powstanie warszawskie** (Warsaw Uprising) of 1944, and after its collapse escaped to **Kraków**. After the war she completed a doctorate in education, became a tenured professor in **Toruń** (the town of her birth), and continually attracted the attention of the police for her activities on behalf of AK war veterans. In the 1980s she was active in the independent trade union **Solidarność**. Zawacka died at the age of one hundred, having five times received the Krzyż Walecznych (Cross of Valor) in addition to the Order Orła Białego (Order of the White Eagle), Poland's highest civilian decoration, and the cross of the **Order Virtuti Militari**, Poland's highest military decoration.

Zawisza Czarny (Black Zawisza). A famous Polish medieval knight (ca. 1370–1428), undefeated in numerous tourneys and battles, whose name is synonymous with dependability. The knight met his untimely death in an ill-conceived campaign against Turkey in today's Serbia while covering the retreat of the Polish army. His black armor is preserved in the **Jasna Góra** monastery. The Polish scout oath calls on his memory, as does the phrase "polegać jak na Zawiszy" (to be as reliable as Zawisza). Zawisza is one of several people out of the past who appear in **Stanisław Wyspiański**'s symbolic play *Wesele* (The wedding). *Zawisza* is also the title of a romantic drama by **Juliusz Słowacki** based on the knight, as well as the name of a famous Polish scouts' training schooner. *Jan Matejko, Zawisza Czarny (a fragment of his Battle of Grunwald)*.

---

zdrowie, opieka lekarska (health, medical care). Foreigners say that Poles talk about their health like the British do about the weather. The saying "zdrowie jest najważniesze" (health is the most important thing) is an oft-expressed Polish truism. Poles "enjoy" universal health coverage administered by the Narodowy Fundusz Zdrowia (NFZ, National Health Fund). The public health sector is notoriously understaffed and underfunded, and seeing a doctor, or getting a reference to a specialist, can require waiting in long lines. Those who can afford to will consult a doctor privately and expensively. Dentistry, generally considered good, is largely in private hands. Not surprisingly, Poles are large consumers of treat-yourself, over-the-counter medications, including herbal. Foreigners often remark that it seems as though every street in Poland has an *apteka* (pharmacy) on it.

---

zespół filmowy (film group). A method of organizing film production more or less unique to Poland, flourishing after the political *odwilż* (thaw) of 1956. Under this system film production was placed under the management of a lead director, screenwriter, and production manager, cutting out the "mogul" level of management typical of Hollywood-style film production. Films produced under this system tended to share common themes, touches, and artistic vision. The *zespół* system was credited for the rise of the internationally respected *polska szkoła filmowa* (Polish film school) as it emerged — especially under the aegis of the Kadr group, headed by Jerzy Kawalerowicz (1922–2007), with some 150 films to its credit. Other important groups were Tor, most recently under Krzysztof Zanussi (b. 1939), and Zebra (logo pictured) under Juliusz Machulski (b. 1955). The zespół (nowadays, "studio") model has come under fire for not being sufficiently competitive in the contemporary international marketplace.

Zielone Świątki (Green Holidays). A relic of a pre-Christian celebration of the leafing out of trees at the beginning of spring, the holiday today is congruent with the Catholic Church holiday of Pentecost, celebrating the Zesłanie Ducha Świętego (descent of the Holy Spirit) onto the disciples of Christ. An official national holiday, it is mobile, falling fifty days after Wielkanoc (Easter). Zielone Świątki are traditionally days for housecleaning, painting, decorating, and airing things out, especially in the countryside. The Kościół zielonoświątkowy (Pentecostal Church), with some twenty-three thousand members, is the country's second-largest Protestant denomination (after Lutheranism).

ziemie odzyskane (recovered territories). After Poland, by the decision of the Big Three, "ceded" to the Soviet Union its former immense territories in the east at the Yalta conference of 1945 (see *kresy wschodnie*; Jałta), the country was "compensated" by being given territory in the west and north (Prusy Wschodnie, East Prussia) formerly belonging to Germany, land which became known self-justifyingly as the *ziemie odzyskane* (recovered territories), since much of it had, at one historical period or another, been under Polish rule. The western border matters were adjudicated at the Potsdam Conference later that year as part of a war-reparations package imposed on Germany. In revanchist action by the Big Three that subsequently has been condemned as a violation of human rights, the ethnically German population — who in many cases had inhabited these lands for hundreds of years — was summarily uprooted, interned, and shipped to postwar Germany without legal rights, compensation, or access to humanitarian aid. Little by little, the legal situation became normalized, first between Poland and East Germany in 1950 under pressure from Joseph Stalin, and finally in a treaty between Poland and the newly reunited Germany in 1990; see Odra.

zjazd gnieźnieński (Gniezno Synod). In the year 1000 Otto III, emperor of the Holy Roman Empire, traveled to Gniezno, seat of the Polanie princes, to obtain relics of Święty Wojciech (Saint Wojciech/Adalbert), who had been martyred while trying to convert the Baltic tribes in the north. He received one of Wojciech's arms. While there, Otto endowed the ruling prince Bolesław I Chrobry with the insignia of royal power, including the crown off his head and a replica of the *włócznia świętego Maurycego* (spear of Saint Maurice); see *polskie regalia królewskie*. The event established the legitimacy of Poland as a royal Christian power, and its church as independent from the archbishopric of Magdeburg.

złota polska wolność (golden Polish freedoms). The rights and privileges enjoyed by the Polish *szlachta* (nobility) under the Rzeczpospolita Obojga Narodów (Polish-Lithuanian Commonwealth), introduced as a condition of the election of Henryk I Walezy in 1573. They included *neminem captivabimus* (no imprisonment without trial, i.e., habeas corpus); *nihil novi* (no new laws without the consent of the nobility); *liberum veto* (the right of any noble to veto a proposed law); *wolna elekcja* (the right to elect kings); *równość stanu szlacheckiego* (the equality before the law of all members of the nobility); *tolerancja religijna* (religious tolerance) throughout the Commonwealth. The golden freedoms gave the Polish szlachta powers not enjoyed by the nobility elsewhere in Europe, but they weakened the power of the central government. Calls to "defend" the golden freedoms by sectors of the Polish upper nobility led to various *konfederacje* (confederations, or noble insurrections) and eventually, toward the end of the eighteenth century, served as a pretext for the intervention in Polish internal affairs of the neighboring great powers: Russia, Prussia, and Austria.

Zmotoryzowane Odwody Milicji Obywatelskiej (ZOMO) (Motorized Detachments of the Citizens' Militia, 1956–1989). A standing paramilitary police force that was placed under the control of the Prezes Rady Ministrów (Chairman of the Council of Ministers, the premier). Its ostensible mission was to provide aid in civilian disasters. However, armed with the latest in clubs, tear gas, and water cannons (pictured), the ZOMO was in practice used in the PRL (communist Poland) to put down riots, street demonstrations, and workers' protests. Dozens were killed in the ZOMO's quelling of the 1970 December events (*grudzień 1970, wydarzenia grudniowe*) on the Baltic seacoast. A 1981 occupational strike at the *kopalnia* Wujek (Wujek coal mine) in Katowice was suppressed by the ZOMO at the cost of nine lives. At its height the ZOMO numbered thirteen thousand recruits and was said to be the best-trained such unit in the entire Soviet Bloc.

znaczek pocztowy (first Polish postage stamp). The stamp Poland #1 celebrated its 150th birthday in 2011. Issued in 1860 by the Królestwo Polskie (Kingdom of Poland) under tsarist Russian rule, it bears Russian insignia. It appeared in an issue of three million, cost ten kopecks, and was good for delivery of a *łót* (approximately ½ oz.) within the Kongresówka (Congress Kingdom) and between it and Russia. The stamp was withdrawn from circulation in 1865 and unsold copies were destroyed, so it is comparatively rare. A distinguished Russian collector, Vladimir Rachmanov, who lived in Warsaw during World War II, bribed his way out of Poland on the eve of the powstanie warszawskie (Warsaw Uprising, 1944) and later arrived in New York with little more than his stamp collection. He died in 1968, and his collection of Poland #1 stamps remained in a bank safe until 2010, when it was auctioned off for over a million dollars.

ZOMO. See **Zmotoryzowane Odwody Milicji Obywatelskiej (ZOMO)**.

ZSRR. See **Związek Socjalistycznych Republik Radzieckich (ZSRR)**.

zupa (soup). A midday meal in Poland is not complete without soup, which is considered to be a meal's *pierwsze danie* (first course). Next to *barszcz* (beet soup), probably the most popular soup is *żurek* (sour rye bread soup, a unique Polish variety), although *zupa pomidorowa* (tomato soup) is also a strong contender. In summer, cold soups are popular, including cream soups made from fruit (*zupa owocowa*). Of Lithuanian origin is *chłodnik* (cold creamed beet-leaf soup with boiled eggs and chives). Other common soups include *rosół* (broth), *grochówka* (pea soup), *jarzynowa* (vegetable, pictured), *kapuśniak* (cabbage soup), *krupnik* (barley soup), *zupa szczawiowa* (sorrel soup), as well as all the familiar types known elsewhere: bean, onion, potato, cucumber, vegetable, mushroom, fish, lentil, and many more. Polish women's magazines are full of soup suggestions to keep the hungry man in the house happy. See also: **"Bo zupa była za słona."**

Związek Socjalistycznych Republik Radzieckich (ZSRR) (Soviet Union, USSR). Because of the negative connotations for Poles of the word *sowiecki* (soviet), the word *radziecki*, based on *rada* (council, the Polish correspondent to Russian *soviet*), was dreamed up by the postwar communists for referring to Poland's "friend" to the east. A particularly grating coinage for referring positively to the USSR was Kraj Rad (Country of Councils). Usually the initials ZSRR were used. The pejorative word *sowiecki* was used routinely by the man in the street, and the adjective *ruski* was (and still is) used similarly pejoratively for referring to things Russian, instead of the neutral word *rosyjski* (Russian). The words *Rusek/Ruska* (Russky) are commonly used even now instead of the neutral *Rosjanin/Rosjanka* (a Russian) to refer derogatorily to a person from Russia. Not that Poles instinctively dislike Russians on an individual basis; quite the contrary.

Zygmunt I Stary (Zygmunt the Old, 1467–1548, reigned from 1506). With his Italian wife, Queen **Bona Sforza**, Zygmunt I was a popular ruler who presided over the beginning of what is sometimes called Poland's *złoty wiek* (golden age, or century), a time of independence, prosperity, and a flowering of the arts and literature. He and his wife were major sponsors of Renaissance art and architecture. Under his forty-two-year reign the **dzwon Zygmunta** (Zygmunt Bell) was cast and the Kaplica Zygmuntowska (Zygmunt Burial Crypt) in **Wawel** was built. In 1525 he received the tribute of the Prussian prince Albrecht Fryderyk Hohenzollern, known as the *hołd pruski* (Prussian fealty), commemorated in verse by **Jan Kochanowski** and in painting by **Jan Matejko**. By this act the Księstwo Pruskie

(Ducal Prussia) became a fief under Polish rule, a situation that was to last until 1657.

Zygmunt II August (1520–1572, ruled 1548–1572). The last of the **Jagiellonian** kings, Zygmunt II conducted his reign in conflict with the Polish nobility over taxes and the support of a standing army. The magnates (*magnateria*) were also scandalized by his marriage to the Lithuanian princess Barbara Radziwiłłówna, a renowned beauty, whom he succeeded in crowning queen in 1550 but who died a year later, most likely of uterine cancer. There is no evidence, as some think, that she was poisoned at the behest of her mother-in-law, Queen **Bona Sforza**, although that would have been her style. In 1569 the king concluded the *unia lubelska* (Union of Lublin), formally creating a combined Polish-Lithuanian Commonwealth, the **Rzeczpospolita Obojga Narodów**. Like his father **Zygmunt I Stary**, Zygmunt II was king during a general flowering of Polish literature and culture during the Polish Renaissance.

"Żeby Polska była Polską" (Let Poland be Poland). A patriotic song composed by Jan Pietrzak in 1976 (pictured reprising the song in 2010). Along with **Jacek Kaczmarski**'s "Mury" (Walls), it became an unofficial anthem of the **Solidarność** (Solidarity) resistance during *stan wojenny* (martial law, 1981–1983). It won Pietrzak first prize at the 1981 **Opole** festival of Polish song. The phrase became known to Americans through President Ronald Reagan's use of it during an American television special condemning martial law and the government clampdown on **Solidarność**. Part of the brilliance of the song was that there was nothing in it censurable, since it referred to sanctified national symbols and events from Poland's past, such as Father **Ściegienny** and *wóz Drzymały*; its spirit of protest was merely implied. The teary-eyed audience in the Kabaret po Egidą (Cabaret under the Auspices) always joined in on the refrain: "Żeby Polska, żeby Polska, żeby Polska była Polską!" (So that Poland, so that Poland, so that Poland can be Poland!).

Żegota (Rada Pomocy Żydom, Council for Aid to the Jews). A conspiratorial organ of the Polish *rząd na uchodźstwie* (government in exile) during World War II whose mission was to bring aid to Jews both inside the ghettos and out. Taking its name from a conspirator in **Adam Mickiewicz**'s Romantic drama *Dziady* (Forefathers' Eve), throughout the war the organization helped to hide Jewish children and to provide medical assistance and *aryjskie papiery* (fake "Aryan" documents) to Jews living outside the ghetto. Best known is the story of

Irena Sendlerowa (1910–2008), who saved 2,500 Jewish children from the Warsaw ghetto. Within concentration camps, Żegota worked to provide food and clothing to prisoners and helped to organize escape attempts. To the outside world, it endeavored to raise the alarm about the extermination of the Jews; see **Jan Karski**. Poland was the only European country in which such an underground organization operated.

Żeromski, Stefan (1864–1925). A novelist and dramatist emphasizing patriotic and social themes, Żeromski was Poland's major novelist in the first years of the twentieth century. Ideologically he belonged to the socially committed positivists, while his rich, exuberant, often impressionistic style places him among the writers of **Młoda Polska** (Young Poland). Among his best-known novels are: *Ludzie bezdomni* (Homeless people, 1899), about social problems at the turn of the nineteenth to the twentieth century; *Popioły* (Ashes, 1902–1903), set in Napoleonic times; and *Przedwiośnie* (Early spring, 1925), about the early years of **Polska Odrodzona** (Reborn Poland) after World War I. All have been made into films. Żeromski's sentimental approach to social problems, combined with heroes who selflessly devoted themselves to solving them at the expense of their own personal happiness, became known as *żeromszczyzna*. A social activist and organizer himself, he founded the Polish section of the international PEN Club. See also: **szklane domy; Judym, Tomasz**.

Żmijewski, Artur (b. 1966). Scarcely an international exhibition of contemporary art anywhere passes without showing work by this Warsaw visual artist, tabbed by US *Newsweek* as one of the ten most promising artists in the world today. Żmijewski photographs and videorecords people in situations contrived to make both the viewer and participants feel deeply uncomfortable (but apparently not the artist). Some critics point to the artist's deep humanity; one could just as easily say that he stretches this concept to the limit. His film *Powtórzenie* (Repetition, 2005) re-creates an experiment designed by Philip Zimbardo at Stanford University, in which participants "play" at being guards and prisoners in a game that turns serious and has to be terminated. In another film, *80064* (2004), he takes a befuddled old Auschwitz survivor to a tattoo parlor and successfully browbeats him into having his camp ID number "refreshed." To illustrate Żmijewski's work, *Newsweek* chose the mysteriously titled *Oko za oko* (An Eye for an Eye, 1998), showing three naked bodies, one an amputee, in an awkward posterior clutch. Another Artur Żmijewski, better known in Poland, is a prolific film and television actor.

Żołnierze Wyklęci (excommunicated soldiers). The informal designation for soldiers of the underground resistance, whether the **Armia Krajowa** (AK, Home Army) or, especially, the **Narodowe Siły Zbrojne** (NSZ, National Armed Forces), who refused to lay down their arms after World War II but continued to engage in active resistance to the Soviet-installed communist government up through the early 1950s. The AK and NSZ had good reason to mistrust the communists, as the Soviets imprisoned or exiled to Siberia their members by the tens of thousands. Some twenty thousand members were executed or died in prisons. As of 2011, March 1 is a designated national day of remembrance for the Żołnierze Wyklęci. *Communist propaganda poster directed against the AK, reading "The giant versus the lickspittle dwarf of the reaction."*

Żółkiewski, Stanisław (1547–1620). Nobleman, magnate, and successful military leader from **Lwów** during the Polish Renaissance, Żółkiewski held many different titles in the **Rzeczpospolita Obojga Narodów** (Polish-Lithuanian Commonwealth), including that of *hetman polny* (field hetman) and *hetman wielki koronny* (Hetman of the Crown). One of the most educated Poles of his time, able to quote the works of Horace from memory (in Latin, of course), Żółkiewski won major victories against the Tatars and Turks across the southeast, and invaded Russia and took Moscow in 1610, withdrawing in 1611. His memoirs of the war with Muscovy, a model of pithy prose, have been compared to Julius Caesar's *Gallic Wars*. Żółkiewski was killed in a battle at Cecora against Ottoman Turks in Moldavia, and his head was cut off as a war trophy, later ransomed by his widow.

żubrówka (bison-grass vodka). A rye vodka lightly flavored and colored with grass of that name growing in the **Puszcza Białowieska** (Białowieża wilderness), a Polish specialty dating back to the seventeenth century. Each bottle of Polish *żubrówka* contains a blade of the grass, named after the *żubr* (European bison), herds of which roam the forest. Because the beverage contains a small amount of the ingredient coumarin (an anticoagulant used in rat poison and blood thinners), the importation of żubrówka was banned in the United States until the recipe was reformulated. One can still get the real thing in Poland. The word itself is a trademark of the Polmos distillery in **Białystok**, which has recently dreamed up the less than compelling brand name "Żu" (supposed to be pronounced "zoo") to market it abroad. A mixed drink consisting of żubrówka and apple juice, the so-called Polish martini, is known in Poland under the name of *szarlotka* (after the Polish name for apple cake). A product feeding off the name, called *biała żubrówka* (white żubrówka, i.e., straight vodka) has recently come on the market.

żupan. The *żupan*, a long-sleeved men's dress, buttoned down the front and was made of usually expensive, brightly colored material. It was not an outer garment (that would be the *kontusz*), but the everyday *sarmacki* (Sarmatian; see *sarmatyzm*) dress of the Polish nobility (*szlachta polska*) in the sixteenth to the eighteenth centuries. The impoverished nobility, distinguishable by the hare-like color of their homespun wool żupan, were condescendingly referred to as *szlachta szaraczkowa* (hare gentry). A crimson żupan, as in Jan Kupecky's portrait of Jan III Sobieski's son Aleksander Benedykt, pictured, signified a member of the *szlachta karmazynowa* (crimson nobility).

żurek (or *żur*, sour rye bread soup). It seems impossible that no other national cuisine has discovered or copied this uniquely Polish wintertime soup, loved by young and old alike. It is made from a rye flour starter left to ferment in water for several days at room temperature by simply adding water, basic seasonings (don't leave out the garlic), and a bit of cream. Absolutely serve with sausage. Its cousin, *barszcz biały*, is made from a wheat flour starter. One can buy *żurek* in bottles or, almost as good, in instant powdered form. On fancy occasions it can be served in a round loaf of bread hollowed into a bowl. In a wonderful scene in Olga Tokarczuk's short story "Żurek," which was turned into a film by Ryszard Brylski in 2003, just to be nasty one of the locals in a store on the Czech-Polish border buys the last bottle of *żurek* out from underneath an ebullient passer-through, who wanted to take a bit of Poland with him on his ski trip to Austria.

Żwirko i Wigura. In 1932 Polish competitive pilots Franciszek Żwirko and Stanisław Wigura perished in an air tragedy in Czechoslovakia two weeks after having won the prestigious international air competition Challenge 1932 in Berlin, flying a Polish-designed RWD-6 aircraft. The country had already followed their flight around Europe in an RWD-2 in 1929. Their names are attached to the road leading from the Warsaw international airport into town, at the end of which stands the prominent Pomnik lotnika (Airmen's Monument).

Żydowski Związek Wojskowy (ŻZW) (Jewish Military Union). An underground military resistance organization in World War II, formed in 1939 and comprised mainly of Jewish former officers in the prewar Polish army. Because of its close ties to the Armia Krajowa (Home Army) and the London-based *rząd na uchodźstwie* (government in exile), knowledge of its activities were suppressed by the postwar communist government, which preferred instead to highlight the deeds of the left-leaning Żydowska Organizacja Bojowa (ŻOB, Jewish Fighting Organization), formed in 1942 primarily out of members of Jewish youth groups in response to the German deportation of the Jews to the death camps.

KALEIDOSCOPE OF POLAND

Both organizations took part in the powstanie w getcie warszawskim (Warsaw Ghetto Uprising), although the ŻOB was the more active in that particular action.

———

Żydzi w Polsce (Jews in Poland). The Museum of the History of Polish Jews (pictured) opened to fanfare in Warsaw in 2013. The first Jews appeared on Polish lands as early as the ninth or tenth century. They arrived in large numbers in the fifteenth through the sixteenth centuries, fleeing persecution elsewhere. Jewish-Polish relations were sometimes better, sometimes worse, but on the whole peaceable. The *statut kaliski* (Kalisz statute) of 1264 granted Jews equal rights alongside Poles. The sixteenth century is considered to be the golden age of Polish Jewry. The eighteenth century saw the rise of various Jewish offshoot movements, including *chasydyzm* (Hasidism) and Frankism (see Frank, Jakub). Rising anti-Semitism characterized the *dwudziestolecie międzywojenne* (interwar period). Nevertheless, Jews had their own members of parliament, and Jewish cultural institutions, including the Yiddish press and theater, flourished. At the beginning of World War II more than three million Jews lived in Poland, in some towns constituting a majority of the population. A relatively small number survived the Holocaust, and a majority of those emigrated after the war out of anxiety over the cultural and political situation in postwar Poland. Additional thousands left after the March events (marzec 1968, wydarzenia marcowe). Today Poland numbers probably fewer than five thousand practicing Jews, although numerous secularized Jews increasingly recognize their cultural roots. The manifold contributions over the ages of Polish Jews to national and international politics and culture can scarcely be overestimated, much less summed up in a brief article; for a hint, see the cross-references in the index.

———

Timeline of Polish Historical Months

1830–1831 listopad powstanie listopadowe (November Uprising). A national uprising against tsarist Russian rule. The insurrection's ultimate failure led to mass cultural repression, deportations, conscription into the Russian army, and emigration.

1863–1864 styczeń powstanie styczniowe (January Uprising). The historically largest and bloodiest Polish national uprising, made against Russian rule. The uprising's ultimate failure led to the confiscation of property, deportations, and mass emigration.

1956 czerwiec wypadki czerwcowe (June incidents). Strikes and street demonstrations in Poznań provoked violent reprisals with numerous fatalities. Their aftermath led to liberalization in the communist party, with Władysław Gomułka now as first party secretary.

1968 marzec wydarzenia marcowe (March events). A crisis brought on by protests over the closing of Adam Mickiewicz's *Dziady* in Warsaw. The government response took on anti-Semitic overtones, leading to the emigration of many people of Jewish background.

1970 grudzień wydarzenia grudniowe (December events). Protests over a rise in food prices broke out along the Baltic seacoast. The army opened fire on protesters, killing at least eighty civilians. Edward Gierek took over as first party secretary. Prices were rolled back.

1976 czerwiec wydarzenia czerwcowe (June events). An increase in food prices provoked strikes and protests especially in Radom and Warsaw. Several thousand workers were jailed or fired, leading to the formation of KOR (Komitet Obrony Robotników, Workers' Defense Committee).

1980 sierpień wydarzenia sierpniowe (August events). Workers' strikes on the seacoast, and eventually across Poland led to the *porozumienie gdańskie* (Gdańsk Accord), signed between Lech Wałęsa and the government, creating the independent trade union Solidarność.

See also: *przewrót majowy* (May coup d'état) under Józef Piłsudski.

Timeline of Polish Literary Figures Cited

Assigned to approximate literary periods

średniowiecze (Middle Ages)
- Kazania świętokrzyskie (Holy Cross sermons)
- Bogurodzica (Mother of God)
- Żale Matki Boskiej pod krzyżem (Lament of the Mother of God beneath the Cross)
- Wincenty Kadłubek (1161–1223)

odrodzenie (Renaissance)
- Jan Długosz (1415–1480)
- Biernat z Lublina (ca. 1460–ca. 1529)
- Mikołaj Rej z Nagłowic (1505–1569)
- Jan Kochanowski (1530–1584)
- Piotr Skarga (1536–1612)

barok (Baroque)
- Mikołaj Sęp-Szarzyński (1550–1681)
- Daniel Naborowski (1573–1640)
- Jan Andrzej Morsztyn (1621–1693)
- Wacław Potocki (1621–1696)
- Jan Chryzostom Pasek (ca. 1636–1701)

oświecenie (Enlightenment)
- Elżbieta Drużbacka (ca. 1695–1765)
- Ignacy Krasicki (1735–1801)
- Jakub Jasiński (1759–1794)

romantyzm (Romanticism)
- Aleksander Fredro (1793–1876)
- Adam Mickiewicz (1798–1855)
- Juliusz Słowacki (1809–1849)
- Zygmunt Krasiński (1812–1859)
- Józef Ignacy Kraszewski (1812–1887)
- Cyprian Kamil Norwid (1821–1883)

pozytywizm (Positivism)
- Eliza Orzeszkowa (1841–1910)
- Maria Konopnicka (1842–1910)
- Henryk Sienkiewicz (1846–1916)
- Bolesław Prus (1847–1912)
- Joseph Conrad (1857–1924)

Młoda Polska (Young Poland)
- Gabriela Zapolska (1857–1921)
- Jan Kasprowicz (1860–1926)
- Zenon Przesmycki (1861–1944)
- Stefan Żeromski (1864–1925)
- Kazimierz Przerwa-Tetmajer (1865–1940)
- Władysław Stanisław Reymont (1867–1925)
- Stanisław Przybyszewski (1868–1927)
- Stanisław Wyspiański (1869–1907)

okres międzywojenny (Interwar period)
- Leopold Staff (1878–1957)
- Zofia Nałkowska (1884–1954)
- Stanisław Ignacy Witkiewicz, "Witkacy" (1885–1939)
- Maria Dąbrowska (1889–1965)
- Maria Pawlikowska-Jasnorzewska (1891–1945)
- Bruno Schulz (1892–1942)
- Julian Tuwim (1894–1953)
- Kazimierz Wierzyński (1894–1969)
- Jarosław Iwaszkiewicz (1894–1980)
- Antoni Słonimski (1895–1976)
- Tadeusz Dołęga-Mostowicz (1898–1939)
- Jan Brzechwa (ca. 1898–1966)
- Konstanty Ildefons Gałczyński (1905–1953)

okres wojenny (World War II)
- Krzysztof Kamil Baczyński (1921–1944)

okres powojenny (Postwar period)
- Jerzy Szaniawski (1886–1970)
- Józef Mackiewicz (1902–1985)
- Witold Gombrowicz (1904–1969)
- Jerzy Andrzejewski (1909–1983)
- Czesław Miłosz (1911–2004)
- Stanisław Dygat (1914–1978)
- Jan Twardowski (1915–2006)
- Stanisław Lem (1921–2006)
- Tadeusz Różewicz (1921–2014)
- Tadeusz Borowski (1922–1951)
- Miron Białoszewski (1922–1983)
- Zbigniew Herbert (1924–1998)
- Tadeusz Konwicki (1926–2015)
- Sławomir Mrożek (1930–2013)
- Jerzy Kosiński (1933–1991)
- Marek Hłasko (1934–1969)
- Edward Stachura (1937–1979)

okres współczesny (Contemporary period)
- Wisława Szymborska (1923–2012)
- Jarosław Marek Rymkiewicz (b. 1935)
- Janusz Głowacki (b. 1938)
- Adam Zagajewski (b. 1945)
- Stanisław Barańczak (b. 1946)
- Stefan Chwin (b. 1949)
- Jerzy Pilch (b. 1952)
- Paweł Huelle (b. 1957)
- Olga Tokarczuk (b. 1962)
- Joanna Bator (b. 1968)
- Jacek Dehnel (b. 1980)
- Dorota Masłowska (b. 1983)

Timeline of Polish Rulers

Dates indicate the reign.

9th century (legendary princes of the Piast dynasty)
Piast
Siemowit
Lestek
Siemomysł

10th Century
Mieszko I (ca. 960–992)
Bolesław I Chrobry (Bolesław the Brave, 992–1025, the first crowned king of Poland)

11th Century
Mieszko II (1025–1034)
Kazimierz I Odnowiciel (1034–1058)

As of 1040, the capital moves from Gniezno to Kraków.
Bolesław II Śmiały (Bolesław the Bold or Generous, 1076–1079)
Władysław I Herman (1079–1102)

12th Century
Bolesław III Krzywousty (Bolesław the Wrymouth, 1107–1138)
The beginning of the *rozbicie dzielnicowe* (division into districts); persons listed were rulers in Kraków.
Władysław II Wygnaniec (Władysław the Exile, 1138–1146)
Bolesław IV Kędzierzawy (Bolesław the Curly-Headed, 1146–1173)
Mieszko III Stary (Mieszko the Elder, 1173–1177)
Kazimierz II Sprawiedliwy (Kazimierz the Just, 1177–1194)
Leszek I Biały (Leszek the White, 1194–1199)
Mieszko III Stary (Mieszko the Elder, 1199–1202)

13th Century
Władysław III Laskonogi (Władysław Spindleshanks, 1202)
Leszek I Biały (Leszek the White, 1202–1227)
Władysław III Laskonogi (Władysław Spindleshanks, 1228)
Henryk I Brodaty (Henryk the Bearded, 1228–1229)
Konrad Mazowiecki (Konrad of Mazovia, 1229–1232)
Henryk I Brodaty (Henryk the Bearded, 1232–1238)
Henryk II Pobożny (Henryk the Pious, 1238–1241)
Konrad Mazowiecki (Konrad of Mazovia, 1241–1243)
Bolesław V Wstydliwy (Bolesław the Chaste, 1243–1279)
Leszek II Czarny (Leszek the Black, 1279–1288)
Henryk IV Prawy (Henryk the Righteous, 1288–1290)
Przemysł II (1290–1291, 1295–1296)

14th Century
Wacław II (1300–1305)
Wacław III (1305–1306)
Władysław I Łokietek (Władysław the Short or Elbow-High, 1320–1333)

As of 1320, the end of the *rozbicie dzielnicowe*.
Kazimierz III Wielki (Kazimierz the Great, 1333–1370, the last of the Piast dynasty)
Ludwik Węgierski (Ludwik the Hungarian, 1370–1382)
Jadwiga (1384–1399), co-ruler with Władysaw II Jagiełło 1386–1399

The beginning of the Jagiellonian dynasty (*Jagiellonowie*)
Władysław II Jagiełło (1386–1434)

15th Century
Władysław III Warneńczyk (1434–1444)
Kazimierz IV Jagiellończyk (1446–1492)
Jan I Olbracht (1492–1501)

16th Century
Aleksander Jagiellończyk (1501–1506)
Zygmunt I Stary (Zygmunt the Old, 1506–1548)
Zygmunt II August (1548–1572)

The end of the Jagiellonian dynasty, and the beginning of the *królowie elekcyjni* (elected kings).
Henryk I Walezy (Henry de Valois, 1573–1575)
Stefan Batory, co-ruler with Anna Jagiellonka (1576–1586)
Zygmunt III Waza (1587–1632)
As of 1596, the capital moves from Kraków to Warszawa.

17th Century
    Władysław IV Waza (1632–1648)
    Jan II Kazimierz (1648–1668)
    Michał Korybut Wiśniowiecki (1669–1673)
    Jan III Sobieski (1674–1696)
    August II Mocny (August the Strong, 1697–1704)

18th Century
    Stanisław I Leszczyński (1704–1709)
    August II Mocny (August the Strong, 1709–1733)
    Stanisław I Leszczyński (1733–1736)
    August III (1733–1763)
    Stanisław II August Poniatowski (1764–1795)
    The end of the Rzeczpospolita Obojga Narodów (Polish-Lithuanian Commonwealth) with the *rozbiory* (the partitions of Poland: 1772, 1793, 1795).

20th–21st Century
Presidents of Interwar Poland
    Gabriel Narutowicz (1922)
    Stanisław Wojciechowski (1922–1926)
    przewrót majowy (May coup d'état); government of Józef Piłsudski, 1926–1935
    Ignacy Mościcki (1926–1939)

Communist Party Secretaries
    Bolesław Bierut (1948–1956)
    Edward Ochab (1956)
    Władysław Gomułka (1956–1970)
    Edward Gierek (1970–1980)
    Stanisław Kania (1980–1981)
    Wojciech Jaruzelski (1981–1989)
    Mieczysław Rakowski (1989–1990)

Presidents of the Modern Polish Republic
    Wojciech Jaruzelski (1989–1990)
    Lech Wałęsa (1990–1995)
    Aleksander Kwaśniewski (1995–2005)
    Lech Kaczyński (2005–2010)
    Bronisław Komorowski (2010–2015)
    Andrzej Duda (2015–)

Major Polish National and Regional Uprisings

insurekcja kościuszkowska (Kościuszko Insurrection, 1794). Led by Tadeusz Kościuszko. A revolt in response to the *drugi rozbiór* (second partition) of Poland among Russia and Prussia. Brutally suppressed by Russia, it led to the third and final partition of Poland in 1795.

powstanie listopadowe (November Uprising, 1830–1831). An uprising against Russian rule in the Królestwo Polskie (Polish Kingdom). The fall of the insurrection led to mass cultural repression, deportations, conscription into the Russian army, and emigration. The Polish army was disbanded.

powstanie krakowskie (Kraków Uprising, 1846). Taking place in the Wolne Miasto Kraków (Free City of Kraków) with sympathetic movements across Galicja (Galicia), the uprising against the three protectorate powers simultaneously (Austria, Prussia, and Russia) led to the annexation of Kraków by Austria and provoked the rabacja galicyjska (Galicia jacquerie).

powstanie styczniowe (January Uprising, 1863–1865). The largest and bloodiest Polish national uprising, made against repressive Russian rule. The uprising's failure led to mass emigration, deportations to Siberia, confiscation of property, and to even harsher cultural repression. The Congress Kingdom ceased to exist, being turned into a province of Russia.

powstanie wielkopolskie (Greater Poland Uprising, 1918–1919). An insurrection around Poznań at the conclusion of World War I, demanding the repatriation to Poland of lands taken by Prussia in the first and third *rozbiory* (partitions). The aims of the uprising were largely achieved, making this one of Poland's few successful armed insurrections.

powstania śląskie (Silesian uprisings, 1919, 1920, and 1921). Three uprisings arising out of the unstable territorial situation in Śląsk (Silesia) following the German defeat in World War I. Upper Silesia became split between Poland and Germany according to a bitterly contested and disputed plebiscite.

powstanie w getcie warszawskim (Jewish Ghetto Uprising, Warsaw, April–May 1943). The first civilian uprising in World War II against German occupation anywhere. Poorly armed and barely supported from the outside, it lasted a surprising month.

powstanie warszawskie (Warsaw Uprising, August 1, 1944–October 3, 1944). An insurrection of the entire Warsaw population against the German occupation. After sixty-three days the uprising was crushed with heavy loss of life, much of it meted out as indiscriminate retaliation against civilians by the Nazis.

See also: **konfederacja barska**; **konfederacja targowicka**.

Important Twentieth-Century Conferences Affecting Poland

1919 konferencja wersalska (Versailles Conference, January 18, 1919–January 21, 1920). Attended by representatives of the "Big Four": Woodrow Wilson (United States), David Lloyd George (Great Britain), Georges Clemenceau (France), and Vittorio Emanuele (Italy), along with representatives of twenty-three other countries, including newly arisen Poland, represented by **Ignacy Paderewski** and **Roman Dmowski**. The conference established the terms of peace after World War I, including the imposition of reparations for damages inflicted by Germany on other countries. Articles creating the League of Nations were crafted. Poland recovered most of the territory lost to Prussia in the second and third *rozbiory* (partitions) but were left with limited access to the Baltic Sea, through the corridor to the newly created entity **Wolne Miasto Gdańsk** (Free City of Gdańsk). The eastern borders of Poland were settled upon only after the *wojna polsko-ukraińska* of 1918 and the *wojna polsko-bolszewicka* (Polish-Bolshevik War) of 1920.

1943 konferencja teherańska (Tehran Conference, November 28–December 1). The first of three wartime conferences of the *wielka trójca* (Big Three), attended by Franklin Delano Roosevelt (United States), Winston Churchill (Great Britain), and Joseph Stalin (Soviet Union). Its main purpose was to divide war theaters into those under Soviet responsibility and those belonging to the Western Allies, with Eastern Europe, the eastern part of Germany, the Baltic countries, and the Yugoslav area falling to the Soviet sphere. The Curzon Line (*linia Curzona*) was agreed to as the eventual border between Poland and the Soviet Union. The Allies committed themselves to opening up a second front in Normandy in 1944, and the idea of the United Nations was put forward.

1945 konferencja jałtańska (Yalta Conference, or — as many Poles would have it, the *zdrada jałtańska*, "Yalta Betrayal" — February 4–11). As was the Tehran Conference, it was attended by Roosevelt, Churchill, and Stalin. At Yalta, Churchill and Roosevelt ceded control of Poland to the Soviet Union, along with approximately one third of Germany. The Western powers, including France, were to be given control over *strefy* (sectors) in the remaining part of Germany. The eastern *kresy* (borderlands) were definitively ceded to the Soviet Union, leaving upwards of eleven million Polish citizens in limbo. In several *kresy* voivodeships they had constituted a majority of the population. Discussion continued on the creation of the United Nations.

1945 konferencja poczdamska (Potsdam Conference, July 17–August 2). Held in Germany and attended by Harry Truman (United States); Churchill, later replaced by Clement Attlee (Great Britain); and Stalin. The purpose was to regulate the shape of the world after World War II, including: matters of German reparations to the Soviet Union and Poland; respective postwar military spheres of influence; and the Polish-German border (although today's Polish-German border was officially ratified only on November 14, 1990). The Potsdam Conference in effect withdrew official recognition from the Polish government in exile in London and inaugurated the postwar political division between East and West that lasted until the early 1990s.

English Index

Some of the headings below refer to headings that are more fully expanded in the Polish Index. All headings in blue text are main headings. Polish terms in black text can be found in the Polish Index.

1905 Revolution. *See* rewolucja roku 1905; "Warszawianka"
ABC book. *See* "Ala ma kota"
accession referendum. *See* traktat ateński
Accursed Soldiers. *See* Żołnierze Wyklęci
actor, actress. *See* Bodo, Eugeniusz; Buzek, Jerzy; Cybulski, Zbigniew; *Czterej pancerni i pies*; Dulska, dulszczyzna; Dymna, Anna; Hanuszkiewicz, Adam; Holoubek, Gustaw; Janda, Krystyna; Kamińska, Ida; Kiepura, Jan; Komorowska, Maja; Łomnicki, Tadeusz; Modrzejewska, Helena; Niemczyk, Leon; Ordonówna, Hanka; Stuhr, Jerzy
Adalbert, Saint. *See* Wojciech, Święty; Mieszko I
Adam Mickiewicz Monument. *See* Kraków
age of majority. *See* wiek
Agora Foundation. *See* Nike
Airmen's Monument. *See* Żwirko i Wigura
Alexander I. *See* Boże coś Polskę; Księstwo Warszawskie
All Saints' Day. *See* Dzień Wszystkich Świętych
Allied forces. *See* Monte Cassino, bitwa pod Monte Cassino; Burza, akcja
amber, amber road. *See* bursztyn

anchor symbol. *See* Polska Walcząca
annual leave. *See* urlop, wakacje
anti-Semitism. *See* dwudziestolecie międzywojenne; Gross, Jan Tomasz; Jedwabne, pogrom w Jedwabnem; Kielce, pogrom kielecki; korporacje akademickie; marzec 1968, wydarzenia marcowe; Narodowa Demokracja, endecja; Żydzi w Polsce
anti-Trinitarian doctrine. *See* arianie, bracia polscy; reformacja
apartment building. *See* kamienica; mieszkania; mieszkania: rodzaje; mieszkanie M1, M2, M3
Arabian horses. *See* araby, polskie konie arabskie
architecture. *See* architektura romańska, gotycka, renesansowa, barokowa
Arianism. *See* arianie, bracia polscy; reformacja
aristocracy. *See* magnateria
armed forces. *See* Siły Zbrojne RP
Art Nouveau. *See* secesja
artist. *See* Bacciarelli, Marcello; Beksiński, Zdzisław; Canaletto; Chełmoński, Józef Marian; Gierymski, Ignacy Aleksander; Grottger, Artur; Kossak, Wojciech; Łempicka, Tamara de; Makowski, Tadeusz; Malczewski, Jacek; Matejko, Jan; Mehoffer, Józef; Michałowski, Piotr; Nikifor; Opałka, Roman; Sasnal, Wilhelm; *Szał uniesień*; Witkacy; Wyczółkowski, Leon; Wyspiański, Stanisław; Żmijewski, Artur
Aryan race. *See* Góral, akcja
Ash Wednesday. *See* ostatki
astronaut. *See* Hermaszewski, Mirosław
Athens Accord. *See* traktat ateński
August 1980 events. *See* Solidarność; Stocznia Gdańska
Augustów Canal. *See* Kanał Augustowski
Auschwitz. *See* Oświęcim
automobile. *See* Fiat 125p, duży Fiat; Fiat 126p, mały Fiat; Polonez; Syrena; Warszawa

bagel. *See* bajgiel
Balcerowicz Plan. *See* Balcerowicz, plan Balcerowicza
Baltic Sea. *See* Bałtyk
Baltic tribes, languages. *See* Bałtowie
baptism of Poland. *See* chrzest Polski; Grunwald, bitwa pod Grunwaldem
Bar Confederacy. *See* konfederacja barska
Barbara, Saint. *See* górnictwo
bard. *See* Wernyhora; Kaczmarski, Jacek

321

baroque. *See* architektura romańska, gotycka, renesansowa, barokowa; barok; epoki (okresy) literackie. *See also* Timeline of Polish Literary Figures Cited

Bartek the oak tree. *See* dąb Bartek

bat sanctuary. *See* Międzyrzecki Rejon Umocniony, Wilczy Szaniec

Battle of Chocim. *See* Chocim, bitwa pod Chocimem

Battle of Grunwald. *See* Grunwald, bitwa pod Grunwaldem

Battle of Monte Cassino. *See* Monte Cassino, bitwa pod Monte Cassino

Battle of Racławice. *See* Racławice; *Panorama Racławicka*.

Battle of Somosierra. *See* Somosierra, bitwa

Battle of Vienna. *See* odsiecz wiedeńska

Battle of Warsaw. *See* Warszawa, bitwy

Battle on Dog's Field. *See* Psie Pole, bitwa

bear soldier; Wojtek the bear soldier. *See* Wojtek, niedźwiedź Wojtek

beauty pageant. *See* Miss Polonia

beer. *See* piwo; pijalnia piwa

Belarus. *See* Bielscy, bracia; Bug; język polski, języki słowiańskie; kasza; kontusz; kresy wschodnie; linia Curzona; mniejszości narodowe i etniczne; Narew; pakt Ribbentrop-Mołotow; pielgrzymki; Podlasie, Polesie; pogoń; ziemie odzyskane

Belgian tapestries. *See* arrasy wawelskie; Wawel

Bellotto, Bernardo. *See* Canaletto

Benedictine monks. *See* cystersi; Tyniec

Berlin–Warsaw–Prague Bicycle Peace Race. *See* Wyścig Pokoju

Beskid Mountains. *See* Beskidy; Karpaty; Wisła

Białowieża Wilderness. *See* Białystok; Podlasie; Białowieża, Puszcza Białowieska; żubrówka

Bible. *See* Biblia

Bielski partisans. *See* Bielscy, bracia

Bieszczad Mountains. *See* Bieszczady; Karpaty

birthdays. *See* imieniny, urodziny

bison-grass vodka. *See* żubrówka

Black Madonna of Częstochowa. *See* Jasna Góra; Matka Boska Częstochowska, Czarna Madonna

Black Sea. *See* Jałta, konferencja jałtańska; Władysław III Warneńczyk

Black Zawisza. *See* Zawisza Czarny

Blackwood. *See* Kochanowski, Jan

Bohemia. *See* chrzest Polski

Bolesław the Bold. *See* Bolesław II Śmiały. *See also* Timeline of Polish Rulers

Bolesław the Brave. *See* Bolesław I Chrobry. *See also* Timeline of Polish Rulers

Bolesław the Pious. *See* Kalisz

Bolesław the Wrymouth. *See* Bolesław III Krzywousty; Płock. *See also* Timeline of Polish Rulers

Bolsheviks. *See* Piłsudski, Józef

Bonaparte, Napoleon. *See* Księstwo Warszawskie; Somosierra, bitwa

book of wishes and complaints. *See* książka skarg i wniosków

bread and salt. *See* chleb i sól

Breslau. *See* Wrocław

Brezhnev Doctrine. *See* Układ Warszawski

bride, bridegroom. *See* oczepiny

Bromberg. *See* Bydgoszcz.

Brothers of the Most Holy Redeemer. *See* Radio Maryja

buckwheat groats. *See* kasza.

bugle call. *See* kościół Mariacki

Bukowina. *See* rabacja galicyjska

Bull of Gniezno. *See* Bulla gnieźnieńska

cabaret. *See* kabaret

cabbage stew. *See* bigos.

café. *See* kawiarnia

cakes. *See* ciasta

Calvinism. *See* Łaski, Jan; reformacja

canals. *See* Bydgoszcz; Kanał Augustowski; Kanał Elbląski; rzeki

canapés. *See* imieniny, urodziny; kanapki

capping ceremony. *See* oczepiny

CARE packages. *See* paczki żywnościowe

carols. *See* kolędnicy

Carpathian Mountains. *See* Beskidy; Bieszczady; Brama Morawska; góral; Karpaty; malarstwo na szkle; Pieniny; Podkarpacie; Rzeszów; strój ludowy; Tatry

Carpatho-Rusyn. *See* Łemkowie, mniejszości narodowe i etniczne

cartoons. *See* "Tango"; *Bolek i Lolek*

carved wooden figurines. *See* kapliczka przydrożna; świątki

castle. *See* Ogrodzieniec; orle gniazda; Wawel; Zamek Królewski w Warszawie

cathedral. *See* Gniezno; Kościół rzymskokatolicki; Wawel

Catherine the Great of Russia. *See* konfederacja barska; Poniatowski, Stanisław II August

Catholic Church. *See* Kościół rzymskokatolicki

cavalry. *See* husaria; ułan

cemetery. *See* cmentarz; cmentarze radzieckie w Polsce; Dzień Wszystkich Świętych

censorship. *See* socrealizm; wydawnictwa drugiego obiegu

Centennial Hall. *See* Hala Stulecia

Certificate of Polish Nationality. *See* Karta Polaka

cheek-kissing. *See* całowanie w policzek; dzień dobry, do widzenia

Chicago. *See* LOT, Polskie Linie Lotnicze LOT
Chopin monument. *See* pomnik Chopina w Warszawie
Christianization of Poland. *See* chrzest Polski; Grunwald, bitwa pod Grunwaldem
Christmas, Christmas Eve. *See* Boże Narodzenie; kasza; kolędnicy; Turoń; Wigilia
Churchill, Winston. *See* Jałta, konferencja jałtańska. *See also* Important Twentieth-Century Conferences Affecting Poland
CIA. *See* Kukliński, Ryszard; Pawłowski, Jerzy
cigarettes. *See* tytoń, papierosy
cinema of moral anxiety. *See* Kieślowski, Krzysztof
circle, triangle. *See* kółeczko, trójkącik
Cistercian monasteries. *See* pielgrzymki
Cistercian order. *See* cystersi
city. *See* miasto i wieś
Clemenceau, Georges. *See* traktat wersalski. *See also* Important Twentieth-Century Conferences Affecting Poland
climate, seasons. *See* klimat, pory roku
cloth hall. *See* Kraków
clothes by weight. *See* odzież na wagę
coat of arms. *See* szlachta polska
coffee house. *See* kawiarnia; cyganeria krakowska.
coffin portrait. *See* portret trumienny
Cold War. *See* Brzeziński, Zbigniew; Miłosz, Czesław
Collegium Novum. *See* Uniwersytet Jagielloński
Colorado potato beetle. *See* czyn społeczny; stonka ziemniaczana
COMECON. *See* Rada Wzajemnej Pomocy Gospodarczej (RWPG)
Commission of National Education. *See* Komisja Edukacji Narodowej; oświecenie
communism. *See* demoludy; komunizm
Communist Party. *See* list 59, Memoriał 59; Polska Zjednoczona Partia Robotnicza (PZPR)
composers, conductors. *See* Chopin, Fryderyk; Górecki, Henryk; Kilar, Wojciech; Komeda, Krzysztof; Lutosławski, Witold; Moniuszko, Stanisław; Paderewski, Ignacy Jan; Penderecki, Krzysztof; Preisner, Zbigniew; Szymanowski, Karol Fryderyk; Wieniawski, Henryk
concentration camp. *See* Majdanek; Oświęcim; "polskie obozy koncentracyjne"; Sobibór; Treblinka; Zamość
concrete slab apartment house blocks. *See* bloki z wielkiej płyty
conductors. *See* composers, conductors
confederation. *See* konfederacja barska; konfederacja, rokosz, zajazd
Congress Hall. *See* Pałac Kultury i Nauki w Warszawie
Congress Kingdom. *See* Królestwo Kongresowe, "Kongresówka"
Congress of Vienna. *See* Królestwo Kongresowe, "Kongresówka"
conspiratorial high-school certificate. *See* tajne komplety
Constantine (Archduke). *See* powstanie listopadowe
Constitution of May 3. *See* konfederacja targowicka; Konstytucja 3 maja; Świątynia Opatrzności Bożej
Constitutional Court. *See* sądownictwo
Copernicus, Nicolaus. *See* Kopernik, Mikołaj
coronation sword of the Piasts. *See* Wawel
Corpus Christi. *See* Boże Ciało; dni wolne od pracy; lajkonik; pielgrzymki
Cossacks, Cossack uprisings. *See* Kozacy, powstania kozackie
Courier from Warsaw. *See* Jeziorański, Zdzisław
courts, administration of justice. *See* sądownictwo
cow-candy. *See* krówki
Cracow. *See* Kraków
Crooked Forest. *See* osobliwości przyrodnicze
crown. *See* polskie regalia królewskie
Crown of the Polish Kingdom. *See* Korona Królestwa Polskiego
Crypt of the Meritorious. *See* Skałka
cult film. *See* filmy kultowe
curiosities of nature. *See* osobliwości przyrodnicze
Curzon Line. *See* linia Curzona; pakt Ribbentrop-Mołotow
Czech. *See* Biblia; chrzest Polski; Lech, Czech, Rus; Mieszko I; mniejszości narodowe i etniczne; Opole; orle gniazda; reakcja pogańska; uczta u Wierzynka; Wrocław
Czech Republic. *See* Beskidy; Brama Morawska; Karpaty; Odra; Sudety; Śląsk; traktat ateński
Czechoslovakia. *See* demoludy; Układ Warszawski; Wyścig Pokoju

dance, folk dance. *See* krakowiak; mazur, mazurek; polonez
Danzig. *See* Gdańsk
December 1970, December events. *See* grudzień 1970, wydarzenia grudniowe. *See also* Timeline of Polish Historical Months
Defense of the Gdańsk Post Office. *See* Obrona Poczty Polskiej
Deluge. *See* potop szwedzki
Demjaniuk, John. *See* Sobibór
Descent of the Holy Spirit. *See* dni wolne od pracy
devil Boruta. *See* Boruta, diabeł Boruta

dialects. See dialekty regionalne
dictionary. See Kopaliński, Władysław; Linde, Samuel Bogumił
Dimitry the Pretender. See Dymitr Samozwaniec
director (cinematic or theatrical). See filmy kultowe; Grotowski, Jerzy; Hanuszkiewicz, Adam; Holland, Agnieszka; Janda, Krystyna; Kantor, Tadeusz; Kieślowski, Krzysztof; Konwicki, Tadeusz; Osiecka, Agnieszka; Polański, Roman; Schiller, Leon; Stuhr, Jerzy; Wajda, Andrzej; Zanussi, Krzysztof; zespół filmowy
districts, division into districts. See Bolesław III Krzywousty
Dobrawa. See chrzest Polski
doctorate. See edukacja
dogs. See owczarek podhalański
Don Cossacks. See Kozacy, powstania kozackie
doughnuts. See ciasta; ostatki
draft (military). see wiek
dragon's cave. See smok wawelski, smocza jama
drinking age. See wiek
Drzymała's wagon. See wóz Drzymały
Duchy of Warsaw. See "Boże coś Polskę"; Księstwo Warszawskie
duck's blood soup. See swaty, zaręczyny

eagles' nests. See orle gniazda
East Germany. See demoludy; Wyścig Pokoju
East Prussia. See Prusy
Easter. See Wielkanoc, Wielki Tydzień
Easter eggs. See pisanki
Easter Monday. See Lany Poniedziałek, Śmigus-dyngus
Easter palm. See palma wielkanocna
Eastern Europe. See Europa środkowa, Europa wschodnia
Eastern Orthodox Church. See unia brzeska; religie

eastern territories. See kresy wschodnie; ziemie odzyskane
eatery. See bar mleczny
educational system. See edukacja
elections of 1947. See wybory 1947
elections of 2011. See wybory 2011
Electoral Gazette. See Gazeta Wyborcza
emigration. See emigracja polska; Wielka Emigracja
end-of-school party. See studniówka
engagements. See swaty, zaręczyny
England. See kampania wrześniowa; Łaski, Jan; odzież na wagę; Polskie Siły Powietrzne w drugiej wojnie światowej
Enigma machine. See Enigma
Enlightenment. See epoki (okresy) literackie; oświecenie. See also Timeline of Polish Literary Figures Cited
Entente. See traktat wersalski
Estonia. See Białystok; Europa Wschodnia i Środkowa; Krzyżacy, zakon krzyżacki
ethnic Germans. See Volksdeutsche
Europa Bazaar. See Jarmark Europa
European Union. See hydraulik polski; Kwaśniewski, Aleksander; traktat ateński
Eye of the Sea. See Morskie Oko

family. See gościnność
Fat Thursday. See ostatki
Faustina, Saint. See Kowalska, siostra Maria Faustyna
Feast at Wierzynek's. See uczta u Wierzynka
festivals. See festiwale filmowe; festiwale muzyczne
Fiat. See Fiat 125p, duży Fiat; Fiat 126p, mały Fiat; Polonez
Fighting Poland. See Polska Walcząca
film festivals. See festiwale filmowe

First Brigade. See Legiony Polskie 1914–1918
First Communion. See Pierwsza Komunia
First Polish Republic. See Rzeczpospolita Polska
first-name basis. See pan, pani, państwo
"fist of Gołota." See Gołota, Andrzej
flag of the Republic of Poland. See flaga
flagship carrier. See LOT, Polskie Linie Lotnicze LOT
Flying University. See Uniwersytet Latający
folk art. See Cepelia (Centrala Przemysłu Ludowego i Artystycznego); malarstwo na szkle; świątki; wycinanki
folk dance. See krakowiak; mazur, mazurek; polonez; tańce ludowe
folk dress. See góral; strój ludowy
food packages. See paczki żywnościowe
food store. See sklep
food-ration cards. See stan wojenny
football. See piłka nożna
forbidden songs. See zakazane piosenki
Forefather's Eve (play). See Dziady (Romantic play)
forest spirit. See Boruta, diabeł Boruta
Fourth Polish Republic. See Trzecia Rzeczpospolita Polska
Four-Year Sejm. See Konstytucja 3 maja
France. See hydraulik polski; Księstwo Warszawskie; Poniatowski, Józef; rząd na uchodźstwie; Walewska, Maria; "Warszawianka"
Frankists. See Frank, Jakub
fraternities. See korporacje akademickie
Free City of Gdańsk. See Wolne Miasto Gdańsk

free Saturdays. *See* wolne soboty
free-land. *See* wola
friend. *See* przyjaciel, przyjaciółka

Galician slaughter. *See* rabacja galicyjska
Gallus Anonymous. *See* Gall Anonim
garden plots. *See* działka
gas chambers. *See* Majdanek; Oświęcim; Treblinka
Gdańsk Accord. *See* Stocznia Gdańska
General Government, General-gouvernement. *See* Generalne Gubernatorstwo
gentry. *See* szlachta polska
George the Hedgehog. *See* Jeż Jerzy
Gerlach. *See* Karpaty
Germans. *See* Grunwald, bitwa pod Grunwaldem; Katyń, zbrodnia katyńska; mniejszości narodowe i etniczne; Opole; Orle Gniazda; powstania śląskie; Psie Pole, bitwa; Volksdeutsche; Wanda; wóz Drzymały; Września
Germany. *See* chrzest Polski; Hala Stulecia; kresy wschodnie, ziemie odzyskane; Nivea krem; pakt Ribbentrop-Mołotow; kampania wrześniowa; Pomorze; Śląsk; Wolne Miasto Gdańsk; zjazd gnieźnieński
Gestapo. *See* Pawiak; Szucha, Aleja Szucha w Warszawie
ghetto. *See* getta żydowskie; granatowa policja; powstanie w getcie warszawskim
glass painting. *See* malarstwo na szkle
Gliwice Provocation. *See* prowokacja gliwicka
Gniezno Cathedral doors. *See* Gniezno
Gniezno papal bull. *See* Bulla gnieźnieńska
Gniezno Synod. *See* zjazd gnieźnieński

gnomes. *See* Wrocław
gods, goddesses: pagan. *See* Marzanna, topienie Marzanny; Perun, Pierun
golden age. *See* Zygmunt I Stary
golden freedoms. *See* Wiśniowiecki, Michał Korybut; złota polska wolność
golden horn. *See* Wernyhora; Wesele
Golden Lion. *See* festiwale filmowe
Golden Palm. *See* Janda, Krystyna; Polański, Roman; Wajda, Andrzej
Goldwyn, Samuel. *See* Gelbfisz, Szmuel
goodbye. *See* całowanie w rękę; dzień dobry, do widzenia
gothic. *See* architektura romańska, gotycka, renesansowa, barokowa; kościół Mariacki; Stwosz, Wit; Wawel
government in exile. *See* rząd na uchodźstwie
grade school. *See* edukacja
grammatical case. *See* przypadki gramatyczne
Grand Duchy of Lithuania. *See* pogoń; Rzeczpospolita Obojga Narodów
Granville, Christine. *See* Skarbek, Krystyna
gray eminence. *See* szara eminencja
Gray Legions. *See* Szare Szeregi
Great Britain. *See* Jałta, konferencja jałtańska. *See also* Important Twentieth-Century Conferences Affecting Poland
Great Emigration. *See* Wielka Emigracja
great field hetman. *See* hetman
Great Orchestra of Christmas Charity. *See* Wielka Orkiestra Świątecznej Pomocy
Great Rafter. *See* Zakopane
Greater Poland. *See* Wielkopolska.
Greater Poland Uprising. *See* powstanie wielkopolskie

Greek Catholics. *See* religie; unia brzeska
Green Holiday. *See* dni wolne od pracy; Zielone Świątki
greeting. *See* całowanie w policzek, podanie ręki; dzień dobry, do widzenia
greetings and wishes. *See* "Sto lat"
Group for Operational Maneuver Reactions. *See* GROM

hall beneath the heads. *See* Wawel
hand-kissing, hand-shaking. *See* całowanie w policzek, podanie ręki
Hanseatic League. *See* Gdańsk; Toruń
Hasidism. *See* chasydyzm; Frank, Jakub
Hel Peninsula. *See* Hel, Półwysep Helski
hello. *See* całowanie w rękę, podanie ręki; dzień dobry, do widzenia, proszę, dziękuję
Hercules' Cudgel. *See* osobliwości przyrodnicze
hero of labor. *See* Przygoda na Mariensztacie
herring day. *See* ostatki
Hetman of the Crown. *See* hetman
high school. *See* edukacja; matura; studniówka
High Tatras. *See* góral; Morskie Oko; oscypek; Tatry; Zakopane; Zakopane: styl zakopiański
higher education. *See* edukacja
highlander. *See* baca; góral; Podhale
highwaymen. *See* ciupaga; Janosik, Juraj
hip-hop music. *See* hip-hop
Hitler, Adolf. *See* Generalne Gubernatorstwo; powstanie w getcie warszawskim; prowokacja gliwicka; rzeź Woli; Wilczy Szaniec
holidays. *See* dni wolne od pracy
Holland (Netherlands). *See* arianie, bracia polscy; Łaski, Jan

Holocaust. *See* Generalne Gubernatorstwo; getta żydowskie; Kielce, pogrom kielecki; Kosiński, Jerzy; Różewicz, Tadeusz; Umschlagplatz; Żydzi w Polsce

Holy Cross Mountains. *See* dąb Bartek; Góry Świętokrzyskie; Kazania świętokrzyskie

Holy Roman Empire. *See* zjazd gnieźnieński

Holy Week. *See* Wielkanoc, Wielki Tydzień

Home Army. *See* Armia Krajowa; Żołnierze Wyklęci

home brew. *See* wódka

honey. *See* miód, miód pitny

honor. *See* honor; szlachta polska.

hospitality, Polish. *See* gościnność

Hungary. *See* Batory, Stefan; Bem, Józef; husaria; demoludy; Jadwiga, królowa; kontusz; Węgry; Władysław III Warneńczyk

hunter's stew. *See* bigos

hunters of skins affair. *See* łowcy skór

hussars. *See* husaria

Independence Day. *See* dni wolne od pracy

Independent Self-Governing Trade Union "Solidarity." *See* Solidarność

Institute of National Memory. *See* lista Wildsteina

intelligentsia. *See* inteligencja

International Chopin Piano Competition. *See* Chopin, Konkurs Chopinowski; Rubinstein, Artur

International Festival of Song. *See* festiwale muzyczne

International Women's Day. *See* Dzień Kobiet

interwar period. *See* dwudziestolecie międzywojenne. *See also* Timeline of Polish Literary Figures Cited

Iron Curtain. *See* demoludy

Islam. *See* religie

Italy. *See* Bona Sforza; Dąbrowski, Jan Henryk; "Mazurek Dąbrowskiego"

Jadwiga of Anjou, Queen. *See* Jadwiga, królowa

Jagiellonian dynasty. *See* Jagiełło, Władysław II; Uniwersytet Jagielloński. *See also* Timeline of Polish Rulers

Jagiellonian University. *See* Uniwersytet Jagielloński

January Uprising of 1863. *See* powstanie styczniowe. *See also* Major Polish National and Regional Uprisings

Jarocin Rock Festival. *See* Jarocin, festiwal w Jarocinie

Jasna Góra Appeal. *See* Apel Jasnogórski

Jasna Góra Monastery. *See* Jasna Góra

Jasna Góra Vows of the Polish Nation. *See* Apel Jasnogórski

Jedwabne Pogrom of 1941. *See* Jedwabne, pogrom w Jedwabnem

Jehovah's Witnesses. *See* religie

jester. *See* Stańczyk

Jesuit order. *See* Kostka, Stanisław; oświecenie; reformacja; Skarga, Piotr

Jesus statue. *See* Świebodzin

Jewish cemeteries. *See* kirkuty

Jewish Fighting Organization. *See* powstanie w getcie warszawskim; Żydowski Związek Wojskowy

Jewish ghettos. *See* Bielscy, bracia; getta żydowskie; powstanie w getcie warszawskim; Sendlerowa, Irena;

Jewish Military Union. *See* Żydowski Związek Wojskowy

Jewish Theater of Warsaw. *See* Kamińska, Ida

Jews in Poland. *See* Żydzi w Polsce

John Paul II (pope). *See* Jan Paweł II (papież)

Jordan Park. *See* ogród (park) jordanowski

JP2 generation. *See* Jan Paweł II (papież)

Judaism. *See* chasydyzm; mniejszości narodowe i etniczne; religie; Żydzi w Polsce

judiciary. *See* sądownictwo

July 1956 events in Poznań. *See* odwilż gomułkowska, październik 1956

July 22 Manifesto. *See* Manifest Lipcowy; Stadion Dziesięciolecia w Warszawie

June 1956 incidents. *See* czerwiec 1956, wypadki czerwcowe. *See also* Timeline of Polish Historical Months

June 1976 events. *See* czerwiec 1976, wydarzenia czerwcowe; Komitet Obrony Robotników (KOR). *See also* Timeline of Polish Historical Months

kabbalah. *See* chasydyzm; Frank, Jakub

Kaliningrad. *See* Prusy

Kalisz Statute. *See* Kalisz

kasha. *See* kasza

Kashubian. *See* Kaszuby, język kaszubski

Katowice Saucer. *See* Spodek w Katowicach

Katyń massacre. *See* Katyń, zbrodnia katyńska

Kazan' school of linguistics. *See* Baudouin de Courtenay, Jan

Kazimierz the Great. *See* Kazimierz III Wielki

Kazimierz the Restorer. *See* Bolesław II Śmiały; Wars i Sawa

kerosene lamp. *See* lampa naftowa

Kingdom of Poland. *See* Królestwo Kongresowe, "Kongresówka"

Konopnicka's Credo. *See* "Rota Marii Konopnickiej"

Kostka, Saint Stanislaw. *See* Kostka, Święty Stanisław

Kościuszko Insurrection. *See* insurekcja kościuszkowska;

Kościuszko, Tadeusz. *See also* Major Polish National and Regional Uprisings
Kościuszko Mound. *See* kopiec
Kozakiewicz's gesture. *See* Kozakiewicz, Władysław
Krak, King. *See* kopiec
Krakovian creche. *See* szopka krakowska
Kraków Academy. *See* Komisja Edukacji Narodowej; Modrzewski, Andrzej Frycz; Nawojka; Parkoszowic, Jakub; Uniwersytet Jagielloński

La Varsovienne. *See* "Warszawianka"
labor day. *See* dni wolne od pracy
ladies' herring night. *See* ostatki
Lady with Ermine. *See* Dama z łasiczką
Laments. *See* Kochanowski, Jan; Treny
landholdings. *See* Lubomirscy, rodzina Lubomirskich; Potocki, Jan
landowner's manor house. *See* dwór szlachecki
language. *See* aspekt dokonany i niedokonany; "Daj, ać ja pobruszę, a ty poczywaj"; dialekty regionalne; język polski, języki słowiańskie; liczebniki polskie; rodzaj męskoosobowy
large Fiat. *See* Fiat 125p, duży Fiat
latifundia. *See* Lubomirscy, rodzina Lubomirskich; Potocki, Jan
Latvia, Latvian. *See* Bałtowie; Krzyżacy, zakon krzyżacki
Lenin, Vladimir. *See* Dzień Kobiet
Leon Schiller State Higher School of Cinema. *See* Łódzka Szkoła Filmowa
Leonardo da Vinci. *See* Dama z łasiczką
Lesser Poland. *See* Małopolska.
Lew Rywin affair. *See* Rywin, afera
life expectancy. *See* palenie papierosów

line, waiting in. *See* kolejka, kultura kolejkowa
literary periods. *See* epoki (okresy) literackie. *See also* Timeline of Polish Literary Figures Cited
Lithuania. *See* Bałtowie; Bielscy, bracia; Bona Sforza; hetman; Jagiełło, Władysław II; Kanał Augustowski; kresy wschodnie; linia Curzona; magnateria; Mickiewicz, Adam; mniejszości narodowe i etniczne; Ostra Brama; Pan Tadeusz; Plater, Emilia; Podlasie, Polesie; pogoń; Suwalszczyzna; Sybir, Sybiracy; Wilno
little Fiat. *See* Fiat 126p, mały Fiat
Lloyd George, David. *See* traktat wersalski. *See also* Important Twentieth-Century Conferences Affecting Poland
Łódź Film School. *See* Łódzka Szkoła Filmowa
London. *See* rząd na uchodźstwie
Lower Silesia. *See* Śląsk; Wrocław
Luftwaffe. *See* Wieluń
Lusatian culture. *See* Biskupin
Lutheran. *See* reformacja; religie
L'viv. *See* Lwów

M1, M2, M3 apartments. *See* mieszkanie M1, M2, M3
Magdeburg law. *See* prawo magdeburskie
magnates. *See* magnateria; szlachta polska
Major Hubal. *See* Hubal
Malbork. *See* Krzyżacy, zakon krzyżacki
manor house. *See* dwór szlachecki
March 1968 events. *See* marzec 1968, wydarzenia marcowe. *See also* Timeline of Polish Historical Months
Mariacki bugle call. *See* hejnał mariacki
Marian Church. *See* kościół Mariacki
Marian cult. *See* Bogurodzica
Mariavite. *See* religie

Marienburg. *See* Krzyżacy, zakon krzyżacki
market hall. *See* targ, hala targowa
Marszałkowska Housing Complex. *See* Marszałkowska Dzielnica Mieszkaniowa
martial law. *See* stan wojenny
masculine-personal gender. *See* rodzaj męskoosobowy
master's degree. *See* edukacja
Masurian Lake District. *See* Mazury, Pojezierze Mazurskie
matchmaking. *See* swaty, zaręczyny
Matołek the Billy-Goat. *See* Koziołek Matołek
Max Factor. *See* Faktorowicz, Maksymilian
May 3 Constitution. *See* Konstytucja 3 maja
May coup d'état. *See* dwudziestolecie międzywojenne; Piłsudski, Józef
mead. *See* miód, miód pitny
meals. *See* posiłki
Memorandum of the 59. *See* list 59, Memoriał 59
memorial mound. *See* kopiec
Metro-Goldwyn-Mayer. *See* Gelbfisz, Szmuel
Michalik's Cavern. *See* cyganeria krakowska
Mickiewicz Monument. *See* Kraków
Middle Ages. *See* epoki (okresy) literackie. *See also* Timeline of Polish Literary Figures Cited
middle school. *See* edukacja
Military Council for National Salvation. *See* Jaruzelski, Wojciech; stan wojenny
military draft. *See* wiek
militia. *See* Ochotnicza Rezerwa Milicji Obywatelskiej (ORMO)
milk bar. *See* bar mleczny
miners, mining. *See* górnictwo
Miracle on the Vistula. *See* Piłsudski, Józef

ENGLISH INDEX

modernism. *See* epoki (okresy) literackie; Młoda Polska. *See also* Timeline of Polish Literary Figures Cited

Modlin Fortress. *See* Modlin, twierdza Modlin

mohair berets. *See* Radio Maryja

Molotov-Ribbentrop Pact. *See* pakt Ribbentrop-Mołotow

money. *See* monety, banknoty

months. *See* miesiące, nazwy miesięcy. *See also* Timeline of Polish Historical Months

Moravian Gate. *See* Beskidy; Brama Morawska; Sudety

Mother of God. *See* Bogurodzica; kult maryjny; Licheń

Mother of God of Częstochowa. *See* Matka Boska Częstochowska

Mother of God of Ostra Brama. *See* Ostra Brama

Mother Pole. *See* Bogurodzica; Matka Polka

motorcycle. *See* SHL

Motorized Detachments of the Citizens Militia. *See* Wujek, kopalnia; Zmotoryzowane Odwody Milicji Obywatelskiej (ZOMO)

mound, memorial mound. *See* kopiec

mountain wind. *See* halny

mountaineer. *See* góral; "Góralu, czy ci nie żal?"; Podhale

mountaineer's ax. *See* ciupaga

Museum of the History of Polish Jews. *See* powstanie w getcie warszawskim

Museum of the Warsaw Uprising. *See* druga wojna światowa: muzea

music festivals. *See* festiwale muzyczne

musicians. *See* composers, conductors; singers

mushrooms. *See* grzyby

mythology, Slavic. *See* Perun

Naliboki massacre. *See* Bielscy, bracia

nameday. *See* imieniny, urodziny

national anthem. *See* "Mazurek Dąbrowskiego"

National Book Award. *See* Nike

National Democratic Movement. *See* Narodowa Demokracja, endecja

National Festival of Polish Song. *See* festiwale muzyczne

National Gallery of Contemporary Art in Warsaw. *See* Zachęta

National Independence Day. *See* jedenastego (11) listopada

national messianism. *See* mesjanizm polski

national minorities. *See* Dmowski, Roman; mniejszości narodowe i etniczne; Narutowicz, Gabriel

National Theater. *See* Hanuszkiewicz, Adam

NATO. *See* Kwaśniewski, Aleksander; Układ Warszawski

natural curiosities. *See* osobliwości przyrodnicze

navy-blue police. *See* granatowa policja

New Horizons Film Festival. *See* festiwale filmowe

new wave. *See* Barańczak, Stanisław

New Year's Eve. *See* dni wolne od pracy; sylwester, noc sylwestrowa

newspapers. *See* gazety

newsstand. *See* kiosk

Nicholas, Saint. *See* mikołajki

nighty-night. *See* dobranocka

Nijinsky, Vaslav. *See* Nyżyński, Wacław

Nivea Creme. *See* Nivea krem

NKVD. *See* Burza, akcja; Majdanek; Operacja Polska NKWD

Nobel Prize. *See* Curie, Maria Skłodowska; Miłosz, Czesław; Nagroda Nobla; *Quo vadis?*; Reymont, Władysław Stanisław; Sienkiewicz, Henryk; Singer, Isaac Bashevis; Szymborska, Wisława; Wałęsa, Lech

nobility. *See* szlachta polska

nomenclature. *See* nomenklatura

November 11, 1918. *See* jedenastego (11) listopada

November Uprising of 1831. *See* powstanie listopadowe. *See also* Major Polish National and Regional Uprisings

numerals. *See* liczebniki polskie

October 1956. *See* odwilż gomułkowska, październik 1956

Office of Security. *See* Służba Bezpieczeństwa (SB)

old town. *See* Stare Miasto; Starówka

oldest Polish sentence. *See* "Daj, ać ja pobruszę, a ty poczywaj"

Olympic Games. *See* Małysz, Adam; Deyna, Kazimierz; igrzyska olimpijskie; Korzeniowski, Robert; Kowalczyk, Justyna; Kozakiewicz, Władysław; Pawłowski, Jerzy; piłka nożna; Szewińska, Irena Kirszenstein

open-faced sandwiches. *See* kanapki; posiłki

opera. *See* Kwiecień, Mariusz

Operation Mountaineer. *See* Góral, akcja

Operation Storm. *See* Burza, akcja; Konwicki, Tadeusz

Operation Tannenberg. *See* Tannenberg, operacja

Order of Military Merit. *See* Order Virtuti Militari; Zawacka, Elżbieta

Order of Reborn Poland. *See* Małysz, Adam

Order of the Teutonic Knights. *See* Krzyżacy, zakon krzyżacki

organized community service. *See* czyn społeczny

Orlen affair. *See* Orlen, afera

Oscar-winner. *See* Polański, Roman; Wajda, Andrzej

Ossoliński National Institute. *See* Ossolineum, Zakład Narodowy imienia Ossolińskich
Our Lady of Sorrows, Queen of Poland. *See* Licheń
Our Lady of the Gate of Dawn. *See* Ostra Brama

Pact of Friendship, Cooperation, and Mutual Assistance. *See* Układ o Przyjaźni, Współpracy I Pomocy Wzajemnej
pagan gods. *See* Perun; Światowid ze Zbrucza
pagan reaction. *See* Bolesław II Śmiały; reakcja pogańska
paid time off. *See* urlop, wakacje
painter. *See* artist
Palace of Culture and Science in Warsaw. *See* Pałac Kultury i Nauki w Warszawie
Palm Sunday. *See* pielgrzymki; Wielkanoc, Wielki Tydzień
papercut art, papercutting. *See* Kurpie; Łowicz; wycinanki
Paris Peace. *See* traktat wersalski
parliament. *See* Sejm; Sejm RP
partitions of Poland. *See* rozbiory
Pawiak prison. *See* Palmiry; Pawiak
Peace Race. *See* Wyścig Pokoju
peasant mania. *See* Młoda Polska
Pen Club. *See* Żeromski, Stefan
Pentecost. *See* Zielone Świątki
Pentecostal. *See* religie
People's Army. *See* Armia Ludowa
people's democracies. *See* demoludy
People's Republic of Poland. *See* Polska Rzeczpospolita Ludowa (PRL); PRL, nostalgia za PRL-em
petty gentry. *See* szlachta polska
Pewex stores. *See* Peweks
Piast dynasty. *See* Mieszko I; Piastowie, dynastia. *See also* Timeline of Polish Rulers
Pienine Mountains. *See* Pieniny; Karpaty
pigeon, pigeon-breeding. *See* gołębie

pilgrimages. *See* pielgrzymki
Pioneer Movie Theater. *See* kino studyjne
playground games. *See* gry podwórkowe
please. *See* proszę
Podhale sheepdog. *See* owczarek podhalański
pogrom. *See* Jedwabne, pogrom w Jedwabnem; Kielce, pogrom kielecki; Lwów, pogrom lwowski
Poland. *See* Polska
Poland the granary of Europe. *See* Polska spichlerzem Europy
Poles abroad. *See* Polonia
police. *See* granatowa policja; Milicja Obywatelska
Polish Air Force in World War II. *See* Polskie Siły Powietrzne w drugiej wojnie światowej
Polish Armed Forces. *See* Bóg, Honor, Ojczyzna; Siły Zbrojne RP
Polish Armed Forces Day. *See* dni wolne od pracy; przysięga Kościuszki
Polish Brethren. *See* arianie, bracia polscy; reformacja
Polish Committee for National Liberation. *See* Manifest Lipcowy
Polish Corridor. *See* Wolne Miasto Gdańsk
Polish Fiat 125p. *See* Fiat 125p, Fiat 126p
Polish Film School. *See* polska szkoła filmowa; zespół filmowy
Polish government in exile. *See* rząd na uchodźstwie
Polish Jazz School. *See* Komeda, Krzysztof
Polish language. *See* language
Polish Legions. *See* Legiony Polskie we Włoszech; Legiony Polskie 1914–1918; Dąbrowski, Jan Henryk; "Mazurek Dąbrowskiego"
Polish National Airlines. *See* LOT, Polskie Linie Lotnicze LOT

Polish national messianism. *See* mesjanizm polski
Polish numerals. *See* liczebniki polskie
Polish plumber. *See* hydraulik polski
Polish Primate. *See* Kościół rzymskokatolicki
Polish road to socialism. *See* Gomułka, Władysław
Polish royal regalia. *See* polskie regalia królewskie
Polish school of mathematical logic. *See* szkoła lwowsko-warszawska logiki matematycznej
Polish school of poster art. *See* plakaty
Polish State Railways. *See* PKP, PKS, MZK
Polish Tourist Organization. *See* hydraulik polski; Polskie Towarzystwo Turystyczno-Krajoznawcze (PTTK)
Polish underground army. *See* Armia Krajowa; Polska Walcząca; powstanie warszawskie; Żołnierze Wyklęci
Polish United Workers Party. *See* komunizm; Polska Zjednoczona Partia Robotnicza (PZPR)
Polish-Bolshevik War. *See* Piłsudski, Józef; wojna polsko-bolszewicka
Polish-Lithuanian Commonwealth. *See* Rzeczpospolita Obojga Narodów
Polish-Ukrainian War. *See* wojna polsko-ukraińska
political parties. *See* partie polityczne
polka. *See* tańce ludowe
polonaise. *See* polonez
Pomerania. *See* Pomorze
poor theater. *See* Grotowski, Jerzy
pope. *See* Kościół rzymskokatolicki
Pope John Paul II. *See* Jan Paweł II (papież)

ENGLISH INDEX 329

poppy. *See* mak
Post Office. *See* Obrona Poczty Polskiej; Wolne Miasto Gdańsk
postage stamp, first Polish. *See* znaczek pocztowy
postcommunists. *See* komunizm
posters. *See* plakaty
postmodernism. *See* epoki (okresy) literackie
Poznań International Trade Fairs. *See* Poznań
Poznań June. *See* czerwiec 1956, wypadki czerwcowe. *See also* Timeline of Polish Historical Months
Prague Linguistics School. *See* Baudouin de Courtenay, Jan
presidential palace. *See* Belweder; Poniatowski, Józef
Primate of the Millennium. *See* Wyszyński, Stefan
printing. *See* drukarstwo
privatization. *See* prywatyzacja
prophet-poet of the nation. *See* wieszcz narodowy
propination. *See* karczma
Protestant Reformation. *See* Łaski, Jan; reformacja
Protestantism. *See* religie
proverbs. *See* przłysowia narodowe
Prussia. *See* insurekcja kościuszkowska; Prusy; rozbiory; saskie czasy, noc saska; wóz Drzymały
Prussian language. *See* Bałtowie
Prussian Partition. *See* Polska A i B; "Rota Marii Konopnickiej"
Prussian tribute. *See* Zygmunt I Stary
pure form. *See* Witkacy

Queen of Poland of Sorrows. *See* Licheń
Queen Zofia's Bible. *See* Biblia

Racławice Panorama. *See* Kossak, Wojciech; *Panorama Racławicka*; Racławice
Radio Free Europe. *See* Radio Wolna Europa

Radio Maria. *See* Radio Maryja
raftsman. *See* flisak; lajkonik
reborn Poland. *See* Druga Rzeczpospolita Polska; Polska Odrodzona
recovered territories. *See* Jałta, konferencja jałtańska; ziemie odzyskane
red and white. *See* flaga
Red Guitars. *See* Czerwone Gitary
Reformation. *See* reformacja
regional dialects. *See* dialekty regionalne
Relief of Vienna. *See* odsiecz wiedeńska; Sobieski, Jan III Sobieski
religions. *See* drukarstwo; religie
religious phrases. *See* "Niech będzie pochwalony Jezus Chrystus"
Renaissance. *See* architektura romańska, gotycka, renesansowa, barokowa; epoki (okresy) literackie; *See also* Timeline of Polish Literary Figures Cited
Republic of Poland. *See* Polska
required readings. *See* lektura szkolna, lektura obowiązkowa
retirement age. *See* wiek
Righteous among Nations. *See* Fogg, Mieczysław; ogrody zoologiczne; Sendlerowa, Irena
rivers. *See* rzeki
roadside chapels. *See* kapliczka przydrożna
Roman Catholic church. *See* Kościół rzymskokatolicki; religie
romanesque. *See* architektura romańska, gotycka, renesansowa, barokowa
Romanticism. *See* epoki (okresy) literackie. *See also* Timeline of Polish Literary Figures Cited
Round Table Discussions. *See* Okrągły Stół, rozmowy Okrągłego Stołu
royal castle in Warsaw. *See* Zamek Królewski w Warszawie
Russia. *See* konfederacja targowicka; Królestwo Kongresowe,

"Kongresówka"; mniejszości narodowe i etniczne; powstanie listopadowe; rewolucja roku 1905; Rokossowski, Konstanty; rozbiory; Sybir, Sybiracy; Związek Socjalistycznych Republik Radzieckich (ZSRR)

Saint Andrew's Eve. *See* andrzejki
Saint Anne's Mountain. *See* pielgrzymki
Saint Catherine's Eve. *See* andrzejki
Saint John's Eve. *See* noc świętojańska
Saint Mary's Basilica. *See* Kraków
Saint Maurice's Spear. *See* polskie regalia królewskie; zjazd gnieźnieński
salt mine. *See* Wieliczka
sandwiches. *See* kanapki
Santa Claus. *See* Boże Narodzenie
Sarmatian. *See* sarmatyzm
satellites. *See* demoludy
sausage. *See* kiełbasa
Saxon Night. *See* saskie czasy, noc saska
scepter. *See* polskie regalia królewskie
scythemen. *See* Plater, Emilia; Racławice
seacoast. *See* Wybrzeże Bałtyckie
Second Polish Republic. *See* Druga Rzeczpospolita Polska
secondary publication outlets. *See* wydawnictwa drugiego obiegu
secret police. *See* Służba Bezpieczeństwa (SB)
secret protocol. *See* pakt Ribbentrop-Mołotow
security service. *See* ochrona
September 1, 1939. *See* kampania wrześniowa
September campaign. *See* kampania wrześniowa
Seven Wonders of Poland. *See* Kanał Elbląski
Seventh Day Adventists. *See* religie
shale gas. *See* gaz łupkowy

Sharp Gate. *See* Ostra Brama

sheep's milk cheese. *See* oscypek

shepherd. *See* baca

shop. *See* sklep

Shrovetide, Carnival. *See* ostatki

Siberia. *See* Sybir, Sybiracy

Silesia. *See* Śląsk

Silesian uprisings. *See* powstania śląskie

singers. *See* Bodo, Eugeniusz; Doda; Fogg, Mieczysław; German, Anna; Grechuta, Marek; Jantar, Anna; Kaczmarski, Jacek; Kiepura, Jan; Kwiecień, Mariusz; Maanam i Kora; Niemen, Czesław; Ordonówna, Hanka; Rodowicz, Maryla; Sabała; Villas, Violetta

sir. *See* pan, pani, państwo

Skamandrites. *See* Skamander

skin hunters. *See* łowcy skór

Slavic languages. *See* język polski, języki słowiańskie

Slavic mythology. *See* Perun

sleigh ride. *See* kulig

Slovak, Slovakia. *See* ciupaga; Karpaty; Łemkowie; mniejszości narodowe i etniczne; Pieniny; Tatry

smoking. *See* palenie papierosów; tytoń, papierosy

Smolensk air disaster. *See* Smoleńsk, katastrofa pod Smoleńskiem

soap opera. *See* telenowela

soccer. *See* Deyna, Kazimierz; piłka nożna

socialism. *See* demoludy; komunizm

socialist realism. *See* "Przygoda na Mariensztacie"; socrealizm;

soda water carts. *See* pijalnia piwa

Solidarity. *See* Solidarność

soup. *See* barszcz; zupa; żurek

Soviet army. *See* Burza, akcja; cmentarze radzieccy w Polsce; Książ, zamek; Majdanek; Międzyrzecki Rejon Umocniony; Oświęcim; powstanie warszawskie; Treblinka

Soviet Bloc. *See* Radio Wolna Europa; Układ Warszawski; Zmotoryzowane Odwody Milicji Obywatelskiej (ZOMO)

Soviet Gothic. *See* Pałac Kultury i Nauki w Warszawie

Soviet NKVD. *See* Majdanek; Burza, akcja; Operacja Polska NKWD

Soviet Politburo. *See* Katyń, zbrodnia katyńska

Soviet Union. *See* demoludy; Jałta, konferencja jałtańska; Karta Polaka; Katyń, zbrodnia katyńska; kresy wschodnie; linia Curzona; list 59, Memoriał 59; odwilż gomułkowska, październik 1956; pakt Ribbentrop-Mołotow; Pałac Kultury i Nauki w Warszawie; Rokossowki, Konstanty; rząd na uchodźstwie; socrealizm; Sybir, Sybiracy; Układ Warszawski; wojna polsko-bolszewicka; wybory 1947; Związek Socjalistycznych Republik Radzieckich (ZSRR)

Soyuz 30. *See* Hermaszewski, Mirosław

Special Action Kraków. *See* Sonderaktion Krakau

special services force. *See* GROM

split-sleeved coat. *See* kontusz

sports. *See* sport w Polsce

Sports Lottery. *See* lotto

Stalin, Joseph. *See* Bierut, Bolesław; Jałta, konferencja jałtańska; Katyń, zbrodnia katyńska; Manifest Lipcowy; odwilż gomułkowska, październik 1956. *See also* Important Twentieth-Century Conferences Affecting Poland

standing in line. *See* kolejka, kultura kolejkowa

Stanislaw, Saint. *See* "Gaude, mater Polonia"; Stanisław ze Szczepanowa, Święty; Skałka

state collective farm. *See* Państwowe Gospodarstwo Rolne (PGR)

state holiday. *See* dni wolne od pracy

statue of Jesus, world's largest. *See* Świebodzin, pomnik Chrystusa Króla

statute of Kalisz. *See* Kalisz

steam locomotives. *See* Parowozownia Wolsztyn

Stettin. *See* Szczecin

store. *See* sklep

stork. *See* bocian

street food. *See* zapiekanka

street roundups. *See* Borowski, Tadeusz; granatowa policja

studio theater. *See* kino studyjne

Subcarpathia. *See* Podkarpacie

Sub-Carpathian voivodeship. *See* Rzeszów

Sudeten Mountains. *See* Brama Morawska; Sudety

summer cottage. *See* działka

summer solstice. *See* noc świętojańska

surnames. *See* nazwiska polskie

Swedish Deluge. *See* potop szwedzki

Swedish kings. *See* Wazowie, dynastia

symbolism. *See* epoki (okresy) literackie

Targowica Confederation. *See* konfederacja, rokosz, zajazd; konfederacja targowicka

Tatar. *See* hejnał mariacki; kościół Mariacki; lajkonik; kresy wschodnie; Podlasie, Polesie

Tatra Mountains. *See* ciupaga; góral; halny; Karpaty; Morskie Oko; Tatry

tavern. *See* karczma

Tehran Conference. *See* Anders, Władysław. *See also* Important Twentieth-Century Conferences Affecting Poland

television. *See* Telewizja Polska, TVP

Temple of Divine Providence. *See* Świątynia Opatrzności Bożej w Warszawie
Tenth-Anniversary Stadium. *See* Jarmark Europa; Stadion Dziesięciolecia w Warszawie
Teutonic Knights. *See* Krzyżacy, zakon krzyżacki
"thank you." *See* całowanie w rękę; dzień dobry, do widzenia
thaw. *See* odwilż gomułkowska, październik 1956
Third Partition. *See* Konstytucja 3 maja
Third Polish Republic. *See* Trzecia Rzeczpospolita Polska
Three Kings Day. *See* kolędnicy; Święto Trzech Króli
Threnodies. *See* Kochanowski, Jan; Treny
Thursday dinners. *See* Poniatowski, Stanisław II August
titles of nobility. *See* szlachta polska
tobacco. *See* palenie papierosów; tytoń, papierosy
toilets, public. *See* kółeczko, trójkącik
Tomb of the Unknown Soldier. *See* Grób Nieznanego Żołnierza
Toruń ginger cookies. *See* pierniki toruńskie
town hall. *See* prawo magdeburskie
town houses. *See* Kraków; prawo magdeburskie; Stare Miasto
towns and cities. *See* miasto i wise; województwo
townships. *See* województwo
trade hall. *See* prawo magdeburskie
trail of Cistercian monasteries. *See* pielgrzymki
trail of wooden architecture. *See* architektura drewniana
transport. *See* PKP, PKS, MZK
Treaty of Tilsit. *See* Księstwo Warszawskie
Treaty of Versailles. *See* traktat wersalski. *See also* Important Twentieth-Century Conferences Affecting Poland

tree, oldest Polish tree. *See* dąb Bartek
Tri-City. *See* Gdańsk; Gdynia; Sopot
Turkey. *See* Bem, Józef; Chocim, bitwa pod Chocimem; husaria; Kamieniec Podolski; kawiarnia; kontusz; Polska przedmurzem chrześcijaństwa; Światowid ze Zbrucza; uczta u Wierzynka; Władysław III Warneńczyk; Żółkiewski, Stanisław
two bared swords. *See* dwa nagie miecze

Ukraine. *See* Beskidy; Bieszczady; Bug; chasydyzm; Frank, Jakub; Jałta, konferencja jałtańska; Kamieniec Podolski; Karpaty; Katyń, zbrodnia katyńska; kresy wschodnie; linia Curzona; Lwów; mniejszości narodowe i etniczne; Ossolineum, Zakład Narodowy imienia Ossolińskich; pakt Ribbentrop-Mołotow; piłka nożna; Polesie; Przemyśl; rzeź wołyńska; Smoleńsk, katastrofa pod Smoleńskiem; konfederacja targowicka; wojna polsko-ukraińska
Ukrainian Insurgent Army. *See* rzeź wołyńska
underground army. *See* Armia Krajowa; Góral, akcja; Karski, Jan; Narodowe Siły Zbrojne; Polska Walcząca; powstanie warszawskie; Zawacka, Elżbieta; Żołnierze Wyklęci
underground publication outlets. *See* wydawnictwa drugiego obiegu
UNESCO. *See* Grotowski, Jerzy; Hala Stulecia; kalwaria; Kraków; Toruń; Wieliczka; Zamość
Uniate. *See* religie; unia brzeska
Union of Brześć. *See* unia brzeska
Union of Combatants for Free-

dom and Democracy. *See* szara eminencja
Union of Lublin. *See* Zygmunt II August
Unitarianism. *See* arianie, bracia polscy
United States. *See* Polonia
universities. *See* uniwersytety
university. *See* edukacja; uniwersytety
university fraternities. *See* korporacje akademickie
University of Lwów. *See* szkoła lwowsko-warszawska logiki matematycznej
University of Warsaw. *See* Kołakowski, Leszek; szkoła lwowsko-warszawska logiki matematycznej
University of Wilno. *See* filomaci i filareci; korporacje akademickie
UPA. *See* Ukrainian Insurgent Army
Upper Silesia. *See* Opole; Śląsk; traktat wersalski

vacation. *See* urlop, wakacje
vampire. *See* strzygoń, strzyga
Vasa dynasty. *See* Wazowie, dynastia
Versailles Conference. *See* Dmowski, Roman; jedenastego (11) listopada; Paderewski, Ignacy; traktat wersalski. *See also* Important Twentieth-Century Conferences Affecting Poland
Via Baltica highway. *See* Białystok
Vienna. *See* kawiarnia; Kostka, Stanisław; Młoda Polska; odsiecz wiedeńska; secesja
Vienna, Relief of. *See* odsiecz wiedeńska; Sobieski, Jan III Sobieski
Vilnius. *See* Wilno
Virgin Mary Queen of Poland. *See* Apel Jasnogórski; kult maryjny; Matka Boska Częstochowska, Czarna Madonna
visas. *See* wizy do USA

Vistula. *See* Wisła
vodka. *See* wódka.
voivodeship. *See* województwo
Voluntary Reserve of the Citizens' Militia. *See* Ochotnicza Rezerwa Milicji Obywatelskiej (ORMO)

Warsaw. *See* Warszawa
Warsaw Autumn. *See* festiwale muzyczne
Warsaw Ghetto Uprising. *See* powstanie w getcie warszawskim
Warsaw mermaid. *See* Syrena warszawska
Warsaw Pact. *See* Układ Warszawski
Warsaw Uprising. *See* powstanie warszawskie. *See also* Major Polish National and Regional Uprisings
waterways. *See* Kanał Augustowski; Kanał Elbląski; rzeki. *See also* individual river names.
Wawel royal castle and cathedral. *See* Wawel
Wawel tapestries. *See* arrasy wawelskie
Way Back, The. *See* Rawicz, Sławomir
Wedding, The. *See* Wesele; Wyspiański, Stanisław
wedding customs. *See* chleb i sól; oczepiny; swaty, zaręczyny
West Prussia. *See* Pomorze; Prusy; traktat wersalski
white eagle. *See* flaga; Orzeł Biały
White Lady. *See* Biała Dama
Wilanów Palace. *See* Wilanów
Wildstein's list. *See* lista Wildsteina
Wilson, Woodrow. *See* traktat wersalski. *See also* Important Twentieth-Century Conferences Affecting Poland
windmill. *See* wiatrak
windstorm. *See* halny
Władysław the Short. *See* Kazimierz III Wielki; Szczerbiec

Wojciech, Saint. *See* Wojciech, Święty; zjazd gnieźnieński
Wojtek the bear soldier. see Wojtek, niedźwiedź Wojtek
Wola massacre. *See* rzeź Woli; powstanie warszawskie
Wołyń massacre. *See* rzeź wołyńska
women in politics. *See* kobiety w polityce
women's day. *See* Dzień Kobiet
wooden architecture. *See* architektura drewniana
wooden figurines. *See* kapliczka przydrożna; świątki
Workers' Defense Committee. *See* Komitet Obrony Robotników (KOR)
World War I. *See* pierwsza wojna światowa in Polish Index
World War II. *See* druga wojna światowa in Polish Index
worry-worn Christ. *See* Chrystus Frasobliwy
writers. *See* Timeline of Polish Literary Figures Cited
Wrymouth's Will. *See* Bolesław III Krzywousty

Yalta Conference. *See* Jałta, konferencja jałtańska
"yes." *See* tak-tak
Yiddish language. *See* chasydyzm; Singer, Isaac Bachevis
Young Poland. *See* Młoda Polska; *Szał uniesień*

Zebrzydowski Revolt. *See* konfederacja, rokosz, zajazd
zoos. *See* ogrody zoologiczne
Zygmunt Bell. *See* dzwon Zygmunta
Zygmunt the Old. *See* dzwon Zygmunta; Kalisz; Modrzewski, Andrzej Frycz; Zygmunt I Stary. *See also* Timeline of Polish Rulers
Zygmunt's Column. *See* kolumna Zygmunta

ENGLISH INDEX 333

Polish Index

Main headings are in blue. Some of the headings below are more fully expanded in the English Index.

II Korpus Polski. *See* Anders, Władysław
III RP. *See* Trzecia Rzeczpospolita Polska
3 × TAK. *See* trzy razy tak
8 marca. *See* Dzień Kobiet
"A-a-a, Kotki dwa". *See* "Kotki dwa"
Adalbert. *See* Wojciech, Święty
Adwentyści Dnia Siódmego. *See* religie
afera Orlenu. *See* Orlen, afera
afera Rywina. *See* Rywin, afera
agencja ochrony. *See* ochrona
Ajdukiewicz, Kazimierz. *See* szkoła lwowsko-warszawska logiki matematycznej
AK. *See* Armia Krajowa
Akademia Krakowska. *See* Jadwiga, królowa; Kazimierz III Wielki; Komisja Edukacji Narodowej; Modrzewski, Andrzej Frycz; Nawojka; Parkoszowic, Jakub; Uniwersytet Jagielloński
akcja Burza. *See* Burza, akcja
akcja Góral. *See* Góral, akcja
"Ala ma kota"
Albrecht Hohenzollern. *See* Zygmunt II August
Alibabki
Anders, Władysław. *See also* Gułag, łagry; kampania wrześniowa; Monte Cassino, bitwa pod Monte Cassino; rząd na uchodźstwie; Wojtek, niedźwiedź

Andrzejewski, Jerzy. *See also* Komitet Obrony Robotników; Wajda, Andrzej
andrzejki
Anielewicz, Mordechaj. *See* powstanie w getcie warszawskim
animacja polska. *See* "Tango"
Antek. *See also* Prus, Bolesław
antysemityzm. *See* dwudziestolecie międzywojenne; Gross, Jan Tomasz; Jedwabne, pogrom w Jedwabnem; Kielce, pogrom kielecki; korporacje akademickie; marzec 1968, wydarzenia marcowe; Narodowa Demokracja, endecja; szara eminencja
Apel Jasnogórski. *See also* kult maryjny
araby, polskie konie arabskie
"Arbeit macht frei." *See* Oświęcim
architektura drewniana. *See also* Podhale
architektura eklektyczna. *See* Łódź
architektura romańska, gotycka, renesansowa, barokowa
arianie, bracia polscy. *See also* reformacja
Arkadia. *See* Łowicz
Arkonia. *See* korporacje akademickie
Armia Krajowa. *See also* Armia Ludowa; Baczyński, Krzysztof Kamil; Burza, akcja; druga wojna światowa; Inka; Jeziorański, Zdzisław; Karski, Jan; Komorowski, Tadeusz; Majdanek; Monte Cassino, bitwa pod Monte Cassino; "Nil," Generał; Polska Walcząca; powstanie warszawskie; Zawacka, Elżbieta; Żołnierze Wyklęci; Żydowski Związek Wojskowy
Armia Ludowa
arrasy wawelskie. *See also* Wawel
Arrinera
Arsenał Artystyczny. *See* festiwale muzyczne
artykuły henrykowskie. *See* Henryk I Walezy
aryjskie papiery. *See* Żegota
aspekt dokonany i niedokonany. *See also* język polski
August II Mocny. *See* Orzeł Biały; saskie czasy, noc saska; Toruń; Warszawa, bitwy
August, Zygmunt. *See* Zygmunt II August
Auschwitz-Birkenau. *See* Oświęcim; Treblinka
autostop
awangarda krakowska. *See* Skamander

Babia Góra. *See* Beskidy
baca
Bacciarelli, Marcello. *See also* Zamek Królewski w Warszawie
Baczyński, Krzysztof Kamil
Bagiński, Tomasz. *See* "Tango"
bajgiel. *See also* obwarzanek
Balcerowicz, Leszek. *See* Balce-

335

rowicz, plan Balcerowicza; prywatyzacja
Balcerowicz, plan Balcerowicza. *See also* Wałęsa, Lech
"Ballada o Janku Wiśniewskim." *See also* grudzień 1970, wydarzenia grudniowe
Baltona. *See* Peweks
Bałtowie. *See also* Wojciech, Święty
Bałtyk. *See also* Bałtowie; bursztyn; Gdańsk; Gdynia; Hel, Półwysep Helski; Sopot; Szczecin; Świnoujście; Wieluń; Wisła; Wolne Miasto Gdańsk; Wybrzeże Bałtyckie
Bamber, Bamberka
Bambrzy. *See* Bamber, Bamberka
Banach, Stefan
banknoty. *See* monety, banknoty
bankowość
bar mleczny. *See also* jadłodajnia; dania barowe
Baranów
Barańczak, Stanisław. *See also* Komitet Obrony Robotników; Nike
Barbara, Święta. *See* górnictwo
Barbórka. *See* górnictwo
Bareja, Stanisław. *See* Polska Rzeczpospolita Ludowa (PRL)
barok, literatura barokowa. *See also* architektura romańska, gotycka, renesansowa, barokowa; epoki (okresy) literackie
barszcz, barszcz biały, barszcz czerwony. *See also* dania barowe; jadłodajnia; zupa; żurek
barszcz litewski. *See* barszcz, barszcz biały, barszcz czerwony
barszcz ukraiński. *See* barszcz, barszcz biały, barszcz czerwony
Bator, Joanna. *See* Nike
Batory, Stefan. *See also* Henryk I Walezy; husaria; ordynacja; Węgry; Wilno; Zamoyski, Jan
Baudouin de Courtenay, Jan
bazyliszek. *See also* smok wawelski, smocza jama
Beck, Józef. *See also* honor

Begin, Menachem. *See* Brzeziński, Zbigniew
Beksiński, Zdzisław
Bellotto, Bernardo. *See* Canaletto
Belweder. *See also* Łazienki Królewskie, Park Łazienkowski; powstanie listopadowe
Bełżec. *See* Zamość
Bem, Józef. *See also* Wielka Emigracja
Ben-Gurion, David. *See* Brzeziński, Zbigniew
berło. *See* polskie regalia królewskie
Berman, Jakub. *See* odwilż gomułkowska, październik 1956; Służba Bezpieczeństwa; szara eminencja
Beskidy. *See also* Karpaty; Wisła
Biała Dama
biało-czerwony. *See* flaga
Białoruś. *See* Belarus *in* English Index
Białoszewski, Miron
Białowieża, Puszcza Białowieska. *See also* Białystok; Podlasie, Polesie; tarpan; Żubrówka
biały orzeł. *See* Orzeł Biały
Białystok. *See also* Podlasie, Polesie; żubrówka
Biblia
Biblia brzeska. *See* Biblia
Biblia królowej Zofii. *See* Biblia
Biblia Tysiąclecia. *See* Tyniec
Biblioteka Narodowa. *See* Warszawa
Biedroń, Robert. *See* wybory 2011
Bielscy, bracia. *See also* Białowieża, Puszcza Białowieska
Bielsko-Biała. *See* Syrena; Śląsk
Biernat z Lublina. *See* drukarstwo; Rej, Mikołaj z Nagłowic
Bierut, Bolesław. *See also* Armia Ludowa; Inka; "Nil," Generał; odwilż gomułkowska, październik 1956; wybory 1947
Bieszczady. *See also* Beskidy; Karpaty
bigos. *See also* dania barowe; jadłodajnia

bimber. *See* wódka
Biskupin
bitwa. *See* Psie Pole, bitwa; Chocim, bitwa pod Chocimiem; Grunwald, bitwa pod Grunwaldem; Monte Cassino, bitwa pod Monte Cassino; *Panorama Racławicka*; Racławice; Somosierra, bitwa; Warszawa, bitwy
bitwa nad Bzurą. *See* kampania wrześniowa
bitwa pod Wiedniem. *See* kawiarnia; Lubomirscy, rodzina Lubomirskich; *see also* odsiecz wiedeńska
Blikle, cukiernia Blikle. *See* Wedel, Fabryka E.
blokersi. *See* bloki z wielkiej płyty
bloki z wielkiej płyty
"Bo zupa była za słona"
Bochnia. *See* Wieliczka
bocian
Bodo, Eugeniusz
Bogurodzica
Bogusławski, Wojciech. *See* oświecenie
bohater trzech narodów. *See* Bem, Józef
Bohomolec, Franciszek. *See* *Monitor*
Bojko. *See* góral; Łemkowie, mniejszość karpatorusińska
Bolek i Lolek
Bolesław I Chrobry. *See also* Mieszko I; polskie regalia królewskie; Szczerbiec; Wojciech, Święty; zjazd gnieźnieński
Bolesław II Śmiały. *See also* Stanisław, Święty
Bolesław III Krzywousty. *See also* Płock; Psie Pole, bitwa; rozbicie dzielnicowe
Bolesław V Wstydliwy. *See* Wieliczka
Bolesław Pobożny. *See* Kalisz
Bolesławiec, ceramika bolesławiecka. *See* Cepelia
Bona Sforza, królowa. *See also* Zygmunt I Stary; Zygmunt II August

Bonaparte, Napoleon. *See* Somosierra, bitwa
Borowski, Tadeusz
Boruta, diabeł Boruta
Boy-Żeleński, Tadeusz. *See* cyganeria krakowska; Miss Polonia
Boziewicz, Władysław. *See* honor
Boże Ciało. *See also* dni wolne od pracy; lajkonik; Łowicz
"Boże coś Polskę"
Boże Narodzenie. *See also* barszcz, barszcz biały, barszcz czerwony; dni wolne od pracy
"Bóg mi powierzył honor Polaków, Bogu go tylko oddam." *See* Poniatowski, Józef
"Bóg się rodzi, moc truchleje." *See* "Kiedy ranne wstają zorze"
Bóg, Honor, Ojczyzna. *See also* honor
Bór-Komorowski. *See* Komorowski, Tadeusz
bracia Bielscy. *See* Bielscy, bracia
bracia polscy. *See* arianie, bracia polscy
Brama Morawska. *See also* Beskidy; bursztyn; Sudety
Branicki. *See* Białystok
Brda. *See* Bydgoszcz
Broniewski, Władysław. *See* Waryński, Ludwik
Bronowice. *See* Wesele
bruderszaft
brukowce. *See* gazety
Brzechwa, Jan
Brześć. *See* Biblia; Podlasie, Polesie; unia brzeska
Brzeziński, Miki. *See* Brzeziński, Zbigniew
Brzeziński, Zbigniew
Buczkowski, Leonard. *See* *Przygoda na Mariensztacie*; Walewska, Maria; zakazane piosenki; "budujemy drugą Polskę." *See* Gierek, Edward
"Budujemy nowy dom"
Bug. *See also* Narew; rzeki
Bulla gnieźnieńska
burmistrz. *See* województwo

bursztyn. *See also* Brama Morawska; Kalisz
Burza, akcja. *See also* Armia Krajowa
Buzek, Agata. *See* Buzek, Jerzy
Buzek, Jerzy. *See also* Komorowski, Bronisław
Bydgoszcz. *See also* Chopin, Konkurs Chopinowski; Kujawy; Popiełuszko, Jerzy; rzeki; Wyczółkowski, Leon

cadyk. *See* chasydyzm
całowanie w policzek, podanie ręki
całowanie w rękę
Canaletto. *See also* Starówka; Zamek Królewski w Warszawie
Caritas. *See* paczki żywnościowe; Wielka Orkiestra Świątecznej Pomocy;
cenzura. *See* socrealizm; wydawnictwa drugiego obiegu
Cepelia (Centrala Przemysłu Ludowego i Artystycznego)
Chałupińska, Barbara Apolonia. *See* Negri, Pola
chart polski. *See* owczarek podhalański
chasydyzm. *See also* Żydzi w Polsce
Chełmno. *See* Wisła
Chełmoński, Józef Marian
chleb i sól
Chłopi. *See* Łowicz; Reymont, Władysław Stanisław
Chmielnicki, Bogdan. *See* Kozacy, powstania kozackie
chochoł. *See* Wesele
Chochół, Andrzej. *See* Brzechwa, Jan
Chocim, bitwa pod Chocimiem
choinka. *See* Boże Narodzenie
Chojnice. *See* Pomorze
Chopin, Fryderyk. *See also* Chopin, Konkurs Chopinowski; mazur, mazurek; polonez (polonaise); pomnik Chopina w Warszawie; Potocka, Delfina; Rubinstein, Artur; Wielka Emigracja; wola

Chopin, Konkurs Chopinowski. *See also* Chopin, Fryderyk; Rubinstein, Artur
choroba filipińska. *See* Kwaśniewskie, Jolanta i Aleksandra
Chrystus Frasobliwy
"Chrząszcz brzmi w trzcinie." *See* Brzechwa, Jan
chrzest Polski. *See also* Mieszko I; Piastowie, dynastia
ciasta, ciastka. *See also* pierniki toruńskie
Cichociemni. *See* Zawacka, Elżbieta
Ciechocinek
cincz many. *See* Peweks
cinkciarze. *See* Peweks
ciupaga
cmentarz. *See also* Dziady
Cmentarz Łyczakowski. *See* cmentarz; Lwów
Cmentarz Orląt Lwowskich. *See* Lwów
Cmentarz Powązkowski. *See* cmentarz
Cmentarz Rakowicki. *See* cmentarz; Grechuta, Marek; Kraków
cmentarze radzieckie w Polsce
Conrad, Joseph
Cud nad Wisłą. *See* Piłsudski, Józef; Warszawa, bitwy; wojna polsko-bolszewicka;
Curie, Maria Skłodowska. *See also* Uniwersytet Latający
Cybulski, Zbigniew. *See also* Potocki, Jan
cyganeria krakowska
Cyrankiewicz, Józef
cystersi
Cytadela lwowska. *See* Cytadela Warszawska
Cytadela Warszawska. *See also* powstanie styczniowe
czapka z piór. *See* Wesele
Czarna Madonna. *See* Matka Boska Częstochowska, Czarna Madonna
czarna polewka, czarnina. *See* swaty, zaręczyny

POLISH INDEX 337

czarna porzeczka

Czarniecki, hetman Stefan. *See* Pasek, Jan Chryzostom

Czarnolas. *See* Kochanowski, Jan

Czartoryska, Izabela. *See* Czartoryscy, rodzina

Czartoryski, Adam. *See* Czartoryscy, rodzina; Wielka Emigracja

Czartoryscy, rodzina. *See also* magnateria; ordynacja

czas okupacji. *See* druga wojna światowa

Czechy. *See* Czech, Czechoslovakia *in* English Index

czepiec. *See* oczepiny

czerwiec 1956, wypadki czerwcowe. *See also* Cyrankiewicz, Józef; odwilż gomułkowska; Rokossowski, Konstanty

czerwiec 1976, wydarzenia czerwcowe. *See also* Jaroszewicz, Piotr; Komitet Obrony Robotników; odwilż gomułkowska, październik 1956

Czerwone Gitary

"Czerwone maki pod Monte Cassino." *See* Monte Cassino, bitwa pod Monte Cassino

Częstochowa. *See also* Apel Jasnogórski; Jasna Góra; Matka Boska Częstochowska, Czarna Madonna; pielgrzymki; potop szwedzki; Warta

Człowiek z marmuru. *See* Wajda, Andrzej

Człowiek z żelaza. See "Ballada o Janku Wiśniewskim"; Janda, Krystyna; Wajda, Andrzej

Czterej pancerni i pies

cztery koła. *See* Fiat 126p, mały Fiat

Czwarta Rzeczpospolita Polska. *See* Trzecia Rzeczpospolita Polska

czyn społeczny

czysta forma. *See* Witkacy

dach polski. *See* karczma

Dadźbóg. *See* Perun, Pierun

"Daj, ać ja pobruszę, a ty poczywaj." *See also* dąb Bartek

Dama z łasiczką (*Dama z gronostajem*). *See also* Czartoryscy, rodzina

dania barowe. *See* bar mleczny

Dar Pomorza

dąb Bartek

Dąbrowska, Maria

Dąbrowski, Jan Henryk. *See also* Legiony Polskie we Włoszech; "Mazurek Dąbrowskiego"; ułan

De Republica emendanda. See Modrzewski, Andrzej Frycz

De revolutionibus orbium coelestium. *See* Kopernik, Mikołaj

Dejmek, Kazimierz. *See* Hanuszkiewicz, Adam; Holoubek, Gustaw

Dekalog I–X. See Kieślowski, Krzysztof

Demarczyk, Ewa

Dembowski, Edward. *See* rabacja galicyjska

demoludy

Deyna, Kazimierz

Dezerter. *See* Jarocin, festiwal w Jarocinie

Dębski, Jacek. *See* Inka

diabeł Boruta. *See* Boruta, diabeł Boruta

dialekty regionalne

diecezja. *See* Kościół rzymskokatolicki

disco polo

Długosz, Jan. *See also* Bogurodzica; Perun, Pierun

Dmowski, Roman. *See also* Narodowa Demokracja, endecja; traktat wersalski

dni wolne od pracy. *See also* jedenastego (11) listopada; wolne soboty

do widzenia. *See* całowanie w rękę; dzień dobry, do widzenia

dobranocka. *See* *Bolek i Lolek*; Rzeszów; "Tango"

Dobrawa. *See* Bolesław I Chrobry; chrzest Polski; Mieszko I

Dobrzański, Henryk. *See* Hubal

Doda

doktorat. *See* edukacja

Dolny Śląsk. *See* Śląsk; Wrocław

Dołęga-Mostowicz, Tadeusz. *See* *Dyzma, Kariera Nikodema Dyzmy*

domek letniskowy. *See* działka

dożynki. *See also* Siwiec, Ryszard

dresiarz. *See* Masłowska, Dorota

Drohobycz. *See* Schulz, Bruno

Druga Rzeczpospolita Polska. *See also* rząd na uchodźstwie; Rzeczpospolita Obojga Narodów; traktat wersalski; Trzecia Rzeczpospolita Polska

druga wojna światowa. *See also* Armia Krajowa; Berling, Zygmunt; Bierut, Bolesław; Burza, akcja; Canaletto; *Czterej pancerni i pies*; Generalne Gubernatorstwo; granatowa policja; Grób Nieznanego Żołnierza; Hel, Półwysep Helski; honor; Hubal; Jeziorański, Zdzisław; kampania wrześniowa; Kolbe, ojciec Maksymilian Maria; Korczak, Janusz; kresy wschodnie; linia Curzona; Monte Cassino, bitwa pod Monte Cassino; obozy koncentracyjne, obozy pracy, obozy zagłady; Ordonówna, Hanka; Ossolineum, Zakład Narodowy imienia Ossolińskich; Oświęcim; Pawiak; Polska Walcząca; "polskie obozy koncentracyjne"; Polskie Siły Powietrzne w drugiej wojnie światowej; powstanie w getcie warszawskim; Prusy; Rokossowski, Konstanty; Sendlerowa, Irena; Sikorski, Władysław; Skarbek, Krystyna; Sybir, Sybiracy; Szare Szeregi; Szczerbiec; Świnoujście; tajne komplety; Umschlagplatz; Volksdeutsche; Warszawa; Westerplatte; Wieluń; Witos, Wincenty; Wolne Miasto Gdańsk; zakazane piosenki; Zamek Królewski w Warszawie; Żegota; Żydowski

Związek Wojskowy; Żydzi w Polsce
druga wojna światowa: muzea
druga wojna światowa: wojna bez zwycięstwa
drukarstwo
Drużbacka, Elżbieta
drzewo, najstarsze polskie drzewo. See dąb Bartek
drzwi gnieźnieńskie. See Gniezno
Drzymała, Michał. See wóz Drzymały
Dulska, dulszczyzna
dulszczyzna. See Dulska, dulszczyzna
Dunajec. See flisak, Pieniny
duży Fiat. See Fiat 125p, duży Fiat
dwa nagie miecze
dwadzieścia jeden postulatów. See Solidarność; wolne soboty
Dwaj mężczyźni z szafą. See Polański, Roman
dwór szlachecki, dworek szlachecki. See also sarmatyzm
dwudziestego drugiego lipca. See Manifest Lipcowy; Wedel, Fabryka E.
dwudziestolecie międzywojenne. See also epoki (okresy) literackie; Gałczyński, Konstanty Ildefons; Gdańsk; Gdynia; Iwaszkiewicz, Jarosław; Kiepura, Jan; Narodowa Demokracja, endecja; Piłsudski, Józef; Polska Odrodzona; *Skamander*; *Trędowata*; Witkacy; Witos, Wincenty; Żydzi w Polsce
Dygat, Stanisław. See polska szkoła filmowa
Dymitr Samozwaniec
Dymna, Anna
dynastia Piastów. See Piastowie, dynastia
Dyzma, Kariera Nikodema Dyzmy
Dziady (Forefathers' Eve)
Dziady (Romantic play). See also Holoubek, Gustaw; Konrad; marzec 1968, wydarzenia marcowe; Żegota

działka
dzielnica, osiedle. See mieszkania: rodzaje
dzień dobry, do widzenia
Dzień Kobiet
Dzień Konstytucji Trzeciego maja. See dni wolne od pracy; Konstytucja 3 maja
Dzień Niepodległości. See dni wolne od pracy
Dzień Trzech Króli. See Święto Trzech Króli
Dzień Wojska Polskiego. See Święto Wojska Polskiego
Dzień Wszystkich Świętych. See also cmentarz; cmentarze radzieckie w Polsce; dni wolne od pracy
Dzień Zaduszny. See Dziady (Forefathers' Eve); See also cmentarz
Dzierżyński, Feliks
dziękuję. See całowanie w rękę; dzień dobry, do widzenia
dzwon Zygmunta. See also Licheń; Zygmunt I Stary
Dżem. See Jarocin, festiwal w Jarocinie

Edelman, Marek. See also powstanie w getcie warszawskim; Robinsonowie warszawscy
edukacja
Eichelbaum, Aaron, Szmul, Hirsz, i Itzhak
Ekstraklasa. See piłka nożna
elementarz. See "Ala ma kota"
Elementarz Falskiego. See "Ala ma kota"
Emaus. See Lany Poniedziałek, Śmigus-dyngus
emigracja polska. See also Wielka Emigracja empik. See also "Budujemy nowy dom"
endecja. See Narodowa Demokracja, endecja
Enigma
ententa. See traktat wersalski
epoki (okresy) literackie

Esperanto. See Baudouin de Courtenay, Jan; Zamenhof, Ludwik
Euro 2012. See also piłka nożna
Europa Środkowa, Europa Wschodnia

Fabryka E. Wedel. See Wedel, Fabryka E.
Fahrenheit, Daniel Gabriel. See Heweliusz, Jan
Faktorowicz, Maksymilian
Falski, Marian. See "Ala ma kota"
Faraon. See Prus, Bolesław
Faustyna, Święta. See Kowalska, siostra Maria Faustyna
Feliński, Alojzy. See Boże coś Polskę
Ferdydurke. See Gombrowicz, Witold
feretrony. See Boże Ciało
ferie. See urlop, wakacje
Festiwal Piosenkiej Polskiej. See festiwale muzyczne; Opole
Festiwal Polskich Filmów Fabularnych. See festiwale filmowe; Gdynia
Festiwal w Jarocinie. See Jarocin, festiwal w Jarocinie
festiwale filmowe
festiwale muzyczne. See also Opole; Warszawska Jesień
Fiat 125p, duży Fiat. See also Fiat 126p, mały Fiat; Kapitan Żbik; Polonez (automobile); Warszawa (automobile)
Fiat 126p, mały Fiat. See also Fiat 125p, duży Fiat
Fieldorf, Emil August. See "Nil," Generał
Filipinki. See Alibabki
filmy kultowe
filomaci i filareci
firma ochroniarska. See ochrona
flaga
Flis. See flisak
flisak
Fogg, Mieczysław
folksdojcz. See Volksdeutsche
Ford, Aleksander. See Hłasko, Marek

POLISH INDEX 339

Francja. *See* France *in* English Index
Frank, Hans. *See* Generalne Gubernatorstwo
Frank, Jakub. *See also* Jankiel; Żydzi w Polsce
fraszki. *See* Kochanowski, Jan
Fredro, Aleksander
Fundacja Batorego. *See* Batory, Stefan
Funk, Kazimierz
furażka. *See* ułan

Gajos, Janusz. *See* *Czterej pancerni i pies*; *Psy*
galerianki. *See* salon
Galicja. *See also* Generalne Gubernatorstwo; powstanie krakowskie; rabacja galicyjska; wojna polsko-ukraińska
Gall Anonim. *See also* Popiel; postrzyżyny
Gałczyński, Konstanty Ildefons
Garbuska. *See* Warszawa (automobile)
"Gaude, mater Polonia"
gaz łupkowy
Gazeta Wyborcza. *See also* gazety; łowcy skór; Nike; Okrągły Stół, rozmowy Okrągłego Stołu; Rywin, afera
gazety
Gdańsk. *See also* bursztyn; Gdynia; grudzień 1970, wydarzenia grudniowe; inni; Kaszuby, język kaszubski; *Medaliony*; Pomorze; Sopot; Stocznia Gdańska; Wolne Miasto Gdańsk
Gdynia. *See also* "Ballada o Janku Wiśniewskim"; *Dar Pomorza*; festiwale filmowe; Pomorze; Sopot;
Gelbfisz, Szmuel
Generalne Gubernatorstwo. *See also* tajne komplety
Geralt. *See* wiedźmin
German, Anna
gest Kozakiewicza. *See* Kozakiewicz, Władysław

Gesta principum polonorum. *See* Gall Anonim
Gestapo. *See* Szucha, Aleja
getta żydowskie. *See also* granatowa policja; Polański, Roman; Sendlerowa, Irena
Giedroyc/Giedroyć, Jerzy. *See* wydawnictwa drugiego obiegu
Gierek, Edward. *See also* grudzień 1970, wydarzenia grudniowe; Polonez (automobile)
gierkówka. *See* Gierek, Edward
Gierymski, Ignacy Aleksander
Giewont. *See* Tatry
gimnazjum. *See* edukacja
Głowacki, Aleksander. *See* Prus, Bolesław
Głowacki, Janusz. *See* Kosiński, Jerzy
Głowacki, Marek. *See* Robinsonowie warszawscy
Głowacki, Wojciech Bartosz. *See* Racławice
gmina. *See* województwo
Gniezno. *See also* Lech, Czech, Rus; Małopolska; Nawojka; Piastowie, dynastia; Polanie; Popiel; Wielkopolska; Wojciech, Święty; zjazd gnieźnieński
Godlewski, Zbigniew. *See* "Ballada o Janku Wiśniewskim"
godzina policyjna. *See* stan wojenny
Godzina "W". *See* powstanie warszawskie
Goldszmit, Henryk. *See* Korczak, Janusz
Goldwyn, Samuel. *See* Gelbfisz, Szmuel
Gollob, Tomasz. *See* sport w Polsce
gołębiarstwo. *See* gołębie
gołębie
Gołota, Andrzej. *See also* sport w Polsce
Gombrowicz, Witold. *See also* Mrożek, Sławomir; wydawnictwa drugiego obiegu
Gomułka, Władysław. *See also*

czerwiec 1956, wypadki czerwcowe; grudzień 1970, wydarzenia grudniowe; marzec 1968, wydarzenia marcowe; odwilż gomułkowska, październik 1956; szara eminencja
gończy polski. *See* owczarek podhalański
Goplana. *See* Kujawy; Popiel
Gorzkie żniwa. *See* Holland, Agnieszka
gościnność
gotyk. *See* architektura romańska, gotycka, renesansowa, barokowa; kościół Mariacki; Pałac Kultury i Nauki w Warszawie; Stwosz, Wit; Wawel
Góra Świętej Anny. *See* pielgrzymki
góral. *See also* baca; Podhale
Góral, akcja
"Góralu, czy ci nie żal?"
Górecki, Henryk. *See also* Warszawska Jesień
Górniak, Edyta. *See* Doda
górnictwo
górnicy. *See* górnictwo
Górny Śląsk. *See* Opole; powstania Śląskie; Śląsk; traktat wersalski
Górski, Kazimierz. *See* piłka nożna
Góry Świętokrzyskie
gra w gumę. *See* gry podwórkowe
granatowa policja
Grechuta, Marek. *See also* Gałczyński, Konstanty Ildefons
grekokatolicy. *See* Przemyśl; religie; unia brzeska
Grodzka, Anna. *See* wybory 2011
GROM
Gronkiewicz-Waltz, Hanna. *See* kobiety w polityce
Gross, Jan Tomasz
grosz. *See* monety, banknoty
Grotowski, Jerzy. *See also* Komorowska, Maja
Grottger, Artur
Grób Nieznanego Żołnierza. *See also* jedenastego (11) listopada; traktat ateński

Grudziądz. *See* Pomorze; Wisła
grudzień 1970, wydarzenia grudniowe. *See also* Cyrankiewicz, Józef; Stocznia Gdańska; Zmotoryzowane Odwody Milicji Obywatelskiej (ZOMO)
Grunwald, bitwa pod Grunwaldem. *See also* Bogurodzica; dwa nagie miecze; Jagiełło, Władysław II; Krzyżacy, zakon krzyżacki; Pomnik Grunwaldzki
Grupa Reagowania Operacyjno-Manewrowego. *See* GROM
gry podwórkowe
grzybobranie
grzyby
Gubałówka. *See* Tatry
Gucwiński, Hanna and Antoni. *See* ogrody zoologiczne
Gułag, łagry. *See also* Bodo, Eugeniusz; Operacja Polska NKWD; Sybir, Sybiracy
gwiazdka. *See* Wigilia
Gwiazdor. *See* Boże Narodzenie; mikołajki

Hala Ludowa. *See* Hala Stulecia
Hala Stulecia
hala targowa. *See* targ, hala targowa
Halik, Mieczysław Sędzimir Antoni. *See* Halik, Tony
Halik, Tony
Halka. *See* Moniuszko, Stanisław
halny
Hansa. *See* Gdańsk; Toruń
Hanuszkiewicz, Adam
harcerstwo. *See* Alibabki; Szare Szeregi
harnaś. *See* ciupaga; Janosik, Juraj
Has, Wojciech Jerzy. *See* Cybulski, Zbigniew; Holoubek, Gustaw; Potocki, Jan; Prus, Bolesław; Schulz, Bruno
Hej. *See* Jarocin, festiwal w Jarocinie
Hejking. *See* Kamieniec Podolski
hejnał mariacki. *See also* kościół Mariacki

Hel, Półwysep Helski. *See also* druga wojna światowa
Henryk I Walezy. *See also* złota polska wolność
Herbert, Zbigniew. *See also* *Tygodnik Powszechny*; wydawnictwa drugiego obiegu
herby polskie. *See also* szlachta polska
Herling-Grudziński, Gustaw. *See* Gułag, łagry
Herman, Władysław I. *See* Bolesław II Śmiały; Płock
Hermaszewski, Mirosław
hetman. *See also* Chocim, bitwa pod Chocimiem; potop szwedzki; Sobieski, Jan III; Zamość; Zamoyski, Jan; Żółkiewski, Stanisław
Heweliusz, Jan
hip-hop
Hłasko, Marek. *See also* Osiecka, Agnieszka; wydawnictwa drugiego obiegu
Hoffman, Jerzy. *See* Kmicic, Andrzej; Kraszewski, Józef Ignacy; Łomnicki, Tadeusz; potop szwedzki; *Trędowata*
Holland, Agnieszka. *See also* Popiełuszko, Jerzy; Janosik, Juraj
Holoubek, Gustaw. *See also* *Dziady* (Romantic play); Walewska, Maria
hołd pruski. *See* Zygmunt I Stary
honielnik. *See* baca
honor. *See also* Anders, Władysław; Bóg, Honor, Ojczyzna; Poniatowski, Józef; szlachta polska
Horeszko. *See* Pan Tadeusz
Hôtel Lambert. *See* Wielka Emigracja
Hubal
Hucuł. *See* góral; Łemkowie, mniejszość karpatorusińska
Huelle, Paweł. *See* inni
husaria. *See also* Chocim, bitwa pod Chocimiem; ułan
hydraulik polski
hymn narodowy. *See* "Mazurek Dąbrowskiego"; Warta

igrzyska olimpijskie. *See* Deyna, Kazimierz; Korzeniowski, Robert; Kowalczyk, Justyna; Kozakiewicz, Władysław; Kusociński, Janusz; Małysz, Adam; Pawłowski, Jerzy; piłka nożna; Szewińska, Irena Kirszenstein
imieniny, urodziny
imiona staropolskie
Inka
inni
Instytut Pamięci Narodowej. *See* lista Wildsteina
insurekcja kościuszkowska. *See also* Dąbrowski, Jan Henryk; Jasiński, Jakub; Racławice; Kościuszko, Tadeusz; Warszawa, bitwy
insurekcja warszawska. *See* insurekcja kościuszkowska
inteligencja
Inwokacja. *See* Pan Tadeusz
Israel Baal Shem Tov. *See* chasydyzm
Iwaszkiewicz, Jarosław. *See also* *Skamander*; Tuwim, Julian
ixi 65. *See* wyliczanki

jadłodajnia. *See* bar mleczny; bigos; dania barowe
Jadwiga Andegaweńska. *See* Jadwiga, królowa
Jadwiga, królowa. *See also* Jagiełło, Władysław II; Kazimierz III Wielki; Radom; Uniwersytet Jagielloński; Węgry
Jadwiga, Święta. *See* Jadwiga, królowa
Jagiellonka, Anna. *See* Batory, Stefan; Henryk I Walezy
Jagiellonowie. *See also* Czartoryscy, rodzina; Jagiełło, Władysław II; Zygmunt II August
Jagiellończyk, Aleksander. *See* Stańczyk
Jagiełło, Władysław II. *See also* Biblia; dwa nagie miecze; Grunwald, bitwa pod Grunwaldem; Jadwiga, królowa; Jagiellonowie; obwarzanek; Pomnik

Grunwaldzki; Uniwersytet Jagielloński
Jak być kochaną. *See* polska szkoła filmowa
Jakub Wujek Bible. *See* Biblia
Jałta, konferencja
Jama Michalika. *See* cyganeria krakowska
Jan I Olbracht. *See* Kazimierz
Jan II Kazimierz. *See* potop szwedzki; Wazowie, dynastia
Jan Paweł II (papież). *See also* Częstochowa; Kowalska, siostra Maria Faustyna; Nowa Huta; Order Uśmiechu; pielgrzymki; Świątynia Opatrzności Bożej; Wadowice
Janda, Krystyna
Janek Wiśniewski padł. *See* "Ballada o Janku Wiśniewskim"
Jankiel
Janko Muzykant. *See* Antek
Janosik, Juraj. *See* ciupaga
Jantar, Anna
Jare Święto. *See* Marzanna, topienie Marzanny
Jarmark Europa. *See* Stadion Dziesięciolecia w Warszawie
Jarocin, festiwal w Jarocinie
Jaroszewicz, Piotr
Jaruzelski, Wojciech. *See also* Cybulski, Zbigniew; stan wojenny
Jasiński, Jakub
Jaskinia Niedźwiedzia. *See* osobliwości przyrodnicze
Jasna Góra. *See also* Apel Jasnogórski; Częstochowa; Matka Boska Częstochowska, Czarna Madonna; pielgrzymki; potop szwedzki; Wyszyński, Stefan; Zawisza Czarny
Jasnogórskie śluby narodu polskiego. *See* Apel Jasnogórski; Wyszyński, Stefan
jedenastego (11) listopada
Jedwabne, pogrom w Jedwabnem. *See also* Gross, Jan Tomasz; Nasza klasa
Jelenia Góra. *See* Sudety

"Jestem za, a nawet przeciw." *See* "Nie chcem, ale muszem"
"Jeszcze Polska nie zginęła." *See* "Mazurek Dąbrowskiego"
Jeziorański, Zdzisław. *See also* Radio Wolna Europa
Jezuici. *See* Kostka, Święty Stanisław; oświecenie; reformacja; Skarga, Piotr
Jezus, największy pomnik Jezusa. *See* Świebodzin, pomnik Chrystusa Króla
Jeż Jerzy
język kaszubski. *See* Kaszuby, język kaszubski
język polski, języki słowiańskie. *See also* aspekt dokonany i niedokonany; dialekty regionalne; przypadki gramatyczne
Jordan, Henryk. *See* ogród (park) jordanowski
Judym, Tomasz. *See also* Żeromski, Stefan
juhas. *See* baca
Jungingen, Ulrich von. *See* Grunwald, bitwa pod Grunwaldem
juwenalia

kabała. *See* chasydyzm
kabaret. *See also* cyganeria krakowska; Grechuta, Marek
Kabaret Piwnica pod Baranami. *See* Grechuta, Marek; kabaret
Kabaret Starszych Panów. *See* kabaret
Kabaret Zielony Balonik. *See* cyganeria krakowska
Kaczmarski, Jacek. *See also* Nasza Klasa; Rejtan, Tadeusz
Kaczorowski, Ryszard. *See* rząd na uchodźstwie; Smoleńsk, katastrofa pod Smoleńskiem
Kaczyńska, Maria. *See* Pierwsza Dama
Kaczyński, Jarosław. *See also* Kaczyński, Lech; "Nie chcem, ale muszem"
Kaczyński, Lech. *See also* Kaczyński, Jarosław; Komorowski, Bronisław; Smoleńsk, katastrofa pod Smoleńskiem; Trzecia Rzeczpospolita Polska
Kadłubek, Wincenty. *See also* Popiel; Psie Pole, bitwa; Wanda
Kadr. *See* zespół filmowy
Kajko i Kokosz. *See* Bolek i Lolek
Kalisz. *See also* Wielkopolska
kalwaria. *See also* pielgrzymki
Kalwaria Zebrzydowska. *See* kalwaria; Wadowice
kalwinizm. *See* arianie, bracia polscy; reformacja
kamienica. *See also* architektura romańska, gotycka, renesansowa, barokowa; Stare Miasto
Kamieniec Podolski
Kamińska, Ida
"Kamizelka." *See* Prus, Bolesław
kampania wrześniowa. *See also* Modlin, twierdza Modlin
Kanał. *See* polska szkoła filmowa
Kanał Augustowski. *See also* rzeki; Suwalszczyzna
Kanał Bydgoski. *See* Bydgoszcz
Kanał Elbląski. *See also* rzeki
kanapki. *See also* posiłki
Kantor, Tadeusz. *See also* Witkacy
Kapitan Kloss
Kapitan Żbik
Kaplica Ostrobramska. *See* Ostra Brama
Kaplica Zygmuntowska. *See* Wawel
kapliczka przydrożna. *See also* Chrystus Frasobliwy; kult maryjny; świątki
"Kapłan i błazen." *See* Kołakowski, Leszek
Kapuściński, Ryszard
Karaim. *See* mniejszości narodowe i etniczne
karczma
Karkonosze. *See* Sudety
karnawał. *See* kulig; ostatki
Karol X Gustaw. *See* potop szwedzki
karp, akcja żywy karp
Karpaty. *See also* Beskidy; Bieszczady; Brama Morawska;

góral; malarstwo na szkle; Pieniny; Podhale; Podkarpacie; Rzeszów; Sudety; Tatry
Karpiński, Franciszek. *See* "Kiedy ranne wstają zorze"
Karski, Jan
Karta Polaka
kartki żywnościowe. *See* stan wojenny
Kasprowicz, Jan. *See* Młoda Polska
kasza, kutia. *See also* dania barowe; Dziady; jadłodajnia
Kaszuby, język kaszubski. *See also* inni; mniejszości narodowe i etniczne; Tusk, Donald; Wolne Miasto Gdańsk
"Katarynka." *See* Prus, Bolesław
katarzynki. *See* andrzejki
katastrofa budowlana na Śląsku. *See* gołębie
katastrofa pod Smoleńskiem. *See* Smoleńsk, katastrofa pod Smoleńskiem
Katedra Wawelska. *See* Wawel; *See also* kościół Mariacki; Sikorski, Władysław
katorga. *See* Sybir, Sybiracy
Katowice. *See also* Gierek, Edward; powstania Śląskie; Spodek w Katowicach; Śląsk; Wujek, kopalnia
Katyń, zbrodnia katyńska. *See also* Sikorski, Władysław; Smoleńsk, katastrofa pod Smoleńskiem; Wajda, Andrzej
kawa zbożowa. *See* Inka; bar mleczny
Kawalerowicz, Jerzy. *See* Iwaszkiewicz, Jarosław; Prus, Bolesław; zespół filmowy
kawiarnia. *See also* cyganeria krakowska; Kazimierz; odsiecz wiedeńska
Kazania gnieźnieńskie. *See* Kazania świętokrzyskie
Kazania sejmowe. *See* mesjanizm polski; Skarga, Piotr
Kazania świętokrzyskie
Kazimierz

Kazimierz, Jan. *See* Jan II Kazimierz
Kazimierz Dolny. *See also* Sandomierz
Kazimierz I Odnowiciel. *See* Bolesław II Śmiały; reakcja pogańska; Wars i Sawa
Kazimierz III Wielki. *See also* dąb Bartek; Kalisz; Kazimierz; Korona Królestwa Polskiego; Matejko, Jan; Orle Gniazda; Piastowie, dynastia; Przemyśl; uczta u Wierzynka; Uniwersytet Jagielloński; Węgry; Władysław I Łokietek
Kazimierz IV Jagiellończyk. *See* Kalisz
"Kiedy ranne wstają zorze"
Kiejstut. *See* Jagiełło, Władysław II
Kielce. *See also* Góry Świętokrzyskie; SHL; Ściegienny, Piotr
Kielce, pogrom kielecki
kiełbasa
Kiepura, Jan
Kieślowski, Krzysztof. *See also* Holland, Agnieszka; Janda, Krystyna; Komorowska, Maja; Łódzka Szkoła Filmowa; Preisner, Zbigniew
Kilar, Wojciech
Kiliński, Jan
kino moralnego niepokoju. *See* Kieślowski, Krzysztof
kino studyjne
kiosk
kirkuty. *See also* cmentarz; Częstochowa
Kisielewski, Stefan. *See* *Tygodnik Powszechny*
Kitowicz, Jędrzej. *See* kawiarnia; saskie czasy
klimat, pory roku
Klonowic, Sebastian. *See* flisak
Kloss, Hans. *See* Kapitan Kloss
klubokawiarnie. *See* kawiarnia
Kmicic, Andrzej
Knabit, Leon. *See* Tyniec
kobiety w polityce
Kobzdej, Aleksander. *See* "Budujemy nowy dom"; socrealizm

Kochanowski, Jan. *See also* noc świętojańska; Treny; wieszcz narodowy; Zygmunt I Stary
Kolbe, ojciec Maksymilian Maria
Kolberg, Oskar. *See* Wlazł kotek na płotek
kolejka, kultura kolejkowa
kolędnicy. *See also* Boże Narodzenie
kolędy. *See* Boże Narodzenie; kolędnicy; Turoń
Kolski, Jan Jakub. *See* Gombrowicz, Witold
kolumna Zygmunta. *See also* Starówka
Kołakowski, Leszek. *See also* *Tygodnik Powszechny*; wydawnictwa drugiego obiegu
Kołłątaj, Hugo. *See* Komisja Edukacji Narodowej; Konstytucja 3 maja
Komeda, Krzysztof
komers. *See* studniówka
Komisja Edukacji Narodowej. *See also* oświecenie
Komitet Centralny. *See* Gomułka, Władysław; Polska Zjednoczona Partia Robotnicza (PZPR)
Komitet Obrony Robotników (KOR). *See also* Barańczak, Stanisław; czerwiec 1976, wydarzenia czerwcowe; Kuroń, Jacek; Michnik, Adam; Uniwersytet Latający
Komitet Samoobrony Społecznej "KOR." *See* Komitet Obrony Robotników (KOR)
Komorowska, Anna. *See* Pierwsza Dama
Komorowska, Maja
Komorowski, Bronisław. *See also* Belweder; Kaczyński, Jarosław; powstanie w getcie warszawskim
Komorowski, Tadeusz. *See also* Burza, akcja; powstanie warszawskie
komory gazowe. *See* Majdanek; Oświęcim; Treblinka

Kompleks polski. See kolejka, kultura kolejkowa; Konwicki, Tadeusz
komuch, komuna, komunistyczny. *See* komunizm
komunizm. *See also* demoludy
koncerz. *See* husaria
Kondrat, Marek. *See Psy*
konfederacja, rokosz, zajazd. *See also* złota polska wolność
konfederacja barska. *See also* konfederacja, rokosz, zajazd; Pułaski, Kazimierz; Rejtan, Tadeusz
konferencja jałtańska. *See* Jałta, konferencja jałtańska; kresy wschodnie; wybory 1947
konfederacja targowicka. *See also* konfederacja, rokosz, zajazd; Konstytucja 3 maja
konferencja teherańska. *See* Anders, Władysław
konferencja wersalska. *See* Dmowski, Roman; Paderewski, Ignacy Jan; traktat wersalski
Kongres futurologiczny. *See* Lem, Stanisław
kongres wiedeński. *See* Królestwo Kongresowe, "Kongresówka"
Kongresówka. *See* Królestwo Kongresowe, "Kongresówka"
Koniaków. *See* Cepelia
Konin. *See* Wielkopolska
Konopnicka, Maria. *See* pozytywizm; "Rota Marii Konopnickiej"
Konrad. *See also Dziady* (Romantic play); Holoubek, Gustaw
Konstytucja 3 maja. *See also* konfederacja, rokosz, zajazd; konfederacja targowicka; oświecenie; Świątynia Opatrzności Bożej
kontusz. *See also* żupan
Konwicki, Tadeusz. *See also* kolejka, kultura kolejkowa; wydawnictwa drugiego obiegu
Kopacz, Ewa. *See* kobiety w polityce
Kopaliński, Władysław

kopalnia soli. *See* Wieliczka
kopalnia Wujek. *See* Wujek, kopalnia
Kopernik, Mikołaj. *See also* Modrzewski, Andrzej Frycz; Toruń; Warmia
kopiec
kopiec Kościuszki. *See* kopiec
kopiec Kraka. *See* kopiec
kopiec Piłsudskiego. *See* kopiec
kopiec Wandy. *See* kopiec
KOR. *See* Komitet Obrony Robotników (KOR)
Korczak, Janusz
Kordecki, ojciec Augustyn. *See* Jasna Góra
Korona Królestwa Polskiego. *See also* Kujawy; Mazowsze; Rzeczpospolita Obojga Narodów; Toruń; unia lubelska; Wilno
koronki z Koniakowa. *See* Cepelia
korporacje akademickie. *See also* filomaci i filareci
korytarz polski. *See* Polska Odrodzona; Wolne Miasto Gdańsk
Korzeniowski, Józef. *See* Conrad, Joseph
Korzeniowski, Robert
Kosiński, Jerzy. *See also Dyzma, Kariera Nikodema Dyzmy*
Kossak, Jerzy. *See* Kossak, Wojciech
Kossak, Juliusz. *See* Kossak, Wojciech
Kossak, Wojciech. *See also Panorama Racławicka*
Kostka, Święty Stanisław
Kostrzyn. *See* Warta
kosynierzy. *See* Plater, Emilia; Racławice
Koszalin. *See* Pomorze
Kościół Greckokatolicki. *See* grekokatolicy
kościół Mariacki. *See also* Kraków; hejnał mariacki; kult maryjny; Matejko, Jan; Mehoffer, Józef; Stwosz, Wit
Kościół rzymskokatolicki. *See also* Boże Ciało; Jan Paweł II (papież); Krzyżacy, zakon

krzyżacki; Pierwsza Komunia; Popiełuszko, Jerzy; Radio Maryja; religie; Święto Trzech Króli; Zanussi, Krzysztof
Kościuszko, Tadeusz. *See also* insurekcja kościuszkowska; Kiliński, Jan; przysięga Kościuszki; Racławice
Kotański, Marek
Kotarbiński, Tadeusz. *See* szkoła lwowsko-warszawska logiki matematycznej
"Kotki dwa"
kotwica. *See* Polska Walcząca
Kowalczyk, Józef. *See* Kościół rzymskokatolicki
Kowalczyk, Justyna. *See also* sport w Polsce
Kowalska, siostra Maria Faustyna
Kozacy, powstania kozackie
Kozakiewicz, Władysław
Kozietulski, Jan. *See* Somosierra, bitwa
Koziołek Matołek
kółeczko, trójkącik
Krajowa Rada Narodowa. *See* Armia Ludowa
Krajowy Festiwal Piosenki Polskiej. *See* festiwale muzyczne
Krak. *See* kopiec; Wanda
krakowiak. *See also* tańce ludowe
Krakowskie Przedmieście. *See* Canaletto; Starówka
Kraków. *See also* bajgiel; Bolesław II Śmiały; cyganeria krakowska; *Dama z łasiczką*; Generalne Gubernatorstwo; Grechuta, Marek; halny; hejnał mariacki; kalwaria; Kantor, Tadeusz; Kazimierz; Kazimierz III Wielki; Kopernik, Mikołaj; kopiec; kościół Mariacki; lajkonik; Małopolska; Matejko, Jan; Miłosz, Czesław; Mitoraj, Igor; Młoda Polska; Nowa Huta; obwarzanek; Orle Gniazda; Oświęcim; pomnik grunwaldzki; pomnik Mickiewicza; prawo magdeburskie; przysięga Kościuszki; Stare Miasto; strój ludowy;

Stuhr, Jerzy; Stwosz, Wit; szopka krakowska; Tyniec; uczta u Wierzynka; Wanda; Wawel; *Wesele*; Wieliczka; Wisła; Jan Wyspiański, Stanisław; Zagajewski, Adam; Zygmunt II August

Krall, Hanna. See Edelman, Marek

Krasicki, Ignacy. See also *Monitor*; oświecenie

Krasiński, Zygmunt. See also mesjanizm polski; Mickiewicz, Adam; Potocka, Delfina; Słowacki, Juliusz; Wielka Emigracja; wieszcz narodowy

krasnoludki. See Wrocław

Kraszewski, Józef Ignacy. See also Paderewski, Ignacy Jan

kresy wschodnie. See also Jałta, konferencja jałtańska; kasza; pakt Ribbentrop-Mołotow; pielgrzymki; Sybir, Sybiracy

Krosno. See Podkarpacie

Królak, Stanisław. See Wyścig Pokoju

Królestwo Kongresowe, "Kongresówka." See also znaczek pocztowy

Królestwo Polskie. See Królestwo Kongresowe, "Kongresówka"; Modlin, twierdza Modlin; powstanie listopadowe

Królewiec. See Prusy

Krótka rozprawa między trzema osobami: Panem, wójtem a plebanem. See Rej, Mikołaj z Nagłowic

krówki

Krynica-Zdrój. See Ciechocinek; Kiepura, Jan; Nikifor

Krypta Zasłużonych. See Miłosz, Czesław; Skałka; Szymanowski, Karol Fryderyk; Wyspiański, Stanisław

Krzemieniec. See Słowacki, Juliusz

Krzeptowski, Jan. See Sabała

Krzywonos, Henryka. See Solidarność

Krzywousty, Bolesław. See Bolesław III Krzywousty

Krzywy Las. See osobliwości przyrodnicze

Krzyż Walecznych. See Zawacka, Elżbieta

Krzyż Zesłańców Sybiru. See Sybir, Sybiracy

Krzyżacy. See Sienkiewicz, Henryk

Krzyżacy, zakon krzyżacki. See also dwa nagie miecze; Grunwald, bitwa pod Grunwaldem; Jagiełło, Władysław II; Kazimierz III Wielki; Kujawy; Mazury, Pojezierze Mazurskie; Prusy; Sienkiewicz, Henryk; Toruń; Władysław I Łokietek

Książ, Zamek Książ

książka skarg i wniosków, książka życzeń i zazaleń

książka życzeń i zażaleń. See książka skarg i wniosków, książka życzeń i zażaleń

Księstwo Pruskie. See Zygmunt I Stary

Księstwo Warszawskie. See also Boże coś Polskę; Poniatowski, Józef

" – Kto ty jesteś? – Polak mały"

Kujawy. See also Biskupin; Bydgoszcz; Kaszuby, język kaszubski; Władysław I Łokietek

Kukliński, Ryszard

Kukuczka, Jerzy

kulig

kult maryjny. See also Bogurodzica; Jasna Góra

kultura kolejowa. See kolejka, kultura kolejowa

kultura łużycka. See Biskupin

Kultura paryska. See wydawnictwa drugiego obiegu

Kunegunda. See Sudety

Kurier z Warszawy. See Jeziorański, Zdzisław

Kuroń, Jacek. See also Komitet Obrony Robotników (KOR)

kuroniówki. See Kuroń, Jacek

Kurpie. See also pielgrzymki; wycinanki

Kurzak, Aleksandra. See Kwiecień, Mariusz

Kusociński, Janusz

kutia. See kasza

Kwaśniewski, Aleksander. See also Orlen, afera; traktat ateński

Kwaśniewskie, Jolanta i Aleksandra

Kwiecień, Mariusz

lajkonik. See also flisak

Lalka. See Prus, Bolesław

lampa naftowa

Landowska, Wanda

lanie wosku. See andrzejki

Lany Poniedziałek, Śmigus-dyngus

las kabacki. See LOT, Polskie Linie Lotnicze

las katyński. See Katyń, zbrodnia katyńska

latyfundia. See Lubomirscy, rodzina Lubomirskich; magnateria

Lech, Czech, Rus. See also Gniezno

Lechoń, Jan. See *Skamander*

Legiony Polskie 1914–1918. See also Dąbrowski, Jan Henryk; Piłsudski, Józef

Legiony Polskie we Włoszech. See also Legiony Polskie 1914–1918; "Mazurek Dąbrowskiego"

lektura szkolna, lektura obowiązkowa

Lelewel, Joachim

Lem, Stanisław. See also *Tygodnik Powszechny*

Leonardo da Vinci. See *Dama z łasiczką*

Leśniewski, Stanisław. See szkoła lwowsko-warszawska logiki matematycznej

liberum veto. See Konstytucja 3 maja; złota polska wolność

licencjat. See edukacja

liceum. See edukacja

Licheń. See also kult maryjny; pielgrzymki

liczebniki polskie

Liga Narodów. See Wolne Miasto Gdańsk

POLISH INDEX 345

Lilla Weneda. See Słowacki, Juliusz
Linda, Bogusław. *See Psy*
Linde, Samuel Bogumił
linia Curzona. *See also* pakt Ribbentrop-Mołotow
lipa czarnoleska. *See* Kochanowski, Jan
list 34
list 59, Memoriał 59. *See also* Zagajewski, Adam
lista kolejkowa. *See* kolejka, kultura kolejkowa
lista Wildsteina. *See also* Służba Bezpieczeństwa
Litwa. *See* Lithuania *in* English Index
LOT, Polskie Linie Lotnicze
lotto
Lubański, Włodzimierz. *See* piłka nożna
Lubaszenko, Olaf. *See Psy*
Lublin. *See also* Generalne Gubernatorstwo; Majdanek; Małopolska; Podlasie, Polesie; socrealizm; Ściegienny, Piotr
Lubomirscy, rodzina Lubomirskich. *See also* Łańcut, zamek w Łańcucie; magnateria; ordynacja; Rzeszów
Lubomirska, Izabela. *See* Biała Dama
Ludwik Węgierski. *See* Jadwiga, królowa; Kazimierz III Wielki; Radom; Węgry
Ludzie bezdomni. See Judym, Tomasz
"Ludzie wolni są braćmi." *See* Legiony Polskie we Włoszech
Luftwaffe. *See* Wieluń
lustracja. *See* lista Wildsteina
luteranizm. *See* reformacja; religie
Lutosławski, Witold. *See also* Warszawska Jesień
Lwów. *See also* Galicja; lampa naftowa; Lwów, pogrom lwowski; Ossolineum, Zakład Narodowy imienia Ossolińskich; wojna polsko-ukraińska; Żółkiewski, Stanisław

Lwów, pogrom lwowski. *See also* wojna polsko-ukraińska
Lwowskie Orlęta. *See* Lwów; wojna polsko-ukraińska
Łańcut, zamek w Łańcucie
łapanki. *See* Borowski, Tadeusz; granatowa policja
Łaski, Jan
Łazienki Królewskie, Park Łazienkowski. *See also* Belweder; pomnik Chopina w Warszawie
Łęczyca. *See* Boruta, diabeł Boruta
Łemkowie, mniejszość karpatorusińska. *See also* mniejszości narodowe i etniczne; Nikifor
Łemkowska Watra. *See* Łemkowie, mniejszość karpatorusińska
Łempicka, Tamara de
Łomnicki, Tadeusz
Łotwa. *See* Latvia *in* English Index
łowcy skór
Łowicz. *See also* Boże Ciało; strój ludowy; wycinanki
Łódzka Szkoła Filmowa. *See also* Łódź
Łódź. *See also* Kosiński, Jerzy; łowcy skór; Łódzka Szkoła Filmowa; mafia pruszkowska, wołomińska, łódzka; Piątek; Piotrkowska, ulica; polska szkoła filmowa; rewolucja roku 1905; Rubinstein, Artur; Schiller, Leon; Tuwim, Julian
Łukasiewicz, Ignacy. *See* lampa naftowa
Łukasiewicz, Jan. *See* szkoła lwowsko-warszawska logiki matematycznej
łużycki. *See* język polski, języki słowiańskie
Łysa Góra. *See* Góry Świętokrzyskie
Łysica. *See* Góry Świętokrzyskie

Maanam i Kora
Machulski, Juliusz. *See Seksmisja*; zespół filmowy
Mackiewicz, Józef
Maczuga Herkulesa. *See* osobliwości przyrodnicze

Madonna z Krużlowej. See also kult maryjny
mafia pruszkowska, wołomińska, łódzka
magnateria. *See also* Białystok; Lubomirscy, rodzina Lubomirskich; ordynacja; Radziwiłłowie; szlachta polska; Wiśniowiecki, Michał Korybut; Zamoyscy, rodzina
Majdanek
mak
Makowski, Tadeusz
Makuszyński, Kornel. *See Koziołek Matołek*
malarstwo na szkle
Malbork. *See* Krzyżacy, zakon krzyżacki
Malczewski, Jacek. *See also* Młoda Polska; rusałka
Malinowski, Bronisław
maluch. *See* Fiat 126p, mały Fiat
Mała apokalipsa. See Konwicki, Tadeusz
mała stabilizacja. *See* Herbert, Zbigniew; Różewicz, Tadeusz
Małopolska. *See also* dialekty regionalne; Kraków; Lubomirscy, rodzina Lubomirskich; Podkarpacie; Wielkopolska
mały fiat. *See* Fiat 126p, mały Fiat
Małysz, Adam. *See also* sport w Polsce; Wisła
małyszomania. *See* Małysz, Adam
Manifa. *See* Dzień Kobiet
Manifest Lipcowy. *See also* jedenastego (11) listopada; Stadion Dziesięciolecia w Warszawie; Wedel Fabryka E.
Manufaktura. *See* Piotrkowska, ulica
Maria Kazimiera d'Arquien de la Grange ("Marysieńka"). *See* Sobieski, Jan III
Marszałkowska Dzielnica Mieszkaniowa
Marysieńka. *See* Sobieski, Jan III
Marzanna, topienie Marzanny. *See also* Perun, Pierun

marzec 1968, wydarzenia marcowe. *See also* Cyrankiewicz, Józef; Gomułka, Władysław; Holoubek, Gustaw; Kamińska, Ida; Kołakowski, Leszek; Michnik, Adam; Ochotnicza Rezerwa Milicji Obywatelskiej (ORMO); szara eminencja; Żydzi w Polsce

Masłowska, Dorota. *See also* Nike

Matejko, Jan. *See also* kościół Mariacki; Mehoffer, Józef; Stańczyk

Matka Boska Częstochowska, Czarna Madonna. *See also* Bogurodzica; Częstochowa; Jasna Góra; kult maryjny; Ostra Brama; potop szwedzki; Wyszyński, Stefan

Matka Boska Królowa Polski. *See* Apel Jasnogórski

Matka Boska Ostrobramska. *See* Ostra Brama

Matka Boża Bolesna Królowa Polski. *See* Licheń

Matka Joanna od aniołów. See Iwaszkiewicz, Jarosław

Matka Polka

matura. *See also* edukacja; Kaszuby, język kaszubski; studniówka; tajne komplety

matura konspiracyjna. *See* tajne komplety

Mauzoleum Walki i Męczeństwa. *See* Szucha, Aleja

Mazepa. See Słowacki, Juliusz

Mazowsze. *See also* Kujawy; Kurpie; Łowicz; Mazury, Pojezierze Mazurskie; Płock

mazur, mazurek. *See also* tańce ludowe

"Mazurek Dąbrowskiego." *See also* Legiony Polskie we Włoszech; mazur, mazurek

Mazury, Pojezierze Mazurskie. *See also* dialekty regionalne; Wilczy Szaniec

mazurzenie. *See* dialekty regionalne; góral

"Mądry Polak po szkodzie." *See* przysłowia o Polsce i Polakach

MDM. *See* Marszałkowska Dzielnica Mieszkaniowa

Medaliony

Mehoffer, Józef. *See also* Młoda Polska

Meir, Golda. *See* Brzeziński, Zbigniew

Memoriał 59. *See* list 59, Memoriał 59; *See also* Kuroń, Jacek

mesjanizm polski. *See also Dziady* (Romantic play); Konrad; Mickiewicz, Adam; Skarga, Piotr

metal, muzyka metalowa. *See also* Jarocin, festiwal w Jarocinie

miasto. *See* województwo

miasto i wieś

Michałowski, Piotr

Michnik, Adam. *See also Gazeta Wyborcza*; Rywin, afera

Mickiewicz, Adam. *See also Dziady* (romantic play); filomaci i filareci; Holoubek, Gustaw; Jankiel; Konrad; Matka Polka; mesjanizm polski; Ordon, Julian; Pan Tadeusz; Pan Twardowski; Plater, Emilia; pomnik Mickiewicza w Krakowie; Schiller, Leon; Telimena; Wielka Emigracja; wieszcz narodowy; Żegota

miecz. *See* polskie regalia królewskie

Miejskie Zakłady Komunikacyjne. *See* PKP, PKS, MZK

miesiące, nazwy miesięcy

miesięczniki. *See* tygodniki

mieszkania

mieszkania: rodzaje

mieszkanie M1, M2, M3

Mieszko I. *See also* Bolesław I Chrobry; chrzest Polski; Gniezno; Kościół rzymskokatolicki; Piastowie, dynastia; postrzyżyny

Mieszko II Lambert. *See* reakcja pogańska

Mieszko III Stary. *See* Gniezno

"między Odrą a Bugiem." *See* Bug

Międzynarodowe Targi Poznańskie. *See* Poznań

Międzynarodowy Dzień Kobiet. *See* Dzień Kobiet

Międzynarodowy Festiwal Piosenki. *See* festiwale muzyczne

Międzyrzecki Rejon Umocniony

Międzywojnie. *See* dwudziestolecie międzywojenne

Mikołaj, Święty. *See* Boże Narodzenie; mikołajki

Mikołaja Doświadczyńskiego przypadki. *See* Krasicki, Ignacy

Mikołajczyk, Stanisław. *See* rząd na uchodźstwie; wybory 1947

mikołajki. *See also* Boże Narodzenie

milicja. *See* Ochotnicza Rezerwa Milicji Obywatelskiej (ORMO)

Milicja Obywatelska. *See also* Armia Ludowa; Kapitan Żbik

Miller, Leszek. *See* Orlen, afera; Rywin, afera

Miłosz, Czesław. *See also* Nike; przesądy i uprzedzenia; *Tygodnik Powszechny*; wydawnictwa drugiego obiegu

"Miłość ci wszystko wybaczy." *See* Ordonówna, Hanka

Ministerstwo Obrony Narodowej. *See* Siły Zbrojne RP

Ministerstwo Spraw Wewnętrznych. *See* Popiełuszko, Jerzy; Służba Bezpieczeństwa

miód, miód pitny

Miriam. *See* Przesmycki, Zenon

Miss Polonia

Mistrzostwa Europy w Piłce Nożnej. *See* Euro 2012

Miś Coralgol. See Bolek i Lolek

Miś Uszatek. See Bolek i Lolek

Mitoraj, Igor

Młoda Polska. *See also* cyganeria krakowska; epoki (okresy) literackie; Mehoffer, Józef; Norwid, Cyprian Kamil; Przesmycki, Zenon; Sabała; secesja; Staff, Leopold; *Szał*

uniesień; Szymanowski, Karol Fryderyk; *Wesele*; Wyczółkowski, Leon; Wyspiański, Stanisław; Żeromski, Stefan
mniejszości narodowe i etniczne. See also Dmowski, Roman; Narutowicz, Gabriel
Mniszkówna, Helena. See *Trędowata*
Moczar, Mieczysław. See szara eminencja
Modjeska. See Modrzejewska, Helena
Modlin, twierdza Modlin
Modrzejewska, Helena. See also "Warszawianka"
Modrzewski, Andrzej Frycz
moherowe berety. See Radio Maryja
monety, banknoty
Monitor. See also oświecenie
Moniuszko, Stanisław. See also "Wlazł kotek na płotek"
Monte Cassino, bitwa pod Monte Cassino. See also Anders, Władysław; mak; Wojtek, niedźwiedź
Montelupi. See Sonderaktion Krakau
Moralność pani Dulskiej. See Dulska, dulszczyzna
Morskie Oko
Morsztyn, Jan Andrzej. See barok, literatura barokowa
Morze Bałtyckie. See Bałtyk
Mościcki, Ignacy. See Beck, Józef; Śmigły-Rydz, Edward
motoryzacja. See Fiat 126p, mały Fiat
mówienie po imieniu. See pan, pani, państwo
Mrożek, Sławomir. See also ogrody zoologiczne
"Mury." See Kaczmarski, Jacek
Muzeum Czartoryskich. See Czartoryscy, rodzina
Muzeum Historii Żydów Polskich. See powstanie w getcie warszawskim; Żydzi w Polsce
Muzeum Powstania Warszawskiego. See druga wojna światowa: muzea
MZK. See PKP, PKS, MZK

"Na wieki wieków! Amen." See "Niech będzie pochwalony Jezus Chrystus!"
Naborowski, Daniel. See barok, literatura barokowa
Nad Niemnem. See Orzeszkowa, Eliza
Nagroda Nobla. See Curie, Maria Skłodowska; Miłosz, Czesław; *Quo vadis?*; Reymont, Władysław Stanisław; Sienkiewicz, Henryk; Singer, Isaac Bashevis; Szymborska, Wisława; Wałęsa, Lech
Najświętszy Sakrament. See Boże Ciało
nalewki. See wódka
Nałkowska, Zofia. See *Medaliony*
namiestnik. See Królestwo Kongresowe, "Kongresówka"
Napoleon Bonaparte. See Hala Stulecia; "Mazurek Dąbrowskiego"; Modlin, twierdza Modlin; Pan Tadeusz; Poniatowski, Józef; Walewska, Maria
Narew. See also Bug; Modlin, twierdza Modlin; rzeki
Narodowa Demokracja, endecja. See also Radio Maryja
Narodowe Siły Zbrojne. See also Żołnierze Wyklęci
Narodowe Święto Niepodległości. See jedenastego (11) listopada
Narodowy Bank Polski. See Balcerowicz, plan Balcerowicza; bankowość
Narodowy Fundusz Zdrowia (NFZ). See zdrowie, opieka lekarska
Narutowicz, Gabriel. See also dwudziestolecie międzywojenne; Narodowa Demokracja, endecja; Zachęta
Nasz Dziennik. See gazety
Nasza Klasa. See also Jedwabne, pogrom w Jedwabnem

"nasza mała stabilizacja." See Herbert, Zbigniew; Różewicz, Tadeusz
Nawojka
nazwiska polskie
nazwiska polskie: pochodzenie
nazwy miesięcy. See miesiące, nazwy miesięcy
Negri, Pola
neminem captivabimus. See złota polska wolność
Netanyahu, Benjamin. See Brzeziński, Zbigniew
Newsweek Polska. See tygodniki
NFZ. See Narodowy Fundusz Zdrowia
"Nie chcem, ale muszem"
"Nie czas żałować róż." See Słowacki, Juliusz
Niebieska Linia. See "Bo zupa była za słona"
Nieborów. See Łowicz
Nieboska komedia. See Krasiński, Zygmunt
"Niech będzie pochwalony Jezus Chrystus!"
Niedziela Palmowa. See palma wielkanocna; Wielkanoc, Wielki Tydzień
niedźwiedź Wojtek. See Wojtek, niedźwiedź
Niemcy, niemiecki. See Germany *in* English Index
Niemczyk, Leon
Niemen, Czesław
Niepokonani. See Rawicz, Sławomir
Niezależny Samorządny Związek Zawodowy "Solidarność." See Solidarność
nihil novi. See Rzeczpospolita Polska; złota polska wolność
Nike. See also Barańczak, Stanisław; Masłowska, Dorota; Matka Polka; Nasza Klasa; Różewicz, Tadeusz; Tokarczuk, Olga
Nikifor
"Nil," Generał
Nivea krem

Niżyński, Wacław
noc listopadowa. *See* powstanie listopadowe
noc saska. *See* saskie czasy, noc saska
noc sylwestrowa. *See* sylwester, noc sylwestrowa
noc świętojańska
nomenklatura. *See also* prywatyzacja
Norwid, Cyprian Kamil. *See also* Bem, Józef; Przesmycki, Zenon; wieszcz narodowy
Norymberga. *See* Generalne Gubernatorstwo; *Medaliony*; prowokacja gliwicka
nostalgia za PRL-em. *See* PRL, nostalgia za PRL-em
Nowa Fala. *See* Barańczak, Stanisław; Zagajewski, Adam
Nowa Huta
Nowak, Jan. *See* Jeziorański, Zdzisław
Nowogródek. *See* Bielscy, bracia; Mickiewicz, Adam; Rejtan, Tadeusz
Nowy Rok. *See* dni wolne od pracy; sylwester, noc sylwestrowa
Nowy Świat. *See* Canaletto
Nowy Targ. *See* Podhale
Nóż w wodzie. See Niemczyk, Leon; Polański, Roman
NSZ. *See* Narodowe Siły Zbrojne
Nysa. *See* Warszawa (automobile)

obiady czwartkowe. *See* Poniatowski, Stanisław II August
OBOP (Ośrodek Badania Opinii Publicznej). *See* tak-tak
obozy koncentracyjne. *See* Majdanek; Oświęcim; Sobibór; Treblinka; *See also* Borowski, Tadeusz; "polskie obozy koncentracyjne"
obozy pracy. *See* obozy koncentracyjne
obozy zagłady. *See* obozy koncentracyjne
Obrona Poczty Polskiej w Gdańsku

Obuchowicz, Danuta. *See* Inka
obwarzanek. *See also* bajgiel
Ochab, Edward. *See* odwilż gomułkowska, październik 1956
Ochota. *See* rzeź Woli
Ochotnicza Rezerwa Milicji Obywatelskiej (ORMO). *See also* marzec 1968, wydarzenia marcowe
ochrona, agencja ochrony, firma ochroniarska. *See also* kamienica
oczepiny
Oddział Wydzielony Wojska Polskiego. *See* Hubal
Odra. *See also* Bug; Opole; rzeki; Szczecin; Warta; Wrocław
odrodzenie. *See* Kochanowski, Jan
odsiecz wiedeńska. *See also* Polska przedmurzem chrześcijaństwa; Sobieski, Jan III
odwilż gomułkowska, październik 1956. *See also* Andrzejewski, Jerzy; Herbert, Zbigniew; Komeda, Krzysztof; socrealizm; Warszawska Jesień; Wyszyński, Stefan; zespół filmowy
odzież na wagę
ogar polski. *See* owczarek podhalański
Ogniem i mieczem. See Sienkiewicz, Henryk
ogrody zoologiczne
Ogrodzieniec. *See* Orle Gniazda
ogród działkowy. *See* działka
ogród (park) jordanowski, park jordanowski
ojczyzna. *See* Matka Polka
Okrągły Stół, rozmowy Okrągłego Stołu. *See also Gazeta Wyborcza*; Kaczyński, Lech; Kuroń, Jacek; Kwaśniewski, Aleksander; Michnik, Adam; prywatyzacja; Rakowski, Mieczysław; Solidarność; Wałęsa, Lech; wybory 1989
okres międzywojenny. *See* dwudziestolecie międzywojenne
Olbracht, Jan I. *See* obwarzanek
Olbrychski, Daniel. *See also* Kmicic, Andrzej; wojna polsko-bolszewicka
Olendrzy. *See* inni
Oleśnicki, Zbigniew. *See* Władysław III Warneńczyk
Olewnik, Krzysztof
Oliwa, pokój oliwski. *See* potop szwedzki
Olsztyn. *See* Orle Gniazda; Warmia
Opałka, Roman
Operacja Polska NKWD
opieka lekarska. *See* zdrowie, opieka lekarska
opłatek. *See* Boże Narodzenie; pisanki
Opole. *See also* festiwale muzyczne; Grotowski, Jerzy; Śląsk; Tokarczuk, Olga
Opór. See Bielscy, bracia
Order Odrodzenia Polski. *See* Małysz, Adam; Opałka, Roman; Order Virtuti Militari
Order Orła Białego. *See* Edelman, Marek; Michnik, Adam; Order Virtuti Militari; Sendlerowa, Irena; Zawacka, Elżbieta
Order Uśmiechu
Order Virtuti Militari. *See also* Zawacka, Elżbieta
Ordon, Julian
Ordonówna, Hanka. *See also* Tuwim, Julian
ordynacja. *See also* magnateria; Zamoyscy, rodzina
organy w Oliwie
Orle Gniazda
Orlen, afera Orlenu. *See also* Kwaśniewski, Aleksander
ORMO. *See* Ochotnicza Rezerwa Milicji Obywatelskiej
ortodoksyjni. *See* unia brzeska
Orzeł Biały. *See also* flaga; Lech, Czech, Rus; Licheń; Rzeczpospolita Obojga Narodów
Orzeszkowa, Eliza. *See also* pozytywizm
oscypek, oszczypek
Osiecka, Agnieszka
osiedla strzeżone

osiedle. *See* mieszkania: rodzaje
osiemnastka. *See* imieniny, urodziny
osobliwości przyrodnicze
Ossolineum, Zakład Narodowy imienia Ossolińskich
Ossoliński, Józef Maksymilian. *See* Linde, Samuel Bogumił; Ossolineum, Zakład Narodowy imienia Ossolińskich
ostatki
Ostatnia Wieczerza. *See* Wielkanoc, Wielki Tydzień
Ostra Brama
Ostrów Lednicki *See* chrzest Polski
oszczypek. *See* oscypek
Ośrodek Badania Opinii Publicznej (OBOP). *See* tak-tak
oświecenie. *See also* epoki (okresy) literackie; Konstytucja 3 maja; Krasicki, Ignacy
Oświęcim. *See also* Borowski, Tadeusz; Kolbe, ojciec Maksymilian Maria; Schiller, Leon
owcarek. *See* baca
owczarek podhalański
Owsiak, Jerzy. *See* Wielka Orkiestra Świątecznej Pomocy
oznaki godności. *See* herby polskie
Ósmy dzień tygodnia. *See* Hłasko, Marek

pacta conventa. *See* Henryk I Walezy
paczki żywnościowe
Paderewski, Ignacy Jan. *See also* Pomnik Grunwaldzki; powstanie wielkopolskie; traktat wersalski
pakt Ribbentrop-Mołotow. *See also* kampania wrześniowa; linia Curzona
Pakt Warszawski. *See* Układ Warszawski
palenie papierosów
Palikot, Janusz. *See* Ruch Palikota
palma wielkanocna
Pałac Kultury i Nauki w Warszawie

pałac w Wilanowie. *See* Wilanów
Pamiętnik z powstania Warszawskiego. *See* Białoszewski, Miron
Pamiętniki. *See* Pasek, Jan Chryzostom
pan, pani, państwo. *See also* bruderszaft
Pan Cogito. *See* Herbert, Zbigniew
Pan Jowialski. *See* Fredro, Aleksander
Pan Kleks. *See* Brzechwa, Jan
Pan Tadeusz. *See also* grzybobranie; Jankiel; Kilar, Wojciech; Mickiewicz, Adam; Ostra Brama; Telimena; Wajda, Andrzej
Pan Twardowski
Pan Wołodyjowski. *See* Kamieniec Podolski; Łomnicki, Tadeusz; Sienkiewicz, Henryk
pani. *See* bruderszaft; pan, pani, państwo
pani Dulska. *See* Dulska, dulszczyzna
pani Walewska. *See* Walewska, Maria
panna młoda. *See* oczepiny
Panny z Wilka. *See* Iwaszkiewicz, Jarosław
Panorama Racławicka. *See also* Kossak, Wojciech
Pańkowska, Magdalena. *See* disco polo
Państwowa Wyższa Szkoła Filmowa, Telewizyjna i Teatralna imienia Leona Schillera. *See* Łódzka Szkoła Filmowa
Państwowe Gospodarstwo Rolne (PGR)
Państwowe Przedsiębiorstwo Eksportu Wewnętrznego. *See* Pewex
papierosy. *See* tytoń, papierosy
papież. *See* Kościół rzymskokatolicki
papież Jan Paweł II. *See* Jan Paweł II (papież)
parafia. *See* Kościół rzymskokatolicki

park jordanowski. *See* ogród (park) jordanowski
Park Łazienkowski. *See* Łazienki Królewskie, Park Łazienkowski
Parkoszowic, Jakub
Parowozownia Wolsztyn. *See also* skansen
partia komunistyczna. *See* Polska Zjednoczona Partia Robotnicza (PZPR)
partie polityczne
pas słucki. *See* kontusz
pas wódczany. *See* wódka
Pasek, Jan Chryzostom. *See also* barok, literatura barokowa; sarmatyzm; Zagłoba, Jan Onufry
Pasikowski, Władysław. *See* Psy
Passent, Daniel. *See* Osiecka, Agnieszka
pasterka. *See* Boże Narodzenie
Pasza, Murat. *See* Bem, Józef
Paw królowej. *See* Masłowska, Dorota
Pawiak. *See also* Kolbe, ojciec Maksymilian Maria
Pawlikowska-Jasnorzewska, Maria. *See* Kossak, Wojciech; *Skamander*
Pawłowski, Jerzy
Pazura, Cezary. *See* Psy
październik. *See* odwilż gomułkowska, październik 1956
pączki. *See* ostatki
pełnoletniość. *See* imieniny, urodziny
Penderecki, Krzysztof. *See also* Warszawska Jesień
Peres, Shimon. *See* Brzeziński, Zbigniew
Perun, Pierun
Pewex
PGR. *See* Państwowe Gospodarstwo Rolne (PGR)
Pianista. *See* Polański, Roman; Robinsonowie warszawscy; Umschlagplatz
Piast Kołodziej. *See* Piastowie, dynastia; postrzyżyny

Piastowie, dynastia Piastów. *See also* Kazimierz III Wielki; Mieszko I; Polanie; postrzyżyny; reakcja pogańska; Szczerbiec; Władysław I Łokietek

Piątek

pielgrzymki. *See also* cystersi; Częstochowa; Jasna Góra; kalwaria; Wadowice; Wojciech, Święty

Pieniny. *See also* flisak; Karpaty

pierniki toruńskie. *See also* ciasta, ciastka

pierogi. *See also* dania barowe; jadłodajnia

Pierwsza Brygada. *See* Legiony Polskie 1914–1918; "Nil," Generał

Pierwsza Dama. *See also* Kwaśniewskie, Jolanta i Aleksandra

Pierwsza Komunia

Pierwsza Rzeczpospolita Polska. *See* Rzeczpospolita Obojga Narodów

pierwsza wojna światowa. *See* Galicja; Grób Nieznanego Żołnierza; Legiony Polskie 1914–1918; Opole; Piłsudski, Józef; Polska Odrodzona; Pomorze; powstania Śląskie; powstanie wielkopolskie; Przemyśl; rozbiory; traktat wersalski; wojna polsko-bolszewicka

pierwszy polski znaczek pocztowy. *See* znaczek pocztowy

pierwszy rozbiór Polski. *See* Galicja; Przemyśl; rozbiory

pierwszy Września. *See* kampania wrześniowa

Pieskowa Skała. *See* Orle Gniazda

Pietrzak, Jan. *See* "*Żeby Polska była Polską*"

pięść Gołoty. *See* Gołota, Andrzej

pijalnia piwa

Pilch, Jerzy. *See* Nike; Wisła

piłka nożna. *See also* Deyna, Kazimierz; Euro 2012

Piłsudski, Józef. *See also* Beck, Józef; Belweder; Druga Rzeczpospolita Polska; dwudziestolecie międzywojenne; jedenastego (11) listopada; kopiec; Legiony Polskie 1914–1918; Narodowa Demokracja, endecja; Polska Odrodzona

Pińczów. *See* Łaski, Jan

piosenki biesiadne

Piotrkowska, ulica. *See also* Łódź; Rubinstein, Artur; Tuwim, Julian

pisanki

piwo. *See also* pijalnia piwa

PKiN. *See* Pałac Kultury i Nauki w Warszawie

PKP, PKS, MZK

PKS. *See* PKP, PKS, MZK

PKWN. *See* Manifest Lipcowy

Plac Piłsudskiego. *See* Grób Nieznanego Żołnierza

plakaty

Plan Balcerowicza. *See* Balcerowicz, plan Balcerowicza

Planty. *See* Stare Miasto

Plater, Emilia

Platforma Obywatelska. *See* partie polityczne; Tusk, Donald

Płock. *See also* Mazowsze; Orlen, afera; secesja; Wisła

PO. *See* Platforma Obywatelska

Poczet królów i książąt polskich. *See* Matejko, Jan

Poczta Polska. *See* Obrona Poczty Polskiej w Gdańsku; Wolne Miasto Gdańsk

podanie ręki. *See* całowanie w policzek; dzień dobry, do widzenia

Podhale. *See also* góral; halny; oscypek; owczarek podhalański; Sabała; strój ludowy; Zakopane

Podkarpacie. *See also* Bieszczady; Łańcut, zamek w Łańcucie; wycinanki

Podkowiński, Władysław. *See* *Szał uniesień*

Podlasie, Polesie

Podole. *See* chasydyzm; Frank, Jakub; Kamieniec Podolski

Podróż za jeden uśmiech. *See* autostop

pogoda. *See* klimat, pory roku

pogoń. *See also* Rzeczpospolita Obojga Narodów

pogrom. *See* Jedwabne, pogrom w Jedwabnem; Kielce, pogrom kielecki; Lwów, pogrom lwowski

pogrom w Kielcach. *See* Kielce, pogrom kielecki

Pojezierze Mazurskie. *See* Mazury, Pojezierze Mazurskie

Pokolenie. *See* polska szkoła filmowa

pokolenie JP2. *See* Jan Paweł II (papież)

pokój paryski. *See* traktat wersalski

pokój tylżycki. *See* Księstwo Warszawskie

pokój wersalski. *See* traktat wersalski

"Polacy nie gęsi." *See also* przysłowia o Polsce i Polakach

"Polak potrafi." *See* przysłowia o Polsce i Polakach

Polak to Katolik. *See* Świątynia Opatrzności Bożej w Warszawie

Polanie. *See also* Kujawy; Mieszko I; Piastowie, dynastia; Popiel; Wielkopolska; zjazd gnieźnieński

Polański, Roman. *See also* Komeda, Krzysztof; Łódzka Szkoła Filmowa; Niemczyk, Leon; Robinsonowie warszawscy

Polesie. *See* Podlasie, Polesie

policja. *See* Ochotnicza Rezerwa Milicji Obywatelskiej (ORMO)

Politbiuro. *See* Jaroszewicz, Piotr

Polityka. *See* Rakowski, Mieczysław; tygodniki

polka. *See also* polonez (polonaise)

Polonez (automobile). *See also* Arrinera; Fiat 125p, duży Fiat

POLISH INDEX 351

polonez (polonaise). See also polka; studniówka; tańce ludowe
Polonia
Polska
Polska A i B
Polska Chrystus narodów. See Skarga, Piotr
polska droga do socjalizmu. See Gomułka, Władysław
Polska Kronika Filmowa, PKF
Polska Ludowa. See Polska Rzeczpospolita Ludowa (PRL)
Polska od morza do morza. See Bug
Polska Odrodzona. See also Druga Rzeczpospolita Polska; Piłsudski, Józef; traktat wersalski; Zamek Królewski w Warszawie; Żeromski, Stefan
Polska Organizacja Turystyczna. See hydraulik polski
Polska Partia Robotnicza. See Armia Ludowa; Polska Zjednoczona Partia Robotnicza (PZPR)
Polska Partia Socjalistyczna. See Polska Zjednoczona Partia Robotnicza (PZPR)
Polska przedmurzem chrześcijaństwa. See also Kamieniec Podolski; mesjanizm polski; Polska spichlerzem Europy
Polska Rzeczpospolita Ludowa (PRL). See also czyn społeczny; druga wojna światowa; Dzień Kobiet; Dzierżyński, Feliks; Jaruzelski, Wojciech; Kapitan Żbik; Katyń, zbrodnia katyńska; kawiarnia; kolejka, kultura kolejkowa; komunizm; Kotański, Marek; książka skarg i wniosków; Kuroń, Jacek; lista Wildsteina; Manifest Lipcowy; mieszkanie M1, M2, M3; nomenklatura; Ochotnicza Rezerwa Milicji Obywatelskiej (ORMO); Peweks; piwo; PRL, nostalgia za PRL-em; sklep; Służba Bezpieczeństwa; socrealizm; Solidarność; Wedel, Fabryka E.; wolne soboty; wydawnictwa drugiego obiegu; Zmotoryzowane Odwody Milicji Obywatelskiej (ZOMO)

Polska spichlerzem Europy. See also Polska przedmurzem chrześcijaństwa
polska szkoła filmowa. See also Konwicki, Tadeusz; Wajda, Andrzej; zespół filmowy
polska szkoła jazzu. See Komeda, Krzysztof
polska szkoła plakatu. See plakaty
Polska Walcząca
Polska Zjednoczona Partia Robotnicza (PZPR). See also Gierek, Edward; Gomułka, Władysław; komunizm; list 59, Memoriał 59
Polski kodeks honorowy. See honor
Polski Komitet Wyzwolenia Narodowego (PKWN). See Manifest Lipcowy
polski owczarek nizinny. See owczarek podhalański
polskie araby. See araby, polskie konie arabskie
Polskie Koleje Państwowe. See PKP, PKS, MZK
Polskie Linie Lotnicze. See LOT, Polskie Linie Lotnicze
"polskie obozy koncentracyjne"
polskie regalia królewskie
Polskie Siły Powietrzne w drugiej wojnie światowej
Polskie Stronnictwo Ludowe. See partie polityczne; Witos, Wincenty; wybory 1947
Polskie Towarzystwo Turystyczno-Krajoznawcze (PTTK)
Polskie Wojsko Podziemne. See Góral, akcja
połonina. See Bieszczady
południca. See rusałka
pomnik Chopina w Warszawie. See also Łazienki Królewskie, Park Łazienkowski
Pomnik Grunwaldzki

pomnik lotnika. See Żwirko i Wigura
Pomnik Małego Powstańca. See Szare Szeregi
pomnik Mickiewicza w Krakowie
pomnik przyrody. See dąb Bartek; osobliwości przyrodnicze
Pomorze. See also Bolesław III Krzywousty; Kaszuby, język kaszubski; Kujawy; Władysław I Łokietek
Pomorze Zachodnie. See Szczecin
Ponary. See Mackiewicz, Józef
Poniatowo. See Treblinka
Poniatowski, Józef
Poniatowski, Stanisław II August. See also Bacciarelli, Marcello; Canaletto; Komisja Edukacji Narodowej; konfederacja barska; Łazienki Królewskie, Park Łazienkowski; Monitor; Order Virtuti Militari; oświecenie; Poniatowski, Józef; Szczerbiec
Popiel. See also Gall Anonim; Kujawy; Piastowie, dynastia
Popiełuszko, Jerzy
Popiół i diament. See Andrzejewski, Jerzy; Cybulski, Zbigniew; polska szkoła filmowa; Wajda, Andrzej
poproszę. See proszę
Pornografia. See Gombrowicz, Witold
porozumienie Gdańskie. See Stocznia Gdańska
portret trumienny. See also sarmatyzm
poseł. See Kuroń, Jacek
posiłki
postkomuniści. See komunizm
postmodernizm. See epoki (okresy) literackie
postrzyżyny. See also Mieszko I
Potoccy, rodzina. See Potocki, rodzina Potockich
Potocka, Delfina. See also Krasiński, Zygmunt; Potocki, rodzina Potockich
Potocka, Julia z Lubomirskich. See Biała Dama

Potocki, Ignacy. *See* Komisja Edukacji Narodowej; Konstytucja 3 maja

Potocki, Jan. *See also* Potocki, rodzina Potockich

Potocki, rodzina Potockich. *See also* Łańcut, zamek w Łańcucie; magnateria; ordynacja

Potocki, Wacław. *See* barok, literatura barokowa

Potop. *See* Łomnicki, Tadeusz; Sienkiewicz, Henryk

potop szwedzki. *See also* Jasna Góra; Sandomierz; Sobieski, Jan III; Warszawa, bitwy

Powązki, Cmentarz Powązkowski. *See* cmentarz

powiat. *See* województwo

powstania kozackie. *See* Kozacy, powstania kozackie

powstania śląskie

powstanie listopadowe. *See also* Belweder; Bem, Józef; Cytadela Warszawska; Lelewel, Joachim; Matka Polka; Mickiewicz, Adam; Ordon, Julian; Plater, Emilia; Stary Wiarus; Sybir, Sybiracy; Ściegienny, Piotr; "Warszawianka"; Wielka Emigracja

powstanie styczniowe. *See also* Boże coś Polskę; dwa nagie miecze; Grottger, Artur; Orzeszkowa, Eliza; Pawiak; Ściegienny, Piotr; Sybir, Sybiracy

powstanie w getcie warszawskim. *See also* Andrzejewski, Jerzy; Żydowski Związek Wojskowy

powstanie warszawskie. *See also* Armia Krajowa; Baczyński, Krzysztof Kamil; Białoszewski, Miron; Burza, akcja; druga wojna światowa; Fogg, Mieczysław; Jeziorański, Zdzisław; Komorowski, Tadeusz; "Nil," Generał; Pawiak; Polska Walcząca; Robinsonowie warszawscy; rzeź Woli; Starówka; Szare Szeregi; Szucha, Aleja; Warszawa

powstanie wielkopolskie. *See also* Wielkopolska

Poznań. *See also* Bamber, Bamberka; Barańczak, Stanisław; czerwiec 1956, wypadki czerwcowe; Nivea krem; marzec 1968, wydarzenia marcowe; powstanie wielkopolskie; rogal świętomarciński; Warta; Wielkopolska; Wieniawski, Henryk; Września

pozytywizm. *See also* epoki (okresy) literackie; Prus, Bolesław

Pożegnanie z Marią. *See* Borowski, Tadeusz

półmetek. *See* studniówka

Półwysep Helski. *See* Hel, Półwysep Helski

Prawo i Sprawiedliwość (PiS). *See* Kaczyński, Lech; partie polityczne

prawo magdeburskie

Prawosławny, Kościół. *See* religie

Preisner, Zbigniew. *See also* Kieślowski, Krzysztof

prezydent miasta. *See* województwo

PRL. *See* Polska Rzeczpospolita Ludowa (PRL)

PRL, nostalgia za PRL-em

propinacja. *See* karczma

proszę. *See also* całowanie w rękę; dzień dobry, do widzenia

"Proszę państwa do gazu." *See* Borowski, Tadeusz

prowokacja bydgoska. *See* Bydgoszcz

prowokacja gliwicka

Prus, Bolesław. *See also* Antek; inteligencja; Orzeszkowa, Eliza; pozytywizm

Prusy. *See also* Krzyżacy, zakon krzyżacki; Mazury, Pojezierze Mazurskie; Pomorze; Warmia

Prusy Zachodnie. *See* traktat wersalski

Pruszków. *See* mafia pruszkowska, wołomińska, łódzka

Prymas Polski. *See* Kościół rzymskokatolicki

Prymas Tysiąclecia. *See* Wyszyński, Stefan

pryszczaci. *See* Borowski, Tadeusz

prywatyzacja

Przasnysz. *See* Kostka, Święty Stanisław

przedmurze chrześcijaństwa. *See* Polska przedmurzem chrześcijaństwa

Przedsiębiorstwo Komunikacji Samochodowej. *See* PKP, PKS, MZK

Przedwiośnie. *See* szklane domy

Przekrój. *See* Gałczyński, Konstanty Ildefons; Świerszczyk; tygodniki

Przemyk, Grzegorz. *See* Popiełuszko, Jerzy

Przemyśl. *See also* Galicja; Podkarpacie

Przerwa-Tetmajer, Kazimierz. *See* Młoda Polska

przesądy i uprzedzenia

Przesmycki, Zenon

przewrót kopernikowski. *See* Kopernik, Mikołaj

przewrót majowy. *See* Beck, Józef; dwudziestolecie międzywojenne; Piłsudski, Józef; Witos, Wincenty

przodownik pracy. *See* *Przygoda na Mariensztacie*

Przybora, Jeremi. *See* kabaret; Osiecka, Agnieszka

Przybyszewski, Stanisław. *See* cyganeria krakowska; Młoda Polska

Przygoda na Mariensztacie

przyjaciel, przyjaciółka. *See also* gościnność

przypadki gramatyczne. *See also* język polski

przysięga Kościuszki. *See also* Kościuszko, Tadeusz

przysłowia o Polsce i Polakach

przyśpiewki. *See* oczepiny

przywilej koszycki. *See* Jadwiga, królowa

POLISH INDEX   353

Psie Pole, bitwa. *See also* Kadłubek, Wincenty
PSL. *See* Polskie Stronnictwo Ludowe
Psy
PTTK. *See* Polskie Towarzystwo Turystyczno-Krajoznawcze (PTTK)
Pudzianowski, Mariusz
Pułaski, Kazimierz. *See also* konfederacja barska
Puławy. *See* Czartoryscy, rodzina
Pustynia Błędowska. *See* osobliwości przyrodnicze
Puszcza Białowieska. *See* Białowieża, Puszcza Białowieska
Pyjas, Stanisław. *See* Komitet Obrony Robotników
PZPR. *See* Polska Zjednoczona Partia Robotnicza

Quo vadis?. *See also* Sienkiewicz, Henryk

rabacja galicyjska
Rabczewska, Dorota. *See* Doda
Racławice. *See also* insurekcja kościuszkowska; *Panorama Racławicka*
Rada Pomocy Żydom. *See* Żegota
Rada Wzajemnej Pomocy Gospodarczej (RWPG)
Radio Maryja. *See also* Rydzyk, Tadeusz
Radio Wolna Europa (RWE), Rozgłośnia Polska. *See also* Jeziorański, Zdzisław; Siwiec, Ryszard; Służba Bezpieczeństwa
Radom. *See also* czerwiec 1976, wydarzenia czerwcowe
radziecki. *See* Związek Socjalistycznych Republik Radzieckich (ZSRR); *See also* Soviet Union *in* English Index
Radziwiłłowie, rodzina. *See also* Łowicz; magnateria; ordynacja
Radziwiłłówna, Barbara. *See* Bona Sforza, królowa; Ostra Brama; Radziwiłłowie; Twardowski, Jan; Zygmunt II August

Raj duszny. *See* Rej, Mikołaj z Nagłowic
Rakowski, Mieczysław
ratusz. *See* architektura romańska, gotycka, renesansowa, barokowa; prawo magdeburskie
Rawicz, Sławomir
reakcja pogańska. *See also* Bolesław II Śmiały
referendum akcesyjne. *See* traktat ateński
reformacja. *See also* arianie, bracia polscy
regalia królewskie. *See* polskie regalia królewskie
Rej, Mikołaj z Nagłowic. *See also* "Polacy nie gęsi"
Rejtan, Tadeusz. *See also* Kaczmarski, Jacek
Reksio. *See* Bolek i Lolek
religie. *See also* drukarstwo; Kościół rzymskokatolicki; unia brzeska; Żydzi w Polsce
renesans. *See* architektura romańska, gotycka, renesansowa, barokowa; epoki (okresy) literackie; Kochanowski, Jan; Orle Gniazda; *Treny*; Wawel; Żółkiewski, Stanisław
Rewers. *See* "Ala ma kota"; Buzek, Jerzy
rewolucja roku 1905. *See also* "Warszawianka"
Reymont, Władysław Stanisław. *See also* Młoda Polska; Łowicz
Rękopis znaleziony w Saragossie. *See* Potocki, Jan
RFE. *See* Radio Wolna Europa, Rozgłośnia Polska
Robak. *See* Pasek, Jan Chryzostom
Robinsonowie warszawscy
Rodowicz, Maryla. *See also* Gałczyński, Konstanty Ildefons
rodzaj męskoosobowy. *See also* aspekt dokonany i niedokonany; język polski, języki słowiańskie; przypadki gramatyczne
rodzina. *See* gościnność

Rodzinne Ogrody Działkowe (ROD). *See* działka
rogal świętomarciński
Rogoszówna, Zofia. *See* "Kotki dwa"
Rokita. *See* Boruta, diabeł Boruta
Rokossowski, Konstanty
rokosz. *See* konfederacja, rokosz, zajazd
rokosz Zebrzydowskiego. *See* konfederacja, rokosz, zajazd
Rom. *See* mniejszości narodowe i etniczne
romantyzm. *See* epoki (okresy) literackie; Schiller, Leon
romańska. *See* architektura romańska, gotycka, renesansowa, barokowa
Rosja. *See* Russia *in* English Index
Rosjanin. *See* Związek Socjalistycznych Republik Radzieckich (ZSRR)
rosyjski. *See* Związek Socjalistycznych Republik Radzieckich (ZSRR)
"Rota Marii Konopnickiej." *See also* Września
rozbicie dzielnicowe. *See* Bolesław III Krzywousty; Piastowie, dynastia; Władysław I Łokietek
rozbiory. *See also* Poniatowski, Stanisław II August; powstanie wielkopolskie; Rzeczpospolita Obojga Narodów; traktat wersalski; unia lubelska; zabór austriacki; zabór pruski; zabór rosyjski
rozmowy Okrągłego Stołu. *See* Okrągły Stół, rozmowy Okrągłego Stołu
Roztocze. *See* Rzeszów
Różewicz, Tadeusz. *See also* Nike
Rubinstein, Artur
Ruch Palikota. *See also* partie polityczne
Rudziński, Witold. *See* Reymont, Władysław Stanisław
rusałka

ruski. *See* Związek Socjalistycznych Republik Radzieckich (ZSRR)
Rutkiewicz, Wanda. *See* Kukuczka, Jerzy
RWE. *See* Radio Wolna Europa, Rozgłośnia Polska
RWPG. *See* Rada Wzajemnej Pomocy Gospodarczej (RWPG)
Rybkowski, Jan. *See Dyzma, Kariera Nikodema Dyzmy*
rycerz. *See* szlachta polska
Rydel, Lucjan. *See Wesele*
Rydzyk, Tadeusz. *See also* Radio Maryja
Rymkiewicz, Jarosław Marek. *See* Umschlagplatz
rynek. *See* prawo magdeburskie; Stare Miasto
Rynek Główny w Krakowie. *See* kościół Mariacki; lajkonik; Matejko, Jan; Mitoraj, Igor; pomnik Mickiewicza w Krakowie; przysięga Kościuszki; uczta u Wierzynka
Rywin, afera. *See also* Kwaśniewski, Aleksander
rząd londyński. *See* rząd na uchodźstwie
rząd na uchodźstwie. *See also* Armia Krajowa; Armia Ludowa; Druga Rzeczpospolita Polska; Jeziorański, Zdzisław; Manifest Lipcowy; "Nil," Generał; Paderewski, Ignacy Jan; Sikorski, Władysław; Zawacka, Elżbieta; Żegota; Żydowski Związek Wojskowy
Rzeczpospolita. *See* gazety
Rzeczpospolita Obojga Narodów. *See also* ordynacja; Potocki, rodzina Potockich; Rzeczpospolita Polska; unia lubelska; Zamek Królewski w Warszawie
Rzeczpospolita Polska. *See* Polska; Polska Rzeczpospolita Ludowa (PRL); rząd na uchodźstwie
rzeki. *See also* Bug; Kanał Augustowski; Kanał Elbląski; Narew; Odra; Warta; Wisła

rzemieślnicy. *See* prawo magdeburskie
rzemiosła. *See* prawo magdeburskie
Rzeszów. *See also* Galicja; Małopolska; Podkarpacie
rzeź galicyjska. *See* rabacja galicyjska
rzeź Pragi. *See* insurekcja kościuszkowska; Warszawa, bitwy
rzeź Woli. *See also* powstanie warszawskie; wola
rzeź wołyńska

Sabała
Sala Kongresowa. *See* Pałac Kultury i Nauki w Warszawie
sala pod głowami. *See* Wawel
Sala Poselska. *See* Wawel
salon. *See also* sklep: rodzaje sklepów
Samozwaniec, Magdalena. *See* Kossak, Wojciech; *Trędowata*
San. *See* Przemyśl
sanacja. *See* Beck, Józef; Dmowski, Roman; Druga Rzeczpospolita Polska; dwudziestolecie międzywojenne; Narodowa Demokracja, endecja
Sanatarium pod klepsydrą. *See* Schulz, Bruno
Sandomierz. *See also* Baranów; Małopolska; San; Wisła
Sanguszko. *See* Baranów
Sanok. *See* Beksiński, Zdzisław
Santor, Irena. *See Przygoda na Mariensztacie*
Sapkowski, Andrzej. *See* wiedźmin
sarmatyzm. *See also* kontusz; mesjanizm polski; Pasek, Jan Chryzostom; Polska spichlerzem Europy; portret trumienny; żupan
saskie czasy, noc saska
Sasnal, Wilhelm
satelity. *See* demoludy
Sąd Konstytucyjny. *See* sądownictwo

Sąd Najwyższy. *See* sądownictwo sądownictwo
Sąsiedzi. *See* Gross, Jan Tomasz; Jedwabne, pogrom w Jedwabnem
SB. *See* Służba Bezpieczeństwa
Schiller, Leon
Schindler, Oskar. *See* druga wojna światowa: muzea
Schulz, Bruno
Secesja. *See also* Mehoffer, Józef
Seifert, Zbigniew. *See* Komeda, Krzysztof
Sejm. *See also* Bierut, Bolesław; Kaczyński, Jarosław; konfederacja, rokosz, zajazd; Konstytucja 3 maja; Królestwo Kongresowe, "Kongresówka"; Kuroń, Jacek; Rejtan, Tadeusz; Rzeczpospolita Polska; saskie czasy, noc saska; szlachta polska; trzy razy tak, 3 × TAK; *Tygodnik Powszechny*; wybory 1947; wybory 1989
Sejm Czteroletni. *See* Konstytucja 3 maja
Sejm RP. *See also* Balcerowicz, plan Balcerowicza; Buzek, Jerzy; Holoubek, Gustaw; kobiety w polityce; Komorowski, Bronisław; Orlen, afera Orlenu; partie polityczne; Polska; Tusk, Donald; wiek; wybory 2011
sejmiki. *See* szlachta polska
Seksmisja
Sendlerowa, Irena. *See also* Order Uśmiechu; Żegota
Sennik współczesny. *See* Konwicki, Tadeusz
Sęp-Szarzyński, Mikołaj. *See* barok, literatura barokowa
Shamir, Yitzhak. *See* Brzeziński, Zbigniew
Shazza. *See* disco polo
SHL
Siemowit. *See* Piastowie, dynastia
Sienkiewicz, Henryk. *See also* Antek; Janko Muzykant; Kamieniec Podolski; Kmicic,

Andrzej; Łomnicki, Tadeusz; Olbrychski, Daniel; Orzeszkowa, Eliza; potop szwedzki; pozytywizm; *Quo vadis?*; Zagłoba, Jan Onufry
Sikorski, Władysław. *See also* rząd na uchodźstwie
Siłaczka. *See* Judym, Tomasz
Siły Zbrojne RP
Singer, Isaac Bashevis
Siwiec, Ryszard. *See also* Stadion Dziesięciolecia w Warszawie; Układ Warszawski
Skałka. *See also* Stanisław, Święty
Skamander. *See also* Iwaszkiewicz, Jarosław; Tuwim, Julian
Skamandryci. *See Skamander*
skansen. *See also* architektura drewniana; wiatrak; wycinanki
Skarbek, Krystyna
Skarga, Piotr. *See also* mesjanizm polski
sklep
sklep: rodzaje sklepów
skrzydła. *See* husaria
skwarki. *See* kanapki; pierogi
SLD. *See* Sojusz Lewicy Demokratycznej
Słobodzianek, Tadeusz. *See* Nasza Klasa; *Nike*
Słonimski, Antoni. *See Skamander*
Słoń. *See* Mrożek, Sławomir
"słoń a sprawa polska." *See* przysłowia o Polsce i Polakach
Słowacja. *See* Slovak, Slovakia *in* English Index
Słowacki, Juliusz. *See also* Hanuszkiewicz, Adam; Kantor, Tadeusz; mesjanizm polski; Wernyhora; Wielka Emigracja; wieszcz narodowy; Zawisza Czarny
Słuck. *See* kontusz
Słupsk. *See* Pomorze
Służba Bezpieczeństwa. *See also* czerwiec 1976, wydarzenia czerwcowe; Pawłowski, Jerzy
smacznego. *See* dzień dobry, do widzenia
smalec. *See* kanapki

smocza jama. *See* smok wawelski, smocza jama
smok wawelski, smocza jama. *See also* bazyliszek; Kadłubek, Wincenty
Smoleńsk, katastrofa pod Smoleńskiem. *See also* Kaczyński, Lech; Pierwsza Dama
Sobibór
Sobieski, Jan III. *See also* Chocim, bitwa pod Chocimiem; Pasek, Jan Chryzostom; Polska przedmurzem chrześcijaństwa; potop szwedzki; Wilanów
socjalizm. *See* demoludy; komunizm
socrealizm. *See also* "Budujemy nowy dom"; Lutosławski, Witold; *Przygoda na Mariensztacie*
Sojusz Lewicy Demokratycznej. *See* komunizm; Kwaśniewski, Aleksander; partie polityczne; Polska Zjednoczona Partia Robotnicza (PZPR)
Solaris. *See* Lem, Stanisław
Solidarność. *See also* "Ballada o Janku Wiśniewskim"; Boże coś Polskę; Buzek, Jerzy; *Gazeta Wyborcza*; Gierek, Edward; Jaruzelski, Wojciech; Kaczmarski, Jacek; Kaczyński, Jarosław; Kuroń, Jacek; Okrągły Stół, rozmowy Okrągłego Stołu; Popiełuszko, Jerzy; Rakowski, Mieczysław; stan wojenny; Stocznia Gdańska; Ściegienny, Piotr; Wałęsa, Lech; wolne soboty; Wujek, kopalnia; Zawacka, Elżbieta; "Żeby Polska była Polską"
Solski, Ludwik. *See* Stary Wiarus
sołtys. *See* województwo
Somosierra, bitwa
Sonderaktion Krakau
Sopot
sowiecki. *See* Związek Socjalistycznych Republik Radzieckich (ZSRR); *See also* Soviet Union *in* English Index
Spanner, Rudolf. *See Medaliony*

Spodek w Katowicach. *See also* Katowice
sport w Polsce. *See also* Gołota, Andrzej; Kowalczyk, Justyna; Małysz, Adam; szalikowcy
Stachura, Edward
stacze. *See* kolejka, kultura kolejkowa
Stadion Dziesięciolecia w Warszawie. *See also* Jarmark Europa; Siwiec, Ryszard
Stadion Narodowy. *See* Stadion Dziesięciolecia w Warszawie
Staff, Leopold. *See also* Młoda Polska
Stalin, Józef. *See* Anders, Władysław; Bierut, Bolesław; Jałta, konferencja jałtańska; Katyń, zbrodnia katyńska; Manifest Lipcowy; odwilż gomułkowska, październik 1956
stan wojenny. *See also* Hermaszewski, Mirosław; Jaruzelski, Wojciech; Kaczmarski, Jacek; Popiełuszko, Jerzy; Rakowski, Mieczysław; Solidarność; Wujek, kopalnia; "Żeby Polska była Polską"
Stanek, Karin. *See* autostop
Stanisław ze Szczepanowa, Święty. *See also* Bolesław II Śmiały; "Gaude, mater Polonia"; Skałka; Wojciech, Święty
Stańczycy. *See* Stańczyk
Stańczyk
Stare Miasto. *See also* Canaletto; Gdańsk; Kazimierz; Kraków; Płock; *Przygoda na Mariensztacie*; Starówka; Zamość
Stargard. *See* Pomorze
starka. *See* wódka
Starokatolicki Kościół Mariawitów. *See* religie
starosta. *See* województwo
Starówka. *See also Przygoda na Mariensztacie*
Stary, Zygmunt I. *See* Bona Sforza, królowa
"Stary niedźwiedź mocno śpi"
Stary Wiarus

Staszic, Stanisław. *See* oświecenie
statut kaliski. *See* Kalisz; Żydzi w Polsce
Stawka większa niż życie. *See* Kapitan Kloss
"Sto lat," życzenia. *See also* imieniny, urodziny
Stocznia Gdańska. *See also* grudzień 1970, wydarzenia grudniowe
stonka ziemniaczana. *See also* czyn społeczny
stopień magistra. *See* edukacja
Straszny dwór. *See* Moniuszko, Stanisław
Striptease. *See* Mrożek, Sławomir
strój ludowy. *See also* góral
strzygoń, strzyga. *See also* wiedźmin
studniówka. *See also* matura; polonez (polonaise)
Stuhr, Jerzy. *See also* Seksmisja
Stwosz, Wit. *See also* kościół Mariacki
styl zakopiański. *See* Zakopane: styl zakopiański
Suchocka, Hanna. *See* kobiety w polityce
Sudety. *See also* Brama Morawska
sukiennice. *See* Kraków; prawo magdeburskie
sukmana. *See* strój ludowy
sumy neapolitańskie. *See* Bona Sforza, królowa
Suwalszczyzna. *See* Podlasie, Polesie
Suwałki. *See* Suwalszczyzna
Swaróg. *See* Perun, Pierun
swaty, zaręczyny
Sybir, Sybiracy
Sygietyński, Tadeusz. *See* Mazowsze
sylwester, noc sylwestrowa
symbolizm. *See* epoki (okresy) literackie
Syrena (automobile)
Syrena warszawska. *See also* Wars i Sawa
system edukacji. *See* edukacja

szabla. *See* husaria
szalikowcy
Szał uniesień
Szaniawski, Jerzy. *See* Holoubek, Gustaw
szara eminencja
Szare Szeregi
Szarik. *See* Czterej pancerni i pies
Szczecin. *See also* kino studyjne; Odra; Pomorze
Szczerbiec. *See also* Bolesław I Chrobry; polskie regalia królewskie; Wawel
Szela, Jakub. *See* rabacja galicyjska
Szewczyk Dratewka. *See* smok wawelski, smocza jama
Szewińska, Irena Kirszenstein
szklane domy
szkoła lwowsko-warszawska logiki matematycznej
szkoła podstawowa, "podstawówka". *See* edukacja
szkoła średnia. *See* edukacja
szkoła wyższa. *See* edukacja
szkoła zawodowa, "zawodówka". *See* edukacja
szlachta polska. *See also*; sarmatyzm; złota polska wolność; żupan
szlak architektury drewnianej. *See* architektura drewniana
szlak bursztynowy. *See* Brama Morawska; bursztyn; Kalisz
szlak cysterski. *See* cystersi; Sandomierz
Szopen. *See* Chopin, Fryderyk
szopka krakowska
Szozda, Stanisław. *See* Wyścig Pokoju
Szpieg w masce. *See* Ordonówna, Hanka
Szpilman, Władysław. *See* Polański, Roman; Robinsonowie warszawscy; Villas, Violetta
Szucha, Aleja
Szurkowski, Ryszard. *See* Wyścig Pokoju
Szymanowski, Karol Fryderyk. *See also* Rubinstein, Artur

Szymborska, Wisława
Ściegienny, Piotr
Śląsk. *See also* Buzek, Jerzy; dialekty regionalne; Gierek, Edward; górnictwo; powstania Śląskie
śledź. *See also* ostatki
Ślub. *See* Gombrowicz, Witold
Śluby panieńskie. *See* Fredro, Aleksander
Śmigły-Rydz, Edward. *See also* Beck, Józef; Sikorski, Władysław
Śmigus-Dyngus. *See* Lany Poniedziałek, Śmigus-dyngus
śniadanie. *See* posiłki
Śniadecki, Jan. *See* oświecenie
Śniadecki, Jędrzej. *See* oświecenie
Śnieżka. *See* Sudety
Śpiący Rycerze
średniowiecze. *See* epoki (okresy) literackie
Środa Popielcowa. *See* ostatki
"*Świadkowie*, albo nasza mała stabilizacja." *See* Różewicz, Tadeusz
Świadkowie Jehowy. *See* religie
Światło, Józef. *See* Służba Bezpieczeństwa
Światowid ze Zbrucza. *See also* kapliczka przydrożna
świątki. *See also* kapliczka przydrożna
Świątynia Opatrzności Bożej
Świebodzin, pomnik Chrystusa Króla
Świecie. *See* Wisła
Świerszczyk. *See also* Jeż Jerzy
święconka. *See* Wielkanoc, Wielki Tydzień
święta państwowe. *See* dni wolne od pracy
Święto Pracy. *See* dni wolne od pracy
Święto Trzech Króli. *See also* kolędnicy
Święto Wojska Polskiego. *See* dni wolne od pracy; przysięga Kościuszki; wojna polsko-bolszewicka

POLISH INDEX 357

Świętochowski, Aleksander. *See* pozytywizm
Świna. *See* Świnoujście
Świnoujście. *See also* Wybrzeże Bałtyckie
świtezianka. *See* rusałka

tajne komplety
tajny protokół. *See* pakt Ribbentrop-Mołotow
tak-tak
Tango (play). *See* Mrożek, Sławomir
"Tango"; animacja polska
Taniec z Gwiazdami. *See* Gołota, Andrzej; Kwaśniewskie, Jolanta i Aleksndra;
Tannenberg, operacja
tańce ludowe. *See also* krakowiak; Kujawy; mazur, mazurek; polonez (polonaise)
targ, hala targowa
Targowica. *See* konfederacja targowicka
Tarnica. *See* Bieszczady
Tarnobrzeg. *See* Podkarpacie; Wisła
Tarnów. *See* Bem, Józef
tarpan
Tarski, Alfred. *See* szkoła lwowsko-warszawska logiki matematycznej
Tatar. *See* mniejszości narodowe i etniczne
Tatarak. *See* Iwaszkiewicz, Jarosław
Tatry. *See also* Beskidy; halny; Karpaty; Morskie Oko; Pieniny; Śpiący Rycerze; Wisła
Tatrzańskie Ochotnicze Pogotowie Ratunkowe. *See* Tatry
Teatr. *See* Schiller, Leon
Teatr Laboratorium. *See* Grotowski, Jerzy; Komorowska, Maja
Teatr Narodowy. *See* Dejmek, Kazimierz; Hanuszkiewicz, Adam
teatr ubogi. *See* Grotowski, Jerzy
Teatr Współczesny. *See* Komorowska, Maja
Teatr Żydowski w Warszawie. *See* Kamińska, Ida

Teatrzyk "Zielona Gęś." *See* Gałczyński, Konstanty Ildefons
telenowela. *See also* Telewizja Polska
Telewizja Polska, TVP
Telimena
Teraz Polska
Tercet Egzotyczny. *See* Czerwone Gitary
testament. *See* Bolesław III Krzywousty
Tłusty Czwartek. *See* ostatki
toalety. *See* kółeczko, trójkącik
Tokarczuk, Olga. *See also* karp, akcja żywy karp; Nike; żurek
Tomek, agent
topienie Marzanny. *See* Marzanna, topienie Marzanny
Tor. *See* zespół filmowy
torcik wedlowski. *See* Wedel, Fabryka E.
Toruń. *See also* Kopernik, Mikołaj; pierniki Toruńskie; Pomorze; Wisła; Zawacka, Elżbieta
Totalizator Sportowy. *See* lotto
Toto-Lotek. *See* lotto
Tour de Pologne. *See* Wyścig Pokoju
Towarzystwo Demokratyczne Polskie. *See* Lelewel, Joachim; Wielka Emigracja
Towiański, Andrzej. *See* mesjanizm polski
traktat ateński
traktat tylżycki. *See* Księstwo Warszawskie
traktat wersalski. *See also* Paderewski, Ignacy Jan; Wolne Miasto Gdańsk
tratwy. *See* flisak
Traugutt, Romuald. *See* powstanie styczniowe
Treblinka. *See also* Korczak, Janusz; powstanie w getcie warszawskim; Umschlagplatz
Treny. *See also* Kochanowski, Jan
Trędowata. *See also* ordynacja
trójkącik. *See* kółeczko, trójkącik
Trójmiasto. *See* Gdańsk; Gdynia; Sopot

Trubadurzy. *See* Czerwone Gitary
Trwam. *See* Rydzyk, Tadeusz
Trybuna. *See* gazety
Trybuna Ludu. *See* gazety; Polska Zjednoczona Partia Robotnicza (PZPR)
trylogia. *See* polska szkoła filmowa; Sienkiewicz, Henryk
Trzaskowski, Andrzej. *See* Komeda, Krzysztof
trzeci rozbiór. *See* Konstytucja 3 maja; rozbiory
Trzecia Rzeczpospolita Polska. *See also* Komorowski, Bronisław; Rzeczpospolita Obojga Narodów
trzy razy tak, 3 x TAK. *See also* wybory 1947
tur. *See also* Białowieża, Puszcza Białowieska
turoń. *See* kolędnicy
Turowicz, Jerzy. *See* *Tygodnik Powszechny*
Tusk, Donald. *See also* Kaszuby, język kaszubski
Tuwim, Julian. *See also* *Skamander*
Twardowski, Jan. *See* *Tygodnik Powszechny*
Twierdza Przemyśl. *See* Przemyśl
ty. *See* bruderszaft; pan, pani, państwo
Tygodnik Powszechny. *See also* tygodniki
tygodniki. *See also* gazety
Tyniec
Tyszkiewicz, Beata. *See* Walewska, Maria
tytoń, papierosy. *See also* palenie papierosów
tytułowanie. *See also* pan, pani, państwo; szlachta polska

UB. *See* Urząd Bezpieczeństwa
uczta u Wierzynka. *See also* Kazimierz III Wielki
Układ o Przyjaźni, Współpracy i Pomocy Wzajemnej. *See* Układ Warszawski
układ Sikorski-Majski. *See* Anders, Władysław; Bodo, Eu-

358   POLISH INDEX

geniusz; rząd na uchodźstwie; Sikorski, Władysław

Układ Warszawski. *See also* Kukliński, Ryszard; RWPG, Rada Wzajemnej Pomocy Gospodarczej; Siwiec, Ryszard

Ukraina. *See* Ukraine *in* English Index

Ukrajin'ska Powstan'ska Armiya. *See* rzeź wołyńska

ulica Piotrkowska. *See* Piotrkowska, ulica

ułan

Umschlagplatz

UNESCO. *See* Grotowski, Jerzy; Hala Stulecia; kalwaria; Kraków; Toruń; Wieliczka; Zamość

unia brzeska

Unia Europejska. *See* traktat ateński

unia lubelska. *See also* Lublin; Radziwiłłowie; Rzeczpospolita Obojga Narodów; Rzeczpospolita Polska; Zygmunt II August

Unicki, Kościół. *See* Przemyśl; religie; unia brzeska

uniwersał połaniecki. *See* Kościuszko, Tadeusz

Uniwersytet Jagielloński. *See also* Jadwiga, królowa; Nawojka; Sonderaktion Krakau

Uniwersytet Latający. *See also* Komitet Obrony Robotników (KOR)

uniwersytety. *See also* edukacja; Uniwersytet Jagielloński

UPA (Ukrajin'ska Powstan'ska Armiya). *See* rzeź wołyńska

Urban, Jerzy

urlop, wakacje

urlop macierzyński. *See* urlop, wakacje

urodziny. *See* imieniny, urodziny

Urszula. *See* Kochanowski, Jan; Treny

Urząd Bezpieczeństwa (UB). *See* Pawłowski, Jerzy; Służba Bezpieczeństwa (SB)

Villas, Violetta
Volksdeutsche

W labiryncie. *See* telenowela
Wadowice
Wajda, Andrzej. *See also* Andrzejewski, Jerzy; "Ballada o Janku Wiśniewskim"; Cybulski, Zbigniew; Holland, Agnieszka; Iwaszkiewicz, Jarosław; Janda, Krystyna; Jankiel; Kantor, Tadeusz; Kilar, Wojciech; Komorowska, Maja; Korczak, Janusz; Łódzka Szkoła Filmowa; Pan Tadeusz; polska szkoła filmowa; *Wesele*

wakacje. *See* urlop, wakacje

Walentynowicz, Anna. *See* Solidarność; Stocznia Gdańska

Walentynowicz, Marian. *See Koziołek Matołek*

Walewska, Maria

Walezy, Henryk. *See* Henryk I Walezy

Wałęsa, Danuta. *See* Pierwsza Dama

Wałęsa, Lech. *See also* Belweder; "Nie chcem, ale muszem"; rząd na uchodźstwie; Stocznia Gdańska; Trzecia Rzeczpospolita Polska; Wajda, Andrzej

Wanda. *See also* Kadłubek, Wincenty; kopiec

Wariat i zakonnica. *See* Witkacy

Warmia. *See also* Krasicki, Ignacy; Mazury, Pojezierze Mazurskie

Wars i Sawa

Warszawa (automobile)

Warszawa (city). *See also* Canaletto; festiwale muzyczne; Generalne Gubernatorstwo; Grób Nieznanego Żołnierza; kawiarnia; kolumna Zygmunta; Królestwo Kongresowe, "Kongresówka"; Łazienki Królewskie, Park Łazienkowski; Marszałkowska Dzielnica Mieszkaniowa; marzec 1968, wydarzenia marcowe; Nike;

Ochotnicza Rezerwa Milicji Obywatelskiej (ORMO); Okrągły Stół, rozmowy Okrągłego Stołu; Pałac Kultury i Nauki w Warszawie; Pawiak; Popiełuszko, Jerzy; powstanie styczniowe; powstanie w getcie warszawskim; *Przygoda na Mariensztacie*; rewolucja roku 1905; Sendlerowa, Irena; *Skamander*; Stadion Dziesięciolecia w Warszawie; Starówka; Szucha, Aleja; Układ Warszawski; Wars i Sawa; Warszawa, bitwy; Wedel, Fabryka E.; Wilanów; wojna polsko-bolszewicka; Zamek Królewski w Warszawie; Żwirko i Wigura

Warszawa, bitwy
"Warszawianka"
Warszawianka (Wyspiański play), *See* Stary Wiarus

Warszawska Jesień. *See also* festiwale muzyczne; Górecki, Henryk; Lutosławski, Witold; Penderecki, Krzysztof

warszawska pielgrzymka. *See* Częstochowa; Jasna Góra

Warta. *See also* Częstochowa; Polanie; Poznań; rzeki

Waryński, Ludwik

Wawel. *See also* arrasy wawelskie; Kaczyński, Lech; Kraków; Orle Gniazda; polskie regalia królewskie; Skałka; smok wawelski, smocza jama; Stanisław, Święty; Szczerbiec

Waza, Zygmunt. *See* Zygmunt III Waza

Wazowie, dynastia
wczasy. *See* urlop, wakacje
Wedel, Fabryka E.
Weisblum, Elimelech. *See* chasydyzm

Wereszczakówna, Maryla. *See Dziady*

Wernyhora
wesele. *See* gościnność; oczepiny
Wesele. *See also* Niemen, Czesław; rabacja galicyjska; Stańczyk;

POLISH INDEX   359

Wernyhora; Wyspiański, Stanisław; Zawisza Czarny

Westerplatte. *See also* druga wojna światowa; Gdańsk; kampania wrześniowa; Wieluń; Wolne Miasto Gdańsk

"Węgier, Polak dwa bratanki, i do szabli i do szklanki." *See* Węgry

Węgry. *See also* Hungary *in* English Index

wianki. *See* noc świętojańska

wiatrak

wiedźmin. *See also* "Tango"

wiek. *See also* imieniny, urodziny

Wieliczka

Wielka Emigracja. *See also* Bem, Józef; Chopin, Fryderyk; Czartoryski, Adam; Mickiewicz, Adam; Norwid, Cyprian Kamil; powstanie listopadowe; Słowacki, Juliusz

Wielka Improwizacja. *See* Konrad

Wielka Krokiew. *See* Zakopane

Wielka Orkiestra Świątecznej Pomocy

Wielkanoc, Wielki Tydzień. *See also* barszcz, barszcz biały, barszcz czerwony; Boże Ciało; dni wolne od pracy; ostatki; pisanki; Zielone Świątki

Wielki Tydzień. *See* Wielkanoc, Wielki Tydzień

Wielki Tydzień. *See* Andrzejewski, Jerzy

Wielkie Księstwo Litewskie. *See* pogoń; Rzeczpospolita Obojga Narodów; Rzeczpospolita Polska

Wielkopolska. *See also* dialekty regionalne; Kujawy; Małopolska; Mazowsze; reakcja pogańska; traktat wersalski

Wieluń. *See also* druga wojna światowa; kampania wrześniowa

Wieniawski, Henryk

Wierzynek, Mikołaj. *See* uczta u Wierzynka

Wierzyński, Kazimierz. *See* Skamander

wieszcz narodowy. *See also* Wyspiański, Stanisław

wieś. *See* województwo

Wigilia. *See also* Boże Narodzenie; karp, akcja żywy karp; kasza; kolędnicy; mikołajki

Wigura, Stanisław. *See* Żwirko i Wigura

Wilanów. *See also* plakaty

Wilczy Szaniec

Wildstein, Bronisław. *See* lista Wildsteina

Wilia. *See* Wilno

Wilno. *See also* Ostra Brama

wino. *See* pijalnia piwaWisła. *See also* Bałtyk; Bug; Kanał Augustowski; Kazimierz Dolny; Kraków; Modlin, twierdza Modlin; Narew; Oświęcim; Płock; rzeki; San; Syrena warszawska; Toruń; Wanda; Wars i Sawa; Warszawa; Wawel

Wisła

Wisła, akcja. *See also* Łemkowie, mniejszość karpatorusińska; Nikifor; rzeź wołyńska

Wisłok. *See* Rzeszów

Wiśniewski, Janek. *See* "Ballada o Janku Wiśniewskim"

Wiśniowiecki, Michał Korybut

Witkacy. *See also* Kantor, Tadeusz; Zakopane

Witkiewicz, Stanisław Ignacy. *See* Witkacy

Witos, Wincenty

wizy do USA

"Wlazł kotek na płotek"

Władysław I Łokietek. *See also* Bolesław III Krzywousty; Kazimierz III Wielki; Szczerbiec

Władysław III Warneńczyk

Władysław IV Waza. *See* kolumna Zygmunta

Włocawek. *See* Kujawy; Wisła

włoszczyzna. *See* Bona Sforza, królowa

włóczek, włóczkowie. *See* flisak, lajkonik

włócznia Świętego Maurycego.

See polskie regalia królewskie; zjazd gnieźnieński

WMG. *See* Wolne Miasto Gdańsk

Wniebowzięcie Najświętszej Maryi Panny. *See* dni wolne od pracy

woda sodowa. *See* pijalnia piwa

Wojciech, Święty. *See also* Bałtowie; Bogurodzica; Gniezno; zjazd gnieźnieński

wojewoda. *See* województwo

województwo

województwo małopolskie. *See* Małopolska

województwo opolskie. *See* Opole

województwo podkarpackie. *See* Rzeszów

województwo świętokrzyskie. *See* dąb Bartek

wojna polsko-bolszewicka. *See also* husaria; kresy wschodnie; linia Curzona; Lwów; "Nil," Generał; Operacja Polska NKWD; Piłsudski, Józef; ułan; Warszawa, bitwy

Wojna polsko-ruska pod flagą biało-czerwoną. *See* Masłowska, Dorota

wojna polsko-ukraińska. *See also* Lwów, pogrom lwowski

Wojsko Polskie. *See* Armia Krajowa; Armia Ludowa; Bóg, Honor, Ojczyzna; Polska Walcząca; Siły Zbrojne RP

Wojskowa Rada Ocalenia Narodowego (WRON). *See* Hermaszewski, Mirosław; Jaruzelski, Wojciech; stan wojenny

Wojtek, niedźwiedź

Wojtyła, Karol Józef. *See* Jan Paweł II (papież)

Wokulski, Stanisław. *See* Prus, Bolesław

wola. *See also* rzeź Woli

wolna elekcja. *See* złota polska wolność

Wolne Miasto Gdańsk. *See also* Gdańsk; Gdynia; traktat wersalski wolne soboty. *See also* dni wolne od pracy

Wolsztyn. *See* Parowozownia Wolsztyn

Wołomin. *See* mafia pruszkowska, wołomińska, łódzka

wódka. *See also* Biała Dama; piwo; żubrówka

wójt. *See* województwo

wóz Drzymały

Wprost. See tygodniki

Wratislavia Cantans. *See* Wrocław

Wrocław. *See also* Bolesław II Śmiały; Grotowski, Jerzy; Hala Stulecia; Nasza Klasa; Odra; Ossolineum, Zakład Narodowy imienia Ossolińskich; *Panorama Racławicka*; Psie Pole, bitwa; Śląsk

WRON. *See* Wojskowa Rada Ocalenia Narodowego (WRON)

Września

wrzosy. *See* miesiące, nazwy miesięcy

Wujek, Jakub. *See* Biblia

Wujek, kopalnia. *See also* Zmotoryzowane Odwody Milicji Obywatelskiej (ZOMO)

Wybicki, Józef. *See* Legiony Polskie we Włoszech; "Mazurek Dąbrowskiego"

wybory 1947. *See also* Bierut, Bolesław; trzy razy tak

wybory 1989

wybory 2011. *See also* partie polityczne; Ruch Palikota

Wybrzeże Bałtyckie. *See also* Bałtyk; grudzień 1970, wydarzenia grudniowe

wybuch, godzina "B". *See* powstanie warszawskie

wycinanki. *See also* Cepelia; Kurpie; Łowicz

Wyczółkowski, Leon. *See also* Młoda Polska

wydarzenia czerwcowe. *See* czerwiec 1976, wydarzenia czerwcowe

wydarzenia grudniowe. *See* grudzień 1970, wydarzenia grudniowe

wydarzenia marcowe. *See* marzec 1968, wydarzenia marcowe

wydarzenia Radomskie. *See* Radom

wydarzenia sierpniowe. *See* Solidarność; Stocznia Gdańska

wydawnictwa drugiego obiegu

wyliczanki

wypadki czerwcowe. *See* czerwiec 1956, wypadki czerwcowe

Wyspiański, Stanisław. *See also* Kantor, Tadeusz; kościół Mariacki; lajkonik; Madonna z Krużlowej; Mehoffer, Józef; Młoda Polska; Stary Wiarus; "Warszawianka"; *Wesele*; wieszcz narodowy

Wyszyński, Stefan. *See also* Apel Jasnogórski; czerwiec 1956, wypadki czerwcowe; Świątynia Opatrzności Bożej

Wyścig Pokoju

"Za naszą i waszą wolność." *See* powstanie listopadowe

zabory. *See* rozbiory

zabór austriacki. *See* Galicja; Polska A i B; rozbiory; tytułowanie; Witos, Wincenty

zabór pruski. *See* Polska A i B; "Rota Marii Konopnickiej"; rozbiory; Września

zabór rosyjski. *See* Piłsudski, Józef; Polska A i B; powstanie styczniowe; rozbiory; Sybir, Sybiracy

Zabrze. *See* Śląsk

Zachęta. *See also* Olbrychski, Daniel; Nikifor; *Szał uniesień*

Zachód. *See* demoludy

Zaczarowany ołówek. *See* Bolek i Lolek

Zaduszki. *See* Dziady (Forefathers' Eve)

Zagajewski, Adam

Zagłoba, Jan Onufry

zajazd. *See* konfederacja, rokosz, zajazd

Zajączek, Józef. *See* Królestwo Kongresowe, "Kongresówka"

zakazane piosenki

Zakład Narodowy Ossolińskich. *See* Ossolineum, Zakład Narodowy imienia Ossolińskich

Zakład Ubezpieczeń Społecznych (ZUS)

Zakopane. *See also* góral; kulig; Małopolska; Młoda Polska; owczarek podhalański; Tatry; Zakopane: styl zakopiański

Zakopane: styl zakopiański

Zamek Królewski w Warszawie. *See also* kolumna Zygmunta; Starówka

zamek w Łańcucie. *See* Łańcut, zamek w Łańcucie

Zamenhof, Ludwik

Zamość. *See also* Zamoyscy, rodzina; Zamoyski, Jan

Zamoyscy, rodzina. *See also* magnateria; ordynacja

Zamoyski, Jan. *See also* Batory, Stefan; Zamość; Zamoyscy, rodzina

Zanussi, Krzysztof. *See also* Holland, Agnieszka; Kilar, Wojciech; Kolbe, ojciec Maksymilian Maria; Komorowska, Maja; Łódzka Szkoła Filmowa; zespół filmowy

zapiekanka

Zapolska, Gabriela. *See* Dulska, dulszczyzna

zapusty. *See* ostatki

zaręczyny. *See* swaty, zaręczyny

"zastał Polskę drewnianą, a zostawił murowaną." *See* Kazimierz III Wielki

Zatoka Gdańska. *See* Gdańsk; Kaszuby, język kaszubski; Sopot; Wisła

Zatoka Pucka. *See* Hel, Półwysep Helski

Zawacka, Elżbieta

Zawadzka, Elżbieta. *See* Zawacka, Elżbieta

Zawisza Czarny

ZboWiD. *See* szara eminencja

zbójnicy. *See* ciupaga

POLISH INDEX 361

zbrodnia katyńska. *See* Katyń, zbrodnia katyńska

zbrodnia naliboska. *See* Bielscy, bracia

zdanie, najstarsze polskie zdanie. *See* "Daj, ać ja pobruszę, a ty poczywaj"

zdrowie, opieka lekarska

Zebra. *See* zespół filmowy

Zebrzydowski, Michał. *See* kalwaria

Zeh, Jan. *See* lampa naftowa

zesłanie. *See* Sybir, Sybiracy

Zesłanie Ducha Świętego. *See* dni wolne od pracy; Zielone Świątki

zespół filmowy

Zielone Świątki. *See also* dni wolne od pracy

Zielonoświątkowy. *See* religie; Zielone Świątki

Ziemia obiecana. *See* Łódź; Reymont, Władysław Stanisław

ziemie odzyskane. *See also* Jałta, konferencja jałtańska; kresy wschodnie; rzeź wołyńska; Wisła, akcja

zimna wojna. *See* Miłosz, Czesław

zjazd gnieźnieński. *See also* Bolesław I Chrobry; polskie regalia królewskie

Złota Palma. *See* Janda, Krystyna; Polański, Roman; Wajda, Andrzej

złota polska wolność. *See also* Wiśniowiecki, Michał Korybut

złoty. *See* monety, banknoty; Polska

Złoty Lew. *See* festiwale filmowe

"Złoty lis." *See* Andrzejewski, Jerzy

złoty róg. *See* Wernyhora; *Wesele*

złoty wiek. *See* Zygmunt I Stary

Zmotoryzowane Odwody Milicji Obywatelskiej (ZOMO). *See also* Ochotnicza Rezerwa Milicji Obywatelskiej (ORMO); "Wujek," kopalnia

znaczek pocztowy

Zniewolony umysł. *See* Miłosz, Czesław

ZOMO. *See* Zmotoryzowane Odwody Milicji Obywatelskiej

ZSRR. *See* Związek Socjalistycznych Republik Radzieckich (ZSRR)

zupa. *See also* dania barowe

Związek Bojowników o Wolność i Demokrację (ZBoWiD). *See* szara eminencja

Związek Socjalistycznych Republik Radzieckich (ZSRR)

Zwierzyniec. *See* kopiec; lajkonik

Zygmunt I Stary. *See* dzwon Zygmunta; Kalisz; Modrzewski, Andrzej Frycz; Stańczyk

Zygmunt II August. *See* arrasy wawelskie; Bona Sforza, królowa; Jagiellonowie; Kochanowski, Jan; Łaski, Jan; Pan Twardowski; Radziwiłłowie; Stańczyk; unia lubelska; Zamoyski, Jan

Zygmunt III Waza. *See* kolumna Zygmunta; konfederacja, rokosz, zajazd; Skarga, Piotr; Warszawa; Wazowie, dynastia

Żabiński, Jan and Antonina. *See* ogrody zoologiczne

Żale Matki Boskiej pod krzyżem. *See* Bogurodzica

Żebrowski, Michał. *See* wiedźmin

"Żeby Polska była Polską"

Żegota. *See also* getta żydowskie; powstanie w getcie warszawskim; Sendlerowa, Irena

żelazna kurtyna. *See* demoludy

Żelazowa Wola. *See* Chopin, Fryderyk; dwór szlachecki; wola

Żerań. *See* Fiat 125p, duży Fiat; Warszawa (automobile)

Żeromski, Stefan. *See also* Judym, Tomasz; pozytywizm; szklane domy

żeromszczyzna. *See* Żeromski, Stefan

Żmij. *See* Perun, Pierun

Żmijewski, Artur

Żnin. *See* Biskupin

Żołnierze Wyklęci. *See also* Armia Krajowa; Narodowe Siły Zbrojne; "Nil," Generał

Żółkiewski, Stanisław

żubrówka. *See also* wódka

żubry. *See* Białowieża, Puszcza Białowieska; żubrówka

Żuk. *See* Warszawa (automobile)

Żuławski, Xavery. *See* Masłowska, Dorota

żupan. *See also* kontusz

żurek. *See also* barszcz, barszcz biały, barszcz czerwony; dania barowe; jadłodajnia; zupa

Żwirko, Franciszek. *See* Żwirko i Wigura

Żwirko i Wigura

Żydowska Organizacja Bojowa (ŻOB). *See* powstanie w getcie warszawskim; Żydowski Związek Wojskowy

Żydowski Związek Wojskowy

Żydzi w Polsce. *See also* bajgiel; Bielscy, bracia; chasydyzm; cmentarz; Częstochowa; Eichelbaum, Aaron, Szmul, Hirsz, i Itzhak; Faktorowicz, Maksymilian; Frank, Jakub; Funk, Kazimierz; Gelbfisz, Szmuel; getta żydowskie; granatowa policja; Kalisz; Kamińska, Ida; Kazimierz; Kiepura, Jan; kirkuty; Kosiński, Jerzy; Majdanek; marzec 1968, wydarzenia marcowe; Mickiewicz, Adam; mniejszości narodowe i etniczne; Oświęcim; Polański, Roman; powstanie w getcie warszawskim; Przemyśl; religie; Rubinstein, Artur; Schulz, Bruno; Sendlerowa, Irena; Singer, Isaac Bashevis; Szewińska, Irena Kirszenstein; Treblinka; Żegota; Żydowski Związek Wojskowy

Żywot człowieka poczciwego. *See* Rej, Mikołaj z Nagłowic

żywy karp. *See* karp

Illustration Credits

Please note that unless specified otherwise, all images were available via the Wikimedia Commons and licensed under the Creative Commons Attribution license (CC BY, versions 2.0–4.0; http://creativecommons.org/licenses/by/), the Creative Commons Attribution-ShareAlike license (CC BY-SA, versions 2.0–4.0; http://creativecommons.org/licenses/by-sa/), or they were in the public domain.

andrzejki. Przykuta (own work).
architektura romańska, gotycka, renesansowa, barokowa. Radomil (own work).
Armia Krajowa. Maciej Szczepańczyk (own work).
autostop. Radosław Drożdżewski (own work).

Baca. © Halina Kraczyńska.
Bamber, Bamberka. Radomil (own work).
bar mleczny. Nejmlez (own work).
Beksiński, Zdzisław. Piotr Dmochowski's collection; Zdzisław Beksiński (copyrights inherited by Muzeum Historyczne w Sanoku).
Belweder. © Marek and Ewa Wojciechowscy.
Białowieża, Puszcza Białowieska. Henryk Kotowski (own work).
Białystok. Sebastian Maćkiewicz (own work).
Bieszczady. Pibwl (own work).
Bigos. Renessaince (own work).
Biskupin. Ludek (own work).
Bona Sforza, królowa. Lucas Cranach the Younger, circa 1553.
Boże Ciało. Politykstargard (own work).
Brzechwa, Jan. Władysław Miernicki.

Bug. Ejdzej (own work).
bursztyn. Anders Leth Damgaard (own work).
Buzek, Jerzy. European People's Party. EPP Congress Bonn.
Bydgoszcz. Waldemar Heise (own work).

chleb i sól. Monika (Leaf_Only).
Chocim, bitwa pod Chocimiem. Palladinus.
Chrystus Frasobliwy. Łukasz S. Olszewski (own work).
"Chrząszcz brzmi w trzcinie." Jacek Krywult.
ciasta, ciastka. Bartosz Senderek.
Ciechocinek. Makary (own work).
cmentarz. Hubert Śmietanka (own work).
cyganeria krakowska. Andrzej Barabasz (own work).
cystersi. Jan Mehlich (own work).
Czartoryscy, rodzina. Based on Tadeusz Gajl's work.

"Daj, ać ja pobruszę, a ty poczywaj." Bonio (own work).
dąb Bartek. Goku122.
Demarczyk, Ewa. Jan Popłoński.
Deyna, Kazimierz. Bundesarchiv, Bild 183-N0706-0039 / Mittelstädt, Rainer.

Dymna, Anna. Marek Kowalski.
Dzień Wszystkich Świętych. Przykuta.
dzwon Zygmunta. Sensor.

Edelman, Marek. Mariusz Kubik.

Gdańsk. www.gdansk.pl, Gdansk City Hall.
getta żydowskie. Adrian Grycuk.
Gniezno. Krzysztof Mizera.
Gołota, Andrzej. Matt Borowick.
góral. Jan Mehlich (own work).
górnictwo. Ewkaa (own work).
Góry Świętokrzyskie. Joasia.
granatowa policja. Jarosław Gdański.

Hala Stulecia. Robert Niedźwiedzki (own work).
Hanuszkiewicz, Adam. **Piotr Szulik**.
herby polskie. Avalokitesvara.
Hermaszewski, Mirosław. http://www.prezydent.pl/, President of the Republic of Poland.
hydraulik polski. www.poland.travel/, Polish Tourist Board.

Jasna Góra. Reytan.
Jeziorański, Zdzisław. TVP.
juwenalia. **Martyna292**.

363

Kaczmarski, Jacek. Paweł Plenzner (own work).
Kaczyński, Jarosław. AAR Gambit.
Kaczyński, Lech. http://www.prezydent.pl/, President of the Republic of Poland.
kalwaria. Ludwig Schneider at the Polish language Wikipedia.
Kamieniec Podolski. Dmytro Sergiyenko (own work).
Kanał Augustowski. © Marek and Ewa Wojciechowscy.
Kantor, Tadeusz. Heinz O. Jurisch.
Kapitan Kloss. Cezary Piwowarski.
kapliczka przydrożna. Eugene Brozda.
Kapuściński, Ryszard. LGPL.
karczma. Merlin (own work).
Kazimierz. Jakub Hałun (own work).
Kazimierz Dolny. Piotr J.
Kilar, Wojciech. Cezary Piwowarski (own work).
kino studyjne. Remigiusz Józefowicz (own work).
kirkuty. Piotr Sereczyński.
kolumna Zygmunta. Ejdzej (own work).
Kołakowski, Leszek. Mariusz Kubik.
Komeda, Krzysztof. Klapi.
Komorowska, Maja. Andrzej Burchard.
Konwicki, Tadeusz. Michał Józefaciuk.
korporacje akademickie. Czestomir.
Korzeniowski, Robert. Bartosz Senderek.
kościół Mariacki. Pgkos (own work).
Kościuszko, Tadeusz. Portrait by Kazimierz Wojniakowski, before 1812.
Kowalczyk, Justyna. Tor Atle Kleven.
Kraków. Michal Ksiazek.

Krzyżacy, zakon krzyżacki. DerHexer (own work).
Książ, Zamek Książ. Spoko ws (own work).
Kukliński, Ryszard. From official page of Polish Senate (http://www.senat.gov.pl/K4/AGENDA/).
Kukuczka, Jerzy. Andrzej Heinrich.
kult maryjny. Robert Wójtowicz, Nowy Targ.
Kuroń, Jacek. Andrzej Iwański.
Kwaśniewski, Aleksander. http://www.prezydent.pl/, President of the Republic of Poland.

lajkonik. ImreKiss (own work).
lampa naftowa. Delimata (own work).
Legiony Polskie we Włoszech. Rose Liliana Baran.
Lem, Stanisław. Wojciech Zemek.
Licheń. Krzysztof Mizera (own work).
lista Wildsteina. Andrzej Barabasz (own work).
Lublin. Marcin Białek (own work).
Lubomirscy, rodzina Lubomirskich. Jolanta Krawczyk (own work).
Lutosławski, Witold. Courtesy of W. Pniewski and L. Kowalski; uploaded by Karol Langner.
Lwów. Gryffindor (own work).
Łańcut, zamek w Łańcucie. Jan Mehlich (own work).
Łazienki Królewskie, Park Łazienkowski. Wojsyl (own work).
Łemkowie, mniejszość karpatorusińska. Aotearoa (own work).
Łempicka, Tamara de. Self-Portrait in Green Bugatti. © 2015, Tamara Art Heritage. Licensed by www.MuseumMasters.com.
Łódź. Jan Mehlich (own work).
Maanam i Kora. Herrzipp (own work).

Madonna z Krużlowej. Photo by Ludwig Schneider.
mak. Michael Maggs.
malarstwo na szkle. Marta Walczak-Stasiowska.
Małysz, Adam. Iwona Erskine-Kellie.
Masłowska, Dorota. Kamil Szewczyk.
Matka Polka. Konrad Strzelecki (own work).
matura. Photo by Oskar Błaszkowski; uploaded by Marcin Otorowski.
mazur, mazurek. Albert Jankowski (own work).
Mazury, Pojezierze Mazurskie. Albert Jankowski (own work).
metal, muzyka metalowa. Krzysztof Sadowski.
Międzyrzecki Rejon Umocniony. Akumiszcza.
Milicja Obywatelska. Hiuppo (own work).
miód, miód pitny. Wzgórze (own work).
Mitoraj, Igor. Photo by Iwona Grabska.
Modlin, twierdza Modlin. Zbigniew Strucki.
Moniuszko, Stanisław. Adolphe Lafosse.
Mrożek, Sławomir. Michał Kobyliński.

Narew. Wojsyl (own work).

Obrona Poczty Polskiej w Gdańsku. Artur Andrzej (own work).
obwarzanek. Ludek (own work).
Odra. Albrecht Conz.
Opole. Marcin Szala (own work).
Orle Gniazda. Tamerlan (own work).
oscypek. Pawel Swiegoda (own work).
osobliwości przyrodnicze. Artur Strzelczyk (own work).
ostatki. Bartosz Milewski (own work).

Ostra Brama. Albertus teolog.
owczarek podhalański. Svenfischer.

Pałac Kultury i Nauki w Warszawie. Nnb (own work).
Panorama Racławicka. Julo.
Państwowe Gospodarstwo Rolne (PGR). Piotrus.
Parowozownia Wolsztyn. Hubert Śmietanka (own work).
Pawiak. Maciej Szczepańczyk (own work).
Penderecki, Krzysztof. Akumiszcza (own work).
Piątek. Merlin (own work).
pielgrzymki. Przykuta (own work).
Pieniny. Jerzy Opioła (own work).
pierniki Toruńskie. Marcin Floryan (own work).
pierogi. Stako (own work).
Pierwsza Dama. MOs810 (own work).
pijalnia piwa. Maciej Misztalski.
Piłsudski, Józef. Library of Congress, Prints and Photographs.
Piotrkowska, ulica. Polimerek.
Płock. Jerzy Strzelecki (own work).
Podhale. Dixi.
Podlasie, Polesie. ŁukaszWu (own work).
Polański, Roman. Georges Biard (own work).
Polska Walcząca. Bastianow.
polskie regalia królewskie. Gryffindor (own work).
pomnik Chopina w Warszawie. Cezary Piwowarski (own work).
postrzyżyny. Josef Peszka, circa 1800.
Potocki, Jan. Alexander Varnek, circa 1810.
powstanie listopadowe. Photo by Maciej Szczepańczyk.
Poznań. Radomił Binek.
prawo magdeburskie. Tcie.
Preisner, Zbigniew. Sławek.
Przemyśl. Merlin.

Pudzianowski, Mariusz. Artur Andrzej (own work).

Radom. Voytek S.
Radziwiłłowie. Bastian, based on Juliusz Ostrowski's work (1897).
religie. Arewicz (own work).
rogal świętomarciński. Radomil (own work).
Rubinstein, Artur. Pawelec (own work).
rząd na uchodźstwie. Cezary Piwowarski.
Rzeczpospolita Obojga Narodów. Olek Remesz.
rzeki. Piotr Trochymiak.
Rzeszów. Betark.

Sandomierz. Piotrus (own work).
Sasnal, Wilhelm. *Anka*, 2001, oil on canvas, 17⅓ x 19 in. Copyright © the artist, courtesy of the Sadie Coles HQ, London.
sądownictwo. C. Szabla.
Schiller, Leon. Hubar.
Sejm RP. Kpalion (own work).
Sendlerowa, Irena. Mariusz Kubik (own work).
Singer, Isaac Bashevis. MCDarchives.
Skałka. Jakub Hałun (own work).
skansen. Silar (own work).
Skarga, Piotr. Anonymous painting, circa 1699.
Słowacki, Juliusz. Władysław Barwicki.
Sobieski, Jan III. Daniel Schultz, *Portrait of Jan III Sobieski in Roman Costume*, circa 1680.
Sopot. Rafal Konkolewski.
Spodek w Katowicach. Halaston (own work).
sport w Polsce. Mwinog2777 (own work).
Stocznia Gdańska. Brosen (own work).
strój ludowy. Jan Mehlich (own work).
Syrena (automobile). Herranderssvensson (own work).

Syrena warszawska. Sculpture by Ludwika Nitschowa; photo by Dixi.
Szczecin. Horvat.
Szewińska, Irena Kirszenstein. Andrzej Barabasz (own work).
szopka krakowska. Rafał Korzeniowski (own work).
Szymborska, Wisława. Juan de Vojníkov (own work).
śledź. Ra Boe (own work).
Śpiący Rycerze. ToSter (own work).
Świątynia Opatrzności Bożej. Wistula (own work).
Świebodzin, pomnik Chrystusa Króla. Mohylek (own work).
Świnoujście. Axe (own work).

targ, hala targowa. Shaqspeare (own work).
Tatry. Tomek Kucharczyk (own work).
Tokarczuk, Olga. Grzegorz Zygadło (own work).
Toruń. DerHexer (own work).
turoń. Łukasz S. Olszewski (own work).
Tyniec. Jerzy Strzelecki (own work).

Uniwersytet Jagielloński. Andrzej Barabasz (own work).

Walewska, Maria. François Gérard, *Portrait of Marie Łączyńska, Countess Walewska*, 1812.
Wałęsa, Lech. MEDEF (own work).
Warmia. Holger Weinnandt (own work).
Warszawa (automobile). Felix O.
Warta. Radomil.
Wawel. Jakub Hałun (own work).
Westerplatte. Holger Weinnandt (own work).
wiatrak. Polimerek (own work).
Wielkanoc, Wielki Tydzień. Marcin Kacper (own work).
Wigilia. Przykuta (own work).

ILLUSTRATION CREDITS 365

Wilczy Szaniec. Przemyslaw (Blueshade) Idzkiewicz (own work).
Wilno. Wojsyl (own work).
Wisła. Wojsyl (own work).
Wiśniowiecki, Michał Korybut. Unknown Polish court painter, seventeenth century.
Witkacy. Self-portrait, 1938.
Wojciech, Święty. Ludmiła Pilecka (own work).
wódka. Kamil Porembiński.
Wrocław. Kolossos (own work).
Wyścig Pokoju. Harald Weber (own work).

Zachęta. © Marek and Ewa Wojciechowscy.
Zagajewski, Adam. Sławek (own work).
Zakopane. Jakub Jura (own work).
Zamek Królewski w Warszawie. Przemysław Jahr (own work).
Zamość. Maciej Ukleja (own work).
Zanussi, Krzysztof. Eva Kröcher (own work).
zapiekanka. Mariuszjbie (own work).
Zmotoryzowane Odwody Milicji Obywatelskiej (ZOMO). Now (own work).
zupa. Paulnasca (own work).
"Żeby Polska była Polską." Silar (own work).
Żółkiewski, Stanisław. Anonymous seventeenth century painting.
żubrówka. Jojo (own work).
żurek. Radosław Drożdżewski (own work).
Żydzi w Polsce. Wojciech Kryński (Museum of the History of Polish Jews).

Kaleidoscope of Poland: A Cultural Encyclopedia was designed and composed in Agmena Pro with Hypatia Pro and FF DIN Offc by Kachergis Book Design, Pittsboro, North Carolina.